£2·00

0003969003

D0613843

THE SUPREME COMMANDER:

The War Years of General Dwight D. Eisenhower

Books by Stephen E. Ambrose

A WISCONSIN BOY IN DIXIE, *Editor*

HALLECK: LINCOLN'S CHIEF OF STAFF

UPTON AND THE ARMY

DUTY, HONOR, COUNTRY: A HISTORY OF WEST POINT

EISENHOWER AND BERLIN

THE SUPREME COMMANDER:

The War Years of
General Dwight D. Eisenhower

STEPHEN E. AMBROSE

CASSELL · LONDON

CASSELL & COMPANY LTD
35 Red Lion Square, London WC1
Sydney, Toronto, Johannesburg, Auckland

Portions of this book were first published in the following periodicals:
American History Illustrated, THE BIG APPOINTMENT and
EISENHOWER'S GREATEST DECISION, Copyright © 1968, 1969
by Historical Times, Inc., respectively; *The National Observer*,
NAILING DOWN D-DAY DETAILS; *American Heritage*, A FATEFUL
FRIENDSHIP, Copyright © 1969 by American Heritage Publishing
Co., Inc.

First published in Great Britain 1971

I.S.B.N. 0 304 93818 1

Reproduced and Printed in Great Britain by
Redwood Press Limited, Trowbridge & London

For Moira with love

INTRODUCTION

This is the story of a soldier. It is told in his terms. I have attempted to describe General Eisenhower's wartime service, his major decisions and activities, and the results from within his frame of reference. For the most part, I examine the alternatives as he saw them, seldom trying to suggest how things might have been done differently or what other approaches to problems were possible. What I have tried to do is to pull together the many facets of his service and to give some sense of the scope of his responsibilities.

This work does not attempt to analyze some basic questions. I do not pretend to deal with the political or moral aspects of the war; with few exceptions, Eisenhower did not try to set policy. He believed that his function was to carry out the policies created by his superiors. Even had Eisenhower not seen himself as an agent and tried to be more active in the formation of policy, it is unlikely that he would have changed much in the basic approach taken by the British and American governments in fighting the war, for he accepted—indeed, heartily endorsed—the mostly unquestioned assumptions held by the governments. As he saw it, he was given a job to do and he did it. How he did it is the subject of this work.

My hope is that it conveys some sense of the magnitude of the task Eisenhower undertook and met, a feeling for the extraordinary charm and deep integrity of the man, a conception of the way in which he operated, a recognition of the manner in which he weighed alternatives, made decisions, and saw to the enforcement of his orders, and some understanding as to the way his decisions affected the outcome of the war.

My debts are deep. Dr. Alfred D. Chandler, Jr., editor of the Eisenhower Papers, was a constant source of encouragement. Dr. Forrest Pogue read the entire manuscript, patiently helped me to avoid pitfalls, and generously gave of his great knowledge of the American high command in World War II. Dr. Robert A. Divine read the chapters dealing with Eisenhower's role in Franco-American relations and provided many useful suggestions. Sir Ian Jacob went through all the chapters, a laborious task in itself, and added to his labors by giving me not only general criticism but also comments drawn from his personal experience, which were always illuminating. In addition, he was kind enough to lend me his personal diary, on which I drew heavily.

The staff of the Eisenhower Project at the Johns Hopkins University, especially Miss Joyce Daidakis and Miss Nellie Wahbe, kept me at the typewriter when I wanted to go duck hunting. Mr. Edwin Alan Thompson, the chief researcher for the Project, provided me with information and documents from sources known only to him. Mrs. Elizabeth Smith was more than an outstanding typist; she was a stern critic and is a good friend. Mrs. Lois Sacks and Mrs. Jean Sample assisted by, among other things, making the work seem worth the effort. I only wish I could properly express my thanks to each member of the staff.

I doubt very much that I could have completed this work without the aid of the staff of the Eisenhower Project; I know that I would not have finished without the support of Joseph P. Hobbs, the assistant editor of the Eisenhower Papers. He read and minutely criticized the first draft of each chapter, which more often than not led to a complete reorganization and revision of the chapter. His great knowledge of General Walter Bedell Smith, whose biography he is writing, and of the events and issues of World War II, was absolutely indispensable to me. Through hundreds of lunch hours and thousands of coffee breaks, he has given me the benefit of his insights and discoveries. I hope that someday I can find a way to repay him.

The dedication is to the one who makes it possible for me to undertake and complete a task. More important, she makes it all worthwhile.

STEPHEN E. AMBROSE
Naval War College
Newport, Rhode Island
December 1969

Contents

BOOK TWO

Supreme Commander, Allied Expeditionary Force

BOOK ONE

The First Two Years

Part I

WASHINGTON TO LONDON

[December 1941–June 1942]

ON December 12, 1941, five days after Pearl Harbor, newly promoted Brigadier General Dwight Eisenhower, chief of staff of the U. S. Third Army in San Antonio, Texas, received a telephone call from the War Department in Washington. Colonel Walter Bedell Smith, Secretary of the General Staff, asked, "Is that you, Ike?" "Yes," Eisenhower replied. "The Chief says for you to hop a plane and get up here right away," Smith ordered. "Tell your boss that formal orders will come through later."

Eisenhower had no idea what the War Department wanted with him, how long he would be in Washington, or what his duties would be. But "the Chief" was Army Chief of Staff George C. Marshall, so Eisenhower asked no questions. He abandoned his plans to visit his son at West Point at Christmastime, packed a single bag, and boarded the next airplane leaving San Antonio for Washington. Mechanical failure forced the craft down at Dallas. Eisenhower shifted over to a train, which got him into Union Station, Washington, on December 14. He immediately reported to Marshall, whose office was in the old Munitions Building.[1]

The two men had met twice before. In 1930, when Eisenhower was working with the American Battle Monuments Commission in Washington, they had talked. Marshall was so impressed with Eisenhower that he asked the young major to join his staff at the Infantry School at Fort Benning. Another assignment made it impossible for Eisenhower to accept, and they had only one additional brief meeting before 1941.[2]

Marshall had ordered Eisenhower to Washington because he wanted him on the War Plans Division of the General Staff to handle the Far East, especially the Philippines, where Eisenhower had served under General Douglas MacArthur for four and a half years. The Chief of Staff wasted no time. He quickly outlined the situation in the Pacific. The Japanese attack on Pearl Harbor had rendered the Navy impotent for some months to come. Although the aircraft carriers were intact they had few supporting vessels. The garrison in Hawaii was weak and an amphibious Japanese landing there was a possibility. The islands had to be strengthened. In the Philippines the ground force consisted primarily of Filipinos and Eisenhower knew full well that their training had not proceeded far enough to make them capable of stopping the Japanese. Marshall had increased the air strength during 1941, giving MacArthur 37 B-17s and 220 fighters, but they had been hit at Clark Field. Marshall did not know the exact extent of the damage but, given the Japanese successes in other areas, he feared the worst. There were serious supply shortages, the Navy was already indicating that it was unwilling to try to break the increasingly tight enemy blockade and was going to write the Philippines off, and the Japanese intended to overrun the islands as soon as possible.

Marshall took about twenty minutes to describe the situation. Suddenly he looked straight at Eisenhower and quietly demanded, "What should be our general line of action?"

Eisenhower was startled. He had just arrived, had not unpacked his bag, knew little more than what he had read in the newspapers and what Marshall had just told him, was not up to date on the war plans for the Pacific, and had no staff to help him prepare a general policy line. Still, he immediately recognized that the assignment was important, not so much because the Chief of Staff had decided to hand over Pacific strategy to a new brigadier general (Marshall, as Eisenhower probably guessed, had already decided upon his policy), but as a personal test. After a second or two of hesitation, Eisenhower asked, "Give me a few hours."

"All right," Marshall replied. His Army had just suffered a humiliating defeat, bad news continued to come in from around the globe, he had problems with expansion, training, supply, strategy, and a hundred other things, and was not going to waste any time. Marshall wanted to know who could do the job for him and who could not, and he wanted to know it immediately. Eisenhower's answer would tell him whether this young general was up to the challenge.[3]

Eisenhower left Marshall's office and went to a desk that had been assigned to him in the War Plans Division. In preparing his answer he had little to work with, for the United States had no specific plan for the war then going on in the Pacific. The official strategy was embodied in

RAINBOW 5, a world-wide program which called for a major effort against the European Axis powers and a defensive effort in the Pacific. Marshall was determined to stick with RAINBOW 5, despite already mounting pressure to turn the full fury of American might, such as it was in December 1941, against the Japanese. The trouble was that RAINBOW 5 contained no settled solution for the defeat of Japan and was based on assumptions that were already crumbling in the face of the Japanese onslaught.

The general idea had been that the Philippines would hold out long enough to allow the fleet to advance across the central Pacific through the Marshalls and the Carolines to save the islands, while the British, Dutch, and Chinese forces contained the Japanese in the Southwest Pacific. But already, a week after the conflict began, the plans were out of date. Except for its carriers, the United States had no fleet. It was apparent that the Philippines would not be able to hold out, nor would the colonial powers south of the Philippines. Willy-nilly the Americans were on the defense in the Pacific; the problem was whether to abandon the garrison in the Philippines, since any material sent there would inevitably wind up in Japanese hands, and build a base to the south, or to make an effort to hold the islands, or to try a combination of both. In addition, agreements had to be reached with the other governments fighting the Japanese.

Eisenhower decided that, for morale purposes, the Philippines could not be abandoned. The War Department would have to make every effort to reinforce the garrison. Sticking a sheet of yellow tissue paper in his typewriter, he tapped out with one finger "Steps to Be Taken." The first requirement was to "build up in Australia a base of operations from which supplies and personnel (air and ground types) can be moved into the Philippines. Speed is essential." This program would not only give heart to the American people and the soldiers in the Philippines but would provide the beginnings of a long-range counteroffensive. Australia appeared fairly safe; with its good harbors, British Commonwealth connections, and English-speaking people, it was the obvious place to build up the base of operations for the Pacific war.

Eisenhower's next paragraph was a simple sentence: "Influence Russia to enter the war." There were great potential benefits. Russian entry would tie down Japanese troops in Manchuria and provide the United States with airfields from which American bombers could hit the home islands of Japan.

For immediate action, Eisenhower recommended sending a carrier with Army pursuit planes, pilots, ammunition, and bombs from San Diego to Australia, and—if possible—saving time by sending a carrier directly from Hawaii to Australia. Another recommendation was to move planes and crews to Australia from the West Coast by the fastest available commercial vessels. Finally, Eisenhower wanted to ferry the planes collected in Australia to the Philippines.[4]

Eisenhower took his written recommendation to Marshall, handed it to him, and said it would be a long time before major reinforcements could go to the Philippines, longer than the garrison could hold out, but the United States had to do everything possible, because "The people of China, of the Philippines, of the Dutch East Indies will be watching us. They may excuse failure but they will not excuse abandonment. . . ." The base should be Australia, and Eisenhower urged that Marshall start at once to expand the facilities there and to secure communications to Australia. "In this last we dare not fail. We must take great risks and spend any amount of money required."

Eisenhower continued to emphasize the importance of making the people of Southeast Asia feel the United States was coming to their aid. He had in mind the British in Greece. A few months earlier, when the Germans threatened that country, the British had felt it was important to send a division there—even though they feared it would do no good— in order to protect their postwar political position in the Mediterranean. Eisenhower felt the Americans had to do at least as much in the Philippines.

Eisenhower's program was exactly what Marshall had in mind. The Chief of Staff said softly, "I agree with you." Then he added, "Do your best to save them." Eisenhower had passed the test; now he was in charge of the Philippines and Far Eastern Section of the War Plans Division.

Then Marshall leaned forward—Eisenhower recalled years later that he had "an eye that seemed to me awfully cold"—and declared, "Eisenhower, the Department is filled with able men who analyze their problems well but feel compelled always to bring them to me for final solution. I must have assistants who will solve their own problems and tell me later what they have done."[5]

CHAPTER 1

Debacle in the Pacific

As Eisenhower left Marshall's office his mind went back twenty years, to the man he had served under in the Panama Canal Zone, Major General Fox Conner. Conner had made a deep impression upon him and was to remain the greatest single influence on his military thought. Even after he was a retired President of the United States and had worked with many of the great men of the century, Eisenhower would say, "Fox Conner was the ablest man I ever knew."

Three things especially that Conner taught stood out. "Always take your job seriously, never yourself," the general emphasized. "In the next war we will have to fight beside allies and George Marshall knows more about the techniques of arranging allied commands than any man I know. He is nothing short of a genius." Conner urged Eisenhower to try for an assignment under Colonel Marshall. Finally, Conner believed that another war was inevitable, that it would be a world war, and that those who directed it would have to learn to think in terms of world rather than single-front strategy.[1]

In meeting his responsibilities as a staff officer for Marshall, Eisenhower could draw upon other experiences. He had never seen combat, a fact he often bemoaned, and indeed had had only limited service with troops, but he had served on the staff of such men as General John J. Pershing, Lieutenant General Walter Krueger, and General Douglas MacArthur. He had a reputation for being a good staff officer. MacArthur said Eisenhower's chief strength was his ability to look at problems from the point of view of the high command and thought him the best drafter of papers in the Army.[2]

Marshall picked Eisenhower partly because of his long service with MacArthur, partly because he was known in the Army as a man who would assume responsibility. Marshall's desire for independent men fitted in with the way he wanted War Plans Division (WPD) to operate. The division, created by the National Defense Act of 1920 as a part of the War Department General Staff, was the principal planning agency and the central operations command post. Through it Marshall controlled the "strategic direction of military forces in the theater of war." WPD's responsibilities grew so large that it became a kind of inner general staff. Eisenhower called it the "Command Post for Marshall."[3]

In the thirties, while he was Chief of Staff, MacArthur had complained that "the War Department has never been linked to fighting elements by that network of command and staff necessary to permit the unified functioning of the American Army."[4] WPD provided the necessary links. The work involved became enormous; just six days after he joined WPD, Eisenhower told his old commander, General Krueger, "The rapid, minute-to-minute, activities of the Army seem to be centered through this place, because no one else is familiar with everything else that has been planned in the past."[5]

The difficulty was, as Marshall had said, that few officers in WPD were willing to assume the responsibility Marshall wanted them to take. Eisenhower felt that everyone in WPD was afraid of Marshall. They either could not or would not speak up when in his presence, and were not making decisions. They passed along the information to Marshall and forced him to decide. One WPD officer, Eisenhower remembered, was a brilliant, capable man. He had just one fault—he got tongue-tied when he was in Marshall's presence.

Marshall had told Eisenhower to make decisions and not bother him about them. Eisenhower did so one day and sent the result up to the division Chief, Major General Leonard Gerow. Gerow changed the decision to a recommendation and passed it on to Marshall for final action. Eisenhower confronted his superior and declared, "Gee, you have got to quit bothering the Chief with this stuff." "I can't help it, Ike," Gerow replied. "These decisions are too important. He's got to make them himself."[6]

Eisenhower grew in Marshall's estimation precisely because he was willing to make the decisions himself. A price was involved, however, one that would increase as the war went on. It was a part of a larger difficulty with the War Department that Marshall created. The Chief of Staff built a streamlined organization that could move quickly and efficiently, but it suffered from the limitations common to most bureaucracies. The emphasis, especially in WPD, was on team play and co-operation. There was little room for individual quirks or brilliance. Marshall would set the objective, which WPD would then implement. There was hardly any internal criticism of Marshall's ideas, since the main function of WPD officers was to provide arguments for Marshall's suggestions or to implement them. Marshall did not surround himself with yes men, nor try to, and he never discouraged criticism and intensive analysis, but the nature of the organization—and Marshall's strong personality—precluded searching examination.

So it was with Eisenhower's relationship with Marshall. Eisenhower was willing to take the responsibility because, in part at least, he was ordinarily confident that his solution was the one Marshall would have arrived at had he worked on the problem. Eisenhower tried to think like Marshall. He was usually successful, which made him less his own man, more Marshall's. This relationship was efficient and probably desirable when Eisenhower was a staff officer; it would be less so when Eisenhower assumed a theater command, but by then the tendency was ingrained and had, indeed, become even more pronounced.

Following his first meeting with Marshall, Eisenhower had decided to "report to the general only situations of obvious necessity." Once he carried that decision to the limit. He needed to transport a division to Australia and found that the British ship *Queen Mary* was available. Eisenhower directed the loading of 15,000 men on her and she started across the Atlantic, without escort, to go around the Cape of Good Hope. The *Queen Mary* was fast enough to avoid submarines, so Eisenhower was not worried until he received an intercepted cable to Rome from an Italian official in Brazil, reading: "The *Queen Mary* just refueled here, and with about 15,000 soldiers aboard left this port today steaming southeast across the Atlantic." Eisenhower envisioned every German submarine in the South Atlantic concentrating on the Cape of Good Hope to send the *Queen* with her 15,000 men to the bottom. For a few days he slept fitfully. He did not tell Marshall, since nothing could be done and there was no point in adding to the Chief's worries.

When the ship arrived safely, Eisenhower told the story to Marshall. The Chief smiled and said, "Eisenhower, I received that intercept at the same time that you did. I was merely hoping that you might not see it and so I said nothing to you until I knew the outcome."[7]

During his first weeks in Washington, Eisenhower spent most of his time working on the day-to-day problem of getting something, anything, into the Southwest Pacific. The biggest source of potential help was the *Pensacola* convoy. When the Japanese struck Pearl Harbor, a convoy of seven ships, carrying men and munitions and escorted by the cruiser *Pensacola,* was en route to Manila. On December 8 the Navy had ordered the convoy to put in at Suva in the Fijis to await further orders. The next day the Joint Board, composed of Army and Navy representatives, agreed to bring the ships back to Hawaii to reinforce that badly battered garrison. Gerow supported this move. Marshall concurred without comment, even though the decision represented the virtual abandonment of the Philippines. On December 10 Marshall had second thoughts and he got the Joint Board to reverse itself and reroute the convoy to Brisbane, the nearest Australian port on the western end of the continent. The Navy agreed but refused to make any promises about its ability to get the convoy from Australia to the Philippines, and the naval officers in the area soon made it clear that they felt it was not even worth attempting. MacArthur disagreed, but without the Navy's co-operation nothing could be done.[8]

The *Pensacola* convoy thus began the implementation of the program Eisenhower had recommended in his "Steps to Be Taken" paper. Designated U. S. Army Forces in Australia (USAFIA), and eventually under the command of Lieutenant General George H. Brett, it was essentially an air and supply base, with the primary task of supporting the Philippines. Marshall put Brett under MacArthur's orders and, in a message Eisenhower drafted, the Chief ordered Brett to arrange for the planes in the *Pensacola* convoy to fly northward, taking with them all the ammunition they could carry.[9]

Eisenhower meanwhile was getting two transports in San Francisco loaded with aircraft and ammunition to send to Brisbane and was arranging for others that could arrive early in January. Via the South Atlantic–Africa route, Eisenhower had two Pan American clippers loaded with 50-caliber ammunition heading for Australia, while the War Department had diverted fifteen heavy bombers from their various destinations to send to Brisbane. Finally, at Eisenhower's suggestion, the War Department made $10,000,000 available to the USAFIA commander to hire blockade runners from private shippers to make the run from Australia to the Philippines.[10]

On paper it was an impressive program of reinforcement, but it meant nothing to the forces in the Philippines unless the airplanes and ammunition got through to them. It did cement the American commitment to defend the Southwest Pacific area, if not the Philippines, and signified the beginning of the huge American build-up in Australia.

On December 22 the *Pensacola* convoy arrived in Brisbane. The same day the Japanese, having secured air bases in the southernmost of the Philippine Islands, thereby assuring their domination of the air, made their major landings at Lingayen Gulf a hundred and twenty miles north of Manila. Within three days the enemy had a firm lodgment. On December 26 MacArthur declared Manila an open city, transferred his headquarters to Corregidor, and began pulling back to the Bataan Peninsula. The Japanese had complete aerial and naval supremacy and had cut the line between the Philippines and Australia.

None of the planes, men, or munitions on the *Pensacola* convoy ever reached the Philippines. When the crews assembled the planes they found that vital combat parts were missing; by the time these arrived from the United States everything had gone smash. A field artillery brigade, together with some ammunition, did manage to reload upon two fast ships and on December 28 left for Darwin, on the north coast of Australia. By the time it got to that port the Japanese had established themselves in Borneo, directly athwart the line of communication northward. In a masterly understatement Eisenhower, in a message he drafted for Marshall, told MacArthur, "It now appears that the plans for reaching you quickly with pursuit plane support are jeopardized."[11]

The pattern of frustration set in the first weeks of the war would continue until the fall of the Philippines. Later, MacArthur charged that had there been sufficient determination in the War Department reinforcements could have reached him. The charge first appeared in Frazier Hunt's *MacArthur and the War Against Japan,* published in late 1944. Eisenhower read it shortly after the liberation of Paris and recommended it to Marshall, with the caveat that "the book practically gave me indigestion." Eisenhower also warned that "you will be quite astonished to learn that back in the Winter of '41/'42, you and your assistants in the War Department had no real concern for the Philippines and for the forces fighting there."[12]

The charge of indifference, encouraged by MacArthur, was grossly unfair. Eisenhower knew many American officers fighting in the islands, had scores of Filipino friends, and if only for personal reasons would have done everything possible to aid the defense. He suffered grievously over his inability to do anything effective. He stayed at the War Department until ten every evening, seven days a week, trying to scrape up something and find a way to get it in to MacArthur.

All Eisenhower's efforts meant nothing to MacArthur. His forces were being beaten back, suffering heavy losses, fighting without enough ammunition, insufficient food and transport, obsolete weapons, and no air support. He received promises from Washington but, except for an occasional submarine loaded with ammunition, no material help. To MacArthur, and to the tired, dirty, hungry men of Bataan, the thought of well-dressed, comfortably housed, well-fed staff officers in Washington was infuriating. The messages from Washington describing the material being sent to Australia became a bitter joke. Washington's encouragement, MacArthur later charged, was deliberate cruel deception. But without the ships to run supplies through the Japanese blockade, and without the planes to challenge the enemy in the sky, there was nothing Marshall and Eisenhower could do beyond building up the forces in Australia.

MacArthur argued that the Japanese blockade was ineffective and urged Marshall to force the Navy to fight its way through to the Philippines. On February 8, 1942, Eisenhower drafted Marshall's reply. He pointed out that the War Department was well aware of the decisive effect a flank attack against Japanese communications could have, not only in breaking the blockade of the Philippines but in stopping the southward thrust of the Japanese, but many factors stood in the way. The Japanese foresight in seizing the islands of Guam, Wake, the Marshalls, and the Gilberts and establishing land-based airplanes on them gave the enemy total air superiority. American and Dutch cruisers had just suffered heavy losses in the Netherlands East Indies from land-based aircraft and the British had lost *Prince of Wales* and *Repulse,* two modern battleships, to land-based aircraft. All this, added to the experiences gained in the Mediterranean, showed conclusively that naval vessels could not operate in regions dominated by hostile aircraft.* The United States, therefore, would continue to hold to a strategy of slowing down, then halting, Japanese advances, while it built a base in Australia from which a massive counterattack could be launched.[13]

One of the reasons Marshall had brought Eisenhower to Washington was to deal with MacArthur. Marshall probably hoped that after all his years with the Far Eastern commander Eisenhower would know how to mollify MacArthur. In this task Eisenhower clearly and completely failed. He drafted nearly every cable Marshall sent to the Philippines; none of them, including the one summarized above, satisfied or convinced MacArthur.

The reason was, perhaps, not so much that Eisenhower was not delivering anything to the beleaguered garrison but rather that the War

---

* In the first six months of the war, when they were on the offensive, the Japanese were always careful to stay within range of land-based fighter cover. Their victories were sensational but their operations were never risky.

Department was sticking to its prewar policy of Europe first. This was partly a strategic decision forced upon the policy makers. Germany was the more dangerous enemy, Europe was closer than the Far East and so shipping men and supplies there was easier, British and Russian troops were already fighting the Nazis, and so on. But it was also a foreign policy decision of the first magnitude, for it meant that in the government's estimation Europe was more important than Asia, at least to Americans living in the middle of the twentieth century.

MacArthur disagreed, violently. He believed that Asia was the key to the future, and that it was on that continent and its offshore islands that America should make her major commitment. The split between MacArthur and Marshall could not have been more decisive. For the immediate future the problem was the moral commitment to the Philippines. MacArthur felt that Americans could never again have any influence among the Filipinos unless they made every effort to save the islands. Eisenhower agreed with this—he had said as much to Marshall his first day in Washington—but he never became a full-fledged Asia-firster, despite his years in the Philippines. For this MacArthur never forgave him.

MacArthur knew full well that not only Eisenhower and Marshall were responsible for what he called his abandonment. The decision was one that nearly every responsible official in Washington agreed to. Time and again MacArthur pleaded with the "faceless staff officers" to make the primary American effort in the Philippines. He argued that the islands could be saved if the U.S. bent every effort to the task. "The yielding of the Philippines by defeat and without a major effort would mark the end of white prestige and influence in the East," he warned, and the United States had to either support the Philippines "or withdraw in shame from the Orient."

But Marshall, Eisenhower, the War Department, and the British had already agreed that the program for the Far East was to hold the Malay Peninsula, if possible, and Australia and Burma, which was another way of saying that they had written off the Philippines. In a staff-prepared memorandum of January 3, WPD reinforced the decision. The fundamental consideration was that help could not be sent to the Philippines in time to save the islands (MacArthur estimated that he could hold on for three months), but beyond that the dispatch of a force that would meet the need would constitute "an entirely unjustifiable diversion of forces from the principal theater—the Atlantic." It would take 1464 aircraft of various types, only half of which were available, to hold the Philippines. Additional airfields in Australia and along the line of advance north would have to be built, along with supporting bases. This would require large naval resources; in addition to the vessels already in the Pacific, the Allies would have to bring in seven to nine battleships, five to seven carriers, about fifty destroyers, sixty submarines, and innumerable small craft. This diversion would cause the loss of the Atlantic supply line to England, jeopardize the Middle East, and limit the defense of the Western Hemisphere. Although no one ever gave formal approval to the abandonment of the Philippines, there was general agreement that saving the islands was not worth the cost and the risk.[14]

Like his colleagues in WPD, Eisenhower had no illusions about saving the Philippines, but he did want a larger commitment to the Far East. On New Year's Day he noted on his desk pad, "I've been insisting Far East is critical—and no other side shows should be undertaken until air and ground there are in satisfactory state." The "side shows" he referred to were plans to ship American forces to Northern Ireland to relieve the British (code name MAGNET), or a possible operation against French North Africa (code name GYMNAST). Both projects were then being discussed by the British and American Chiefs of Staff, meeting in Washington. On January 17, noting that the whole situation in the Pacific was critical, he scribbled on his pad, "My own plan is to drop everything else—Magnet, Gymnast, replacements in Iceland—and make the British retire in Libya. Then scrape up everything everywhere and get it into NEI [Netherlands East Indies] and Burma."[15]

On January 14 Eisenhower got a convoy scheduled to take American troops to Northern Ireland reduced in size. He used the space saved to ship Air Force personnel, supplies, and aircraft to the Southwest Pacific.[16] This slowed down MAGNET and GYMNAST, but. it did not mean "dropping everything else" and did little to help the situation in the Far East, since it took weeks to reload the ships, turn them around, and get them to their destination. The reinforcements made no practicable contribution to the defense of the Netherlands East Indies. Eisenhower's efforts to get B-17s into Java, the most directly threatened of the NEI islands, were likewise piecemeal and for the most part unsuccessful. There were a variety of reasons; the most important were simple absence of planes and crews and the tremendous distances involved.

Always present in Eisenhower's mind was the problem of shipping. The United States, unprepared for the scope of the Japanese onslaught, was incapable of meeting the enemy effectively with the forces available to it. The British, in their first meetings with the Americans, were shocked to find how little shipping their new allies had. The maximum American troop lift for January was 25,000 men, for February, 18,000 and for March 15,000.[17] In the middle of January Eisenhower scraped up 21,000 men with ships to carry them to Australia but he noted on his desk pad, "I don't know when we can get all their equip. and supply to them. Ships! Ships! All we need is ships!" Then, as an afterthought, he added, "Also ammunition—A.A. guns—tanks—airplanes."[18]

Two events in February illustrated the frustrations inherent in the attempt to hold onto something north of Australia in the Southwest Pacific. By the middle of the month everyone except the Dutch had given up on holding Java, but it seemed that something should be done. Eisenhower and WPD got the aircraft tender *Langley,* with a cargo of thirty-two P-40s, ordered to Tjilatjap, on the south coast of Java, along with the freighter *Seawitch,* which had twenty-seven P-40s in her hold. When *Langley* was almost within sight of Java, Japanese patrol planes spotted and sank her. *Seawitch* arrived in Java on the eve of the final invasion and had to dump her cargo of P-40s, still crated, into the sea to prevent their capture.[19]

Under the circumstances, the tension in the War Department could almost be heard. "Tempers are short!" Eisenhower noted in January. "There are lots of amateur strategists on the job—and prima donnas everywhere." A little later he complained, "There's a lot of big talk and desk hammering around this place—but very few *doers!*· They announce results in advance—in a flashy way and make big impressions but the results often don't materialize and then the workers get the grief."[20]

As the stopgap measures failed to work and the pattern of Japanese aggression became clearer, Eisenhower began to have second thoughts about his plan to drop everything else and go all out in the Pacific. In the middle of January he talked with Major General Joseph T. McNarney, a West Point classmate and Army Air Corps officer who had recently returned from London to join the War Department. McNarney had no involvement in the Far East and would only talk to Eisenhower about Europe. He was most convincing. On January 22 Eisenhower noted the results on his pad: "The struggle to secure the adoption by all concerned of a common concept of strategical objectives is wearing me down. Everybody is too much engaged with small things of his own"—which was as true of Eisenhower as it was of anyone else.

Eisenhower then announced his full conversion to the Europe-first doctrine. "We've got to go to Europe and fight," he declared, "and we've got to quit wasting resources all over the world—and still worse —wasting time. If we're to keep Russia in, save the Middle East, India and Burma; we've got to begin slugging with air at West Europe; to be followed by a land attack as soon *as possible*."[21] This was also, of course, the trend of Marshall's thinking.

Eisenhower spent the rest of his tour in the War Department working assiduously for the Europe-first program. It did not mean that he was abandoning the Pacific, but rather that he had recognized the futility of piecemeal reinforcements and the need to draw back to Australia, lick the wounds, establish a workable defensive line, and meanwhile go over to the offensive in Europe. The temptations to change the basic RAINBOW 5 concept were always great, and it was difficult not to yield to them as the Japanese advance carried the enemy far beyond the points the Allies had imagined the Japanese could attain, but for the most part Eisenhower and WPD held firm. Events strengthened his hand, for short of Australia there was not much left to be saved. On the day Eisenhower wrote of the necessity to start an air campaign in West Europe, MacArthur fell back to his final defensive position on the Bataan Peninsula and the outer defenses of Singapore collapsed. The Japanese were gathering their strength for the final assault on the Netherlands East Indies and none of the governments resisting them had anything like the forces needed to hold out.

On January 22 Eisenhower wrote that he, Colonel Thomas Handy of WPD, and McNarney "stick to our idea that we must win in Europe." Eisenhower realized "it's going to be one hell of a job—but, so what?" In a sharp criticism of WPD's action up to that time, he pointed out "we can't win by sitting on our fannies giving our stuff in driblets all over the world—with no theater getting enough."[22] The scope of Japanese success had forced the planners to reconsider RAINBOW 5—no one had counted on losing Singapore, for example—and gave added weight to MacArthur's program of turning full force on the Japanese first. The argument would continue throughout the war, but under Marshall's strong direction the War Department never wavered after the first couple of months.

In any case it is hard to see what more Washington could have done to save the Philippines. Long after the situation on Bataan had become irretrievable the War Department sent whatever reinforcements became available to the Pacific. As late as April 1942 no American forces of any size had gone to the British Isles. By the time sizable American forces were available for deployment overseas, the Philippines had already fallen. The Japanese had sealed their fate on the first day of the war by eliminating the Navy's striking force. Even had the Navy gotten through, however, the Army had practically nothing to send. MacArthur could have held on longer with more equipment and especially air support, but the necessary units to retrieve the situation simply were not available. Money could not buy them—they had to be built and trained, and that took time.

Later that spring Eisenhower explained the predicament to his brother Edgar, who had said he wanted to get the war over with in a hurry. Eisenhower replied that he too was anxious to end it, but "there are so many things that we didn't do in the past twenty years that their accomplishment now is a matter of weeks and months. It cannot be done in a minute. There is no use going back over past history either to regret or condemn; although I was one of those that for the past two years has preached preparedness and tried to point out the deadly peril into which the United States was drifting." Eisenhower saw no point in an "I told you so attitude," especially since "we have got a fearful job to perform and everybody has got to unify to do it." The only consideration, he added, was the defeat of the Axis powers, for "if they should win we would really learn something about slavery, forced labor and loss of individual freedom."[23]

Eisenhower did try to use money to save the Philippines. Marshall had sent former Secretary of War Patrick J. Hurley to Australia with a brigadier general's star on each shoulder and orders to use the $10,-000,000 cash he carried to hire blockade runners. Eisenhower sent Hurley a series of messages, urging him to set prices high enough "to insure utmost energy and daring" on the part of ship commanders, and demanding redoubled efforts. The risks, however, discouraged most sea captains, and few ships could be found at any price. Despite liberal monetary offers and feverish activity, Hurley got only six ships started; of these only three got through. One reached Mindanao and two got to Cebu, but only 1000 of the 10,000 tons the ships carried reached the garrison in Luzon.[24]

It took weeks to convince the enthusiastic Hurley that he was not helping his old friend MacArthur, but finally he recognized what the War Department had seen all along. "We did not have the ships, the

air force or ground forces necessary to make the operation successful,"
Hurley declared. "We were out-shipped, out-planed, out-manoeuvred, and
out-gunned by the Japanese from the beginning."[25]

Manuel L. Quezon, President of the Philippines, could not accept
that conclusion. Dying of tuberculosis on a cot in the crowded tunnel
of Corregidor, humiliated at the thought of Japanese troops in the
presidential palace in Manila, frenzied because he would never live
to see his country a free republic, Quezon blamed Washington for his
desperation and decided that only shock action could retrieve the situation and force the United States to send help. If the United States
did not intend to defend its colony, he told Roosevelt, it and Japan
should be invited to withdraw troops, with the islands being neutralized.
Since the Japanese already held Manila and badly needed the ports
of the Philippines, the suggestion was absurd. Quezon knew that; so
did MacArthur. But, like Quezon, MacArthur was ready to try anything. In forwarding Quezon's proposal, MacArthur neglected to say that
he disagreed with it. Rather, he said the plan "might offer the best
possible solution of what is about to be a disastrous debacle." If the
Japanese accepted, the United States would lose no military advantage,
and if the Japanese rejected the proposal it would be a psychological
gain for the United States.[26]

On February 9 Marshall and Secretary of War Harry Stimson dis-
cussed the proposal with President Roosevelt. "We can't do this at all,"
Roosevelt firmly declared, and asked Marshall to prepare a reply.[27]
Marshall had Eisenhower draft one for the President's signature.

Eisenhower began by authorizing MacArthur to arrange for the capitulation of the Filipino units but declining even to consider the neu-
tralization of the islands. MacArthur should keep the flag flying "so
long as there remains any possibility of resistance." Eisenhower emphasized that the duty and necessity of resisting Japanese aggression to
the last transcended in importance any other obligation facing the United
States in the Philippines. Eisenhower had the President express great
sympathy for the plight of those on the island (Quezon and Eisenhower
were close friends), then declare that the service the troops on the
Philippines could render to the country in the struggle then developing
"is beyond all possibility of appraisement."[28]

MacArthur replied, with some heat, that he had no intention of
surrendering the Filipino units and planned to fight on until his forces
in Bataan were destroyed.[29] He would then take up the struggle on
the island of Corregidor. Marshall, horrified at the idea of MacArthur

going down with the garrison, decided to order him to leave the islands and go to Australia. The whole thing had to be handled with some care, for there was always a possibility that MacArthur would strike a pose, refuse to leave, and fight until killed or captured. Eisenhower took care of the delicate arrangements, and eventually MacArthur agreed to leave.[30]

In the second week of March MacArthur made his dramatic escape on a PT boat from the Philippines. On March 17 he arrived in Darwin, from whence he proceeded to Melbourne. The trip signified an end and a beginning; the end of the Allied attempt to hold onto anything substantial in the Southwest Pacific north of Australia, as well as the end of a policy of meeting Japanese thrusts with haphazard measures, and the beginning of the implementation of a well-thought-out, comprehensive, world-wide strategy.

It did not mean the abandonment of MacArthur's successor, Lieutenant General Jonathan Wainwright, to his fate. Eisenhower kept trying, despite increasing feelings of helplessness, to get aid into the islands. "For many weeks—it seems years—I've been searching everywhere to find any feasible way of giving real help to the P.I.," he noted in his desk pad. "We've literally squandered money; we wrestled with the Navy, we've tried to think of anything that might promise even a modicum of help. I'll go on trying, but daily the situation grows more desperate."[31]

Marshall had asked Eisenhower to see what he could do about saving the Philippines and, by implication, to mollify MacArthur. In addition, Marshall had wanted Eisenhower to attempt to retrieve the situation in the Southwest Pacific. In none of these objectives had Eisenhower achieved success. But he had never thrown up his hands at the herculean task, had shown himself willing to assume responsibility, and had made himself invaluable to Marshall not only in handling details but in dealing with larger policy questions. Eisenhower had done as much as any man could have, but his efforts were fruitless.

CHAPTER 2

Establishing the Organization and the Strategy

The American problems in 1942 were to build an army, secure the shipping to get it overseas, establish an organization through which agreement could be reached with the British on a strategy to defeat Germany, and resist the pull of the Pacific. The Army's contribution to the solution to these problems was Marshall's responsibility and therefore Eisenhower's job. The way in which Eisenhower carried it out would depend, in part, on the nature of his relations with the Chief. Establishing an intimate relationship would not be easy, for the Chief was a stern man.

George Marshall's back had no bend to it. He carried himself lightly, with great dignity. His movements were deliberate, his shoulders square, his dress immaculate. His face looked as if it were chisled out of stone. Quietly handsome, a little too thin, he had a determined jaw, a firm mouth, and deep-set, penetrating eyes. The Chief of Staff commanded attention.

He was a cold, aloof person who forced everyone to keep his distance. Franklin Roosevelt had tried at their first meeting to call him "George," but Marshall let the President know the name was "General Marshall," and "General Marshall" it remained. He had few intimate friends. When he relaxed he did it alone, watching movies or puttering in his garden. His sense of humor was limited at best and he kept a tight grip on his emotions. If he had a weakness, it was that his sense of duty was so highly developed that he seemed almost inhuman, a sort of intellectual superman, and made small allowance for failings in others. Throughout his career he kept a little Black Book in which he listed the names of officers who had, at one time or another, disappointed him. When war came he used the book ruthlessly, shucking aside dozens of high-ranking officers without explanation or apology.[1]

To those who could do the work and who shared his sense of duty, Marshall was intensely loyal. He also felt deep affection toward them, but something, perhaps a natural shyness, or a fear of indulging in emotion, or a half-thought-out notion that it would make him appear weak, prevented him from ever showing his feelings, even to someone as close to him as Eisenhower came to be. Hardly anyone could resist Eisenhower's infectious grin and he was known throughout the Army by his catchy nickname "Ike." Eisenhower worked under Marshall for four years. For the first six months they met several times a day; thereafter they communicated almost daily and met often. Eisenhower was Marshall's personal protégé, and in four years the younger man never let the Chief of Staff down on a major matter. Yet in all that time Marshall never called him anything but "Eisenhower." (Only one time did Marshall slip and call him "Ike"; to make up for it he used "Eisenhower" five times in his next sentence.[2])

Once, when Eisenhower was in Marshall's office, a detail arose about an officer's promotion. After settling it, Marshall leaned forward and explained to Eisenhower his attitude toward promotion. "The men who are going to get the promotions in this war are the commanders in the field," he declared, "not the staff officers who clutter up all of the administrative machinery in the War Department. . . . The field commanders carry the responsibility and I'm going to see to it that they're properly rewarded so far as promotion can provide a reward." In the last war, Marshall explained, the staff had gotten everything. This time he was going to reverse the process.

"Take your case," he continued, looking right at Eisenhower. "I know that you were recommended by one general for division command and by another for corps command. That's all very well. I'm glad they have that opinion of you, but you are going to stay right here and fill your position, and that's that!" He had already made Eisenhower head of WPD, but no promotion accompanied the advance in status and responsibility.

Preparing to turn to other business, Marshall muttered, "While this may seem a sacrifice to you, that's the way it must be."

Eisenhower's sense of duty was almost as keen as Marshall's and he had already reached a rank he had not thought possible. He resented being singled out for the lecture, so impulsively he blurted out, "General, I'm interested in what you say, but I want you to know that I don't give a damn about your promotion plans as far as I'm concerned. I came into this office from the field and I am trying to do my duty. I expect to do so as long as you want me here. If that locks me to a desk for the rest of the war, so be it!"

Pushing back his chair, Eisenhower strode toward the door. It was a big office and a long walk. By the time he reached the door his anger had subsided. He turned, looked at Marshall, and grinned. As he closed the door he thought he detected a tiny smile at the corners of Marshall's mouth.

Two weeks later Marshall recommended Eisenhower for promotion to major general. In his recommendation to the President, Marshall explained that Eisenhower was not really a staff officer, but was his operations officer, a sort of subordinate commander. On March 27 Eisenhower got his second star.[3]

Eisenhower knew enough about the Chief not to try and thank him. When other promoted officers did try, Marshall would brush them aside with a terse "Thank yourself; if you hadn't earned it you would not have received it." After the war Eisenhower recalled, "The nearest that he ever came to saying [anything] complimentary directly to my face was, 'You are not doing so badly so far.' "[4]

There was a father-son quality to the Marshall-Eisenhower relationship, but it had a nineteenth- rather than twentieth-century flavor to it. They were never "pals." To the Chief's face, and in discussing him with others, Eisenhower always called him "General." Marshall was proud of Eisenhower and tried to guide him. Eisenhower respected the general, who had an enormous influence on his thought—there was never any doubt, throughout the war, that Marshall's was the guiding hand behind the broad policies.

Marshall's strengths were in the higher levels of policy, organization, and strategy. In these areas Eisenhower followed, for he was an operator rather than a theoretician, the perfect man to take Marshall's concepts and translate them into practice. The Supreme Allied Command in Europe would never have come about had it not been for Marshall's thought, driving force, and persuasive powers, but it would not have worked had it not been for Eisenhower.

The partnership began during the first weeks of the war; symbolically it took on the form it was to assume for much of the remainder of the conflict—a fight for American versus British ideas. Right after Pearl Harbor the British Prime Minister, Winston Churchill, and his Chiefs of Staff came to Washington to discuss grand strategy. The meetings began on December 4 (code name ARCADIA) and lasted until the middle of January. There were twelve meetings in all, several of which Eisenhower, as Gerow's deputy, attended.[5]

The conference was essentially an exploration. Each side was feeling the other out, for the extent of American mobilization was not yet known with any degree of accuracy and the Americans were preoccupied with the crushing events in the Pacific. What stood out was the agreement on grand strategy. The British had feared that the Americans would react to Pearl Harbor and the impending loss of the Philippines by abandoning RAINBOW 5 and turning full force on the Japanese. The Americans laid those fears to rest at the opening of the conference.

It was a great achievement and must always be kept in mind, for it is easy enough to present a picture of the Grand Alliance as being not so grand, to concentrate on the disagreements and to argue that the real story of World War II is British-American infighting, with the climax coming when the Americans imposed their will on the British. Any account of Eisenhower and the alliance will inevitably lean toward a picture of Anglo-American irritation, harassment, bitterness, and disagreement, because it was the issues the two sides did not agree upon that they talked about.

But this was the firmest alliance in history. The partners agreed upon the broad goal and the broad strategy—the total defeat of the Axis powers brought about by first assuming a defensive role in the Pacific and an offensive one in the Atlantic. That they stuck to the agreement was their greatest accomplishment. Agreement on implementation was never easily reached, however, and except for Operation OVERLORD it is difficult to find an operation in the war about which both sides were enthusiastic. The disagreements began at ARCADIA.

In December 1941 Marshall and the Americans were willing to bide their time. They did not intend to defer to the British, but in the first wartime meeting they were ready to keep their own ideas in the background. The British had been at war for more than two years and had gained invaluable experience. Britain was fully mobilized and in terms of striking forces available much more powerful than the United States. American potential loomed in the background, but it would be a year or more before the country was tooled up for the war. The British were engaged with the European Axis; the Americans were not. Under the circumstances, the Americans allowed the British to take the initiative and to make the proposals, contenting themselves with commenting upon them.

The British proposed, in briefest terms, to close and tighten a ring around Germany and then, when all the signs were favorable, plunge in the knife. They were detailed and exact in their proposals about closing the ring, vague about the final battle in northwestern Europe. Churchill argued that for the final attack "it need not be assumed that great numbers of men are required," and contended that 600,000 troops would be sufficient. He did warn that enormous amounts of material would be required. He thought one of the Allies' greatest advantages was the population of western Europe; especially France, and a major task of the British and Americans would be to get arms into the hands of these people. It was traditional British strategy writ large— England (and the United States) would supply the money and arms, while the Continentals did their own fighting. The program "was tailored to suit scattered interests, a small-scale economy and limited manpower for ground armies, and to exploit sea- and air-power."[6]

For the immediate future, the British proposed operations in the Middle East and on the North African coast, looking toward a 1943 invasion of Europe "either across the Mediterranean or from Turkey into the Balkans. . . ." Churchill felt that the Vichy French could be persuaded to co-operate with the British and Americans, and offered as an initial step an invasion of North Africa by 100,000 men, mostly British. The idea had a great appeal for Roosevelt, who laid it down as a principle to Marshall that it was "very important to morale, to give this country a feeling that they are in the war, to give the Germans the reverse effect, to have American troops somewhere in active fighting across the Atlantic" in 1942.[7]

The War Department position differed radically. WPD had classified as subsidiary theaters not only the Far East but also the Iberian Peninsula, the Scandinavian Peninsula, Africa, and the Middle East. The American premise, which was Marshall's and from which he never wavered, was that the plains of northwestern Europe constituted the main theater, where "we must come to grips with the enemy ground forces."[8] It soon became apparent that the difficulty was that no attack on the main theater could be launched in 1942, so if the President's dictum was to be met it would have to be elsewhere.

Much of the next two years would be taken up with arguments about Marshall's conception of the quickest and surest way of defeating Germany. During ARCADIA, however, the Americans did not push. They agreed to study GYMNAST, the North African operation, and to begin implementing MAGNET, which sent American troops to Northern Ireland, allowing the British to release troops in the home islands for the Middle East.

At ARCADIA, Marshall was more concerned with organization than with strategy. Where to fight the war could be worked out later, but how to fight it had to be settled immediately. The *sine qua non* of Allied success, Marshall felt, was the adoption of the concept of unity of command.

This concept differed radically from the British practice. In their most active theater, the Middle East, as elsewhere, the British worked with a committed system. The senior army, air, and naval officers formed a group called the Commanders in Chief and directed the war in that theater, subject to close supervision from London. The system had the advantage of avoiding any instance in which a general gave an order to an admiral, or vice versa, while it had the inherent disadvantage of most committees trying to operate in a crisis situation.

Following the first ARCADIA meeting, Eisenhower wrote a memorandum for Marshall on the subject of unity of command. He did not intend to influence Marshall's thinking, but rather to supply him with arguments, since the Chief was going to make his bid for agreement in principle at the next day's meeting. Eisenhower began by pointing out that in the Southwest Pacific there were several separate forces operating, each independent of all the others—the American Air Force, the American Asiatic Fleet, the Australian Forces (which consisted of three separate arms), the British Army, Navy, and Air Force, and the Dutch land, sea, and air forces. It was obvious, Eisenhower said, that "the strength of the allied defenses in the entire theater would be greatly increased through single, intelligent command." He realized that with the number of independent national interests involved, as well as the separate organizations represented, "real unity of command cannot be achieved suddenly," but did feel that it could be achieved in small localities such as Singapore, where "the paramount interest and the vast majority of the forces concerned are British." He pointed out that "unification of British forces could be accomplished by a single order from the head of the government," while the forces of the other powers in the area could be directed to report to the British supreme commander for orders.

Eisenhower was trying to slip in the principle through the back door by getting the British to adopt it in their current hot spot (in return for dropping their committee system, the British would get command of the small American forces in the area). Hopefully, then, the British would not object when the principle was applied elsewhere, over a broader area.

Marshall, however, felt there was no hope of success in Singapore—the old salts in the Admiralty would never allow a British general to direct their fight, and the British Army felt the same way about the Royal Navy. In any case Marshall was after bigger game, and he therefore rejected Eisenhower's recommendation.[9] Instead, at the Christmas afternoon meeting, which Eisenhower attended, Marshall used the opportunity presented by a discussion on the question of reinforcements for MacArthur to broach the larger issue. He said it was too early to make a decision on aid for the Philippines and in any case it was not an appropriate topic for the Chiefs of Staff. If they were to become involved in the details on what went to each local commander it would take all their time. By the same token no local commander could see the situation whole and each would be demanding everything he could think of for his particular locality. In a world-wide war this was intolerable. The Allies needed someone in between the Chiefs and the local commanders—they needed, in short, a supreme theater commander.

The most important consideration before the ARCADIA conference, Marshall maintained, was unity of command. "I am convinced," he said, "that there must be one man in command of the entire theater—air, ground, and ships. We cannot manage by cooperation. Human frailties are such that there would be emphatic unwillingness to place portions of troops under another service. If we can make a plan for unified command now, it will solve nine-tenths of our troubles." Marshall realized there were objections but felt they were "much less than the hazards that must be faced" by the Allies if they failed to achieve unity of command. He wanted one man, operating under instructions from a combined body in Washington, to direct operations in each theater. "We had to come to this in the First World War," he concluded, "but it was not until 1918 that it was accomplished, and much valuable time, blood and treasure had been needlessly sacrificed."[10]

Raising the specter of World War I failed to move the British. They had not expected Marshall's proposal and were unwilling to discuss it until they had an opportunity to sound out the Prime Minister. Realizing that he had made a tactical blunder by not preparing the ground, Marshall closed the meeting, cornered Eisenhower, and told him to draft immediately a letter of instruction for the prospective supreme commander of the Pacific area, the only theater in which combined (multinational) forces were then operating. By showing the British something concrete, Marshall hoped to convince them that "no real risk would be involved to the interests of any of the Associated Powers, while on the other hand great profits should result."

Eisenhower, made cautious by Marshall, placed drastic limits on the supreme commander. In his draft he said that the commander had no authority to move ground forces from one territory to another within the theater and could move only those air forces that the governments concerned chose to put at his disposal. He had no power to relieve national commanders or their subordinates, to interfere in the tactical organization and disposition of their forces, to commandeer their supplies, or to control their communications with their respective governments. These limitations, as severe as those under which Marshal Foch operated in 1918, were drastic. Eisenhower and Marshall defended them on the grounds that they represented the best that could be accomplished. Marshall declared, "If the supreme commander ended up with no more authority than to tell Washington what he wanted, such a situation was better than nothing, and an improvement over the present situation." The command would be called ABDA—Australian, British, Dutch, American.[11]

Marshall showed Eisenhower's draft to the President, who approved. To sweeten the pill for the British, Marshall proposed that General Sir Archibald Wavell, a British ground commander, become Supreme Commander, ABDA. The United States Navy objected to Wavell, but Marshall won them over. He then presented the proposal to the next ARCADIA meeting. The British Navy "kicked like bay steers," but after some backing and hedging, Marshall received their assent. He had achieved his main goal for ARCADIA—agreement on unity of command.[12]

A long discussion over who should give directives to Wavell followed; eventually, following the British lead, the Chiefs agreed that Wavell should report to and receive his directives from a committee—the Combined Chiefs of Staff (CCS). It would be composed of the Chiefs of Staff of the two nations, and would sit permanently in Washington, where the British Chiefs of Staff (BCOS) would be represented by a permanent Joint Staff Mission, headed by Field Marshall Sir John Dill, former Chief of the Imperial General Staff. In international conferences—such as ARCADIA—the BCOS members would act for themselves.[13] To

create a parallel organization to BCOS, the Americans created the Joint
Chiefs of Staff (JCS), composed of Marshall, General Henry H. Arnold
of the Army Air Forces, the Commander in Chief, U. S. Fleet, and
soon to be Chief of Naval Operations Admiral Ernest King, and—
somewhat later—Roosevelt's personal Chief of Staff, Admiral William
Leahy. The JCS would be responsible for the higher direction of the
American war effort.[14]

This meant, in practice, increased work for WPD, for Marshall was
the dominant personality on the JCS. He would now be involved daily
in discussions of world-wide strategy, and it was to WPD that he looked
for help. The work load was already great enough; as Eisenhower told
a friend who was coming to Washington to join the War Department,
"Just to give you an inkling as to the kind of mad house you are
getting into, it is now eight o'clock New Year's Eve. I have a couple
hours' work ahead of me, and tomorrow will be no different from
today. I have been here about three weeks and this noon I had my
first luncheon outside of the office." Usually he ate a hot dog at his
desk. He lived with his brother Milton, a government employee who
had a home in Falls Church, Virginia, and not once did he see the
house in daylight. He would arrive after dark, have a drink and dinner,
play with Milton's children for a few minutes, and fall into bed. In the
morning he left before daylight.[15]

Despite the daily strain and tension under which he worked, Eisenhower
bore up well, presenting the appearance of a faceless, tireless staff
officer. The mask came off, briefly, when on March 10 his seventy-
nine-year-old father died. Eisenhower confessed that he felt terrible.
"I should like so much to be with my Mother these few days." He could
not, for "we're at war! And war is not soft—it has no time to indulge even
the deepest and most sacred emotions." On March 11 his father was
buried. For thirty minutes Eisenhower closed his office door and shut
off all business, "to have that much time, by myself, to think of him."
Eisenhower thought of his five brothers, of his mother, of his father's
reputation in Abilene, of how proud he was to be his father's son. "He
was a just man," Eisenhower said, "well liked, well educated, a thinker.
He was undemonstrative, quiet, modest, and of exemplary habits. . . .
He was an uncomplaining person in the face of adversity, and such
plaudits as were accorded him did not inflate his ego." Finally, the only
regret: "It was always so difficult to let him know the great depth of my
affection for him."

At 7:30 P.M. Eisenhower noted simply, "I love my Dad," closed his office, and went home. "I haven't the heart to go on tonight."[16]

On February 16 Gerow assumed a field command and Eisenhower took charge of WPD. At the time Marshall was in the midst of a reorganization of the War Department. For Eisenhower, the result was increased responsibility. After noting in his desk pad that "The Joint and Combined staff work is terrible! Takes an unconscionable amount of time," he declared. "We are faced with a big reorganization of W.D. We need it! The [General Staff] is all to be cut down, except W.P.D.—which now has all the Joint and Combined work, all plans and all operations so far as active theaters are concerned!" Continuing to pour out his frustrations, he added, "Fox Conner was right about allies. He could well have included the Navy!"[17]

The key feature of the reorganization as a whole (completed on March 23) was the unequivocal grant of broad power over the entire Army to the Chief of Staff. Inevitably in practice this resulted in placing power in the hands of Eisenhower's division, renamed the Operations Division (OPD), since it was to that agency that Marshall turned for strategic plans and directives and the transmission of orders to theaters.[18]

Although Eisenhower headed OPD, although OPD was Marshall's command post, and although Marshall had enormous powers, neither Eisenhower nor Marshall nor anyone else was, at any time, solely responsible for the strategic direction of the war. The conflict was too vast, the commitment of men and material too great for anyone to have the situation as a whole complete in his mind. It took dozens of men to work out the details of allocation of resources, industrial priorities, shipping space, and supply problems, to plan and execute operations involving hundreds of thousands of men, ships, and planes. All big offensives needed a lead time of from three to six months to prepare. In the first two years of American participation, shortages of everything compounded the problem. "It's a back breaking job to get a single battle order out," Eisenhower noted, "and then it can't be executed for from 3–4 months!!!"[19]

Even had there been someone in the War Department trying to run the entire show himself, he would have met constant frustration. Marshall, Eisenhower, and OPD were not working in a vacuum; their solutions often did not agree with those of the U. S. Navy or the President and seldom were they in complete accord with the British. Eisenhower put it succinctly: "In a war such as this, where high command invariably involves a Pres., a Prime Minister, 6 Chiefs of Staff and a horde of lesser 'planners' there has got to be a lot of patience—no one person can be a Napoleon or a Caesar!" Still, it was frustrating. "My God," he declared, "how I hate to work by any method that forces me to depend on anyone else."[20]

All of which does not mean that OPD played a minimal role in the war. Marshall's authority over the United States Army was complete, and he exercised it mainly through OPD. His voice carried great weight with the President, the Prime Minister, and on the CCS, and he relied upon OPD for background material and detailed planning. Marshall set the goals, while OPD prepared the studies that showed how they could be accomplished.

In February 1942 what Marshall wanted was a coherent statement that he could present to the President and to the CCS which would outline a general strategy for the war. Eisenhower prepared it for him toward the end of the month. It began with a question. "What are the vital tasks that must be performed by the United Nations in order to avoid defeat [during the period while they prepared for an offensive]?" Eisenhower's answer was to secure the North American citadel, maintain England, assist Russia to stay in the war, and secure the Indian-Middle East position. He realized that there were many other tasks that would contribute greatly to the goal, but classified them as "highly desirable" rather than as a "must," resting his classification on a rule used in OPD: "Will the loss of the particular area render our strategic situation so desperate as to make an eventual victory practically impossible?" Under that criterion, the Southwest Pacific was only very important, not vital.

Eisenhower's second question was, where could an eventual offensive be launched that would do most toward defeating the Axis? His answer was short: "An attack through Western Europe." He then developed the detailed reasoning behind the proposal. The major Allied problem was shortage of ships and an attack through western Europe involved the shortest possible sea routes, thus placing *a minimum strain upon shipping.* The sea lanes to England had to be maintained in order to feed the British whether or not an American build-up in England took place, so creating a theater in western Europe did not involve dispersion of escorting vessels for ships. The base for the proposed theater would be England; if the United States immediately began building up air and ground forces on the island it would constitute a threat which Germany could not ignore, thus forcing the enemy to leave some of its divisions in France and thereby aiding the Russians. Land communications in western Europe were superior to those available "in any other area from which either enemy can be attacked." England already had airfields from which a large air force could operate to secure air superiority, a *sine qua non* of a successful assault. "Nowhere else is there such a base, so favorably situated with respect to either of our enemies."

In conclusion, Eisenhower emphasized that the recommendation offered "the only feasible method for employing offensively a major portion of the British combat power." If a large offensive were attempted else-where, the British would have to keep a large proportion of their forces at home, "useless, except for the protection of that island." Finally, Eisenhower scribbled by hand, "It attempts to attack our principal enemy while he is engaged on several fronts; hence speed in preparation is important."

Eisenhower's plan was bold and imaginative, and—for 1942 at least—impossible. Like his countrymen, when he was confronted with a problem Eisenhower tended to overcome it through the most direct and quickest method possible. The United States had been in the war for only three months, had no combat-ready divisions in England, could expect to get no more than a dozen there by the end of the year, had a quarter-trained, inadequately equipped air force that had practically no combat experience, a Navy whose principal fighting ships rested at the bottom of the sea and which had hardly any assault landing craft, and a General Staff that was in the midst of a badly needed reorganization. Yet Eisenhower was proposing that this nation immediately plan to come to grips with the mighty Wehrmacht and Luftwaffe in an all-out campaign on the plains of northwestern Europe.

Eisenhower did recognize certain possible objections, chief of which was "the difficulty of organizing, on the shores of Western Europe, a force of sufficient strength to meet the hostile opposition that could be brought against it." To be successful, he realized, the plan needed the complete and enthusiastic support of the CCS, overwhelming air support, ample landing craft, and sufficient shipping to support the operation. And, the Allies would have to husband their combat power "to acquire the necessary strength, and avoid the evils of unjustified dispersion." In short, Eisenhower wanted to skip that part of Churchill's program that called for closing the ring before engaging the bulk of the Wehrmacht on the Continent.

Since planners could not plan unless they had a definite target, Eisenhower argued that, if the British did not agree, "we must turn our backs upon the Eastern Atlantic and go, full out, as quickly as possible, against Japan!" This threat to abandon the British if they refused to follow American strategic conceptions would later be used by Marshall and King. It had a hollow ring to it. Commander in Chief Roosevelt never gave it serious consideration and it is doubtful if even the War Department did. Certainly there was never enough detailed planning done to make the threat believable. The Americans were simply too impressed by the logic of their own arguments about the strategic advantages of fighting in Europe, Germany was so obviously the major threat, Japan's resources were so clearly limited, and American historic, cultural, and economic interests were so much more important in Europe than in Asia, that it would have been inconceivable for the United States to turn its back upon Europe "and go, full out, as quickly as possible, against Japan!"

There were, to be sure, deep emotional currents in the United States that would have supported such a switch in grand strategy. The country had been humiliated at Pearl Harbor. The men of Bataan had evoked a response of admiration and a determination to avenge them. The racist overtones to the war in the Pacific made that conflict, in the eyes of millions of Americans, more important than the war in Europe. Finally, at the time Eisenhower made the threat, the Japanese were winning everywhere. But none of these factors, real as they were, negated the basic arguments Eisenhower developed earlier about the advantages of Europe as the main theater.

In his late February memorandum, Eisenhower emphasized the over-riding reason for a Europe-first strategy. The fundamental fact of World War II, from June 21, 1941, onwards, was the Russo-German war. Here was where the major forces were engaged, where the greatest killing was done, where the stakes were highest. Whoever won on Germany's eastern front would win the war. On the banks of the Volga, where Germany had made by far her largest commitment, and not in the South China Sea or in the central Pacific or even in the desert around Tobruk, the issue would be decided. Under the circumstances, the first priority for the Western Allies was to keep Russia in the war.

To do so, Eisenhower declared, it was necessary to provide maximum material aid through lend-lease and to "conduct such operations as will directly and indirectly assist in taking the pressure off of the Russian Armies." The threat of the build-up in England would help accomplish this, as would direct support of the Middle East, by keeping Germany and Japan separated and denying to Germany badly needed oil. But the major help the Allies could give would be in opening a second front. Eisenhower felt that if this could not be done in the summer of 1942, then the Allies should send more of their major strength into the Middle East. He realized this would delay the opening of the second front, but "if the diversion must be made, we should realize it promptly and act accordingly."[21]

Nothing in Eisenhower's program was new. Marshall had long since been advancing its major provisions. The memorandum did swing the War Department's attention back to Europe, and at Marshall's request Eisenhower, on February 28, submitted a fuller, more formal study. He included most of his arguments from his earlier memorandum but made significant additions. He began by pointing out that "time works in our favor. The hostile power is now at its maximum, ours will grow—provided none of the principal members of the United Powers is defeated and forced to capitulate."

The main thrust of Eisenhower's argument was to differentiate between operations which were *"necessary* to the ultimate defeat of the Axis Powers" and those which "are merely *desirable."* In the first category he placed the maintenance of the United Kingdom, the retention of Russia in the war, and the safety of the India-Middle East theater. Things which were merely desirable were, in order of priority, security of Alaska, holding bases west and southwest of Hawaii, security of Burma, security of South America, security of Australia, and maintaining the trans-African air route. Eisenhower insisted that the distinction between the necessary and the desirable had to be "rigidly observed," and that the Allies hold strictly to the principle that *"minima* should be diverted to secondary or merely desirable objectives, while *maxima* are to be striven for in primary, essential, operations."

In the case of helping Russia, Eisenhower argued that it would not be sufficient to urge upon the Soviets the indirect advantages that would accrue to them from Allied operations in remote theaters, nor would it suffice to step up lend-lease. The United States could not expect to win the war by paying others to do the fighting. *"Russia's problem is to sustain herself during the coming summer,"* Eisenhower declared, "and she must not be permitted to reach such a precarious position that she will accept a negotiated peace, no matter how unfavorable to herself, in preference to a continuation of the fight." The Western Allies had to initiate operations that would draw off sizable portions of the Wehrmacht; the operations had to be *"so conceived, and so presented to the Russians, that they will recognize the importance of the support rendered."* An immediate air offensive from England against Germany, with a ground offensive to follow, *"is indicated."*

The Eisenhower program represented a compromise between two schools of thought then current in Washington. Some War Department officers, especially in the Army Air Force, were arguing that the United States should abandon Australia and New Zealand, pull all the way back to Hawaii, build a passive defense there, and throw everything else into Europe. In the Navy there was strong sentiment, shared to a certain extent by Admiral King, to leave Europe to the British and go all out in Asia. Eisenhower's middle way became the accepted strategy, partly because it reflected Marshall's and Roosevelt's thinking, partly because it was the most logical—what was the point of using dreadfully scarce shipping to pull troops out of an unthreatened Australia?

Eisenhower used his strongest arguments against the Asia-first advocates. He pointed out that both the War and Navy Departments had long ago agreed that in case of a two-ocean war the United States would make its major offensive effort in Europe. He realized that some Navy Department officials now wanted to change that commitment. Their latest argument was that it was a strategic axiom that, when a divided enemy was encountered, the weaker portion should be attacked and defeated first, and in this war the European Axis was far stronger than the Japanese. Eisenhower denounced such reasoning as "without validity." Military estimates, he pointed out, were based on *"relative power at a particular point* of actual or possible contact." Japan was relatively stronger in Asia than Germany and Italy were in Europe, both because of the Japanese geographical position and because of the relatively small force that could be brought to bear and maintained against her. "This is particularly true as long as Russia is in the war."

If the Russo-German war was the first fact of World War II, until 1944 the second was to be the relative scarcity of British-American shipping, because it made it difficult for America to exert her great strength. Thus, in addition to all the other arguments in favor of a European rather than Asian offensive, the final, unanswerable one was, "To conduct a war in East Asia requires, for the same number of troops to be maintained there by U.S. and England, at least three, possibly four, times the shipping needed for a force of similar strength in the Western Atlantic." The United States had to "seek for the shortest possible line of overseas communication to our major effort."[22]

Marshall read and approved Eisenhower's memorandum. It, and other studies, became the basis on which the Joint U. S. Strategic Committee, an agency of the JCS, considered future strategy. On March 6 the committee accepted Eisenhower's arguments and declared itself in favor of the general principle, "If the war is to be won in Europe, land forces must be developed and trained which are capable of landing on the continent and advancing under the support of an overwhelming air force." This required "strict economy of force in other theaters."[23]

The United States now had a strategic solution to the problem of victory in World War II. The British had accepted the major organization concepts, an over-all directing committee composed of the Chiefs of Staff, and unity of command within a theater. The task now was to throw out the rather vague agreements about closing the ring that the Americans had accepted at ARCADIA and get the British to adopt Marshall's strategic formulation of an early assault on the Continent. To that task the War Department began to devote its energies.

CHAPTER 3

BOLERO: The Build-up in England

If the Americans had a program, so did the British, and they had no hesitation about criticizing Marshall's ideas. In the middle of March 1942 the British Joint Staff Mission in Washington presented for planning use a study that called for landing British forces near Le Havre, France, early in the summer of 1943, but only "under conditions of severe deterioration of German military power." The British flatly stated that the operation would have to be postponed if the enemy had not already been "weakened in strength and morale."[1] Thus while the Americans saw the cross-Channel assault as the chief method to defeat Germany, the British viewed it as a mopping-up operation which would follow the closing and tightening of the ring.

The conceptual difference was crucial, for the Americans could not even dream of going it alone. Any cross-Channel assault in 1942, and even in 1943, would have to be primarily British. OPD estimates were that by July 1 the United States could ship to the British Isles exactly no ground forces, by October 1 some 70,000, and by January 1, 1943, only 207,000. Since Marshall, Eisenhower, and all others concerned agreed that it would take 600,000 ground troops to cause a material diversion of German forces from the Russian front, there was no doubt that the American "force available for the European Theater is not adequate immediately for a major offensive."[2]

Or at least for a major offensive in western Europe. Other areas, notably Norway and North Africa, were available. Churchill was a strong advocate of either or both theaters and the War Department had additionally to operate under the constant pressure of Roosevelt's dictum that American troops had to be fighting Germans somewhere in 1942. The great advantage of the peripheral theaters was that the Germans could not bring much strength to bear in them, so fewer American forces would be needed. The great difficulty was that, once involved in a theater other than France, the United States would find its resources being drained and the second front delayed.

Marshall and Eisenhower had a complicated task. They had to convince the British of the feasibility of a cross-Channel attack before Germany was seriously weakened while simultaneously fending off the President. For Roosevelt's benefit they had to act as if a 1942 invasion was their objective, but because they recognized that this was almost impossible, even with British support, when presenting their plans to London they had to soft-pedal 1942 and argue for the possibilities in 1943. Marshall, Eisenhower, and OPD tried to carry water on both shoulders, but the lack of candor made them vulnerable and led to their eventual failure.

The first OPD official to urge realism about 1942 was one of Eisenhower's most capable subordinates, Colonel Thomas T. Handy, a Virginia Military Institute graduate who would become a full general and Eisenhower's successor as head of OPD. Handy insisted that Eisenhower and OPD—and by inference Marshall—accept the fact that America could make no important contribution to a 1942 invasion and that the British, deeply involved in the Middle East, could hardly do it alone. Other problems, principally the absence of shipping and landing craft, also had to be faced.[3]

Facing tactical reality did not mean abandoning strategic concepts.[4] Marshall continued to ask Eisenhower for staff studies that would emphasize the importance of the second front and the British soon proved temporarily willing to accept Eisenhower's conclusions. Agreement on a second front sometime in the future, after all, could and did lead to an immediate build-up of American forces, especially air forces, in the British Isles, which released British troops for the Middle East. Churchill and his advisers recognized as one of their major problems the need to keep Marshall and the American Army reasonably content, for Marshall could always threaten to turn away from Europe and go to the Pacific. Through the late winter and spring of 1942 each side was, in a sense, toying with the other, making concessions when necessary, insisting on fundamental points when they had to. It was a frustrating time for everyone, but especially for the Americans, since their potential power was so great, their actual strength so small, and their firmly held ideas so different from those of the British. It did not help that the role they were forced to play was that of supplicant.

The crucial problem was to obtain immediate agreement on the objective, both in order to aid Russia and to give some coherence to the American build-up. The United States was planning to raise two hundred divisions and the world's largest air force. If this were done in a strategic vacuum the result would be chaos. As Eisenhower put it in a memorandum he prepared for Marshall on March 25, setting an objective would "govern training and production programs and will constitute a basis on which subsidiary decisions, involving necessary dispersion of forces, will be made."

Eisenhower's March 25 memorandum contained all of the arguments he had earlier advanced in favor of a Europe-first strategy and an early opening of the second front, but this time Eisenhower put the emphasis upon the need for decision. "The question of time is, of course, of the utmost importance," he said. "Manifestly if all United Nations unified their most strenuous efforts toward preparation for a single agreed upon purpose the results that can be accomplished will bear no comparison to those that will follow disorganized, unintensive and diverse activity."[5]

After reading the memorandum, Marshall penned a note on a separate slip of paper: "Hold for me. GCM." He then went to have lunch at the White House with Stimson, Secretary of the Navy Frank Knox, Admiral King, General Arnold, Harry Hopkins, the President's adviser, and Roosevelt. Marshall presented Eisenhower's arguments for a cross-Channel attack. Roosevelt played the devil's advocate, arguing for more intensive activity in the Pacific, but Marshall finally won him over. The President told the Chief to get the details worked out.[6] By March 27 the OPD planners had outlined an invasion scheme indicating an April 1943 assault somewhere between Le Havre and Boulogne. Eisenhower and Handy, the head of OPD's new Strategy and Policy Group, carefully reviewed the proposal before submitting it to Marshall on April 1.

The memorandum, entitled "Operations in Western Europe," was thus a staff product, but throughout it carried Eisenhower's personal touch. The main conclusions were his and of course they represented Marshall's thought. The object of the plan was to convince the British that something could be done on the Continent before the Germans were on the verge of collapse and to satisfy the President that American troops would be fighting Germans before the end of the year.

The paper began with a restatement of the advantages of making western Europe the theater in which to stage the first Allied offensive. A new advantage concerned timing, on which OPD, at Roosevelt's insistence, was becoming more specific. France offered "a unique opportunity to establish an active sector . . . this summer, through steadily increasing air operations and by raids or forays all along the coasts." These operations would have the major advantage of providing "some help to Russia and immediate satisfaction to the public." Even more important, OPD felt, they would make experienced veterans of the air and ground units and prevent the deterioration in morale which might otherwise come about as a result of prolonged inactivity. Much of the remainder of the paper consisted of detailed recommendations for the size and area of these raids.

The other main theme was what could be done by the Allies in 1943. Continuous staff study had shown that the United States could have, by the early spring of 1943, more than enough planes, troops, and equipment for an invasion. The two bottlenecks were shipping and landing craft. If the British would take up sixty per cent of the shipping, that problem could be solved; through intensive effort, the United States should be able to produce enough landing craft.

Assuming that the British were prepared to supply at least half the combat forces, OPD was prepared to recommend "an attack, by combined forces of approximately 5,800 combat airplanes and 48 divisions, against Western Europe as soon as the necesssry means can be accumulated in England—estimated at April 1, 1943, provided decision is made *now* and men, material and shipping are not further dispersed." The attack would begin with a six-division assault between Le Havre and Boulogne.

OPD's plan assumed that Russia, with the assistance of the raids against the French coast and lend-lease aid, could stay in the fight. If this assumption proved unfounded, the entire plan was academic. To deal with a changed situation, OPD included in the memorandum a modified plan, one which would be justified only if the situation on the Russian front became desperate, or the German situation in western Europe deteriorated. "Because of the emergency basis on which a modified plan would be undertaken," OPD emphasized, "it is impossible to predict the time for its execution" or even the minimum scale on which it could be initiated. The only thing that was clear was that nothing could be done before September 1942.

The modified plan called for a suicide operation against France. The Allies would attempt to establish and hold a beachhead with what amounted to a large-scale raiding party. The major purpose would be to draw the German Air Force into a battle of destruction with the Royal Air Force and whatever American planes were available, under conditions favorable to the Allies, and thus relieve pressure on the Russians.[7]

The plan for an emergency landing in 1942 came to be known as SLEDGEHAMMER, the one for a permanent landing in 1943 became ROUNDUP. As soon as Eisenhower handed Marshall the OPD study the Chief, accompanied by Stimson, took it to the President. Roosevelt endorsed the proposal. Hopkins suggested that Marshall should take the plan directly to London. Roosevelt agreed, and directed Marshall and Hopkins to go at once to obtain support from Churchill and his military advisers. In early April they left for England.

For six days Marshall met daily with the British Chiefs of Staff to present the American plan.[8] On April 14 the Bristish accepted the American proposal. The Japanese had just stepped up their activities in the Indian Ocean area and the British insisted that all necessary measures be taken to prevent a German-Japanese link-up in the Middle East. This was consistent with OPD thinking and the Americans readily agreed. Marshall was elated, but he recognized certain danger signs, reporting back to the War Department, "Everyone agrees . . . in principle but many if not most hold reservations regarding this or that."[9]

The British had agreed to accept and implement Operation BOLERO, the build-up of American resources in the United Kingdom, aiming toward SLEDGEHAMMER (if necessary or possible) and more specifically toward ROUNDUP. British agreement meant OPD had won a great victory, but Eisenhower, like Marshall, was restrained. On April 20 he noted, "I hope that—at long last, and after months of struggle . . . we are all definitely committed to one concept of fighting! If we can agree on major purposes and objectives, our efforts will begin to fall in line and we won't just be thrashing around in the dark."[10]

The day he made the note, Eisenhower had a conference with Marshall to discuss organization for BOLERO planning. Major General James E. Chaney was already in London as commanding general of the U. S. Army forces in the British Isles. Marshall decided, for the present, to keep Chaney there to carry on the necessary negotiations with the British government for arrangements for the arriving American troops. Chaney would have serving under him an air commander, a ground crops commander for England, another corps commander for Northern Ireland, and an over-all Services of Supply (SOS) commander. Marshall wanted the corps commanders to spend some time in OPD before going over in order to familiarize themselves with the operation.[11]

With the organization presumably set, OPD began its detailed work. It quickly became clear that the fears Marshall and Eisenhower had expressed were real. On May 5 the War Department learned that the

President, giving in to pressure from the Australian government, the Navy, and MacArthur, had decided to increase the U.S. ground forces in Australia by 25,000 men and the air forces there by 100 planes. Marshall asked Eisenhower to draft a memorandum to the President. Eisenhower had it ready that afternoon. Speaking for Marshall, Eisenhower began: "My mission to England was greatly embarrassed by the fact that we could propose only 2½ divisions to participate in a cross-channel operation by September 15th. Not only was this a very small force but in order to gather even that number of troops in the British Isles we were forced to set the late date of mid-September." If 25,000 men went to Australia, it would make "it impossible for us to contribute more than a division and a half for the cross-channel operation. . . ."

The War Department would spend much of its time in the first year of the war pointing out to the President the implications of his meddling in military matters. Roosevelt had a tendency to thrust himself into the middle of a situation, give it a casual study, and then order this or that action. He often threw the whole operation into chaos. On the domestic front, during the New Deal, the practice had worked, even though it created a tizzy among the bureaucrats. During the war, when operations needed a lead time of six months for planning and involved millions of men and thousands of ships, interference in the middle of a situation meant the end of the operation.

Eisenhower made this perfectly clear. He emphasized that the two and a half divisions the Americans had offered the British for BOLERO were "insufficient" and had to be increased. If the President's decision to send troops to Australia were implemented the result would be to cut the number of men available for BOLERO by fifty per cent. Eisenhower told Roosevelt that if his decision were carried out "our recent proposal to the British Government for 1942 has, in effect, largely been cancelled." Roosevelt was, in short, making a decision against BOLERO.[12]

The next day the Navy entered the fray. Admiral King wrote Roosevelt to say that, "important as the mounting of BOLERO may be, the Pacific problem is no less so, and is certainly the more urgent—it must be faced *now*." He said the United States needed enough force there "to hold what we have against any attack that the Japanese are capable of launching against us." Marshall got a copy of King's note and replied the same day. After reviewing the strategic debate that led to BOLERO and arguing that it "is impossible to make every point in the island chain impregnable," he asked the President to make a decision between BOLERO and Australia.

Roosevelt was an expert in taking care of bickerings between agencies. As soon as he was aware of the issues involved he adroitly handled the Marshall-King dispute. On May 6 he told Marshall he had never issued a directive calling for an increase of strength in Australia, but had only asked if "this could properly be done." He understood now that it was "inadvisable." The President concluded bluntly, "I do not want 'Bolero' slowed down."[13]

The incident had been settled in two days, but it left a heritage of apprehension in the War Department. Eisenhower noted that "Bolero is *supposed* to have the approval of the Pres and Prime Minister. But the struggle to get everyone behind it, and to keep the highest authority from wrecking it by making additional commitments of air-ships-troops elsewhere is never ending." Turning to a more general theme, he sadly reflected, "The actual fact is that not 1 man in 20 in the Govt. (including the W. and N. Depts) realizes what a grisly, dirty, tough business we are in! They think we can buy victory!"

The President was not the only source of frustration. As early as February, Eisenhower had complained about the relative lack of urgency in the landing craft program. In May the problem was still there. The Navy had given top priority to building escorting vessels for convoys, a decision with which Eisenhower had no quarrel—there could be no BOLERO if the Americans could not get their convoys to England. Many of the nation's shipyards concentrated on building merchant ships; again, Eisenhower obviously approved. The trouble was that the Navy also wanted to rebuild its capital ship fleet and as a result the landing craft program, despite verbal agreement as to its necessity, was stuck in a rut. From Eisenhower's point of view there was no point to bringing men and equipment to England unless the landing craft were available to carry them the last few miles across the Channel. Even had he forgotten it, the British had not and would make sure the question remained at the fore, since their arguments against SLEDGEHAMMER and even ROUNDUP would center around the lack of landing craft.

Eisenhower, along with Hull and Wedemeyer of OPD, was a member of a subcommittee of the Washington BOLERO committee, called the "Special Committee on Landing Craft for the Continent." On May 6, the day Roosevelt reiterated his support for BOLERO, Eisenhower attended a meeting of the subcommittee. The results were disappointing and at noon Eisenhower returned to his desk to ask, on his pad, some questions: "Who is responsible for bldg. landing craft? What types are they bldg? Are they suitable for cross channel work? Will the number of each type be sufficient? etc?" And finally, "How in hell can we win this war unless we can crack some heads?"[14]

On May 11 Eisenhower was able to turn his attention away from details and concentrate on the question of command structure in England. Major General Joseph T. McNarney, Marshall's deputy chief of staff, had just submitted a proposed organizational chart under the heading "U.S. Set-up for Administrative Purposes." McNarney's chart showed, for the United States, the commanding general, and under him the commanders of U.S. ground forces, air forces, SOS, and naval forces. McNarney put the entire BOLERO operation under the BOLERO Task Force commander, presumably British, who would report to the CCS. Marshall asked Eisenhower to study McNarney's chart and comment on it.[15]

Eisenhower began by questioning the advisability of McNarney's use of the word "administrative," since it implied definite limitations upon the authority of the officer. Eisenhower insisted that he should be "a Theater Commander in every sense of the word" with full responsibility. In the American Army the tradition was to delegate almost complete authority to the field commander, but this was not the British practice. He felt it was important to emphasize to the British the powers of the chief Army officer in England, so that the British would not be turning to Washington whenever an important question arose. This could be accomplished most easily by calling the top-ranking officer what he was, "Commander."

In the bulk of his paper, Eisenhower commented on the type of officer needed to command the U.S. forces in England. The first requirement was that he have the full confidence of the Chief of Staff and be in full agreement with Marshall's basic ideas. He had to be able to exercise command, for all activities of U.S. forces in the British Isles *"must* be cleared through him; otherwise his position will be intolerable." Next, he had to be flexible, capable of playing any one of several roles, and able to "fit perfectly into the final organization—no matter what that may be." BOLERO could take many forms, and Europe might become a sceondary theater. In that case, the commanding general would unquestionably continue to serve as theater commander. If BOLERO developed as planned, and Europe became the critical theater, it was possible that the President would send Marshall himself to assume command, so the officer who had been serving as commanding general should be able to act as Marshall's deputy or chief of staff. The officer should be selected immediately, and "the whole task of preparation in the United Kingdom should be turned over to him as rapidly as possible, and he should be allowed to carry out his task *with a minimum interference from this end.*"[16]

Marshall did not make an immediate selection; he evidently wanted to see how Chaney would work out. By May 21 he was concerned at the lack of progress, which he felt might be due to an absence of communication between Chaney and OPD. Marshall decided to send Eisenhower to London to bring Chaney up to date and to come back with recommendations on future organization. Eisenhower left on May 2, noting that he had "an uneasy feeling that either we do not understand our own C.G. and Staff in England or they don't understand us. Our planning for Bolero is *not* progressing!"[17]

On Saturday, May 23, Eisenhower left Washington for Montreal. At 11:30 A.M. he flew on to Goose Bay, Labrador, leaving there in the late afternoon for England. Three hours out the weather forced his pilot to turn back, and he spent the night at Gander, Newfoundland. There was no break in the weather the next day, so he killed the time shooting skeet, his first day off in half a year. On May 25 he made it to Prestwick, Scotland, where he watched landing craft in operation, talked with some British officers, and visited the birthplace of Robert Burns.[18] That evening he took the train to London, arriving early Tuesday morning, May 26.

He spent the next day in conference with Chaney and his staff, going in the evening to a dinner given by Air Chief Marshal Sir Charles F. Portal. The next day he observed a field exercise in the Kent-Sussex area, under the direction of the Army Commander in the Southeast, Lieutenant General Bernard Montgomery. Later he attended a lecture at which Montgomery explained the exercise. While the British general talked, Eisenhower lit a cigarette. He had taken about two puffs when Montgomery broke off in the middle of a sentence, sniffed the air without looking around, and in a loud voice demanded, "Who's smoking?"

"I am," Eisenhower replied.

"I don't permit smoking in my office," Montgomery said sternly. Eisenhower put out the cigarette. When he returned to the United States, Eisenhower reported that Montgomery was "a decisive type who appears to be extremely energetic and professionally able."[19]

On the morning of May 28 Eisenhower met with the BCOS to discuss over-all command organization for ROUNDUP. The British submitted two proposals, one of which called for a supreme commander, while the other called for a committee system. Eisenhower explained that the Americans believed "that single command was essential and that committee

command could not conduct a major battle." There was no need to hurry
the selection of a supreme commander, however, since ROUNDUP was
nearly a year away, and if SLEDGEHAMMER went off, it would
be under a British officer. The British then asked with whom they
should deal in the meantime. Eisenhower, astonished, replied that Chaney
was the theater commander, Marshall's representative and the operational and administrative commander of all U.S. forces in the United
Kingdom. "This idea had apparently never occurred to the British,"
Eisenhower noted.

None of Eisenhower's answers satisfied the British. They wanted a
command organization agreed to at once, and they were not impressed
with Chaney (neither was Eisenhower, who found Chaney and his
·staff still wearing civilian clothes, working an eight-hour day, and taking
weekends off). On the main point, Eisenhower noted, "It is quite apparent
that the question of high command is the one that is bothering the
British very much and some agreement, in principle, will have to be
reached at an early date in order that they will go ahead wholeheartedly
to succeeding steps."

That afternoon Eisenhower met with Vice-Admiral Lord Louis Mountbatten, Chief of Combined Operations. At this first meeting with the
admiral, Eisenhower was so impressed with the way in which he had
created a joint staff and made it work that he asked permission to send
some American officers over to join Combined Operations. Eisenhower
also discussed landing craft with Mountbatten and found that the admiral
was . as concerned about the subject as he was. Eisenhower had not
thought in any detail about types of landing craft and was a willing
listener when Mountbatten explained that he wanted the largest ones he
could get since he believed that strong ground formations had to hit the
beaches suddenly and simultaneously. This could not be accomplished in
small boats because the required density was not possible in them. At
the conclusion of the meeting Eisenhower may have felt as if he had
been at school. Within a year he would be assuming the teacher's role,
with Mountbatten as student. But neither man felt anything stiff or formal
about their relationship, and they were well on the way to becoming
close friends.

That was not the case with Eisenhower's relationship with General
Alan Brooke, Chief of the Imperial General Staff (CIGS), with whom
Eisenhower had a session on May 29. Brooke, a fiery Irishman with
impressive battle credentials, carried throughout the war the handicap of
a prejudice against the Americans. After his first meeting with Marshall,

Brooke had commented that the American Chief of Staff was "rather overfilled with his own importance," a unique judgment. Brooke admitted that Marshall was "a pleasant and easy man to get on with" (a conclusion he would later change), "but I should not put him down as a great man."[20] Brooke's comments on Eisenhower, from beginning to end, were similar but more scathing. He put Eisenhower down as an affable type with no strategic sense or practical ability.

Eisenhower's practice was either to say something nice about an associate or not mention him, and he seldom mentioned Brooke.

At their first meeting the contemptuous British officer lectured to the diffident American. In view of the difference in their ranks and positions, Eisenhower had to listen and, occasionally, raise an objection, but he could not speak for himself—his responsibility was to relay Marshall's opinions. The results of the meeting, in which high command and the organization of American forces in England were discussed, were inconclusive.

On June 3 Eisenhower returned to America filled with dissatisfaction. The British seemed to know what they were about and where they were going, but their idea, shared by everyone except Mountbatten, that the attack would be risky and it would take at least three months to build up a beachhead and launch a major offensive, seemed to Eisenhower to be unnecessarily timid. He was even more disturbed by what he had seen of the American contingent in London, which seemed hardly to know that the United States was in the war. The low opinion the British held of Chaney and his staff and the British desire to go over Chaney's head directly to Marshall emphasized the point. The day after his return to his desk in OPD, Eisenhower noted, "It is necessary to get a punch behind the job or we'll never be ready by spring, 1943, to attack. We must get going!"[21]

Upon his return to Washington, Eisenhower sent a memorandum to Marshall saying it was "immediately necessary" to send to England the officer who would command the American ground forces in ROUNDUP. He recommended for that position Major General Mark Clark. Marshall agreed, but he rejected Eisenhower's next recommendation. Eisenhower said he had given "a great deal of study" to the problem of who should be the commanding general of all American forces in England, and suggested McNarney. "I believe that General McNarney has the strength of character, the independence of thought, and the ability to fulfill satisfactorily the requirements of this difficult task." Marshall, however, wanted McNarney to stay on as his deputy chief of staff.[22]

Three days later Eisenhower added another thought on the subject of command in England. He felt that whether Marshall decided to retain Chaney or replace him, the officer in command should be promoted to lieutenant general, so that the British would pay him a little more respect than they were currently giving Chaney. Eisenhower realized that the question of promotion might appear trivial, but in this case he thought it imperative. Then he tried again to get Marshall to appoint McNarney, pointing out that McNarney was familiar with British organization and methods and had the outstanding characteristic of patience, "which he possesses to a noticeable degree at no sacrifice of energy and force." In a prophetic statement, Eisenhower concluded, "Patience is highly necessary because of the complications in British procedure."[23]

On June 8 Eisenhower took to Marshall a draft directive he had prepared in early May for the commander of the European Theater of Operations. It was essential, Eisenhower argued, in view of the distance between the European Theater and the United States, "that absolute unity of command should be exercised by the Theater Commander." The officer himself should be able to organize, train, and command the combined forces of all arms and services set up in the BOLERO plan, and should also be qualified to assume the duties of chief of staff to the eventual ROUNDUP commander (it was widely assumed by now that this would be Marshall).

The draft called for a European Theater of Operations (ETO), with a commanding general who would "command all U. S. Army forces and personnel" in the theater and would "exercise planning and operational control, under the principle of unity of command, over all U. S. Navy forces assigned to that theater for participation with U. S. Army operations against Western Europe." Remembering Pershing's fight in World War I to keep the British and French from absorbing American units into their corps, Eisenhower said that, although the commanding general was required to co-operate with the British, "the forces of the United States are to be maintained as a separate and distinct component of the combined forces."[24]

When Eisenhower handed the draft to Marshall he asked the Chief to read it carefully because it could be an important document in the further waging of the war. Marshall replied, "I certainly do want to read it. You may be the man who executes it. If that's the case, when can you leave?"[25]

Eisenhower was thunderstruck. He had resigned himself to spending the war in Washington with OPD and had no idea that Marshall had been grooming him for command. The appointment put him in the unusual position of having written his own directive (he later spoke of the directive as "the Bible").

In sending Eisenhower to England in June 1942, Marshall did not expect that Eisenhower would remain in command until Germany's unconditional surrender. Rather, he wanted Eisenhower to put some energy into the BOLERO program, much of which Eisenhower had created and which he understood thoroughly, and to prepare the way for the eventual Supreme Commander. When that man was appointed, and Marshall probably shared the general view that he himself would be it, Eisenhower would become chief of staff to the Supreme Commander. Marshall's association with Eisenhower had convinced him that Eisenhower would work perfectly in that assignment.

After the war, when asked about Eisenhower, Marshall remarked, "If he hadn't delivered he wouldn't have moved up." The London trip had been, in part, a test. "I sent Eisenhower and some others over so the British could have a look at them," Marshall recalled in 1956, "and then I asked Churchill what he thought of them. He was extravagant in his estimate of them, so then I went ahead with my decision on Eisenhower."[26] Marshall's memory was faulty on this point. While in England Eisenhower met only with British Army and Navy officers and did not see the Prime Minister, and Marshall himself did not see Churchill from the middle of April until June 19. Marshall probably did check with Field Marshal Sir John Dill, head of the British Joint Staff Mission in Washington, who could have relayed the information that the BCOS had a favorable impression of Eisenhower.

Leaving Marshall's office after receiving the momentous news, Eisenhower returned to his desk and noted what Marshall had told him. He was flattered, for he knew "It's a big job—if U.S.-U.K. stay squarely behind Bolero and go after it tooth and nail, it will be the biggest American job of the war." Then, being a realist, he continued, "Of course command now does not necessarily mean command in the operation—but the job before the battle begins will still be the biggest outside of that of C/S himself."[27]

Eisenhower spent the next two weeks preparing for his departure. He spent much of his time with General Handy, his successor, and talked with government officials whose duties included some part in BOLERO. A short talk with Secretary Stimson convinced him that Stimson was the most active backer of ROUNDUP in Washington. He visited with the blunt and abrupt Chief of Naval Operations, Admiral King, who emphasized that in England the United States was, for the first time in her history, attempting to create a unified command in the field for an indefinite period. King promised to give Eisenhower full support, to see to it that he was "commander" of the U. S. Navy in the British Isles in fact as well as name. If any naval officer violated the unity of command concept by questioning Eisenhower's single authority, King asked Eisenhower to report him at once.[28]

On June 19 Eisenhower had to interrupt his last-minute preparations, leave bag-packing to his wife, and attend a meeting between Marshall, Dill, Brooke, and General Hastings Ismay, Churchill's personal representative on the BCOS. The British had come to Washington to have another discussion on strategy. While the soldiers talked, Churchill and Roosevelt met at Hyde Park, New York. It was a sweltering hot day in Washington. The generals, sitting around a table in the Munitions Building, fumed, wilted their collars, and anxiously imagined all sorts of wild schemes their heads of government might be dreaming up in Hyde Park. Brooke and Marshall had little in common, but they equally dreaded the possible consequences of a Roosevelt-Churchill meeting when they were not present to keep the politicians from making impossible commitments.

Churchill, in fact, was trying to swing Roosevelt away from BOLERO and back to North Africa (he was also pushing Norway, a prospect that horrified all the soldiers). While they talked at Hyde Park, the soldiers in the Munitions Building—Eisenhower, who was present, kept the minutes—reiterated their commitment to BOLERO and ROUNDUP. They also denounced any operation in French North Africa, Brooke because it would take strength away from the Middle East, Marshall because it would make ROUNDUP impossible. Brooke even agreed that SLEDGEHAMMER was preferable to North Africa.[29]

The next day, at a formal meeting of the CCS, Brooke explained that, since they had North Africa out of the way, he wanted to express his opposition to a "so-called 'sacrifice' operation on the Continent" in 1942, for even if a bridgehead was gained it could not be followed up. Eisenhower replied that "there was a possibility at least of securing a bridgehead and holding it as Malta or Tobruk had been held. If the air forces in Great Britain were concentrated for the operation, the Germans would certainly have to bring back air forces to deal with the situation." He realized that the circumstances in which such an operation might be feasible were unlikely to arise, but felt that the Allies should be ready to seize any favorable opportunity.[30]

Churchill, meanwhile, was swinging Roosevelt around to North Africa. The American President had promised the Russians some aid in 1942 and it was easy enough for Churchill to demolish SLEDGEHAMMER. He intimated to Roosevelt that he could sell the Russians on the idea that North Africa constituted a second front. Roosevelt made no promises, but his interest was aroused.

On the night of June 20–21 Churchill and Roosevelt took the train to Washington. Shortly after their arrival, they learned of the fall of Tobruk, the symbol of British resistance to the Germans in Libya. It was one of the heaviest blows Churchill suffered during the war.[31] He used it immediately, however, to step up his arguments for a North African invasion. The British-American talks reached no firm conclusions, but a North African invasion was once again very much alive as an alternative to SLEDGEHAMMER-ROUNDUP.

When Eisenhower left for England the strategic situation was in a state of flux. He was not taking over as commander of a going concern with a firm objective. Instead of being able to concentrate on building up his forces, training them, and planning for their employment, he would have to engage in still another strategic debate. His son John came down from West Point for two days, and Eisenhower had a brief vacation, but he probably did not enjoy it fully, since the uncertainties loomed so much larger than the certainties.

Of one thing Eisenhower was sure and the knowledge was to sustain him not only in his first trying months in England but throughout the war. It was that as long as he did his job Marshall would stand behind him. Just before leaving, Eisenhower took time to write to Brigadier General Spencer Akin, a friend who was on MacArthur's staff. Summing up his experience in OPD, Eisenhower said it had been a "tough, intensive grind—but now I'm getting a swell command and, of course, am highly delighted that I got away with this job sufficiently well to have the Chief accord such recognition to me." This meant everything to Eisenhower, because he felt "the Chief is a great soldier." Enumerating his characteristics, Eisenhower said Marshall was "quick, tough, tireless, decisive and a real leader. He accepts responsibility automatically and never goes back on a subordinate." Eisenhower thought the United States was "particularly fortunate in having him for a Chief of Staff," and declared that it had been a "pleasure to work directly under him."[32]

Marshall had almost as high an opinion of Eisenhower, for the younger man had fulfilled all his expectations and met all his tests. But Eisenhower's achievements, to date, had been as a staff officer, usually serving under strong-willed superiors. All of the men under whom he had worked, including MacArthur, thought he would be a success as an independent commander, but that was only prediction. No one really knew how he would react when commanding on his own, away from the daily influence of a decisive superior. Eisenhower still had to meet that test.

Part II

LONDON TO GIBRALTAR

[June 1942–December 1942]

CHAPTER 4

The Theater Commander

On June 24, 1942, Eisenhower arrived in England. There were no bands to greet him, no speeches at the airport, no ceremonies. He quietly climbed into a car and had his driver take him to his office at 20 Grosvenor Square, an apartment building that served as headquarters for the U. S. Army in Europe. A kitchen in the basement put forth a constant odor of boiled cabbage and Brussels sprouts, an odor strong enough to remind all inhabitants of 20 Grosvenor that they were in England and England was at war.[1]

On his first full day in London, Eisenhower began his career as theater commander by meeting with his staff and impressing on them that their job was to have an army in the field ready to attack the coast of France. He told them that he wanted every American officer in the British Isles to cultivate an attitude of determined enthusiasm and optimism and warned them that he would not tolerate pessimism or defeatism. Eisenhower said that any officer who could not rise above the recognized obstacles should ask for instant release from ETO.

Most of Chaney's officers had regarded their positions as unimportant and had fallen into the habit of referring anything big back to Washington for decision. Eisenhower informed them that all policy making applying to ETO lay with his headquarters. He urged the officers to adopt the greatest informality, learn to solve their own problems, and stop passing the buck.[2] Following his meetings with Chaney's officers, Eisenhower wrote Marshall, "I am quite certain that this staff and all commanders now realize that we have unique problems to solve, that we have full opportunity and freedom of action in solving them, and that no alibis or excuses will be acceptable. . . ."[3]

Eisenhower liked to describe himself as a simple Kansas small-town boy and his typical expressions, such as "Determined enthusiasm and optimism," certainly struck some observers as pure corn. On the face of it, it was ridiculous for Eisenhower to come into a wartime headquarters and tell cynical, able officers that they had to work hard, assume responsibility, and be cheerful. But something had to be done, for the job was not being accomplished. Eisenhower's way, at least when applied by Eisenhower, worked.

One reason Eisenhower ran an efficient office was that he knew how a staff should function. He once said that he suspected he had been a chief of staff, either to a division, corps, or army, longer than anyone else in the U. S. Army, so he knew how to run an organization. He emphasized the positive. When he was dissatisfied with or disappointed in an officer, he seldom wasted time criticizing him, but instead sent him back to the States. He preferred to praise and encourage, to give a man a task and then leave him alone, resisting the temptation to look over his shoulder or to guide him to the correct solution. When the work was well done, he saw to it that the man got credit for his accomplishment.

Support from Marshall helped too. Eisenhower was not particularly good at bringing forth hidden talent; instead he gave up on officers who disappointed him and asked Marshall for a proven replacement. After August, when it was clear that Eisenhower was the permanent theater commander and Marshall was going to stay in Washington, Marshall gave Eisenhower the men he wanted.

Eisenhower had spent much of his time in the twenties coaching football teams and he adopted most of the ideas about morale that football coaches had developed through the years. He wanted the emphasis on the team rather than upon the star, co-ordination of effort rather than flashy individual performances. He said that one of the reasons he wanted to move his headquarters out of London was to get the staff living "together like a football team" so that the officers could "think war, plan war, and execute war twenty-four hours a day, or at least all of our waking hours."[4] On a great football team everyone's responsibility intertwined and all pulled together. Success came through team effort. Eisenhower wanted his headquarters to operate on the same basis.

"War has become so comprehensive and so complicated that team-work seems to me to be the essence of all success," Eisenhower once declared. "Each bureau, each section, each office . . . has to be part of a well-coordinated team." Because he thought that "no successful staff can have any personal enmities existing in it," he insisted "on having a happy family. . . . I want to see a big crowd of friends around here." This had been important to Eisenhower since the twenties, when Fox Conner told him that a commander should never have a personal enemy on his staff, since he would sabotage the commander.[5]

In the summer of 1942 Eisenhower could go only so far in shaping his staff, since practically none of the officers was hand-picked. At the end of July he was still growling about the inability of the staff to function. He wondered if his own drive was causing his officers to leave all decisions and initiative to him, a tendency he regarded as near disastrous. "Too many staff officers are merely pushing paper," Eisenhower declared, "and we can't win this war pushing paper. It takes imagination and initiative and a lot of it."[6] He did simplify his task, and that of his headquarters staff, by divesting himself of most administrative responsibilities, turning them over to the head of the Services of Supply (SOS) organization in England, Major General John C. H. Lee, a martinet who was both willing and able to handle the thousands of details connected with the presence of the American Army in England. Lee freed Eisenhower and his staff for more important work.[7]

Eisenhower forcibly impressed his presence upon his staff, but with the British and even with the U. S. War Department his position still seemed temporary. BOLERO was not making great strides and Eisenhower did not have a large command. European Theater of Operations, United States Army (ETOUSA), consisted of a total of 55,390 officers and men. Headquarters at 20 Grosvenor had 105 ground officers, 20 air officers, 18 attached officers, and 12 enlisted men. The U. S. Eighth Air Force had 918 officers and 10,047 enlisted men, while there were 37,226 ground force enlisted men in ETO (which contained the British Isles and Iceland).

Common talk around the War Department reflected the general opinion that Eisenhower's appointment was an interim one, an opinion which he shared but which he was beginning to resent. In late July, when he received a chatty letter from Lieutenant General Brehon Somervell, head of SOS in Washington, he came close to admitting his feelings of uncertainty. After telling Somervell that he could not imagine how much his letter had meant, Eisenhower added, "It is so easy to lose contact with the War Department that frequently I am overcome by a 'lost' feeling, and have a desperate desire to jump on a fast plane and come over for a twenty-four-hour visit."[8] The basic trouble was that no one really knew how important the job in London was going to be. If BOLERO went forward and was followed by ROUNDUP, it would be the biggest command in the war, but the British were dragging their heels and ROUNDUP was by no means certain. Marshall was not going to step down as Chief of Staff for a minor post, and he certainly could not retain his position as head of the American Army while serving in London as theater commander. On the other hand, even if BOLERO-ROUNDUP did go forward, Marshall could not appoint himself to the command—only Roosevelt could, and Roosevelt had not revealed whether or not he was willing to give up Marshall's services as Chief of Staff. The result was that everyone had to mark time until final decisions were reached, which was irritating—especially to Eisenhower—but unavoidable.

There was nothing Eisenhower could do about the ambiguous situation, but he could and did make sure that until a change was made the War Department looked upon him as the Commanding General, ETO. Just two days after his arrival in London he told Somervell to "straighten out for me" certain aspects of the assignment of personnel to his theater. The War Department had been sending officers to ETO with an assignment to a specific branch, and Eisenhower had just discovered that the department had transferred a man from SOS to the Eighth Air Force. Although Somervell was his superior in rank and experience, Eisenhower informed him that "such a move involves only the authority of the theater commander," and told him in the future to see to it that such assignments were made only to the theater commander. He concluded by admitting that this was a minor matter, "but I am simply trying to keep the strings all tied together so that no loose ends are flopping around."[9]

Eisenhower was insistent that his authority and the position of his headquarters be recognized by all Americans in the United Kingdom. In July, when he learned that an American civilian agency in London had suggested that the British take over the rationing of food for U.S. troops, Eisenhower told Somervell that "this suggestion strikes me as just another sample of the things that plague a commander in a world capital, where there are all kinds and descriptions of U.S. governmental representatives. These people form contacts with a complete maze of local civil agencies that seem to have little coordination before the Prime Minister." Time and again, Eisenhower said, he got news of propositions being discussed between British and U.S. civil officials "which impinge directly upon the responsibilities of this Headquarters." The reason, he thought, was that the headquarters had been just a mission before his arrival, "just another of the many agencies that dealt with important matters in a very uncoordinated and haphazard manner." The civil agencies had as a result gotten into the habit of proposing to the British "far-reaching plans and schemes without taking the trouble to see that this headquarters approves." Eisenhower promised to overcome the problem, "or else."[10]

Establishing ETO's importance was not easy. Two days after his complaint to Somervell, Eisenhower learned that Ambassador Winant wanted to create a Bomber Objective Committee at the embassy, and that he had developed the plan with the aid of members of Eisenhower's staff without Eisenhower's knowledge. Eisenhower patiently explained to Winant that the committee idea would not work at all, but it took time and gave emphasis to his statement to Handy: "It is not an exaggeration to say that, right this minute, I could profitably place fifteen additional top-notch officers if I had them."[11]

Eisenhower was satisfied with his naval aide. His closest associate in London was Navy Reserve Captain Harry Butcher, a Columbia Broadcasting System vice-president who was a family friend of the Eisenhowers. Just before leaving Washington Eisenhower had requested Butcher's services as "naval aide," and Admiral King had acceded to the unique request. Eisenhower wanted Butcher around because he was a good bridge player, pleasant company, and knew something of public relations. He asked "Butch" to keep a diary, which Butcher did throughout the war. Eisenhower told a friend once, "Sometimes I get back to quarters and I just want to curl up in a corner like a sick dog. Butch won't let me." He went on, "Butcher's job is simple. It is to keep me from going crazy."[12]

One of Butcher's first jobs was to find a weekend retreat. He selected Telegraph Cottage, a tiny, quaint house twenty-five minutes from London. It fit Eisenhower's needs perfectly. The slate-roofed cottage was off the beaten track, nestled in a ten-acre wooded tract near Richmond Park. It had a private road leading into it, a high wooden fence, and a small rose garden. The living room had ceiling-to-floor windows opening out onto the lawn, a fireplace for heat, and an old oak table. Butcher got it for thirty-two dollars a week, complete with the services of a gardener. The grounds fringed on a golf course and Eisenhower frequently stepped out and played the adjacent holes. At other times he and Butcher would engage in .22 pistol practice shooting in back of the cottage, or Sergeant Mickey McKeogh, an aide, would get out a baseball and some gloves and play catch with the general.[13]

Eisenhower spent as many weekends at Telegraph Cottage as he could, lounging around the living room in G.I. slacks, an old shirt, a half-suede, half-leather jacket, and a shabby pair of straw slippers left over from Manila. He refused to look at newspapers, books, or general magazines. Instead, he devoured paper-backed cowboy magazines, which Sergeant Mickey scrounged up for him. Mrs. Kay Summersby, his driver, thought it disgraceful that one of the most important men in the world read pulp magazine junk, and once told Eisenhower exactly what she thought of his habit. He replied that he came to the cottage to rest, and when he read Westerns, "I don't have to *think*."[14]

He did not often have that luxury. One of his major immediate tasks was preparing for the Americans who were coming to his theater— eventually 2,000,000. In an island only slightly larger than Colorado these men had to be sheltered, fed, trained, and organized, all in the midst of a local people who were underfed, had already placed even submarginal ground under intense cultivation, and were suffering in nearly every conceivable way. From the moment he first stepped on the island, Eisenhower felt that one of his major tasks was to ensure good relations with the English people, a task for which he had no background. The problem was acute because the American soldier was just as un- prepared.

The G.I. came onto the islands viewing himself as a privileged crusader who had come to pull Britain out of a hole, in much the same way as the World War I doughboy who explained that AEF stood for "After England Failed." The British people saw themselves as the saviors of democracy, the ones who had held the fort while waiting for the Ameri- cans to make up their minds, and they were hardly ready to welcome the cocky Americans as their rescuers. Differences in pay scale and the quality and quantity of rations did not help. The American G.I. was the best-paid soldier in the world. In the early stages of the war a majority of those who went overseas were unmarried, so they had no responsibilities back in the States and felt no compunction about blowing their pay as soon as they received it. It bothered the British to see young men throwing so much money around. They could accept the fact that the Americans got more and better food, but even here there was a problem, for American habits of waste led to garbage cans being filled with food that British citizens could have used. As one Englishman put it, the trouble with the Yanks was that they were "overpaid, over-sexed, over-fed, and over here."

Eisenhower urged his subordinates to conduct "sustained and vigorous campaigns" to induce officers and men to save their pay by buying war bonds, so as to cut down on the "lavish expenditure of money."

He insisted upon eliminating waste and made each commander responsible for the inspection of kitchens and mess halls before and after every meal.

In July the number of Americans in the British Isles was not overwhelming; aside from the 34th Infantry Division in Northern Ireland they were mostly Eighth Air Force personnel. Eisenhower managed to talk with almost all senior commanders, stressing to each one the need for good relations. He ordered the officers to conduct constant educational programs, designed to explain to the G.I. conditions and customs in Britain. Most of all, Eisenhower wanted the G.I. to learn of the sufferings the British had endured since 1939. One of his programs took newly arrived American personnel on a short tour of London's bombed areas.[15]

The total Army program, which of course began in the initial training stages in the U.S., was a success. Although for three years hundreds of thousands of young Americans jostled the British public for elbow room, there were few major incidents. By 1945 Anglo-American relations were better than they had been since 1763. Surely those G.I.s who lived side by side, day by day with the English deserved some of the credit.

In a letter he sent to all his senior subordinates, Eisenhower made a number of suggestions beyond the pay, food, and visiting questions to help improve relations. Most important of all, he felt, was good discipline. If the Army had it, it would convince "the British that we are here not as muddling amateurs but as earnest, competent soldiers who know what we are about." The British had signed agreements with the U. S. Government which gave the Army the right to punish criminals who violated British law. Eisenhower wanted punishment in such cases to be adequate and swift, and he wanted the British authorities notified. But this line of action was only negative; he was more concerned with avoiding serious offenses through the development of good discipline.

Eisenhower recognized that "it is trite indeed" to say that discipline is "a matter of leadership, but evidence of failures along this line are so common in military experience as to warrant the continuous and earnest attention, even of very senior officers." He believed that there were certain constants by which the state of discipline could be judged: standards of military courtesy, bearing and carriage of soldiers, and neatness in clothing and appearance. He had just visited the 34th Division in Ireland and thought that the infantrymen there made a good appearance. The Air Force and staff officers in London, however, disappointed him. The worst offenders were majors, captains, and lieutenants. On one motor tour of the city, which was filled with newly commissioned

Air Force personnel, Eisenhower received just one salute—and that from a British officer. Eisenhower told Major General Carl Spaatz, commanding the Eighth Air Force, that if the young officers did not improve they should be sent home.

All of his professional life Eisenhower had dealt with Regular Army soldiers; now he was being called upon to lead what would soon be the largest civilian army the nation ever put into the field. The G.I.s in it were a cross section of the nation. By European standards, most of them were educated, independently minded men who had been conscripted into the service and who were contemptuous of most of the ways of the old Army. They had certain obvious strengths—their knowledge of motor vehicles, their general mechanical ability, their cocky optimism—and certain obvious weaknesses, chief of which was a tendency to be soft and to grouse, not only at the big things like the bad luck that sent them instead of their neighbor overseas, but at any meal that was not hot. In theory they were supposed to be trained, disciplined, of good morale, and ready to fight when they reached Eisenhower, but in fact he had to assume much of the responsibility for getting them prepared.

Eisenhower thought the first requirement was constant, intensive training. Time was short, the war demanded trained personnel, and "our men must be toughened and hardened physically to stand the most rigorous operations." Eisenhower felt that the training should be understandable to everyone involved. He recognized that he would never turn the average American soldier into a Prussian-type automaton, that to hope for unquestioned obedience was to hope for too much. Besides, he wanted his soldiers to retain their initiative. He therefore told his subordinates to give constant explanations during field exercises, so that the last private in the ranks could "understand the reasons for the exertions he is called upon to make." Eisenhower declared that "any commander should be summarily relieved who neglects this important phase of training intelligent, patriotic Americans."

He felt that morale was "the most highly important of any military attribute." It could never be obtained through pampering the men or lowering the standards of discipline to permit easier living, but rather through self-respect, intensive training, and adequate leadership. He recognized the importance of proper recreational facilities and reasonable pass privileges, but insisted that "they themselves are not the answer to the problem." Field exercises were his favorite method for achieving high morale, and he visited divisions operating in the field whenever possible. As he told his subordinates, "I cannot overemphasize the concern I feel about all these things . . . because of my deep conviction that we must form, here, the best army that the United States has ever put into the field. . . ."[16]

In the two years preceding the war, Eisenhower had visited a number of divisions engaged in field exercises, and he continued to do so throughout the war. One result, he told a West Point classmate, Brigadier General Vernon E. Prichard, was that he had "developed almost an obsession as to the certainty with which you can judge a division, or any other large unit, merely by knowing its commander intimately." Eisenhower knew that Prichard had been told that hundreds of times, but confessed that he himself had never realized fully "how infallibly the commander and unit are almost one and the same thing."

At the time Prichard had not gone high up the rank or command ladder (he later had an armored division in Italy), and partly to buck up his spirits, partly to say some things that he felt deeply, Eisenhower continued: "This is a long tough road we have to travel. The men that can do things are going to be sought out just as surely as the sun rises in the morning. Fake reputations, habits of glib and clever speech, and glittering surface performance are going to be discovered and kicked overboard." For a man to make it in this war, he had to be a leader with "inexhaustible nervous energy . . . and iron-clad determination to face discouragement, risk, and increasing work without flinching. . . ." He would also need imagination—Eisenhower confessed he was "continuously astounded by the utter lack of imaginative thinking among so many of our people that have reputations for being really good officers." Finally, the man had to be able to forget himself and his personal fortunes.

Promotions to date, Eisenhower told Prichard, had been based on personal propinquity, wild guesses, school records, past friendships, and other unimportant factors. "But the stark realities of distress, privation and discouragement will bring character and ability into their own," and all those with ability would rise to high command. "I am almost ashamed to send this letter," he concluded, and only dared unburden his soul to Prichard because he was sure Prichard would understand "that I am talking sincerely and am not indulging a bombastic ego."[17]

Selecting the right commanders, creating an efficient staff, maintaining good relations with the British and preparing his men for combat were parts of Eisenhower's task, but his objective was the defeat of the Axis. Had he ever been tempted to forget it, a July issue of *Life* that gave him his first personal publicity would have reminded him. In cutting language that took much of the pleasure from his own publicity, *Life* began its story on Eisenhower by saying, "The U. S. Army, nearly eight months after Pearl Harbor, has yet to deliver an offensive land attack on any enemy anywhere," even though it had 3,500,000 men and 80 divisions in the Army and 225 battle squadrons in the Air Force. The same issue carried a story on the Russian front, which pointed out that the Russians were buying time for the Western Allies at a cost of "tens of millions of its people." *Life* commented, "Compared with this awful sacrifice, the war effort of the Anglo-Saxon nations is so far pitifully puny."[18] On July 16 Eisenhower read three editorials in American newspapers urging a second front in 1942.[19] This kind of reporting, widespread in the U.S. that summer, put enormous pressure on Roosevelt and the Army to get something going somewhere. It was the same kind of pressure Horace Greeley had brought to bear on President Lincoln in July of 1861 with his "On to Richmond" cry, and it would soon have a direct effect on the commander of ETO.

CHAPTER 5

The Blackest Day in History

In the middle of July, just as Eisenhower was settling into a routine, the fundamental question of where to strike the Germans arose again. Eisenhower and his staff had been preparing for SLEDGEHAMMER and ROUNDUP, but it had become obvious to them that they were getting neither co-operation nor encouragement from the British. On June 30 Eisenhower had confessed to Marshall that he could "discover little if any real progress in the formulation of broad decisions affecting the operation as a whole" and said he had undertaken, as his principal task, to force decisive action. He had visited with most of the British officers involved but, perhaps because of the unsettled command situation, could not get to Brooke, "who has been practically incommunicado. . . ." Summing up, Eisenhower noted "there seems to be some confusion of thought as to the extent of the British commitment toward a 1942 operation."[1]

Over the next week and a half Eisenhower had daily meetings with Mountbatten, General Sir Bernard Paget, commanding the Home Forces, Admiral Sir Bertram H. Ramsay, Air Chief Marshal Sir Sholto Douglas, commanding the British Expeditionary Air Forces, and their staffs. The British more and more openly criticized SLEDGEHAMMER, as did the Prime Minister, who had always been opposed to a 1942 invasion. For Eisenhower the meetings were frustrating since he could not talk with the man who was really making British policy and the British officers simply raised objections to SLEDGEHAMMER while offering nothing constructive. Since no one was in over-all command of the proposed invasion, no decisions could be made.[2]

Churchill, meanwhile, was mounting his own campaign. He had, he later confessed, "made a careful study of the President's mind and its reactions for some time past" and now he prepared to use his knowledge to influence grand strategy.[3] SLEDGEHAMMER, he told Roosevelt, could not work, and even if it did it would exert no influence on events on the Russian front, since the Allies could send no more than nine divisions to France and the Germans already had twenty-five divisions there.[4] On June 20 Churchill had thrown in a requirement that, as far as he and his staff were concerned, doomed SLEDGEHAMMER—the British laid it down as a condition that they would undertake no landings in France in 1942 unless they could stay ashore.[5]

Eisenhower and his staff made some proposals to meet the requirement, but none of them convinced the British, who were unwilling to go through with a suicide operation no matter how desperate the situation on the Russian front became. Besides, Churchill insisted that nothing should be done to halt ROUNDUP, and he argued that SLEDGEHAMMER would probably end in disaster, which "would decisively injure the prospect of a well-organized large-scale action in 1943."[6] This argument put Churchill in the ideal position of opposing SLEDGEHAMMER because of his keen desire for ROUNDUP. It also allowed him to add that it was a pity nothing was being done in 1942.

On July 11 Eisenhower wired Marshall to say that the BCOS and the Prime Minister had "decided that SLEDGEHAMMER can not repeat not be successfully executed this year under the proposition that the invading force must be able to remain permanently on the continent." The BCOS, Eisenhower added, "are most fearful that in making this decision they may be giving you a feeling that they have partially let you down," but they hoped Marshall would understand and agree with their conclusions. For his part, Eisenhower thought "an attempt at SLEDGEHAMMER in spite of its obvious risks and costs would be preferable to GYMNAST or other major expedition intended to open up an entirely new front unrelated to this theater."[7]

Inasmuch as the Americans had always thought of SLEDGEHAMMER as an emergency operation, the decision to drop it did not abandon anything (unless an emergency arose) and in any case, since the British would have to supply the bulk of the forces for the operation, there was nothing the Americans could do. For Marshall and Eisenhower the danger was that, having abandoned the SLEDGEHAMMER concept, the British would want to use their force elsewhere to open a new theater, which would so deeply commit the Allies that they would not be able to mount ROUNDUP. For Marshall, holding to the concept of SLEDGEHAMMER was essential to getting the reality of ROUNDUP, and he did not for a minute believe Churchill's protestations that the British were dropping SLEDGEHAMMER to ensure ROUNDUP.

At all times the key to the debate was the probable effect of a North African invasion (GYMNAST) on ROUNDUP. Both heads of government wanted ROUNDUP, or so at least they said. Churchill argued that the only way to get it was to drop SLEDGEHAMMER and go for GYMNAST. Marshall felt that GYMNAST would kill off ROUNDUP. Roosevelt had the deciding vote, and he agreed with the Prime Minister that a diversion to the Mediterranean in 1942 would not rule out a cross-Channel operation in 1943.[8]

Marshall wired Eisenhower on July 13 to say he thought it important to continue SLEDGEHAMMER planning, as it would be useful for ROUNDUP and would keep the British from attempting other operations. Eisenhower knew all this, but he may have been surprised at the depth of Marshall's anger over what the Chief regarded as a double-cross. Marshall said that if the British were going to abandon SLEDGE-HAMMER he would advise the President to turn to the Pacific and make the major U.S. offensive there.[9]

In the history of World War II, Marshall's threat to drop the Germany-first strategy if the British would not do it his way has gone down as "something of a red herring." Marshall himself was the first to use those words.[10] It may have been bluff, but the head of the British Joint Staff Mission in Washington, Field Marshal Sir John Dill, who was close to Marshall, thought the Chief was serious. In a cable to his superiors, Dill warned that if the BCOS continued to push GYMNAST at the expense of BOLERO the result would be to drive the U.S. into a "we are finished off with the West and will go all out in the Pacific" attitude. Dill noted that such a reversal in strategy would be "immensely popular" with the U. S. Navy, Australia, New Zealand and China, and sections of the American population. Dill had just talked with Marshall, who claimed that the switch from the Atlantic to the Pacific would be comparatively easy to make.[11]

Marshall, in short, felt more strongly about dropping SLEDGEHAM-MER than he did about any other issue in the war. The British made the strength of their feelings equally clear by ignoring Dill's warnings. Nor did the BCOS pay any attention when Eisenhower told them of the "transcendent importance of keeping Russia in the war" and said that it was his opinion "that the collapse of Russia would force the United States to go on the defensive throughout the Atlantic and to build up offensive operations against Japan."[12] The British could afford to ignore the warnings, threats, and angry outbursts because they knew that Marshall and Eisenhower were not setting American policy, and they were always confident that Roosevelt would not let the Army turn away from Europe.

On July 16 Eisenhower learned that Marshall, King, Harry Hopkins, and various aides were on their way to London. Roosevelt was sending them over with instructions either to get the British to agree to SLEDGE-HAMMER or else to find a 1942 alternative. In the next few days the Western Allies made their most important strategic decision of the war, with the possible exception of the agreement to defeat Germany first. The decision the CCS made was to invade North Africa; it is still controversial. Marshall died convinced that a mistake had been made. Churchill was always sure he had been right. After the war Eisenhower, who had supported Marshall throughout the debate, decided that "those who held the Sledgehammer operation to be unwise at the moment were correct in their evaluation of the problem," and he admitted that greater results came from the North African landings than could have come from SLEDGEHAMMER.[13]

Since operations in 1943 flowed directly from the decision reached in July 1942, and operations in 1944 were drastically influenced by that decision, it must be examined in some detail. In simplest terms, the British were willing to gamble that the Russians would hold on in 1942 without a second front (and even with a cut in lend-lease—one convoy was called off to supply North African forces), while the Americans were not willing to take the risk. The British were not so foolish as to hope for a Russian defeat, as right-wing admirers and left-wing critics have said, nor did they have better information than the Americans. To the Prime Minister and the BCOS, it just looked impossible to do anything in Europe to help the Russians.

There was a difference in emphasis between the Allies. For the Americans, a chief requirement was to keep Russia in the war, and beyond that to get an Allied land army operating in France. The British gave verbal agreement to this, but their hearts belonged to the Middle East. For them, Egypt was the main theater, and it was in as much danger as Stalingrad or Moscow. Especially after the fall of Tobruk, the British were determined that by the end of 1942 the Middle East would be secure. To the Americans this seemed foolish. At the time the Germans had taken Sevastopol, encircled Rostov, crossed the Don River, and were preparing for their assault on Stalingrad. They were poised for a sweep into and beyond the Caucasus Mountains, which would give them the bulk of Russia's oil fields. By comparison, the importance of the British Eighth Army in Egypt or of French North Africa seemed minuscule.[14]

Another difference was the way the two sides looked at the situation. The Americans, with no experience of defeat, felt they were quite capable of taking on the German Army and were anxious to do so. They also felt the pressure to end the war in Europe so that the full fury of the United States could be turned against Japan. The British mood differed. Under no circumstances did they want to be chased in disgrace from the Continent again. They had held on, alone, for a year; the Russian and then American entry into the anti-Axis coalition ensured Hitler's defeat—as long as no mistakes were made.

General Sir Ian Jacob has expressed the British feeling best. "The general war situation in July, 1942," he recalled in 1946, "was by no means favourable." Rommel had just inflicted a severe defeat on the British, the Japanese were threatening Australia, while the Germans in Russia rolled forward unchecked. At sea the submarines raised havoc with Allied shipping, and in the air the RAF Bomber Command could deliver only small attacks against the German homeland. The war production potential of the United States was still comparatively undeveloped. There was, for example, no flow of modern tanks from the assembly line. Jacob points out that, under 'the circumstances, "Everyone could see the need for early action in the West to influence the developments on the Eastern fronts, and to draw off German forces, but it was not so easy to see how action could be taken. A landing in Northern France was the accepted goal of the Anglo-American strategy, but nothing could be more fatal to the Allied cause than an unsuccessful attempt."

The British found it difficult to believe the Americans were serious about SLEDGEHAMMER. While Eisenhower and Marshall tried to concentrate on the future potential of the Western alliance and the current danger to the Russians if something were not done, the British—whose men would have to carry out the attack—quite naturally concentrated on practical problems. These were nearly insurmountable. Again quoting Jacob, "The Atlantic wall was not to be despised, even in 1942. Moreover, the Allies had had no experience of carrying out large opposed landings under modern conditions. The technique of assault forces, of bombardment, of air support, of off-shore protection and of administrative organisation was unknown and untried. There were no battle-trained troops available, and, except in the Middle East, there had been no opportunity for commanders to handle large forces in battle. On the other side, the Germans had plenty of troops standing ready in France and the Low Countries to oppose a landing without drawing on the Russian front. . . . There would have to be no doubt about the power to support the subsequent operations with ample reinforcements of men, equipment and supplies. There was grave doubt, to say the least of it, about this in 1942."[15] After a long look at SLEDGEHAMMER, the BCOS refused to participate.

Once the British had turned down SLEDGEHAMMER, they could open other possibilities for action in 1942 that could satisfy Roosevelt's desire to get troops into combat. Churchill offered three alternatives— JUPITER, an operation in Norway; reinforcement of the British Eighth Army in the Mid-East with American troops; an invasion of French North Africa. Almost every professional soldier in both countries opposed JUPITER, while Marshall was loath to put Americans under a British commander in Egypt, so it came down to North Africa.

As Marshall's plane flew toward England he determined to make one last effort to convince the British that SLEDGEHAMMER was feasible. Failing that, he could try to convince them—and, more important, Roosevelt—that the proper strategy was to continue progress on BOLERO, increase bombing raids against Germany, and wait until 1943 before doing anything on the ground. The worst possibility was North Africa, since the drain that would impose on Allied resources would kill off ROUNDUP.

Eisenhower and the ETO staff were all Marshall could count on for help. His traveling companions, except for a couple of officers from OPD, did not share his views. The British were well aware of this and were prepared to exploit the divided American councils. Brooke noted in his diary on July 15, "It will be a queer party, as Harry Hopkins is for operating in Africa, Marshall wants to operate in Europe, and King is determined to stick to the Pacific."[16] Brooke knew how strongly Marshall felt, for Dill had warned Churchill that there was no possibility of changing Marshall's mind. "Marshall feels, I believe, that if a great businessman were faced with pulling off a *coup* or going bankrupt he would strain every nerve to pull off the *coup* and would probably succeed."[17]

Churchill was not overly worried because he knew that the key man, Roosevelt, was on his side. In a series of telegrams to the President, Churchill made SLEDGEHAMMER seem ridiculous, argued that an operation in North Africa would help the Russians, said that North

Africa "is the true 2nd front of 1942," and urged the President to mount the operation while going "full steam ahead on ROUNDUP."[18]

On July 16, while Marshall and his party proceeded to their first stop, the airport at Prestwick, Scotland, Eisenhower and his staff worked on a position paper. Eisenhower began by reviewing the history of SLEDGEHAMMER. He pointed out that it was designed to keep Russia fighting and added that ROUNDUP, which the British claimed to support, would be a feasible operation only if the Russians were still fighting in 1943. "The only real test of SLEDGEHAMMER's practicability," Eisenhower emphasized, "is whether or not it will appreciably increase the ability of the Russian Army to remain a dangerous threat to the Germans next spring." The trouble was no one really knew the situation in Russia and there was a sharp difference of opinion on the ability of the Red Army to hold out. Speaking for himself and his staff, Eisenhower thought "the Russian situation is at least sufficiently critical to justify any action on our part that would clearly be of definite assistance." A successful SLEDGEHAMMER would give the Russians a morale lift and, eventually, material help. "Unsuccessful attack may depress and discourage the Russians—but even this should convince them that we are trying to assist."

After presenting the background, Eisenhower considered the alternatives. JUPITER was impossible, since it required three to four hundred carrier-based fighter airplanes and they were not available. GYMNAST was "strategically unsound" as an operation either to support ROUNDUP or to aid the Russians. If undertaken, *"it should be done on the theory that the Russian Army is certain to be defeated"* and designed to improve the Anglo-American defensive position in the European Theater. As far as Eisenhower was concerned, in other words, the only real alternatives were SLEDGEHAMMER or nothing ("nothing" meaning BOLERO merging into ROUNDUP), and Roosevelt's orders to Marshall eliminated nothing as a possibility.

For Eisenhower, then, the task was to convince the British that SLEDGEHAMMER could work. He examined various possible landing sites and recommended Le Havre, with a later operation against Cherbourg. He said that the operation should be under British command, with participating U.S. troops attached to appropriate British formations. If the attack went on September 15, the U.S. could contribute two infantry divisions (the 1st and 34th), four tank battalions, and some scattered units.

Estimating the probability of success, Eisenhower warned, was difficult. Landing craft shortages limited the initial landing to one division, aircraft cover would be minimal, and even if the assault force got ashore the Germans might be able to drive it back into the sea. "I personally estimate that, favored by surprise, the chances of a fairly successful landing by the leading division are about 1 in 2," Eisenhower said, while the chances of establishing a force of six divisions in the area were about 1 in 5.

Following the gloomy prediction, Eisenhower declared and then underscored, *"But we should not forget that the prize we seek is to keep 8,000,000 Russians in the war."*

Before a conclusion could be reached, Eisenhower said, two questions had to be answered. Was the Russian situation so desperate as to justify an operation whose costs would reduce readiness for ROUNDUP? And would a partially successful SLEDGEHAMMER help the Russians? Eisenhower felt that if the answer to both questions was yes, then SLEDGEHAMMER was "a practical operation and should be launched at the earliest possible date," while if the answer to both questions was no, then the Allies should forget SLEDGEHAMMER. If they dropped the 1942 invasion, then the Allies should redouble the BOLERO program. If Russia was defeated that fall the Western Allies should "go immediately on the strategic defensive in the Atlantic" and prepare to assume the offensive against Japan.[19]

On Saturday, July 18, and the following morning, Marshall, Eisenhower, King, Clark, Admiral Harold Stark, the commander of the U.S. naval forces in the British Isles, and various staff officers from Washington and London talked over Eisenhower's recommendation. Marshall adopted them with only one important change: the site of the attack should be Cherbourg, not Le Havre. The Chief of Staff then asked Eisenhower to prepare a formal memorandum that he could present to the BCOS the next day.

Eisenhower had a memorandum ready that night. Much of his paper repeated what he had already said in the notes he had handed Marshall. He did attempt to make the British see what was at stake by declaring that, if the Western Allies allowed the Germans to "eliminate an Allied army of 8,000,000 men, when some stroke of ours might have saved the situation," then they "would be guilty of one of the grossest military blunders of all history." He therefore recommended that preparations for SLEDGEHAMMER go forward and that in early September an evaluation of the Russian situation be made. At that time a final decision on SLEDGEHAMMER could be reached. This proposal had the great advantage of stalling Churchill while holding out to Roosevelt the promise of some action in 1942. If in September the decision was not to go on with SLEDGEHAMMER, it would be too late to mount a North African expedition.[20]

On Sunday night, July 19, Marshall, King, Eisenhower, and Clark worked on the memorandum. The final version, which Marshall presented to the BCOS and Churchill on Monday morning, was much shorter than the one Eisenhower had written. Marshall dropped most of the strategic arguments and simply concentrated on proposing that an attack be made on Cherbourg. He argued that the assault force, once ashore, could remain and would draw Germans from the Russian front.[21]

All day Monday and again on Tuesday the British argued with Marshall. Eisenhower noted that "the decisions to be made are not only highly secret but momentous. There is an atmosphere of tension that will disappear once the decisions are completed and we actually know what we are to do."[22]* Marshall held out for SLEDGEHAMMER, carefully and fully answering all British objections. Eisenhower and Clark stayed up until after midnight each night providing their Chief with information on American landing craft production, delivery schedules, intelligence estimates of German strength, and so on. But time and again the British rejected Marshall's arguments and made it clear that they were absolutely against the attack. As Eisenhower summed it up, the British believed SLEDGEHAMMER "would have no beneficial effect on the Russian situation" and in addition felt "the chances of tactical disaster are very great."

The American officers, Eisenhower noted, "sat up nights . . . and have tried to open our eyes clearly to see all the difficulties and not to be blinded by a mere passion for doing something." The last factor, he added, could not be ignored, for the British and American people "need to have the feeling that they are attempting something positive." An added irritation to the Americans was their feeling that only Churchill, not the British professional soldiers, stood in their way. "I have held earnestly to the opinion that any fight this year should be within the general scope of the ROUNDUP objectives, and designed to forward and facilitate ROUNDUP when it can occur," Eisenhower reported

---

* As Eisenhower told his brother on July 24, "We are living under conditions of considerable strain and pressure. It has been particularly bad for the past week and shows no promise of letting up for another week." To Edgar Eisenhower, EP, No. 391.

to a friend in the War Department. "In spite of the fact that a great many of the British Air and Army officers agree to this view in private, the government itself was dead against it."[23]

On Wednesday, July 22, the climax came. Eisenhower sat in his office and chatted with an aide, admitting that it had been a tough grind and that he was worried about his recommendation to mount SLEDGEHAMMER. If it was adopted, he said, "I sincerely hope that it works out with reasonable success."[24] Marshall and King met with Churchill and the BCOS. After a heated debate, the Americans "admitted defeat" and abandoned SLEDGEHAMMER. The British were unalterably opposed, and that was that.[25]

Marshall cabled Roosevelt to admit that he and the British were deadlocked. Roosevelt sent back orders for Marshall to develop plans to bring American ground troops into action against the Germans in 1942. He said Marshall could choose from an offensive against French North Africa in combination with the British, or one carried out by Americans alone, or JUPITER, or sending American troops into Egypt to fight under the British Eighth Army, or an operation through Iran into the Caucasus.[26]

Before deciding, Marshall turned to Eisenhower, asking him to prepare yet another paper. By this time Eisenhower may have wondered what was the point of his leaving OPD. He was, in addition, depressed. At breakfast on Thursday morning, July 23, he and Clark talked about the end of SLEDGEHAMMER. "Well, I hardly know where to start the day," Eisenhower said. "I'm right back to December fifteenth." He thought that Wednesday, July 22, 1942, could well go down as the "blackest day in history." Despite his mood he gathered together his staff and "they settled down to assemble pieces of the wreckage of their plans."[27] By evening Eisenhower had an eleven-page "Survey of Strategic Situation" ready for Marshall.

It began with a list of assumptions—no cross-Channel attack in 1942, no offensive in the Pacific, and so on. After a long review of the German, British, and American military situations, Eisenhower considered three possible operations: reinforcement of the Middle East, an attack in northwestern Africa (GYMNAST), or the seizure of the Azores and the Cape Verdes. He listed the advantages inherent in a reinforcement of the Middle East but pointed out that the operation "is purely negative in purpose" and involved much costly shipping. The idea of operating against Atlantic islands was also negative and defensive, so was not worth serious consideration.

This brought Eisenhower to GYMNAST, another defensive operation "designed to limit German exploitation in Africa" and to relieve the situation in the Mediterranean. If successful, it could deny North Africa to the Axis, protect sea communications in the South Atlantic, provide air bases, ease the shipping crisis by opening the Mediterranean, and provide direct support to the Middle East. The disadvantages were obvious, especially the most important one—if Marshal Henri Pétain ordered Vichy's troops to resist, he could delay or jeopardize the operation and Vichy would become actively allied with the Germans. GYMNAST would pull American naval forces from the Pacific, open a new theater, and possibly bring Spain into the war on the German side. Most of all, like the option of reinforcing the Middle East, mounting GYMNAST would mean postponing ROUNDUP.

In the end, therefore, the only major operation Eisenhower liked was ROUNDUP. What he and Marshall really wanted was to get by in 1942 doing as little as possible. One way to do that and still satisfy the President might be to send what would amount to a token force to the Eighth Army, which would alleviate the "On to Richmond" type of pressure while causing minimum interference with ROUNDUP. Eisenhower's final recommendations, therefore, were to make no cutback on BOLERO, to send one U.S. armored division to Egypt, and to undertake no major operation which would interfere with ROUNDUP.[28]

The proposal to send a token force to Egypt and to delay making any other decisions might have satisfied the President, who had listed such action as one of the alternatives available to Marshall. In addition, on July 15, Marshall had had his planners in OPD prepare a study on the same subject, and they had reached the same conclusion as Eisenhower. Given the vehemence with which Marshall had attacked GYMNAST, it would have been consistent for him to agree.

But Marshall rejected the recommendation. His experiences with Pershing in World War I, when the British and French had tried to gobble up the American Army piecemeal, may have made him leery of sending American divisions into British armies. He may have been suspicious of Eighth Army leadership—certainly the British record in the desert would not have filled him with confidence in British methods or made him anxious to place his soldiers under British command. He may also have doubted that he could get away with sending just one division to Egypt, as Eisenhower had hoped, since the President wanted to get at least five American divisions into action before Christmas. Still, the proposal to reinforce the Eighth Army in the desert

represented a most intriguing alternative to the over-all strategy of World
War II. The British quite possibly would have been satisfied with one
armored and one infantry division, which would have made ROUNDUP
feasible. The Eighth Army alone, in the end, proved strong enough
to drive the Germans across Africa. Opening a new theater in North
Africa not only required more shipping, it dictated the strategy of 1943
in a way that reinforcing the Eighth Army would never have done.
Marshall's decision to ignore the recommendation was a crucial one;
surprisingly, it is ignored by almost all historians, including Marshall's
official biographer. Perhaps the reason for the neglect is that Eisenhower and Handy, awed as always by Marshall, did not push. As
soon as the Chief announced his decision, they accepted it, abandoning
their own brain child.

On July 24 Marshall and King met with the British. Marshall proposed to invade North Africa that fall, although he wanted the final
decision delayed until September 15, when a study of the Russian
situation would be made. The British agreed, and when Marshall left
London shortly thereafter he thought nothing would be done before
September 15.[29]

Churchill thought otherwise and so, it turned out, did the President.
Both men ignored the contention that GYMNAST meant the end of
ROUNDUP, both professed their eagerness to go ahead with a 1943
cross-Channel attack, both paid no attention to the September 15 decision date, and both were delighted to have a firm agreement. They
exchanged joyful telegrams and before Marshall even got back to Washington it was all settled. Operation TORCH, as it was rechristened,
would be the first Anglo-American offensive since the French and Indian War.

July 22, 1942, was hardly history's blackest day, but of course Eisenhower had said it might have been, not that it was. There are two
unanswerable questions with regard to the decision for TORCH. First,
was the gamble of leaving the Russians to their own devices justifiable? Since Russia did win, it would seem so. In the West, however,
not enough is known of the true Russian situation that summer. It
seems fair to say that the Red Army was in dire straits, and certainly many German generals later felt that had Hitler adopted a more
orthodox plan the Germans could have forced a general Soviet collapse.

Marshall was quite right in arguing that TORCH made ROUNDUP

impossible, so the second question is, did TORCH delay the final victory? This is even more speculative than the first, for it really asks, could ROUNDUP have worked? German coastal defenses in 1943 were not as strong as they were in 1944, but then Allied air power in 1943 was not what it would become in 1944. Most of the Allied air effort in 1943, however, had gone into the Mediterranean—it could have been used against Germany. The Nazis did not reach total mobilization until 1944, but neither did the Americans. U.S. troops were neither fully trained, equipped, nor blooded in 1943. The Allies did not have the landing craft in 1943 that they would have in 1944. The German eastern front in 1943 was farther into Russia than it would be a year later, so the Wehrmacht would have found it more difficult to transfer troops from one front to the other.

The argument can go on and on and on; each advantage for either side in 1943 is balanced by a disadvantage. Looked at from another point of view, the question is, what contribution did TORCH make to the final victory? Since Erwin Rommel's Afrika Korps was to be defeated at El Alamein *before* the Allies launched TORCH, the major accomplishments of TORCH and later Mediterranean operations were to (1) free shipping and (2) drive Italy out of the war. But TORCH took up as much shipping as it freed, and the Germans—paying a high cost—occupied Italy before it left the war. TORCH did give the British a better political position in the Mediterranean immediately after the war, but in the long run that was not worth much.

One advantage of TORCH often overlooked is that it gave the American Army battle experience and provided Marshall and Eisenhower with a better idea as to which generals were going to be successful as combat commanders. A number of the ground force commanders for TORCH proved wanting and had to be sent home; by the time of OVERLORD the American team was settled and Eisenhower had few disappointments with his subordinates. Had the cross-Channel attack gone in 1943, the Americans would have hit the beaches with raw troops fighting under untested leaders, which would have been costly and could have been disastrous. Finally, TORCH did give the Americans a 1942 offensive against the Germans, which presumably helped morale in the U.S.

There can be no authoritative answer to the question, did TORCH delay the end of the war? One thing does seem clear: the only chance the British and Americans had of winning the war sooner was to mount the cross-Channel attack earlier. The risks would have been greater, but so would the rewards. If successful, ROUNDUP might have led to a link-up of Western troops with the Red Army somewhere near the old Polish-Russian frontier sometime in 1944. The implications of a Western liberation of central Europe are enough to justify Butcher's comment on July 16: "Upon the discussions to take place in the next few days may rest the future history of the world."[30]

The speculation can and will go on forever. For Eisenhower, in the summer of 1942, the point was that everything he had worked on for the preceding six months was in the ashcan, and it was time to start all over.

CHAPTER 6

The Transatlantic Essay Contest

The atmosphere at 20 Grosvenor during the week of Marshall's visit had been tense; over the next three weeks it became confusing. Organization, plans, even basic decisions were up in the air. The confusion resulted from the CCS statement that no decision should be made until September 15 and Marshall's refusal to accept the President's rejection of that statement. At the July 25 meeting of the CCS the Chiefs had faced the problem of appointing a commander for TORCH, for although they felt that the operation was still tentative it was necessary to get on with the planning. The British wanted an American to take the position of Supreme Commander, but Marshall was hesitant to move without consultation with the President. At this point Admiral King remarked, "Well, you've got him right here. Why not put it under Eisenhower?"[1] The British agreed, their idea being that Eisenhower would be in charge of planning until Marshall or someone else could take over.

Marshall then remarked that he wished to avoid competition for resources between ROUNDUP and TORCH and Brooke suggested that initially the Supreme Commander should be responsible for both so that he could shift resources from one to the other in line with later decisions. The Americans accepted the proposal and the meeting broke up. Marshall then went back to his suite at Claridge's and asked Eisenhower to come to his room. When Eisenhower arrived Marshall was in the washroom. Through the closed door he called out that Eisenhower was now in charge of planning for TORCH and that he and King favored him for command of the expedition.[2]

By August 2 Marshall was back in Washington and the somewhat confused arrangements began to become clearer. The BCOS, uncertain as to Eisenhower's role, had wired their Joint Staff Mission in Washington for clarification; the reply indicated that Eisenhower was to assume "immediate executive authority" for TORCH planning.[3] The same day Eisenhower met with the BCOS, who said they objected to the title "Supreme Commander" and suggested in its place "Commander in Chief." Eisenhower had no objection. He also agreed with a British recommendation that an American become his deputy so that the American character of the expedition would be maintained even if the original commander were disabled. In effect, this meant Eisenhower now commanded TORCH.

The British also said they wanted to increase the size of the total force from seven to twelve divisions, which meant that TORCH's objectives and importance were increased. Marshall and King had proposed the old GYMNAST to the British, but TORCH had now become an expedition designed to go far beyond the occupation of French North Africa. Its new aim was to drive the Axis from Africa altogether. This increase in scope made Eisenhower's responsibilities far too broad for one man to handle. He was Commanding General, ETO, in charge of planning for BOLERO-ROUNDUP and TORCH, had to furnish an American detachment for a combined planning team, control the team once it was established, and in accordance with the July 25 decision of the CCS present as soon as possible an outline plan for TORCH. His first move to clear his desk was to assign Major General Russell P. Hartle as deputy theater commander, ETO, and turn most ETO problems over to him. He then appointed Clark deputy Allied commander in chief for TORCH and put him in direct charge of all TORCH planning.[4]

One of Eisenhower's major tasks was to build a staff for Allied Force Headquarters (AFHQ). He chose the American delegation from among planners at ETO. Under the direction of Brigadier General Alfred M. Gruenther, an old friend of Eisenhower's (and the best bridge player in the Army), the Americans met with their British opposite numbers and began to study British plans already developed. On August 4 they moved over to Norfolk House on St. James's Square to begin their combined deliberations. On August 10 Clark took command of the planning.

In building AFHQ Eisenhower decided that since both the commander and his deputy were American he would use the American staff system of G-1, G-2, and so on. He also decided that at AFHQ he would follow the principle of balanced personnel, which meant that whenever the assistant chief of staff for an operational staff section was of one nationality his opposite number was of the other and had the title of deputy assistant chief of staff. Below the heads of sections the rest of the personnel was recruited as equally as possible from American and British sources. As Eisenhower noted, "there was no historical precedent upon which to base" the organization of AFHQ, and he considered his decisions in setting up his headquarters as "among the most important and far-reaching . . . of the campaign."[5]

The integration was complete. At AFHQ British soldiers worked in daily contact with American sailors, while Army Air Force officers struggled over problems with British sailors. At first, Eisenhower recalled, they came together like a bulldog meeting a cat, but all realized that the job had to be done and they made valiant efforts to understand each other's accents, slang usages, and administrative ideas. In most offices the co-operation was so complete that British officers joined their American opposite numbers for a coffee break in the morning, while the Americans joined the British for tea in the afternoon.

The system worked, mainly because of the determination of the participants to make it work, partly because of Eisenhower's leadership. He was, by his own description, fanatic on the subject of Anglo-American solidarity, and he shipped home immediately any American officer who could not co-operate with the British. When asked, long after the war, about his emphasis on the need for Allied unity, Eisenhower said that he had read a considerable amount of military history and had talked at length about it with Fox Conner. Neither he nor Conner had any respect for coalition commands as they had existed in the past. This was the reason, he added, that he supported the CCS system, for it made it possible for theater commanders to look to one source for orders. The CCS system was as close as one could get, Eisenhower felt, to having one government giving the orders. But even with the CCS, Eisenhower knew that as Allied commander in chief he had an enormous responsibility to make the alliance work.[6]

Soon after AFHQ came into existence, General Hastings L. Ismay, Churchill's Chief Staff Officer and a member of the BCOS, reported to Eisenhower that he had heard of an American officer who when drinking boasted that the Americans would show the British how to fight. Eisenhower "went white with rage." He summoned an aide and told him to arrange for the officer in question to report the next morning. As the aide left the room, Eisenhower hissed to Ismay, "I'll make the son of a bitch swim back to America." The officer was sent home— by boat. Sometime later, Eisenhower learned of a fracas between an

American and a British officer on the AFHQ staff. He investigated, decided that the American was at fault, ordered him reduced in rank, and sent him back to the States. The British officer involved called on Eisenhower to protest. "He only called me the son of a bitch, sir, and all of us have now learnt that this is a colloquial expression which is sometimes used almost as a term of endearment." To which Eisenhower replied, "I am informed that he called you a British son of a bitch. That is quite different. My ruling stands."[7]

AFHQ's initial problems were not only in the area of national prejudices. It was almost as difficult to force soldiers and sailors to work together as it was British and American officers. Eisenhower had asked King for two of the U. S. Navy's most capable officers to serve on the staff. When they arrived on August 10 they were welcomed with the statement that there were a thousand questions the Navy could answer. One of the officers replied, "We are here only to listen." Eisenhower was furious. He said that if King himself were in London there would be no difficulty, "but we have a one-man Navy." Eventually the Navy officers pitched in and did their share, but it took time.[8]

Given Eisenhower's own professional experiences and the practice in the American Army, it was inevitable that he should regard the choice of his chief of staff as crucial. The man he wanted was Brigadier General Walter Bedell Smith, whom Eisenhower had known in the War Department as Secretary of the General Staff, but Marshall wanted him to stay in Washington. The tug of war did not end until the first week in September, when Marshall finally allowed Smith to join Eisenhower in London. By then Marshall realized that TORCH was going to go, and that Eisenhower would command it. For the first American offensive in Europe the Chief wanted his commander to have the best.

Smith remained with Eisenhower throughout the war. He was close to indispensable. His square jaw and Prussian appearance dominated Eisenhower's headquarters. He decided who could see Eisenhower and who could not, handled much of Eisenhower's civil affairs and diplomatic duties, had almost unlimited responsibility and authority in all matters except promotion of officers and operational directives, was the "no" man in the office, and frequently represented Eisenhower at meetings. Sir Ian Jacob, Ismay's deputy, thought Eisenhower was lucky to have Smith, because Smith was tough while Eisenhower used to bend somewhat with the wind. Eisenhower trusted Smith completely and regarded him as a "godsend—a master of detail with clear comprehension of the main issues." Years later Eisenhower said he was like a crutch to a one-legged man.

Smith was also, as Eisenhower politely expressed it, "strong in character and abrupt by instinct." Or, as he put it more directly to a British officer, "Remember Beetle is a Prussian and one must make allowances for it."⁹ Smith suffered from an ulcer, and although he could be suave and conciliatory when on a diplomatic mission, he was a terror in his own office. He reduced his subordinates to a bundle of shaking nerves. Once when he was holding a conference in his office his secretary, Ruth Briggs, a gracious lady who later ran for governor of Rhode Island, stuck her head in the door. Smith bellowed, "Get the hell out of here." Without pausing for breath, and before the startled Miss Briggs could withdraw, Smith turned to the officers around the table and declared, "You'll have to excuse her, gentlemen. She's an idiot." He then picked up the conversation exactly where he had left it.¹⁰*

Smith's most important duty was to be the channel through which the assistant chiefs of staff communicated with Eisenhower. He handled them without strain or fuss. Smith "is a natural-born chief of staff and really takes charge of things in a big way," Eisenhower told Gailey right after Smith arrived. "I wish I had a dozen like him. If I did, I would simply buy a fishing rod and write home every week about my wonderful accomplishments in winning the war." Smith had two deputies, General Gruenther and the British Brigadier John F. M. Whiteley, who like Smith stayed with Eisenhower through the war. One of Smith's first acts was to add to Eisenhower's organization a new section, the Secretary, General Staff (SGS). Because he had held the same post himself under Marshall, Smith knew exactly what he wanted from SGS and was so demanding that he tried five different men in

---

* At the end of the war, when Eisenhower's deputy, Air Chief Marshal Sir Arthur Tedder, was going to Berlin, he needed a piece of information from Smith. Tedder sent an aide to get it. The aide found Smith in a conference with the British and American ambassadors to France but barged right in since Tedder was in a hurry. "What the hell do you want?" Smith shouted. The aide explained. Smith told him to clear out. The aide refused and said he must have the information. "You're under arrest!" Smith yelled. The aide came to full and stiff attention and said that in any case he had to have the information. Smith relented, made a telephone call, got the information, and repeated it to the aide. He then returned to his conversation with the ambassadors, who had watched the exchange openmouthed. Looking up a few moments later, Smith noticed Tedder's aide still standing at attention. "What the hell are you doing?" "I haven't been released from arrest, sir." "Get the hell out of here," Smith bellowed. Interview with Eisenhower, December 7, 1965.

the office and was never satisfied—except once, and that officer came to Eisenhower and begged to be sent out of the theater because he could not stand working for Smith. An astonished Eisenhower explained that he was the first SGS to impress Smith, but the officer insisted upon leaving. The function of SGS was to maintain an office of temporary record, receive and record all proposals of new policies or changes in existing policies, directives, and operations plans, to route papers to their proper destinations and to ensure prompt action on them. SGS was the cement holding the headquarters together.[11]

On the operational side Eisenhower's major worry was the degree of control he would have over the fighting forces. British and American air, ground, and sea forces would be making three widely separated landings, each under a naval officer while at sea and a soldier when they hit the beaches. Eisenhower wanted all the strings to lead up to him. "Alliances in the past," he observed, "have often done no more than to name the common foe, and 'unity of command' has been a pious aspiration thinly disguising the national jealousies, ambitions and recriminations of high-ranking officers, unwilling to subordinate themselves or their forces to a commander of different nationality or different service."[12] That this was a danger in 1942 became clear when the BCOS dug out Marshal Foch's old directive of April 3, 1918. Foch had been charged "with the duty of coordinating the action of the Allied Armies on the Western Front" and had "strategic direction of military operations." The British, French, and American Armies continued to exercise "in full the tactical conduct of their armies," and each had "the right to appeal to his Government, if in his opinion his Army is placed in danger by any instructions received from General Foch."[13]

In their first directive to the British ground force commander, the BCOS strengthened but did not essentially change the old Foch directive. On the crucial point, the British general still had the right to appeal an order of Eisenhower's to his government if he thought his army was placed in danger by it. Eisenhower protested, and the BCOS responded handsomely. Under their revised directive, the British ground force commander was told that Eisenhower was his commander and "you will carry out any orders issued by him."[14]

Concurrently with the organization of his headquarters and the establishment of unity of command, Eisenhower got on with the task of selecting his field commanders. For the head of the American Army forces he wanted Major General George S. Patton, Jr., an experienced cavalry and armored officer who was an old friend. Patton was Eisenhower's senior and back in 1940 Eisenhower had hoped to command a tank unit under him. Now he sought to get the flamboyant, unpredictable Patton to serve in TORCH. Patton was widely regarded as an officer who caused more headaches than he was worth, but Eisenhower was willing to put up with almost anything from Patton in order to reap the benefit of his fighting qualities. A handsome man who dressed expensively and who usually put on an act for dramatic effect, Patton liked to wear flashy pistols on his hips, used obscene language in his high, squeaky voice in any company, bragged incessantly, and had vague ideas about being the reincarnation of earlier generals. Independently wealthy, with no problems of personal security, he was embarrassingly outspoken, especially on political subjects, about which he was hopelessly naïve. But Eisenhower was willing to take all this because he recognized that most of it was an act and that Patton's "one ambition was to be a great soldier."[15]

For his British commanders, Eisenhower turned to "Pug" Ismay for help. On August 6 he asked that the BCOS name an air commander and a naval commander so that work could go forward. They had already assigned the ground commander, General Sir Harold Alexander, one of Churchill's favorites. Before the month was out, however, Churchill had decided to shake up the Middle East command and put Alexander in charge there. His replacement was General Montgomery, but when the commander of the Eighth Army in the Middle East died in an airplane crash, Churchill sent Montgomery to Egypt. Eisenhower ended up with Lieutenant General Sir Kenneth Anderson, a Scot who —everyone assured Eisenhower—had a fine reputation. If Eisenhower was irritated when the British sent their first team to Egypt while leaving him with the substitutes, he never complained about it.

In any case, Eisenhower did get the best the Royal Navy had to offer. The BCOS assigned Admiral Sir Andrew B. Cunningham to command the British naval forces in TORCH, with subordinate commanders for each of the three landing forces. Cunningham was the embodiment of the traditions of the Royal Navy, a man of enormous dignity, efficient and cool in action, whose only thought was to send his ships out in order to fight and sink the enemy. Eisenhower came to admire, almost to the point of adulation, many of his British associates, but none ever made quite the impression upon him that Cunningham did. He was, Eisenhower felt, "vigorous, hardy, intelligent, and straightforward . . . a real sea dog." Later in life, when asked about a man, Eisenhower would use Cunningham as a standard. Thus Ismay was "almost as good as Cunningham."[16]

Under the arrangements, Eisenhower had direct contact with his two ground commanders, Anderson and Patton, but he dealt with naval commanders through Cunningham. The air forces organization followed that of the ground forces. There were two groups, the Eastern Air Command composed of RAF units under Air Marshal Sir William L. Welsh and a Western Air Command under Brigadier General James H. Doolittle, already a legend because of his raid on Tokyo. Doolittle's force was known as the Twelfth Air Force and consisted primarily of units he took from the Eighth Air Force in England. Both Welsh and Doolittle reported directly to Eisenhower.

With his staff picked and functioning and his commanders selected, Eisenhower could give his full attention to operational planning. It had been going along at a brisk pace; as Eisenhower later pointed out, "Any narration of the problems that faced us during the late summer and fall of 1942 must take them up in turn; but solutions had to evolve together. . . . [Everything] had to be handled progressively and simultaneously. Difficulty in [one area] produced at once difficulties in all the others."[17] But organization came before all the others. As Butcher noted, "Ike is most worried when he is uncertain about an organizational pattern. Once the pattern clarifies in his mind, his brow unwrinkles."[18] With his organization set, Eisenhower could concentrate on the transatlantic essay contest.

In planning the grand strategy of 1942 the Americans had been bold, the British cautious. When the time came to work out in detail the plans for Operation TORCH, the British were prepared to take great risks while the Americans advocated the safer course. Although by mid-August the CCS had not written Eisenhower's directive and had not yet set an objective, clearly the aim of TORCH was to drive the Axis from North Africa. Half of the North African coast belonged to a neutral, Vichy France. Axis possessions began with Italian Libya and extended on to Rommel's lines in Egypt. To drive the Axis out, the Allies had to go through French Morocco, Algeria, and Tunisia. Enormous distances were involved; it was nearly a thousand miles from Casablanca on the Atlantic coast of Morocco to Algiers, another four hundred from Algiers to Tunis. The Allies had to expect, in addition, that TORCH would lead the Germans to pour troops into Tunis, which they could reach from Sicily, Sardinia, and Italy with relative ease. The Allies could hope that

Vichy would resist German movements into French North Africa, but they could hardly count on it in view of the German domination of Marshal Pétain's government.

Tunis was the main prize. With it Eisenhower's troops could launch operations into Libya against Rommel's rear, without it they would have to fight in the mountains of Tunisia and Algeria against an enemy operating with an excellent port close to his main source of supply. The Allies could reduce the distance they had to advance by landing as far east in the Mediterranean as possible, thus placing themselves closer to Tunis and giving them at least a fair chance of getting the city before the Germans could react. The problem was Spain. General Franco had so far resisted Hitler's urgings that he join the Axis but, given his Fascist sympathies and his concern over Spanish Morocco, it was entirely possible that he might come into the war when the Allies invaded North Africa. Spain could take Gibraltar, close off the Mediterranean, and provide the Germans with air bases from which they could pound the Allied troops in Algeria. The result would be disaster. The way to reduce, even eliminate the threat was to take Casablanca, a good port with a railroad line running to Algiers, and make it the major supply depot. This would provide a secure, if lengthy, supply line.

The planners in OPD were more impressed by the dangers than they were by the possibilities and proposed to take Casablanca, seize the railroad to the east, secure all the approaches to Gibraltar, and consolidate the position in French Morocco before moving eastward into Algeria. They estimated that the program would take three months. Planners in the British armed services had a different idea, brought about because they were responding to a different urgency. For the Americans the main object of TORCH was to get troops into action, and as far as they could see it really did not matter much to the President where or against whom they fought. For the British, the objective was to free North Africa, which meant in practice to drive Rommel out of the continent. They therefore advocated the bold course, driving deep into the Mediterranean with the initial landings and seizing Tunis. The American plan horrified them. There was no point to the operation if three months were frittered away consolidating positions a thousand miles from Tunis while the Germans established themselves there. Such a result would make Rommel's position stronger, not weaker.

In the debate the British stressed the relative softness of the Algerian coastal area as compared with Casablanca. Algeria had more favorable weather and tide, more numerous and better ports, and was of course much closer to Tunis. At Casablanca the surf was enormous, so high that even the Americans admitted that on four days out of five it would be impossible to land there. The British also argued that landings at Casablanca would threaten Spanish Morocco and thus be more likely to bring the Spanish into the war.[19]

One obvious solution to the disagreement was to compromise by combining the two plans, which was what Eisenhower did in his first meeting with the British planners. Together they explored the possibility of landings both "inside" (Algeria) and "outside" (Casablanca) and decided there was not sufficient shipping to do it simultaneously. Eisenhower therefore tentatively agreed to a plan that called for a landing by four divisions (two American) in the Mediterranean, to be followed by a later operation against Casablanca. Follow-up troops could enter the theater through either Casablanca or Algiers, or both, depending upon Axis reaction.[20]

On August 1 Marshall said he objected to sending four divisions through Gibraltar to Algeria, both because it was too large a force and because a troop movement of that size was sure to be spotted and the Allies would lose the element of surprise. Eisenhower, who never liked to cross Marshall, hastened to reassure the Chief. He said he had not made it "sufficiently clear . . . that the tentative and temporary plan outlined . . . represented exclusively the exploratory opinions of the British joint planners." No one was willing to "express definite opinions" but the British, Eisenhower pointed out, disagreed with Marshall's thought that the danger was Spain and the possible closure of Gibraltar. Even if Marshall was right, it would take the Germans weeks to establish airfields in Spain. Eisenhower himself felt that moving into the Mediterranean without protecting communications through Gibraltar was "a highly dangerous affair" and that Casablanca should be taken quickly. Eisenhower also passed on, without comment, the British view that the movement of a large convoy through Gilbraltar would not forfeit the element of surprise, since the Germans would assume it was headed for the Near East. The British also agreed that a simultaneous assault on Casablanca would be ideal, but lack of naval vessels precluded it.[21]

On August 9 Eisenhower submitted the first formal plan for TORCH. It called for an "approximately simultaneous" assault against the Mediterranean coast of Algeria and the west coast of French Morocco. The plan included landings at Oran, Algiers, and Bône, with an assault against Casablanca coming five to ten days after the inside landings.[22]

When Eisenhower sent the August 9 plan on to Marshall, who he knew favored more emphasis upon Casablanca, with at least a simultaneous landing there, he included a covering letter justifying the plan. He said that the attack against Casablanca would have to wait because of the lack of air cover. If he had had aircraft carriers available, Eisenhower added, he could make simultaneous inside and outside landings, but the carriers were not available and the only airfield he had was at Gibraltar. Its capacity was so limited that planes could not be passed through at a sufficient rate to meet minimum demands on both the north and west coasts. He could not build up the air facilities on Gibraltar beforehand, because "the airfield there literally lies on the Spanish border and there is no hope of concealing activity from spies and agents."[23]

Marshall's reaction was that without a simultaneous landing at Casablanca the operation had less than a fifty-fifty chance of success and was too risky. "A failure in SLEDGEHAMMER, for which the public has been adequately prepared, could have been accepted," he explained, "but failure in TORCH would only bring ridicule and loss of confidence."[24]

The British did not like the plan either, but they wanted to drop Casablanca altogether. In commenting on the August 9 plan, the BCOS said that the threat from Spanish Morocco was not serious and reiterated that not only were there not enough aircraft for simultaneous inside and outside landings, naval support was also insufficient. They then repeated that they were concerned about the early occupation of Tunisia. Eisenhower, commenting on the British paper, wrote in the margin, "The milk of the whole coconut." Where the British declared, "We do not in any way wish to magnify the difficulties involved," Eisenhower scribbled, "My God!"[25]

Eisenhower was closer to the British than to the American position. He warned Marshall that if the Germans beat him to Tunis "their later capabilities for building up strength will far exceed our own and will reduce the campaign to another futile and costly defensive venture." This situation, Eisenhower said, "clearly calls for deferment of the Casablanca attack." An added advantage of an inside attack only would be that he could push forward the assault date to October 7, and the British, like Roosevelt, thought the sooner the attack the better. Eisenhower concluded that he, Patton, Clark, and the staff agreed that this plan "represents the maximum degree of security, coupled with reasonable opportunity for attaining prescribed objectives, that can be developed out of the means and assets now in prospect."[26] Marshall was not at all happy with the prospect, but planning went ahead in London on the basis of no Casablanca operation.

Things were beginning to get well muddled. Later in the war, when everyone had more experience, a major amphibious operation needed a lead time of three to five months and a much larger staff than AFHQ had to work out all the details of troop and ship movement, air cover, naval support, assault objectives, D-Day movements, and so on. In 1942 the British and the President were urging Eisenhower to mount his attack in two months, this at a time when there was no high-level agreement as to immediate or final objectives, or even landing sites.

The lack of experience came forcibly to Eisenhower's attention at this time; the first shipment of material for TORCH arrived in England without one crate or box properly labeled. His supply men had to go through every package, item by item, before AFHQ knew what was on hand and what was missing.[27] On the day Eisenhower got the bad news that the navies could not provide enough ships for simultaneous assaults, he also learned that Rommel had been reinforced by two divisions. "The way things are going," he complained, "the war will be over before we get in it!"[28]*

On August 14 Marshall asked Eisenhower for his "completely frank view" on the chances for a successful TORCH. Eisenhower replied with a long list of the difficulties and potential dangers, then concluded that he felt "the operation has more than fair chances of success provided Spain stays absolutely neutral and the French forces either offer only token resistance or are so badly divided by internal dissension and by Allied political maneuvering that effective resistance will be negligible." He was not, however, hopeful about the French, so "the chances of overall success in the operation . . . are considerably less than fifty percent."[29] After composing the message Eisenhower walked with Butcher from 20 Grosvenor back to his apartment. Butcher said that as far as he could tell Marshall wanted to call the whole thing off. Eisenhower thought that was a real possibility.[30]

Two days later Eisenhower wrote one of his long personal letters to Marshall. He said time had been lost because the failure to establish

---

* The daily planning sessions revealed more and more difficulties; one evening in the apartment Eisenhower told Butcher he wished someone would give him some good news. Among other things, the constant work meant a definite end to the social front. On August 10 Lady Astor phoned to invite Eisenhower to dinner. Her prize guest was to be George Bernard Shaw, and Butcher wanted very much to go. "To hell with it," Eisenhower growled. "I've work to do." Butcher, *My Three Years*, p. 48.

clear command arrangements had made planning difficult. Once Clark had been appointed to command the planning staff, "a tremendous upsurge in progress has been noticeable." When Clark set to work the shortages, especially in naval vessels and aircraft, began to show up. The staff began to wonder if it was all worth it. The objections the British had raised against SLEDGEHAMMER could now be applied to TORCH, especially the most important one—it might lead to disaster.

Eisenhower fought against the tendency to feel that TORCH ought to be dropped. "From the instant that I was authorized to assume executive charge of the proposition," he assured Marshall, "I laid down a specific charge to all subordinates ‧ that the time for analysing the wisdom of the original decision had passed—that we were going to accept, without question, whatever the two governments could make available and that our problem was first to make the best possible plan within the framework of visible assets, then by leadership, organizing ability and intensive preparation to do all that lay within our power to insure success." When Marshall asked for a frank evaluation, Eisenhower had dropped that attitude temporarily—thus his estimate of a less than fifty per cent chance of success. Clark and Patton had wanted him to add a statement that, regardless of that calculation, "we have no other thought except that of carrying this operation through to the utmost of our abilities," but Eisenhower had refused to add the sentence "on the grounds that you needed no reassurance of this particular kind; that unless you took these sentiments for granted you would not have named any of us to our present posts."[31]

Marshall may have wished that Eisenhower would stall on the planning a little; the British were afraid that he was doing so. On August 19 Ismay told Eisenhower that Churchill, who was in Moscow to explain TORCH to Stalin, had been cabling often to say he wanted TORCH lit as soon as possible and that he expected "superhuman efforts." Churchill had heroically taken it upon himself to tell the hard-pressed Russians that there would be no second front in 1942. To soften the blow, he pictured TORCH in glowing terms. Stalin was still unhappy, so Churchill wanted TORCH to be as big and as soon as possible. "I am sure that on his return he will expect to hear . . . all about the state of planning," Ismay told Eisenhower. To reinforce the point the BCOS sent a formal note to Eisenhower, saying that they were aware of his difficulties and did not want to embarrass him, but that they were "extremely anxious to get the plan settled. . . ."[32]

Eisenhower and his staff had been working for hours every day and by

August 21 had the new plan ready. It took into account the British objections to the August 9 plan and the lack of naval escorts. The objective was defined as an assault against Algeria "with a view to the earliest possible occupation of Tunisia." The assault forces were to come in two convoys, one from Norfolk, Virginia, commanded by Patton, to land at Oran, and the other from the United Kingdom. Once inside the Mediterranean, the latter force would split, with the main force landing at Algiers and a small force going on to Bône.[33]

Eisenhower sent the plan to the British on August 22, along with a covering letter for Ismay. He told Ismay that in several ways the plan was tentative. The D-Day date of October 15 was probably too early since planning for the Patton force was not far advanced and too little was known about the schedules for U.S. convoys bringing men and equipment for the 1st and 34th Divisions to England. His available naval support continued to be cut, which required the reduction of the force to the point where it would no longer be strong enough to deal with the resistance the French could offer. Eisenhower said his personal opinion was that simultaneous landings inside and outside would make a great difference.[34]

General Handy, Eisenhower's successor at OPD, had meanwhile arrived in London to take a close look at the plans. He provided Eisenhower with the first direct contact with War Department thinking he had had since Marshall left. Handy thought the whole thing much too risky. The British had continually emphasized the dangers involved in landing at Casablanca because of the heavy surf. Handy's view, reflecting Marshall's, was that it was better to take a chance on the surf at Casablanca than on the closing of the Strait of Gibraltar. He proposed that if sufficient naval vessels could not be found for simultaneous landings, then either Patton be sent to the Middle East to join the British there or the objective of TORCH be reduced.

Influenced by Handy, Eisenhower became more cautious. On August 22 Butcher noted, "Ike torn between desire to go ahead and do the job with the tools available and the necessity of stating his military belief that the assignment is ultra-risky. . . ."[35] Eisenhower was not, however, impressed by Handy's alternative of sending an American force to Egypt, since Marshall had already turned that down. He therefore tried to get the objective reduced. On August 23 he told the CCS that it was his opinion that TORCH was not "sufficiently powerful to accomplish . . . the purpose prescribed by the Combined Chiefs of Staff." He explained why he felt that way, implied that if his forces could not be increased the objective should be decreased, but did not actually say he wanted to shift from an inside to an outside attack. He concluded with what amounted to a fervent plea to the CCS to look again and see if they could not find some more ships for him, so that he could launch a simultaneous assault. As long as the CCS directive made Tunis the objective, however, and his force was limited, he would stand by his August 21 plan.[36]

Eisenhower's caution caused the BCOS to reconsider the whole operation. On August 24 they had a conference with Eisenhower and indicated that they too would like to make a simultaneous attack at Casablanca. The First Sea Lord commented that the British Navy was doing everything it could to provide Eisenhower with the ships he needed. Under the circumstances, Admiral Pound thought that the U. S. Navy "may be able to find additional escorting and supporting vessels so that the Casablanca attack might be staged along with those planned inside." To get such help from the U. S. Navy, the British were willing to postpone the attack to November 7.[37]

This put it up to the U. S. Navy, which meant Admiral King. He said no. His fleet could barely hold its own in the Pacific with what it had, was deeply engaged in the Solomons, and had just lost one of its few operational aircraft carriers.

While the BCOS moved to new positions, so did the War Department. The same day that Eisenhower met with the BCOS, Marshall wired him to say that he was proposing to the CCS a new directive, limiting the objective to French Morocco and Oran. This would eliminate landings east of Oran. Marshall asked Eisenhower for his opinion. Eisenhower replied that, though it would "provide maximum possible degree of security," it still risked bringing Vichy France and Spain into the list of active enemies "while it sets up no obtainable objective to balance either those risks, or the possibility of tactical defeat. . . ." The dangers were thus just as great but "we do not have a gambling chance to achieve a really worthwhile strategic purpose." Eisenhower admitted that if the real purpose of TORCH was simply to get American troops into action at an early date, Marshall's plan was preferable, but if the purpose was to take a tactical risk in the hope of gaining something worth while the Allies should go as far east as possible.[38]

Eisenhower was growing weary of the debate. After sending his message off to Marshall, he told Butcher that as he engaged in the frequent exchanges of messages he felt as if he was "in a transatlantic essay contest."[39] The British were willing to give Eisenhower Casablanca if

King would provide the ships, but King would not. Marshall would not accept Algiers without Casablanca, while the British saw no point to the operation without Algiers. Eisenhower tended to side with the British, but without CCS agreement nothing could be done. It was like July and SLEDGEHAMMER versus TORCH all over again, and once again it was necessary for the heads of government to step in.

Churchill returned from Moscow on August 25. Eisenhower and Clark dined with him, and he talked all night. Eisenhower reported to Marshall that the "Former Naval Person feels completely committed to launching TORCH at the earliest possible date, on as grand a scale as possible and with ambitious objectives."[40]

When Churchill felt strongly about something, few could resist him. He was an impressive sight, with his jutting chin, round shoulders, and fat cigar. With his cherubic face and bulldog head he was capable of portraying grumpiness incarnate. He was a great talker, able to switch moods instantly, crying one minute, laughing the next, engaging in a tirade immediately afterward. The Prime Minister was an accomplished actor who enhanced his ability to persuade through his thorough knowledge of the facts of a situation. He also never gave up. When the "Prime" got an idea into his head, he would argue for it until everyone with whom he came into contact was heartily sick of the subject. When his fertile imagination developed a new scheme and his professional subordinates did not immediately embrace it, he could be a most irritating person. He was well versed on military affairs, considered himself to be a military expert, and refused to accept the conclusions of his soldiers. He therefore meddled in every plan and operation of the war. He also would use whatever tools he could find to get his way. He knew that Eisenhower admired and liked him, and he never hesitated to use that knowledge to bring Eisenhower around when they had an argument. On the other hand the BCOS knew how Churchill felt about Eisenhower, so when they could not argue Churchill out of a project they would appeal to Eisenhower for help.

The two men had a number of violent disagreements during the war, but their friendship was never affected. Eisenhower later paid tribute to Churchill's ability to forget the arguments once a decision had been reached: ". . . in countless ways he could have made my task a harder one had he been anything less than big, and I shall always owe him an immeasurable debt of gratitude for his unfailing courtesy and zealous support, regardless of his dislike of some important decisions."[41]

Churchill's hours were strange and all those who served with him had to adjust. His day began late and ended in the small hours. The evening Eisenhower and Clark dined with him they talked about TORCH, and all the back-and-forth planning that had gone on, well past midnight. Churchill snorted that it was ridiculous to think that Franco would enter the war and said the Americans were making too much of the Spanish threat. Eisenhower agreed with him.[42]

Churchill suddenly decided, around 1 A.M., that he had to talk to Pound and Mountbatten, so he called them in for the conference. When they arrived, rubbing their eyes, he told them to cut down the time element in preparing the British contingent for TORCH so that it could go by mid-October. Shaking his finger at Pound, he said the Royal Navy would have to bring back to England "every available piece of equipment." Since the U. S. Navy was so heavily engaged in the Pacific, he told Pound, he was perfectly willing to strip the Indian Ocean to give Eisenhower more escort vessels. Turning to Eisenhower, he said that if necessary he would fly to Washington to convince Roosevelt and Marshall of the need to get TORCH moving. He wanted it started by October 15, and wanted Eisenhower to go beyond the August 21 plan and land as far east as Philippeville. The next morning Eisenhower summed up the results of the meeting for Marshall, then added in an understatement, "He is putting his tremendous energies and enthusiasm behind the project. . . ."[43]

Churchill began to take over. He fired off messages to Roosevelt, telling him what he wanted, summoned his service chiefs to his side to tell them what to do, and had Eisenhower join him often for conferences. On Friday, August 28, he had Eisenhower and Clark come to his country estate at Chequers for the weekend. On Saturday morning Churchill told Eisenhower that he was willing to drop the attacks against Bône and Philippeville, but said that the British would "go it alone" at Algiers if necessary.[44] While Eisenhower was at Chequers, an aide delivered to him a cable from Marshall. Tearing it open, Eisenhower learned that Roosevelt, as a result of his exchange of views with Churchill, was going to propose that landings be made at Oran and Casablanca only. Eisenhower had Clark put the staff to work on that proposal; Clark commented that "this football team of planners must be dizzy trying to follow all the signals for the play called by the several quarterbacks."[45]

Roosevelt did not send his proposal to Churchill until August 31; upon receiving it the Prime Minister immediately called Eisenhower and Clark to a conference. He told the Americans that it was a mistake to put half the strength of the operation onto a coast where the surf might make it impossible to land and that he was seriously concerned with the omission of Algiers. As a counter, he was interested in eliminating the Bône and Philippeville attacks, reducing the force at Casablanca, and making the two main American attacks against Algiers and Oran. Roosevelt had insisted that all the initial landings be American; Churchill thought the President was greatly exaggerating the French hostility toward the British but was willing to go along. Eisenhower, who by now was primarily engaged in passing on information, did give the War Department his own opinion, which was that "every possible chance of including Algiers in the first attack should be explored." He was, however, convinced that this could be done only if the U.S. provided more ships.[46]

As the heads of government worked out details and changed objectives and landing sites, Eisenhower confessed to Patton, "I feel like the lady in the circus that has to ride three horses with no very good idea of exactly where any one of the three is going to go." He was in an irritable mood, he said, "because last night, when I hit the bed, I started thinking about some of these things all over again and at two-thirty I was still thinking."[47] That evening, August 31, Eisenhower climbed into bed at ten-thirty and went right to sleep. At eleven the phone rang. Churchill's secretary wanted to know if Eisenhower could come to 10 Downing later "that evening." Eisenhower said he could and went back to sleep. An hour later the secretary called back, waking Eisenhower again to tell him he did not need to come around until the next morning.[48]

On the morning of September 3, Butcher brought a message to Eisenhower, saying that it looked as if the British and Americans were getting together. Eisenhower took the message and grumbled, "There'll be something impossible in it."[49] The message was from Marshall. On September 1 Churchill had cabled Roosevelt, suggesting in effect a trade. He would agree to Casablanca if Roosevelt would add Algiers.[50] This set off a flurry of activity in the War Department. On September 2 Marshall cabled Eisenhower to say that the JCS had found that the U.S. could provide all the shipping and escort vessels needed for the Casablanca operation, while U. S. Navy ships already in the Atlantic could be used inside the Mediterranean.

Admiral King, in short, after standing up to Eisenhower, Marshall, Pound, and Churchill, had yielded to Roosevelt's pressure and found that he could, after all, spare a few ships. This broke the impasse and made three landings possible. Marshall said the President was going to propose to Churchill simultaneous landings at Algiers, Oran, and Casablanca. Churchill received the President's suggestions that afternoon and called

Eisenhower and Clark to 10 Downing for a conference at 5 P.M., where they worked out the details.[51]

On the morning of September 5 Eisenhower attended a meeting of the BCOS. They agreed to accept Roosevelt's proposal "without qualification."[52] Churchill cabled Roosevelt, "We agree to the military layout as you propose it." Roosevelt responded the same day with a one-word telegram, "Hurrah!" to which Churchill replied, "O.K., full blast."[53] TORCH was finally settled. There would be three landings, at Casablanca, Oran, and Algiers.

It had been a long time coming, and it left everybody a little shaken. No one seemed to trust anyone else, except at the very top. Later in the war the CCS would give Eisenhower as theater commander a directive that set an objective for him, then let him work out plans as he saw fit. In the spring of 1943, for example, they gave him the task of knocking Italy out of the war, leaving the decision on how to accomplish this (to invade Italy or not) up to Eisenhower. But that kind of confidence came only after the Chiefs had learned to trust him and, equally important, each other. During the essay contest the Chiefs had, for the second time in six weeks, reached an impasse. As with the decision for TORCH, they had been forced to throw up their hands and turn to the heads of government for solution. The CCS-theater commander system still was not working. The Allies had much to learn about making global war, but with the inside-outside debate finished, Eisenhower could go to work and begin the process of fighting Germans.

CHAPTER 7

Preparing the TORCH

"I liked him at once. He struck me as being completely sincere, straightforward and very modest. In those early days I rather had the impression that he was not very sure of himself; but who could wonder at that? He was in supreme command of one of the greatest amphibious operations of all time, and was working in a strange country with an Ally whose methods were largely unfamiliar. But as time went on Eisenhower grew quickly in stature and it was not long before one recognized him as the really great man he is—forceful, able, direct and far-seeing, with great charm of manner, and always with a rather naive wonder at attaining the high position in which he found himself."

ADMIRAL CUNNINGHAM[1]

Dwight Eisenhower thought of himself as an apolitical being. He felt that he knew nothing about politics, did not like either the subject or its practitioners, had no political ambitions, and based all his decisions on military necessity. He was a straight-from-the-shoulder, single-minded soldier who especially abhorred the subtle niceties of international diplomacy and intrigue. Unfortunately for his personal desires, he would spend a large part of the war engaged in political and diplomatic activities and would be forced to make many political decisions. By 1945 he was as adept at politics as any professional diplomat, but he never learned to like it.

The diplomatic education of the soldier began with TORCH. The United States was preparing to invade the territory of a neutral nation without a declaration of war, and that was only the beginning of the complications. The Western Allies wanted what amounted to transit rights in Algeria and Tunisia. They had no desire for territorial gain and did not want to make war against Vichy. Ideally, they would have preferred to take Pétain's government into their confidence and make an alliance, but it was impossible for Vichy to join their cause because the Germans lived on Vichy's doorstep. The Allies could hope for Pétain's surreptitious support but nothing more.

Vichy was no ordinary government. Spawned in defeat, it lived at the sufferance of the Germans and had little popular support. It was Fascist in orientation by choice. Most of France's colonial administrators and soldiers had remained loyal to it, but their commitment was less than complete. The Allies counted on being able to shake the colonies loose. To do that, they needed to produce a man around whom the French colonial army could rally. Here there were two alternatives—the British and Americans could support a high Vichy official who would defect to their side, or they could find a leading figure in France not associated with Vichy.

Actually there was a third alternative, but the Americans rejected it from the start. In 1940 General Charles de Gaulle had formed in England the Free French, an organization that refused to accept the Franco-German armistice, denounced the Vichy government for treason, and asked all true Frenchmen to rally to it. Few colonies joined the Free French and the total number of Frenchmen who had thrown in with De Gaulle was small. He was entirely dependent upon the British. Still, he did represent an alternative to Vichy, and an effort could have been made to get the North African colonies and Algeria to rally to him. The British were willing to try, but the Americans were adamant about avoiding De Gaulle. The reasons were diverse and complex, but they revolved around Roosevelt's personal feelings toward De Gaulle.[2]

It would have been difficult in any case to get the French Army in the colonies to follow De Gaulle, because from the point of view of French officers, if De Gaulle was right in rejecting Vichy's orders and carrying on the struggle, then they had been wrong to obey the surrender notice. If De Gaulle was the true patriot, they were traitors; if he was the hero, they were cowards.

Finding either a Frenchman within the Vichy hierarchy or one who could assume leadership in North Africa was difficult, but a State Department employee named Robert Murphy was sure he could do it. Murphy had been serving in North Africa since the Franco-German armistice, knew everyone of importance in the colonies, had arranged an economic accord between the United States and Algeria, and had long advocated that the United States launch an offensive there. A conservative Catholic, Murphy was basically pleased with the Vichy government's domestic policies. He of course condemned collaboration with the Nazis, but that part of Pétain's program that emphasized work, family, and country appealed to him. He blamed France's troubles on the Popular Front and liked Pétain's stability. His French friends were aristocrats, Roman Catholics, and authoritarian in politics. He was impressed by the skill with which French administrators kept the native populations of North Africa under control and was sure that if the Allies came into the region they would have to use the existing administrative structure to keep order. He detested De Gaulle and thought Free France was dangerously radical. Murphy, in short, felt the Allies would have to make a deal with the Vichy French. Because he was the senior State Department representative in the area and because he became Eisenhower's chief civil affairs adviser, his views were decisive.[3]

Murphy was sure of himself, even cocky. He exuded confidence. His manners and dress were perfect, his smile disarming, his head full of plots and intrigues. Even though he made promises he could not keep and predictions that were hopelessly mistaken, even though he got the United States to back the wrong forces in North Africa, he always bounced back and ended up on top.

For nearly two years he had been telling the State Department that the North African French were anxious to join the Allied cause. His reports played a role in Roosevelt's thinking, adding to the President's desire to mount the North African expedition. When TORCH was decided upon, Roosevelt had Murphy fly from Africa to Washington, where the President briefed him on the operation. Murphy also saw Marshall, who asked him to fly on to London to explain the political situation in North Africa to Eisenhower.

Murphy arrived in England on September 16. Bedell Smith met him at the airport and drove him to Telegraph Cottage, where he spent a day and a night in a series of conferences with Eisenhower and high-ranking military officers and diplomats. Eisenhower listened with "horrified intentness" as Murphy described the various French factions and the possible political complications. Murphy tried to cheer him up by practically promising that he could arrange things so that the French would not resist. Aside from his contacts with local commanders, Murphy had gotten in touch with General Henri Giraud, who he said could rally the French Army in North Africa to the Allied banner.[4]

Giraud had lost a leg to the Germans in the First World War, had escaped from an enemy prison camp in 1917, and had escaped again in May 1942. He was living in the unoccupied section of France. He had let Murphy know that he was ready to come to North Africa and co-operate with the United States in an invasion.[5] The potential gain from collaboration was great, for although the French Army in Africa lacked modern equipment, it did have 120,000 men (55,000 in Morocco, 50,000 in Algeria, and 15,000 in Tunisia).[6]

Giraud had Pétainist sympathies, had no place in the hierarchy of the French Army, no popular following, no organization, no social imagina-tion, no interest in politics, no program, and no administrative abilities.[7] None of this was known to Eisenhower, and none of it bothered Murphy. Major General Charles E. Mast, of the North African Army, told his friend Murphy that the Army would obey Giraud, and that was enough.[8]

The Murphy-Eisenhower discussions at Telegraph Cottage covered a number of points—proclamations to the French, the need to impress upon them the size and power of the Allied force so that they would feel resistance was hopeless, and so on. Murphy raised one potentially dan-gerous point when he explained that Giraud would want to be the Su-preme Commander. Eisenhower, taken aback, said the question of com-mand would have to wait. In due time he would see to it that the French got modern arms and equipment, and he would insist that the French take charge of their own army, but only under his supreme command. After all, he explained to Murphy, the Allies would eventually be sending half a million men into North Africa—surely Giraud could not expect to command them all?[9]

The next morning, September 17, Murphy flew back to Washington, where he had more conferences, and then on to Algiers. Eisenhower, usually a shrewd judge of military men, was not so good outside his field. He had formed an excellent impression of Murphy. "I have the utmost confidence in his judgment and discretion," Eisenhower told Mar-shall, "and I know that I will be able to work with him in perfect harmony." Still, he was unhappy with Murphy's directive, which was vague on Murphy's relationship to the commander in chief. The President had written the directive, so Eisenhower was hesitant to raise the issue, but he felt it was "essential that final authority in all matters in that theater rest in me." Unless Murphy was clearly under him, Eisenhower said, there was a possibility that the French might think there was a division of authority between the American civil and military officials.[10] Marshall talked to Roosevelt about Murphy's status and three days later the President issued a new directive, telling Murphy that he would operate under Eisenhower.[11]

Murphy had wanted to tell the French when the attack was coming; Eisenhower had refused. One reason was that he did not know himself. The complexities involved in an operation that called for three separate landings, with one of the forces starting its journey from the United States and other two from Great Britain, were enormous. The target date was October 31; as one example of Eisenhower's problems, if he were to meet that date he had to begin combat loading in the United Kingdom by September 26. The beginning of combat loading would mean an end to training, because of the lack of equipment. Nothing that left the United States after September 12 would arrive in the U.K. soon enough to be loaded, but as of mid-September AFHQ planners had no master list in hand that told them what had arrived, what was on the way, and what was scheduled. Eisenhower toyed with the idea of substituting British equipment for the American assault units, but that was impractical because there was not time to give the men training with the weapons. All he could do was ask Somervell for a master list "as soon as possible."[12]

The date of D-Day was worrying everyone. President Roosevelt was especially concerned because congressional elections were coming up and a successful TORCH would give a great, and needed, boost to the Democratic Party. Under the circumstances, he preferred to have the operation go before the elections. Later, the idea that Roosevelt insisted upon TORCH in preference to SLEDGEHAMMER-ROUNDUP in order to influence the elections gained wide currency, but there is no evidence to support this charge. Roosevelt never tried to get Eisenhower to push the date forward, although the President did tell the general in late 1943 that it had been a "disappointment" for him that the African invasion came just after, instead of just before, the November 3 elections (in which the Democrats took a bad beating).[13]

But if Roosevelt did not interfere with Eisenhower's choice of a date, he was interested, like everyone else. On September 8 Marshall asked Eisenhower to let Washington know what date he had selected. Eisenhower replied that the best he could do was November 4 and that a more realistic date was November 8. Churchill, Eisenhower added, had reluctantly accepted the fact that TORCH would not go before November 4.[14]

Since Churchill's return from Moscow, Eisenhower had been having dinner with him at 10 Downing Street every Tuesday evening.[15] Eisenhower was also spending his weekends at Chequers, and one Friday evening the Prime Minister, along with Brooke and Pound, questioned Eisenhower about the date. They knew that November 4 was the earliest TORCH could go, but they were concerned about the latest possible date. The Allies had stopped a lend-lease convoy for Russia (PQ-19, due to leave October 4) in order to provide ships and supplies for TORCH, but Churchill felt that if TORCH was not going to begin before November 15, then PQ-19 ought to go ahead. Eisenhower repeated that his best guess was November 8.[16] Churchill wanted a guarantee. Eisenhower explained that it was impossible to prepare complete loading schedules until the equipment had actually arrived and been properly sorted, and until this was done no exact date could be given.[17]

A little more than a week later Eisenhower had a Monday morning staff conference with Churchill and the BCOS. Churchill again raised the question of running PQ-19. Two days earlier PQ-18 had reached Archangel, but it had suffered heavy losses. The Prime Minister was worried about the Russian situation. The Allies had already taken, to use in TORCH, some lend-lease P-39 fighters that had been scheduled for the Russians, and Stalin was displeased generally because TORCH made a second front in 1942 impossible. Churchill was so concerned that he told Eisenhower he might recommend a two-week delay in mounting TORCH in order to run PQ-19.

The discussion about Russian reactions to TORCH brought up the subject of a second front in 1943. Eisenhower casually remarked that because of TORCH it would be impossible to mount ROUNDUP. Churchill was thunderstruck. All of Marshall's arguments against TORCH had revolved around its cost to ROUNDUP, but they evidently had made no impression on the Prime Minister. He told Eisenhower he was "very much astonished" to learn that TORCH eliminated ROUNDUP.

Throughout the morning Churchill kept coming back to the subject. Jutting out his chin, he glowered at Eisenhower and said it simply could not be so. After all, the Allies had been planning to employ fifty divisions in ROUNDUP, and at the most TORCH would take only thirteen. He found it amazing that this small force could have such a profound effect on ROUNDUP. Eisenhower later reported, "I again went over with him all the additional costs involved in the opening of a new theater, in establishing a second line of communications, in building up new port and base facilities and in the longer turn-around for ships," but it made no impression.

Churchill was terribly put out. He said the Allies "must resume at the earliest possible moment a concentration of force" for ROUNDUP. The whole thing was intolerable. The United States and United Kingdom could not possibly confess that the best they could do in an entire year was one thirteen-division attack. Turning to his own chiefs, he told them to get started on plans for an operation in Norway (JUPITER) and added that he was asking Stalin to co-operate.

The conference lasted for more than two hours and left Eisenhower shaken. He reported to Marshall, "The serious implication is that either the ·original TORCH decision was made without a clear realization of all its possible adverse consequences or that these considerations were ignored in the anxiety to influence the TORCH decision. It is also very apparent that the Former Naval Person has no conception of the terrific influence ·the situation in the Southwest Pacific exerts on our own strategy."[18]

The questions that the conference left in Eisenhower's mind were long-range ones about the nature of British leadership; the immediate problem of the date was soon settled. Roosevelt and Churchill agreed to cancel PQ-19 and use the "trickle method" of sending supplies to Archangel—unescorted merchantmen would move out from Iceland singly or in pairs. Regular convoying began again in mid-December.[19] On September 26 the CCS gave Eisenhower formal responsibility for the final choice of a D-Day date, and he settled on November 8.

Eisenhower planned to go to Gibraltar before the attack began and he would need a deputy theater commander for ETO. The man he wanted was his old boss in WPD, Gerow, currently commanding the 29th Division in England. Eisenhower told Marshall that he was "quite well aware that you do not fully share my very high opinion of General Gerow's abilities," but he felt that Gerow's "loyalty, sense of duty, and readiness to devote himself unreservedly to a task, are all outstanding." Clark and Smith agreed with his estimate of Gerow, and he hoped Marshall would give his concurrence.

Marshall said he would accept Gerow; he also gave Eisenhower a little lecture. He wanted to be dealt with on the "frankest possible basis," the Chief said, indicating that he felt Eisenhower had tried too hard to please him in the past and had not stood up for his own ideas. "When you disagree with my point of view, say so, without an apologetic approach; when you want something that you aren't getting, tell me and I will try to get it for you. I have complete confidence in your management of the affair, and want to support you in every way practicable." Before Eisenhower could appoint Gerow, however, Clark made a trip to Washington. When he returned he reported that Marshall had privately expressed his doubts about Gerow. Eisenhower, unhappy, decided he would ignore Marshall's invitation to be frank and make someone else his deputy. He noted that Gerow had never clicked with Marshall, and once an officer was on the bad side of the Chief he could never get right again.[20]

The staff, meanwhile, was working fourteen hours a day on loading schedules, intelligence estimates, air cover, and the thousands of details involved. Progress seemed, at times, to be so slow that "impatience . . . irritation and irascibility" set in. Eisenhower confessed to Marshall that "it has been a trifle difficult to keep up, in front of everybody, a proper attitude of confidence and optimism." Still, he was doing his best and by taking a long view was fairly well satisfied. His own estimate as of October 12 was that the plan would develop "almost perfectly up to the point of departure." After that, of course, the unknown factors of the surf at Casablanca and the French reaction made prediction impossible. Eisenhower's own conviction was that, with a break in the weather, "we should get on shore firmly and quickly and, at the very least, should find divided councils among the French. . . ." Then if the governments sent in enough follow-up troops, the campaign would proceed effectively.[21]

Eisenhower kept to a tight schedule. On Sunday, September 27, he tried to take the day off—it would have been one of his first since December 14, 1941—but he had to go to 20 Grosvenor in the morning and spend four hours in the office. During ordinary days he was there from eight until seven, usually had twelve to fifteen appointments, and had AFHQ officers coming and going all day long. He did get to take the Sunday of October 4 off. He spent it at Telegraph Cottage resting and shooting his pistol.[22]

Eisenhower did get to relax with idle conversation after dinner. Talking with Smith and Butcher at Telegraph Cottage one evening, Eisenhower said he had heard that MacArthur had asked again that Southwest Pacific be made the main theater of war. MacArthur had added that if he were not given all the equipment he demanded he "would refuse to accept responsibility for the consequences." Turning to Smith, Eisenhower remarked that "come hell or high water" he would never use such phrases. When the plan was set he intended to go ahead with the equipment available and he would not whine to the War Department about his needs.

Smith and Eisenhower then talked about how tough Marshall's job was and how well he did it. Eisenhower said, "I wouldn't trade one Marshall for 50 MacArthurs." He thought a second, then blurted out, "My God! That would be a lousy deal. What would I do with 50 Mac-Arthurs?"[23]

While planning in London went forward, Murphy was busy in Algiers. On October 15 he wired Washington to say that a new possible leader for the French was available, Admiral Jean Darlan. The admiral was commander in chief of Vichy's armed forces. He had served in Pétain's cabinet and was an enthusiastic collaborator. But he was, next to Pétain himself, the most important French official in the hierarchy and Murphy recommended that the Allies make a deal with him, even though Giraud and his Algerian contact, General Charles E. Mast, would have nothing to do with Darlan.

Murphy was running into other difficulties. Mast was not at all happy with the idea of Giraud serving under Eisenhower and proposed instead that Eisenhower retain command of the American forces while Giraud became Supreme Commander. In this connection Mast pointed out that the French knew all the details of the terrain, and added that with Giraud in command the Allies could enter "practically without firing a shot." Finally, Mast insisted that the Americans immediately send five officers from Eisenhower's staff to Algeria to meet their French opposite numbers for an exchange of information.[24]

On October 16 Marshall passed Murphy's messages on to Eisenhower, asking for his comments and remarking that he did not trust Darlan. Eisenhower immediately arranged for a conference with Churchill and the BCOS. Before going, he gave Marshall his early reactions. He thought "a possible formula affecting the delicate command situation" could be worked out, primarily on the basis of what amounted to bribery. He would retain his position while making Giraud governor of all French North Africa, responsible for all French civil and military affairs. Eisenhower would support Giraud in this position with the British and American armies. But under the Eisenhower formula Giraud, like all puppets forced onto a people, would not have a free hand. Eisenhower would "request" him to make "proper contacts" with Darlan and to appoint Darlan commander in chief of French military or naval forces in North Africa "or in some similar position that will be attractive to Darlan."

Eisenhower thought the Allies would have to decide whether they wanted to make Darlan or Giraud "our chief collaborator," but he was anxious to "secure the advantages accruing to us" if both would co-operate. In order to satisfy the French on command arrangements, Eisenhower was willing to promise that eventually the entire military command in the area would pass to them, but he would retain the right to decide himself when to make the switch. If, meanwhile, the campaign went well, and the Allies moved through French territory toward Libya, Eisenhower would organize an American army under Clark and make either Giraud or Darlan the deputy Allied commander.[25] For the immediate future, Eisenhower was sending Clark and some other staff officers to meet with Mast's representatives in Algeria.

Churchill readily accepted Eisenhower's proposals,[26] which indicated how much importance the Prime Minister attached to TORCH. Darlan stood for everything Churchill and his friends had denounced at Munich and again when the French quit in 1940. The French admiral had accepted the armistice and was eager to join Hitler in building a New Order in Europe. He had always hated the British and his feelings were even stronger after the British sank part of the French fleet in Oran. Darlan had played a prominent role in the proclamation of Vichy's anti-Semitic decrees and was a willing collaborationist.

There were broader foreign policy issues involved in the selection of a North African leader. The United States had maintained its diplomatic relations with Vichy while the United Kingdom had thrown its support to De Gaulle. For Churchill, the Free French movement "was the core of French resistance and the flame of French honour."[27] Postwar France, the Prime Minister held, would have to be purged of all the Vichy scum and reconstituted under De Gaulle's leadership. Churchill had his problems with De Gaulle throughout the war, as the two egotists often rubbed each other wrong, but the alternative of the hated Vichy, with its supine creatures who had left England in the lurch in 1940 and accepted surrender and dishonor, made Churchill gag.

The United States State Department took the view that one could do business with Vichy. It rejected De Gaulle, in large part because he had hurt Secretary of State Cordell Hull's and Roosevelt's feelings, in part because he represented the unknown. De Gaulle did not help by constantly denouncing the United States for its Vichy policy. There were those who professed to see a conspiracy in America's policy, and the leader of the conspiracy school was De Gaulle himself, who thought that arrangements with men like Pétain and Darlan were "not completely

disagreeable to certain parties in the United States which are playing
for a new Europe to oppose the Soviet Union and even England."[28]

That there was a split in Anglo-American relations with regard to
French policy was clear enough, as was the line-up, with De Gaulle
being the British nominee for postwar power while the Americans were
prepared to back Giraud, Darlan, or anyone other than De Gaulle
with whom they could work. But that there was a conspiracy to make
France into some sort of American puppet state was simply not so.
American policy toward France was shortsighted, often mistaken, ineffective, and frequently ludicrous, but it was not based on conspiracy.
Roosevelt neither liked nor trusted De Gaulle and in any case wanted
to be the savior of France himself, directing free elections for a government after his armies had liberated and occupied it. The President was
convinced that France was a second-rate country that would never again
amount to anything in world politics; De Gaulle embodied a very different
image of postwar France. Hull hated De Gaulle, Murphy did too, and
besides they found it easier—more convenient, really—to work with
the established Vichy officials.

Eisenhower, for his part, knew practically nothing of the political
complexities and was only interested in finding a Frenchman who could
deliver up Algeria and allow his armies to move on into Tunis. Murphy
said Giraud or Darlan could do just that, and Eisenhower agreed to
work with them. Churchill, more anxious to keep his promise to Stalin
and to attack Rommel's rear than to maintain his French policy, went
along.

With Churchill's blessing, Clark prepared to set out on October 17
for Gibraltar, then North Africa, where he would meet secretly with
Murphy's French friends. Eisenhower went to Scotland the next day to
inspect a field exercise. The next few days, while Clark was off on his
mission, Eisenhower fretted. Visiting troops helped him get through the
waiting period—he had not been away from the desk in what seemed
like months. "Sometimes I feel like a politician and at others like an
errand boy," he confessed to a friend in OPD, "but I get so little chance
to go out and be with the troops that it is only infrequently that I can
gain a personal sense of feeling like a soldier."[29]

While Eisenhower was watching the exercise he managed to forget
about Clark and his dangerous mission. When he returned to London
the worries came back with him. "I do not need to tell you," he confessed to Marshall, "that the past weeks have been a period of strain

and anxiety." He could imagine a hundred different things that could happen to Clark, and that got him to thinking about the various aspects of the operation as a whole. "If a man permitted himself to do so, he could get absolutely frantic about questions of weather, politics, personalities in France and Morocco, and so on," Eisenhower said. He refused to do so. "To a certain extent," he explained, "a man must merely believe in his luck and figure that a certain amount of good fortune will bless us when the critical day arrives."[30] Throughout the war Eisenhower trusted in his luck along with his preparations, and it never failed him.

But even those upon whom Dame Fortune smiles get tense, and Eisenhower was no exception. Two days after Clark left, Eisenhower learned that he had arrived off the Algerian coast too soon and would have to lie around in a submarine, submerged, for a full day waiting for his rendezvous. Eisenhower kept himself as busy as he could, but it did little good. Finally he shut up the office and announced he was going to drive himself out to the cottage that night. He was not sure of the way, had never driven in England before, and had no driver's license, but he started the car and zoomed off. "When last seen," Butcher reported, "he was going down the middle of the road, veering a little bit to the right and a bit uncertain."[31]

Around midnight Saturday, October 24, one of Eisenhower's staff officers called to say that they had just received a message from Clark. The police had broken up his meeting with Mast, Clark reported, and he had been forced to hide in an "empty, repeat empty wine cellar." In getting into the rubber boat for his trip out to the submarine, Clark had lost his pants and the bribe money he had taken with him. But he was safe in Gibraltar and would be in London late Sunday.

All Sunday morning Eisenhower fretted at the office. At 1 P.M. Butcher drove him out to Telegraph Cottage, where Clark and Smith soon joined him. Clark was jubilant. Mast had given him exact details on the location of troops, batteries, and installations at Oran and Algiers, assured him of French co-operation, and emphasized the importance of moving on Tunis before the Germans could get there.

Clark reported that the most troublesome problem was the question of eventual command. Mast insisted upon Giraud's assumption of over-all command, which Clark would not accept. Eventually they were able to agree on a draft letter which proposed the restoration of France to its 1939 boundaries, the acceptance of France as an ally by the U.S. and the U.K., and the assumption of the supreme command in North Africa by the French "at the appropriate time." As Eisenhower clarified the phrase, it meant that he retained command of the area as a base of operations against the Axis, while giving the French charge of the defense as soon as the area was secure. That problem aside, Eisenhower was delighted with Clark's report. He immediately recommended him for a Distinguished Service Medal and congratulated him on the amount of detailed military information he had gathered.[32]

Clark's brief visit with Mast was the only contact anyone at AFHQ had had with the French, and it illustrated what a chancy undertaking TORCH was. The Allies were preparing to invade a neutral country where they had only a single source of information, without a declaration of war and with the hope that the inhabitants would not resist them. If Murphy's predictions about French reaction were wrong the whole operation might fail. The only Frenchman in any position of authority to whom the Allies had talked was Mast, who was only a division commander. Although Giraud's name was supposed to be something to "conjure with" in North Africa, no one knew that for sure. Besides, no Allied officer had talked with Giraud, so Eisenhower did not really know what that Frenchman would do.

The Allies wanted French co-operation, but only Mast had any idea of when the invasion was coming. No one had discussed the operation with the Spanish, so their reaction was also a mystery. The unpredictable included the weather—the surf at Casablanca might force one third of Eisenhower's total force to lay off shore for a day or even more, and he had no strategic reserve. The Allies were taking chances in TORCH, in short, that later in the war they would not dream of taking.

Despite the risk, as October came to an end and D-Day approached Eisenhower exuded confidence. Patton's force had already set out from Norfolk and so far there had been no mishaps. The Eighth Air Force was pounding away at the German submarine bases in the Bay of Biscay. Mast had "committed himself so far that there is no chance of his double-crossing us." Montgomery had launched on October 23 his attack at El Alamein, and initial reports indicated that he was enjoying success. The troops for the Oran and Algiers landings were loaded and ready to go. Churchill and the BCOS were giving Eisenhower their full backing.

Eisenhower had problems, but he was sure he would overcome them all. Taking his last long view of strategic developments before departing for his forward command post at Gibraltar, he suggested to Marshall that in so far as port capacity in North Africa was limited, they ought to begin thinking about what they were going to do with the mass army being built in the U.S. Some of the troops could be used profitably in the Southwest Pacific, but most of them should come to Europe. As Eisenhower saw it, "the spring of '43 may see the ROUNDUP idea revived with the purpose of launching a decisive blow in the spring of '44, with the summer of '43 used for building up the necessary forces in Great Britain, firmly establishing ourselves in favorable position in the Southwest Pacific and exploiting TORCH to the point that the whole region" was secure.

With Mast safely in the Allied camp, Eisenhower thought "everything for TORCH is well in hand." He feared "nothing except bad weather and possibly large losses to submarines." These dangers were real enough but, given a little luck, he told Marshall, "you may rest assured that the entry will go as planned and that we will have good news for you by the morning of November 9th."

The nagging problem was Giraud's demand for command. Mast had made it clear to Clark that since the battle was on French territory, since Giraud was senior to Eisenhower and a distinguished commander in his own right, and since it was through his influence that the landings would be unopposed, Giraud should have the supreme command. Eisenhower was willing to go to great lengths to satisfy Giraud—for example, Mast had said Darlan could not be trusted and that Giraud would have nothing to do with him, so Eisenhower dropped the idea of working with Darlan—but not so far as to give him supreme command. The question of over-all command "is going to be a delicate one," Eisenhower recognized, and he knew he would "have to ride a rather slippery rail on this matter." But here, as with all his other problems, Eisenhower was sure he could handle it. He told Marshall not to worry.[33]

CHAPTER 8

The Invasion of North Africa

Eisenhower planned to go to Gibraltar on Monday, November 2, take command of the Rock, the best communications center in the area, and direct the invasion from there. By Saturday, October 31, everything that could be done in London had been done, so the commander in chief went to Chequers for a final weekend. Sunday evening he and Butcher watched a movie. It was a private showing. Eisenhower was supposed to be in Washington, this having been announced to the press as cover for his imminent absence from London. The cover plan may have helped lull the Germans into thinking no invasion was coming, but it made Eisenhower a trifle nervous, for not even Mrs. Eisenhower knew it was a cover plan and she was expecting him in Washington. He tried to fly to Gibraltar on Tuesday, but the weather prevented it. The weather was still bad the next morning and Eisenhower's pilot, Major Paul Tibbets (who later piloted the plane that dropped the first atomic bomb on Japan), did not want to fly. Eisenhower ordered him to take off, after taking the precaution of putting Clark on another B-17.

After a bumpy passage and landing, Eisenhower went right to his head-quarters, which were in the subterranean passages under the Rock. Feeble electric light bulbs only partially pierced the darkness of the tunnels. Water dripped from the walls. Offices were caves where the cold damp air stagnated and stank. It was, Eisenhower declared years later, "the most dismal setting we occupied during the war."[1]

For three days Eisenhower fretted. He tried to work on plans for operations after the capture of North Africa, but he could not concentrate. The talk in the Gibraltar tunnels centered around Giraud.[2] He had finally agreed to leave France on the date selected by the Allies and was now on a submarine. He thought he was headed for Algiers to take command there; actually the submarine was bringing him to Gibraltar, for Eisenhower wanted to make sure he would co-operate before turning him loose in North Africa. Eisenhower's staff meanwhile prepared a message for Giraud's approval, announcing that he had made an alliance with the Allies to liberate French Africa and urging the Army not to resist. The idea was to send it by radio to Giraud on the submarine, have him approve, then print it and drop it from planes over Morocco and Algeria.

Admiral Cunningham suggested that, since Giraud was safely in Allied hands, they might as well proceed to issue all the statements, pamphlets, and so on, they pleased, all in Giraud's name. Eisenhower said that was too "double-crossy."[3]

That evening Eisenhower, Clark, and Butcher sat around in Eisenhower's room and had a bull session. It would not be long, Clark said, before they were either lions or lice. Eisenhower mused that he would rather be leading an invasion directly into France. Clark cursed at all the politics involved in TORCH. Eisenhower declared that he would be happier commanding a division but added that he was thankful he had an opportunity to make some mark in history, an opportunity few men ever had. Clark, who was scheduled to fly to Algiers and set up an advanced headquarters there, said that if things went badly he intended to fly right on into central Africa and parachute out, keeping the gobs of gold he would be carrying with him for contingency use. He promised to let Eisenhower know where he was but said that if the commander in chief wanted to join him he had to bring his own gold along.[4]

Such nonsense helped to pass the time, as did dictating letters. The day before the invasion Eisenhower sent a long letter to Marshall. There was little else he could do, since the troops were all at sea and he could not visit with them. He was caught in that period in a commander's life in which all he could do was wait. The plans were finished, the operation in motion. Until it succeeded or failed, events were out of his hands. Eisenhower would go through that waiting period a number of times during the war, but he never got used to it.

Dictating a message to Marshall was, in a way, like talking to the Chief, and Eisenhower drew some reassurance from it. He recounted all his worries, which centered on the German submarines, mentioned Murphy's "case of jitters" and wondered if Murphy was developing "a bit of hysteria." Eisenhower had just received a message from Murphy saying that unless the Kingpin (code name for Giraud) was in Algiers by the night of November 6–7 "the success of the operation could not be assured." Murphy had also asked for diversionary attacks against Norway, western France, and southern France.

In contrast to Murphy, the AFHQ staff had stayed calm. Eisenhower was especially impressed with his British subordinates. Growing expansive, he described to Marshall the congestion on Gibraltar, then gave a detailed account of his trip from London to Gibraltar.

As he talked, Eisenhower's mind jumped from subject to subject. He mused about the Spanish, weather conditions at Casablanca, and promotions for the American Army officers involved. He explained that bad weather had forced him to cancel a proposed paratrooper drop on Tunisia. While Eisenhower was talking a flash report came in that one of the combat loaders for Algiers had been torpedoed about three hundred miles east of Gibraltar. Eisenhower passed the information on, along with the hope that the ship could make it safely to shore. (It did.)

When he ran out of minor details, Eisenhower began to talk about the meaning of TORCH. "We are standing, of course, on the brink and must take the jump—whether the bottom contains a nice feather bed or a pile of brickbats!" He was satisfied that he had done his best to assure a successful landing. Looking back over the "high pressure weeks since July 24th," Eisenhower could not think of a major decision that he would change. He told Marshall that every member of the AFHQ staff, British and American, had "slaved like a dog," and added that he felt strongly that "we have established a pattern for Combined Staff operation that might well serve as a rough model" for future expeditions.

Analyzing the reasons for the successful teamwork, Eisenhower said the most important was unity of command. Next was the attitude of the British government, which had made "absolutely certain" that none of the British officers had any "mental reservations about their degree of responsibility to the Supreme Commander." The way in which the CCS had allowed AFHQ to work out its own problems helped, too, as had the quality of the officers assigned to AFHQ by both countries.

Eisenhower was proud of what he had achieved at AFHQ. Waiting now for the troops to hit the beaches, he told Marshall that it was always possible some unforeseen development might cause TORCH to fail. If so, he was afraid that "much of the work that has been done will be discredited by unthinking people, and the methods that have been followed [at AFHQ] will be cited as erroneous." Eisenhower hoped that would never happen, because he was convinced that an integrated staff operating under unity of command was the only way to make the alliance work. If TORCH failed it would be because of political factors beyond AFHQ's control; the lessons AFHQ had to teach would remain valid.[5]

As Eisenhower finished his dictation an aide ran in with news that Giraud had arrived on the Rock. A seaplane had picked him up off the submarine and brought him to Gibraltar. Giraud demanded to see Eisenhower—he would talk to no one else. While the secretary, with the dictated notes, left the cave that served as an office, Eisenhower sat down and waited for Giraud. Colonel Julius Holmes joined him to interpret.

The tall Frenchman burst into Eisenhower's cave and slapped down on the desk a memorandum for "The American General Staff." In it Giraud demanded that he be taken to Algiers, be given a good radio transmitter and an airplane, some qualified American staff officers, and facilities for an advance command post. Eisenhower brushed aside the demands and said all he wanted Giraud to do was to issue a statement that could be broadcast that night to Morocco and Algeria. Giraud flatly refused. He said he could not participate in the operation unless he was made Allied Supreme Commander. He wanted to change the direction of the convoys and invade the south of France. Eisenhower told Holmes to tell Giraud that both demands were impossible. Giraud replied categorically that by November 10 all forces ashore must come under his command, and thereafter all forces landing in North Africa would have to come under him immediately upon debarking. He added that Eisenhower could retain control of base and administrative arrangements near the ports. He himself, however, "would make all decisions respecting the tactical and strategical employment of the troops."

Again and again Eisenhower said that Giraud could take command in Algeria after the Allies had moved on to Tunisia but it was simply impossible to change commanders in the middle of the operation. Each time Giraud paced the room and said he must have the command. Eisenhower promised him eventual command as soon as possible, but Giraud was "completely deaf" to the promises. He shook his head and repeated his demands. At one point he said he would not, as Supreme Commander, be responsible to the CCS. Eisenhower could deal with them on supply matters while Giraud directed the war. That was preposterous, Eisenhower replied. Very well, Giraud responded, he would stand aside, the French Army would fight, and the Allies would not even get ashore.

Eisenhower conceded every point he could to get Giraud to come over. He offered Giraud "the governorship, virtually the kingship, of

North Africa," with money to build an army and an air force, but Giraud kept saying *non*. He had to have the supreme command.

After about an hour of argument Eisenhower left the cave and told Clark to take over. Clark argued for an hour and gave up. Eisenhower went back. Giraud repeated that he had to be the Supreme Commander.

Eisenhower found the conversation tiring and confusing. It was irritating to have to wait for Holmes to translate. Eisenhower thought Murphy had explained all the command arrangements to Mast, and that through Mast they had been explained to Giraud. The Frenchman's idea of diverting the convoys to southern France was madness—obviously Giraud knew nothing of amphibious warfare, of the enormous complexity of Operation TORCH, or he would never have even made such a suggestion—and caused Eisenhower to question Giraud's military ability. Eisenhower wanted to go to the communications room and listen for news from the assault convoys, but instead he had to stay in his cave and argue with a supposed ally. Giraud had no governmental backing, no infantry, no airplanes, no navy, no political following, nothing. Yet he was demanding the supreme command of the major Anglo-American operation in the war to date. The setting, in a dark, dripping cave with an air raid going on overhead, lent an Alice in Wonderland quality to the meeting.

The Allied commander in chief could neither accept Giraud's demands nor understand the man who was making them. From Giraud's point of view, on the other hand, it was simple and logical. His country was being invaded by foreigners, who wanted him to lend his name to their aggression while withholding from him all real power. He was being asked to fight against his own government and army in a subordinate role under a plan elaborated by foreigners, with command in the hands of younger and less experienced commanders than he. To this proposition Giraud could only say *non*.

While Eisenhower and Giraud talked, in the tunnels of the Rock there was "hubbub and bustle . . . like election eve." Butcher burst into Eisenhower's office with a message and came out to report that "Ike was red-faced from talk." Clark guessed that Giraud was going to sit on the fence for forty-eight hours to see how the assaults went, then make up his mind. At 8 P.M. the meeting broke up. It had started at 4 P.M. and nothing had been accomplished.[6] Eisenhower called in his secretary and added a postscript to his letter to Marshall. "I've had a 4 hour struggle with Kingpin," he said. Giraud "says 'Either I'm Allied C-in-C or I won't play!; He threatens to withdraw his blessing and wash his hands of the affair." Then, as a final note, Eisenhower added, "I'm weary!"[7]

Even dinner was a problem. The governor of Gibraltar had asked Giraud and Eisenhower to be his guests, but if both went there would be a seating problem. Eisenhower decided to eat with Clark at the Royal Navy mess so that Giraud could sit in the position of honor at the governor's right. At ten-thirty Eisenhower and Giraud went back into the caves. They argued for another two hours and again failed to reach any agreement.[8]

By the end of the evening Holmes was too tired to interpret any longer, so Clark took over. His French was not good, but everyone got along without any difficulty because, as Eisenhower put it, "each of us merely repeated, over and over again, the arguments he had first presented." Eisenhower finally said they might as well get some sleep. As they shook hands, Giraud's good-night statement was, "Giraud will be a spectator in this affair."[9]

By the time the meeting broke up, the assault forces were on their way in. Butcher jubilantly reported that Eisenhower's luck was holding— the surf on the Morocco coast was down to three to five feet. Patton's men could go ashore and he would not have to bombard Casablanca. As Eisenhower dictated a long cable to CCS on the results of his meeting with Giraud, news came in from Oran. The landings there were unopposed. A message from Admiral Hewitt, naval commander in Patton's force, said the operation was proceeding on schedule. There was no news from Algiers. Satisfied and exhausted, at 4:30 A.M. Eisenhower unfolded a cot in his office and went to sleep.[10]

He was up at seven, reading messages and dictating cables. The situation was unclear, partly because the messages he was receiving were frequently garbled, but as far as he could tell everything was going ahead about as he anticipated. The French were beginning to resist, but Eisenhower could not tell how actively. "I'd give a month's pay for an accurate report this minute from each sector," he told Smith, who was in London, at 9:30 A.M. He did know that his troops were fairly solidly ashore at Oran and Algiers.[11]

Giraud came in and the AFHQ staff gave the Frenchman exaggerated reports of the success of the landings. Somewhat subdued, he went into Eisenhower's office at 10 A.M. for a conference. He must have sensed the hostility around him, perhaps even realized the potential danger he was in if he refused to co-operate. Butcher reported that "all felt something had to be done with him . . . even a little airplane accident. . . ." The governor of Gibraltar had told Eisenhower that "he had a good body disposal squad if needed."[12]

Eisenhower opened the meeting. "It is impossible for me to serve two masters," he said. Giraud admitted that was true and declared he had no intention of asking for command of the air and sea forces. But the bulk of the ground forces, in any fight with the Germans, would be French, and they would only obey him. Eisenhower demurred, discussion followed, and no progress was made. Eisenhower finally agreed to "consult" with Giraud on the big decisions, making him in effect a co-commander for ground action. Giraud said that made him much happier.

After a few more minutes of polite talk Giraud concluded a gentlemen's agreement with Eisenhower. As the commander in chief reported to the CCS, "The basis of the agreement is exactly what I offered Kingpin throughout the long conference of yesterday." Eisenhower would recognize Giraud as the commander in chief of all French forces in North Africa and as governor of the area. Eisenhower based his right to make this appointment on military conquest, although he hoped to keep up the fiction that it represented the real desire of the French people. Giraud agreed to go to Algiers the next day to begin organizing the French forces for employment against the Germans.[13]

Tired but happy, Eisenhower had lunch, then took an hour's nap on the field cot in his cave. Giraud woke him to ask for a radio-equipped plane for himself and modern fighters to train French pilots. Eisenhower said he would see what he could do. Giraud then returned to the subject of a landing in the south of France and Eisenhower had to calm him down again.[14]

When Giraud left, Eisenhower sat down at his desk, took a sheet of paper, and began to write. He scribbled "Worries of a Commander" at the top of the page, then listed ten points. He was uneasy because Spain was "ominously quiet." The French opposition, which had been half-hearted, had "blazed up, and in many places resistance is stubborn." Three of his points centered around his troubles with Giraud, and another with the fact that no Frenchman, "no matter how friendly toward us," was able to stop the fighting. The reports he was receiving were "few and unsatisfactory"; in fact "we cannot find out anything." Indications were, however, that the Algiers force was being held up and the push for Bône and Bizerte delayed.[15]

Eisenhower was beginning to realize that none of Murphy's elaborate schemes got off the ground. In Oran the chief of the conspiracy lost his nerve and the American troops met a hostile reception and had to fight their way ashore. French resistance was fierce and effective. In Casablanca one of Mast's friends, General Emile Béthouart, did act. He had his collaborators surround the house of General Auguste Noguès, the resident general, and issued orders to Army units not to fire on the invaders. But Béthouart moved too soon, for Patton's men were still hours away. When news of the invasion of Oran and Algiers came in, with the information that the French in those cities were resisting, Noguès turned the tables on Béthouart, had him arrested, and told the troops to fight. They did.

In Algiers the situation resembled a bad musical comedy. Shortly after midnight on November 8 Murphy went to the suburban residence of General Juin and solemnly announced that an invasion was in progress. He added that it had Giraud's sanction. Juin was unimpressed by Giraud's name but conceded that an American success was vital to the salvation of France. A tough, practical man, Juin was easily the best soldier in the French Army. He was also a patriot who wanted above all to liberate his country from Germans. He would have ordered the French in Algiers to lay down their arms, but he could not because by coincidence his superior, Admiral Darlan, was himself in the city, having come there to see his son, who was in the hospital. Darlan could quickly overrule Juin.

At Juin's suggestion Murphy went to see Darlan, roused him from his bed, and persuaded him to come to Juin's villa with him. Mast had meanwhile used his irregular forces to place Juin under house arrest and take over the city. When Murphy arrived with Darlan in tow, Juin implored Darlan to send out orders to Oran to stop the bloodshed. Juin himself had already ordered the troops in Algiers to withdraw before the invaders. Darlan said he could do nothing without Pétain's authority, and Murphy gave him permission to send a message to Vichy.

The regular troops in Algiers, meanwhile, disregarded Juin's and Mast's orders, sent Mast's irregulars flying, and placed Murphy under house arrest. The Americans had landed but they were floundering about in confusion on the outskirts of the city. The two sides soon clashed and blood began to flow. Juin sent out repeated orders to cease fire while the Americans broadcast statements from Giraud that had no effect at all.

About nine that morning Darlan heard from Pétain—the Vichy head of state told him to act freely. Darlan then arranged for a cease-fire in Algiers but refused to act for all French North Africa until he had a meeting with Eisenhower.[16] As Eisenhower wrote his "Worries of a Commander," resistance in Oran and Casablanca continued.

After Eisenhower finished writing he called Butcher into his cave, handed him the sheet of paper, and began to talk about where they should eat. Cunningham walked in with a message from Algiers. Eisenhower learned that Darlan was in the city and was willing to negotiate about all of North Africa. "Ike spluttered," Butcher recorded. Someone asked about Giraud. "What I need around here is a . . . good assassin!" Eisenhower said. Cunningham reminded Eisenhower of what Churchill had told him: "Kiss Darlan's stern if you have to, but get the French navy."[17]

The message from Algiers indicated that Darlan would not meet with any Frenchman, but only Eisenhower or his representative. Since Darlan had been told that Giraud was in Gibraltar, that meant he would not deal with Giraud. Eisenhower informed Giraud of Darlan's presence in Algiers and Giraud said he would not deal with Darlan, whom he distrusted and hated. Eisenhower explained to Smith that Giraud "wants to be a big shot, a bright and shining light, and the acclaimed saviour of France," and so did Darlan. Eisenhower was caught in the middle. He had promised to push Giraud to the top, and now had "to use every kind of cajolery, bribe, threat and all else to get Darlan's *active* cooperation." Disgusted, he exclaimed, "All of these Frogs have a single thought —'ME.'" He said he was tired, but not because of the operation—"it's the petty intrigue and the necessity of dealing with little, selfish, conceited worms that call themselves men."

Eisenhower was prepared to send Clark to Algiers to talk to Darlan. The situation, as he understood it, was that Mast had done the job in the Algiers area and the city was in Allied hands. At Oran Major General Lloyd R. Fredendall had enough strength ashore to launch a decisive attack. Patton was facing resistance everywhere, and one report indicated that he had re-embarked at one beach. Eisenhower refused to believe it.[18]

Eisenhower slept well the night of November 8–9; the best night's sleep, he wrote Marshall, he had had in fourteen weeks. He was satisfied with the way the American troops were fighting, even though it infuriated him that the French were resisting. Every bullet that was expended against the French was "that much less in the pot with which to operate against the Axis." Worse, every minute lost meant a week of reorganization and straightening out later, and "I am so impatient to get eastward and seize the ground in the Tunisian area that I find myself getting absolutely furious with these stupid Frogs."[19] It was already clear, moreover, that Murphy had been "completely mistaken" about Giraud. The proclamations in Giraud's name had done absolutely no good. As

far as Eisenhower could tell, not a single French soldier had quit fighting because of them.[20] Eisenhower had made a deal with Giraud and
would live up to it, but increasingly it looked as though the man to work
with was Darlan.

The reason was that Darlan had a place in the French hierarchy
while Giraud did not. There was no single reason why any French officer
who had stuck with Vichy this far should suddenly go over to Giraud.
None of Eisenhower's promises to Giraud had any legal backing. Except
through *force majeure,* there was no justification for Eisenhower's forcing
Giraud on North Africa as commander in chief or governor or anything
else.

Darlan had an established position. He had just come from Vichy
and could be presumed to possess Pétain's "secret thoughts," the thoughts
the marshal would have expressed had more than half his country not
been occupied by the Germans. Darlan could issue orders and claim they
really came from Pétain, and even if they did not he, Darlan, was commander in chief of French armed forces and thus his orders, unless
countermanded, were legal. French soldiers could follow their natural
inclinations and join with the Americans only if Darlan ordered them to
do so, for only then would they be acting legally. To obey Giraud was to
engage in mutiny.

Eisenhower and AFHQ were beginning to see all this. Around 11
A.M. on November 9 Clark flew to Algiers. Eisenhower's instructions were
to come to terms with Darlan. While Clark was flying, Hitler was putting
pressure on Pétain. The German leader was furious with the French,
whom he accused of making a deal with the Allies. To appease him, Pétain
authorized German use of Tunisian aerodromes and gave him permission
to move large bodies of troops into Tunisia to aid the French in defending
against Allied attack. When Eisenhower learned of Pétain's action, he
cabled Clark in Algiers, telling him to put the pressure on Darlan to
"urge all Tunisian forces and leaders to destroy Axis planes and resist
Axis invasion."[21] Darlan, however, had already sent his own orders
to Tunisia, telling the commanders there to co-operate with the Germans.
Murphy could not bring him around, nor could Clark, who arrived in
the late afternoon. Giraud got into Algiers shortly after Clark, but Darlan
simply ignored his countryman.

On the morning of November 10, in a small room in the Hotel
St. Georges, Clark met again with Darlan. Before a tense, perspiring
crowd of American and French officers, Clark told Darlan he would force
him to come to terms. Towering over the tiny admiral, Clark said his

alternatives were action or prison. Darlan, quivering though he was, said he would have to await Marshal Pétain's orders. Clark flew into a rage. Juin saved the situation by calling Darlan aside and lecturing him on the senselessness of the battle at Oran and Casablanca. Darlan finally decided to go halfway. He told Clark he would order the troops to lay down their arms, but not to fight against the Germans. That meant Oran and Casablanca were now in Allied hands, but the Germans had Tunisia.

Immediately after the meeting broke up, Pétain declared from Vichy that he had removed Darlan from office. Clark hurried back to Darlan's side. Darlan said he would have to cancel the armistice. Clark said in that case he would throw Darlan into prison. Darlan decided to let the cease-fire stand.

The next day, November 11, Hitler announced that he was going to march into southern, unoccupied France. Darlan then announced that this meant Pétain was no longer free to express himself and claimed that he had secret orders from Pétain (which he never produced) that gave him authority to act under such circumstances. At midday he declared that he was going to exercise the powers of the government in the marshal's name. He again ordered a cease-fire and this time told the French in Tunisia to resist the German landings. Pétain stripped Darlan of his authority, transferring it to Noguès in Morocco, who nevertheless threw in with Darlan.

French officers in Tunisia did not know what to do, but the Germans soon took away their freedom of action. As early as November 9 the Axis had men and planes in Bizerte and Mateur. The only troops Eisenhower had in the area were the floating reserve of the Eastern Task Force, part of the British 78th Division. On November 11 he sent it ashore at Bougie, about a hundred miles east of Algiers. He might have taken a long shot and thrown everything he had into Bizerte, but the risk—especially after the fighting at Oran and Casablanca—seemed too great. Meanwhile Clark and Darlan did everything they could to encourage the French in Tunisia, but the Army commander there, General Georges Barre, threw up his hands in despair and took the easy way out, withdrawing his forces westward into the mountains, refusing either to fight the Axis or to follow Vichy orders and collaborate with them.

The French naval commander in Tunis, Admiral Jean Pierre Esteva, was an old friend of Cunningham's, and Cunningham sent him an appeal in Eisenhower's name to "use his forces to throw out the German." Cunningham said that if Esteva would act, Eisenhower would "rush every type of support to his assistance without delay." But German troops were arriving daily by air and the first sea-borne convoy was on its way. Esteva contrasted the German reality with Eisenhower's promises and decided to do nothing.[22]

By November 11 Eisenhower was afraid that the chance of TORCH being a strategic success had already vanished. The Allies were ashore and were getting ready to push east, but they were going to have to fight for Tunisia and it would probably be a long campaign. There was still a slim possibility of getting Tunis cheaply, but it depended upon the French, especially Esteva. If he "would only see reason at this moment, we could avoid many weeks of later fighting and have exactly what we will then gain at the cost of many lives and resources," Eisenhower said, but he guessed that the French had "been brow-beaten too long—they are not thinking in terms of a cause but of individual fortunes and opportunities."

Esteva had the equivalent of three divisions available. It would take the Germans two weeks to get even one division into Tunisia. If Esteva would act he "could cut the throat of every German and Italian in the area" and Eisenhower could afford to rush every fighter airplane he had into Tunisia. "A situation such as this creates in me so much fury," he told Smith, "that I sometimes wish I could do a little throat-cutting myself!"[23]

The morning of November 12 Eisenhower tried to get to Algiers, where he wanted to put more pressure on Darlan so that Darlan would put more pressure on Esteva and the fleet. The weather prevented him from flying. Clark, meanwhile, had managed to conclude a tentative agreement with the French. As a matter of principle the U.S. had decided that the French colonies were not to be treated as conquered provinces but as friendly territories and Roosevelt had explicitly promised Giraud that the U.S. would not interfere in domestic affairs in North Africa. Murphy said that without the experienced French administrators the area would be chaos and Eisenhower did not have the organization or the personnel to establish a military government. Clark was happy to make a deal with Darlan, the only requirement being that Giraud have an important position—which showed a rather astonishing loyalty to Giraud in view of his lack of effectiveness. On November 13 Darlan took on the title of High Commissioner and assumed the civil powers in North Africa. Giraud became commander in chief of French forces, with Juin as his deputy in charge of ground troops. Darlan explained that he had new secret orders from Pétain ratifying the arrangement and absolving all officers of their personal oath of fidelity to Pétain.[24]

On November 12 Eisenhower sent a note to Clark saying that he approved of everything Clark had done and including instructions for the organization of the area. He wanted Clark to hire all the labor he could, paying at least ten per cent more than the prevailing wage. He also warned Clark not to create any dissension among the Arab tribes "or encourage them to break away from existing methods of control." The Allies would have to use the existing French officials to keep the area under control and Eisenhower did not want "any internal unrest or trouble."

Around midday on November 12 Eisenhower received a cable from Smith that shocked him. The commander in chief had been only mildly satisfied with results so far and was deeply upset at the failure to get any force into Tunisia, where the German build-up continued. Although Eisenhower was far from thinking of himself as a hero or TORCH as a great success, Smith told him that the CCS were so enthusiastic with Eisenhower's quick victories and the agreements that had been reached with the French that they were broaching the idea of broadening operations in the Mediterranean. Smith said the Chiefs wanted Eisenhower to consider the possibility of invading Sardinia. They questioned the necessity of building up TORCH to the strength originally contemplated and felt Eisenhower should return to London for a general strategy conference.[25]

The CCS position sounded for all the world like Giraud's demand that Eisenhower invade southern France. He immediately set out to straighten out their thinking. "I am unalterably opposed to any suggestion at this time for reducing contemplated TORCH strength," Eisenhower told Smith. The situation had not crystallized. In Tunisia it was "touch and go," the port of Oran was blockaded with sunken ships, and the country was not completely pacified. "Moreover, every effort to secure organized and effective French cooperation runs into a maze of political and personal intrigue and the definite impression exists that neither Kingpin nor any of the others really wants to fight nor to cooperate wholeheartedly." Without local co-operation, the Allies would have "a tremendous job on our hands in this sprawling country." Eisenhower wanted to move ahead in an orderly fashion "but for God's sake let's get one job done at a time." Instead of talking about reduction of forces, the CCS should be contemplating building up TORCH so that Eisenhower could do something effective in Tunisia.

Eisenhower was more upset at the apparent lack of understanding in London by the CCS than he was at the actual suggestions they had made.

He could not understand how they could be so ignorant about the situation. "I am not crying wolf nor am I growing fearful of shadows," he explained, but he had to insist that "if our beginning looks hopeful, then this is the time to push rather than to slacken our efforts." This certainly was no time for him to come to London, but he wanted Smith to dispel the "apparently bland assumption that this job is finished." If one of the Chiefs would spend just five minutes on the ground, he would lose his illusions.[26]

After dictating the message to Smith, Eisenhower decided to eliminate the middleman and sent a nearly identical cable to the Chiefs themselves. In a note he dictated to Smith later in the day, Eisenhower said, "Don't let anybody get any screwy ideas that we've got the job done already."[27]

By D-Day plus five Eisenhower had pressures on him from his front and rear. In Algiers, despite their agreement, Darlan and Giraud were still bickering. Clark had gotten about as much out of the French as he was capable of getting, and so far that had not included co-operation at Tunisia or the French fleet. In London, the CCS were displaying a disturbing lack of understanding. But in London Eisenhower had Smith, who could handle things there. He decided to go to Algiers and see what could be done. On the morning of November 13 he climbed into a B-17 and set out for Algiers and a meeting with Darlan.

CHAPTER 9

The Darlan Deal

Eisenhower went to Algiers to ratify the deal that Clark and Murphy had made with Darlan, to try to get Darlan to save the French fleet, and to see what could be done in Tunisia. The deal was a simple military pact written to suit the convenience of the conqueror. It confirmed Darlan as the chief administrative officer in North Africa but denied him the status of political recognition.

All Eisenhower had to do was say no and the deal was dissolved. American and British troops now held the key points in Algiers, Oran, and Casablanca. Darlan could have complained about a double-cross, but with his record as a collaborationist and former member of the Nazi New Order he would not have received a sympathetic hearing. There were plenty of experienced colonial administrators among the Gaullists in London who would have been delighted to come to Algiers and take up the reins of government.

Eisenhower, however, probably never even considered dumping Darlan. Murphy and Clark felt that the admiral was a man you could do business with, and there was still the French fleet at Toulon to consider. Roosevelt wanted Eisenhower to get the French port of Dakar in French West Africa, which De Gaulle had unsuccessfully assaulted earlier in the war. Darlan was the man who could deliver it. Murphy insisted that only Darlan and the Vichy-appointed officials in Algiers could keep order among the Arabs, and Eisenhower had to have a secure rear for his drive on Tunis. Most important of all, Eisenhower had no real sense of what the political reaction in the United States and the United Kingdom would be to a deal with Darlan. He expected some complaints but thought that as long as Darlan delivered the goods the deal would be accepted on the grounds of military necessity.* Murphy agreed. The basic factor in the Darlan deal was political naïveté. Eisenhower could not comprehend the depth of feeling against men like Darlan, just as he was incapable of understanding the motives of French Army officers.

On the morning of November 13, when Eisenhower and Cunningham flew to Algiers, Clark met them at the airport and took them to his headquarters at the Hotel St. Georges. Eisenhower immediately went into session with Clark and his staff. Murphy arrived "somewhat breathless," carrying a copy of the Clark-Darlan agreement. It was a conqueror's dictate, giving the Allies control and command of airports, harbor and port defenses, fortifications, and so on, with wide emergency powers in case the internal situation threatened disorder. But there was much in it for Darlan. The French armed forces would remain intact under French command, and the Vichy administration remained. Nothing in the agreement even hinted that the French would be required to expunge the Fascist elements in the governmental structure. The Americans agreed to distribute food supplies in Algeria.

The agreement would not go into effect until Eisenhower gave it his approval. He looked to Murphy for political guidance, but all Murphy could say was, "The whole matter has now become a military one. You will have to give the final answer." Years later Eisenhower remembered, "While we were reaching a final decision he stepped entirely aside except to act upon occasion as interpreter. It was squarely up to me. . . ."

As Eisenhower saw it, the local French officials who would retain their offices were still members of a neutral country and unless the United States and U.K. chose to declare war on France "we have no legal or other right arbitrarily to establish . . . a puppet government of our own choosing."[1] This after-the-fact reasoning, however, did not coincide with the Allies' attitude less than a week earlier, when Eisenhower had been quite willing to impose Giraud on the French administration, nor with Roosevelt's intentions.

One of the things that Clark and Murphy impressed upon Eisenhower was the need to keep order in Algeria. Only the established officials could do that, they insisted. Like American Southerns dealing with Negroes, they argued that only French colonial officers knew how to

---

* Eisenhower would never admit the reaction to the Darlan deal caught him by surprise. Three months later he told his brother Edgar, "The only thing that made me a little peeved about the matter was that anyone should think I was so incredibly stupid as to fail to realize I was doing an unpopular thing, particularly with those who were concerned with things other than winning the war—which is my whole doctrine and reason for existence." To Edgar Eisenhower, February 18, 1943, EP, No. 825.

"handle" the Arabs. The Allies had hoped to use men like Mast and Béthouart, but the French Army would not co-operate with them because they had been "traitors" and helped the Americans ashore. Mast was in hiding, afraid of being shot, while Noguès had thrown Béthouart in jail. Eisenhower could not consider using De Gaulle's followers because Roosevelt would not have allowed it. It had to be Darlan.

At 2 P.M. Darlan, Giraud, Noguès, and Juin came to the St. Georges to meet with Eisenhower. Through his interpreter, Colonel Holmes, Eisenhower told them that he accepted the Clark-Darlan agreement and would "acknowledge" Darlan as the chief civil official in North Africa. He emphasized that he was representing Great Britain and the United States. Eisenhower demanded one thing: signing the agreement meant that the French would attack the Germans. Darlan replied, saying he accepted the agreement and would respect it "scrupulously." He "heartily" agreed with the objective of beating Germany, but offered an additional objective— the reconstruction of France. Eisenhower endorsed the objective but reminded the French that they would have to "get in and pitch."[2]

The diplomatic niceties over, the gentlemen repaired to lunch. The Darlan deal had been made.

After lunch Eisenhower flew back to Gibraltar, arriving around 7 P.M. He sent a message to Smith, asking him to tell the CCS that he had reached an agreement incorporating Darlan, Kingpin, Noguès, and others but warning Smith to caution the Chiefs to release no publicity on the agreement. The reason was that Giraud's name had to be withheld. It turned out that he was so unpopular among the French officers that it would be unwise to let them know that Giraud was their new commander.[3]

Eisenhower's report raised the first storm over the Darlan deal. The British were thunderstruck. Darlan represented everything they had been struggling against for three years, and in many cases even longer. Darlan epitomized the spirit of Munich and stood first among the Frenchmen who had deserted the British in 1940. "Is this then what we are fighting for?" Churchill's friends, those who had stood with him at the time of Munich and after, asked him.[4] Beyond the moral question, the deal raised practical questions for the British. They had agreed to ignore De Gaulle in TORCH, but only with Giraud, who had no Vichy connections, as the French leader. Churchill felt he could sell Giraud to De Gaulle but knew he could never get De Gaulle to co-operate with Darlan, who had even outdone Pétain in denouncing the Free French leader.[5]

Smith wired Eisenhower to tell him of the intensely hostile British reaction. Eisenhower, probably for the first time, began to realize how far out he had stuck his neck. He had made a political blunder. Roosevelt could well disavow him and cancel the deal. Aside from the liberal uproar in the United Kingdom and the United States, there was the question of the Soviets. What would Stalin say? Within hours of its first combat operation of the war, the United States had made a deal with a German collaborator. Stalin might very well conclude that the Americans would do the same with Hitler when the opportunity presented itself, and were not to be trusted. Eisenhower had to convince the President, the Prime Minister, and Stalin that the deal was an absolute military necessity.

"Can well understand some bewilderment in London and Washington with the turn that negotiations with French North Africans have taken," Eisenhower wired the CCS on the morning of November 14. "The actual state of existing sentiment here does not repeat not agree even remotely with some of prior calculations," he explained. "The following salient facts are pertinent and it is extremely important that no repeat no precipitate action at home upset such equilibrium as we have been able to establish."

The first fact about life in North Africa was that "the name of Marshal Pétain is something to conjure with. . . ." All French officials tried to create the impression that they lived and acted "under the shadow of the Marshal's figure." The second fact was that all Frenchmen agreed that only one man had a right "to assume the Marshal's mantle," and "That man is Darlan." The French initially resisted the Allied landings because they believed it to be the marshal's wish; it ended when Darlan told the troops to stop fighting. The French would follow Darlan "but they are absolutely not repeat not willing to follow anyone else."

The Allied hope of an early conquest of Tunisia could not possibly be realized unless the governments in London and Washington accepted the Darlan deal. "The Kingpin is now so fully aware of his inability to do anything by himself, even with Allied moral and military support, that he has cheerfully accepted the post of military chief in the Darlan group," and Giraud agreed that his own name should not be mentioned for several days. If the governments refused to accept the Darlan deal, the Allies would have to undertake a complete military occupation of North Africa. The cost in time and resources "would be tremendous." In Morocco alone, Patton estimated it would take 60,000 troops to keep the tribes quiet.

Eisenhower assured the CCS that Giraud was "honest and will watch Darlan." In addition Murphy, "who has done a grand job, will . . . practically live in Darlan's pocket." Eisenhower realized that "there may be a feeling at home that we have been sold a bill of goods," but he explained that the deal had been made only "after incessant examination of the important factors and with the determination to get on with military objectives against the Axis. . . ." Eisenhower said he was not attempting to extend the agreement beyond North Africa, which meant he had made no promises to Darlan about the eventual, post-liberation government of France. He pointed out that Darlan thought he could bring Dakar into the Allied camp and said that, after a talk with Cunningham, Darlan had sent an appeal to the French fleet at Toulon to come to Algiers and join the Allies.

With the assistance of Cunningham, Clark, and Murphy, Eisenhower said, he had made what he considered to be the only possible workable arrangement. "I am certain that anyone who is not repeat not on the ground can have no clear appreciation of the complex currents of feeling and of prejudice that influence the situation." Eisenhower said that if, after reading his message, the two governments were still dissatisfied, they should send British, American, and even Free French representatives to Algiers "where, in ten minutes, they can be convinced of the sound-ness of the moves we have made."[6]

Upon receipt of Eisenhower's message, the CCS sent it on to Roosevelt, who was at Hyde Park. Robert Sherwood, playwright and Office of War Information official, who was there, reported, "Roosevelt was deeply impressed by it and, as he read it with the same superb distribution of emphasis that he used in his public speeches, he sounded as if he were making an eloquent plea for Eisenhower before the bar of history."[7] Churchill too was impressed. Eisenhower had won the first round, but neither of the heads of government had yet decided to support him publicly.

After dictating his message to the CCS, Eisenhower sent one to Churchill. "Please be assured," he told the Prime Minister, "that I have too often listened to your sage advice to be completely handcuffed and blindfolded by all of the slickers with which this part of the world is so thickly populated."[8] Eisenhower then sent another letter to Smith, asking him to impress upon the British the fact that the Allies were very weak in North Africa. Without French help, the situation would be impossible. Allied strength was building up, but "it will be a long time before we can get up on our high horse and tell everybody in the world to go to the devil!" He asked Smith to make sure that the "bosses" understood this.[9]

Reaction to the deal, meanwhile, grew in intensity. Neither Roosevelt nor Churchill had made any public statements in support of Eisenhower.

Under the circumstances, radio and newspaper commentators felt free to criticize. The most important of these was Edward R. Murrow, the CBS newsman based in London and perhaps the most respected commentator in the United States. Murrow blasted the deal. What the hell was this all about? he asked. Were we fighting Nazis or sleeping with them? Why this play with traitors? Didn't we see that we could lose this war in winning it? De Gaulle's supporters in New York were adding fuel to the flame. Wendell Willkie, Republican nominee for the presidency in 1940, denounced Darlan, and press comments became increasingly critical.[10]

Correspondents were beginning to filter into Morocco and Algeria and what they saw there did not make them likely to praise the deal. The vast population of underprivileged natives had no political rights, and Frenchmen continued to beat Arabs at the slightest provocation. The Jews were still persecuted. Communists, Jews, Spanish Republicans, and anti-Vichy political prisoners filled prisons and concentration camps. Fascist organizations were effectively bullying the population and carrying on their petty graft while all the Vichy-appointed officials, who had allowed this system to flourish for two years while they got rich, were still in office.[11]

The British found it difficult to reconcile themselves to the deal. On November 17 Churchill wired Roosevelt, "I ought to let you know that very deep currents of feeling are stirred by the arrangement with Darlan," and said he was convinced it could "only be a temporary expedient justifiable solely by the stress of battle."[12] The same day the Foreign Office told the British Embassy in Washington that it might "well be that Darlan's collaboration is indispensable for military reasons as an interim measure," but his record was so odious that he could not be considered for the permanent head of the North African administration. "There is above all our own moral position," the message concluded. "We are fighting for international decency and Darlan is the antithesis of this."[13]

As the criticism of Eisenhower mounted,* his friends began to rally to his defense. Admiral William D. Leahy, former ambassador to Vichy

---

* It naturally bothered Eisenhower to be so extensively criticized, but he tried to keep the criticism in perspective. On December 20 he wrote his son, "From what I hear of what has been appearing in the newspapers, you are learning that it is easy enough for a man to be a newspaper hero one day and a bum the next. The answer is that just as one must not let his head get swelled too much by a bit of acclaim, he must not be too upset and irritated when the pack turns on him." He added that a soldier had to do his duty as he saw it "and not be too much disturbed about popularity or newspaper acclaim." To John Eisenhower, December 20, 1942, EP, No. 731.

and now the President's Chief of Staff, told Roosevelt that it was necessary to give Eisenhower a free hand in the matter.[14] The State Department had proposed that Roosevelt send Eisenhower a telegram ordering him not to retain Vichy officials "to whom well-founded objections might be taken." Marshall realized that this was aimed at Darlan, and the Chief of Staff rushed to stop the cable. He pointed out to State that Darlan was "the man to whom General Eisenhower must look for immediate results in the Tunisian operation and the matter of the French fleet," and asked that the message be withdrawn. State reluctantly agreed.[15]

Secretary Stimson did more. He barged into the White House and told Roosevelt that he, as President, absolutely had to speak out in Eisenhower's defense. Roosevelt's tendency was to say nothing—he had never publicly defended his Vichy policy, despite intense criticism, and saw no reason to act now. He tried to joke his way out of the mess by telling Hull that his idea of a solution would be to put Darlan, Giraud, and De Gaulle in one room by themselves "and then give the government . . . to the man who came out."[16] But Marshall joined Stimson in demanding action and so did two of the President's close advisers, Samuel I. Rosenman and Harry Hopkins. Even Churchill added his voice.

The President gave in. He asked an OWI official who happened to be the Allied commander in chief's younger brother, Milton Eisenhower, to draft a statement. Roosevelt changed the draft extensively—to Milton Eisenhower's disgust, he used the word "temporary" to the point of redundancy[17]—and issued it at his regular press conference on November 18. Roosevelt said he had accepted Eisenhower's political assignments in North Africa but that he did so only as "a temporary expedient, justified solely by the stress of battle." The purpose of the "temporary assignment" was to save American, British, and French lives and to provide time by making unneccessary a mopping-up period in Algeria. The United Nations, Roosevelt insisted, would never make a "permanent arrangement" with Darlan. He then stated his basic French policy. "The future French Government will be established, not by any individual in Metropolitan France or overseas, but by the French people themselves after they have been set free by the victory of the United Nations."[18]

The most immediate result of Roosevelt's statement was a note from Darlan to Clark. The tiny admiral was hurt. Mustering what dignity he could, he declared, "Information coming from various parts tends to give credit to the opinion that 'I am but a lemon which the Americans will drop after it is crushed.'" Darlan explained that he had acted "neither through pride, nor ambition nor intrigue, but because the place I held in my country made it my duty to act." He claimed that only around his name could French North Africa rally and said it would be better for the Americans if they did not create the impression that his authority was temporary.[19]

Marshall continued to smooth things over in the United States. In order to give some positive weight to the claim that the deal was a military necessity, Marshall asked Eisenhower for permission to release the casualty figures for the assault. Eisenhower agreed. The Americans had lost 1800 men. Planning estimates had declared that the loss might go as high as 18,000, so the Darlan deal had the theoretical advantage of saving 16,200 American casualties, and Marshall emphasized this to the press. He also called a press conference, and, according to one reporter who was there and who had attended a number of Marshall's conferences, "I have never seen him so concerned as he was on this occasion." Marshall told the press they were incredibly stupid if they did not see what the outcome of their expression of shock and amaze-ment at the deal would be. Press criticism would play into the hands of the British, who would demand Eisenhower's replacement by a Brit-isher, and American leadership of an Allied expedition would have such a black eye that there would be great difficulty in getting an American into such an enviable position again. So, Marshall concluded, the press was criticizing American leadership which, if successful, would put the United States into a position of world prestige beyond anything the country had previously enjoyed. As a result of the conference a number of American newspapers refused to print critical statements coming from De Gaulle and from his Washington representatives.[20]

The political turmoil was beginning to wear Eisenhower down. He confessed to Marshall that he was feeling the strain and had an acute urge to play hooky for a couple of days.[21] A little later, after a trip in an armored Cadillac to the front to check with Anderson on the offensive, Eisenhower got a miserable cold complicated by severe diarrhea. He spent a day in bed, reading messages and dictating replies.

Dictating messages was, in fact, practically his sole occupation. He received directives, advice, and queries from Marshall, the CCS, Roosevelt, and Churchill, and had to answer them all. Since Roosevelt chose to ignore the State Department, Eisenhower became in effect the ambassador to French North Africa and had to handle all the re-sponsibilities involved. He also had to communicate with Churchill and the BCOS. Smith's presence in London was a great help, for Eisenhower could send candid messages to his chief of staff and let Smith then explain the position to the British, but frequently Smith's statements were not enough to satisfy the Prime Minister and Eisenhower had to communicate directly with him. In addition, Eisenhower sent Marshall two, sometimes more, messages a day. The result of all this was an enormous volume of correspondence.

Most of it concerned the Darlan deal. "I regret that I must use so much of my own time to keep explaining these matters," Eisenhower told Smith. He was also irritated at the seemingly rampant attitude that he was a naïve soldier who was being taken in by shrewd politicians like Darlan. He said he could not understand how anyone could think he was being used by Darlan "or why it should be thought I fail to realize crookedness or intense unpopularity of Darlan."[22]

In a later message to Smith the same day, November 18, Eisenhower said he was now turning his entire attention to the military campaign for Tunisia. When he had captured it, he said, Churchill "can kick me in the pants and put in a politician here who is as big a crook as the chief local skunk."[23]

Eisenhower's hopes of concentrating on soldiering, however, could not be realized. When he arose the next morning he found a message from Marshall. The State Department wanted to know exactly what Darlan's position was and Eisenhower had to send another lengthy cable to Washington.[24]

On November 19 Eisenhower got out from under sole responsibility for the Darlan deal. He forced his superiors to approve it and thus commit themselves. "Protocol No. 1," the original Clark-Darlan agreement that gave the Allies military rights and kept the Vichy French in power, had been typed up at Algiers after Eisenhower made minor changes. It was ready to be issued. Eisenhower wanted to send it back to Clark and tell him it was in effect, but his staff protested. They advised Eisenhower to send it to the CCS for approval. Eisenhower felt this would look like an attempt on his part to escape his responsibility for the deal, which was exactly what the staff had in mind. He was ready to ignore them when Cunningham, whom Eisenhower considered "as bold a man as I know of," joined in the chorus. Eisenhower "caved in" and sent the Protocol on to the Chiefs for approval.[25]

The Chiefs simply turned the problem over to the heads of government and Churchill indicated he would follow Roosevelt's lead. The President thus had one more opportunity to repudiate the deal. He knew that if

Protocol his liberal, New Deal supporters would accuse
with Fascists, of selling out the honor of the United
campaign of the war. For many Americans, and even
Bush, accepting Darlan implied a basic change in the nature
the war. The Four Freedoms, the Atlantic Charter, would be forgotten. No longer would it be a struggle against Fascism. Instead, the
war would be an old-fashioned balance-of-power conflict in which the
Western Allies took help wherever they could find it, no questions asked.

Roosevelt realized what the reaction would be. He may even, at this
late date, have considered repudiating the deal. But Eisenhower's explanations of its necessity, plus the pressure from Stimson, Hopkins,
and Marshall, kept him from acting. He told the CCS that he accepted
the terms of the agreement but wished to eliminate the word "Protocol,"
as it implied recognition. The President preferred that it take the form
of an "announcement" with a statement from Darlan on his "concurrence." Roosevelt's squeamishness over words aside, the Darlan deal
had been ratified.[26]

The President was fairly safe, for most of the critics denounced
Eisenhower and ignored Roosevelt. In public, Eisenhower made no
defense of himself, aside from pointing to the advantages the deal had
brought. He was deeply hurt, however, by some of the names news-
papermen had called him.* To his son John he said, "I have been
called a Fascist and almost a Hitlerite." The fact was that he had one
earnest conviction about the war: "It is that no other war in history has
so definitely lined up the forces of arbitrary oppression and dictatorship
against those of human rights and individual liberty." His single passion
was to do his full duty in helping "to smash the disciples of Hitler."[27]

Fortunately for all concerned, Darlan began to deliver. On November
24 he told Eisenhower he would conduct the affairs of North Africa
on a "liberal and enlightened basis and in accordance with the principles
on which the French Republic was founded." He intended, as soon as
possible, to restore property and individual rights to Jews, who under
current law were not citizens, could not practice the professions of law
and medicine, own property, and so on. Darlan had to go slowly, he
explained, because of the anti-Semitism of the Arabs, but he promised
progress. The admiral was also making arrangements to bring Dakar

* "I can't understand," he told Harold Macmillan, "why these long-haired, starry-
eyed guys keep gunning for me. I'm no reactionary. Christ on the mountain! I'm as
idealistic as Hell." Harold Macmillan, The Blast of War, 1939–1945 (New York,
1968), p. 174.

over to the Allied camp.[28] Eisenhower had earlier told the CCS that although French West Africa was outside his theater he would assume responsibility for dealing with Pierre Boisson, the governor general, if the Chiefs wanted him to. The Chiefs gave Eisenhower the authority, and Darlan arranged for a meeting for November 28.

The meeting threatened to break up in a shambles. Boisson held some British sailors in his prisons and British officials present shouted at him that he had to release them. Boisson, meanwhile, loudly demanded that the British make the Free French stop sending into French West Africa radio propaganda denouncing him. Darlan was simultaneously making his own suggestions.

Eisenhower quietly took Boisson off into a corner. He told the governor general that it would take weeks to straighten out details and he could not afford to waste the time. If Boisson would sign an agreement, Eisenhower promised on his honor as a soldier to do everything possible to see that general arrangements were carried out on a co-operative basis. Eisenhower added that as long as he held his post Boisson could be sure that "the spirit of our agreement will never be violated by the Allies." Without another word Boisson walked over to Eisenhower's desk and, while the chatter continued in various parts of the room, sat down and signed. The port and airfield of Dakar, which the Allies had long desired, were safely in hand.[29]

Darlan could take partial credit for the achievement, and he needed it, since his efforts to bring the French fleet over to the Allied side had failed dismally. On November 25, as the Germans prepared to board the warships, the French admirals at Toulon ordered their captains to scuttle. Three battleships, seven cruisers, and 167 other ships went to the bottom.[30]

The Allies had, in short, paid a high political price for a minor material gain. By the time Darlan had ordered the cease-fire in Algiers, Casablanca, and Oran the French soldiers there had satisfied their honor and were ready to quit anyway. He had been of no help where it counted, in Tunisia, and Eisenhower's promises were more important than Darlan's orders in bringing Dakar over to the Allied camp. The French fleet was resting on the bottom of the sea. Darlan did deliver those "proven administrators" whom Murphy felt to be essential to domestic tranquillity in North Africa, but that was all. The Darlan deal had little to recommend it, but Eisenhower could not see then, or later, what he could have done differently. The CCS had not given him enough troops to impose a military occupation, and Roosevelt would not let him work with De

Gaulle's Free French, who provided the only alternative to the Vichy officers. Giraud was hopeless. Before the invasion Murphy had talked at length about working with Darlan and no one had cautioned Eisenhower at that time about possible political complications. The commander in chief had not been well served by his political advisers. He was beginning to learn that he would have to make his own decisions, based on his own observations. He was also learning about the complexities of foreign policy, especially in wartime.

What stood out was the amount of time taken up in explaining the Darlan deal. Through the first two weeks of the invasion, Eisenhower could give only cursory glances at the battlefield situation. The result was a certain lack of direction to the campaign. Now that Roosevlet had finally ratified the Darlan deal, Eisenhower could turn his attention to Tunisia.

CHAPTER 10

The First Campaign

Eisenhower had never commanded men in combat. Like the American troops and their officers, he had much to learn. The education began in Tunisia; it was long, painful, and expensive.

When Marshall selected Eisenhower to command TORCH he did so on the basis of qualities that had little or nothing to do with leading men in battle. Eisenhower's orderly mind, his intelligence, his experience in administration, his ability to get along with others, and his penchant for making others get along with each other—these were some of the traits that impressed Marshall. The Chief knew that if unity of command were to work in an Allied theater the commander in chief had to be a man who could force a mixed staff to work together. Eisenhower was outstanding at the job.

But strengths can be weaknesses when operating in different areas. Eisenhower's desire to be liked and his inner need to have others co-operate were essential to forming and heading a staff. Precisely because he had these virtues, however, he lacked that ruthless, driving force that would lead him to step into a tactical situation and, through the power of his personality, extract the extra measure of energy to get across the final barrier. He never forced his subordinates in the field to the supreme effort, and as a result until almost the very end of the war there would be, at critical moments, an element of drift in the operations he directed. It is entirely possible, of course, that had Eisenhower been as hard-driving as Patton he could not have held the Allied forces or the AFHQ staff together.

The tendency toward drift first showed up in Tunisia. On November 24 Eisenhower decided that the communications system in Algiers was far enough advanced to allow him to move his headquarters there. When he arrived he found that things were not going at all the way he wanted them to. Clark had been busy at Algiers dealing with Darlan, so he had given no direction to the battle. As a result the whole operation toward Tunis was disorganized and getting nowhere. Eisenhower blamed the British, who had the bulk of the fighting forces in the area, reasoning that they had reverted to their traditional practice of fighting through "co-operation" between land, sea, and air officers. Not realizing that the trouble was the absence of over-all leadership and the hesitancy of subordinates to take risks unless the commander in chief encouraged them to do so, Eisenhower decided the thing to do was to "take the British by the horns. . . ."[1]

The British thought the difficulty lay elsewhere. Ian Jacob, Ismay's deputy, who visited AFHQ, decided that Clark was the disturbing factor. Clark imposed himself on Eisenhower "in the most extraordinary way," refusing to work through the staff, causing immense irritation throughout the branches. Jacob believed that the U.S. officers were terrified by Clark, who "has all along been the evil genius of the [Allied] Force [Headquarters]." Clark wanted the command of the troops in Tunisia, who were operating under Anderson, which led him to an anti-British attitude.

In Jacob's view, the fact that Clark had been allowed to hold his position and create such havoc was a reflection on Eisenhower. "Though a man of decisive mind in immediate issues," Jacob recorded in his diary, "General Eisenhower is far too easily swayed and diverted to be a great commander in chief." Jacob admitted that Eisenhower had been forced to grapple with a baffling political situation and his "downright and honest character has been of great value in this task," but his lack of experience "and his naturally exuberant temperament prevent him from preserving a steady course towards a selected goal."[2] Given the lack of progress in the campaign, it was inevitable that Jacob, and other British officers, would be critical—Eisenhower himself was deeply dissatisfied. But Jacob was exaggerating in blaming everything on Eisenhower. Circumstances were against the commander in chief. He did not have the men or equipment to do the job against the Germans, who in any case moved with great efficiency and speed.

The weather, too, was working against the Allies. It had rained so hard the past week that the American B-17s had to be propped under the wings to prevent them from sinking hopelessly into the quagmire. The Germans had good, hard-surfaced airfields on Sicily, Sardinia, Tunis, and Bizerte from which to operate, but the Allies were mainly limited to small, muddy fields. The Anglo-American air forces had to park their planes close together because of inadequate facilities, which made them profitable targets for German bombing raids. They took a heavy toll of Spitfires. It did not help that the absence of strong central command had led to a lack of co-operation between the anti-aircraft gunners and the air forces and even to a certain confusion between the American and British air forces. Eisenhower saw an air raid soon after arriving in Algiers and thought the air defense shameful.

He set to work to get his organization functioning. He crystallized the staff and the widely separated commanders into co-ordinated action, a job that had been beyond Clark. He also began to force his services into shape, concentrating at first on the air forces. He asked the British Chiefs to send him more fighters and replacement parts, explaining that his needs were excessive because "in rushing forward into Tunisia with every bit of available tactical strength that could be moved, we have been forced to do so without the methodical preparation and prior defense of bases and lines of communication that are normally the first concern of a commander."[3] The Chiefs sent the material Eisenhower wanted; equally important, they sent him for consultation an expert on the employment of air forces.

Air Marshal Sir Arthur Tedder headed the Middle East Command of the RAF. A suave, handsome man, Tedder had strong prejudices and concepts which he never hesitated to express. He usually had a pipe stuck in his mouth and the amount of smoke it gave forth was a good indication of the amount of emotion he was feeling. He was an intensely loyal man who stuck with a friend or a superior without question or fail. His dedication to Anglo-American solidarity was as strong as Eisenhower's. His World War I experiences had been in the Army (he joined the RAF in 1919), and perhaps as a result he had a wider view of the proper use of air forces than many of his colleagues in the RAF. He was by no means convinced that strategic bombing could win the war and felt that, at least in certain instances, the most efficient way to employ air power was in close tactical support of the infantry. He was also an organizational genius.

Tedder, in short, had a great deal to offer Eisenhower. The Allied commander in chief had never met him but they quickly hit it off and became close friends. When they were introduced, Eisenhower gave his big grin and thrust out his hand. "Well, another Yank," Tedder thought to himself. Once Eisenhower started to talk, however, Tedder decided "he made a great deal of sense."[4] Tedder eventually became

Eisenhower's deputy and the Englishman who had the most influence on his thinking. After their first meeting Eisenhower asked the British Chiefs to lend Tedder to AFHQ for an indefinite period, a request that the authorities in London soon granted. Following a general reorganization early in 1943, Tedder became Commander in Chief, Mediterranean Allied Air Forces, under Eisenhower.

In the Middle East Tedder had learned to arrange for close co-operation between air, ground, and naval units, to deploy air forces to make the best use of meager facilities, and to select air targets in a non-industrialized region. All this experience was valuable on the Tunisian front. After listening to Tedder, Eisenhower made some changes in his own procedures to apply the lessons learned in Egypt. For example, he had Air Marshal Sir William L. Welsh of the Eastern Air Command send a liaison officer to General Anderson's headquarters and told Welsh that Anderson's needs and desires would take precedence over everything else in determining missions. Eisenhower also placed all American air units in the area under Welsh's command—they had been operating under Doolittle's. Tedder insisted that all air units stationed on forward fields had to be subject to direct call from Anderson and Eisenhower saw that it was done.[5]

After dealing with the air force problem, Eisenhower turned his attention to the ground forces. Anderson needed more of everything, but especially armor. Eisenhower's staff in Algiers had denied Anderson's request that half-tracks (personnel carriers with light armor and machine guns) be sent eastward under their own power on the grounds that the half-tracks would use up one third of the life of their treads in the march. When Eisenhower discovered this he boiled. "What are we saving them for?" he thundered. "To hell with the life of the half-tracks!" While the staff piddled around waiting for trains to carry the vehicles forward, Anderson's men were stuck. Eisenhower told the staff to have the half-tracks move under their own power, reminding them that wars were won by marching and had been throughout history.[6]

After two days in Algiers, Eisenhower grew itchy. He convinced himself that he could do no more in Algiers until he had seen the conditions at the front for himself. On November 27 he and Clark set out for the front in a semi-armored Cadillac, with a jeep and a scout car leading the way. At Anderson's headquarters they learned that the Germans were falling back into their bridgehead covering Tunis and Bizerte, but the Allied advance was slow. One reason was German air control and the terrifying effect German planes had as they roared out of the skies on strafing missions. The fighters did not do that much actual damage, but by forcing the troops to dash off the road and seek shelter they slowed up the advance. In addition the Germans were experts in leaving booby traps and road mines behind them.

Anderson was in the middle of an attack, but his forces were so stretched out and so small that he felt it had little chance of success. He had only three brigades of infantry and one brigade of tanks, known somewhat hopefully as the British First Army. American forces were coming forward to reinforce Anderson but so far only insignificant numbers had arrived. Still, some progress was being made. The main reason was that General Walther Nehring, the German commander of the Axis forces, was defense-minded and was excessively concerned with strengthening his bridgehead. Instead of ordering his men to push westward over the high ground beyond Bizerte and Tunis, he had indicated to them that they should fall back when they encountered the enemy. German defenses would toughen when they got closer to base.[7]

Eisenhower spent two days at the front, talking to Anderson, junior officers, and men. When he returned to Algiers he was fairly well satisfied. Anderson had pushed forward and almost secured the line Mateur–Tébourba. On his right, the French who had fled Tunis had finally decided to throw in with the Allies and were protecting Anderson's flank. Anderson, Eisenhower told Marshall, "is apparently imbued with the will to win, but blows hot and cold. . . ."

Eisenhower's major worry was the weakness of his forces driving on Tunis and his inability to get more help to Anderson. He could run only nine trains a day eastward from Algiers and two of those had to haul coal to operate the railroad. One had to carry food to keep the civilian population from starving. That left six for military purposes, and most of those were taking troops forward. The result was that reserves of munitions and rations were almost "at the vanishing point." The logistical situation, Eisenhower confessed to Marshall, was so bad it would "make a ritualist in warfare go just a bit hysterical." Eisenhower had no motor transport to speak of, "in spite of impressing every kind of scrawny vehicle that can run," and shipping by sea was impractical because of the German control of the air over the Mediterranean. The danger was that some of Anderson's small columns might get chewed up by the Germans, who had a much more secure base and shorter line of communications, but Eisenhower had realized the risks involved when he made the decision to move into Tunisia as rapidly as possible. Whatever happened now, Anderson was well into Tunisia and although the

Germans might hold onto Tunis and Bizerte, it was unlikely that they would throw the Allies out of western Tunisia.[8]

The Axis were going to try, however. Pushed by his superiors, Nehring decided to launch local counterattacks. They met with limited success. On December 2 Anderson radioed Eisenhower that if he did not take Tunis or Bizerte within the next few days he would have to withdraw. The primary reasons were the enemy's air superiority and his rate of reinforcement, added to the poor administrative situation of the Allied forces (systematic command structures had been deliberately disregarded during the dash for Tunis). The next day Nehring attacked: the results, Anderson reported, were "a nasty setback for us." German dive bombing had been especially effective and there was little the Allies could do to stop it.[9]

On the morning of December 3, Eisenhower met with Cunningham and members of the AFHQ staff to discuss the situation. They agreed that the time had come to pay the bill on the pell-mell race for Tunisia. British First Army did not appear to be strong enough, at present, to drive the Germans into the sea. Anderson needed more of everything, especially air. The best chance for an early success, a sea-borne assault against the east coast of Tunisia, in Nehring's rear, had been abandoned because Eisenhower and the BCOS agreed it was too risky.

The reports of staff officers who had been at the front lines, plus Anderson's messages, indicated that the present scale of air support was not sufficient to keep down the hostile strafing and dive bombing that were breaking up every attempted ground advance. The Allies needed advanced operating airfields, air maintenance troops well forward, stocks of spare parts, and more anti-aircraft. To get them, there had to be a breathing space. Eisenhower agreed to cut down on all air operations for the next few days and tell Anderson to "consolidate" his position.

To prevent the enemy from taking advantage of the pause, Eisenhower decided to order bombers from Eighth Air Force in England to North Africa, where they could operate against German-held ports and airfields. He also pulled some of his fighter planes back from the front, hoping thereby to cut down plane losses on the ground and to build up reserve supplies of gasoline and ammunition for a sustained effort later. Eisenhower set the target date for the renewal of the offensive at December 9. In reporting these decisions to the CCS, Eisenhower said he felt he "still retained a fair chance of getting the big prize," and concluded, "It is noticeable that it is the Hun and not the Wop that is defending this particular spot."[10]

A few days later Eisenhower had a few spare moments and decided to dictate a letter to Handy. "I think the best way to describe our operations to date," he began, "is that they have violated every recognized principle of war, are in conflict with all operational and logistic methods laid down in textbooks, and will be condemned, in their entirety, by all Leavenworth and War College classes for the next twenty-five years."[11] The CCS had told Eisenhower that "large initial losses in a determined assault were much preferable to the wastage inherent in a war of attrition," which was tantamount to accusing him of being too cautious in ordering a pause in the offensive. Eisenhower bristled at the implication. He had pushed as hard as possible, he felt, but a continuing offensive was impossible.

On December 9 Eisenhower again had to postpone the offensive "for a week or ten days," as Anderson said he did not have enough strength to move forward. Eisenhower accepted the delay but it made him irritable. When Doolittle came to lunch and recounted his problems with the German air force, Eisenhower snapped, "Those are your troubles—go and cure them. Don't you think I've a lot of troubles, too?" Butcher reported that Eisenhower was "like a caged tiger, snarling and clawing to get things done."[12]

Continuing political problems did not help Eisenhower's mood. Darlan was taking on all the appearance of a genuine head of government. During the first week in December he asked Marcel Peyrouton, former Minister of the Interior in the Vichy government and a man closely connected with Vichy's anti-Semitic laws, to serve as his "accredited political representative" to the Argentine government. Darlan also asked other chiefs of French missions for their support.[13] All this upset Roosevelt and the State Department and they told Marshall to tell Eisenhower to have Darlan stop it. Marshall did so and Eisenhower replied that he would see what could be done, but added, "I feel it is a mistake to demand cooperation and a friendly attitude on the one hand and on the other to act like we have here a conquering army which enforces its will by threat and views with intense suspicion every proposal of these people."[14]

The next day, December 4, Eisenhower learned that Darlan intended to announce that since Pétain was a "prisoner" he, Darlan, was assuming the prerogatives of a head of state as the "repository of French Sovereignty" and setting up an Imperial Council. This went directly against Roosevelt's policy of non-recognition of any Frenchman until after liberation and was the very thing Churchill had feared, since it froze De Gaulle out of the French picture. Eisenhower put a censorship stop on the announcement, called Darlan in, and forced the admiral to change it so that it indicated that Darlan's authority was only local and that he was "in no sense" head of the French state. Eisenhower emphasized that the Allies were dealing with Darlan only as a de facto head of a local administration, but did allow Darlan to set up an Imperial Council with the admiral as its head.[15]

In the middle of his political activities, Eisenhower took time to write an old friend. "I think sometimes that I am a cross between a one-time soldier, a pseudo-statesman, a jack-legged politician and a crooked diplomat," Eisenhower began. "I walk a soapy tight-rope in a rain storm with a blazing furnace on one side and a pack of ravenous tigers on the other." If he got safely across, Eisenhower said, his greatest possible reward would be a quiet little cottage "on the side of a slow-moving stream where I can sit and fish for catfish with a bobber." Still, he confessed, the job had certain compensations, chief of which was that it was always interesting.[16]

Press and radio criticism of Darlan, meanwhile, continued. He had done nothing to liberalize the administration of North Africa and American and British presence had made no practical difference in day-to-day life in Algiers. Eisenhower had Murphy talk to Darlan about the situation. Darlan promised, informally, to alleviate the condition of the Jews by restoring them their property and returning to them the right to practice the professions. Darlan did ask for time, as he claimed that if "sensational steps to improve the lot of the Jews" were taken there would be a violent Moslem reaction which the French could not control. Eisenhower had made the deal with Darlan in large part because the French could "control" the Arabs, so it was consistent for him to grant the delay.

On December 7, however, Marshall cabled Eisenhower to report that there was a "real desire" in Washington and London to withdraw the anti-Semitic decrees. Marshall added that Roosevelt was aware of the Jew-Moslem problem and wanted Eisenhower's approval before moving. Eisenhower talked to Darlan, who said he was ready to issue a public announcement that would place him on "the side of liberal government," opposed to the Axis and all they stood for. Eisenhower drew up a statement for Darlan to make to the press, which finally went out on December 15. The next day Darlan disclaimed any postwar ambitions and said the French people should elect their own government. There was, however, no change in the anti-Semitic laws.[17]

With the conclusion of what most hoped would be the final phase of the Darlan deal, Marshall told Eisenhower that he had "not only my confidence but my deep sympathy" in having to fight a battle, organize one sixth of a continent, and carry on "probably the most complicated and highly supervised negotiations in history," all at the same time. Marshall said Eisenhower's judgment had been sound and his actions completely justified. Eisenhower, deeply touched, replied, "No other person's complete understanding of this complicated situation and commendation for its handling to date could possibly mean so much to me as yours."[18]

Marshall's praise helped put things in perspective. The criticism of the Darlan deal, the maddening delays in getting the offensive going again, and the political problems were all irritating, but "through all this," Eisenhower declared in a note he dictated on December 10, "I am learning many things." The first was that waiting for other people to produce "is one of the hardest things a commander has to do." The second was that, in a modern armed force, organizational experience and "an orderly, logical mind are absolutely essential to success." The flashy, ambitious soldier or sailor "can't deliver the goods in high command." On the other hand, neither could the slow, methodical, ritualistic officer. There had to be a fine balance, which was difficult to find.

Most of all, a successful commander had to have "an inexhaustible fund of nervous energy," since he was called upon day and night "to absorb the disappointments, the discouragements and the doubts of his subordinates. . . . The odd thing about it is that most of these subordinates don't even realize that they are simply pouring their burdens upon" their superior.[19]

Despite his remarks, Eisenhower was finding it increasingly hard to keep up an attitude of optimism and cheerfulness. After the war his staff officers and subordinate commanders remembered him as a constantly smiling, considerate, and encouraging commander, but they forgot what December 1942 in North Africa was like. The dripping heavens and depressing poverty of Algeria and Tunisia were a fitting background to the general mood. Criticism of the Darlan deal continued. Anderson was unable to make any progress. The air forces remained snarled and accomplished nothing. The French fought among themselves and with everyone else. The Americans and British fought with each other and snapped at the French. Jacob later recalled that everyone he talked to agreed that things would be better if the others were not there. Each of the three Allies disliked the other two.[20] The only man who could hold them together was Eisenhower, and he was beginning to succumb to the atmosphere around him.

The tone in the office was bad. Morale had dropped measurably. Smith had come in a week earlier and taken up his duties as chief of staff, but his ulcer was acting up and he blistered anyone who came within range. He was supposed to handle the problems of dealing with the French but was not and they ended up on Eisenhower's desk. Butcher complained that, despite Smith's reputation, "he's just a neurotic with an aching ulcer." More disturbing was Eisenhower's habit at lunch of ending a discussion by saying, "Anyone who wants the job of Allied Commander-in-Chief can have it." The saying began as a joke, but it seemed that he was beginning to mean it.[21]

But, as Eisenhower realized, he was learning as he went along, getting better at the job each day. Perhaps the best example was his ability to deal with the French. In mid-December Giraud demanded permission to move some French colonial troops into the front lines. Eisenhower was unwilling to comply, since the units had no anti-aircraft and would be a burden on the supply lines. He realized, however, that "blunt refusal might cause repercussions in the region his light forces are covering for us," and explained to Churchill that this was typical of the political-military problems he had to deal with. "These people are poor and have suffered much humiliation," Eisenhower pointed out, "and are therefore excessively proud." The matter "cannot be handled on a straight military basis." The commander in chief had learned much since November 8, when he regarded all Frenchmen who would not immediately do his bidding as Frogs. Now he was beginning to be able to see things from their point of view and to act accordingly.[22]

Relations with the French were improving, but unfortunately at the front they were not. On December 22 Eisenhower started for the front, where he wanted to see conditions for himself. Traveling incessantly, stopping only to talk to troops he saw by the side of the road, he reached Anderson's headquarters early on December 24. He and Anderson together then visited the units in the field. It had been raining all across North Africa when Eisenhower left Algiers and continued to do so. The entire countryside was a vast quagmire. To test it, Eisenhower had armored commanders send tanks or half-tracks over the ground. At no point was it possible to maneuver any type of vehicle off the roads. Coming upon a group of men trying to extricate a motorcycle from the mud thirty feet off the road, Eisenhower had his driver stop and watched for a few minutes. The soldiers pushed and pulled, sweated and swore, but only managed to get the motorcycle more deeply bogged down. When they finally gave up they needed help themselves in getting out.

Eisenhower decided to call off the attack. He told the CCS he would reorganize and try later to mount an offensive south of Tebessa, where the terrain was firmer.[23]

The last hope of getting Tunis before winter really set in was gone and TORCH had failed of complete success. In calling off the attack, Eisenhower was agreeing to engage the Germans in a logistical marathon and fight a battle of attrition. It was a bitter decision that he hated to make, but he was sure that to mount the offensive under the current conditions was to court disaster.

As darkness fell on Christmas Eve, Eisenhower returned to the farmhouse that served as V Corps headquarters. He reported to the CCS, concluding with the confession that "the abandonment for the time being of our plan for a full-out effort has been the severest disappointment I have suffered to date."[24] It was a cautious but courageous decision —many commanders would have found it easier to attack, and hang the losses. Eisenhower was certainly right in deciding it was too late to put the necessary energy into the offensive.

After reporting to the CCS, he sat down at the mess table to eat his Christmas Eve dinner. A messenger rushed in from the communications tent. Darlan had just been assassinated. Mumbling to himself, Eisenhower got into his car. After thirty hours of non-stop driving through rain, snow, and sleet, he got back to Algiers.[25]

His first act was to write a letter expressing his sympathy to Madame Darlan. He then had the staff brief him on what had happened. The story was simple enough. Fernand Bonnier de la Chapelle was a member of a conspiracy of five young Frenchmen of anti-Nazi royalist inclination that a Free French organizer had formed in Algiers. The group had drawn lots to decide which of them would have the honor of killing the admiral, De la Chapelle won, and he walked up to Darlan and shot him dead. He expected to become a national hero, but much to his surprise Giraud had him tried and executed within forty-eight hours.[26]

Darlan's death was, taking it all in all, the best possible thing that could have happened. Eisenhower was leery by now of all Frenchmen and said that while Darlan's removal solved one problem, he feared it would create many more. It did, but the Allies were now over the big hurdle. The embarrassment of dealing with Darlan was finished. Eisenhower saw to it that Giraud replaced him at the head of the Imperial Council,[27] and Giraud had none of the tar from the Vichy brush on him. It pleased Roosevelt to have Giraud finally on top and it delighted the British, for they had always been more sensitive to the moral stigma of dealing with Darlan. Besides, De Gaulle had hated Darlan but was only contemptuous of Giraud and could work with him. French unity was now possible, which in turn could mean a unified Anglo-American policy with regard to the French.

As Clark put it, "Admiral Darlan's death was, to me, an act of Providence. . . . His removal from the scene was like the lancing of a troublesome boil. He had served his purpose, and his death solved what could have been the very difficult problem of what to do with him in the future."[28]

Spirits at AFHQ immediately rose. With Darlan gone, a new start could be made. The tension disappeared, too, for Eisenhower was no longer living under the constant pressure of trying to get an offensive started. The decision to call it off meant that he and his staff could now settle down to manageable tasks—building up the force, creating a reserve, constructing a line of communications, and straightening out the command situation, which was almost hopelessly confused because of the mixture of American, British, and even some French units in Anderson's First Army.

On December 22 Marshall had told Eisenhower to "delegate your international diplomatic problems to your subordinates and give your complete attention to the battle in Tunisia. . . ."[29] With Darlan gone, Eisenhower felt he could now afford to do just that. Although the failure to get Tunis and Bizerte hurt, he had much to be proud of, especially in diplomacy. He had brought Dakar into the Allied camp, arranged matters so that Frenchmen were once again fighting on the Allied side, and most of all commanded the largest amphibious operation history had ever seen. Despite setbacks that put a strain on the alliance, he had held together the largest allied force that ever operated under one man's command. He himself was gaining experience and learning to command men in battle. He could look forward with confidence.

Part III

OPENING THE MEDITERRANEAN

[January 1943–July 1943]

A S 1943 opened, the initiative everywhere lay with the Allies. A year earlier Germany, Japan, and Italy had decided where and when to fight. The United States, Russia, and Great Britain had reacted to their thrusts. By January 1, 1943, the situation was reversed. This was due primarily to the courage, fortitude, and effort of the British and Russian people, for the United States was not yet totally mobilized and had less than one field army in contact with the enemy throughout the world. But at Stalingrad, El Alamein, Tunisia, and Midway the Allies had stemmed the flow of the Axis advance. Now the Allies could decide the time and the location of the battles, and the Americans were almost ready to play their full role.

CHAPTER 11

Conference at Casablanca

The first month of 1943 was devoted to preparation. In Tunisia, both sides worked to build up their force, with Eisenhower additionally struggling to improve the quality of the American troops in the theater. On a higher level the CCS and heads of government met to plan a strategy for 1943 and to create an organization that could implement it. By the end of the month the tasks were almost complete and the Allies were nearly ready to resume the offensive.

The day of Darlan's death Eisenhower had decided to abandon all hope of getting Bizerte and Tunis before spring, but he did not intend to fall back. He feared the psychological effects of a retreat and he wanted to keep the troops in place on a line that would cover the forward airfields at Thélepte, Youks-les-Bains, and Souk-el-Arba. With the airfields, Eisenhower could send air attacks against the Germans in Bizerte and Tunis, while remaining in position on the ground for a final offensive when Allied strength and the weather permitted. These positive advantages seemed to him to be greater than anything that could be gained by falling back toward the supply bases at Oran and Algiers.

From the forward line, Eisenhower told his commanders to engage the enemy with probing attacks, especially on the right (to the south), where the flank was in the air. He planned to concentrate the U. S. 1st Armored Division in the Tebessa area and give it a tentative objective of Sfax. If it captured that port on the Gulf of Gabès, small detachments might push south toward Gabès while the main force struck north toward Sousse. This operation, if successful, would secure Eisenhower's right flank and, more important, interpose 1st Armored between

Rommel's forces retreating from Libya and Generaloberst Juergen von Arnim, who succeeded Nehring in Tunisia.

It was an ambitious plan for one division, even a reinforced armored one. What made it possible was the nature of the countryside. Mountainous or hilly and sparsely settled, southern Tunisia was devoid of a modern communications network. Roads were dry and dusty or muddy and impassable and there were only a couple of small railroads. Later in World War II the Americans could have handled such terrain with relative ease because of their motor transport, but this was an item in which AFHQ was deficient. So were the Germans. The result was that neither side could maintain large forces in southern Tunisia. At this time in all of Tunisia south of Enfidaville neither side had more than light patrols. The Germans were attempting to build up forces at Sousse, Sfax, and Gabès, supplying them by sea. For the Allies, transportation problems were so bad that Eisenhower was afraid that even if he took Sfax "we may later find it impossible to hold the place permanently," not because of German counterattacks, but because of supply difficulties. Still, he would try.[1]

His major concern was the inadequacy of motor transport. He needed it so badly that he had stripped rear units of their transportation in order to restore some effectiveness to the troops on the fighting line. Adding to Eisenhower's worries, the 50,000 French in the center of the line were not equipped to stand up to a tank-air attack and the Germans were concentrating their probing thrusts in that area. The air situation was critical, mainly because of the lack of suitable forward landing fields. Eisenhower could construct them, but each landing strip required two thousand tons of perforated plate and to move it forward tied up his transport for days, at the expense of everything else.

The outlook was gloomy, but on January 4 Eisenhower assured the CCS, "Personally, I do not consider the picture to be excessively dark, providing always of course that no great catastrophe overtakes us." He felt that by conducting aggressive operations on the right he could divert German strength and attention while building up Anderson on the left. The key to the situation was transportation and equipment for the French, which brought him up against the same problem he had wrestled with a year earlier while in OPD—shipping. If the U.S. devoted cargo space to material for the rebuilding of the French Army, it could not bring trucks, aircraft, tanks, and other material to the U.S. forces.[2]

The absence of needed equipment was disheartening to the troops as well as to Eisenhower, but they at least could complain about it. The commander's position required him to maintain a façade. "On the whole," he reported to OPD on New Year's Day, "I think I keep up my optimism very well, although we have suffered some sad disappointments." Actually, he could not call them disappointments, "because they were only things to be anticipated in the event that the enemy reacted aggressively and strongly." He realized that "none of this business is child's play and only the sissy indulges in crying and whimpering. . . ." The need now was to "get tougher and tougher," to take losses in stride "and keep on everlastingly pounding until the other fellow gives way."[3]*

The war, in short, would have to be slugged out. Getting the troops into the right place at the right time, with the right amount of the proper equipment in their hands, was an essential part of the soldier's job. But even logistical considerations were secondary to the human factor. The industrial might of the United States, the efficiency of American supply officers, the strategic brilliance of American generals—all this would count for nothing if the enlisted men in the field could not outfight the Germans. Eisenhower knew this and he was unhappy with what he had seen on his trips to the Tunisian battlefield.

When German troops took up a defensive position, they had their mine fields laid, their machine guns emplaced, and troops located in ready reserve within two hours. Americans, on the other hand, took two or three days to do the same thing. The British had been at war for three years, but whenever their troops were out of the line they trained for the next operation; the Americans tended to go to the nearest city and relax. This in turn reflected a national attitude, an almost casual approach to the war based on the cockiness seemingly inherent in the American character. Eisenhower could hardly overcome it by himself, but he feared that it would lead to disaster and he did what he could to change the attitude.

On January 15 he sent a letter that amounted to a lecture to his senior commanders. He said that nothing had impressed him in North Africa more strongly than American "deficiencies in training." This was

---

* Jacob spent New Year's Eve with Eisenhower at a dinner party at Eisenhower's villa. Jacob decided to make a small speech to cheer Eisenhower up, for "he has such an exuberant and emotional temperament that he goes up and down very easily, and a small thing like this might well have a large effect in restoring his self-confidence." The speech went well, Jacob thought; afterward, Eisenhower played bridge. "He finished the evening at 1:30 A.M. by calling and making a grand slam vulnerable, which put the seal on his happiness." Jacob diary, January 1, 1943.

not a result of poor doctrine or methods, for they were sound. Rather, it stemmed from the failure to "impress upon our junior officers, on whom we must depend in great measure, the deadly seriousness of the job, the absolute necessity for thoroughness in every detail. . . ."

One of the major deficiencies was discipline. The G.I. and the junior officer, coming into the Army from one of the most permissive societies in the world, had scoffed at the professional soldier's concept of discipline. To the average soldier the idea that a speck of dust on his bedpost might have anything to do with the job of fighting Germans or Japs was so ludicrous that he developed a contemptuous attitude toward discipline as a whole. The result was reflected on the battlefield. Officers failed to carry out orders, men failed to construct foxholes or slit trenches, drivers neglected to use vehicle blackout lights and ran their road columns closed up. As a result men—many men —died needlessly.

The newly commissioned officers were primarily responsible, for like their men they could not take the Army's petty discipline seriously and winked at minor infractions. Eisenhower said he would no longer tolerate such an attitude. "Every infraction, from a mere failure to salute, a coat unbuttoned, to more serious offenses, must be promptly dealt with, or disciplinary action taken against the officer who condones the offense."

On the basic tactical level, the principal mistakes in North Africa had been the tendency to make frontal instead of envelopment attacks, diversion from the objective by minor incidents, poor communications between units, and inadequate reconnaissance. These could have been avoided had there been more small unit training. Eisenhower ordered his commanders to require frequent combat exercises involving the squad, platoon, and company, and wanted each one followed by complete critiques. He ordered, and underscored, *"An exercise should be repeated until proficiency is attained."*

A major difficulty was that the troops, and their officers, being Americans, were tied to their vehicles and the roads. They were uncomfortable when they were away from either. This was reflected in training, for most exercises revolved around road networks, and in practice, for in battle the Americans tended to remain road-bound. Eisenhower wanted them to get off the roads and out into the countryside.

The American soldier came from a specialized society. This had obvious advantages, but a price had to be paid for technological sophistication. A part of the bill was that the men did not know how to take care of themselves in the field, how to reserve rations, how to live off the countryside, how to make themselves inconspicuous in wild terrain. Eisenhower wanted them taught. Surprisingly, the Americans were also showing an inability to co-ordinate the use of modern arms. Air and ground forces were not co-operating in battle. Eisenhower wanted it emphasized in training (it was, and became one of the strengths of the U. S. Army).

He had been shocked at the softness of his men. Their physical endurance did not come close to that of the British and was even below that of the undernourished French. "Troops must be hard," he told his commanders, capable of marching up to twenty-five miles a day while going without sleep and subsisting on short rations. He ordered frequent cross-country runs and *"real* exercise," not some perfunctory calisthenics, during sea voyages.

Eisenhower's conclusion was clear and direct. "Perhaps the above may appear elementary," he declared. "It is so intended. The defects in training in elementary subjects are the most outstanding of the lessons learned in this campaign. The mistakes made in maneuvers nearly two years ago are now being repeated on the battlefield—almost without variation—but this time at the cost of human life instead of umpire penalties." His last words were those of a professional soldier thoroughly proficient in his trade: "I cannot urge too strongly that emphasis be placed on individual and small unit training. Thoroughness —thoroughness achieved by leadership and constant attention to detail —will pay maximum dividends."[4] Training can accomplish only so much, however, and most of the deficiencies Eisenhower enumerated would disappear only when the G.I. became a veteran soldier. Still, his efforts did help prepare the G.I. for the test of meeting the Wehrmacht in combat.

Strategic, tactical, and organizational problems are the meat of a soldier's life, the tasks for which he has prepared himself throughout his career. No general commanding alliance forces, however, can escape politics. On December 30 Boisson called on Eisenhower to complain about the treatment he had received from the British. When Boisson brought Dakar over to the Allied side, he had done so as a result of Eisenhower's personal promise that the British would release the French West Africa prisoners they held and would cease sending anti-Boisson propaganda into West Africa via radio. In return, Boisson had promised to release the British prisoners he held and make his air and port facilities available to the Allies.

Boisson had carried out his part of the bargain but, he reported to Eisenhower in some excitement, the British had not. They continued to hold his men prisoner and to beam into West Africa radio propaganda boosting De Gaulle and attacking Boisson. He reminded Eisenhower that he had signed the agreement only because "I have found and all other French leaders tell me that you will not lie or evade in any dealings with us, even when it appears you could easily do so."

Although Eisenhower had no official or unofficial connection with French West Africa, he reported the conversation to Churchill and asked the Prime Minister to do something to satisfy Boisson. Eisenhower justified interfering in matters outside his theater by pointing out, "I engaged my personal word and honor" in making the original commitments to Boisson. "My whole strength in dealing with the French . . . has been based upon my refusal to quibble or to stoop to any kind of subterfuge or double dealing."[5] Churchill promised to patch things up with Boisson "in spite of his bad record." He ordered the French internees released and curbed the Gaullist propaganda.[6]

Obviously, co-ordination between the British government and AFHQ was lacking. In the Boisson case it had hurt AFHQ: earlier, in the Darlan deal, when the British had been confronted with a *fait accompli,* the lack of communication had damaged His Majesty's Government. On New Year's Eve Churchill took steps to improve co-ordination by sending Harold Macmillan, Tory MP and Under Secretary of State, Colonies, to AFHQ to report to the Foreign Office on the political situation and to represent to Eisenhower the views of the British government on political matters.[7]

Macmillan arrived in Algiers on January 2 and went immediately to see Eisenhower in his office. "Pleased to see you," Eisenhower said, "but what have you come for?"

Macmillan tried to explain that the appointment had been arranged between the President and the Prime Minister. "But I have been told nothing of it," Eisenhower declared. "You are a minister, but what sort of a minister are you?"

"Well, General," Macmillan replied, "I am not a diplomatic minister; I am something worse."

"There is nothing worse," Eisenhower pointed out.

"Perhaps you will think a politician is even more troublesome," Macmillan warned.

"Well, I don't know about that. Perhaps so. But anyway what are you going to do?" Eisenhower asked.

"I will just do my best," Macmillan replied.[8]

Churchill meanwhile answered an Eisenhower query about Macmillan's status. He stressed that "We meant Macmillan to be in the same relation to you as Murphy, who I presume reports on political matters direct to the President as Macmillan will to me." Although Macmillan would not be a member of the AFHQ staff, Churchill said he would fully accept Eisenhower's authority "and has *no* thought but to be of service to you." It was the Prime Minister's hope that Macmillan and Murphy would work together to relieve Eisenhower of the burden of local politics.

There was more to Macmillan's appointment than he or Churchill indicated. As Allied commander in chief in a war zone, Eisenhower was the only man through whom a whole variety of British and American agencies could implement their policies in North Africa. Eisenhower was responsible to Roosevelt as commander of American forces in North Africa and to Churchill (through the CCS) as commander in chief of Allied forces. Both the U. S. State Department and the British Foreign Office were dependent on him for their policies in North Africa. Thus Eisenhower received directives and advice from the CCS, the JCS, the State Department, the War Department, the Foreign Office, Roosevelt, and Churchill. Although Eisenhower officially represented a combined command, Roosevelt frequently sent him direct instructions on political matters, with copies to Churchill. The Prime Minister wished to avoid clashes with the United States and so nearly always concurred, even when in disagreement. Macmillan, Churchill felt, would be useful as an agent to make sure British views were put before Eisenhower on all questions.[9]

Roosevelt had already provided Churchill with the best possible argument for placing a British political representative at Eisenhower's side. On New Year's Day, while the Macmillan appointment was being discussed, Roosevelt described his attitude on North Africa to Churchill, making explicit what had already been implicit. "I feel very strongly that we have a military occupation in North Africa and as such our Commanding General has complete charge of all matters civil as well as military," the President said. "We must not let any of our French friends forget this for a moment." If they did not "play ball," Roosevelt warned, "we will have to replace them." This interpretation gave Eisenhower enormous power and made it imperative that the British have some political influence with him.[10]

If the President's policy alarmed Churchill, it distressed Eisenhower. He did not want all that power, not only because it brought extra problems with it but more because he feared it would lead to a show-down between Giraud and himself. If Giraud refused to continue to co-operate and withdrew his support, it would force the Americans to take on the "man-wasting" job of providing civil administration for North Africa. Further, it could mean the withdrawal of French troops guard-ing the lines of communication and require large Allied replacements. Instead of active assistance from the French, Eisenhower feared that there would be "probably passive resistance à la Gandhi or possibly resumption of French fighting against Americans and British 'pour l'honneure' [sic]."

Eisenhower received a copy of the President's telegram from the War Department and could not reveal that he had seen it. Still, he felt he had to act. In a note to Smith, he wondered if Murphy could work up a cablegram to the State Department, *"but not on the basis of the President's telegram,"* pointing out the facts of the situation. Eisenhower also wanted Murphy to confer with Macmillan "to determine upon a course of long-distance education that might make our governments un-derstand . . . actualities." Finally, he thought he might send "a very personal and secret telegram" to Marshall, warning him that if AFHQ disregarded the "Allied" principle, there was a "very definite possibility that we shall have to retreat hastily out of Tunisia."[11]

Eisenhower turned to Marshall for help, and the Chief saw to it that Eisenhower's wishes were taken into account in Washington. Not even Marshall could guarantee anything, however, for the stakes were too high. North Africa itself was immensely valuable, and in addition whoever controlled Algiers and Tunisia at the conclusion of hostilities would have the inside track to take over in France. No one—not Churchill, not Roosevelt, not De Gaulle, not even Giraud—was going to allow the future of North Africa and France to be decided upon the basis of the military requirements of what was, if the truth be told, a secondary campaign on the eastern coast of Tunisia.

Eisenhower recognized this. On New Year's Day he told his old friend in OPD, Colonel Charles Gailey, that no matter what was done in his theater, "it is bound to remain one in which intrigue and cross-currents of opinion are always going to prevail and, in many cases, will be most difficult to combat." But as far as possible Eisenhower wanted to eliminate the long-range political considerations and concentrate on the battle. His personal responsibility was to drive the Germans out of Tunisia and his duty required him to recommend to his government whatever action he thought necessary to accomplish this task.[12]

Fortunately, Eisenhower would soon have an opportunity to meet face to face with Roosevelt, Churchill, Marshall, and his other superiors, for they were all coming to Casablanca for a conference. Then, one would hope, they could see the problems for themselves.

Roosevelt and Churchill and their staffs arrived in Casablanca the second week in January. Marshall came to the meeting hoping to close down operations in the Mediterranean and to revive ROUNDUP. As Ian Jacob put it, he regarded "the Mediterranean as a kind of dark hole," and feared that the British would want to go on after Tunisia had been cleared to an invasion of Sicily and then Italy. All this would delay the major invasion of France. But Marshall was arguing from a position of weakness. One of his fellow American Chiefs, Admiral King, was interested mainly in the Pacific, while another, General Arnold, participated in discussions only when the air forces were mentioned. The President rather liked the idea of invading Sicily and Italy.

The British, by contrast, were solidly in favor of extending operations in the Mediterranean. They were better prepared to present their case in other ways, too. They sent out in advance to Casablanca a 6000-ton liner equipped as a headquarters and communications vessel, complete with technical details on all possible aspects of any proposed operation. It was, in fact, a floating file cabinet. "What was completely lacking in the American party," Jacob noted, "was any kind of staff who could tackle the problems that were bound to arise in the course of the conversations." They "had left most of their clubs behind."[13]

The result was inevitable. The Allies agreed to push operations in the Mediterranean in 1943, making the first objective after the fall of Tunisia the invasion of Sicily. This meant that the men and equipment needed for ROUNDUP would come to North Africa and it would be 1944 before a cross-Channel attack could take place. Admiral King, who wanted to get the European war over with so he could turn full force on the Japanese, was furious. He growled that the invasion of Sicily was "merely doing something just for the sake of doing something." Sicily led nowhere and its conquest would accomplish nothing of significance. Going into Sicily meant avoiding an invasion of France, but there was no CCS agreement on the matter of the Mediterranean versus cross-Channel strategy, no agreement on what to do after the capture of Sicily, no agreement even on what to do about Italy once Sicily fell.

The decision was a serious blow to Marshall, and even more to his staff. OPD was bitterly disappointed. Generals Albert Wedemeyer and John Hull and Colonel Gailey, who represented OPD at the conference, returned to Washington feeling that they had suffered a major defeat. "We came, we listened, and we were conquered," as Wedemeyer put it.[14]

Eisenhower had great sympathy for the members of OPD. Six months earlier he had been in the same position, arguing for the same strategy they had advanced and, like them, losing to the British. Now, however, he had changed his strategic views. The build-up in North Africa was so vast that it seemed to him to be foolish to waste it, and he generally agreed with the British views. Still, he knew how Handy and the rest of the OPD staff felt, and after the conference he wrote them a long letter trying to soften the blow. "Frankly, I do not see how the 'big bosses' could have deviated very far from the general course of action they adopted," he declared. If operations in the Mediterranean ceased and the Allies pointed toward ROUNDUP, then for the most part the Allies would be inactive in 1943. That was intolerable.

Eisenhower's main fear was that OPD would develop an attitude of bitterness toward the British. He pleaded with Handy to refuse "to deal with our military problems on an American vs. British basis." He said he was not so naïve as to hope for complete objectivity, "but one of the constant sources of danger to us in this war is the temptation to regard as our first enemy the partner that must work with us in defeating the real enemy." He asked Handy to be frank and honest with the British and to avoid a purely national attitude. "I am not British and I am not ambidextrous in attitude," Eisenhower concluded. "But . . . I am not going to let national prejudice or any of its related evils prevent me from getting the best out of the means that you fellows struggle so hard to make available to us." He said the problem was "never out of my own mind for a second."[15]

Tactical questions, not coalition strategy, were Eisenhower's main concerns at Casablanca. He arrived on January 15, had lunch with Marshall and King, then went to a meeting with the CCS. Mountbatten, Dill, Wedemeyer, Somervell, and other staff officers also attended. Eisenhower gave, from memory and without the aid of notes, a detailed account of operations in North Africa. Alexander followed with an account of Eighth Army operations. He said Montgomery was on the verge of driving Rommel from Libya, but after that a period of stagnation would ensue until Montgomery could repair the port of Tripoli and restore his supplies. He expected Rommel to stand on the Mareth Line, a defensive position in southern Tunisia prepared earlier by the French.

Eisenhower asked Alexander what Rommel's position would be if the Eighth Army captured Tripoli and Fredendall captured Sfax. Could Eighth Army keep Rommel engaged so that the forces at Sfax could neglect their right flank and turn toward the north? Alexander warned Eisenhower that if Rommel found hostile forces at Sfax he "would react like lightning and his plan would be the best possible." Brooke thought it "might be unfortunate" if Fredendall arrived at Sfax just at the time that Montgomery reached Tripoli and was immoblized for lack of supplies. The upshot was that Eisenhower decided to call off Fredendall's offensive because his newly organized II Corps was not strong enough to stand up to German attacks from both sides. Instead, Eisenhower proposed to build up his mobile forces in southern Tunisia and prepare to hit Rommel's rear when the Germans made their stand at the Mareth Line.[16]

Apart from grand strategy and politics, the Casablanca meeting provided the CCS with an opportunity to make needed organizational changes. On Eisenhower's suggestion the Chiefs separated ETO from North Africa. More important were the changes the CCS made in North Africa. With Eighth Army coming up to southern Tunisia, it was necessary to provide a new structure that would cover both Eisenhower's and Alexander's forces. The CCS decided to place Alexander under Eisenhower and to provide for co-ordination by making Alexander Eisenhower's deputy in charge of ground operations. Tedder would become commander in chief, Mediterranean Air Forces. Cunningham remained as commander in chief of the naval contingent. Eisenhower was Supreme Commander. These changes would take place when Eighth Army reached the Tunisian border.

Marshall was happily surprised. Since the British had the preponderance of force in the Mediterranean, he thought they would insist on subordinating Eisenhower to Alexander. There were two major reasons why they did not. First, Eisenhower had a functioning Allied headquarters, Alexander did not. Under the arrangement, AFHQ would continue to function, and Brooke especially was most impressed by AFHQ.

Thanks to Eisenhower, he felt, "there was remarkably little friction at [AFHQ] between the staff officers of the two nations. . . ." Second, Brooke felt he was losing nothing and gaining much. Unimpressed by Eisenhower's handling of the campaign to date ("he had neither the tactical nor strategical experience required for such a task," the CIGS said of Eisenhower), Brooke felt that by giving Alexander command of the ground forces he could take advantage of Eisenhower's strength in molding an integrated staff while at the same time avoiding his weaknesses on the battlefield. "We were carrying out a move which could not help flattering and pleasing the Americans," he declared, "in so far as we were placing our senior and experienced commander . . . under their commander who had no war experience. . . ."

The move also allowed the British to achieve a return to a situation in which day-to-day operations would rest with Alexander, Cunningham, and Tedder, operating as co-equals. As Brooke put it, "We were pushing Eisenhower up into the stratosphere and rarefied atmosphere of a Supreme Commander, where he would be free to devote his time to the political and inter-allied problems, whilst we inserted under him one of our own commanders to deal with the military situations and to restore the necessary drive and co-ordination which had been so seriously lacking."[17]

Eisenhower was sure he could make the new system work. For one thing he had a long talk with Alexander and was impressed. What Churchill called Alexander's "easy smiling grace" and "contagious confidence" charmed Eisenhower, as it did everyone else. Eisenhower's relations with Cunningham were close and friendly, and he was delighted to have Tedder to run the air forces. Other generals who were still lieutenant colonels on the permanent list, as Eisenhower was, might have looked at the distinguished and awe-inspiring line-up of Alexander, Tedder, and Cunningham and shuddered at the thought of leading them. When all together in full uniform, they looked the personification of British tradition and habit of command. But Eisenhower thought only that these were men of proven ability who had a great deal to offer. He intended to work with them, not by imposing his will but through persuasion and co-operation, and draw on their talents. He was confident he could do it and become the Supreme Commander in fact as well as in name.

The rosy glow did not last long, as there was an almost immediate test of strength. On January 20 and again on the twenty-second, the CCS issued directives as to how and what his subordinates were to do. The first concerned air force organization, which was set forth in some detail, and included the statement that "further details will naturally be left to the Air Commander-in-Chief." The second concerned organization for the invasion of Sicily. It directed Alexander to take charge of planning details, telling him to "cooperate" with Cunningham and Tedder in executing the project. It also said that in Tunisia Alexander should "coordinate the operation of all three armies. . . ."[18]

These directives left Eisenhower "burning inside." He dictated a "hot message challenging such intrusion into the organizational set-up of an Allied Commander," saying that the tendency was to dull the principle of unity of command. Smith pleaded with him to moderate the message, and Eisenhower let his chief of staff rework it and tone it down.[19]

Eisenhower felt that both planning and organization were his responsibility and should be under his control. He wanted Alexander to command, not to "coordinate," but he also wanted Alexander to limit himself to handling the troops in contact with the enemy. Strategic reserves and rear-area troops were, he believed, directly responsible to him. He had other objections. "As far as I am concerned," he told Marshall in reference to the directive that said Tedder would create his own organization, "no attention will be paid to it. It is my responsibility to organize to win battles and while I do not anticipate, ever, any difficulty with a man of Tedder's ability, it is still quite evident that only a man of [Air Chief Marshal] Portal's turn of mind would have thought of inserting such a statement."

The whole affair represented "the inevitable trend of the British mind toward 'committee' rather than 'single' command," and the "British tendency toward reaching down into a theater" from London to dictate events. Eisenhower did not think there was anything "vicious or even deliberate" in this attempt to by-pass him; it simply reflected British training and doctrine.

Eisenhower would never allow himself to be made into the chairman of the corporation, the man who maintained contact with the outside world while letting a board composed of Cunningham, Alexander, and Tedder run the show. The British wanted him to deal with the French and the U. S. War Department, while turning operations over to a committee of British generals and admirals. It would have been easy enough for Eisenhower to accept that role, to spend the war pacifying Giraud and De Gaulle, entertaining visiting dignitaries, holding press conferences, and announcing victories. But he was convinced that the British system was inadequate to the demands of modern war, that whatever decisions had to be made the Supreme Commander should make, freely, "under the principle of unified command." He promised Marshall, "I will be constantly on my guard to prevent any important military venture depending for its control and direction upon the 'committee' system of command."

Eisenhower's personality reinforced his organizational views. As long as he was *supposed* to be the commander, he was determined to *be* the commander. "Manifestly, responsibility . . . falls directly on me," he said.[20] If the British wanted to change the system, let them do so openly, not through the back door. He, meanwhile, intended to act like a Supreme Commander. The structure that emerged from Casablanca seemed to him adequate and even logical. He would work through the existing structure—always making sure that directives like those of January 20 and 22 were resisted—and through the power of his personality see to it that Cunningham, Tedder, and Alexander recognized him for what he was, the Supreme Commander.

Eisenhower spent only one day at Casablanca. On January 16 he returned to Algiers and the more mundane problems of the battle in Tunisia. The next day Von Arnim launched an attack against the undermanned French sector, near Pichon. After heavy fighting the Germans secured numerous penetrations. On the eighteenth Eisenhower went to his advance command post at Constantine, moved reinforcements into the French sector, and ordered parts of the U. S. 1st and 34th Divisions into the line to relieve the French. He also reviewed with Juin, Fredendall, and Anderson the developments at Casablanca.[21]

When he returned to Algiers, Eisenhower wrote a memorandum for the AFHQ G-3, covering the results of his talks with the battlefield commanders. He wanted to know when AFHQ could get more tanks to Anderson, how much equipment could be gotten to the French and when, what was being done to improve the line of communication, when a mobile reserve could be established "so that a minor attack by Bosche" would be stopped, what was being done to co-ordinate air and artillery activity, and so on. To his G-3, Eisenhower wrote, "Supplies: Let's pile them in—dispersed but handy. When we start we want to go to town." He thought the use of camouflage had been "sadly neglected," and concluded: "*Alertness* by ALL troops: We must STRESS this," and "TRAINING —all the time—all the time!!"[22]

Nothing could be done immediately, and the French continued to reel under German armored blows. On January 21 Eisenhower made another quick trip to Constantine. He decided that with their inadequate equipment the French would never be able to stop the Germans. The only solution was to phase them out of the line by having Fredendall move north and Anderson south until the British and Americans had a common border. After spelling out the details of the necessary movements, he put Anderson in charge of the whole front.[23]

On January 24 Marshall, King, and Somervell came to Algiers to see for themselves America's largest overseas base. Somervell brought with him the best possible news—he had five thousand trucks which he could ship to North Africa if King could provide a convoy for them. King said he could, and the gears began to grind back in the War and Navy Departments in Washington. Within three weeks the first trucks began to arrive. When the last one had been shipped, one of Somervell's assistants at SOS cabled the news to Eisenhower. In a final sentence that summed up the amount of work involved, he declared, "If you should happen to want the Pentagon shipped over there, please try to give us about a week's notice."[24]

Marshall's visit went well. He was glad to see and talk with Eisenhower, delighted at getting out of Washington, and anxious to see his men. Marshall had been slaving at building the U. S. Army since 1939, but this was his first opportunity to see it in the field facing the enemy. He flew to the front, then returned to spend the night in Algiers, where he and Eisenhower discussed command arrangements, strategy, and the performance of the American soldier. Marshall asked Eisenhower to have a talk with Clark and see what could be done about toning down Clark's ambition. He also mentioned that he was putting Eisenhower in for a fourth star. Butcher noted that Marshall's "whole attitude toward Ike was almost that of father to son." The Chief told Butcher to see to it that Eisenhower got more rest, had a masseur who would give him a rubdown every evening, and got some horseback riding for exercise. "He may think he has had troubles so far, including Darlan," Marshall said, "but he will have so many before this war is over that Darlan will be nothing."[25]

When Butcher produced a masseur soon after, Eisenhower protested that he had no time for such nonsense. Butcher said he was acting under orders, so Eisenhower, grumbling, submitted to one rubdown. He then fired the masseur. He did let Butcher acquire a villa for him fifteen miles outside Algiers, a secluded place which overlooked the sea and provided access to a wooded area. A British officer obtained three Arab stallions for Eisenhower, and he went riding frequently.[26]

Shortly after Marshall left, Churchill, Brooke, and entourage arrived. The Prime Minister had been flying all over North Africa and the eastern Mediterranean. He had been to Cairo, then on to Turkey, where he talked with the Turks in an effort to induce them to enter the war (this will-of-the-wisp continued until 1945, but the Turks' price, equipment for over forty divisions, was always too high), returned to Cairo and then on to Tripoli, where he reviewed the Eighth Army.

On February 5 Churchill came to Algiers. Eisenhower had a luncheon for him, with all the leading French, British, and American personalities in the theater present. In the evening Eisenhower, Cunningham, and Churchill had dinner together. Eisenhower thought that finished his obligation, but to his dismay the Prime Minister announced that he was so pleased with the sunshine and comfortable quarters that he had decided to stay overnight. Rumors of possible assassinations abounded in Algiers, and Eisenhower did not like the responsibility.

Churchill rested and talked the next day. That evening he was supposed to fly to Gibraltar, but when he got to the airport a magneto failed on one of his motors and he had to stay yet another day. One of Eisenhower's staff officers suspected that Churchill liked quiet, peaceful Algiers so much that he had sent one of his aides out to the airport to remove the magneto wire. On the morning of the seventh, Butcher had wakened Eisenhower to tell him the Prime Minister was still in Algiers; throwing on his clothes, Eisenhower hurried over to Cunningham's villa to entertain the unwelcome guest. Churchill shut off the storm of protests Eisenhower raised at his remaining in Algiers by filling Eisenhower with praise. He told the general to take care of himself, that he was doing a magnificent job, that there was no one in sight who could possibly replace him except Marshall, and Marshall was needed in Washington.

Eisenhower let him run on for an hour or so. Finally the general exclaimed that, while the Prime Minister was worth two armies to the Allies when he was in London, when he was in Algiers or any other unsafe place he was just a liability. Churchill liked that. He left at noon on a happy note.[27]

With Churchill's departure the last of the Casablanca visitors was gone. Eisenhower was pleased with the results. His theater would remain the center of Allied activity. With the inclusion of the Middle Eastern forces, his command would be a large one. He had Cunningham, Tedder, and Alexander under him and was confident he could work out the command structure to his satisfaction. On the Tunisian front, his forces were building. The trucks Somervell was delivering would be a great help. His talks with Marshall, Roosevelt, and Churchill had all gone well and he felt he had solid support at home, the best evidence being Marshall's promise of a fourth star. At Casablanca De Gaulle and Giraud had taken the first step toward getting together. January had been a good month.

CHAPTER 12

Kasserine Pass

War is many things, but to those who fight it is above all a learning experience. Professional soldiers cannot practice their trade in peacetime and war games are at best a poor substitute for active combat. Many soldiers feel that they can learn or teach more in one week of combat than in months of training. The process was called "blooding" the troops. It sounded harsh, but the officers who used the phrase realized that until their men had been blooded they could not fight the Wehrmacht on equal terms.

The Battle of Kasserine Pass matched veterans against neophytes. Since the German veterans had local numerical superiority, an American defeat was almost inevitable. The real problem, before and during the battle, was whether or not the Americans could prevent a tactical defeat from turning into a strategic disaster. In this they succeeded. The problem after the battle was whether or not they could learn from their mistakes. From the top to the bottom, from Eisenhower to the lowest G.I., they did. The Army—and its leader—that emerged from Kasserine was far superior to the one that went into the battle.

For Eisenhower, there was an element of frustration about the battle, for he could sense it coming and foresaw some of the results, but he could do little or nothing about it. While Rommel was moving into Tunisia, Montgomery was pausing at Tripoli to repair the port. He was a week or so behind the Germans and in the pursuit from El Alamein had failed to hurt Rommel significantly. With a prepared position waiting for him at the Mareth Line, Rommel could afford to combine his forces with Von Arnim in Tunis and strike out against Eisenhower's forces.

"I anticipate that the enemy will continue to make a series of limited attacks in Tunisia," Eisenhower told the CCS in early February. The

Germans' aim was to widen the bridgehead. Eisenhower ordered Anderson to concentrate his mobile forces in the south so that he could "counter any enemy move immediately," but this was difficult because of the lack of transportation, both to get the troops near the front and to support them once there.[1]

On February 2 Eisenhower flew to one of his small forward airfields to have a conference with Anderson. Both men were worried because the line was thin everywhere. The major immediate threat was that the Germans would break through the passes of the Eastern Dorsal and get into the rear of the British and American forces. Eastern Tunisia is divided into two parts by the Eastern and Western Dorsals of the Atlas Mountains, which form an inverted "V" running southwest from Tunis. Eisenhower's forces were along the line of the Eastern Dorsal; in the plain between the two dorsals the Allies had supply bases and forward airfields. If the Germans could push through the passes of the Eastern Dorsal they could raise havoc in the central plain. If they could then move through the passes of the Western Dorsal, of which Kasserine was one, they could conceivably continue right on to Bône or even Algiers itself, cutting off the entire British First Army.

Von Arnim was not thinking in such ambitious terms. His attacks against the French, which had gained him the Eastern Dorsal passes at Fondouk and Faid, were designed to gain room, not to destroy the enemy. He only wanted to make sure that the Allies could not use the passes to descend on his flank or to break through to the Gulf of Gabès or Sousse and cut him off from Rommel. With Rommel moving into Tunisia, however, the Germans might be tempted to try something bigger than limited, spoiling attacks against the French.

Eisenhower was also fearful that Fredendall would strike out against the enemy and get himself and his men into a tenuous position. On February 4 Eisenhower cautioned him not to get too involved with the Germans, especially since he was not sure the American troops could handle the Wehrmacht yet. "I particularly would like to avoid, during the coming weeks, the joining of battle on terms that will result in a bitter and indecisive fight," Eisenhower said. "My motto is to take a regiment to whip a squad, if you can get the regiment together."

Although Eisenhower had told Marshall that he was generally satisfied with Fredendall, certain characteristics about the general bothered him. Fredendall had made some pointed cracks about the British, something Eisenhower would never stand for in his command. He warned Fredendall that "our Allies have got to be partners and not people that we view with suspicion and doubt" and reminded him that so far the Americans had done nothing to brag about. He asked Fredendall to so conduct II Corps operations "as to enhance the reputation of the American Army with the British . . . and create in them a confidence in our armed forces that will have a beneficial effect throughout the remainder of the war."[2]

Another disturbing feature about Fredendall's behavior was his excessive concern with the safety of his command post. American doctrine was to place command posts near crossroads and close enough to the front so that visits back and forth would be convenient. Near Tebessa, however, Fredendall had placed his command post miles to the rear and far up a canyon in a gulch that could be entered only by a narrow, twisting road constructed by his corps engineers. Down between towering mountains he had dug or blasted underground shelters for himself and his staff. Two hundred engineers worked at the project for three weeks. "Most American officers who saw this command post for the first time," an observer later wrote, "were somewhat embarrassed, and their comments were usually caustic."[3] Fredendall rarely left it. When Eisenhower paid a visit he asked an engineer who was working on a tunnel if he had first assisted in preparing front-line defenses. A young II Corps staff officer accompanying Eisenhower spoke up: "Oh, the divisions have their own engineers for that!"[4]

Eisenhower tried to lead through persuasion and hints rather than direct action, and although he was worried about Fredendall's burying himself outside Tebessa, all that he did about it was to tell Fredendall that "one of the things that gives me the most concern is the habit of some of our generals in staying too close to their command posts," and asking him to "please watch this very, very carefully among all your subordinates." Eisenhower then gave a brief lecture on the advantage of knowing the ground, knowledge which could come only through personal reconnaissance and impressions. Eisenhower did point out that "generals are expendable just as is any other item in an army." The lecture did no good. Fredendall did not change his habits, and within two weeks the American forces would pay for it dearly.[5]

On February 12, Eisenhower left Algiers for Tebessa. His G-2 officer, British Brigadier Eric E. Mockler-Ferryman, reported that Von Arnim intended to beef up his forces with Rommel's troops in order to make a major attack through the pass at Fondouk. This was at the dividing line for British and French troops and thus represented a weak position in the line.

Eisenhower was also worried about the II Corps, which stretched from Gafsa on the south to near Fondouk on the left flank. The corps had moved all the way south to Gafsa on Eisenhower's orders; he later felt this was one of his major mistakes.[6] He had ordered the move to protect his forward airfield at Thélepte, which was just south of Kasserine and just east of the Western Dorsal. Thélepte was the best airfield the Allies had. It lay in a well-drained sandy plain and operations from it were never interrupted by rain. Still, it could have been protected by sending small detachments to Gafsa, keeping larger formations farther to the north. As it was, holding Gafsa in strength seriously weakened other portions of the II Corps line. The situation did not seem to be serious, however, since G-2 information indicated that the German attack would come north of the II Corps line.

Eisenhower planned to spend a few days at the front to personally see to the disposition and prepare for Von Arnim's attack. On the afternoon of February 13 Eisenhower arrived at Fredendall's head-quarters. After a talk with Anderson and Fredendall, Eisenhower left for an all-night tour of the front. He was disturbed by what he saw. The American troops were complacent. The men of the 1st Armored, 1st Infantry, and 34th Infantry were green and unblooded. They had not received intensive training in the United States, as they were among the first divisions to go to the United Kingdom in 1942. It had taken months for their equipment to catch up with them so training in England was difficult. Then they shipped out for North Africa, where operations were just active enough to prevent training but not enough to provide real battlefield experience. Officers and men alike showed the lack of training.[7]

Eisenhower was also upset at the disposition of the 1st Armored Division. It had been split into two major segments, Combat Command A and Combat Command B (CCA and CCB), and was incapable of operating as a unit. Anderson had insisted upon keeping CCB near Fondouk to meet the expected attack there, while CCA was to the south near Sidi-bou-Zid, just west of the Faid Pass. The division commander, Major General Orlando Ward, had practically nothing left under his own command. The problem of a split division was compounded because Fredendall had told Brigadier General Paul M. D. Robinett of CCB to keep in close touch with corps headquarters. This meant that Ward often did not know what Robinett was doing, while Robinett himself never knew whose command he was under. During the week that followed, he alternately thought he was under Eisenhower, Anderson, Fredendall, Ward, or Juin.[8]

In addition to all this confusion, Robinett was sure that the information Mockler-Ferryman had was wrong. When Eisenhower visited him during the night of February 13–14, Robinett said he did not expect an attack at Fondouk and pointed out to Eisenhower that his patrols had penetrated all the way across the Eastern Dorsal without encountering any major enemy build-up. Robinett said he had reported these facts to his superiors, but they did not believe him. Eisenhower did, and promised to change the dispositions the next day.[9]

After his talk with Robinett, Eisenhower went on to visit CCA. Everything seemed to be in order and just after midnight he went for a short walk into the desert at Sidi-bou-Zid. The moon shone on a quiet desert. Looking eastward, he could just make out the gap in the black mountain mass that was the Faid Pass. Nothing moved.

Shaking off the mood of the desert, Eisenhower returned to CCA headquarters and then returned to Tebessa. He reached Fredendall's headquarters around 5:30 A.M. The Germans, he learned, had attacked out of Faid Pass toward Sidi-bou-Zid an hour and a half earlier.

It was said to be only a local, limited attack, however, and CCA would hold with no difficulty. Climbing into the car, Eisenhower drove back toward Constantine. He stopped along the way to visit the famous Roman ruins at Timgad and did not reach Constantine until the middle of the afternoon.

The news he received when he reached his advanced command post was bad. The German attack out of Faid turned out to be a major one. The enemy had destroyed an American tank battalion, overrun a battalion of artillery, isolated two large segments of American troops, and driven CCA out of Sidi-bou-Zid back toward Sbeitla. Eisenhower immediately abandoned his plans to return to Algiers and said he would remain at Constantine until the situation was crystallized.[10]

For most of St. Valentine's Day confusion reigned. Anderson still insisted that Mockler-Ferryman was right and the main attack would come at Fondouk. He refused to release Robinett's CCB. The result was that CCA, badly outnumbered, had to try to stand off the Germans alone. Eisenhower spent most of February 14 trying to speed the flow of men and equipment to the front. His main strategic reserve was the U. S. 9th Infantry Division, but it was unable to move with any speed because he had taken its organic truck transport earlier to give to front-line units.[11]

Because the Allied reserves could not participate and because the inexperienced American troops could not match their German opponents, CCA suffered badly. German attacks on February 15 again drove CCA troops back with heavy losses, although the situation was so confused that Ward could report to Fredendall that night, "We might have walloped them, or they might have walloped us." It soon became clear as to who had walloped whom. CCA had lost 98 tanks, 57 half-tracks, and 29 artillery pieces. It had, in effect, been destroyed.[12]

On the afternoon of February 15 Anderson telephoned Eisenhower and asked permission to evacuate Gafsa. The "very exposed southern flank," he said, threatened the whole Allied force. He wanted to withdraw to the main ridge of the Western Dorsal, starting first in the Fondouk area. Anderson felt that holding the Western Dorsal would be impossible if the Allies lost heavily while being driven out of their positions. Eisenhower asked if First Army could launch a diversionary attack in the north to lighten the enemy pressure in the south. Anderson said no, he did not have enough resources. Eisenhower gave Anderson permission to pull back, establishing a new main line of resistance from Feriana, just south of Thélepte, to Sbeitla. He ordered Anderson to hold there at all costs, since any further withdrawal would lose the Thélepte airfields.[13]

Eisenhower had, in short, given up the plain between the two Dorsals and established his troops along the eastern slope of the Western Dorsal. If the Germans could force a breakthrough they would not only get the Thélepte airfields but, more important, would be through the last major barrier between them and the great Allied supply base at Le Kef. Beyond Le Kef, Bône and even Algiers itself were possible targets. The Germans could begin to think in terms of turning a tactical advantage into a strategic triumph. They might even destroy the II Corps and isolate First Army, thereby reversing the entire position in North Africa. If all went well, the Germans could accomplish their objectives before Montgomery got up to the Mareth Line; by the time he arrived, Rommel and Von Arnim could combine their forces and concentrate on him.

There were many "ifs" involved, undoubtedly too many, but Rommel had pulled off miracles before, and Rommel was directing this attack. Fortunately for the Allies, however, the German command situation was as muddled as theirs. Rommel and Von Arnim operated, to all intents and purposes, independently. Von Arnim wanted to confine himself to limited attacks, one of which would hit Fondouk. Rommel was after much bigger things. But Von Arnim was a vain, ambitious man who refused to co-operate. Higher headquarters had ordered him to give his best Panzer division, the 10th, to Rommel for the attack, but he had stalled and it was not committed. In a way, however, this helped Rommel, for as long as the 10th Panzer was not engaged the Allies felt they had to keep their strongest mobile reserves, CCB, in the north.[14]

Despite the threat to the Allies, there was no panic at higher headquarters. Anderson was sure Rommel lacked the necessary supplies for a breakthrough all the way to the Mediterranean coast. The enemy would have to succeed quickly, if at all, because Montgomery was coming up on his rear. Anderson wanted to let the Germans expend their energy in a short-term offensive, then counterattack. Eisenhower agreed.

The evening of February 15 Eisenhower reported to Marshall. After giving a realistic presentation of the situation and saying that he intended to "strain every nerve" to hold Thélepte, he discussed the long-range significance of the battle then in progress. "Our soldiers are learning rapidly," he said, "and while I still believe that many of the lessons we are forced to learn at the cost of lives could be learned at home, I assure you that the troops that come out of this campaign are going to be battle wise and tactically efficient."[15]

The first two days of the battle Eisenhower carried a heavy load of work. Smith was in Tripoli seeing Montgomery, Clark was sick, and Alexander and Tedder had not assumed their commands. "I was really busy!" Eisenhower later told Marshall.[16] He got the 9th Division artillery started on a 735-mile march for the battlefield, stripped the 2d Armored and 3d Infantry of equipment to send to Fredendall, and cannibalized other units then in training for the invasion of Sicily in order to get trucks, tanks, weapons, and ammunition to the Western Dorsal.[17] On February 16 he ordered infantry, anti-tank guns, trucks, and even tanks from CCA sent south to beef up the line. He also told Fredendall "that every position to be held must be organized to max. extent—at once—mines, etc. *Emphasize reconnaissance.*"[18]

While the battle around the Western Dorsal raged, Eisenhower had to deal with a serious personnel problem. Fredendall and his subordinates were at loggerheads. Robinett charged that no one at II Corps was co-ordinating the units in the field, no one knew what unit boundaries had been assigned, no one knew who was on the flanks or in support, no one was co-ordinating defensive fire or providing military police in the rear areas, and the piecemeal commitment of small units was causing great confusion.[19] Ward was even angrier at Fredendall for splitting his division and for his interference with the commanders of CCA and CCB.

For his part, Fredendall wired Eisenhower on February 19, "At present time, 1st Armored in bad state of disorganization. Ward appears tired out, worried and has informed me that to bring new tanks in would be the same as turning them over to the Germans. Under the circumstances do not think he should continue in command. . . . Need someone with two fists immediately."[20]

The situation was nearly intolerable. Eisenhower could try to patch things up, relieve Fredendall, or relieve all of Fredendall's subordinates. The last alternative was hardly feasible, and Eisenhower did not want to relieve Fredendall in the middle of a battle. Later in the war, when more was at stake and he had more confidence in himself, he would relieve commanders at the first sign of uncertainty in battle, and Fredendall had already shown many signs of uncertainty. But Fredendall was Marshall's personal selection and Eisenhower had not yet relieved any officers so he had no precedent. He decided to try to patch things up. He sent Major General Ernest N. Harmon, commander of the 2d Armored Division, to II Corps headquarters. Fredendall could use him in any way that he saw fit. Eisenhower wanted Ward left in command of 1st Armored.[21]

An hour or so later Eisenhower did ask for the relief of one of his staff officers. He decided that Mockler-Ferryman was too wedded to one type of information, had ignored too much evidence about the build-up around Sidi-bou-Zid, and had to go. He asked Brooke to provide a substitute; eventually Brigadier Kenneth W. D. Strong came to Algiers, to remain with Eisenhower through the remainder of the war as Eisenhower's G-2.

The same day, February 20, Rommel finally got control of the 10th Panzer Division and attacked Kasserine Pass. By February 21 he was through the pass and in a position to drive west toward Tebessa or north to Le Kef. Eisenhower heard the news just as he finished dictating a letter to Marshall. In a postscript, he assured the Chief of Staff that although he expected Rommel to drive toward Le Kef, "we have enough to stop him. . . . I am disappointed but nothing worse. We'll do it—even though it is obviously a major job."[22] His biggest regret was that Anderson had decided he had to abandon the Thélepte airfields.

By evening of the twenty-second it was clear to Eisenhower that Rommel had shot his bolt. The Germans were not going to be able to exploit their breakthrough at Kasserine and, in fact, were now in a perilous position, with all their supplies coming through the narrow gap in the mountains. Eisenhower wanted an immediate counterattack and urged Anderson and Fredendall to hit the Germans with everything they had that night. Both battlefield commanders disagreed. They felt Rommel had enough force for one more offensive and they wanted to keep the troops around Tebessa together to meet it. Eisenhower did not have a firm grip on the battle and he did not insist on his views or galvanize his subordinates to action. As a result, a fleeting opportunity was lost. Rommel had already decided to withdraw, and that night his troops began to pull back. It was a successful retreat.[23]

Harmon had, meanwhile, arrived. After a short conference with Eisenhower he went by jeep to Tebessa. He got there the morning of the twenty-third, a few hours after Rommel began his withdrawal but before the Americans knew that the Germans were pulling out. The first thing Fredendall asked Harmon was whether he thought the headquarters ought to move to the rear. Harmon thought that was a strange question to ask someone who had just arrived, but replied, "Hell, no."

"That settles that," Fredendall told his staff. "We stay." He then gave Harmon an envelope and said, "Here it is. The party is yours." Harmon opened it and found a typewritten order placing him in command of "the battle then in progress." Fredendall, having turned everything over to Harmon, then went to bed and slept for twenty-four hours.[24]

By the time Fredendall woke up the Battle of Kasserine Pass was over. Rommel had returned to the Mareth Line to await Montgomery's attack. The American casualties in killed, wounded, and missing numbered over 5000, but they had not lost the battle. Rommel had made no strategic gain, nor had he imposed a sense of inferiority on the American troops, as he had wanted to do. He had felt that if he could hit them hard before they were prepared he could permanently destroy their morale. In this he failed. In the last days of the battle the Americans fought well and the G.I.s decided that they could, after all, stand up to the best the Wehrmacht had to offer.

The soldiers and their commanders learned many lessons from the battle, which was what made it significant. The coalition command had not stood up well to the test of fighting on the defensive. Anderson and Fredendall did not get along nor did they communicate with each other. On a lower level, British and American officers made constant jibes at each other, the British sneering at the Americans' fighting qualities while the Americans charged that the British stood by and refused to help during the crisis. Over the weeks that followed Alexander did much to improve this situation.

For the G.I.s, Kasserine provided experience. "All our people," Eisenhower reported to Marshall, "from the very highest to the very lowest have learned that this is not a child's game and are ready and eager to get down to the fundamental business of profiting by the lessons they have learned and seeking from every possible source methods and means of perfecting their own battlefield efficiency." Eisenhower had asked Alexander to provide experienced British officers to American units as liaison officers, something he could not have done before the battle because of national pride. Now, however, American officers realized they had something to learn from the British veterans. The troops, Eisenhower said, were "in good heart. . . . They are now mad and ready to fight." The complacency he had noticed just before the battle was gone.

Eisenhower himself had learned much. He was going to make it a fixed rule, he promised, that until the war was won no unit in his theater "will ever stop training," including units in the front line. He also realized that his previous insistence on unity of command, which had been more or less theoretical and which he had ignored when Giraud refused to place French troops under Anderson, had to be achieved. A major cause of the early losses was the lack of co-ordination on the battlefield. He also learned that the combat command teams did not work, and thereafter kept his divisions together, fighting as a single unit.

The biggest benefit to the Allies from the battle was the shakedown of the command. Harmon stopped off at Algiers after the battle, to see Eisenhower before returning to 2d Armored. Eisenhower asked for his impressions of the generals at the front. Harmon said Ward was all right but Fredendall ought to go. Alexander had already told Eisenhower the same thing. Still Eisenhower hesitated. He had a long talk with General Lucian Truscott, an assistant, and with Smith; both wanted Fredendall relieved. Then Eisenhower went to the front and conferred with the divisional commanders and liaison officers of II Corps and the senior staff people in Constantine. They were all in agreement on the need for a change. Eisenhower decided he could no longer put it off and offered the command to Harmon, but Harmon said he could not take the II Corps after recommending Fredendall's relief. Harmon suggested Patton. Eisenhower agreed, and finally, on March 4, got rid of Fredendall.[25]*

When Patton arrived, Eisenhower gave him a task he himself had been unable to perform. "You must not retain for one instant," Eisenhower warned Patton, "any man in a responsible position where you have become doubtful of his ability to do the job. . . . This matter frequently calls for more courage than any other thing you will have to do, but I expect you to be perfectly cold-blooded about it."[26]

---

* Fredendall returned to a hero's welcome and a promotion to lieutenant general, but he never held a combat command again.

Eisenhower was determined that he himself would do as well as he wanted Patton to do. He told Gerow, training an infantry division in Scotland, that "officers that fail . . . must be ruthlessly weeded out. Considerations of friendship, family, kindliness and nice personality have nothing whatsoever to do with the problem." If nothing else, generals owed it to the men to see that they were well led.

Eisenhower said that he knew Gerow would do a good job, so "the only thing on which I would venture to give the slightest advice is that you must be tough." He told Gerow to get rid of the "lazy, the slothful, the indifferent or the complacent," even if he had to spend the rest of his life writing letters explaining his actions.[27] That was the great lesson of Kasserine Pass.

CHAPTER 13

Climax in Tunisia

Following the Battle of Kasserine Pass, the Axis fate in Tunisia was sealed. Eisenhower's forces were increasing in men and equipment every day, while Montgomery, with the port of Tripoli to draw upon, also grew stronger. The Axis had good ports in Tunis and Bizerte and could, for the present, maintain their existing force, but the growing Allied air power was taking a larger and larger toll of enemy shipping. At Kasserine the Axis had failed to widen their bridgehead or cut Anderson's supply lines and had thus lost their last opportunity to reverse the strategic situation in North Africa. The end was now in sight.

Impending victory was not without its problems. The traditional time for alliances to disintegrate is during a successful advance, as the partners fight over the spoils and claim the credit for themselves. Indications that this might happen in North Africa appeared as early as the beginning of March, with the arrival of Alexander and the Eighth Army on the front. Previously the nationalistic strains had been at a minimum, in large part because neither Anderson nor Fredendall had a preponderance of the ground strength, and neither had achieved any great victories that placed the other in the shadows. Now, however, the British were far stronger than the Americans, and the Eighth Army, fresh from its desert triumph, was boastful, given to making scornful remarks about the military prowess of the Americans. Alexander was inclined to share this attitude. He did not trust the Americans and wanted to give them only easy—and thus insignificant—objectives, saving the really hard jobs for British soldiers.

On the higher levels these and other strains were handled without undue difficulty. Eisenhower and Cunningham were already close friends, and Eisenhower quickly established a similar relationship with Tedder and Alexander. Churchill and Roosevelt devoted a large part of their time and considerable skills to cementing the alliance. At AFHQ, by personal direction and example, Eisenhower had created a truely integrated staff and nationalistic problems almost never emerged there. In the field, however, among the line officers, where nerves were tighter, tempers shorter, and the need to keep the alliance running smoothly not so clear, trouble was bound to come. Dealing successfully with this problem was one of Eisenhower's primary tasks. It was on the battlefield that the success of the alliance could be seen most easily and counted the most. Eisenhower's job was to see to it not only that the Allies won in North Africa but that they won as allies.

"Circumstances bring about odd situations," Eisenhower told an old friend on the first day of March, "and I sometimes think that one of the oddest of all is the picture of a western Kansan, with all his profanity and outspokenness, being in command of an Allied organization where tact, suavity and diplomacy are all supposed to be essential weapons."[1] Eisenhower could have emphasized the "supposed to be," for he never tried to become a top-hat-and-tail-coat type of statesman. The British liked him precisely because of his outspokenness and the honesty that went with it. Equally important was his recognition of the political problems inherent in the situation. He liked to say that he never let politics interfere with his conduct of a campaign and insisted that his staff make all decisions on military grounds only. But despite his penchant for portraying himself as a naïve soldier unaware of the complexity of statecraft, he was a keen and insightful politician who was sensitive to any danger that threatened the alliance. Eisenhower felt that the war could not be won if the alliance did not work and that it would not be worth winning if the British and Americans split after victory. He made his basic decisions, therefore, on the grounds of political as well as military necessity.*

Holding to a concept of Allied unity and establishing and maintaining good relations with senior British military and political leaders, important as they were, did not by themselves insure success. Eisenhower had to instill in the line officers of both countries the same spirit he had brought

---

* There is much confusion over the terms used here, and I have perhaps been guilty of overstressing the difference between political and military decisions. Our vocabulary is geared to discussing political-military relations in a way that emphasizes either one side or another—that is, a decision is "political" or it is "military." Actually, it is difficult to distinguish between a political and a military decision. What we really need is a new word that can combine both military and political decisions into a single word, as a single concept.

about at AFHQ. He wanted American and British officers to respect, trust, and even like one another. "I realize," he told Marshall, that the task would be difficult, because "the seeds for discord between ourselves and our British allies were sown, on our side, as far back as when we read our little red school history books." But he was sure it could be done, and without tricks, gimmicks, force, or propaganda. "My method is to drag all [disagreements] into the open," he said, "discuss them frankly, and insist upon positive rather than negative action in furthering the purpose of Allied unity."[2]

Eisenhower was not only Allied commander—he was also theater commander of the American Army in North Africa, and with his American subordinates he could use the direct methods of giving orders and relieving offending officers to achieve his aims. One of the reasons Fredendall went was his habit of criticizing the British. To his replacement, Patton, Eisenhower gave as a first task "the intelligent direction of opinion in our Army so that there is created a spirit of partnership between ourselves and the British forces." He insisted that "negative measures will not answer the purpose; without being extravagant and without indulging in blatant propaganda, we can produce the result desired by sound leadership and the exercise of good sense."

Over the next two months one of the objectives toward which Eisenhower strove was building up the American Army in the eyes of the British. After Kasserine, and British remarks about the American performance there, this was essential. Eisenhower chose to accomplish his objective by the most direct means available—giving the II Corps a difficult mission and hoping that by successfully carrying it out the corps would restore its pride in itself and its image with the British. Before that could be done, however, he had to get Patton firmly in command and have Patton rebuild the II Corps. Eisenhower ordered Patton to rehabilitate the American forces and prepare them for an attack. He wanted intensive training that would take into account all the lessons learned at Kasserine.

On the personal side Eisenhower kept a tighter grip on Patton than he had on Fredendall. He knew Patton better and had personally selected him for the command. He had tried to get Fredendall to go to the front more often; with Patton the problem was recklessness. "Your personal courage is something you do not have to prove to me," he assured Patton, and "I want you as a Corps Commander—not as a casualty." He had told Fredendall that the need for a commander to be at his command post was overemphasized; he now told Patton that "in actual battle under present conditions a Commander can really handle his outfit from his Command Post."

Finally, Eisenhower reminded Patton that II Corps would operate under Alexander's command. "I expect you to respond to General Alexander's orders exactly as if they were issued by me," he warned. "I want no mistake about my thorough belief in unity of command."[3]

With Alexander, meanwhile, Eisenhower was working on a project that would bring II Corps into the offensive against Rommel. The Germans were building up their defenses along the Mareth Line while Montgomery was preparing the Eighth Army to attack it. Eisenhower met with Alexander on March 7 and persuaded the British general to give Patton the objective of seizing and holding Gafsa. Montgomery's offensive was scheduled to begin on March 20; Patton's should go off a few days earlier. Patton's movement was designed to draw off reserves from Rommel, to gain control of forward airfields in order to give assistance to Montgomery, and to establish a forward maintenance center from which Eighth Army could draw supplies to maintaim its expected advance.

Patton was unhappy with his assignment. He insisted that II Corps could do much more than simply take Gafsa and make feints toward Maknassy. He wanted to drive all the way through to Sfax, thus splitting Rommel and Von Arnim. Alexander, however, felt the II Corps was not strong enough or experienced enough to accomplish this. Eisenhower was more inclined to give Patton and II Corps credit than Alexander was, but even the commander in chief wanted to avoid another American reversal and thus he accepted Alexander's plan with its limitation on Patton's operations.

Although he agreed with his deputy's plans, Eisenhower also made it clear to Alexander that more was involved in the final campaign in Tunisia than simply military victory. Repeatedly he warned Alexander to keep Allied unity high on his priority list. On March 9 he said he had noticed that reporters were beginning to use Kasserine to start an argument about "blame and credit as between British and Americans." American reporters were saying that the British had been slow in coming to the aid of U.S. troops, while British papers criticized the American fighting ability. Eisenhower called a press conference and gave "a rather heated lecture." He said that any attempt to initiate a British-American argument "would be completely and invariably censored" and warned that he would order the offending reporter out of the theater. Eisenhower had also heard that German propaganda was trying to convince the world "that British and Americans are at each other's throats in this theater." Eisenhower passed this on to Alexander and commented, "We'll show them."

On March 17 Patton got his attack off on schedule. As he had predicted, it went well. He took Gafsa and began probing to the east, pinning down the 10th Panzer Division on his front. Rommel had left Africa, a sick man, and Von Arnim, now in command of the whole front, ordered a counterattack. The U. S. 1st Infantry handily repulsed the panzers; Patton then drove on to take Maknassy. On March 20 Montgomery launched his offensive along a narrow front; despite a tremendous artillery bombardment and a four-to-one superiority in tanks, he made little or no progress against the strong entrenchments. The New Zealanders then swung around the left flank, got up to El Hamma, and threatened the German rear, forcing the enemy to withdraw. Patton tried to break through at Fondouk and Maknassy to the coastal plain, but his attacks made little progress against stubborn resistance.

Up to this point the operation had been a success. The American troops were regaining their confidence in themselves, the Germans were pulling back, and the Allied ship was tight. Suddenly the joints began to creak. On April 1 Patton's G-3 issued a situation report (sitrep) in which he protested that "total lack of air cover for our units" permitted the German Air Force to "operate almost at will." Air Marshal Sir Arthur Coningham, who headed the Allied Air Support Command, replied that Patton was using the Air Force "as an alibi for lack of success on ground." Coningham continued, "If sitrep is earnest, it can only be assumed that II Corps personnel concerned are not battleworthy. . . ." He added that he had instructed his flyers "not to allow their brilliant and conscientious support of II Corps to be affected by this false cry of wolf."[4]

The exchange of messages was a bomb with a short, fast-burning fuse. Before Eisenhower even knew of its existence, Coningham's reply to Patton was circulating among most of the headquarters in Tunisia. Eisenhower received a copy and got Tedder, now air commander in chief, on the telephone. Tedder promised to order Coningham to withdraw and cancel his message, but it was too late for that to do much, if any, good. Tedder also promised to take Coningham with him to Gafsa to meet with Patton and make a personal apology. Eisenhower was so upset that he drafted a message to Marshall saying that since it was obvious he could not control his subordinates he should be relieved. Smith talked him out of sending it.[5]

Before Patton met with Coningham, Eisenhower did what he could to see to it that the meeting was amicable. Patton had complained about the wide distribution given to Coningham's criticism and demanded a public apology. Eisenhower told Patton he understood completely, but added that *"the great purpose of complete Allied teamwork must be achieved in this theater."* This purpose, he pointed out, "will not be furthered by demanding the last pound of flesh for every error . . . ," and he asked Patton to go easy on Coningham. Eisenhower reminded Patton that his sitrep had also been widely and unwisely distributed and asked him in the future to make sure that anything that smacked of criticism be reported to his superiors only. Even better was "a friendly and personal conference with the man responsible."

"In carrying out my policy of refusing to permit any criticism couched along nationalistic lines," Eisenhower added, he did not want Patton to make the mistake of not passing on his views to Alexander. One of Patton's obvious responsibilities was to keep Alexander fully informed. It all came down to a simple statement: "True cooperation and unification of effort will come about only through frank, free and friendly understanding amongst all."[6]

Patton took Eisenhower's advice. When he met with Coningham and Tedder he declared peace. After everything was settled, and the three generals were enjoying a drink, three German aircraft flew overhead and strafed the headquarters building. Tedder looked at Patton, who was grinning, and said, "I always knew you were a good stage manager, but this takes the cake." Patton responded, "If I could find the sonsabitches who flew those planes I'd mail them each a medal."[7]

The problem of maintaining relations was never ending. As Montgomery pushed forward from the Mareth Line, the U. S. 34th Division at Fondouk failed to break through to the coast and the bulk of the Axis forces escaped. Montgomery took Sfax on April 10, Sousse on the twelfth, and Enfidaville on the thirteenth. He was disappointed at his failure to bag any large numbers of Axis prisoners and tended to blame it on the 34th Division. For the purpose of the attack the division had been assigned to Eighth Army, and the plans under which it operated had been drawn up by British officers. Major General Charles W. Ryder, commanding the 34th, agreed with his subordinates that the trouble was that the division had been committed to a faulty plan.[8]

The British plan had sent the 34th Division through a valley at end of which was a high cliff, protected by German artillery, and on the left of which was another high hill with dug-in fortifications and artillery. The American troops were pinned down by a cross fire, but the British said that they could have moved and the failure to advance caused unnecessary casualties among the Eighth Army troops. Eisenhower took some of the blame on himself, saying that he was afraid that his orders to get along with the British had been taken so literally that the American commanders had been too meek in acquiescing in British plans. They had hesitated to insist on their own views.[9]

Before Eisenhower had an opportunity to deal with the grousing he received a message from Marshall. The Chief of Staff said it was widely believed in the United States that the failure of the 34th Division to co-operate with Eighth Army spoiled a chance to trap the retreating Germans. Columnists in the States were playing up stories that American units were being used to clean up the battlefields. Publicity favorable to the American soldier was practically non-existent. Public relations officers, Marshall said, reported a "marked fall in prestige of American troops in minds of pressmen and in reaction of public."

Alexander's plan for the final elimination of the Axis from their Bizerte–Tunis bridgehead called for shifting the U. S. 1st and 9th Divisions to the Mediterranean coast on the north and putting them under Anderson. The other two American divisions in II Corps would be squeezed out of the line as Eighth Army moved north and linked up with First Army. This was a logical military arrangement which allowed for the most efficient use of resources, but Marshall told Eisenhower that he was opposed to relegating the Americans to such a minor role. The Chief feared "that in this vital matter you might give way too much to logistical reasons with unfortunate results as to national prestige."[10]

Eisenhower also had his doubts about the plan, saying it seemed "to be a bit on the slow, methodical side." He was beginning to wonder about Alexander, too. He explained privately to Marshall that Alexander was most unfair to II Corps. Eisenhower had twice been in II Corps headquarters with Alexander when the British general cautioned Patton to avoid pitched battles because the Americans "might get into trouble." Like Patton, Eisenhower thought the II Corps could have done much more in the Gafsa–Maknassy area had not Alexander held it back.[11]

Over the next few days Eisenhower applied himself to correcting the past record and ensuring that the Americans would play a key role in the future. He held a press conference in which he emphasized the American contribution to the offensive, giving facts and figures on the losses inflicted upon the enemy by II Corps in the Gafsa area. He convinced Alexander to publish an order giving II Corps credit for holding off two German armored divisions plus other units during the Mareth Line fighting. He was angry with his censors for letting British criticisms of the 34th Division be made public. He had issued an order that no criticism of himself should be censored; as he told Marshall, "the fool censor extended this to include troop units, although how he reasoned that one out is beyond me." Eisenhower had done everything possible to make sure the Americans got the credit they deserved for the campaign and said that "to find myself defeated by the stupidity of a subordinate censor was perfectly infuriating." He did not often get discouraged, he added, "but I must say that last night was a bad one." He relieved the censor and asked for the best man available in the War Department for the job.[12]

On April 14 Eisenhower went to the front to confer with Alexander, Anderson, Spaatz, Patton, and the American division commanders. He bluntly told Alexander that, whatever the military requirements, it was absolutely essential that the Americans have their own sector in the final phase of the Tunisian battle. He wanted II Corps to fight as a unit on the north coast, with Bizerte as its objective. Alexander demurred, saying that the terrain was difficult, implying that he thought the job was beyond the capabilities of the Americans. He said that the 1st Armored had failed at Kasserine and the 34th Infantry at Fondouk, and that he thus wanted II Corps in the rear.

Eisenhower explained some realities to Alexander. The United States had given much of its best equipment, such as the Sherman tanks, to the British. If the American people came to feel that their troops had not played a substantial part in the campaign, they would be even more insistent upon prosecution of the war in the Pacific and less interested in the Europe-first strategy. On the local level, he argued that American divisions would surely carry a heavy load in Sicily and in all future European campaigns, and that it was therefore obviously necessary that American troops feel confident of their ability to fight the Germans.

Alexander admitted that Eisenhower was right and agreed to send all of the II Corps north, where it would fight as a unit.[13] The trucks that Somervell shipped over in March made the move possible, and in an operation that showed the Americans at their logistical best 100,-000 troops, along with supporting units, shifted to the north, moving behind the British lines, in two days.

The II Corps now had a new commander. Eisenhower had not wished to put Patton in command originally because he wanted Patton to devote himself to planning for the Sicily invasion. So at this first opportunity he pulled him back from II Corps and put his West Point classmate, Omar N. Bradley, in command. It was in no sense a demotion for Patton; Eisenhower had been intending to make the switch since early March. He did relieve Ward, putting Harmon in his place. Ward seemed to Eisenhower to be tired out and unprepared for the rigors of another campaign.[14]

As Bradley took command, Eisenhower sent him some instructions. He pointed out that, while the 1st and 9th Infantry had established themselves as first-class fighting units, "there is no blinking" that the 1st Armored and 34th Infantry had left themselves open to justifiable criticism. Although it was true that there were extenuating circumstances, and also true that the British in the early days in the desert also did poorly, Eisenhower wanted the American units improved. He realized that the sector in which Bradley would be fighting was not well suited for an offensive. Anderson had been forced to use mules for transporting supplies in the area. But Bradley had to overcome the difficulties and prove to the world that the American "can perform in a way that will at least do full credit to the material we have." He wanted Bradley to plan every operation "carefully and meticulously, concentrate maximum fire power in support of each attack, keep up a constant pressure and convince everyone that we are doing our full part. . . ." Since the whole armored division could not be used simultaneously, Eisenhower said, Bradley had an opportunity to deploy his armor in great depth and use a maximum portion of the division's supporting arms to insure success.

Eisenhower concluded by warning Bradley to be tough. He said he had just heard of a battalion of infantry that had suffered a loss of ten men killed and then asked permission to withdraw and reorganize. That sort of thing had to cease. "We have reached the point where troops *must* secure objectives assigned," Eisenhower said, and "we must direct leaders to get out and *lead and to secure the necessary results.*"[15]

"Ike's position just now is something like that of a hen setting on a batch of eggs," Butcher recorded on April 25. "He is waiting for the eggs to hatch, and is in the mental state of wondering if they will ever break the shell."[16] The shell was the German bridgehead at Bizerte–Tunis, and three separate beaks—the British Eighth and First

Armies and U. S. II Corps—were trying to break it. Eighth Army had made one attempt on the night of April 19–20, but it had only made a dent in the German lines and Montgomery had called off his offensive in order to regroup and concentrate along the coast near Enfidaville. Anderson's attack jumped off from Medjez el Bab on April 22. The Germans concentrated against him because they were contemptuous of the II Corps in the north and because Montgomery was presenting no immediate threat in the south. As a result, First Army scored only limited gains. This put it up to the Americans.

Bradley had four American divisions on the II Corps front; from north to south, they were the 9th Infantry, 34th Infantry, 1st Infantry, and 1st Armored. Eisenhower spent the last week in April touring the battlefront and came away with favorable impressions. He thought Bradley was "doing a great job" and was delighted to hear from a British veteran that the 1st Infantry was "one of the finest tactical organizations that he had ever seen." He was also satisfied with the 9th Infantry and the 1st Armored. The 34th Infantry, however, still had to prove itself. It had been involved, without distinction, at Kasserine, and had failed in its offensive at Fondouk. Its morale seemed low.[17]

Alexander had agreed to use the division, and Bradley had complied with Eisenhower's wishes and given the 34th strategically important Hill 609 as its objective. The hill, almost a mountain, was the key to the German defensive line facing II Corps. Von Arnim used it for artillery fire and observation, and from it the Germans could prevent movement by both the 1st Division to the south and the 9th Division to the north. From Hill 609 Tunis could be seen. It was protected not only by its own height and artillery but by fire from nearby high ground, which gave the Germans a cross fire on the slopes leading up to it. Altogether, Hill 609 was the most difficult objective in Tunisia.

On April 30 the attack went forward. The troops slogged up the hill, falling before the cross fire but advancing relentlessly. "I sincerely hope the 34th takes Hill 609 today," Eisenhower told Alexander. "It would do worlds for the division and for the campaign."[18] By the next morning, the Americans had the hill. The Germans counterattacked furiously all through the day but the division, its self-respect restored and its confidence high, repulsed the enemy. Eisenhower's patience and insistence paid huge dividends, not only in the campaign but for the future. The 34th Division went on to compile one of the best combat records in the American Army, making the assault at Salerno, holding the beachhead at Anzio, and leading the drive through Italy.

The fall of Hill 609 broke the shell of the German defense in front of the Americans. To the north the 9th Division got into the hills behind Jefna and on May 1 the Germans pulled out, retreating to Mateur. The 1st Division, meanwhile, moved eastward along the southern slopes of Hill 609, while the 1st Armored drove along the Tine River valley to Eddekhila, then turned north toward Mateur. On the afternoon of May 3 it pushed the Germans out of Mateur and was in position for the final drive on Bizerte. Most important of all, the American attack had eliminated the bulk of Von Arnim's mobile reinforcements. Montgomery had meanwhile launched another flanking attack, which was successful.

On May 4 Anderson joined in the general offensive. Within two days the Germans in front of Anderson were in full retreat, and on May 7 the British moved into Tunis. The same day Bradley sent Eisenhower a two-word message—"Mission accomplished." His II Corps had captured Bizerte.[19] Only mopping-up operations remained to clear the Axis completely out of Tunisia and North Africa.

Eisenhower spent the last week of the campaign at the front, and it made a deep impression on him. He spoke of it in a letter he dictated to his brother Arthur on May 18. He had just learned that a reporter had done a story on their mother, who was a member of the Jehovah's Witnesses. The story stressed the pacifism of the religious group and the irony of Mrs. Eisenhower's son being a general. After telling Arthur that their mother's "happiness in her religion means more to me than any damn wisecrack that a newspaperman can get publicized," Eisenhower said of pacifists generally, "I doubt whether any of these people, with their academic or dogmatic hatred of war, detest it as much as I do." He then spoke of his experiences on the Tunisian front and said the pacifists "probably have not seen bodies rotting on the ground and smelled the stench of decaying human flesh. They have not visited a field hospital crowded with the desperately wounded." Eisenhower said that what separated him from the pacifists was that he hated the Nazis more than he did war. There was something else. "My hatred of war will never equal my conviction that it is the duty of every one of us, civilian and soldier alike, to carry out the orders of our government when a war emergency arises," Eisenhower told his brother. "As far as I am concerned, Stephen Decatur told the whole story when he said: 'Right or wrong, my country.'" Or, as he put it to his son, "The only unforgivable sin in war is not doing your duty."[20]

Immediately after the fall of Bizerte, Eisenhower recommended Bradley for promotion to lieutenant general (it was approved the following month) and told Marshall that he had been at the front nearly all week, "tremendously busy." When the last Axis forces had surrendered, he declared, "I am going to take a 24-hour leave where no one in this world will be able to reach me."[21]

The work, however, drove him on. After the Tunisian campaign, Eisenhower wrote a memorandum to himself with a paragraph on each of his leading commanders, "for reference when I may need them at a later date." He put Cunningham at the top of the list, ranking him first "in absolute selflessness, energy, devotion to duty, knowledge of his task, and in understanding of the requirements of Allied operations."

Tedder was a close second in every respect, although Eisenhower did wonder if Tedder was not a bit too much the airman, "not quite as broad-gauged as he might be," a little too inclined to see problems only from the air point of view. Alexander had "a winning personality," energy, and sound tactical conceptions. "The only possible doubt that could be raised with respect to his qualifications is a suspected unsureness in dealing with certain of his subordinates," which was a polite way of saying that Alexander could not control Montgomery. Eisenhower thought Montgomery himself was "a very able, dynamic type" who "loves the limelight." This was not necessarily a weakness, although Eisenhower usually frowned upon publicity seekers. Still, he found Montgomery to be intelligent, a good talker with "a flare for showmanship," and said, "I personally think that the only thing he needs is a strong immediate commander."

Eisenhower had worked most closely in the campaign with Anderson, a soldier who had the virtues of being "an earnest fighter completely devoted to duty." His trouble was that he instinctively thought in smaller terms, of battalions and brigades rather than divisions and corps, and thus was not really qualified to run an entire army.

Turning to the Americans in North Africa, Eisenhower began with Mark Clark, "the best organizer, planner and trainer of troops I have yet met in the American Army." Clark was orderly and logical. Eisenhower had once thought that "he was becoming a bit consumed with a desire to push himself," but "all that has disappeared. . . ." Clark's only drawback was his lack of combat experience. In the early days in Tunisia, Eisenhower had offered him command of II Corps, but Clark "rather resented taking any title except that of Army Commander" and declined.

"This was a bad mistake on Clark's part," Eisenhower concluded, "but I still think that he could successfully command an army in operations."

Patton, as Eisenhower knew better than most, "believes in showmanship to such an extent that he is almost flamboyant." He talked too much and too quickly and often "creates a very bad impression." He was not a good example to subordinates. But he was the best fighting general America had, and Eisenhower intended to keep him, whatever the cost. Bradley, on the other hand, never gave Eisenhower any worry. He "is about the best rounded, well balanced, senior officer that we have in the service." Bradley's judgments were always sound and he was respected by British and Americans alike. "I feel that there is no position in the Army that he could not fill with success," Eisenhower declared.[22]

Eisenhower's considered judgment on his subordinates revealed, among other things, his abilities to see a man's strengths and weaknesses quickly. He had known Cunningham for less than a year, Tedder, Montgomery, and Alexander for only a few months. He had known Patton and Bradley for years but had seen each in action only briefly. He did not know how Clark would react to combat. Yet all his judgments remained valid and he never had cause, in the campaigns that followed, to change any of them.

Eisenhower's memorandum was as revealing about himself as it was about the men he discussed. There was, first of all, the obvious prejudice of the ground officer toward the airmen, especially those airmen who wanted a separate air force. More important was what the memorandum showed about Eisenhower's value structure. The key words were selflessness, energy, duty, and the allegiance to alliance. The thing he abhorred most was publicity seeking.

He never sought publicity for himself. On May 13 the last Axis forces in Tunisia surrendered and the continent of Africa was in Allied hands. Eisenhower's forces had captured 275,000 enemy troops, a bag of prisoners even larger than the Russians had gotten at Stalingrad. Eisenhower saw to it that the men responsible got their full share of credit, but failed in a final press conference to mention his own role. As a result the British and American press hardly mentioned his name. This upset Marshall, who ordered the director of public relations, Major General Alexander Surles, to see to it that Eisenhower be given his proper credit for the "magnificent job" he had done. "You can tell some of these newsmen from me," Marshall told Surles, "that I think it is a damned outrage that because [Eisenhower] is self-effacing and not self-advertising that they ignore him completely when, as a matter of fact, he is responsible for the coordination of forces and events. . . ."[23]

If the press ignored Eisenhower, others did not. Congratulations poured in on him from all sides—from the President, the Prime Minister, Anderson and the rest of the British, the Russians, and soldiers, sailors, and private citizens throughout the world. Eisenhower claimed not to be impressed. He told Marshall he wished he had a disposition that would allow him to relax and enjoy a feeling of self-satisfaction, but he did not. "I always anticipate and discount, in my own mind, accomplishment," he said, "and am, therefore, mentally racing ahead into the next campaign" before the current one was complete. "The consequence is that all the shouting about the Tunisian campaign leaves me utterly cold."

He said that he was so impatient and irritated because of the slowness with which HUSKY* was being developed that "I make myself quite unhappy." He suffered physically for every additional day that the Axis had to perfect and strengthen the Sicily defenses, so much so that his "chief ambition in this war" was to get to a place where the next operation would not be amphibious, "with all the inflexibility and delay that are characteristic of such operations."[24]

Despite his protests, Eisenhower was not "utterly cold" to his own accomplishments or the praise they brought forth. He was proudest of the progress he had made in welding the Allied team together, not only at AFHQ but among the field units. He was most pleased by the way II Corps had fought in the final phases of the campaign, with the proof it offered that American troops, once blooded, would be able to take on the best Germany had to offer and win.

His deepest personal satisfaction came from having won Marshall's praise. The Chief sent his congratulations to Eisenhower. In reply, Eisenhower said that, since he had been given the mission of clearing North Africa almost ten months earlier, "my greatest source of inspiration and strength has been my confidence in your understanding of the intricate problems involved and the generosity of your support.

"Praise from no other individual could mean so much to me as yours," Eisenhower told his Chief, who hardly ever praised anyone. "I thank you from the bottom of my heart. . . ."[25]

* Code name for the invasion of Sicily.

CHAPTER 14

The Local Political Mess

Conceived in the disaster of the fall of France, born out of wedlock in London, with no national state to support it and thus an orphan as a child, it was inevitable that Free France would be a juvenile delinquent. The forms that the delinquency took, however, would depend in large part on the actions of others, especially the United States and the United Kingdom.

Roosevelt's attempt at Casablanca to bring De Gaulle and Giraud together had failed. Something simply had to be done to bring De Gaulle to Algiers and into an alliance with Giraud.[1] In February, in furtherance of his aims, Roosevelt sent Jean Monnet to Algiers to be Giraud's adviser and to work for unity. Monnet had been the first deputy secretary-general of the League of Nations and was an internationally known banker. He had been in London when France surrendered but had not rallied to De Gaulle's Free French cause; thus Roosevelt felt he was safe. But Monnet's only interest was in France, not personalities, and he refused to be the President's tool. He quickly assessed Giraud and found him wanting. "When the general looks at you with those eyes of a porcelain cat," Monnet said of Giraud, "he comprehends nothing!"[2] Since this was also the view of most of the leading British and Americans in Algiers, the only thing supporting Giraud was the influence and power of the President of the United States.

Monnet, Eisenhower, Murphy, and Macmillan set to work to draft a formula that would allow De Gaulle to come to Algiers and join with Giraud. Everyone was for this, for different reasons. Monnet was sure that De Gaulle would quickly overshadow Giraud, which would be good for France. Macmillan agreed, for he too wanted a strong France in postwar Europe and felt that only De Gaulle could provide one. Churchill, at least at times, seemed interested only in getting De Gaulle out of London. Murphy on the other hand thought that Giraud and Monnet could control De Gaulle and, like Eisenhower and Smith, felt that bringing De Gaulle into Algiers would ease political problems there. Roosevelt evidently thought that in Algiers, surrounded by visible evidence of America's military might, De Gaulle would be more tractable.

The basis of the formula was the creation in Algiers of a provisional government based on cabinet responsibility rather than personal rule. Monnet insisted upon this, and together with Macmillan and Murphy worked out a formula that called for a committee of seven leading Frenchmen, with De Gaulle and Giraud as co-presidents, to assume office as "the central French power." In May, Macmillan flew to London to present the proposal to De Gaulle. After much discussion, De Gaulle agreed to come to Algiers.³

The only difficulty in bringing De Gaulle and Giraud together, so it seemed on the surface, was their individual, monumental egos. But, as Macmillan also later admitted, "many of us did not altogether realize the fundamental difference between the position of [De Gaulle] and that of Giraud and his friends."⁴ De Gaulle represented a new France, while Giraud stood for the old. De Gaulle believed that France had to be reconstituted from top to bottom. All the Vichy scum—the police chiefs and their brutality, the clerks and their petty graft, the generals and their lust for glory and position—had to be flushed out. "It is not our fault," he declared, "if France is undergoing a virtual revolution at the same time as being at war."⁵ Thus when Macmillan proposed to De Gaulle that he join with Giraud, De Gaulle said one of his conditions would be that Giraud dismiss from office all Vichy "capitulators and collaborators" and announce that the armistice was null and void. Giraud bristled at this. For him, the armistice was fact. He had his duty to perform. The danger was Communism, and he would not yield to it. This point had not been settled when De Gaulle came to Algiers.⁶

Aside from the immediate problem of whether of not to dump the Vichy administrators, there were long-range differences between the two that would have to be settled. For Giraud, what mattered was to maintain order and stability, to keep competent officials at their posts, to insure that pensions for officers and civil servants remained intact, and most of all to keep the forces of radicalism within France under control. All this could best be done by co-operating with the Americans, who seemed to have essentially the same aims. Like many soldiers, Giraud contended that he was apolitical, which in his case meant that he would do nearly anything to support the status quo.

Roosevelt's policy toward De Gaulle, with its strong element of personal bitterness, has mystified many observers. No adequate analysis, taking into account all the factors, has been made. One thing is clear—something more than personal pique was involved. Roosevelt's view of the world was complex, and no one as yet knows what he intended for his postwar program. At times he seemed to favor collective security, modeled on Wilson's concept of the League of Nations and later implemented through the United Nations. On other occasions he advocated a traditional spheres-of-influence doctrine, best seen in his "Four Policemen" expression, which would have Russia and America rule the world, with some help from Britain and China. Within either context, Roosevelt wanted a stable France. Given American determination to withdraw the G.I.s from Europe once Germany was defeated, stability in France was essential to stability on the Continent.

But how could this be achieved? The great fear was that the French people would, as they had done in the past, run to an extreme. Either the weak, inefficient, radical governments of the Popular Front type would take over, with consequences neither Roosevelt nor Churchill liked to think about, or there would be a man on a white horse, a Boulanger or even a Napoleon. Either result would be a disaster.

De Gaulle was dangerous on both counts. He had the aura of the man on the white horse about him. Without any mandate whatsoever from the French people, he had set himself up as head of the French state. He carried himself like a dictator, deliberately insulted foreigners and Frenchmen who did not agree with him, was totally ruthless in his relations, and used personal loyalty rather than efficiency as a criterion for advancement within his organization. What made him even more dangerous was the way he flirted with the forces of the left. From Roosevelt's point of view, this made De Gaulle dangerous. "France faces a revolution when the Germans have been driven out," the President once said, and he felt that the man most likely to profit from it would be De Gaulle. He would ride whatever popular mood existed into power. That Roosevelt was wrong is obvious—there was no fundamental revolution in France and De Gaulle, within a year of the end of the war, held free elections and relinquished his power. But there was in De Gaulle's behavior a real basis for the President's fears, which in any case nearly every member of the European section of the State Department shared.

Roosevelt spent much effort trying to find an alternative to De Gaulle. The best hope was the French Army, more specifically Giraud, who represented the forces of stability and conservatism without carrying in addition the tar of the Vichy brush. The trouble here was Giraud's political innocence, and he soon fell by the wayside. This left the President without a candidate and, because of his tendency to personalize, meant that the United States had no definite policy regarding France. Under the circumstances, the most the President could do was to try to buy time and hope for the best, which in practice meant he followed the dubious course of attempting to stop De Gaulle.

The President expressed his views most clearly in a May 8, 1943, message to Churchill. He said De Gaulle was becoming "well-nigh intolerable," for he was stirring up strife between various elements in Algiers, making promises to the Jews that incited the Arabs, "expanding his present group of agitators," and so on. "I am inclined to think that when we get into France itself we will have to regard it as a military occupation run by the British and American generals," Roosevelt said. "The top line, or national administration, must be kept in the hands of the British or American Commander-in-Chief."[7]

As Milton Viorst has put it, "Roosevelt, irritated by French politics, without deep understanding of French history, with no experience in European diplomacy, took a condescending view of France and its prospects as a nation." The Americans were already working out a program to bring democracy to Germany; Roosevelt evidently thought that the United States would have to show France the way too. Hull was in "complete agreement" with this policy, which he felt was needed to "prevent anarchy."[8]

Eisenhower was caught in the middle of this plethora of political conflicts, which were far more complex than the summary above indicates. Roosevelt instructed him to act in North Africa as the military governor of a conquered province, but if he did that even Giraud would balk, and Eisenhower would be forced to use invaluable manpower to maintain order in North Africa. Nonetheless, the President wanted to keep De Gaulle out of power and made Eisenhower responsible for achieving this end. This ran counter to British wishes, and if Eisenhower was ever tempted to forget that he had more than one master Macmillan was there to remind him. Both Churchill and Roosevelt wanted Eisenhower to bring De Gaulle and Giraud together, a nearly impossible task because they wanted it accomplished on different terms. De Gaulle, in turn, wanted Eisenhower's help in freeing France of the Vichy administrators, while Giraud and Roosevelt wanted Eisenhower to see to it that the administrators stayed and the army was re-equipped. The De Gaulle faction put pressure on AFHQ to get the British and American governments to recognize the committee in Algiers as the provisional government of France, while the Giraud group wanted something altogether different. Eisenhower's personal wish was to escape from politics altogether, and his official desire was to get the issue settled so that he could get on with the war. But the stakes were high, the problem complicated, and there was no easy or quick solution. There was simply no way for Eisenhower to escape a deep and lasting involvement in the politics of war-torn France, especially as he became more and more accomplished as a diplomat and the leading actors came to look to him for solutions.

On May 30 De Gaulle arrived in Algiers. Churchill and Foreign Secretary Eden were already there. The Prime Minister had come, along with Brooke and Marshall, to discuss post-HUSKY strategy with Eisenhower, but Churchill also wanted to be a witness to the French union. He no longer flattered himself with the belief that he had undue influence with De Gaulle, who he knew was going to go his own way whatever the Prime Minister thought, but Churchill did feel that along with Eden he could play some sort of role. De Gaulle had declared that if Giraud wished to continue as commander in chief of the French armed forces he should not serve as a member of the prospective committee. Churchill was a strong advocate of civilian control of the military, but in this case he did not agree with De Gaulle. He talked about the problem with Eisenhower, calling De Gaulle an "ego-maniac" and a "Prime S.O.B." These were welcome words to American ears, and Eisenhower ventured to say that Giraud was a capable leader of the French Army who had done what he was told. Eisenhower declared that he intended to continue to back Giraud as commander in chief of the French armed forces and would expect the governments to do the same.[9]

Behind the scenes, meanwhile, De Gaulle's supporters were building their strength for the showdown. Some two thousand Fighting French enlisted men and officers, who had fought through the desert with the Eighth Army, had gone AWOL (the British had ordered them to stay in Tripoli) and come into Algiers, where they were proselytizing among Giraud's French troops and officers, with great success. Giraud's police tried to herd up the Free French, but they simply scattered to the homes of friends outside Algiers.

With, in effect, two French armies in Algiers, one responsive to Giraud and the other to De Gaulle, and with the eventual government of

France at stake, the atmosphere was tense. A Fighting French officer boasted that De Gaulle had enough troops to take control of the city in a coup. With Darlan's death fresh in everyone's mind, the possibility of assassination could not be ignored. Eisenhower quietly checked on the number of American and British troops available for combat in the city and found there were almost none. There were, however, two British battleships and an aircraft carrier in the harbor and, of course, the air forces. Eisenhower felt that De Gaulle could probably take Algiers with an organized putsch but would be unable to hold it long. He did promise his aides one day he would start wearing a pistol, but he forgot it the next.[10]

The French, it turned out, were doing a better job of keeping calm than the British and Americans. On June 3 De Gaulle and two of his Free French representatives met with Giraud and two of his followers. Monnet was the seventh member of the committee. The proposal before them was to constitute themselves into what was in effect a provisional government of France. Giraud at first balked at the proposal. He wanted to keep all the power Eisenhower and the Americans had given him for himself, but Monnet advised him to yield and he ultimately agreed. Thus the French Committee of National Liberation (FCNL) was born. After discussion, the FCNL proclaimed itself the central French power. At Monnet's urging, the committee was careful to state definitely that it would "relinquish its power" when France was liberated. De Gaulle and Giraud were co-presidents of the Committee, and Giraud remained as head of the armed forces.[11]

Eisenhower was delighted. Although neither the British nor the American government recognized the FCNL as a provisional government, they did agree to deal with it as an administrative agency for French interests. This meant, Eisenhower hoped, that all relations with the French would now be on an impersonal basis. When Churchill or Roosevelt wanted something, Macmillan or Murphy could discuss it with the FCNL. The old days, in which Eisenhower personally had to talk everything over with Giraud, hopefully were gone.[12]

The members of the FCNL, however, soon began bickering with each other. De Gaulle wanted to dismiss the old Vichy administrators, starting with Boisson at Dakar. Giraud would not agree. De Gaulle wanted control of the armed forces taken out of Giraud's hands and placed in those of the FCNL, and he was furious with Giraud for the supine way in which he accepted the "constant and unjustified interference by the Allies in French affairs." De Gaulle was also upset because the

Americans had prevented some of his followers in London from coming to Algiers.

Everything came to a head at a meeting on the morning of June 10. De Gaulle stated his position, failed to carry a majority, and thereupon indulged in a calculated outburst. "Shrouded in sorrow," he declared he could "no longer associate with the Committee" and resigned.[13]

Whatever illusions Eisenhower had had about being free of French political troubles now disappeared. The day after De Gaulle's outburst Roosevelt sent Eisenhower three cables. In the first he said he was not displeased, for he felt "this De Gaulle situation was bound to come to a head sooner or later" and better now than a month hence. In the second cable Roosevelt repeated a message he had sent the same day to Churchill, insisting that Giraud must have complete control of French troops in North Africa. He said he would send "several regiments to Dakar and also naval vessels if there were any sign that De Gaulle proposes to take things over in French West Africa."

In the third message Roosevelt referred to De Gaulle's intention of dumping Boisson. Churchill had given Boisson an oral promise, and Roosevelt a written one, that he would not be punished for co-operating with Vichy. Thus Roosevelt ordered Eisenhower to pass an important message to both Giraud and De Gaulle, a message that was to come from the general, not the President. Eisenhower was to say that he was pleased by the expression of French unity shown in the formation of the FCNL and then to express his concern over reports of the possibility of the removal of Boisson from his West Africa post as a violation of this very spirit of unity and co-operation. He was then to ask for reassurances that the reports were unfounded. Roosevelt told Eisenhower to "go as far as you like in carrying out" these orders.[14]

Eisenhower spent the morning in conference with Murphy and Macmillan. He ruefully commented that Marshall and others had advised him "to get out of the political machinations, and yet the President had plunged him back into them."[15] Because Eisenhower did not speak French he asked Murphy to deliver the message to Giraud. Murphy did so, and Giraud replied, *"Tres bien."*

De Gaulle was pleased with the hornet's nest he had stirred up and when Murphy saw him was in a "most amiable state of mind." He talked for an hour. He told Murphy the United States should make more of an effort to understand him and his movement. He had realized from the first, he said, that Great Britain could not win the war alone and that therefore France's future would hinge on the efforts of the

Americans. He realized that the British were "traders capable of quick shifts of policy to meet their own interests and that they wished to use France for the purpose," so he felt no compunction about using the British "as a convenience." He expected from the United States "better comprehension" of the new France which he was building. Again and again he referred to the American attitude on Boisson, saying "it presented him with the gravest kind of problem on a matter of principle concerning French Sovereignty. If he yielded . . . he was lost."[16]

Monnet, meanwhile, oiled the wheels and got the FCNL rolling again. De Gaulle returned to the committee, which expanded from seven to fourteen members, with a permanent subcommittee composed of De Gaulle, Giraud, Juin, and two others to control military affairs. Giraud had gone along because Monnet advised him to do so, but by June 16 it was clear that De Gaulle dominated the larger committee. Giraud charged that Monnet had betrayed him and threatened his own resignation. Murphy insisted that he remain in office. Eisenhower was out of town on a three-day inspection trip to Clark's Fifth Army, and in reporting these developments to Roosevelt, Murphy was most pessimistic. The diplomat saw no way to prevent a Gaullist takeover.[17]

The President's response was immediate and sharp. On June 17 he cabled Eisenhower to insist that "we will not tolerate control of the French Army by any agency which is not subject to the Allied Supreme Commander's direction . . . nor are we interested in the formation of any government or committee that in any way presumes to indicate that it will govern in France." In even stronger language, he added, "It must be absolutely clear that in North and West Africa we have a military occupation and, therefore, no independent civil decision can be made without your full approval."[18]*

In another cable of the same day Roosevelt told Eisenhower, "for your very secret information . . . we may possibly break with De Gaulle in the next few days." The President also cabled Churchill to point out that "it is an intolerable situation. . . . We must divorce ourselves from De Gaulle because . . . he has been interested far more in political machinations than he has in the prosecution of the war. . . ."[19]

Late on June 17 Eisenhower returned to Algiers. The next morning he tried to get Washington to calm down a little. He told the President

---

* How Roosevelt got it into his head that the Allies had a military occupation of French West Africa is a mystery. Boisson had invited Allied representatives into Dakar and allowed the Allies to use the facilities at Dakar of his own free will. There was never any pretense of military conquest, as there was in Algiers, Morocco, and Tunisia.

that the "local French difficulties . . . have been magnified." Much of the "acrimonious discussion" between De Gaulle and Giraud was more indicative of typical French politics than anything else. He had arranged to meet with De Gaulle and Giraud the next morning "to lay down in definite terms my minimum requirements" on the control of the French armed forces, and he expected to be successful. The question of Boisson was not on the agenda of the FCNL and Eisenhower advised Roosevelt not to make an issue of French West Africa, since to do so would give De Gaulle "the opportunity of breaking on an issue which he might falsely publicize as interfering in French civil administration. . . ." Eisenhower respectfully suggested to Roosevelt that nothing be done in Washington about breaking with De Gaulle until after the meeting. "I assure you, Mr. President," he concluded, "that I am fully alive to the potentialities of the situation. . . ." In a cable to Marshall, Eisenhower pointed out that "De Gaulle has other and bigger fish to fry" and asked that the Chief, at an opportune moment, present his case to the President.[20]

More clearly than Roosevelt, in short, Eisenhower recognized De Gaulle's strength. De Gaulle was enormously popular among French civilians in Algiers and had at least as much influence in the army as Giraud. To break with him and try to throw him to the wolves would, at the very least, touch off serious civil disorder in Algiers. HUSKY was only three weeks away and Eisenhower had no troops in the area to keep order.

Eisenhower also realized—as Roosevelt did not—that De Gaulle could not be intimidated or bribed. He was far stronger now than he had been in January at Casablanca, when the Allies had in effect offered him a secure position, a sort of recognition, and funds to carry on his work. If he had yielded to please them and joined Giraud, he could have become an important part of a Giraud government, probably the Minister of Defense. He would have had to follow Eisenhower's orders and agree that France, when liberated, would be run by an Allied military government until the British and Americans chose to hold an election on their terms. But he would have received in return security, honor, prestige, and the friendship of the United States. By standing off at Casablanca he risked losing all. He had rejected the offer then, holding out for bigger prizes. There was no question but that he would do the same now.

But though Eisenhower saw these facts, he did have his orders from the President to carry out. The key to the Eisenhower-Giraud-De Gaulle meeting of June 19 would be Eisenhower's ability to hold his temper.

De Gaulle was sure to make policy statements which would amount to insults. Eisenhower would have to try to soothe his feelings and keep smiling himself.

De Gaulle purposely arrived last and spoke first. He strode into the room in full uniform, his tall frame ramrod stiff, his Roman nose suspiciously sniffing the air. "I am here in my capacity as President of the French government," he announced. "For it is customary that during operations the chiefs of state and of the government should come in person to the headquarters of the officer in command of the armies they have entrusted to him."

De Gaulle looked around. No one could think of a response to his preposterous opening gambit, so he plunged on. "If you wish to address a request to me concerning your province," he said to Eisenhower, "be assured that I am disposed beforehand to give you satisfaction, on condition, of course, that it is compatible with the interests in my charge."

Eisenhower then politely asked De Gaulle to leave Giraud in charge of France's armed forces. De Gaulle replied that "the organization of the French command is the province of the French government, not yours." Eisenhower repeated his request, whereupon De Gaulle asked, "You who are a soldier, do you think that a leader's authority can subsist if it rests on the favor of a foreign power?" Eisenhower spoke of his responsibilities and his need to have his line of communications through North Africa secure and in the hands of a man he could trust.

De Gaulle thought Eisenhower was acutely embarrassed to have to demand assurances from a head of government about his army leaders and did so only because of the pressure from Roosevelt. He admitted that Eisenhower was playing a strong hand insofar as the American general was directing the rearming of the French Army with American equipment. But he recalled World War I, when the Americans had fired only French cannon, driven only French trucks, flown only French airplanes. "Did we," he asked, "in return . . . demand of the United States that they appoint this or that leader or institute this or that political system?" He then demanded that Eisenhower reduce his statements and demands to writing, and Eisenhower agreed to do so.

At this point Giraud, for the first time, spoke up. He began to discuss French problems and emphasized how utterly dependent upon the Americans the French were. De Gaulle mumbled that he had heard all this before and stalked out of the room.[21]

Eisenhower chatted with Giraud for a few more minutes, then went to confer with Cunningham and Alexander. They agreed that the best thing to do was nothing. Any unrest or disturbances in Algiers at the present time would only have the most deplorable effect on HUSKY, and the chances were good that in time the French would find their own way out of the tangle. "I hope you will say to the President," Eisenhower concluded in his report of the meeting to Marshall, "that I beg of him to avoid any action that could increase our local difficulties until after HUSKY is at least a week old."[22]

The President responded by insisting on the retention of Giraud and, returning to his old obsession, declaring, "I want it distinctly understood that under no circumstances will we approve the removal of Boisson from Dakar." He added that he expected Eisenhower to accomplish the goals of his government in this area.[23]

On June 22 Eisenhower sent a long analysis of the situation to Marshall. He emphasized that "when the HUSKY forces begin loading within a very few days, there will be practically no repeat no troops west of Tunisia that could be employed for insuring tranquility." He again begged Marshall to see to it that Roosevelt did not force matters to a crisis. Monnet had told him that any attempt to depose De Gaulle would be disastrous, and Eisenhower added that he felt De Gaulle could be controlled. Giraud, Eisenhower said, had strength in the FCNL because of his record of co-operation and more important because Roosevelt had personally given him support. "His great weakness is the uneasy feeling throughout the region, including the Army and the civil population, that he is reactionary, old fashioned, and cannot be persuaded to modernize the forces already organized. It must be admitted that he moves with ponderous slowness. He had no repeat no political acumen whatsoever."[24]

The next day the situation brightened. The FCNL met and reached a compromise agreement. Giraud would be commander in chief of all French forces in North Africa, while De Gaulle would command all French forces elsewhere. Both were part of but responsible to a war committee that was in turn responsible to the FCNL. At AFHQ everyone was delighted, mainly because the officers there greatly misjudged De Gaulle's political abilities. Eisenhower said he and his advisers had gone over the terms of the compromise "very carefully" and were "convinced that it assures the conditions prescribed" by the President. Eisenhower promised to watch the situation to make sure nothing was changed "by subterfuge, or otherwise except in the direction desired by us."[25] Smith wired Marshall to say that he had just talked with Giraud's chief of staff, who was delighted with the decree and considered it "a definite victory." Smith commented, "From every point of view we are certain that the new arrangement is all that we could ask for and I am still surprised that it was put across without a flare-up."[26] The Americans, in short, thought that De Gaulle had been had.

The truth was that De Gaulle accepted the arrangement because he was sure he could bend the committee to his will. AFHQ officers saw what they wanted to see and, despite all evidence to the contrary, kept assuring themselves that De Gaulle was through. In reporting on the "local political mess" to Marshall, Eisenhower said, "I am quite sure that De Gaulle is losing ground, but strangely enough this is not resulting in a strengthening of Giraud." He sensed a "growing weariness by the majority with the bickerings of individuals," and thereby came close to putting his finger on one of the key elements in De Gaulle's success— his persistence. De Gaulle was in it for the long haul. Unlike ordinary men, he would never get weary until he got his way.[27]

De Gaulle was certain things would begin to fall into place, and they began to do so almost immediately. On the morning of June 24 Boisson wired to Giraud to announce his resignation. This came as a great surprise. Giraud, fearing that Boisson had sent a similar resignation to De Gaulle, "and not wanting to be outfoxed" by having De Gaulle assume the prerogatives of government and accept the resignation, accepted it himself. Eisenhower rushed over to see Giraud and urged him to defer any action on Boisson until the FCNL could meet.[28] Giraud thereupon withdrew his acceptance of the resignation.

Murphy meanwhile told the American government that, if Boisson insisted upon resigning, it should make the best of it. Roosevelt, who earlier had been ready to send regiments of infantry into Dakar to keep Boisson, had by now lost interest. Neither Murphy nor Eisenhower received instructions from Washington. The FCNL, meanwhile, met and decided to ask Boisson to remain at his post until a successor could be found. The Americans asked only that the successor be *persona grata* to them, and he was. By July 1 the whole thing was settled.[29]

De Gaulle then began to press for recognition of the FCNL as the sole French administrative body. This issue was far more important than Giraud's position. Recognition would force Eisenhower and American officials to deal with the committee rather than the commander in chief, it would open the way for representatives of the FCNL to participate in Allied committees, it would permit the FCNL access to French credits held in the United States (estimated at a billion dollars in gold), and most of all it would simplify the situation when the day of liberation came. If there were no recognition of the FCNL, nothing would prevent the Allied commander from signing another Clark-Darlan accord with some Pétainist official or with Pétain himself, from ignoring the Resistance, or from setting up a military occupation.[30]

Macmillan thought the committee ought to be recognized, and he was gradually converting the Americans at AFHQ to his view. He felt that the committee was acquiring a collective authority, that De Gaulle was by no means its master, and that it would make dealings much less complicated if AFHQ could deal with the FCNL instead of with personalities. Besides, he feared that if the committee broke down, as it was likely to do without recognition, De Gaulle would become the sole figure around whom patriotic Frenchmen could rally.[31]

Churchill agreed with Macmillan. He was deeply concerned about De Gaulle because De Gaulle's conduct had alienated Hull and Roosevelt so badly that the two Americans could hardly speak rationally about the man. The Prime Minister thought the solution was to submerge De Gaulle in the committee and allow it to demonstrate its value.[32] On July 21 Churchill urged Roosevelt to help solidify Anglo-American relations with the FCNL. "What does recognition mean?" he asked. "One can recognize a man as an Emperor or as a grocer. Recognition is meaningless, without a defining formula." The formula he wanted amounted to a recognition of the FCNL as the provisional government of France. Churchill added that Macmillan "reports that Eisenhower and Murphy both agree with this. . . ."[33]

Roosevelt's response was to send a blistering cable to Eisenhower demanding to know what was going on. "Under no condition are you to recognize the Committee . . . ," Roosevelt warned.[34]

Eisenhower was "astonished" at the suggestion that he had intended to recognize the FCNL on his own authority. He assured Marshall, "I am quite well aware of the exclusive authority of the President in such matters, and I am sometimes disturbed that any rumor of such a kind can gain such force or atmosphere of validity as to create an impression that I would step out of my own proper sphere to this extent, or could impel, as in this case, the President himself to send me orders on the subject." He then added that he, Murphy, and Macmillan felt that "some kind of limited recognition . . . would be helpful."[35]

A period of negotiation between Churchill and Roosevelt followed. Eventually, in August, they reached an agreement of sorts. Roosevelt, roundly declaring that he would not "give De Gaulle a white horse on which he could ride into France and make himself master of a government there," chose to "recognize" the FCNL "as administering those French overseas territories which acknowledge its authority." He went to great pains to emphasize that "this statement does not constitute recognition of a government of France or of the French Empire by the Government of the United States."

Churchill's government gave the FCNL a much broader and less circumscribed recognition. Both governments insisted that, "in view of the paramount importance of the common war effort, the relationship with the French Committee of National Liberation must continue to be subject to the military requirements of the Allied Commanders," although the British couched their statement in more polite language.[36]

For Eisenhower, what mattered was that there had finally been a settlement of French affairs, and, it must be added, generally along the lines he had recommended. He could, he believed, expect political tranquillity in Algiers. With Giraud and De Gaulle functioning as loyal members of a committee that was beginning to take its position as a provisional government seriously, Eisenhower could look forward to a relationship with the French free from personal animosity or difficulty. Or so he at least fondly hoped. If trouble did come, however, he could cope with it, for he had learned much since Murphy first introduced him to French political affairs. He had indeed become an expert in the field.

CHAPTER 15

Preparing HUSKY: March–July 1943

As the end of the campaign approached in Tunisia, planners began the detailed work on HUSKY, the invasion of Sicily. As had been the case with TORCH, the attempt to reach agreement on a date and landing sites led to confusion and disagreement. "The HUSKY thing has gotten planners really in a turmoil," Eisenhower told Somervell as early as March 19.[1] The next day he confessed to Handy that HUSKY was bringing on "terrific headaches." Unlike the TORCH argument, however, the HUSKY dispute did not follow national lines. "I do not allow, ever, an expression to be used in this Headquarters in my presence that even insinuates a British vs. American problem exists," Eisenhower told Handy. "So far as I am concerned, it doesn't."[2] There were differences of opinion on when and where to land, but at the center of the argument were three British officers, with Montgomery on one side and Tedder and Cunningham on the other.

About some things there could be no argument, since availability of equipment was the determining factor. The possible dates for the invasion were limited by the phases of the moon. The army men wanted darkness for their trip to the landing sites, while the paratroopers who would land inland to seal off the beaches wanted some light for their drop. This meant the assault had to come when the moon was in its second quarter, either between June 10 and June 14 or during a similar period in July. The CCS wanted the attack to come in June, but on March 13, following a meeting with his three deputies, Eisenhower decided that he could not mount it until July. The main reason was that landing craft would not arrive before May. In addition, Eisenhower needed time to train the HUSKY contingent in assault tactics.[3]

A brief glance at a map of the Mediterranean indicated that the best landing site would be at or just south of Messina. Possession of that area would cut off Sicily from the Italian mainland. The Allies could then throw up a defensive line and force the Axis troops to attack them. Messina, however, received no serious consideration because all the commanders thought it too risky. The Axis could bring too much strength to bear, the approach was narrow, and the sea rough. Most of all, it was out of range of fighter cover. Next best was anywhere north of Mount Etna, followed by a northward move to Messina, but again the risks seemed too great. The truth was that, both at AFHQ and at Alexander's headquarters, planners were cautious to a fault. Their major —sometimes, it seemed, sole—concern was getting ashore. Montgomery and his staff shared this concern.

The easiest place to get ashore was on the southeastern portion of Sicily. It was closest to Allied ports in North Africa and had the softest beach. The trouble here was that the supply people insisted that without port facilities they could not support the nine divisions that would participate, and even if Syracuse was captured early there would not be enough port capacity. The operation would thus fail, they felt, because of lack of reinforcements, ammunition, and other supplies.

The alternative was to make the major attack in the southeast with smaller attacks elsewhere to gain the needed ports. As long as only Italians were on the island, the relative weakness of the minor attacks did not matter much, for the planners did not expect the Italians to put up a serious fight. But if German troops came onto the island in any number, each assault force would have to be large enough to maintain itself or face annihilation.

At a March 13 meeting of the commander in chief and his deputies, the Allies decided to make three separate landings. The first and largest would be in the southeast, the second in the southwest, and the third in the northwest, near the excellent port of Palermo. One of the major concerns was air cover and the need to eliminate the Axis striking force; under the echelon plan, captured airfields from the first landing would be used to provide air support for the second, and so on. Meanwhile ports would be opened, and an inland parachute drop would take place opposite the southeastern landing site.

The risks seemed great. The plan was complicated, involved a serious diversion of strength, and called for successive rather than simultaneous assaults. If the Germans got onto the island in a strength of two divisions or more, the Allies felt the Axis could defeat any one of their landing forces in detail, thus throwing the whole program out of kilter. But the commanders felt they had to trust their experts. The supply people said they had to have the ports, especially Palermo, so the final decision was made.[4]

The assault forces would consist of the Eastern Task Force, composed of five divisions of Montgomery's Eighth Army, and the Western Task Force, the U. S. Seventh Army, under Patton.[5] All would come under Alexander's Fifteenth Army Group. Eisenhower personally selected Patton, while the British insisted on Montgomery, even though during the main planning stage he was busy in Tunisia.

When Montgomery studied the first plan, he immediately declared that his force was not strong enough to take all its objectives, which included Syracuse and the airfields at Catania and Gela. To achieve this, he declared, he had to have at least one more division. Alexander and Eisenhower went over the problem and decided they would have to eliminate the southwestern landings, since there was no possibility that the CCS would give them more men or landing craft. This would bring an American division to the east and place it under Montgomery, with Gela as its objective.[6]

Neither Cunningham nor Tedder liked this alternative plan. They wanted as many landings as widely scattered as possible in order to capture Axis airfields. To Tedder this was the cheapest and quickest way to gain control of the air; to Cunningham, worried about his ships in the area, it represented insurance against enemy air strikes on his naval forces. Both were inclined to feel that Alexander gave in to Montgomery too easily.[7]

At the beginning of April Eisenhower paid a visit to Montgomery. He wanted to inspect the Eighth Army, visit the Mareth battlefield, and talk about HUSKY. It was his first long meeting with the British general and his impression was unfavorable. Eisenhower told Marshall that although Montgomery had ability he was conceited. Eisenhower thought Montgomery was so proud of his achievements that he would never attack until victory was certain. He thought Montgomery intended to preserve the reputation he had won at El Alamein.[8]

Caution was widespread that spring. As Eisenhower prepared for the first Allied assault against an Axis position in Europe, his major thought continued to be getting ashore safely. On April 7 he told the CCS that if more than two German divisions were present in Sicily "the operation offers scant promise of success." The assault was a frontal one devoid of strategical or tactical surprise, with nine Allied divisions hitting eight Axis divisions. It could succeed against the poorly-equipped

Italians, but not against a garrison with a high proportion of German troops.[9]

The next day an agitated Churchill discussed Eisenhower's message with the BCOS. He pointed out, with some heat, that Eisenhower's caution contrasted oddly with the confidence the Americans had shown the previous summer about invading France across the Channel, where they would have to meet a great many more than two German divisions. If two German divisions were to be decisive against the operations of the million men now in North Africa, the Prime Minister felt, he could not see how the war could be carried on. "Months of preparation, sea power and air power in abundance and yet two German divisions are sufficient to knock it all on the head," he growled.

To Churchill it was "perfectly clear that the operations must either be entrusted to someone who believes in them, or abandoned. I trust the Chiefs of Staff will not accept these pusillanimous and defeatist doctrines from whoever they come." He reminded the BCOS that the Allies had told the Russians that lend-lease convoys could not be run for the sake of HUSKY. Now HUSKY was to be abandoned if there were a mere two German divisions in the neighborhood. "What Stalin would think of this when he has 185 German divisons on his front, I cannot imagine."[10]

Churchill's chiefs agreed with him and immediately sent a telegram to the JCS in Washington. The JCS accepted the view of the BCOS, and a telegram in the same sense as Churchill's remarks, but in less vehement language, came to Eisenhower on April 10. His reply, in full, read: "Operation HUSKY will be prosecuted with all the means at our disposal. While we believe it our duty to give our considered and agreed opinion of relative changes under conditions as stated in our previous messages, there is no thought here except to carry out our orders to the ultimate limit of our ability."[11]

Eisenhower's British deputies, meanwhile, continued to argue about HUSKY (which ultimately went through eight separate plans). Eisenhower did not officially participate in the argument, since under the command structure created at Casablanca he was supposed merely to approve or disapprove of the plan his deputies sent up to him. Unofficially, however, he was deeply involved, primarily by paying visits to the various headquarters and talking things over with the commanders.

The situation began to come to a head in late April. Montgomery went to Cairo, where his own planning headquarters was working on HUSKY, and came away convinced that everything should be concentrated on the southeastern corner of Sicily. He flew to Algiers to present his plan. Eisenhower refused to discuss it with him unless Alexander was present, and Alexander was busy conducting the Tunisian battle. Montgomery then proposed to Smith that AFHQ give up the Palermo landing and put Patton's force ashore on Eighth Army's left flank, near Gela. Smith agreed and called a staff conference, at which Montgomery presented his case.

"I know well that I am regarded by many people as being a tiresome person," Montgomery began. "I think this is very probably true. I try hard not to be tiresome; but I have seen so many mistakes made in this war, and so many disasters happen, that I am desperately anxious to try and see that we have no more; and this often means being very tiresome. If we have a disaster in Sicily it would be dreadful." The way to avoid disaster, he continued, was to be strong at the point of landing, which meant putting Seventh and Eighth Armies ashore side by side.[12]

Montgomery felt he convinced Eisenhower, to whom Smith related the plan, but Eisenhower refused to come to a decision until the plan was recommended to him by the three deputies. When they came to Algiers the next day, agreement was finally reached. Tedder felt that Montgomery would take "no risks" and was "shaken at the thought of the risks inevitable in an operation of this sort," but since the plan would give the air forces the fields at Gela and Catania, Tedder agreed to go along with it. Cunningham was agreeable, too, since at least his naval forces would have concentrated air cover. Alexander, according to Tedder, did whatever Montgomery wanted him to do. When Eisenhower gave his approval, the plan was set.[13]

The final plan was based on anticipation of strong Italian and German resistance. As the official American historians note, "The whole approach toward Sicily was cautious and conservative," with the emphasis on ensuring success and avoiding calculated risk. The plan reflected the planner—Montgomery—and like him it was cautious. "No one except Montgomery was particularly happy with it."[14]

With the concentrated assault, the Allies were avoiding the risk of dispersion and accepting another. Montgomery's plan had long been discussed and always rejected on the grounds that the Allies could not supply the Western Task Force over the beaches. Montgomery insisted that the technicians would have to find a way. What convinced Eisenhower was the presence of additional LSTs that the CCS brought in, and the quantity production of the DUKW, or "duck," an amphibious vehicle that could bring in supplies over the beach. With the DUKW,

Eisenhower's supply people told him, they could maintain Patton. This assurance made up Eisenhower's mind.[15]*

In May the CCS were scheduled to meet again (at Washington, code name TRIDENT) to review strategy for the remainder of 1943 and 1944. Before the meeting Eisenhower took up with Marshall the future of AFHQ. He wanted Marshall's views on future operations in the Mediterranean under various assumptions: HUSKY proving to be a difficult operation; HUSKY going according to plan; or the defenses in Sicily collapsing suddenly and completely.

Under the last assumption, Eisenhower thought the follow-up troops for HUSKY should be sent into Sardinia and Corsica, with a long-range objective of invading the west coast of Italy. He realized that such a proposal ran counter to Marshall's views. Taking Italy would force the Allies to take care of the civilian population there. Estimates were that 10,000,000 tons of coal a year alone would be required, along with vast quantities of other supplies. Allied soldiers would also have to be supported. All this would tie up Anglo-American shipping and thus delay the build-up in England for the cross-Channel attack. The only real military advantage the Allies would gain would be possession of airfields capable of handling heavy bombers closer to Germany.

"I personally have never wavered in my belief that the ROUNDUP conception is the correct one," Eisenhower assured Marshall, but he pointed out that it would take nearly a year to prepare for it. For political if not military reasons the Allies had to do something in the meantime. The Mediterranean was a major theater, with supply bases and troops already there. They had to be maintained anyway, so with a relatively minor additional expenditure in shipping the Allies could keep the pressure on Germany by continuing operations in the Mediterranean.[16]

Marshall replied that if HUSKY went according to plan Eisenhower should be ready to exploit his victory. If there was a sudden collapse, he should have plans ready to seize Sardinia, Corsica, and the heel of the Italian boot. Marshall, as expected, reminded Eisenhower that an all-out invasion of Italy would present serious consequences and prevent

* In an interview on October 7, 1965, Eisenhower commented, "The reason the 'concentrated' attack was now deemed preferable was logistical in character. Originally all staffs were adamant in refusing to try to supply too many troops over one beach. Fixed formulae were accepted as inviolate by such staffs. Then came the DUKW—the swimming truck. This made all the difference; an almost unlimited number of troops could now be supplied over a single beach."

major operations elsewhere, but nevertheless the Chief realized that "we must include such an operation in our planning."

"You will understand that the operations outlined above are not in keeping with my ideas of what our strategy should be," Marshall said in conclusion. "The decisive effort must be made against the Continent from the United Kingdom sooner or later." He warned Eisenhower to be prepared to transfer some of his forces to Great Britain and implied that he was going to do his best to shut down operations in the Mediterranean before they drained more resources.[17]

The CCS met for two weeks. The arguments were interminable. On May 19 an agreement of sorts was reached. The CCS declared in favor of a cross-Channel attack in 1944 and made the goal for 1943 the elimination of Italy from the war. On the key question—whether to invade the mainland of Italy or Sardinia and Corsica—the Chiefs could not agree. The plan they finally transmitted to Eisenhower, who had been patiently waiting for guidance, directed him "to plan such operations in exploitation of HUSKY as are best calculated to eliminate Italy from the war and to contain the maximum number of German forces." How to accomplish this (whether to invade mainland Italy or not) was left up to Eisenhower. He could use the forces he had in the Mediterranean, less seven divisions that would go to the United Kingdom on November 1, 1943.[18]

No one was very satisfied with this result, least of all Churchill. Since Eisenhower would make the final decision, the Prime Minister decided to fly to Algiers and try to talk Eisenhower into accepting an invasion of the Italian mainland. He told Roosevelt that he would "feel awkward" if a high-ranking American did not accompany him, for he might then be charged with having exercised "undue influence." Roosevelt therefore told Marshall to go along with Churchill to represent opposition to the plan for the mainland invasion of Italy.[19]

Churchill and Marshall, along with Brooke, Ismay, and entourage, arrived in Algiers on Friday afternoon, May 28. Churchill got right down to business, and what came to be known as the Algiers Conference was under way. He began by saying that he feared the Sicilian campaign might proceed too rapidly, thereby causing an embarrassing interlude of Allied inactivity. Eisenhower said that if that happened he would be willing to go straight into Italy. If the campaign in Sicily dragged on, however, the question of post-HUSKY operations would have to remain unsettled. Much would turn on the strength of Italian resistance and German intentions.[20]

The discussions went on for days. Churchill told Eisenhower that "his heart lay in an invasion of Southern Italy." The choice of Italy over Sardinia represented the difference between "a glorious campaign and a mere convenience." The glory would come from the capture of Rome, which "would be a very great achievement for our Mediterranean forces," a fitting climax to the Eighth Army's odyssey. Rome had no particular strategic or economic importance, but the ancient capital did offer psychological rewards, and the Prime Minister was enough of a nineteenth-century romantic to value such rewards highly. Besides, the prospect of sweet revenge on Mussolini appealed to the Prime Minister.[21]

"The PM recited his story three different times in three different ways last night," Eisenhower complained on May 30. All during the Algiers Conference Churchill talked continuously, trying to wear down the last shred of opposition. On Sunday night, May 30, he called after dinner to ask if he could come over to Eisenhower's villa at 10:45 P.M. Eisenhower wanted to sleep and he was tired of going over the same ground again and again, but he said it would be all right. Churchill arrived fifteen minutes late, then talked steadily for two hours. Butcher finally had more or less to push him out the door.[22] Brooke saw the "very sleepy Eisenhower" the next day and enjoyed the situation immensely. "I smiled at his distress, having suffered from this type of treatment repeatedly."[23]

Despite the late hours, having Churchill and Marshall around was profitable. Eisenhower took advantage of the opportunity to talk at length with Marshall about such problems as promotions, organization, and equipment. Marshall had spent some of his time in Algeria touring the recent battlefields and inspecting troops. On one occasion the Chief and Eisenhower had joined Bradley to watch a practice landing by the 1st Division. Patton was there. As the first wave came up the beach, Patton marched to the water's edge and confronted a squad of startled riflemen.

"And just where in hell are your goddamned bayonets?" he shouted. While the soldiers stood helplessly before him, Patton showered them with curses. Eisenhower and Marshall looked on in embarrassed silence. One of Eisenhower's staff officers, standing next to Bradley, nodded toward Marshall and whispered, "Well, there goes Georgie's chance for a crack at higher command. That temper of his is going to finish him yet."[24]

Formal meetings and casual conversations about the future continued. Marshall was steadfast in his refusal to make further commitments in the Mediterranean which would draw troops and material from the 1944 cross-Channel invasion. He wanted to delay making any decision until the German reaction to HUSKY was clear. He suggested that Eisenhower set up two separate headquarters, each with its own staff, to plan post-HUSKY operations. One would plan for operations against Sardinia and Corsica, the other for operations against southern Italy.

Eisenhower agreed. He suggested there might be three possibilities: (1) if the enemy collapsed quickly in Sicily, he would immediately undertake operations against the Italian mainland (a reflection of Churchill's persuasive powers since Marshall preferred Sardinia); (2) if the enemy offered prolonged resistance in Sicily, the Allies would have no resources available for immediate post-HUSKY operations and the whole campaign in the Mediterranean could then be rethought; (3) if resistance was stubborn but could be overcome by the middle of August, no decision could be made in advance. He thought the third possibility the most likely, and therefore having two separate headquarters to plan separate operations would give him alternatives from which to choose. The Algiers Conference thus ended without a clear-cut decision; in Churchill's words, "post-HUSKY would be in General Eisenhower's hands."[25]

On the afternoon of June 2 Eisenhower hosted the last meeting of the conference. Montgomery and Tedder joined the British contingent and both outlined the development of HUSKY plans. Montgomery exuded confidence. There were risks involved, he said, but they were justified and he would overcome them. He expected ten days of hard fighting, then a sudden end, after which he would cross the Strait of Messina and get the windpipe of Sicily into his hands. After that he wanted to move up the Italian peninsula.[26]

Tedder and Churchill then talked about bombing Rome. The Allies had held off so far for fear of hitting the Vatican, but now they wanted a crack at the Eternal City. The railroad yards would be the target, and they were on the opposite side of the river from the Vatican. With precision daylight bombing, the airmen felt they could hit the railroads without endangering the Vatican. Eisenhower wanted to launch the operation because the railroad bottleneck at Rome was a key in the supply line to Sicily. Churchill promised to get permission from the War Cabinet, while Marshall said he would try to get Roosevelt to authorize Eisenhower to order the bombings.[27]

The meeting then turned into a love fest. Churchill grew expansive. In his best oratorical manner he declared that he was satisfied at the great measure of agreement he had found, and full of confidence in

Eisenhower and his team. Eisenhower replied that any praise which might be given belonged to the officers around the table. While there might be differences of opinion and discussions in his headquarters, he added, they were never based upon national differences. Marshall then stood and said he wanted to reinforce the Prime Minister's tribute to Eisenhower and his team. He said that the support the British gave Eisenhower was deeply appreciated and highly significant, because in his opinion the Germans' greatest discomfort came not so much from their loss of troops as from the fact that Great Britain and the U.S. had worked so well together.[28]

"Cunningham commands the naval forces, Tedder commands the air forces, and Alexander commands the ground forces. What in hell does Eisenhower command?" a group of touring American senators demanded to know of Secretary Stimson. The answer was, he commanded Cunningham, Alexander, and Tedder. Eisenhower brought this about, not through any structural change, but by holding weekly meetings with the three British officers, by having frequent casual conversations with them individually, by acting as referee to settle their inter-service disputes, and most of all by the force of his personality. As he explained to his son on June 19, "The one quality that can be developed by studious reflections and practice is the leadership of men. The idea is to get people to working together, not only because you tell them to do so and enforce your orders but because they instinctively want to do it for you." Eisenhower said a man did not need to be "a glad-hander nor a salesman" to be successful as a leader, but "you must be devoted to duty, sincere, fair and cheerful."[29]

The capture of the tiny island of Pantelleria showed what Eisenhower was talking about. Alexander was thoroughly against the operation. He feared it would fail and that the failure would have a disheartening effect on the troops to be committed against Sicily. Cunningham was not sure, but he was inclined to agree with Alexander. Tedder had his doubts, but he was the first to swing around to Eisenhower's view because he wanted the airfield on Pantelleria. Eisenhower never wavered in his insistence that the operation go forward, and soon brought Cunningham around to agreement with him.

Because of the rocky coast line, the only place troops could come ashore in their assault boats was at the tiny harbor. Eisenhower hoped to smash it into submission and concentrate the attacks on the eastern portion of the island. For nearly three weeks the air forces blasted away.

Despite the pounding, the Italians showed no sign of quitting. The British general assigned to lead the assault protested to Eisenhower that the plan would never work and that the casualties would be awful. Eisenhower disagreed and decided to carry on.

Objections from Alexander and other ground commanders continued. They classed Pantelleria as a miniature Gibraltar bristling with guns, and they filled Algiers with their "dismal forebodings."[30] Eisenhower decided to make a personal reconnaissance immediately prior to the assault date to make sure the defense had been sufficiently softened to assure success. He set out on the morning of June 7, along with Admiral Cunningham, on H.M.S. *Aurora,* as a part of a fleet that was going to Pantelleria to bombard the island. The *Aurora* sailed right up to the beaches and blasted away, with Cunningham directing some of the fire. ("More to the right," he would say, or "Try a bit to the left." He did not use starboard and port, to Eisenhower's great amusement.) Only two Italian shore batteries replied, and neither of them with any accuracy. Eisenhower was confident that morale on the island was low and thus was confident of success.

On June 11 the British troops set sail, with H-Hour set for twelve noon. Eisenhower had not slept well the night before; Butcher noted that "he has been going through the same type of jitters and worries which marked the days immediately preceding our landings in North Africa." Eisenhower fretted all morning, but the finale was anticlimax. Shortly after noon, Cunningham sent word to Algiers that Pantelleria had surrendered before a single British soldier set foot ashore. The Italians had cracked. There was one casualty; a British Tommy was bitten by a mule. The Allies rounded up 11,199 prisoners of war.[31]

Eisenhower was elated. "I am afraid this telegram sounds just a bit gloating," Eisenhower confessed in reporting the success to Marshall. He felt so good that he added, "Today marks the completion of my twenty-eighth year of commissioned service and I believe that I am now legally eligible for promotion to colonel," that is, colonel in the Regular Army.[32]

The airfield on Pantelleria would now be most helpful in providing fighter cover for HUSKY, but that was only part of the reason for Eisenhower's gay mood. He took deep personal satisfaction in the results. It had been his plan all along, he was the one who insisted upon it, and despite the numerous and highly placed doubters, some of whom were senior to him in rank and experience, it had worked. It was a command decision which showed that the experts were not always right and it gave him confidence in his own abilities and judgment. In later years he would talk of Pantelleria with as much pride as OVERLORD.[33]

Now full-scale planning for HUSKY could proceed. "Everybody is tremendously keyed up," Eisenhower told Marshall on July 1. "Whenever I have a short conference with a staff section, my whole effort is to get the attending individuals to relax a bit." The planners had been working on HUSKY since January and they were showing the strain.[34] It was natural enough, considering the complexity of the operation and the size of the force involved.

HUSKY was the largest amphibious assault in all history. At dawn on July 10 seven divisions, preceded by airborne operations involving parts of two airborne divisions, would go ashore simultaneously along a front of one hundred miles. Both the frontage and initial assault forces were larger than those at Normandy a year later.[35] The amount of detailed planning involved defied belief. Since every step was related, one mistake by one planner or one unit commander would have repercussions that would spread throughout the entire operation. Much depended upon the weather and on the enemy. No one of course could predict the wind force, and this was crucial for the Americans, since they would be making a shore-to-shore invasion, crossing the Mediterranean in their assault boats. How well the Italians would fight was another open question, as was the number of German troops on the island.

Despite the risks, Eisenhower was confident. In the last week of June he had a two-day conference with all the principal commanders and went over the plans with "great thoroughness. I know that everything that careful preparation and hard work can do, has already or is being done."[36]

On July 7 Eisenhower arrived at Malta, Cunningham's command post and the best communications center in the Mediterranean. Eisenhower said he felt "as if my stomach were a clenched fist." He had done all he could do and for the next two days there was nothing to do but fret.[37] Everything was now out of his hands—except for the most important decision of all. He still had to decide whether to go ahead with the operation or call it off.

All continued to go smoothly, however, and confidence grew. Then, on D-Day minus 1—July 9—the weather turned bad. The wind came up from the west and increased in force. It began piling up whitecaps in the Mediterranean, tossing about the boats in which Patton's men were crossing and throwing up a heavy surf on the western beaches. The wind would have little or no effect on Montgomery's landing, since his area was on the lee shore, but if it continued at its present rate of forty knots it would ruin Patton's landing. Staff officers suggested to Eisenhower that he postpone the invasion before it was too late. Because of the size and complexity of the forces involved, such a postponement would have meant a two- or three-week delay before the invasion could be mounted again.

Eisenhower conferred with Cunningham's meteorological experts, who had good news for him. They said the velocity of the wind would likely fall around sundown, and that conditions by midnight should be satisfactory. Marshall sent a wire asking if the invasion was on or off. As Eisenhower later put it, "My reaction was that I wish I knew!" He and Cunningham went outside to look at the wind indicators, which showed that the wind force was dropping as predicted, and to catch a glimpse of some of the troop carrier aircraft towing the gliders filled with men of the British 1st Airborne Division. Eisenhower rubbed his ever present seven lucky coins and silently prayed for the safety and success of all the troops under his command.[38]

Eisenhower then went inside. He had made up his mind. He wired Marshall, "The operation will proceed as scheduled."[39]

Hours later someone turned on a little table radio and picked up BBC. The Allied commander in chief and his deputies gathered around it to wait for the latest news—it seemed much the best way of finding out when and if the troops got ashore, since the ships were maintaining radio silence. BBC was playing popular music. Eisenhower, more and more worried, began pacing the floor. Suddenly BBC said, "We interrupt this programme to give you a flash message from General Eisenhower— he reports that the first waves of his landing craft have just landed successfully in Sicily."

Eisenhower looked at the others, smiled, and said, "Thank God—*he* ought to know!"[40]

CHAPTER 16

Sicily

When the Axis generals went to bed on the night of July 9 the wind had been howling and the surf was high. They assumed that no invasion fleet could cross the Mediterranean in such weather. This assumption worked to the great advantage of the Allies, who felt they had to have surprise, since they were invading with 478,000 men and the enemy had almost 350,000—hardly a sufficient margin for a sea-borne invasion. Luckily for the Allies, everything was working. The wind, as predicted, died down during the night and on the morning of July 10 the sea was calm. It was perfect weather for an invasion.

The Axis forces were also caught unawares by the location of the landings. General Alfred Guzzoni, the Italian who was in theory in supreme command, had wanted to concentrate the two German divisions on Sicily on the eastern half of the island, find out where the Allies were landing, and then launch a strong counterattack. Field Marshal Albert von Kesselring, commanding all German forces in the Mediterranean, overruled Guzzoni. Von Kesselring thought the way to defeat an invasion was to meet it on the beaches and had Guzzoni locate most of his divisions along the coast, with the greatest strength on the western tip, where Von Kesselring expected the invasion to come. Von Kesselring did allow Guzzoni to hold the Hermann Goering Panzer Division in reserve south of Mount Etna. The upshot was that all Guzzoni had available to defend the southeastern and southern coasts were two coastal divisions, composed of Sicilian reservists who hated the Germans and thought the war was already lost. They had no intention of putting up even token resistance.

The combination of surprise, low quality opposition, and divided counsels in the Axis high command meant that Eisenhower's fears were seemingly unwarranted and that the invasion of Sicily was in fact comparatively easy. The night of July 9–10 two parachute units, an American regiment and a British brigade, made inland landings. The high winds blew the planes off course and the paratroopers were scattered all over the southeastern end of the island. Nevertheless the Americans managed to seize high ground near Vittoria, where they set up road blocks and helped keep the Hermann Goering Division away from the beaches. The British captured a bridge near Syracuse and held it long enough to allow sea-borne troops to take and hold the port itself. The assault divisions hit the beach at dawn, encountered no serious opposition, and by nightfall had secured their D-Day objectives.

Eisenhower knew practically nothing of these developments.[1] The generals and admirals leading the assault wave were too busy to send reports back to higher headquarters. At another step up the chain of command the JCS and BCOS were as anxious as Eisenhower to know what was happening, but all he could report was that the troops seemed to be getting ashore without difficulty.[2]

During the morning, while waiting for news, Eisenhower went for a walk with an aide. He expressed the fear that the Germans would breathe a sigh of relief when they realized the Allies were only going after Sicily, not something bigger. Eisenhower thought the enemy would destroy the airfields and the ports on the island, build up a defensive cordon around Messina, and let the Allies "sweat out" the slow approach to the Continent. The Germans would wear the Allies down, absorb Eisenhower's forces, and proceed with their offensive in Russia.[3]

By evening Eisenhower had managed to shake the mood and the night of July 10 he got a good sleep, his first in a week. When he woke the news was encouraging. He learned of Montgomery's success in taking Syracuse and of Patton's at Gela and Licata. Naval losses, however, were fairly high. The HUSKY plan had failed to provide for a fighter umbrella over the beaches and Allied planes were going after inland targets. The Luftwaffe had a free hand at the beaches, bombing the incoming ships almost at will. German accuracy was poor, fortunately, and only one U.S. destroyer was sunk. Two others were damaged, along with two combat loaders and an LST. Tedder was seeing to it that more fighters covered the beaches, and a lesson had been learned.[4]

On the ground, July 11 was the critical day. Guzzoni directed a counterattack against Patton's force at Gela, and the Hermann Goering Panzers rumbled down the road intent upon throwing the Americans back into the sea. Terry Allen's 1st Division, the Big Red One, received and repulsed the attack.[5] The Germans made another attempt that evening, but it too failed. Guzzoni, with Von Kesselring's approval, then ordered most of his remaining mobile elements out of western Sicily and concentrated his strength around the Catania plain. From now on his tactics would be those of delay and attrition, which meant that he had given up any attempt to hold the island.[6]

The Axis had, in effect, changed the nature of the campaign. It would no longer be a struggle for control of Sicily, but rather one for time and prisoners. The Axis aim was to delay the Allies as long as possible with a minimum sacrifice in casualties and prisoners. The Allies wanted to overrun the island as quickly as possible while preventing the escape of any significant number of Axis troops. For both sides, the key to the campaign was Messina. The direct road to it was on the Catania plain, past Mount Etna, and along the east coast. This was Montgomery's route, and it was all up to him. Montgomery, however, could attack only on a narrow front over difficult ground. He was unwilling to commit his men to a blood bath and did not get to Messina in time.

But if Montgomery did not push his men, neither did Alexander push him, nor in turn did Eisenhower push Alexander. The reason was that the Allies had not been able to readjust their thinking as quickly as the Germans. AFHQ and Alexander's Fifteenth Army Group had spent months working intensively on the problem of getting ashore; once there, they congratulated themselves and there was an inevitable letdown. Guzzoni and Von Kesselring, meanwhile, were adjusting to the new situation and making realistic plans. By the time the Allies caught on, it was too late.[7]

Indicative of the Allied inability to adjust was a trip Eisenhower made to the beaches on July 12. He did not go ashore at the crucial sector near the Catania plain to see what could be done about getting Montgomery moving. Instead, he paid a visit to Patton, whose headquarters were still on a destroyer off Gela. Eisenhower spoke "vigorously" to Patton about the inadequacy of Seventh Army reports to AFHQ. He said that because of his ignorance he could not determine just what assistance, particularly in the air, Patton needed. "Ike stepped on him hard," an observer reported. "I didn't hear what he said but he must have given Patton hell because Georgie was upset."[8] Patton was more than upset—he was angry. After visiting more troops on the quiet beaches, Eisenhower returned to his headquarters. He had made no attempt to galvanize any of his subordinates to action. The Allied force, like its commander, remained passive.

On the ground the campaign soon bogged down, even though the Italian divisions in Sicily had virtually ceased to exist. Thousands of Italians were happily sitting in Allied POW cages, while other thousands had simply doffed their uniforms and melted into the civilian population. The Germans had at most 60,000 men in Sicily and were thus outnumbered between six and ten to one. The Allies could not take advantage, however, because Montgomery was still reluctant to launch a costly frontal attack. By the end of the first week of the campaign he had reached the Catania plain and could not drive on.

One reason was malaria. The plain was highly infected and the casualty list was serious. Still, despite malaria, the intense, humid heat, and the dust, the campaign was not too bad for the British soldier. The Eighth Army "enjoyed Sicily after the desert." There were wine and roses in profusion; as Montgomery described it, it was "high summer; oranges and lemons were on the trees, wine was plentiful; the Sicilian girls were disposed to be friendly." At the front, as at headquarters, there was no sense of urgency.[9]

Eisenhower recognized that the Germans intended to abandon the western end of Sicily "and would attempt to take up a line running northwestward from Mount Etna," a line which "with German troops alone . . . he could hold for a considerable time."[10] The need was clear—get around Mount Etna and into Messina before the Germans could complete their defensive preparations. If Montgomery could not do it on the coastal road, then it would have to be done by moving around the western side of Mount Etna. Patton's Seventh Army was in perfect position to carry out such a maneuver, and Patton was the perfect commander to lead such a drive.

Alexander, however, remained skeptical of the Americans' ability, and was thus responsive when Montgomery proposed that Eighth Army make the move. Montgomery said he would launch one of his "left hooks" around Mount Etna. To do so, he needed the road leading north from Vizzini. It had already been assigned to Patton, but on July 15 Alexander gave it to Montgomery. Bradley protested, because it meant his columns had to turn back almost to the beaches before they could push on northward again. But Alexander did as Montgomery wished. He gave Montgomery the road and Seventh Army the passive mission of guarding Montgomery's rear.[11]

The Germans held Montgomery on the west of Mount Etna just as easily as they had done on the east through their skillful use of mines and the way they took advantage of the good defensive terrain. Montgomery took heavy casualties but could not break through. His left hook, meanwhile, had the effect of pushing Bradley westward, which in turn pushed the remainder of Seventh Army into central Sicily. Weeks later Patton complained to Montgomery about the injustice of losing the only road that led through central Sicily to Messina. "George," Montgomery replied in an answer that foreshadowed a whole series of events in the 1944–45 campaign in northwest Europe, "let me give you some advice. If you get an order from Army Group that you don't like, why just ignore it. That's what I do."[12]

In effect Patton had already taken the advice. When Alexander gave the Vizzini road to Montgomery, Patton sent Truscott, commanding the 3rd Infantry Division, on a "reconnaissance in force" to the northwest, toward Palermo. If Montgomery was to have the glory of taking Messina, Patton at least wanted the satisfaction of capturing Palermo. He was, therefore, "mad as a wet hen" when on July 17 Alexander issued a directive that limited Seventh Army to objectives in central Sicily. He decided to protest and prepared an alternative plan to present to Alexander, one that gave the Seventh Army the objective of Palermo. The best thing that could be said of it was that it in no way impinged on Montgomery's operations, since it led the Americans westward, away from the Germans and the main action.

On July 17 Patton went to Tunisia and met with Alexander. He argued forcefully for his plan, and Alexander, who "appeared to be more of a conciliator than a firm leader," reluctantly agreed.[13] The real basis for the decision was American unhappiness. When Patton made his case, Alexander realized for the first time how indignant American officers were at being assigned a passive role.

Allowing Patton to dash off to the west satisfied the Americans and may have helped the Alliance, but it brought no military return. Alexander's policy was essentially one of "Have a go, Joe," for there was no co-ordination of effort. All Patton's capture of Palermo did was to give him some headlines and the Germans more time to prepare their defense protecting Messina.

On July 18 Patton organized the Provisional Corps, put Major General Geoffrey Keyes in command, and sent it off to Palermo. The corps made the hundred-mile advance by foot in four days—a magnificent achievement. But, as mentioned above, there was no strategic gain. The Germans still held Messina, Montgomery had not advanced, and all the Allies could do now was drive the enemy off the island. There was no chance to capture any significant numbers of prisoners or to take Sicily in a hurry.[14]

Confusion over aims and purposes, reflecting the absence of an over-all plan, was probably inevitable in Sicily. One reason was that it was difficult for Eisenhower to get all the commanders together. Cunningham's headquarters were on Malta, Tedder's at La Marsa on the Tunisian coast, and in early August Alexander moved to Sicily. Eisenhower's permanent base was in Algiers, where he was frequently needed to handle diplomatic and strategic problems. When he could, he visited the commanders, but it was never a very satisfactory way to co-ordinate operations.

Eisenhower made the best of it. As he explained to Mountbatten, the commander in chief had more independence of movement than his deputies. In an "academically perfect procedure" the commander in chief and his deputies "must always be in the same locality," but perfect solutions were not always possible.

Eisenhower did not ordinarily give advice to senior British officers, but Mountbatten had just been appointed Supreme Allied Commander, South-east Asia Theater, and had asked Eisenhower for help. He realized that he would not have to face the "appalling political problems" which took up so much of Eisenhower's time, but he did feel there was much Eisenhower could tell him about being an Allied commander. He said he would appreciate it if Eisenhower would find time to dictate some notes "on the pitfalls to avoid and the line to take."[15] The result was the most thorough document on the theory and practice of Allied command that Eisenhower produced in the war.

The basis for an Allied command, Eisenhower began, was in the "earnest cooperation" of the senior officers in the theater, co-operation which depended upon "selflessness, devotion to a common cause, gen-erosity in attitude, and mutual confidence." Actual unity, therefore, de-pended "directly upon the individuals in the field," especially since the commander in chief had no disciplinary powers over officers of a different nationality.

Turning to procedure, Eisenhower warned Mountbatten that his senior commanders would be named by the CCS. Eisenhower felt this was an error, for the commander in chief should pick his own deputies, but it could not be helped. He reminded Mountbatten that each of his three deputies would be accustomed to dealing directly with his own ministry or department at home, and that each would also have a senior subordinate from the opposite nationality who would also deal directly with his own national authorities. Eisenhower thought that "these channels of communication should be interfered with as little as possible," but warned Mountbatten to guard jealously his privileged communications with the CCS: "No one else must be allowed to send communications to that Body." This meant, Eisenhower added, "that final recommendations as to operations to be undertaken and requests for the needed resources must likewise pass through you."

Mountbatten would also have to co-ordinate the efforts of his staff, which would have sections dealing with public relations, censorship, operations, logistic problems, communications, and civil affairs. "To form your staff," Eisenhower advised, "start from the bottom up. Make sure that in every section and in every sub-section are officers of both nationalities and *never permit any problem to be approached in your staff on the basis of national interest.*"

The personal bearing, manner, and decisions of the commander in chief were one key to a successful Allied command, Eisenhower felt. He told Mountbatten that he would have to strive for mutual respect and confidence among the seniors in his theater, and gave him some practical advice on how to achieve it. First, "all of us are human and we like to be favorably noticed by those above us and even by the public." An Allied commander in chief, whose opportunities for personal publicity were unlimited, "must more sternly than any other individual repress such notions." He had to be self-effacing, quick to give credit to others, ready to seek and take advice, and willing to decentralize. "On the other hand," Eisenhower continued, "when the time comes that he himself feels he must make a decision, he must make it in clean-cut fashion and on his own responsibility and take full blame for anything that goes wrong; in fact he must be quick to take the blame for anything that goes wrong whether or not it results from his mistake or from an error on the part of a subordinate."

Eisenhower realized that the picture of an Allied commander in chief that he had painted differed from the old-fashioned image of a soldier. An Allied commander in chief did not lead a charge up a hill, or direct planes to their targets, or command a battle fleet. But that did not mean that the Allied commander was a figurehead or a nonentity. "He is in a very definite sense the Chairman of a Board, a Chairman that has very definite executive responsibilities. . . . He must execute those duties firmly, wisely and without any question as to his own authority and his own responsibility." In Eisenhower's view, however, his battlefield duties were minimal; the implication was that making the alliance work came first. Eisenhower's definition of his role almost precluded active participation in battle—he felt that a Supreme Commander who did intervene might in fact jeopardize the alliance.

In conclusion, Eisenhower pointed out that it would never be possible to say that the problem of establishing unity in an Allied command had been solved. "This problem involves the human equation and must be met day by day. Patience, tolerance, frankness, absolute honesty in all dealings, particularly with all persons of the opposite nationality, and firmness, are absolutely essential."[16]

Eisenhower's advice to Mountbatten, dictated at odd moments by a man whose responsibilities were enormous and whose working day never had enough hours, remains today what it was in 1943—the best description in military literature of what an Allied commander should strive to be in his non-battlefield capacity. Its weakness, reflecting Eisenhower's, was vagueness about how the Supreme Commander should take control of a battle. This was, perhaps, inevitable. Any firm battlefield decision Eisenhower made in a situation involving an American and a British army would inevitably anger one side. Given Eisenhower's priorities, it is difficult to see how he could have acted differently, how he could have afforded or seen fit to intervene to direct the battle. Decisions could not be made solely on military grounds, as Alexander's experience in Tunisia illustrated. Pulling the Americans, especially the 34th Division, out of the line in Tunisia was the best military policy, but Alexander could not do it because of the alliance. Eisenhower felt such pressures even more than Alexander did.

Comparisons between Eisenhower and other commanders cannot be made, because the role he played was unique. No one before or since has commanded such a thoroughly mixed force, had such wide responsibilities, or took orders from so many different superiors. Later in the war Montgomery, recognizing this, suggested that Eisenhower leave the land battle to someone else, concentrating his attention on diplomatic, logistical, and strategical matters. Montgomery believed that this would allow the general who ran the land battle to make his decisions on solely military grounds. But if Montgomery had studied Alexander's actions in Tunisia, he would have known better. Whoever might be in charge would feel the same pressures Eisenhower did, for giving the real command to someone under Eisenhower would not change the nature of the role. The other difficulty with Montgomery's proposal was that the land commander would not carry the prestige the Supreme Commander did. Once the decision was made to put first the holding together of the alliance, a price had to be paid in a lack of over-all direction on the battlefield. The alternative was to put affairs in the hands of someone like Montgomery or MacArthur. Given the vehemence with which Brooke and Marshall defended the interests of their respective armies, even when commanded by Eisenhower, such a move would have been courting disaster. All of this indicates that Eisenhower's passivity about battle may have been a reflection not so much of his personality as of his role.

On Sicily the battle continued. While Patton raced for Palermo, away from the enemy, Bradley, whose II Corps was operating almost independently, undertook the much less glamorous but far more meaningful task of pushing eastward through central Sicily. This campaign, which never received much publicity, was one of the toughest for American soldiers in the war. At Troina, for example, the ground was rocky and broken and the Germans augmented the rugged terrain with mine fields, road blocks, and demolitions. The Germans also launched twenty-four separate counterattacks during the battle. Several days after the capture of the position by the 1st Division, American soldiers were astonished to find in one small valley a field with several hundred German dead, victims of American artillery fire.[17]

By the time Bradley took Troina (August 5) he had significant help from Keyes' Provisional Corps, which had moved out from Palermo and was racing eastward along the northern coast. It was too late, however. At the end of July Guzzoni had decided to evacuate what Italian troops there were left on the island and turned the battle over to German General Hans Hube. Hube had already selected five positions upon which he would base his delaying actions while the evacuation took place, and nothing Patton did was enough to upset his delaying schedule or evacuation.

Nearly all military historians condemn the campaign in Sicily. The landings should have been made, according to the critics, closer to Messina. Failing that, a plan to exploit the bridgehead and get into Messina quickly should have been available. It was inexcusable, in view of Allied air, sea, and land superiority, that it took so long to take the island and that the bulk of the German defenders escaped.

Postwar German comments were filled with references to Allied "caution." The Germans were amazed that the Allies did not land near Messina or at least at Catania. Eisenhower himself came to agree with this; Butcher reported on August 14, "Ike now thinks we should have made simultaneous landings on both sides of the Messina Strait, thus cutting off all Sicily and obtaining wholesale surrender and saving time and equipment, particularly landing craft, which would have permitted a rapid rush on the mainland itself." Von Kesselring spoke of the "exceptionally systematic actions of the Allied forces" and "the slowness of the Allied advance." The German field marshal was astonished that "strong forces had been dispersed to the western part of Sicily which . . . just marched and captured unimportant terrain, instead of fighting at the wing where a major decision had to be reached."[18]

Sicily did pay some dividends, however; perhaps the most important being the lessons it taught. Aside from purely tactical considerations, it was a proving ground for the decisive invasion of Europe across the English Channel, especially in the selection of commanders. Eisenhower had known Patton and Bradley long enough to have a good idea of each man's strengths and weaknesses. Sicily reinforced his impressions. Patton was seen as excellent in the pursuit, in driving his own troops to the limit, but his strategic sense was limited and his tendency to dash off after the spectacular instead of settling for the necessary was disturbing. He had reached his limit as an army commander. Bradley, on the other hand, was, in Eisenhower's view, capable of almost anything.[19]

Eisenhower himself played practically no role in the development of the campaign. From July 25 on he was deeply involved in political and diplomatic affairs, and he left the ground to Alexander. In late July, Smith made a trip to Sicily for Eisenhower and conferred with Montgomery, Patton, and Alexander. Smith returned in a pessimistic mood; Montgomery had said it would "take another month." Eisenhower was irritated at the delay. He said he could not see why, with overwhelming air support and naval bombardment from the sea, 500,000 Allied troops could not settle the issue with 60,000 Germans more quickly. He was inclined to take some drastic action but Smith, after visiting the scene, was just as cautious as the commanders on the spot and urged him to leave the planning to Alexander.[20] Eisenhower agreed; it was simply too late for him to take a tight grip on the battle.

A few days later Eisenhower was upset when his G-2, the British General Strong, reported that in his opinion Montgomery could have taken Catania on the first or second day if he had made a bid for it. Strong said there had been only one regimental combat team against the Eighth Army at the outset, and if Montgomery had been "less conservative and his forces more mobile, he could probably have been to Messina during the first week."[21] Eisenhower tended to agree with Strong's estimate. On

August 5 he passed Strong's report on to the CCS, but in accordance with the advice he gave Mountbatten he took the blame for Montgomery's mistake himself. "I did not sufficiently appreciate the situation," Eisenhower declared.[22]

In Sicily, meanwhile, Montgomery's and Patton's slow advance toward Messina continued. The Germans used every rock, every piece of high ground, every obstacle nature had put on the island to delay the Allies. The Provisional Corps had to channel its attack along the single coastal road and at times was reduced to moving forward in single file. Patton was a bundle of energy. He spent most of his time either at the front or in various divisional headquarters, urging his men onward. In co-operation with the Navy, he made three end runs, landing troops along the coast behind German lines. Each was a tactical success, but the landings were not large enough or far enough behind German lines to achieve a strategic victory. The Americans were getting closer to Messina, but they were getting there on German terms, not their own.

By August 16 Eisenhower could report to the CCS that the "campaign is now drawing rapidly to a close." The Germans were pulling out, retreating to the toe of Italy, but in spite of "every effort by all three services" were succeeding in getting most of their men and material evacuated.[23]

It was a rather dismal conclusion to a campaign that had already taken too long. Eisenhower had little time to worry about it, however, for just at this time he received a report about Patton's personal conduct that was "shocking in its allegations."[24] On August 10 Patton, who at that time was almost beside himself because of the slowness of the advance, visited a forward hospital. After talking with some of the wounded men, he lost his self-control when he saw a soldier who apparently had nothing wrong with him. Patton asked what the trouble was. The soldier replied, "It's my nerves," and began to sob. Patton screamed at him, "What did you say?" The soldier replied, "It's my nerves. I can't stand the shelling any more." He continued to sob. "Your nerves hell," Patton yelled. "You are just a Goddamn coward, you yellow son of a bitch." He slapped the man. "Shut up that Goddamned crying. I won't have these brave men here who have been shot seeing a yellow bastard sitting here crying." He struck the man again, then turned to the Receiving Officer and ordered him not to admit the soldier to the hospital.

The slapping incident had taken place in the II Corps area. Two days after it occurred the doctors sent a full report to Bradley. After reading the report, Bradley decided to do nothing and had it locked in the safe. A copy of the report reached Alexander, who also pigeonholed it. The doctors, however, were not willing to let Patton off so easily. The Seventh Army's surgeon sent the report to Brigadier General Frederick A. Blessé, Eisenhower's surgeon general. Blessé took it to T. J. Davis, the adjutant general, who took Blessé in to see Eisenhower.

It was 10:30 A.M., August 17, and Patton's men had just entered Messina. Eisenhower was feeling friendly toward Patton and after reading the report said mildly, "I guess I'll have to give General Patton a jacking up." He then praised Patton for the "swell job" he had done in Sicily. Eisenhower did order Blessé to go to Sicily and conduct a full investigation, but warned him to keep it quiet. "If this thing ever gets out," Eisenhower said, "they'll be howling for Patton's scalp, and that will be the end of Georgie's service in this war. I simply cannot let that happen. Patton is *indispensable* to the war effort—one of the guarantors of our victory."[25]

After giving Blessé his orders, Eisenhower sat down and wrote by hand a personal letter to Patton. By now he was beginning to see the enormity of Patton's offense and to realize that more than a "jacking up" was required. "I clearly understand that firm and drastic measures are at times necessary in order to secure desired objectives," Eisenhower wrote, "but this does not excuse brutality, abuse of the sick, nor exhibition of uncontrollable temper in front of subordinates." Eisenhower said it was "acutely distressing" to learn of such charges on the very day that an American army under Patton's leadership had attained a success "of which I am extremely proud," and added that he did not intend to institute any formal investigation. Eisenhower did warn that if the reports were true he would have to "seriously question your good judgment and your self-discipline." This would "raise serious doubts . . . as to your future usefulness." In the meantime, Eisenhower ordered Patton to submit a full report of his own and to apologize to the soldier he had struck and to the nurses and doctors in the forward hospital.

Eisenhower would go to almost any length to keep Patton. He knew Patton's shortcomings better than almost anyone else in the Army, and dealing with a safe, quiet, dependable leader like Bradley was much easier than handling the wild, unpredictable, coarse Patton. But Patton had something to offer too. No one else in the American Army could drive so hard in the pursuit, keeping the troops moving and the enemy off balance. When the decisive test came, Eisenhower wanted Patton with him.

"In Allied Headquarters," Eisenhower assured Patton, "there is no record of the attached report or of my letter to you, except in my own secret files." He promised to keep Patton's reports secret. In short, there would be no official reprimand. Patton's record would remain immaculate.

In conclusion, Eisenhower declared, "No letter that I have been called upon to write in my military career has caused me the mental anguish of this one, not only because of my long and deep personal friendship for you but because of my admiration for your military qualities." But, Eisenhower warned, "I assure you that conduct such as described in the accompanying report will *not* be tolerated in this theater no matter who the offender may be."[26]

Eisenhower gave the letter to Blessé and told him to hand-deliver it to Patton. He then sent Dr. Perrin H. Long, the theater medical consultant, to Sicily to make a separate investigation "for my eyes only." Eisenhower also ordered Major General John Lucas, an assistant, to undertake a third investigation, this one strictly from the soldier's point of view.[27] With that, he hoped, the incident could die.

But when a general slaps a private the story does not die easily. The next day the press corps in Sicily got hold of it. The reporters made their own investigation, found the truth, and prepared to file the story. Someone suggested that they ought to take it up with Eisenhower first, and Demaree Bess of the *Saturday Evening Post* (who had recently done a flattering profile on Eisenhower), Merrill Mueller of NBC, and Quentin Reynolds of *Collier's* came to Algiers. On August 19 they handed Smith a complaint against Patton along with a full description of the incident. "If I am correctly informed," Bess wrote, "General Patton has subjected himself to general court-martial by striking an enlisted man under his command." The reporters offered what amounted to a deal—they would refrain from filing the story if Patton was removed from command. "I might have to send Georgie Patton home in disgrace after all," Eisenhower sadly told Smith.[28]

Eisenhower would not quit without a fight. He called Bess, Mueller, and Reynolds into his office and confessed that he was doing everything he could to keep Patton. "His emotional tenseness and his impulsiveness are the very qualities that make him, in open situations, such a remarkable leader of an army," Eisenhower explained. "The more he drives his men the more he will save their lives. He must be indifferent to fatigue and ruthless in demanding the last atom of physical energy." Eisenhower pleaded with the correspondents to keep the story secret so that Patton could be "saved for the great battles facing us in Europe."

Smith, meanwhile made a similar plea to the correspondents based in Algiers. The effort worked. The correspondents entered into a gentlemen's agreement to sit on the story.[29]

Patton, meanwhile, acted abject. He humbly apologized to the soldier he had struck, and to the nurses and doctors. He wrote Eisenhower, "I am at a loss to find words with which to express my chagrin and grief at having given you, a man to whom I owe everything and for whom I would gladly lay down my life, cause for displeasure with me."[30] The incident was closed, or so Eisenhower hoped.

So was the campaign in Sicily, although it offered nothing to boast about either. The Germans had won a moral victory. Their few divisions had surmounted their Italian ally's defections and rout, and for thirty-eight days some 60,000 Germans had held off an Allied force of 500,000. Then, despite overwhelming Allied air and sea superiority, the Germans carried out a successful evacuation. The total German loss was around 12,000, while the Allies lost 20,000. Eisenhower and his commanders, as will be seen, were busy with other matters, and this was perhaps the main reason that the evacuation was so successful. Still, the record—especially in the air—was poor. Tedder was more concerned with strategic bombing than he was with interfering with the evacuation, so the air forces tended to ignore Messina. The Germans began by moving troops to Italy only at night, but they soon found that Allied interference was so ineffective that they also moved by day.[31]

There were some bright spots. The Allies had won Sicily and were ready to go after the Italian mainland. Everyone had learned from the campaign. Once Patton began moving toward Messina, his men had done well in an arduous campaign. They kept marching, Eisenhower reported to Marshall, "when no skin was left on the bottom of their feet," and they "fought magnificently and successfuly in one of the most unrelenting offensives in which American troops have ever participated." The men of the Seventh Army had established themselves as a "completely worthy teammate for the famous British Eighth Army."[32]

The American generals also learned and improved. A week after the campaign ended Eisenhower sent a report on his subordinates to Marshall, for Marshall's use in selecting his army commanders for the invasion of France. Eisenhower said that Patton's chief characteristics were energy, determination, and unflagging aggressiveness. He kept the troops going when anyone else would have let them stop and rest. Nevertheless, "George Patton continues to exhibit some of those unfortunate personal traits of which you and I have always known and which during this

campaign caused me some most uncomfortable days." Eisenhower had not
reported the slappings to Marshall; in his recommendation he hinted at
them by saying that Patton's "habit of impulsive bawling out of subordinates" had extended to "personal abuse of individuals." Eisenhower
said he had taken "the most drastic steps; and if he is not cured now,
there is no hope for him."

Eisenhower believed that Patton was cured, partly because of his
"personal loyalty to you and to me" but mainly because "he is so avid for
recognition as a great military commander that he will ruthlessly suppress
any habit of his own that will tend to jeopardize it." Patton was, in sum,
an excellent combat commander. By implication, that was his limit; commanding an army group was beyond his capabilities.

Bradley was an intelligent leader with a thorough understanding of
the requirements of modern battle. "He has never caused me one moment
of worry," Eisenhower said, in a sentence that summed up the relationship of the two men. Eisenhower believed that no job was beyond Bradley—by implication, therefore, he could handle an army group.

At this time it was assumed that Marshall would command Operation
OVERLORD, the 1944 invasion of France. Eisenhower said that if
Marshall had to take a British ground commander from the Mediterranean, he should take Alexander. "He is broad-gauged and should perform excellently. . . . He works on the 'Allied' basis." Eisenhower would
be content to keep Montgomery "because during these months I have
learned to know him very well, feel that I have his personal equation,
and have no lack of confidence in my ability to handle him."[33]

A few hours after Eisenhower finished dictating his recommendation
to Marshall, he received a message from the Chief asking for suggestions
as to who should command the American army preparing for the cross-
Channel invasion.[34] Eisenhower sent a long cable in reply, repeating
most of what he had already put into the letter. He did add that, of the
three seniors in the theater, Bradley was "the best rounded in all respects,"
although it was true that Bradley had little experience in planning amphibious operations. Clark on the other hand had the advantage of being
the ablest and most experienced planner of amphibious operations, and
Eisenhower told Marshall that, if he picked Clark for OVERLORD,
Bradley could take command of Fifth Army.[35]

The next day Eisenhower decided that he had been subconsciously
trying to hold onto Bradley. He knew that this was not fair of him, both
for Bradley's sake and for the Allied cause, since OVERLORD was the
most important operation of the war, and that he had therefore better

make a clear and forceful recommendation. He sent a short cable to Marshall: "The truth of the matter is that you should take Bradley and, moreover, I will make him available on any date you say. I will get along." Less than a week later Bradley had his orders, and on September 8 left for England and command of the U. S. First Army.[36] His slug fest at Troina and his deliberate choice of the unspectacular advance through central Sicily cost him the headlines, but it got him the most coveted combat command in the U. S. Army.

Eisenhower, meanwhile, had dozens of other worries. One of the main reasons the Sicilian campaign went so slowly was that the higher commanders never had the time to give it their full attention. A great deal was going on in the Mediterranean in the summer of 1943.

Part IV

THE ITALIAN CAMPAIGN

[*July 1943–December 1943*]

T HE story of the second half of 1943 in the Mediterranean is one of missed opportunities. Because the Allies were unwilling to abandon Roosevelt's unconditional-surrender formula, deal once again with a Fascist like Darlan, or even move quickly, the Italian campaign was long, slow, bloody, and sterile.

The caution of the Allied governments on the diplomatic front was matched by the caution of the Allied soldiers on the battlefield. One of the reasons Eisenhower and his deputies were unwilling to take risks in Italy was the steady relegation of the entire Mediterranean theater to a secondary status. For a year the Allied warriors in the Mediterranean had been directing the major offensive in what had then been the primary theater and for the most part they were accustomed to getting from the CCS the men and supplies for which they asked. From the early fall of 1943 onward, however, preparations for OVER-LORD took precedence over operations in the Mediterranean, a situation which Eisenhower and his subordinates found frustrating. This, however, was only a psychological factor that could not be accurately measured. What could be counted were acute shortages in vital equipment, especially bombers and landing craft. Eisenhower could not persuade the CCS to provide him with his minimal needs and therefore had constantly to reduce his objectives—in short, to be cautious. The key figure in the refusals of support was George Marshall, who would do almost anything for Eisenhower except provide him with equipment that would have to be taken from the cross-Channel build-up.

The best thing that could be said for the campaign was that in the end the Allies did conquer the Italian Peninsula. The generals and admirals involved, especially Eisenhower, gained experience in amphibious operations that would prove invaluable later in the war.

CHAPTER 17

The Beginning

For the officers at AFHQ, as for the Allied soldiers fighting on Sicily, the last two weeks of July and the first two weeks of August were marked by nearly unbearable heat and constant frustration. Fortunately for the sake of internal harmony, the source of the frustration came from outside North Africa. Eisenhower and his officers, British and American, could do nothing about the merciless sun, but they could join together in their feelings of irritation at the CCS and both of their governments. These were good targets for a needed release of emotion, the CCS because the Chiefs would not give AFHQ the material it needed, the governments because they would not set a clear policy line and then let AFHQ handle all the details. The result was that neither of the two major objectives—preparing for the invasion of Italy and taking advantage of the political possibilities opened in Italy following a change in government—could be worked through. Eisenhower and his subordinates, both military and diplomatic, felt they could have done a better job if left alone.

On July 17, 1943, Eisenhower had Cunningham, Tedder, and Alexander come to Algiers for a meeting to consider post-HUSKY operations. Although HUSKY was only a week old, Eisenhower feared that Sicily would not be cleared of the enemy until mid-August. His commanders agreed with him, but they also agreed that Italian morale was so low that an invasion of the mainland of Italy would drive the Italians out of the war or, failing that, at least cause the overthrow of Mussolini.

But the Italians were not the only enemies, not even the most important ones. Eisenhower warned his deputies that they could not discount the possibility of a substantial German reinforcement of southern Italy.

He thought that the way to minimize its effects was to get onto the peninsula quickly. Alexander pointed out that, while this was theoretically sound, no firm plans for an invasion could be made until the Sicilian campaign had progressed further. Cunningham added that only events could tell what landing craft losses in Sicily would be. Seventh Army was still being supplied by the craft over open beaches. Other unknown factors included German and Italian movements, both on Sicily and Italy, and Tedder added that he had no idea as to how much aircraft the CCS would give him for an invasion.

With so many questions open it was impossible to make definite plans. After a long discussion, Eisenhower ordered his staff to study a series of alternatives, including a movement across the Strait of Messina into the Italian toe and from there a drive up the peninsula, a British invasion of southern Italy at Crotone, repeated outflanking movements by small amphibious forces up the Italian shin, an invasion by the U. S. Fifth Army at Taranto, and an assault on Naples.

The overrriding conclusion of the meeting was clear—immediately upon the capture of Sicily, the Allies should take the war to the Italian mainland. Eisenhower so recommended to the CCS.[1] How immediately such an invasion could take place, however, depended upon many factors. Eisenhower had already explained to the CCS that it would be necessary to withdraw landing craft from Sicily thirty days before any assault could be mounted. Since most of the craft in the Mediterranean were involved in supplying the Seventh Army, that meant there would have to be a pause between the fall of Sicily and the invasion of Italy.[2]

But Churchill wanted to speed up the operations. On July 18 he asked the theater commander to do everything he could to get onto the Italian mainland quickly, and he urged him to think on a grand scale. The Prime Minister was disturbed by the cautious approach of the Mediterranean commanders. An invasion of the toe, or even at Naples, struck him as insignificant. In support of his conviction he passed along a message he had received from Field Marshal Jan C. Smuts, Prime Minister of South Africa and a man with an uncommonly large influence on Churchill. Smuts said that the next Allied operation should be directed against Rome, for "we should attempt only vital blows at this stage of the war and side shows should be avoided."[3]

Eisenhower replied, "I always find my sentiments in full accord with any suggestion that seeks to avoid nibbling and jabbing in order to leap straight at the vitals of the enemy," but he pointed out that no one could long be engaged in the business of conducting modern war without becoming convinced of the "absolute necessity" of keeping his shipping under the protection of shore-based fighter aircraft. He agreed with Churchill that German strength was the only real problem on the mainland and that the way to beat the Germans was to get there quickly. But to send a large invasion force directly to Naples or northward, where it would be without fighter cover, "would certainly be asking for trouble." Eisenhower promised to do everything humanly possible to take Rome in a hurry; he added that he and his commanders agreed that the way to do it was to get established on the toe, take Naples, and then drive north overland.[4]

Although Rome was beyond fighter range, it was well within bomber range, and because it was a railroad bottleneck it was a constant temptation to the Allies. There were obvious drawbacks: the Eternal City had a special meaning for artists, architects, historians, and others, not to mention Catholics, throughout the world. Tedder's staff had made intensive studies, however, which indicated that the railroad marshaling yards and outlying airfields were far enough away from the historical buildings, and especially the Vatican, to guarantee that the military targets could be bombed without any danger of damage to sensitive areas. After talking with Eisenhower in Algiers in early June, Churchill had received permission from the War Cabinet for a raid on the city, and Marshall got Roosevelt's approval.

The operation was handled with the greatest possible care. Eisenhower saw to it that the crews were specially trained, that the targets were only the most essential railroad objectives, and that the margin for error was sufficient to prevent damage of any kind to historical or religious edifices. The press was completely briefed before the raid.[5] On July 15, after the crews had had two weeks of training, Eisenhower set July 19 as the target date. Four hundred heavy bombers would drop more than a thousand tons of bombs on the railroad yards; in a subsidiary operation medium bombers would hit airfields south of Rome.[6]

The raid went as scheduled and it was a success. Except for the Basilica of San Lorenzo, no major religious or historic shrine was damaged. Spaatz reported to Arnold that the raid had "very little interest" from an Air Force standpoint because it was "too easy."[7] But as Eisenhower had hoped, Italian morale was further shaken. Mussolini, who was in conference with Hitler about the situation in Sicily, returned to Rome on July 20 to find fires raging and the King "frowning and nervous."[8]

All of Italy now became a seething hotbed of intrigue and conspiracy. Plot after plot was planned; most had abortive births. The one that counted came on July 25, when the Fascist Grand Council met and had what amounted to a vote of no confidence in Mussolini. That evening a group of the conspirators arrested Mussolini. The King, who was himself involved, turned to Marshal Pietro Badoglio, an old soldier who had been dismissed by Mussolini in 1940 following the Greek disasters, and gave him the task of forming a new government.

The next day Badoglio broadcast the news of Mussolini's fall to the world. In his radio speech Badoglio stated "The war continues. Italy, cruelly hurt in its invaded provinces, in its destroyed cities, keeps faith to its pledged word." But the statement convinced neither the Germans nor the Allies and only bewildered the Italian people.[9]

Statesmen and leaders throughout the world reacted swiftly to Mussolini's fall. The day the news came out Hitler began rushing troops into northern Italy (two divisions in France received their marching orders the very night of July 26) and began planning to occupy the South. Roosevelt wired Churchill, saying he thought the Italians were ready to give up the battle and that the terms the Allies offered should be "as close as possible to unconditional surrender." The President did feel that Italy should be treated leniently so that the Italian armed forces could be used against the Germans in the north and so that the Allies could use Italian airfields. Roosevelt also told Churchill, "In no event should our officers in the field fix any general terms without your approval or mine."

Churchill remembered the Darlan deal as well as Roosevelt and agreed at once to the policy of limiting Eisenhower's authority. The Prime Minister did indicate, however, that he was inclined to deal more gently and freely with the Italians than the President. "I do not think myself that we should be too particular in dealing with any non-Fascist government, even if it is not all we should like. Now Mussolini is gone, I would deal with any non-Fascist Italian government which can deliver the goods." Roosevelt took a stronger line. In a radio broadcast on July 28 he reassured his audience by emphatically affirming that "our terms to Italy are still the same as our terms to Germany and Japan—unconditional surrender. We will have no truck with Fascism in any way, shape, or manner." And to the Prime Minister he cabled, "There are some contentious people here who are getting ready to make a row if we seem to recognize the House of Savoy or Badoglio. They are the same element that made such a fuss over North Africa."[10]

On Monday, July 26, Eisenhower was at breakfast in Tunis when the news of Mussolini's fall reached him. He called Macmillan on the telephone and asked him to come right over; when Macmillan arrived he found Eisenhower in a "state of considerable excitement and full of plans and ideas for exploiting the situation created by Mussolini's fall."[11]

Eisenhower told Macmillan that he wanted to build strong public sentiment among the Italians to encourage the King to negotiate quickly for peace, a peace that would eliminate Fascism and turn the Italians against the German soldiers on their soil. The emphasis was on the latter goal. Not much was known about Badoglio's politics, but obviously he must have been a Fascist or he would not have headed the Italian Army in 1940. But in view of the potential military profit, this did not bother Eisenhower. He was far enough along in planning the invasion of Italy to realize how difficult an operation it was going to be. He knew how effectively the German could fight on the defensive in mountainous country. The CCS had already made it clear that, with OVERLORD approaching, AFHQ could no longer count on unlimited supplies and reinforcements. A quick pact with the Italian government, no matter how odious its personnel, would allow the Allies to occupy the mainland and to use Italian airfields, release troops for OVERLORD, save landing craft and time, and, most important of all, save lives.

To attain these objectives, Eisenhower was willing to pay almost any price, including a public censure for another Darlan deal. Although the King of Italy, Victor Emmanuel III, was widely regarded as a Fascist because of his long association with Mussolini, Eisenhower was concerned with victory, not ideological purity. He told Macmillan that the King should be assured that the House of Savoy might "stay as a symbol of Italian unity" if Italy sued for peace.[12]

Eisenhower wanted to broadcast an immediate proposal to the Italians, but Murphy pointed out that AFHQ lacked the authority to make a political offer. Eisenhower replied wearily that in the old days generals were free to do whatever they thought best. Still, he knew Murphy was right, and agreed to consult his superiors.[13]

Eisenhower and Macmillan drafted a message to the CCS outlining their ideas. "We regard it as of the utmost importance that full opportunity should be taken immediately of the dismissal of Mussolini," they began, and warned that if the King remained as head of a country still at war with the Allies "full odium in our two countries now concentrated on Duce will be transferred to the King." This would make it difficult, perhaps impossible, to work with the King, and there was no other responsible authority in Italy to deal with. Eisenhower and Macmillan therefore suggested that a propaganda message be "immediately and constantly" broadcast to Italy from AFHQ. The message would "commend" the Italians and the King on ridding themselves of Mussolini and point out that "the greatest obstacle which divided the Italian people from the United Nations has been removed by the Italians themselves." The only remaining obstacle to peace was the German Army on Italian soil.

The message would promise the Italians immediate and honorable peace and say the Allies would come to Italy as liberators to "rid you of the Germans and deliver you from the horrors of war." Soldiers and prisoners of war would return to their homes, while the "ancient liberties and traditions of your country will be restored."[14]

Even as he helped compose the message, Eisenhower had a sinking feeling that while he waited for government approval he would lose the opportunity. He knew that Roosevelt especially would tread carefully in an area which involved Italy because of the hundreds of thousands of Italian-American voters, and that neither the President nor the Prime Minister was particularly anxious to have another Darlan deal on his hands.

After two days, exchange of a number of messages, and modifications of the Eisenhower-Macmillan draft to eliminate such words an "honorable peace" and promises about the return of prisoners of war, the governments gave AFHQ permission to make the propaganda broadcast. By then it was more or less academic, as AFHQ was already preparing firm armistice proposals.[15]

Eisenhower spent most of July 26 working with his staff on the problem of what AFHQ should do if the Badoglio government asked for an armistice. By July 27 they had a policy ready, but it needed CCS approval before it could be put into effect. Eisenhower therefore sent a long cable to the CCS, requesting that he be authorized to offer the Italians the general terms he outlined. He explained that he had to be "prepared to announce at once the conditions under which a general armistice would be granted" if Badoglio approached him. Eisenhower admitted that he had not had a chance to talk to his deputies about the problem and recognized that further details would have to be worked out by the governments.

One of the key questions was disarming German troops in Italy. Eisenhower thought the Allies should not require this, partly because the Italians would consider it "completely dishonorable" to make such an about-face, mainly because the Italians "would not be getting the only thing in which they are interested, which is peace." To insist on disarming the Germans "might prevent us from obtaining great advantages."

The list of requirements Eisenhower drew up was fairly stern, but two things stood out: the Italians could have peace, and the Italian government would remain in power. It was a long way from an unconditional surrender.

The terms, Eisenhower declared, "are submitted in the hope that they may serve as a basis for an immediate directive to me by the Combined Chiefs of Staff." Most important, he wanted authority to broadcast the terms to the Italian people, since they promised a peace under honorable conditions and after the people heard them "no Italian government could remain in power if it refused to request an armistice."[16]

Eisenhower's request for approval of surrender terms took a long and circuitous route before being met. On July 28 Churchill approved Eisenhower's provisions except that terms should more expressly provide for the release of Allied prisoners. The Prime Minister also thought that the Italians should be required to force the German garrison in Italy to surrender and implied that he hoped for a future alliance with Italy against Germany. He spoke of turning the "fury of the Italian population" against the Hun.[17] In reply, Eisenhower said it was his conviction "that there is no fury left in the population unless it is aroused by desperation. The people are tired and sick of the war and want nothing but peace."[18] On July 29 Marshall warned Eisenhower that his authority was limited to concluding local surrenders.[19] Eisenhower replied that he was "perfectly aware of the fact that there are many implications and corollaries that far transcend military considerations as well as my own authority," and asked Marshall to inform the President that he had only military contingencies in mind. He added that Churchill had sent him a similar reminder.[20] By July 31 Eisenhower had received four more long cables from London and Washington, each asking for some modification of the terms.

On July 29 Macmillan summed it all up: "I spent from 9 to 12 going backwards and forwards between my own office and A.F.H.Q. and conversation with General Eisenhower and Bedell Smith. . . . Poor Eisenhower is getting pretty harassed. Telegrams (private, personal and most immediate) pour in upon him from the following sources:

(i) Combined Chiefs of Staff, his official masters.

(ii) General Marshall, Chief of U. S. Army, his immediate superior.

(iii) The President.

(iv) The Secretary of State.

(v) Our Prime Minister (direct).

(vi) Our Prime Minister (through me).

(vii) The Foreign Secretary (through me).

All these instructions are naturally contradictory and conflicting. So Bedell and I have a sort of parlour game in sorting them out and then sending back replies saying what *we* think ought to happen. As this rarely, if ever, coincides with any of the courses proposed by (i), (ii), (iii), (iv), (v), (vi), or (vii), lots of fun ensues. But it gets a bit wearing, especially with this heat."[21]

The Germans also had divided counsels. Rommel wanted to pull back to northern Italy; Hitler wanted to seize the Badoglio government and put Mussolini back in power; Von Kesselring argued that the Germans should maintain correct relations with Badoglio while reinforcing southern Italy, which he felt could be held. But though the Germans disagreed among themselves, they were capable of acting. While the Allied governments and soldiers debated, the Germans started four more divisions on the road to Italy—they even went to the extreme of withdrawing two SS Panzer divisions from the eastern front.[22]

The Allies, meanwhile, continued to bicker. Churchill cabled Eisenhower to inform him that he had told Roosevelt that no armistice terms should be broached until a responsible Italian government approached the Allies with a request for an armistice. That ended all hope of broadcasting a peace feeler from AFHQ, and meant as far as the Italians were concerned that unconditional surrender was all they could hope for. If a request for terms were made to Eisenhower, "you would naturally refer it to both Governments." The Prime Minister said he liked Eisenhower's draft, but "we feel that more precision is needed and that the document must be drawn up between Governments and must include civil as well as military terms." Churchill thought the terms should be "cut and dried" rather than "attractive and popular."[23]

Eisenhower told Churchill that he did not think it necessary to repeat "that I am ready to carry out in detail any instructions that the two governments may choose to give me." He did suggest that Roosevelt and Churchill "should give me a general directive on this subject couched in as accurate terms as they can now foresee as applicable," so that he would be ready if Badoglio did ask for an armistice. Any delay, he reminded Churchill, would only work to the advantage of the Germans. "All I urge," Eisenhower concluded, "is that the Governments decide quickly on what to do in a certain contingency and give me a suitable directive by which my actions may be guided."[24]

Clear directives, however, seemed to be beyond the two governments' capacities, as an incident in the first week of August emphasized.

"When things are going rather badly," Eisenhower told Marshall on August 4, "the troubles of an Allied Commander-in-Chief are wholly at the front." At such times the CCS provided him with everything he asked for, while the commanders at the front plagued him with demands for more of everything. When the battle was going well, however, the people in front were quite happy, "but some of the individuals who are responsible for running the war begin to take an enormous interest in its detailed direction."[25]

The incident that Eisenhower had in mind, and that upset him so much, had its origins with the British Political Warfare Executive at AFHQ. On July 24 the Allied bombers had reached a state of near exhaustion and Tedder and Spaatz had decided to give the crews a short rest. The propaganda staff decided to make the hiatus appear voluntary and proposed to announce to the Italians that the Allies were giving them a breathing space to allow them to unite "for peace and freedom." The Joint Propaganda Planning Board and Macmillan agreed, and the announcement went out over Eisenhower's name. Eisenhower was in Malta at the time, but as he later told Marshall, "I accept full responsibility for the actions of a staff in which I have confidence."[26]

Churchill, always sensitive to the intrusion of soldiers into political affairs, felt the announcement went much too far. He protested to the President, reminding Roosevelt that while it was necessary for low-level propaganda "to be pumped out by the machines," when the Supreme Commander spoke it involved the governments. "Speaking broadly," the Prime Minister told the President, "it is quite right that politicians should do the talking and generals the fighting." He hoped Roosevelt would agree that no pronouncements should be made by AFHQ over Eisenhower's name until they had been agreed to by the British.[27]

It was the first time Churchill had protested to the President about an action of Eisenhower's. Previously, when unhappy, he made his complaints directly to AFHQ. Eisenhower learned about the protest on August 4, a bad day for him. Montgomery's attempt to get around Mount Etna had failed, Patton was making no real progress, the interminable discussion over armistice terms was at its height, the CCS had just turned down a request for more bombers, and the heat in Algiers was ungodly. "I spent rather a difficult couple of hours with the C.-in-C. and Chief of Staff," Macmillan noted that afternoon. "Ike is beginning to get rather rattled by the constant pressure of telegraphic advice on every conceivable point."[28]

After discussing the situation with Smith and Macmillan, Eisenhower dictated a long cable to Marshall. As he talked his irritation grew. He could not see why the broadcast was considered harmful in conception, Eisenhower began; in fact he felt it was "a very good statement and one that appears appropriate in the circumstances." He pointed out that the entire statement dealt with the employment of forces in his theater and did not even hint at any broad Allied foreign policy.

"The Combined Chiefs of Staff have provided me with personnel who are presumably expert in the business of using propaganda," Eisenhower declared. He said that these staff officers had tried to keep up the closest possible contact with the appropriate agencies in Washington and London so that they would always know the policies of the two governments, "so far as these policies have been promulgated." No statement had ever gone out from AFHQ without Macmillan's approval, and Churchill had assured Eisenhower that Macmillan represented his, Churchill's, personal views on political matters. Problems arose daily in a theater of war on which the commander had to act swiftly, Eisenhower felt; indeed, the governments expected him to act and not procrastinate.

"I do not see how war can be conducted successfully if every act of the Allied Commander in Chief must be referred back to the home government for advance approval," Eisenhower said. In an oblique reference to the discussion over armistice terms, he added that AFHQ could act much more effectively if the governments would agree upon a policy and then let the commander in chief know what it was. If he then failed to carry out the directive successfully, the CCS should relieve him of his command, "but the authority and responsibility of his office should not repeat not be diminished." Eisenhower concluded by recommending that Churchill's specific proposal—to have all AFHQ statements cleared with both governments—be emphatically rejected. Marshall agreed with Eisenhower, and the Prime Minister dropped the proposal.[29]

The most troublesome aspect of the endless exchange of messages, both on the propaganda and on armistice terms, was that after a week of debate the Allies were no closer to agreeing upon terms to offer the Italians than they had been at the beginning. Nothing, meanwhile, had gone out to the Badoglio government to indicate that it could expect anything more than unconditional surrender. Roosevelt and Churchill, in fact, had both publicly said that the only terms were unconditional surrender. No Italian representatives, therefore, showed up at AFHQ, and Eisenhower's hands remained tied.

Plans for the invasion of Italy, meanwhile, went forward. Eisenhower had anticipated German reinforcement of Italy in reaction to the change of government, and it made him even more anxious to get the invasion started. The day Mussolini fell he met with his deputies to try to settle the vexing question of where and when to invade. Just before the meeting Eisenhower's planners told him that after intensive study they had decided that, because of the shortage of landing craft and the commitment of these craft to supply duty on Sicily, it would be impossible to launch an attack before September 10. Eisenhower was disappointed, but facts were facts. For three hours he and his deputies went over the list of available equipment; in the end the planners, "as usual, backed by stern reality, won the day." Eisenhower did get the date advanced to September 7, but he was "obviously disappointed at the inability to move ahead."[30]

The commanders were unable to settle upon a landing site; they wanted to wait a few days to determine "the military significance of recent political changes in Italy." Eisenhower and his deputies did narrow the range of choice down to two alternatives: BUTTRESS, a British invasion of the toe at Gioia, and AVALANCHE, an invasion of Salerno, twenty-five miles south of Naples, with one British and one American corps, both under Clark's Fifth Army. They also ordered plans prepared to rush two divisions into Naples, one by sea and one by air drop, in the event of a complete Italian collapse.[31]

The independent strategic air war, meanwhile, continued. Immediately upon the conclusion of the attack on Rome, the air forces began training for Operation TIDALWAVE. The target was the Ploesti oil refineries in Rumania. Oil had always had a high priority in the planning of the Combined Bomber Offensive but Ploesti, the most inviting of all oil targets, lay beyond the reach of planes based in the United Kingdom. Bombers from North Africa, however, could hit Ploesti. It was heavily defended but since it provided one third of Germany's total supply of oil was obviously worth attacking. Eisenhower was an enthusiastic proponent of the operation.[32]

Marshall had his doubts. On July 19 he had urged Eisenhower to co-operate with the British-based Eighth Air Force in a raid on the German fighter airplane factories in Austria, even if it was done at the expense of TIDALWAVE. He also urged Eisenhower to return to Lieutenant General Ira Eaker, commander of the Eighth Air Force, three B-24 groups that the Ninth Air Force in the Mediterranean had borrowed.[33] Eisenhower called in Tedder and Spaatz to discuss the situation. They agreed with him that TIDALWAVE was important, but that it should follow the raid against the fighter factories, mainly because it was the more dangerous of the two missions and would have higher losses.

When he reported this conclusion to Marshall, Eisenhower went on to discuss the broader policy of withdrawing bombers from the Mediterranean for use in England. In so doing he began a debate that was to be one of the most exasperating of the entire war. Eisenhower said he could understand Eaker's desire to get his bombers back, but pointed out that the operations scheduled for the Ninth Air Force would have a direct effect upon the whole European situation. "In other words," Eisenhower said, "both these operations are in support of the raids now being carried out from the U.K. and it merely happens that we have the more practicable bases from which to execute them." He wanted the borrowed groups to stay with Ninth Air Force until TIDALWAVE was completed, and warned that one raid against Ploesti would not be enough—there would have to be a follow-up. Finally, he assured Marshall that he was not simply trying to retain forces in his theater at the expense of OVERLORD. Neither the fighter factories nor Ploesti, he reminded the Chief, "is a specific or particular objective for this theater."[34]

Marshall would not agree. He did allow the Ploesti raid to go ahead, but he told Eisenhower to launch it first, then make the attack against the fighter factories, and then return the three borrowed groups to England. TIDALWAVE went on August 1. In one of the most controversial actions of the war the Ninth Air Force lost 54 planes while destroying forty per cent of Ploesti's total refining capacity. By activating idle units at Ploesti, however, the Germans quickly made up for their losses. Because there was no follow-up raid, TIDALWAVE was a failure.[35]

So, it seemed, was Eisenhower's attempt to keep Eighth Air Force's bombers, but he would not give up the two hundred or so planes involved without a fight, and even went so far as to expand his demand. Marshall had not accepted his strategic argument, so on July 28 Eisenhower shifted to a tactical one. Tedder had pointed out that the Germans were rushing fighters and bombers into Italy along with the ground divisions, which made AVALANCHE a risky undertaking, since Salerno was at the extreme limit of fighter aircraft range. Eisenhower told the CCS that the tenor of the messages pouring in on AFHQ from London and Washington indicated that everyone expected great results from Mussolini's fall. AFHQ would like to meet the expectations, but it could take "bold and rapid advantage" of the situation only if it had the strength necessary to assure reasonable success in AVALANCHE. Specifically, Eisenhower said he and Tedder believed that, if they could keep the borrowed bombers for three or four more weeks and use them in Italy, "we could practically paralyze the German air effort in all southern Italy and almost immobilize his ground units."

Then, expanding his claim, Eisenhower said that if the CCS would send three or four more bomber groups from Eighth Air Force to North Africa the chances for achieving a decisive success in AVALANCHE "would be tremendously enhanced." While on the surface such a shift would mean taking away from the central effort against Germany, Eisenhower felt that it was strategically sound. One of the purposes of the Mediterranean campaign was to secure bases for continuation of the bombing offensive against Germany, a purpose which would be furthered by using Eighth Air Force bombers on tactical missions in Italy. Eisenhower said that if the CCS agreed to the shift General Eaker should "lead his formations here in person in order that there may be no misapprehension as to the temporary and specific nature of the reinforcement."[36]

Lieutenant General Jacob Devers, the commanding general of ETO, saw a copy of Eisenhower's request and protested bitterly. He argued that a diversion of bombers from ETO to AFHQ would be a mistake for a number of reasons: the Eighth Air Force was already too small to carry out its mission; August and the first half of September were critical for the Combined Bomber Offensive; the RAF was counting on a maximum effort from Eighth Air Force; and maintenance crews and bases were already established in the United Kingdom. Summing up, Devers said he had to consider "the overall war effort. I must be guided by the greatest damage to the German enemy and I must never lose sight of the imminence of OVERLORD." The German high command would be delighted if the shift were made, Devers declared, and added that he felt the Eighth Air Force should "never be diverted" from its "primary task."[37]

Eisenhower received a copy of Devers' protest; he contented himself with sending a short cable to Marshall saying that he found Devers' arguments unconvincing. Around the office, however, he made no attempt to hide his feelings. "Ike is furious with Devers," an aide recorded, "and feels that the much flaunted mobility of our Air Force has been exposed as talk rather than action."[38]

On July 31 Marshall entered the fray. He sent a message to both Devers and Eisenhower, saying that he had decided that Devers was right and the heavy bombers had to stay in England. He did ask Devers if he could spare four groups of medium bombers, and asked Eisenhower if mediums would meet his needs.[39] Eisenhower replied that, while mediums would not really answer the requirements of the theater, still he could certainly use them. But Devers said he could not spare even those planes, and on August 4 Marshall told Eisenhower that after full consideration he had decided against the transfer.[40]

Eisenhower then tried another tack. The three B-24 groups that had participated in TIDALWAVE were waiting for good weather to return to the United Kingdom. On August 12 Eisenhower again asked the CCS to be allowed to retain them. "We consider that at this juncture every available force should be brought to bear against Italy and the German in Italy," he declared.[41] Again Devers protested, and again Eisenhower's superiors said the planes would have to be returned.

Eisenhower was not accustomed to having his requests to Marshall turned down and he found it difficult to accept. After getting off his cable to the CCS, he sent a fervent plea to Marshall. "I am not submitting any detailed argument on the point," he began, "because I am sure you understand that we are not asking, from this theater, for anything we do not believe to be absoluely necessary to carry out our mission." He asked that before Marshall gave any adverse decision, "I first be given further opportunity to describe the situation in detail. The hostile bomber strength has been steadily building up in this theater for some days and we simply must be on top of this matter if AVALANCHE is to be a success."[42]

Arnold replied for Marshall. He told Eisenhower that the Eighth Air Force was engaged in a "critical battle" for air supremacy over Germany and the three groups would provide Eaker with another long-range striking force "which might well account for an aircraft factory each week." These actions, he emphasized, turning Eisenhower's original argument end to end, would help the Mediterranean forces as much as those in England. The three groups returned to Eighth Air Force that week.[43]

It was a victory for the advocates of strategic bombing, a defeat for those who felt the air forces made their greatest contribution by working in close co-ordination with the needs of the ground campaign. It was also a decision which, within a month, Eisenhower's superiors would sadly regret, and one which they would have to reverse.

The decision also emphasized that Marshall remained wedded to OVERLORD. He would do nothing that even hinted at reducing the commitment to the cross-Channel invasion, even for his protégé. The incident also showed that Eisenhower did not handle affairs with his usual smoothness when his theater was relegated to a secondary status. When it came to stripping AFHQ of material he protested as vigorously as MacArthur in his Pacific domain. He did so, however, only after convincing himself that he would be using the planes on operations that would help OVERLORD as much as AVALANCHE. Still, he was a long way from the position he had taken a year earlier, when he promised Marshall he "would not be adding to your troubles by insistently clamoring for more than you can furnish. . . ."[44]

Eisenhower could not resist firing one parting shot. He told the CCS that, despite the adverse decision, he was going ahead with AVALANCHE "with whatever forces we have at the moment. But I think it only fair to the Combined Chiefs of Staff to give them the essential factors on which risks must be calculated." There was a German corps of three divisions in the Naples area, plus the Hermann Goering Division, which had just evacuated Sicily. German bomber strength was increasing daily, while AFHQ's was diminishing. The way to keep air activity over Salerno down on D-Day was to bomb German airfields, but there were not enough Allied bombers in the Mediterranean to do this. Salerno was at the extreme range of fighter cover: "As a consequence of these things our convoys will have to anticipate higher losses from air attack while at sea and while lying offshore." Tedder and Spaatz, Eisenhower added, agreed with his view. "I repeat," Eisenhower ended, "that my plans for attack will not repeat not be altered as a result of this transfer."[45]

Despite the statement, Eisenhower was disturbed at his apparent inability to get the CCS to understand his needs. He felt that the Chiefs still did not appreciate the precariousness of the air situation in the Mediterranean. In addition, they apparently were not aware of the high replacement rate required for landing craft. Most important of all, neither the Chiefs nor the governments seemed to have a sense of urgency about the Italian situation. Because of his material shortages, Eisenhower was still extremely anxious to take advantage of Mussolini's fall and make a deal with the Italians, but he had been unable to get even a directive on armistice terms. He would very soon have need of one.

CHAPTER 18

The Italian Surrender Negotiations

"The first Italian-Allied exchanges resembled two persons talking to each other in their sleep, each the victim of his own hallucination. In the nightmare of German occupation, Italy gasped, 'Help, I am not free.' After a long pause, the Allies replied, 'Say Uncle.' "[1]

One of Eisenhower's major characteristics was his desire to simplify. Faced with a complex situation, he usually tried to separate it into its essentials, extract a principal point, and then make that point his guiding star for all decisions. The defeat of Germany's armed forces was his aim and anything that contributed to that end was good, while anything that did not was, if not bad, at least superfluous. Thus, since the Allies could defeat Germany more quickly and easily if they fought together, Eisenhower bent every effort to make the alliance work. Or, equally pragmatically, since the greatest contribution the French could make to victory would be to provide a secure rear in North Africa for the Allied forces, Eisenhower's sole criterion for picking a French leader was simple: "Who can control?" At first it was Darlan, then Giraud, and finally De Gaulle, and Eisenhower worked smoothly with each one.

What Eisenhower wanted from the Italians was help in getting ashore and up to the Po Valley, where there were airfields in striking distance of the heart of Germany. He would gladly deal with any Italian government that would co-operate.

It has been argued that Eisenhower's approach represented not so much a desire to simplify as simple-mindedness. He had forgotten his Clausewitz, critics charged, and did not realize that in war the real objective is not the defeat of the enemy but rather the political end of the continuing security of the nation, which involves much more than victory on the battlefield. In the critics' view, Eisenhower's political naïveté cost the Americans dearly in the postwar world.

What the critics have failed to recognize was the political motivation inherent in Eisenhower's thought. The decision to defeat Germany was not his, but he heartily agreed with it, for the obvious reason—too easily forgotten during the Cold War—that the *sine qua non* of American security in 1943 was the defeat of the armed forces of Nazi Germany. Within that context, anything that speeded up the process was a political gain, since it would save American lives and money and would also allow the United States to turn its full might against the Japanese sooner.

In the case under consideration, the Italian surrender negotiations, Eisenhower was the man on the spot, responsible not only for victory but also for the lives of the men entrusted to him. He saw clearly that which Churchill and Roosevelt always failed to recognize—that the Italians had something to offer and to get it the Allies had to give them some positive inducement, not just the sterile and negative formula of surrender and occupation.

Eisenhower also realized that success in war can justify almost anything. In their national capitals, close to the critics, Roosevelt and Churchill could not help but take into account the liberal sentiment that permeated the Allied world throughout the war. When an Italian double-cross of the Germans became a real possibility, the soldier leading the Allied forces thought only of the advantages offered, while the heads of government thought of the reaction at home. "The merest suggestion of recognition of the Badoglio government," Robert Sherwood noted, "brought down more and more opprobrium on the State Department which by now was regarded in liberal circles as the very citadel of reaction. . . ."[2]

Churchill and Roosevelt were perfectly aware that it would have been supreme folly not to exploit the Italian situation, but they also felt that it was impossible to make an open deal with the King and Badoglio on the Darlan model. Their solution was to ignore Eisenhower's pleas for an easy armistice and demand unconditional surrender, then give that surrender an elastic implementation. They would ultimately allow the Italians to prove their worth by joining in the crusade against the Nazis. This had the advantage of keeping morale at home high and satisfying public opinion and, somewhat later, of getting Italian help.[3]

The only trouble was that it took so long in coming. By the time the agreement was concluded to everyone's satisfaction, the Germans had nineteen divisions in Italy. The bill for the delay was paid in blood at Salerno, Anzio, and Cassino.

The tangled story began on the morning of August 17. Eisenhower had just returned from Sicily to Algiers. When he got to his headquarters he found copies of three messages from Eden, in London, to Churchill, who was in Quebec for the QUADRANT Conference of the CCS. Eden reported that General Giuseppe Castellano, assistant to the chief of the Italian high command, had arrived in Madrid and talked with the British ambassador there. Castellano had no credentials from his government to work out an armistice, but he did want to negotiate with Allied military representatives in order to arrange an Italian double-cross. He wanted the Allies to first land on the Italian mainland in force, to be followed by Italy's joining the war against the Germans.

Eden was the first high official to react to the Italian offer and his attitude set the tone for the Allies throughout the negotiations. "Although at first sight this offer of cooperation sounds tempting," Eden told Churchill, "I feel that if we accept it it will land us in all sorts of difficulties both military and political with few if any corresponding advantages. . . . I am sure we ought to stick to our present policy of refusing to make the Italian government any promises or enter into any bargain with them in return for their surrender."[4]

Eisenhower took the opposite view. After consulting with his G-2, Brigadier Strong, and Macmillan, he sent a message to the CCS at Quebec. He said he wanted to send Strong, in civilian clothes, to Lisbon (where Castellano was headed) with instructions to get all the military information he could from Castellano. The proposal was that Strong should tell the Italian general that if Italy was anxious to speed up the day when an Allied force would land on the mainland, the Italians should undertake widespread sabotaging operations. Eisenhower also wanted Strong to tell Castellano that the Italians "have no recourse except to depend upon the decency and sense of justice of the Allied Governments when once we have arrived in Italy." In short, Eisenhower wanted to avoid all the complications of any formal negotiations, make a simple military agreement with the Italians, and deal with the political aspects of the situation once the Allies were firmly ashore.[5]

The CCS replied the next day, August 18, in what became known as the Quebec Memorandum. The Chiefs told Eisenhower to send two staff officers—Strong and an American—to meet Castellano. They should tell Castellano that the Allies would accept the unconditional surrender of

Italy on the basis of the "short terms," which followed closely the terms Eisenhower had outlined and wanted to offer the Italians on July 27. Churchill and Roosevelt, meanwhile, would work out at Quebec the "long term" agreements, which would include economic, political, and financial terms and which the Italians would eventually also be required to sign. Under the short terms, the Italians were to announce the armistice at once and to send their fleet and air force to Allied territory. The army was to "collaborate with the Allies and resist the Germans." If the Italians complied, Eisenhower had the authority to soften the armistice terms proportionately to the scale of the assistance the Italians rendered to the Allies.[6]

The Quebec Memorandum was a strange document. Eisenhower was supposed to require Italian collaboration, but he was specifically forbidden to reveal his military plans to Badoglio's representative. How, under such circumstances, could the Italians collaborate? Eisenhower was supposed to demand "unconditional surrender" on the conditions of the short terms, in itself a comment on the logic being used. In addition the question of to whom Badoglio was to surrender was open. There were no Allied troops in Italy, much less in Rome, to accept a surrender. The Chiefs gave Eisenhower the power to accept a surrender, but he— the man on the spot—could not negotiate.

The Chiefs ignored the reality of the Italian situation. Italy was caught between the hammer and the anvil. Germany had lost the military momentum and it was time for Italy, never fully mobilized and absolutely unable to carry on, to get out. Allied troops in Sicily were poised for invasion, while Allied planes pounded Italian cities from the skies. But the Germans were already in Italy in large numbers, with more coming in every day. If Italy surrendered to the Allies before Eisenhower's divisions occupied the peninsula at least up to Rome, the Germans would overthrow the government and occupy the country.

The Italians scarcely knew where the greater threat lay. Their key question to Eisenhower, the one on which their decision would have to be based, was: Are you able to occupy Rome and protect us from the Germans? If so, the Italians would do all they could to help, and do it immediately. But in the Quebec Memorandum the Chiefs told Eisenhower that under no circumstances should he answer the Italian question. All he could do was send Smith and Strong to see Castellano in Lisbon to demand surrender.

One reason the Chiefs were so hesitant to let the Italians have any information, and one which would later play a role in Eisenhower's decisions, was that they felt they could not afford to have the Italians discover how weak the Allies were in the Mediterranean. As far as the Italians knew, the Mediterranean was still the main theater of war for the Allies, and Eisenhower had unlimited resources. Castellano, for example, was thinking of a landing of fifteen divisions in the Rome area; in fact Eisenhower did not have enough resources to land three divisions. The Chiefs wanted to keep the Italians ignorant so that they would continue to overestimate Allied strength. In short, they did not allow Eisenhower to answer the key question because the answer would have been "No, we cannot occupy and protect Rome." Eisenhower was still unhappy because he felt that with generous terms he could get Italian co-operation and occupy the peninsula before the Germans built up their strength.

Smith and Strong flew to Lisbon on August 19 and held a nine-hour conference with Castellano. Smith told Castellano that the Allies were prepared to accept an unconditional surrender. Castellano, taken aback, replied that the purpose of the meeting was to discuss the question of how Italy could join the Allies in operations against the Germans, and more specifically to ask what help the Allies could give the Italians on the mainland. Smith said that he was only prepared to discuss surrender and read to Castellano the "short terms." Castellano tried to make it clear that such matters were irrelevant; what he needed to know was something quite different and in any case he had no authority to discuss any terms. Smith understood well enough, but his hands were tied because of the orders Eisenhower had received from the CCS. He did manage to emphasize to Castellano the statement in the Quebec Memorandum that declared that the armistice terms would be modified in favor of Italy in accordance with the amount of help the Italians gave the Allies. Castellano grasped at the straw and said he would take the short terms back to Rome for governmental approval. He and the AFHQ representatives arranged to meet again on August 31.

Smith returned to Algiers on August 20 and helped Eisenhower prepare a report to the CCS. Castellano had given much useful military information on German formations and positions in Italy, and it all matched what AFHQ G-2 already knew. Eisenhower emphasized to the CCS that Castellano had given the impression of "intense hatred and intense fear of Germans" and said the Italians seemed completely willing to co-operate "if they have reasonable assurance of protection and support."[7]

During the next week Castellano made his way home; because of the need to keep his mission a secret from the Germans, he took extreme precautions and did not reach the capital until August 27. The CCS, Churchill, and Roosevelt, meanwhile, discussed Eisenhower's cable and prepared their position. The result was approval of the comprehensive surrender document, known as the "long terms," which were transmitted to Eisenhower on August 27.

The long terms contained forty-one tightly worded paragraphs covering military, civil, social, economic, and political affairs. Macmillan called the long terms "a planner's dream and a general's nightmare."[8]

Eisenhower, meanwhile, was pushing ahead with preparations for AVALANCHE. He was not at all happy about the prospects, since he was undertaking the operation with limited forces and resources, especially in landing craft and bombers. In addition he had learned from Castellano that the Germans had 400,000 men in Italy, with more coming every day. His G-2 confirmed this estimate, which meant that the Germans were far stronger than AFHQ had thought they would be when AVALANCHE was planned. Eisenhower thus could use all the help he could get from the Italians and was willing to make any concession to get it.

The CCS and heads of government were not, and on August 27 ordered Eisenhower to use the long terms in all future negotiations with the Italians. Aside from the fact that the sternness of the long terms would cause the Italians to hesitate before accepting them, the situation was doubly complicated because the day Eisenhower received his orders Castellano was in Rome showing his government the "short terms."[9] At Eisenhower's urging, Macmillan told his government that it was possible that Castellano might not return to meet his August 31 date with Smith but would simply send over the radio the Italian government's acceptance of the short terms. If the Italians did do this, Macmillan said, Eisenhower should be empowered to proceed to conclude a military armistice. The British War Cabinet agreed.

Eisenhower passed this information on to the CCS and added that, if the Italians took only the short terms, "I strongly urge that the matter be closed on the spot." He would then transmit the long terms to Castellano and tell him that "these are the complete surrender terms which will be imposed by the United Nations."[10]

The imposition of the long terms had not helped a confusing situation; neither did the actions of the Italian government. Unknown to Castellano and the faction backing him, another negotiator had shown up at Lisbon, General Giacomo Zanussi. Zanussi represented General Mario Roatta, the Army Chief of Staff, a man thought to be pro-German. AFHQ did not know if Zanussi had come to check on Castellano, if he had come to support Castellano, or if Roatta had sent him in good faith, not knowning about Castellano's mission (the last interpretation was the correct one). Eisenhower ordered Zanussi brought to Algiers. The trouble was that the British ambassador in Lisbon, acting upon previous instructions from the War Cabinet, had already shown Zanussi the long terms.[11] This caused Eisenhower "grave apprehension," since he feared it would delay the armistice at best and make it impossible at worst. He hoped to straighten this out with Zanussi when he arrived in Algiers.

All of which emphasized the importance of letting AFHQ go ahead on the basis of the short terms. Eisenhower told the CCS that he was perfectly willing to accept the risks inherent in AVALANCHE but wanted to point out that the risks would be "minimized to a large extent if we are able to secure Italian assistance just prior to and during the critical period of the actual landing. Even passive assistance will greatly increase our chances of success and there is even some possibility of the Italians being willing to immobilize certain German Divisions." Eisenhower concluded, "It is these factors which make me so very anxious to get something done now."[12]

The CCS passed Eisenhower's request on to the heads of government, who relented and gave Eisenhower authorization to proceed with the surrender negotiations on the basis of the short terms.[13] Zanussi, meanwhile, had proved to be most co-operative. After a discussion with Eisenhower, he agreed to send his aide back to Italy with a letter to General d'Armata Ambrosio, chief of *Comando Supremo*. The letter would make four points: (1) that there was need for immediate acceptance of the short terms; (2) that the long terms dealt "with political, economic and other questions of only relative importance" and that the question at issue "was not one of formulas but of the general Italian attitude"; (3) that the Italians should "believe in the good faith of the Allied governments"; (4) that either Zanussi or Castellano should remain in Sicily in permanent contact with AFHQ. Then Eisenhower decided he would not let Zanussi send the long terms with his aide, for he feared that they might fall into German hands. This later led to additional confusion.

Zanussi and Eisenhower then discussed the political situation in Italy. Zanussi pointed out that a major difficulty was that Italy was dominated by "used men" like the King and Badoglio, who had for years submitted to the Fascists. He warned Eisenhower not to expect any spectacular initiative on their part. They were terrified of the Germans, the more so because of the slowness of the negotiations with the Allies, which had given the Germans time to prepare plans to take over the Italian government. The Germans might move on Rome, Zanussi said, within days or even hours. He also pointed out that the House of Savoy had "acted as a stabilizing influence in Italy for the past six centuries," which made it a "peg on which a transition regime may be attached." The King and Badoglio, he added, were managing to keep comparative order and tranquillity in Italy, which should work to the benefit of the Allies. Zanussi confided that, although the Italians had told the Germans that they were moving troops to meet the expected Allied landing, in fact the movements were intended to protect Rome and its airfields. He pleaded with Eisenhower to hurry and get as many divisions into Italy as possible.[14]

The Allied governments shortly showed that they could be almost as troublesome as the Germans or Italians. In the midst of the negotiations, messages began to pour in on AFHQ from London asking what arrangements were being made for representatives of governments of the Dominions and other United Nations to attend the surrender ceremony. The British wanted to celebrate their first official victory in the war in a grand manner, with appropriate ceremony and publicity. They even wanted De Gaulle informed.[15] Macmillan "kept sending back protests at this folly," and Eisenhower and Murphy together told Marshall and Secretary of State Hull it was absurd. "At what seems to us a very premature stage of an extremely delicate negotiation with emissaries who have come to us at a great risk of precipitating German seizure of the present Italian Government," they declared, "we are astounded that any thought may be entertained of something in the nature of a public armistice ceremony. . . ." The CCS saw to it that the matter was quietly dropped.[16]

On August 31 Smith and Alexander met with Castellano and Zanussi at Alexander's headquarters in Cassibile, Sicily. Castellano reported that his government would not announce the armistice until the Allies had landed in massive force. The Italians wanted fifteen Allied divisions north of Rome; any lesser force would be insufficient. The Germans would pour into the capital and take over the government, and under those circumstances the Italians would have gained nothing by surrendering. Smith bluntly replied that this was unacceptable—the Italians could either take the short terms or reject them, but they could not bargain. He would not tell Castellano when the Allies were landing, or in what force. Smith's attitude aroused Castellano's suspicions—perhaps, he began to think, the Allies were not as strong as they should be. Much as the Italians yearned to be rid of the Germans, they could not afford to commit themselves without some guarantees about their own safety.

After long discussions, with Murphy, Macmillan, and Alexander all trying to convince Castellano to accept the armistice on the basis of the short terms, Castellano proposed an alternative. Would the Allies at least help hold Rome by sending some assistance to the Italians there? Smith said that it might be possible to bring in an airborne division on the day of the invasion. Could the Italians hold an airfield for the Allied airborne troops? Castellano thought they could. On that note, Castellano returned to Rome. He promised to urge Badoglio to accept the short terms, with the proviso that an airborne division would land in Rome. The announcement of the armistice would be made the evening before the Allied landings.[17] Smith, meanwhile, flew to Algiers to brief Eisenhower.

The next day, September 1, Eisenhower sent a full report to the CCS. Italy, he began, "is in fact an occupied country and its government has no freedom of independent action." The best the Allies could hope for from the Italians was a general strike, which would increase the Germans' transportation problems. The Italians were "far more frightened of the German strength and reprisals within the country than they are of our threat of invasion or even of our bombing operations." They were particularly concerned about Rome, so Eisenhower had accepted Smith's suggestion and agreed to fly the 82d Airborne Division into Rome on the eve of AVALANCHE. This had to be done because the Italians were "merely frightened individuals that are trying to get out of a bad mess in the best possible way. . . ." Eisenhower intended to do all he could to help them; at the same time he assured the CCS that "nothing that I am doing now or will do in the future implies any promises to any particular government or heads of government with respect to their status after occupation by Allied forces.

"I have no repeat no thought of abandoning plans for AVALANCHE," Eisenhower declared, but he did want the CCS to know the extent of the risks, which he felt justified his doing everything possible to get Italian help. Castellano thought the Allies needed fifteen divisions landing north of Rome to secure the peninsula. AVALANCHE in fact projected an initial Allied landing of only three divisions nearly a hundred and fifty miles south of Rome, with a build-up over two weeks to a maximum of eight divisions. The Germans had nineteen divisions in Italy. If the Italians, fighting on their own soil, stayed with the Germans, the Allies would face a major disaster, one that would have catastrophic repercussions in England and the United States. Thus sending the 82d into Rome was a "good gamble," since it would reassure the Italians. Unfortunately, Eisenhower concluded, "my own belief is that the Italians will probably allow this situation to drift and will not seek a formal armistice. They are too badly demoralized to face up to consequences and are not sufficiently assured of the safety of Rome." Still, if the Italians did nothing, even that was better than having them oppose the landing.[18]

Castellano and Zanussi, meanwhile, had gotten back to Rome. So far only Zanussi knew of the long terms—when he tried to tell Castellano about them Castellano brushed him off—and the government thought that after signing the short terms all disagreements would end and preparations to fight beside the Allies could begin. On this basis, and encouraged by Eisenhower's willingness to bring the 82d into Rome, Badoglio decided to continue the negotiations. AFHQ received a radio message to that effect around 11 P.M., September 1.[19] Castellano was returning to Sicily, where he would meet with Smith.

The CCS had instructed Eisenhower to sign the formal armistice agreement, and on September 2 he told Smith he was ready to "come any place any time to do this." He felt, however, that anything Castellano (rather than Badoglio) signed would be a "preliminary document," and thought that Smith should sign for AFHQ.[20]

Smith, meanwhile, discovered that Castellano wanted to discuss military co-operation and had no authority to sign an armistice. Smith suggested that Castellano wire Rome for permission; after a long discussion and much confusion, Castellano did so and received authority to sign. One of the deciding factors was that Montgomery's Eighth Army had begun to cross the Messina Strait that morning, September 3. The British met with no serious opposition. Allied troops were back on the continent of Europe.

At Smith's urging, Eisenhower flew to Sicily the next day to witness the signing. After Smith and Castellano affixed their signatures, which was done quickly and quietly, the two sides arranged to announce the armistice late in the evening of September 8, a few hours before Clark's Fifth Army hit the beaches at Salerno. Eisenhower told the CCS that a final signing would take place later, when he was able to get together with the King and Badoglio, and begged the Chiefs to keep everything secret for the time being.[21]

After the signing, Smith calmly handed Castellano a copy of the long terms. Castellano had so far managed to avoid the humiliating unconditional surrender phrase in all his negotiations and he was painfully surprised to read the opening line: "The Italian Land, Sea and Air Forces wherever located, hereby surrender unconditionally." He protested violently, which in turn surprised Smith. He said that surely Castellano knew about the long terms, since Zanussi had received a copy in Lisbon. Castellano replied that not only did he not know about them, his government did not either, and that this development put a whole new light on the armistice. Smith reminded him of the modifying force of the Quebec Memorandum, but Castellano was not impressed, since it contained only general promises. Smith then sat down and made a promise in writing. "The additional clauses," he declared, "have only a relative value insofar as Italy collaborates in the war against the Germans."[22]

Finally on September 6, after two days of continuous discussion between Castellano and the staff, Eisenhower made a series of adjustments to his plans to take advantage of Italian aid. These adjustments satisfied the Italian leaders. The most important was pulling the 82d out of AVALANCHE (the paratroopers had been scheduled to be used as a floating reserve) and flying it into Rome. Half the division would go in on the night of September 8, with the remainder following over the next few days. Castellano said that the Italians would be able to open the ports of Taranto and Brindisi to the Allies, and Cunningham said that as soon as the Italian fleet came under Allied control, in accordance with the armistice terms, he could release some cruisers and destroyers for escort duty. Eisenhower therefore decided to take the British 1st Airborne Division, which was in North Africa awaiting transportation to Britain, and rush it to Taranto, on the Italian heel, on D-Day. Last, Eisenhower and Badoglio would simultaneously announce the armistice on the radio at 6:30 P.M. on September 8.[23]

The over-all picture, in short, was suddenly rosy. Eisenhower would be entering Italy from four different directions, with Montgomery coming north from the toe, the British paratroopers on the heel, the 82d Airborne in Rome, and Clark's Fifth Army at Salerno. The prospects for AVALANCHE looked especially good, since taking the 82d Airborne out of floating reserve released some landing craft, and the absence of opposition in the toe against Montgomery had released additional craft.

With the 82d in Rome, the Germans would find it difficult to move reserves into the Salerno area to oppose the Allies. If everything worked out, and the Italians stuck to their agreements, the Allies could count on being north of Rome in a matter of days.

All of these developments had happened so quickly that it seemed too good to be true, and Eisenhower curbed his optimism. On September 6 he told Marshall that the Italian negotiations were complete, "and I hope that something real will come from them. If we can only produce a situation that will force the Germans in the south to become fearful and retire rather than to counterattack us quickly and seriously, my greatest concern will be alleviated." Even if the campaign on the ground stalled, however, getting the Italian fleet would be a major gain. Eisenhower said he was encouraged at the absence of opposition on the toe, but "the AVALANCHE operation is a horse of a different color and I am frank to state that there is more than a faint possibility that we may have some hard going." But the commanders and troops were in good spirits, and "I am determined to hit as hard as I can."[24]

Two days later Eisenhower's caution became justified as the high hopes began to fall. Castellano conferred with his government and reported that Badoglio wanted a larger force in Rome, with at least an armored division supporting the 82d Airborne. This request came on the eve of the invasion, but neither Castellano nor Badoglio knew how imminent AVALANCHE was.

Eisenhower flatly refused. Castellano then asked if the Italians could keep a portion of their fleet for the use of the King. As soon as the armistice was announced, the King decided he wanted to put to sea and stay there until the situation had crystallized. Eisenhower agreed to give them one cruiser and three gunboats, but for a few days only. Castellano had other requests, all of which Eisenhower turned down.[25]

By far the most disturbing aspect of the requests was Italian nervousness about Rome. Fortunately, Eisenhower already had officers there who could keep Badoglio in line. On September 6 Eisenhower met with Major General Maxwell Taylor, commanding the 82d's artillery, and Colonel William T. Gardiner. He was sending the two officers into Rome to make last-minute arrangements with Badoglio and to recommend changes as needed. An elaborate code system was worked out; the key word was "Innocuous." If for any reason Taylor thought the airborne operation should be canceled, he would radio the word "innocuous" to AFHQ. Taylor was a West Point graduate with a reputation for brilliance and an ability to keep his head in a crisis. Eisenhower was sure he could trust him.

On the morning of September 7 Taylor and Gardiner traveled by PT boat to the Italian coast, splashed some water on their uniforms to give the appearance of aviators shot down and rescued from the sea, and rode by automobile to Rome, passing German troops along the way. They reached the city at nightfall and entered into a series of discussions with lower-ranking Italian Army officers. All the Italians seemed apprehensive. The American force coming into Rome was too small to hold the city; the Italians could not hold the airfields for them; they could not supply material, as promised, for the 82d; final preparations had not been made; the Allied landings at Salerno were too weak and too far south and would do the Italians no good at all. As one officer put it to Taylor, "If the Italians declare an armistice, the Germans will occupy Rome, and the Italians can do little to prevent it." They wanted GIANT II, code name for the 82d's move to Rome, canceled and the armistice announcement and AVALANCHE postponed.

Taylor demanded to see Badoglio. Around midnight he got to Badoglio's villa and found that Badoglio was just as frightened as his subordinates. Like them, he wanted the whole operation postponed. Taylor argued to no avail. As the official American historians put it, in a grand understatement, "Badoglio's bland disregard of the terms signed by his accredited representative, Castellano, and his unwillingness to oppose the Germans were extremely disconcerting. . . ."[26] Taylor finally gave up, and Badoglio wrote a message to Eisenhower. Badoglio said that "due to changes in the situation . . . it is no longer possible to accept an immediate armistice," since it would provoke the Germans. The 82d's move to Rome "is no longer possible because of lack of forces to guarantee the airfields." Taylor wrote a message of his own recommending that GIANT II be abandoned.[27]

Both messages had to be encoded, transmitted, and decoded. The process took hours. GIANT II was scheduled to take off from Sicily at 6:30 P.M., September 8. Around noon of that day Taylor, anxious to make sure GIANT II was canceled, sent a two-word message, "Situation innocuous." That evening he and Gardiner returned to Sicily on an Italian airplane.[28]

On the morning of September 8 Eisenhower had wakened early, dictated some messages, and then left Algiers to go to Amilcar, his advance command post near Tunis. Shortly after he left Badoglio's message renouncing the armistice came in and was decoded. It threw Smith off balance. After sending a copy to Eisenhower at Amilcar, Smith sent a message to the CCS asking whether or not to proceed with the armistice announcement.[29]

Eisenhower was enraged. His annoyance with Smith for having referred the problem to the CCS was almost as great as his anger at Badoglio for backing down. He grasped a pencil, broke it, and began dictating a message to Badoglio. When he was finished he had Castellano, who was in Bizerte, brought to Amilcar.

The stage managing was excellent. Eisenhower had Castellano wait in a courtyard for half an hour, with officers of all' ranks scurrying past, paying no attention at all to Castellano. Eisenhower then had Castellano ushered by armed guards into his office. Eisenhower sat at a table, flanked by Alexander and Cunningham, and with other awe-inspiring Allied officers to the right and left. Castellano came to attention and saluted. No one returned it. He felt as if he were at his own court-martial.

Eisenhower read to Castellano his message to Badoglio, which was then being encoded for transmission. "I intend to broadcast the existence of the armistice at the hour originally planned," Eisenhower's message began, and that hour was 6:30 P.M., that day, less than twelve hours away. "If you or any part of your armed forces fail to cooperate as previously agreed I will publish to the world the full record of this affair." Eisenhower refused to "accept" Badoglio's message postponing the armistice, pointed out that an accredited representative had signed it, and warned: "The sole hope of Italy is bound up in your adherence to that agreement." Athough Eisenhower was sure that the Italians had sufficient troops near Rome to hold the city, on Badoglio's "earnest representation" he was canceling GIANT II.

In his last paragraph, Eisenhower let out all the stops. "Plans have been made on the assumption that you were acting in good faith and we have been prepared to carry out future operations on that basis," he declared. His voice rising, he continued to read to the quaking Castellano. "Failure now on your part to carry out the full obligations to the signed agreement will have the most serious consequences for your country. No future action of yours could then restore any confidence whatever in your good faith and consequently the dissolution of your government and nation would ensue." Eisenhower then dismissed Castellano, sending him to Tunis with the hope that he could do something to bring Badoglio around. The whole explosive scene probably made Eisenhower and his deputies feel better, but it had little practical value, since Badoglio was not there to see it. If Badoglio was to relent, Eisenhower's message alone would have to persuade him.[30]

With the message on its way to Badoglio and Castellano properly terrified, the next step was to make sure GIANT II had been canceled. AFHQ had sent a message to the division headquarters in Sicily, but it would take so long to encode, transmit, and decode that a quicker method was needed. Eisenhower therefore sent Brigadier General Lyman Lemnitzer by plane to Sicily. The pilot got lost, and only when he almost crashed into Mount Etna was he able to identify his location. The 82d's commander, Major General Matthew Ridgway, was meanwhile waiting near a radio. Eisenhower was scheduled to broadcast the armistice at 6:30 P.M. and that broadcast was the 82d's signal to go. Sixty-two of the 150 troop-carrying planes were already circling into formation to prepare to go to Rome when Lemnitzer landed. GIANT II was off.[31]

At 6:30 P.M., on schedule, although no word had been received from Badoglio, Eisenhower went on the air on Radio Algiers. "This is General Dwight D. Eisenhower, Commander in Chief of the Allied forces," he began. "The Italian government has surrendered its armed forces unconditionally. As Allied Commander in Chief, I have granted a military armistice." The terms had been approved by the Allied governments, he added, and "the Italian government has bound itself by these terms without reservation." The armistice became effective "this instant. Hostilities between the armed forces of the United Nations and those of Italy terminate at once." Finally, "Italians who now act to help eject the German aggressor from Italian soil will have the assistance and support of the United Nations."

When Eisenhower finished, technicians at Amilcar quickly turned their dials to pick up Radio Rome. No announcement came from Badoglio. After waiting ten minutes, Eisenhower told the technicians to broadcast over Radio Algiers the text of Badoglio's proclamation. This had been cleared earlier with Eisenhower and declared that an armistice was in effect. It ordered Italian soldiers to cease all acts of hostility against the Allies while urging them to "oppose attacks from any other quarter."[32]

That finished it. There was nothing more Eisenhower could do. He had gambled heavily, and now he had entered the waiting period before an invasion, that maddening time when he could only sit and pray. Clark's men were on their way to the beaches. The Germans were undoubtedly moving to take Rome, which would clear their transportation routes to get reinforcements down to Salerno. No one knew what Badoglio was going to do or even where he was; presumably he and the King, along with other government officials, would flee Rome.

Eisenhower had always insisted on announcing the armistice before the invasion, hoping that this would induce the Italians to at least commit acts of sabotage against the Germans. He recognized, however, that the terms the Allies had insisted upon were hardly likely to induce the Italians to become wholehearted advocates of the Allied cause. All the Allies had given the Italians was a crushing set of terms depriving them of all authority, all independence, and even the basic means of defense. In return, the Allies would not even recognize them as co-belligerents. But except at Taranto, no plans for co-operation had been made.[33]

From the first, however, Eisenhower had not expected much positive help from the Italians. He had told Churchill all along that there was "no fury left in the Italian population." What he absolutely had to have was passive neutrality. If the Italians chose to ignore the armistice announcement, pulled another double-cross, and fought beside the Germans, AVALANCHE would be a bloody failure. The situation was risky enough as it was, since Clark was invading with less than four divisions, while the Germans had almost twenty divisions on the mainland, and their ability to rush reinforcements to the Salerno area was greater than that of the Allies. It all hinged on Badoglio.

CHAPTER 19

Salerno

While the landing craft plowed forward through the Mediterranean, carrying Clark's men to their landing sites around Salerno, Eisenhower and his AFHQ staff sat beside a radio, waiting to hear whether Badoglio would broadcast over Radio Rome. Finally, at 7:45 P.M., Badoglio came on and announced the armistice.*

Eisenhower grunted his satisfaction. He had "played a little poker," as he put it, and won. By the time the Italians realized that the Allies had only a few divisions available for operations in Italy, it would be too late to back out.** He had done everything he could. It was now up to Clark—really, the men of the British X and the American VI Corps—and there was nothing the commander in chief could do until the situation on the beach clarified. Eisenhower was getting better at these waiting periods. This time, instead of fidgeting, he went to sleep.[1]

When he awoke at 6:45 A.M. the news was good. Clark's first waves had gotten ashore successfully, even though the Germans had pinpointed

---

* Badoglio had had a long conference with the King and merely reported that the alternatives were staggering. The Italians could refuse to make any announcement, in which case Eisenhower would carry out his threat to make public the negotiations, which would leave them in an impossible position vis-à-vis the Germans, or they could make the announcement, in which case the Germans would take over their capital and probably their country. The King finally made the decision. He declared that Italy could not change sides once again and ordered Badoglio to make the announcement. Garland and Smyth, *Sicily,* pp. 512–13.

** Eisenhower told McNarney a week later, ". . . when the results eventually justify the decision most people think it was obviously an easy one to make," but in fact it was not. There had been "a lot of guess work" involved. Eisenhower said that he had decided that if Badoglio did not make the announcement, "there was no use fooling with him any more." The big worry was the Italian fleet, and Eisenhower was willing to gamble to get it. Eisenhower to McNarney, September 16, 1943, EP, No. 1262.

the general site of the landing. Secrecy was minimal because Salerno Bay was the only point between the toe and Naples with beaches that would support a landing, and the Germans knew that the Allied land-based fighter aircraft could not operate north of Naples. The enemy had assigned the 16th Panzer Division to the defense of the region. The defense was a mobile one, designed to hold up the Allies until the German divisions in the south of Italy could extricate themselves from combat with the Eighth Army and come to the aid of the 16th Division. Von Kesselring's plan was to bring together every force he had and, on the third or fourth day of the invasion, drive the Allies into the sea.

Eisenhower hoped to upset Von Kesselring's plan by putting pressure on him at so many different points that concentration of forces would be impossible. The Allies already had Eighth Army coming north from the toe, and Clark was ashore at Salerno. In addition, Eisenhower had directed the British 1st Airborne Division into Taranto as soon as Badoglio announced the armistice. By early morning on September 9 the 1st Airborne was on its way. The 82d Airborne's operation at Rome had been a part of this over-all plan, but it of course had been abandoned. Still, on the morning of September 9, the situation looked bright.[2] An important factor was Italian neutrality, now insured thanks to Badoglio's announcement. AFHQ could even begin to hope for active Italian assistance, which might be considerable, for even though the Italian Army was ill equipped, it did contain 1,700,000 men.

But the hope that something could be accomplished by the Italians soon died. After announcing the armistice, Badoglio, the King, and the leaders in the government spent the next few hours debating whether or not they should leave Rome. They had hoped that the Germans would accept the armistice, and some even dreamed of the Germans agreeing to an Italian demand that they lay down their arms. But when the Germans made it clear that they would fight their way into Rome if necessary, the government panicked. At 5 A.M., as Clark's men came ashore, the King, Badoglio, and the most important military leaders piled into private automobiles and fled the capital, headed for the south and safety under Allied protection. No one bothered to send any orders to units in the field, and for the most part the Germans merely disarmed the Italian soldiers. Within a matter of days the Italian Army ceased to exist and Italy was an occupied country.[3]

Much of this was already known to Eisenhower by noon of September 9, when he dictated a long situation report to the CCS. He said that information received from Castellano indicated that nothing could be expected from the Italians. On the positive side, the Italian fleet had started out of Taranto and the British 1st Airborne had started in. Eisenhower was also rushing troops to Brindisi, for the Germans seemed to have no ground strength on the heel. Montgomery was making progress from the toe, but he was not moving fast enough to hold the Germans in the area, so Eisenhower expected them to turn up on Clark's front shortly.

At the main point, Salerno, the initial success was already beginning to give way to disturbing developments. The British X Corps, to the north, had three separate beachheads, one at Maiori, eight miles west of Salerno, another at Salerno itself, and a third to the south. The American VI Corps had one beachhead, twenty-five miles to the southeast, around Paestum. Beach conditions had forced the dispersal of troops. The immediate object was to link up. Resistance everywhere was heavy, but it was especially marked on the VI Corps front. It was beginning to look as though the link-up would be difficult to achieve and once made difficult to hold. Clark wanted to rush the 82d Airborne into the beachhead, and Eisenhower was trying to find landing craft with which to to the job.

"I feel that AVALANCHE will be a matter of touch and go for the next few days," Eisenhower told the CCS. If he had enough landing craft to put another division ashore immediately "the matter would be almost a foregone conclusion," but as it was "we are in for some very tough fighting." Eisenhower admitted that he looked for a "very bad time in the AVALANCHE area," but declared that he believed that "the enemy is sufficiently confused by the events of the past 24 hours that it will be difficult for him to make up a definite plan. . . ."[4]

It was a poor prediction. Even though German divisions in central Italy were fully engaged in disarming the Italian forces there and though those in southern Italy had long distances to march, over poor roads, Von Kesselring's reaction was swift and strong. After building up his forces to the north of the beachhead to protect his communications with Naples, he concentrated on the center of Clark's line to prevent the British and Americans from meeting. By nightfall of the tenth, although both the British and Americans had made some progress inland, they had not achieved a firm link-up. The ground just to the left of the Sele River was disputed, with the situation highly fluid. The next day Von Kesselring got five additional divisions into the area and prepared to destroy the Salerno beachhead.

Von Kesselring attacked all through the day of September 12, driving the Allies back. The fighting continued throughout the night and into the next day. The American commander decided to strengthen his left flank in order to close the gap between his corps and X Corps. He began shifting troops northward. While this sliding maneuver was going on the Germans attacked the exposed troops along the north bank of the Sele River. They overran an American battalion, forded the river, and drove southeast for a ford on the Calore River. In the process the Germans inflicted heavy losses on the Americans, scattering many units. If they got across the Calore they would be loose in the American rear areas along the beaches.

Eisenhower did what he could to rush reinforcements to Clark. Since there were no landing craft available, he had a part of the 82d Airborne dropped into the beachhead. He urged Montgomery to speed up his movement, which would have the effect of putting pressure on Von Kesselring's left flank. Constant prodding had some effect on Montgomery, but real improvement came when Eighth Army got to better terrain. Initially it had only one mountain road to move on, and every bridge was blown, every defile blocked. It had traveled only forty-five miles in the first seven days in Italy; it covered twice that distance during the next week. Clark had constructed a small airfield in VI Corps beachhead, capable of handling fighters, but German artillery on the high ground inland dominated the area and the airfield took a constant shelling. Eisenhower nevertheless rushed planes in, willing to take the losses in order to get some air protection. He prepared another infantry division to go into the beachhead as soon as landing craft were available.[5]

As a result of some fervent pleas to the CCS and after many refusals from them, Eisenhower finally secured eighteen additional LSTs, but they were of no immediate help. They had been transiting through the Mediterranean on their way to India, and were loaded with steel rails. Eisenhower cursed every minute it took to unload them. "If we could have had the use of these for the past two weeks," he complained to Wedemeyer, "we would be sitting rather well in Salerno Bay." By the same token if he had had the three B-24 groups he had begged for, there would have been no crisis. "I would give my next year's pay for two or three extra heavy groups right this minute," Eisenhower said on the afternoon of September 13.[6]

It was the most dangerous moment of the entire war for the Allied armies in Europe. An army of two corps, with four divisions, was on the verge of annihilation. AFHQ received a message from Clark that indicated that he was making plans to put his headquarters on board ship in order to control both sectors and to continue the battle in whichever one offered the greatest chance for success. The message made Eisenhower almost frantic. He told Butcher and Smith that the headquarters should leave last, that Clark ought to show the spirit of a naval captain and if necessary go down with his ship. The Fifth Army should emulate the spirit of Stalingrad, Eisenhower said, and stand and fight. He wondered if it had not been a mistake to give Clark the command—perhaps he should have selected Patton. The message from Clark, it turned out, had been garbled in transmission, and Clark had no intention of withdrawing.[7] Still, it left everyone a little shaken.

Eisenhower managed to keep up a front, no matter how bad the news. "My optimism never deserts me," he declared on September 13th. He thought the efficiency of the air forces, the fact of the Germans unsureness about the possibility of another attack still farther north, and the fighting quality of the allied troops would eventually turn the trick.[8]

Eisenhower's confidence stemmed in part from the command structure, which was geared to quick decisions and rapid action and could concentrate enormous fire power on one spot in a hurry. Eisenhower's deputies were with him at his advanced command post at Amilcar. He had insisted on this after the HUSKY experience, when they had been divided, and the new arrangements worked well. "We meet daily and it is astonishing how much we can get done to keep our staffs operating at full tilt to execute needed projects," Eisenhower told Marshall on September 13. Everyone was currently working on saving the beachhead at Salerno. Tedder had his air forces "flat out" in support, while Alexander was prodding Montgomery. Cunningham was rushing capital ships into Salerno Bay, where they could fire in direct support of the ground forces. Eisenhower and the staff completely juggled the scheduled movements from the Mediterranean to OVERLORD, put into Salerno men who had been loaded to go to England, built up the 82d Airborne on the beachhead to full strength, and sent the 8th Indian Division into Brindisi.[9]

The situation was still uncertain, but Eisenhower thought Clark could hold on. If he did not, Eisenhower told Marshall, "I would . . . merely announce that one of our landings had been repulsed—due to my error in misjudging the strength of the enemy at that place." But he had "great faith that even in spite of currently grim reports, we'll pull out all right."[10]

Even as Eisenhower was dictating, the American G.I.s were proving him correct. At the critical point, along the Calore River, American artillerymen stood to their guns and prevented a German breakthrough. The situation was still critical but not desperate.

All the next day, September 14, the Germans attacked. Eisenhower sent a note of encouragement to Clark, told Tedder to put "every plane that could fly" over Salerno, including all the Strategic Air Forces, and supported Cunningham in his decision to bring the ships up close to shore so that they could pound the Germans.[11]

While the battle raged, Eisenhower dictated a memorandum for the diary. He admitted that, when the CCS withdrew his B-24s, Alexander and others had wanted to call off AVALANCHE. The decision to go ahead "was solely my own, and if things go wrong there is no one to blame except myself." Eisenhower did point out that in the end all three deputies supported AVALANCHE, but he was not building up an excuse for the record. His deputies, as well as the staff at AFHQ and at Fifth Army, had "striven in every possible way" to make AVALANCHE work, and "I have no word of complaint concerning any officer or man in the execution of our plans." Eisenhower thought the position could be held because "I think that our air force will finally disorganize the attacks against the Fifth Army. . . ."[12] Shortly after he dictated the memorandum, word came in that the German attacks had failed and the situation was stabilizing. The combined Allied air and naval bombardment had stopped the enemy. Eisenhower, like most soldiers, tended to give the credit to the air forces. In speaking of the battle later, he would usually praise the fliers in the highest terms, then add almost as an afterthought that the Navy had done well too. In fact, although the air attacks were more spectacular, with planes sweeping out of the skies and swarming over German positions, or dropping bombs from on high which the G.I.s could watch coming down, it was the naval fire that was decisive in the victory. While the air forces were dropping 3020 tons of bombs, the naval forces—mostly Royal Navy—delivered more than 11,000 tons of shell in direct support of the ground forces on the beachhead, and the naval fire was immeasurably more accurate.[13]*

By the fifteenth the crisis was over. The next day lead elements of the Eighth Army made contact with a Fifth Army patrol forty miles southeast of Salerno. Von Kesselring recognized that his attempt to push the Allies into the sea had failed. On September 18 he began a deliberate disengagement and withdrawal.

* "A German commander at Salerno reported to Kesselring on the 14th: 'The attack this morning . . . had to endure naval gunfire from at least 16 to 18 battleships, cruisers and large destroyers. . . . With astonishing precision and freedom of maneuver, these ships shot at every recognized target with overwhelming effect.' " Quoted in Samuel Eliot Morison, *The Two-Ocean War, A Short History of the United States Navy in the Second World War* (Boston, 1963), p. 356.

Just as the AFHQ officers were beginning to breathe sighs of relief, offers of support began to pour in on them. The CCS declared that "we are most anxious to give all the help possible at the earliest moment," and told Eisenhower to "state clearly" what he wanted.[14] Churchill, meanwhile, wired Alexander: "Ask for anything you want and I will make allocation of necessary supplies with highest priority irrespective of every other consideration." Alexander passed the offer along to Eisenhower.[15]

Considering his superiors' earlier refusals to give him the equipment that would have made AVALANCHE a sure thing, Eisenhower may have been more inclined to cry than to laugh. Still, he tempered his response, resisting the temptation to say, "I told you so." In replying to Churchill, he pointed out that the crisis was over, so there was really nothing that could be done from London.[16]

But he did not let the CCS off completely by any means. He said he wanted some bombing raids by Eighth Air Force against German communications in northern Italy, and that he wanted the three B-24 groups that had been in the Mediterranean returned, even if only for a period of two weeks. "I would appreciate an early reply," Eisenhower said in conclusion. "I have complete faith that we are going to solve this problem but I feel it my duty to let you know that any possible temporary assistance of the kind indicated would mean a great deal to us."[17]

The CCS responded handsomely. That night, within twenty-four hours of Eisenhower's request, some 340 RAF heavies and five B-17s bombed the railroad yards at Modane in southwestern France in an effort to close the northern end of the Mont Cenis tunnel. The CCS also told Devers to get some B-24s down to AFHQ, and Devers had them there within the week.[18]

Eisenhower decided to press his advantage, and on September 18 pointed out to Marshall the benefits available to the Allies if they used Italy as a major base for the strategic air offensive against Germany.[19] Once the fields at Foggia were available, Eisenhower said, the advantages would be considerable. The Allies could reach targets beyond the reach of bombers operating from the U.K.; there were better weather conditions with less German fighter and anti-aircraft opposition; they would force the Germans to spread their defenses, and the air forces could have some flexibility in meeting cyclic weather changes.[20]

By this time, however, it was as clear in Washington as in Algiers that the crisis was over and Marshall would not accept this argument. After the B-24s from Eighth Air Force made some raids in Italy, Marshall told Eisenhower to return them to Devers.[21] Smith remarked that AFHQ ought to set up a special section whose sole job would be to keep the home front frightened, since that was the only way AFHQ seemed to be able to get material from the CCS.[22]

On the front, by September 22, the situation showed marked improvement. After two weeks of battle, the British X Corps was on the high ground surrounding its beachhead, ground which the German artillery had used before with great effectiveness. The American VI Corps had a firm link-up with X Corps and with Eighth Army, which in turn had joined with the British V Corps coming from Taranto. The Allies had a continuous line across Italy. Losses had been high but unevenly distributed—Clark had suffered 14,000 casualties to Montgomery's 600. The drive for Naples and the airfields at Foggia, on the east coast, was under way.

At this juncture Marshall sent Eisenhower a criticism of his recent tactics and a suggestion for the future. On September 23 Marshall told Eisenhower that he had been talking with Field Marshal Dill, and they agreed that if AVALANCHE had been started before the operations in the toe of Italy the Germans would have been caught unprepared and probably would have fallen back beyond Naples. More to the point, Marshall said he and Dill feared Eisenhower was about to repeat the mistake. If Eisenhower took the time to develop a secure position around Naples, Marshall said, the Germans would have time to prepare their defenses and thus make the road to Rome long and difficult. He wondered if Eisenhower had considered the possibility of halting Fifth and Eighth Army efforts in Naples once it was "under the guns" and making a dash for Rome, perhaps by amphibious means.[23] These thoughts coincided with Eisenhower's wishes; as he told Handy, "I would give my last shirt to be able to push a strong division landing into the Gulf of Gaeta," which was north of Naples.[24]

Eisenhower took any criticism from Marshall seriously and went through a "great deal of mental anguish" while dictating his reply. His usual practice was to pace the room, talking rapidly, or else to shift from chair to chair. This time he became so engrossed in getting the answer just right that he walked right out the open door into the hallway and kept on dictating. His secretary scurried after him, taking shorthand all the while.[25]

Eisenhower began his reply by saying that the subject of Marshall's message had been the chief topic of discussion at the Commanders' Conference the previous day. Eisenhower and his deputies had searched for the means to make a landing behind the German flanks because they knew it would offer great results, but that they had been unable to come up with anything that promised even a fair chance of success. He reminded Marshall that the Germans had a Panzer division in the Gulf of Gaeta area, another in Rome, and a reserve division that could reinforce either one. Eisenhower felt that if he landed a small force it would be quickly eliminated, while a force large enough to sustain itself could not be mounted "for a very considerable period."

"I cannot repeat not agree that the Salerno operation could have logically preceded" the landing on the toe, Eisenhower said. It came hard, after the tense days at Salerno, to be obliquely accused of excessive caution, and Eisenhower dictated a full two pages defending his program. AVALANCHE could not have begun any sooner even if there had been no landings at the toe, he said, and added that Montgomery's drive northward played in fact a considerable role in saving the day at Salerno. Marshall had also expressed disappointment at AFHQ's failure to seize Rome initially; Eisenhower said that he and his subordinates had given a complete study to a Rome operation and had to reject it because the port there was inadequate and because it was beyond the range of fighter cover.

"As a final word," Eisenhower concluded, "I want to say that we are looking every minute for a chance to utilize our air and naval power to turn the enemy positions and place him at a disadvantage. I do not see how any individual could possibly be devoting more thought and energy to speeding up operations or to attacking boldly and with admitted risk than I do. My staff is imbued with this same attitude and I should like to reassure you that nothing that offers to us a chance for a successful stroke will be ignored."

As Eisenhower was dictating, a message came in from Churchill. The Prime Minister congratulated Eisenhower on the landing and deployment in Italy and commented, "As the Duke of Wellington said of the battle of Waterloo, 'It was a damned close-run thing.'" Churchill said he was proud of Eisenhower for his policy of "running risks." Eisenhower passed the message along to Marshall and commented, "I feel certain that some of his [Churchill's] correspondents in this area look upon me as a gambler."[26]

Gambler or not, by September 26 Eisenhower was committed to the slow, direct, overland approach to Rome. The basis of his decision was G-2's reading of German intentions, reinforced by Allied shortages in landing craft. G-2 had learned of Hitler's plan to withdraw into northern

Italy, and without the landing craft to make wide sweeping end runs, or the aircraft to block the German retreat, Eisenhower and Alexander felt there was little they could do beyond staying on the Germans' heels. There had been some talk about shutting down operations once Naples and Foggia were secure; Eisenhower rejected this idea because he wanted to stay on the offensive, because he was aware of the political prestige of Rome, because there were airfields around Rome which AFHQ could use, and most of all because if the Allies ceased any initiative the Germans might launch a counteroffensive which could wipe out the hard-won gains.

The trouble was that the G-2 information was dated. Hitler had wanted to withdraw to northern Italy, but Von Kesselring convinced him that he could wage a successful defense for a considerable period south of Rome. Von Kesselring was also acting on a misreading of his enemy's intentions, for he reasoned that once the Allies had Foggia they would halt their Italian campaign and launch a major invasion of the Balkans. But unlike Eisenhower's, his misreading was not of serious consequence. Hitler was much concerned with the Balkans, and Von Kesselring found it fairly easy to convince him that the Germans should stay as far south as possible in order to prevent an invasion of Yugoslavia. Thus Hitler duly authorized Von Kesselring to build a "Winter Line," a series of defensive lines, organized in depth, along the general line of the Garigliano and Sangro rivers. By October 1 Fifth Army had Naples and the British had Foggia, but from that point on resistance began to stiffen.

As always, Eisenhower found it impossible to devote his full attention to the battle. Both the French and the Italians were making trouble. When the German garrison withdrew from Corsica, Giraud had put some French troops onto the island. De Gaulle sent his commendations to Giraud for his conduct of operations, but then he learned that Giraud had for months been secretly dealing with the Communist underground on the island. Disturbed at Giraud's naïveté, De Gaulle decided to bring the army commander directly under his control. He could not chance a repetition of the Corsican experience in Metropolitan France, where the Communists were even stronger. Eisenhower said he did not care how the trouble ended as long as Giraud stayed in command of the army.[27] On September 25 De Gaulle proposed to the FCNL that a single, strong executive replace the existing system of dual command. Giraud protested, but he was heavily outvoted, and the FCNL proceeded to deprive him of all but nominal powers as commander in chief. Giraud, priding himself on his political innocence, then committed political suicide by co-signing the measure that removed him from the co-presidency of the FCNL. A month later he had been ousted from the committee.[28]

All this made Roosevelt most unhappy. "I have very distinct feelings," he told Marshall, "that we should not send further equipment of munitions to the French army in North Africa if our prima donna is to seize control of it from the old gentleman." Marshall dissented from this view, as did Eisenhower, on the grounds that Eisenhower needed the French divisions for forthcoming operations in the Mediterranean.[29] De Gaulle continued to receive supplies and increased his hold over the FCNL.

One of the reasons De Gaulle was able to get away with ousting Giraud with only mild protests from the U.S. was American preoccupation with Italian affairs. Immediately after the invasion, having secured Italian neutrality, Eisenhower tried to urge the Italian Army into activity against the Germans. He cabled Badoglio, who had made it to Brindisi, urging him to take action. "The whole future and honour of Italy depends upon the part which her armed forces are now prepared to play," Eisenhower said. He asked Badoglio to issue a clarion call to all patriotic Italians to "seize every German by the throat."[30]

It did no good. Asking the Italian armed forces to act was like beating a dead horse. There were no Italian armed forces left. All the Allies had gotten out of the armistice was a symbol of leadership in the King and Badoglio, and as a symbol they were approximately as valuable as Mussolini, whom Hitler had rescued from his Italian captors. Neither symbol had any appeal at all to the Italian armed forces or people.

But the Allies, like Hitler, had to make do with what they had. Eisenhower did what he could to establish regular relations with Badoglio. He decided to send Lieutenant General Sir Noel Mason-MacFarlane (the governor of Gibraltar), Macmillan, and Murphy to Brindisi. A visit from these high-ranking officials would give some prestige to the Brindisi government. When Badoglio learned of their selection he told Eisenhower he was pleased, but suggested that it would be more profitable for him to meet with Eisenhower and his staff "to discuss further operations in Italy, a theater of war which we [Italians] naturally know perfectly."[31]

Considering the history of his past dealings with Badoglio, Eisenhower was hardly anxious to confide his plans to members of the Italian government. In addition, Eisenhower commanded large and powerful armed forces, while Badoglio commanded nothing. Why should Eisenhower subject himself to listening to Badoglio telling him how to wage the war? Still, conversation might help to clear the air, and in any case Eisenhower's superiors wanted him to get Badoglio's signature on the long terms, a task Eisenhower regarded with repugnance but which had to be done. He therefore agreed to a meeting, but to stall said it would have to be in Tunis. The Mason-MacFarlane mission could work out the details.[32]

In reporting these developments to Marshall, Eisenhower said that Badoglio wanted to bring along some of his general staff. "I can't make out what his general staff can possibly be directing just now," Eisenhower laconically commented.[33] The first reports from Mason-Mac-Farlane, who arrived in Brindisi on September 15, reinforced this con-tempt for the Italians. "They all say we should have landed north instead of south of Naples," Mason-MacFarlane said. "On this point I tell them they know nothing about it and to shut up." He found the King to be "pathetic, very old, and rather gaga," while Badoglio was "old, benevolent, honest and very friendly." The Italian Army could be "written off." As for the government itself, its only importance was that except for Mussolini and his gang, who had announced from Ger-many the organization of a Fascist Republican Party, no one had chal-lenged its authority.[34]

Two days later Murphy and Macmillan returned from Brindisi, and Eisenhower and Smith, who had become AFHQ's expert on Italian affairs, conferred with them. Smith then drafted a long cable on the situation to the CCS. He said that AFHQ wanted to use the Italian divisions that were intact on Sardinia and Corsica for coastal defense and the Italian Navy to transport troops and supplies. The trouble was that such activity, although desirable and even necessary to the Allies, was inconsistent with the terms of the armistice, which called for the Italian armed forces to be disarmed and disbanded. Smith asked for a new Allied policy toward Italy, granting the Badoglio administration "some form of *de facto* recognition . . . as a co-belligerent or military associate." He added that the meeting with Badoglio could not be de-layed for more than ten more days, so instructions were needed im-mediately. And because he realized that his suggestion would "provoke political repercussions," and perhaps "arouse considerable opposition and criticism," he recommended that "the burden be placed upon us, on the ground of military necessity, which I am convinced should be the gov-erning factor."[35]

The next day, September 19, Eisenhower—who had gone to Tunis—

decided that Smith's telegram was indecisive and drafted a new one. He sent it to Smith at Algiers, asking him to send it along to the CCS if he agreed with it (a typical illustration of how closely the two men worked). Smith sent it on to the CCS on September 20. The message was brief. Eisenhower said that in future relations with Italy there were only two courses: (1) to accept and strengthen the government and to regard it as a co-belligerent, or (2) to sweep Badoglio aside, set up an Allied military government, and accept the very heavy commitments involved. "Of these two courses," Eisenhower commented, "I strongly recommend the first."[36]

Eisenhower's recommendations forced the Allied governments to make a decision. On September 23, after an exchange of messages with Churchill, Roosevelt laid down a basic policy for Eisenhower's guidance. Eisenhower was to withhold the long-term armistice provisions until a later date to allow the Italians to fight beside the Allies, and to permit the Italian government to assume the status of a co-belligerent if it declared war on Germany and promised to give the people the right to decide the form of government they wished. Eisenhower immediately passed this on to Mason-MacFarlane and told him to arrange for a meeting in Malta between Badoglio and the AFHQ heads.[37]

The possibility of this simple proposal's approval seemed too good to be true, and it was. Macmillan sent a private message to Churchill saying that he thought Badoglio would sign the long terms, and Churchill convinced Roosevelt. On September 25, Roosevelt gave his assent to using the long terms if Badoglio's signature could be obtained quickly. Eisenhower reluctantly accepted the switch in policy, and told Smith to go to Brindisi to prepare for the Eisenhower-Badoglio conference, set for September 29.

A rift in the Italian government added to the complications. Badoglio saw clearly the need for Italy to declare war on Germany, both to regularize the status of Italian soldiers who fell into German hands and as a prerequisite for improving Italy's position with the Western powers. But the King disagreed. He told Mason-MacFarlane that he alone could declare war on Germany and he did not think it wise to do so until the Germans were ousted from Rome. The King added that he was anxious to drop Badoglio, as it would be difficult to form a representative anti-Fascist government under him. He stressed the danger of the Communist Party in Italy and said "he thought it would be most dangerous to leave the choice of post-war government unreservedly in the hands of the Italian people."[38]

The royal political acumen was somewhat limited. As if to illustrate this, Victor Emmanuel III signed his first proclamation from Brindisi as "His Majesty the King of Italy and Albania, Emperor of Ethiopia." Mason-MacFarlane tried to point out that all these situations were changed, but the King grandly replied that he could not surrender his titles without an act of parliament.[39]

In the face of such gaucherie it was difficult for AFHQ officers to keep from laughing. After he returned from Brindisi, Smith told reporters that "the Italian Government, at the present time, consists of the King, Marshal Badoglio, two or three generals, and a couple of part-time stenographers. The day that 'I was there, a couple of cheap help from the Foreign Office came down from Rome on foot (an Under-Secretary or two)." He said the King was not too bad after he had had his breakfast and before lunch, but "after that he is a little bit slow on the uptake." For this reason he used the one typist the government had in the morning, while Badoglio had the typist's services in the afternoon.[40]

While he was at Brindisi, Smith carefully laid the groundwork for the Eisenhower-Badoglio meeting on Malta. He was able to get complete agreement from Badoglio, but the King remained stubborn. He did authorize Badoglio to sign the long terms, but he refused to declare war on Germany, to pledge to broaden his government, or to promise to permit the people to choose their own form of government at the end of the war.[41]

At 11 A.M., September 29, aboard the British battleship H.M.S. *Nelson* at Malta, Eisenhower finally met Badoglio. Ambrosio, Roatta, Murphy, Macmillan, Alexander, Smith, Cunningham, Mason-MacFarlane, and a whole bevy of lesser officials were there. Eisenhower and Badoglio stiffly shook hands and signed the long terms.

Then Eisenhower handed Badoglio a letter which said, in effect, that the terms of the agreement they had just signed were already out of date and could be disregarded. "They are based," Eisenhower said, "upon the situation obtaining prior to the cessation of hostilities. Developments since that time have altered considerably the status of Italy, which has become in effect a co-operator with the United Nations." Eisenhower continued that his governments "fully recognized . . . that these terms are in some respect superseded by subsequent events and that several of the clauses have become obsolescent. . . ."[42] It was, most agreed, a strange form of unconditional surrender. Some wondered why they bothered to sign the terms at all.

A conference followed. Badoglio said that if the title of the document he had just signed ("Instrument of Surrender of Italy") and the first clause, which contained the phrase "surrender unconditionally," became known, his government would be "overwhelmed by a storm of reproach and he would be forced to resign. . . ." Eisenhower promised to use his strongest efforts to get it changed, and said if he could not he would keep the whole thing confidential. He was as good as his word, sending a recommendation the next day to the CCS that the title be changed to read "Additional Conditions of the Armistice with Italy," and that the phrase "surrender unconditionally" be omitted.[43] After a week's discussion the heads of government agreed.

The wording settled, Eisenhower turned to other matters. He asked Badoglio if the government could promptly be given a definitely anti-Fascist character. Badoglio avoided a direct answer, even when Eisenhower made it clear that the government would have to adopt an anti-Fascist complexion before it could join the Allies in combat. Eisenhower asked when the declaration of war would be made. Badoglio wanted to make it as soon as the Italian government returned to Rome. Eisenhower said he wanted it right away and would be willing to turn over the administration of Sicily to Badoglio as soon as the Italians declared war on Germany. Badoglio lamely replied that only the King could declare war.

It then became Badoglio's turn to ask the direct questions and Eisenhower's to be evasive. Badoglio wanted to be initiated into Allied plans and requested that Italian troops participate in the entry into Rome. Eisenhower said he would see what could be done. The two soldiers exchanged pleasantries, promised continued co-operation, remarked on how pleased they were with the outcome of the conference, and separated. Two weeks later the Italians, expecting the Allies to be in Rome shortly, declared war on Germany.[44]

Eisenhower had carried out his orders—to knock Italy out of the war—and through his careful handling of the negotiations achieved even more, since Italy was now a partner. He had not, however, occupied Italy.

He was well aware of the limitations of his achievement. "The King-Badoglio government is a pretty weak affair," he confessed to Dill on September 30, "yet it is the only medium through which Italians can be inspired to help us. . . ." On the by now far more important point of German resistance, Eisenhower was optimistic. "We are getting along," he said, "and in my opinion will be in Rome" before the end of October.[45] The test would come on the battlefield. Eisenhower's troops were in Naples, restoring the port and building in strength. AFHQ's forces were poised for the dash to Rome.

CHAPTER 20

Stalemate in Italy

"The long drawn out and exhaustive campaign [in Italy] may be divided into three stages: (1) The reasonable, to the capture of Naples and Foggia. (2) The political, to the occupation of Rome. (3) The daft, from the occupation of Rome onwards."[1]

By early October 1943, AFHQ had achieved the objectives set for it in Italy. The country itself had left the Axis and joined the Allies. The Germans had evacuated Sardinia and Corsica. The Allies occupied Naples, and American engineers soon had it in workable order. The capture of Foggia gave the Allies excellent airfields from which they could carry out strategic bombing raids against Germany. The Germans had put twenty-four divisions into Italy, including some crack Panzer and Panzer Grenadier divisions, which would be sorely missed on other fronts, so AFHQ was in addition tying down German forces. From a strategic point of view, there was nothing more of substance to be gained in Italy and it was time to call a halt to operations there.

From a tactical point of view a further offensive also seemed ill advised. The hundred miles between the Volturno River (which Clark reached on October 12) and Rome was a maze of jumbled mountains cut by swift streams that ran east and west, across the Allied line of advance. The country was ideally suited for defensive warfare and Eisenhower had no divisions trained for mountain operations. The fall was the wettest season in Italy, with coastal areas flooded and the mountain streams running in torrents. Although Cunningham's ships controlled the seas, the absence of landing craft made it difficult for the Allies to exploit this advantage through amphibious end runs. Finally, the best American and

British divisions in the Mediterranean were scheduled to go to England
for OVERLORD.[2]

Despite the limitation, Eisenhower and his deputies wanted to press on
in Italy. The doctrine and tradition of the Anglo-American armies emphasized the importance of the offensive. Rome beckoned. Its political
significance was tempting, and it had airfields around it that Tedder
could use. Intelligence reported that the Germans were prepared to pull
back north of Rome anyway, and Eisenhower could not afford to leave a
no man's land between his forces and the Germans, as that would allow
Von Kesselring to shift divisions to other theaters or mount a counterattack. Thus even with his limited forces and the adverse conditions,
Eisenhower decided to drive on.

The week Naples fell, Eisenhower was made painfully aware of just
how limited his forces were. The lesson had its origins in plans made in
August by the British commanders in chief in the Middle East. General
Henry Maitland Wilson, the Army commander in the Middle East, popu-
larly called "Jumbo" because of his enormous bulk, large, bald head, and
bushy mustache, wanted to make an assault on Rhodes. The island
was the largest and most strategically significant in the Dodecanese and
was occupied by the Italians. Wilson had been unable to mount the
operation because of inadequate forces, however, and when Italy switched
sides the Germans quickly overpowered the Italians on Rhodes and reinforced their garrison there. Unable to capture the main island, on September 14 the British landed small parties on Cos, Samos, Leros, and
still lesser islands. Wilson's forces were so limited, however, that on none
of the islands did he have enough strength to withstand a determined
German attack.

On September 26 Churchill took up the subject with Eisenhower. The
Prime Minister wanted AFHQ to send additional troops to the Middle
East, some to reinforce Leros and Cos and others to participate in an
attack on Rhodes. He said Rhodes was the key to both the Aegean and
the eastern Mediterranean and thought it was worth one tenth of the
total Allied effort in the Mediterranean. Another tenth should go to the
Adriatic, with the remaining four fifths to be used in Italy. Churchill
assured Eisenhower both that Rhodes would fall easily and that it was
important, because of its airfields and because Allied possession of the
island might bring Turkey into the war.[3] Eisenhower had not had time
to study the implications but he did not want to dampen Churchill's enthusiasm. He made his reply noncommittal but nevertheless hopeful.

AFHQ was examining its resources, he said, and "we feel sure that we can meet minimum requirements of Mideast."[4]

Eisenhower now found himself in the same position vis-à-vis Wilson as Devers earlier had been vis-à-vis AFHQ. The most immediate help Eisenhower could give was through air power, but Tedder did not want to take his bombers away from the Italian campaign. Nor did Eisenhower want him to, but when Wilson reported on October 3 that German bombers based in Greece were pounding his men on Leros and Cos, the commander in chief decided he had to act. One reason for Eisenhower's decision was additional pressure from Churchill, who wired on October 3 to say he was much concerned about Cos, since the airfield there was necessary to provide fighter cover for an invasion of Rhodes. The Prime Minister wanted to be assured "you will do all in your power to prevent a vexatious injury to future plans occurring through its [Cos's] loss."[5] Eisenhower sent bombers and P-38s from Twelfth Air Force against German airfields in Greece, Crete, and the Dodecanese on raids that spanned a four-day period.[6]

Tedder was unhappy, not so much about the temporary diversion as its implications, especially since Wilson now demanded more. On October 4 he received a request from Wilson asking for air support for ACCOLADE (code name for the Rhodes operations). Tedder told Eisenhower that it was impossible to help and he protested against Wilson's having planned an operation without consulting with the people who would have to supply the material. Tedder needed all the aircraft he could get for Italian operations and told the air commander in the Middle East that the procedure by which the Mideast commanders "launch operations without full consultation with me and Eisenhower is, I feel, most dangerous."[7]

Eisenhower told Tedder not to worry. He would not make any commitments to ACCOLADE beyond bombing German airfields in Greece, which helped the forces in Italy anyway. "All our experience has shown that when the land forces undertake a major move," Eisenhower said, "a period of most intensive work devolves upon the air force," and since the push to Rome was about to begin, Eisenhower wanted Tedder's forces available for use in Italy.[8]

Immediately after Eisenhower completed his message to Tedder, two telegrams from Wilson came in. Wilson reported that the Germans were counterattacking in the Dodecanese and Cos would fall within a matter of hours, with Leros sure to follow soon after. He wanted immediate air and sea assistance that would enable him to hold Leros until Rhodes was attacked and captured, from which island he could then provide adequate air facilities for his forces in the Middle East.[9] Eisenhower talked with General John Whiteley of the AFHQ staff and some Mideast representatives who were in Algiers and then had Whiteley draft a reply. Whiteley said AFHQ was afraid of a continuing drain on its resources and could not justify such a commitment.[10]

Churchill saw the message and was much distressed. He communicated directly with Eisenhower, stressing the importance of the Aegean, both in itself and in relation to Italy, and asked Eisenhower to approve the diversion of a division to Mideast, along with ships and planes, to insure the capture of Rhodes. He contended that the diversion that would be forced upon the enemy would be greater than that Eisenhower would have to produce, and added that an operation against Rhodes would give the Allies an opportunity to engage and wear down the enemy's air power in a new region. It might even bring Turkey into the war.[11]

Eisenhower handled the whole thing with the utmost care, since the tone of Churchill's messages indicated that he was clearly upset and since reports from London implied that he was almost in a frenzy. An offensive, once started, would generate its own momentum, and Churchill, always expansive in his thinking, had already projected operations beyond Rhodes into the Balkans, with the Allies moving on the left flank and the Turks on the right. What Churchill sometimes spoke of as Germany's soft underbelly would fall into Allied hands and perhaps there would not be any need for OVERLORD and an expensive campaign in northern France. "He seemed always to see great and decisive possibilities in the Mediterranean," Eisenhower later recalled, "while the project of invasion across the English Channel left him cold." Churchill had often said, in speaking of OVERLORD, "We must take care that the tides do not run red with the blood of American and British youth, or the beaches be choked with their bodies." Eisenhower thought there were two additional reasons for Churchill's advocacy of attack on Rhodes; the first was his desire to have a strong political position in the Balkans after the war, and the second was to vindicate the disastrous World War I campaign at Gallipoli.[12]

Whatever Churchill's motives,* it was obvious that he regarded Rhodes as an issue of primary importance, and Eisenhower thus had to treat it as such. He called for a full-scale meeting between all the senior AFHQ officers and the commanders in chief, Middle East, to be held

---

* Sir Ian Jacob maintains that Churchill's main motive was to open a supply line to Russia by bringing Turkey into the war. Jacob to author, October 15, 1968, author's possession.

on October 9 in Tunis. The whole issue could be thrashed out then. What had begun as a fairly small affair in a fairly remote corner of the war had blown up into a strategic situation requiring a major decision. To American eyes it was "scatteration" all over again, with the British wanting to open up a new theater and move even farther eastward in the Mediterranean.[13] But in fact it was only the British in London and in the Middle East who wanted to move in that direction; not a single British member of AFHQ supported ACCOLADE.

Churchill however certainly did, and Eisenhower gave his views full consideration. On October 7, Eisenhower informed Marshall of the coming conference at Tunis and asked for guidance from the War Department. His own view, he said, was that the greatest contribution AFHQ could make to OVERLORD was through a fall and winter offensive that would carry the Allies into northern Italy. From there they could attack the south of France in the spring of 1944 as a diversion for OVERLORD. To reach northern Italy, however, Eisenhower needed all his resources and could spare none for ACCOLADE.[14] If OVERLORD retained priority, in short, there was nothing to argue about—ACCOLADE should be canceled. If there were new priorities or a shift in world-wide strategy, Eisenhower wanted to be informed, and he requested a new directive.

Marshall talked with Roosevelt, who had also been subjected to Churchill's pressure for ACCOLADE, and they agreed that Eisenhower was right—no diversion should be made. Roosevelt cabled this conclusion to Churchill, with a copy to Eisenhower.[15] Not satisfied, Churchill contacted the President again, repeated his strategic arguments, and said he was willing to come with the BCOS to Eisenhower's headquarters to discuss plans with Eisenhower and Marshall, whom Roosevelt should send over for the conference. The President thought that such a trip was unnecessary and by transatlantic telephone Hopkins informed the Prime Minister that there was little chance of Marshall's coming to such a meeting. Tedder meanwhile expressed the view to Portal that a visit from Churchill was "most dangerous and might have a disastrous effect on Anglo-American relations."[16]

The next day, October 8, an intelligence discovery made the whole issue academic. G-2 reported that the Germans had moved three additional divisions that were in Italy south of Rome. It suddenly became obvious that Von Kesselring intended to make the campaign a real fight, and the Allies would have to pay a high price to take Rome.[17] Churchill's assumption that Rome would be won cheaply and that the Allies could afford the diversion to the Aegean was shattered. Still, the Prime Minister was not willing to give up, even though his commanders in the Middle East had departed from his view.

The meeting at Tunis on October 9 was, Eisenhower later recalled, "the simplest, most unargumentative of any . . . I attended during the war." Eisenhower outlined the situation and announced his decision, which was to make no diversion for ACCOLADE. Every officer present, including Wilson, agreed.[18] Churchill, however, deserved and would demand a complete explanation, so after the meeting Eisenhower dictated a two-part, six-page, single-spaced report for the CCS that could be handed to the Prime Minister. He concluded by saying that ACCOLADE could be re-examined after Rome was captured.[19] Then he sent a special, personal message to Churchill in which he stressed that his decision had been unanimously supported by all the commanders in chief from both theaters, all of whom were British. "It is personally distressing to me to have to advise against a project in which you believe so earnestly," Eisenhower concluded, "but I feel I would not be performing my duty if I should recommend otherwise."[20]

Churchill however was not ready to give up his favored plan. He asked if the decision had been affected by Roosevelt's view that no diversion should be made; Eisenhower said it had not. To back up Eisenhower the British officers present at the meeting all sent their own cables to the Prime Minister, assuring him that they had examined the possibilities of ACCOLADE fully, fairly, and without prejudice and agreed with Eisenhower. Churchill finally conceded the issue, but not gracefully. In a long cable to the President he said he recognized that the activation of his plan was hopeless, and added, "I will not waste words in explaining how painful this decision is to me." Years later he was still bitter. "The American Staff had enforced their view," he wrote in his memoirs; "the price had now to be paid by the British."[21]

What Churchill meant was the immediate price in lives lost on Leros. But Eisenhower could have answered, with justice, that both British and American troops in Italy were suffering heavy losses, losses which would have been even higher without the air forces. The mountain fighting had become slow, tedious, and bloody. The Germans were amazingly proficient with demolitions, mines, and booby traps. The Allies had respected their opponent's tactical performance in Sicily; in Italy, they almost stood in awe of Von Kesselring's and his men's abilities. In one sense Eisenhower could congratulate himself on his own performance in the new role of commander of a secondary theater, because he certainly was attaining his main objective: to threaten the enemy and force him to make a relatively heavier commitment to the battle than AFHQ had to make. By mid-October Eisenhower's eleven divisions were engaging twenty-five German divisions, but the final offensive would have to wait until spring, when AFHQ could use its air superiority effectively. That meant a winter campaign in Italy, with carefully planned minor offensives that would seemingly have every chance of success.[22]

But under the circumstances progress was exasperatingly slow. Because Von Kesselring needed time to get his Winter Line constructed, he ordered the Volturno River held until October 15. Fifth and Eighth Armies pushed forward in bitter fighting but they did not reach the Volturno until October 12. That night Clark sent each of his corps on a frontal assault with three divisions abreast. He gained some bridgeheads, but German artillery firing from high ground north of the Volturno delayed the construction or repair of bridges, and not until October 15 did Fifth Army make any real progress. From the fifteenth on, the Germans gradually fell back from one natural strong point to another, until they reached the Winter Line, which ran along the Garigliano River on the west across the high ground south of the Sangro River on the east. Tedder's air forces proceeded to make the winter difficult but not impossible for the defenders, the chief limiting factor on air operations being the weather.

Obviously an inferior force was going to have difficulty pushing back a superior one that was skilled in defensive operations, especially along a narrow peninsula cut by mountains and rivers. Eisenhower's advantages over Von Kesselring were command of the air and sea, but bad weather prevented effective use of the air and a lack of landing craft limited the advantage of control of the sea. The apparent way to defeat the Germans was seemingly to outflank them, force them out of their prepared positions, and hit them while they were on the move. Along the Winter Line, however, Von Kesselring was so strong that there was no possibility of forcing a breakthrough which was needed to create flanks. An amphibious operation was the only answer.

The trouble was that, again, the landing craft were not available. At Quebec the CCS had decided to concentrate the craft in England in preparation for OVERLORD and ordered Eisenhower to send eighty per cent of his LSTs and LSIs and two thirds of the remaining landing craft in the Mediterranean to the U.K. between the middle of October and early December. Eisenhower protested, to no avail. But after the capture of Foggia he decided the CCS had been right—OVERLORD should have priority. He told Alexander he did not intend to bother the CCS with any more requests for landing craft for Italy.

Alexander had accepted Eisenhower's view, but he had done so during the period when the Allies were sure they would get Rome without a major fight. The situation brought about by Von Kesselring's decision to stand on the Winter Line changed the entire situation. On October 13 Alexander told Eisenhower that, while he was aware "you have decided to accept Combined Chiefs of Staff decision," it was his duty to point out that the shortage of landing craft "will force us into frontal attacks which will undoubtedly be strongly contested and prove costly." Eisenhower passed Alexander's views on to Smith, who had gone to Washington to confer with Marshall about future strategy, and commented, "I refuse to raise again with the Combined Chiefs of Staff this question . . . but you might make personal inquiries to discover whether the production situation has improved sufficiently to warrant our asking for more."[23] Smith replied that the production situation had not improved, "but all concerned are aware of the great advantages that would accrue to us through additional equipment of this kind."[24] It emerged that the only way AFHQ could get landing craft support was by delaying departure of the vessels scheduled to go to England, and Eisenhower did not want to request such a delay since he knew it would have an adverse effect on OVERLORD.

On October 21 Eisenhower had a Commanders' Conference. Alexander held the floor, giving a full review of the battle situation and making his recommendations for the future. He argued persuasively for the retention of some landing craft for a month or so and convinced Eisenhower and his fellow deputies that the request had to be made. Alexander's main point was that the most help AFHQ could give OVERLOAD would be to retain the initiative in Italy and prevent Von Kesselring from withdrawing divisions from the area, divisions which could be used to oppose OVERLORD. In view of the two-to-one German manpower superiority on the ground, there was a certain danger in this, as Von Kesselring might change his program to an offensive. Eisenhower was not particularly worried about that possibility, however, because of his faith in the air forces, and Alexander pointed out that if Von Kesselring did attack "the better it will be for OVERLORD and it then makes little difference what happens to us if OVERLORD is a success."

To retain the needed initiative, Alexander proposed a three-pronged thrust. He would begin by having Montgomery seize the high ground north of the Pescara River, then turn to his left (southwest) and drive up the valley of the Pescara River, threatening Rome from the rear. To give Montgomery a fair chance of success, Alexander wanted a sea-borne attack by an infantry brigade around the Germans' east flank. Thus, while Montgomery was moving forward, Alexander wanted Clark to launch a frontal attack aimed at Rome. The third prong of the offensive would be an amphibious attack by an infantry division northwest of Rome. The crucial governing factor in the entire proposal, Alexander recognized, was landing craft. He urged Eisenhower to ask the CCS for a delay in the movement of the craft to the U.K., saying it simply had to be permitted "if we are to capture Rome in the near future and avoid a slow, painful and costly series of frontal attacks."[25]

Eisenhower thought about Alexander's proposal for a week, then discussed it again with his deputies at another Commanders' Conference. He finally decided that Alexander was right. On October 31 he asked the CCS to be allowed to retain some sixty-eight LSTs until January 5, or three weeks beyond their scheduled departure date. He said he was certain that a favorable decision from the CCS would lead to success in Italy, "which will have a great effect on OVERLORD." He was reluctant to make the request, "but the enormous value to us of being able to use these additional LST's for a comparatively short period . . . is so impressive from our local viewpoint . . ." that he felt he had to do it.[26]

Churchill and the BCOS supported Eisenhower and Marshall gave in. On November 5 the CCS told Eisenhower that he could retain sixty-eight LSTs until December 15. Eisenhower immediately protested that the December deadline still made effective amphibious assaults difficult, and Alexander made a similar protest to Brooke.[27] On November 7 Brooke privately told Alexander to plan on the assumption that the LSTs would remain until January 15. Brooke, however, had no authority to make any promises. Eisenhower meanwhile had talked to Clark, who wanted to lower the sights a little. Instead of an amphibious landing north of Rome, Clark thought it ought to be to the south, around Anzio. From that point the troops could drive inland and take the Alban Hills, which dominated the surrounding countryside and would cut Von Kesselring's communications between Rome and the front lines. If everything worked, the Allies might even cut off and destroy the Germans facing Fifth Army. Clark also felt there was no point in launching the attack on Anzio until Fifth Army was farther north. Eisenhower agreed with him and adjusted the plan accordingly.

Everything still hinged on availability of landing craft. "The situation appears to me to hang in the balance," Eisenhower told the CCS, in asking once again to be allowed to keep the LSTs until January. "Naturally I do *not* wish to interfere with the preparations for OVERLORD but I have felt it my duty to lay before you my requirements, leaving it to you to judge the priorities."[28]

Until the CCS said otherwise, however, Eisenhower had to proceed on the assumption that the orders stood and that the LSTs would sail for England in mid-December. On November 9 he told Alexander that although he had sought in every possible way "to avoid a mere slugging match along a wide front," he had come to the conclusion that Alexander should try to build up Fifth and Eighth Armies "while depending upon our air forces to make the enemy's maintenance more and more difficult." Small end runs might be possible, and Alexander should keep the possibility of a stronger sea-borne operation in mind, "but for the present it would seem to be more advantageous to continue an intensive buildup than to set aside craft hoping to make an attack by a reinforced division."[29] The next day Eisenhower learned that the CCS would be meeting in two weeks at Cairo and that he and his deputies would be going there to testify. The whole question of world-wide strategy could be reviewed; as a part of the review, of course, the CCS would deal with AFHQ's request for help in landing craft. Eisenhower thought a verbal presentation of AFHQ's case "by far the best way of raising the question again," and so advised Alexander.[30]

The Anzio operation, in short, was still uncertain. Alexander meanwhile took Eisenhower's advice and decided to start the first two thrusts in his over-all plan. On November 20 Eighth Army opened its offensive. Montgomery quickly established some small bridgeheads on the north bank of the Sangro River, but then torrential rains held him up for a week. Not until December 2 was his whole army across the Sangro. Then both the rains and German resistance increased. Ammunition resupply in the mountains became difficult, casualties mounted, tanks and artillery bogged down in the mud. Montgomery had few reserves, so when his men did win small local victories he could not exploit them. The weather prevented the air forces from helping. In mid-December Montgomery called off the offensive. The Pescara, which Alexander had hoped to reach in late November, was not crossed until June of 1944.[31] Clark's offensive, which began on December 1, ran into similar difficulties. Eisenhower made a series of trips to the front, inspected the positions, talked to officers and men, brought in what supplies he could, but was unable to get the offensive rolling. Von Kesselring had imposed a stalemate.

The relative inactivity on the Italian front allowed Eisenhower to catch up on other matters, including his personal correspondence. He even managed to take a full day off and go partridge hunting with Smith. He had to do a great deal of entertaining, as VIPs poured into Algiers. In October alone Secretary of the Navy Frank Knox, Donald Nelson, chairman of the War Production Board, James Landis, director of the Office of Civilian Defense, Secretary of the Treasury Henry Morgenthau, Secretary Hull, W. Averell Harriman, ambassador to the U.S.S.R., Mountbatten, Field Marshal Smuts, and others passed through Algiers. Eisenhower grumbled about it, but managed to have at least one meal with each of them. He did feign illness in order to avoid having to dine with a group of touring senators.[32]

He decided that one way to escape the VIPs was to move his headquarters closer to the front lines. He wanted to keep AFHQ on the march anyway, because he did not want the staff digging in at one location, particularly in a large, comfortable city like Algiers. The staff did not get its required work done when the officers had comfortable billets and social obligations, and the troops resented it when they saw staff officers living in splendor. Eisenhower told Smith to set up an advanced headquarters at Naples and to be prepared to move the AFHQ headquarters there when it was captured. It took more than a month to arrange the move, and when it did come it accomplished none of Eisenhower's purposes. Smith had picked a sumptuous villa for himself, Butcher had found another for Eisenhower (Prince Umberto's hunting lodge), and other officers had equally palatial billets. Headquarters itself was the Caserta Palace north of Naples. Eisenhower's office was a room large enough to serve as a railway station. He protested, in vain. A conqueror's complex had settled on the staff, and the members insisted on living in accordance with their rights.[33]

One officer who could not enjoy the fruits of victory in this manner was Admiral Cunningham. Churchill had selected him to replace Pound, who was ill, as First Sea Lord. The admiral was due to leave Algiers on October 17; Eisenhower arranged a ceremony for him, complete with a band playing "Rule Britannia." As Cunningham's plane took off, Eisenhower had a member of the crew hand a letter to the admiral. "It is a sad day for the North African Theater that sees you leave us," Eisenhower wrote. Every man in AFHQ had come to look on Cunningham "as one of the solid foundation rocks upon which has been built such success as we have achieved." The real purpose of the letter, however, was to give Eisenhower an opportunity to express his personal "profound sense of loss" at Cunningham's departure. He thanked the admiral for his unfailing support, his wise counsel, and his brilliant leadership, and wished him "good luck and Godspeed."[34]

After the ceremony Eisenhower returned to the St. Georges Hotel. There he found a letter for him from Cunningham, thanking him for all he had done. Two weeks later Cunningham wrote again. He told Eisenhower it had been a great experience for him to see the forces of two nations, made up of men with different upbringings, conflicting ideas on staff work and basic "apparently irreconcilable ideas," brought together and knitted into a team.

In a final tribute, Cunningham declared: "I do not believe any other man than yourself could have done it."[35]

CHAPTER 21

The Big Appointment

By September 1943 it was clear that Operation OVERLORD was to be one of the largest military undertakings in man's history. For eight months nearly all human and material resources of two great nations would be directed toward the one objective of mounting an amphibious assault on a small bit of the coast of western France. OVERLORD's needs came before all else, as Eisenhower and the other commanders in the Mediterranean, as well as the Allied leaders in the Pacific and elsewhere, were discovering. From July 1943 onward, Eisenhower geared his operations to the question, Will this help or hinder OVERLORD?

Command of OVERLORD was the most coveted in the war, perhaps in all history. The commander would have tremendous forces at his disposal. His fighting men would be highly trained and magnificently equipped. He could call on all the mighty air and sea power the Allies had. The field commanders would be the best the U.S. and the U.K. had to offer. To serve him on his staff, the Supreme Commander could pick the most talented men available. If the operation was a success he could take much of the credit for the defeat of Nazi Germany and would go down in history as one of the great captains. No reward would be too great for the commander of OVERLORD.

Fittingly, the story of the selection of the commander is one of high purpose, resolve, and thoughtful consideration. It involved little intrigue or back-door Army politics. In theory, the choice of the commander rested with the CCS, but in fact, since members of the CCS were candidates, the Chiefs deferred to the heads of government. Churchill in turn bowed to Roosevelt, since the Americans would ultimately be making twice the commitment in men and material as the British. So it came down to Roosevelt, a man who had the reputation of often being haphazard in his administrative arrangements and remarkably casual in picking his top officials.

One favorite Roosevelt technique of decision-making was to leak a story to the press and then gauge the reaction. The obvious choice for the position was Marshall. He had been the force behind OVERLORD, the one responsible for its birth, the one who insisted upon its importance all along. In early September 1943 stories began to appear in American newspapers stating that his appointment as OVERLORD commander had been decided upon. Many commentators took this as a matter of course, but two important objections did appear. First, political opponents of the President charged that he was trying to replace Marshall as Chief of Staff with a political general who would manipulate the awarding of war contracts in such a way as to insure Roosevelt's re-election. The criticism was so widespread that Stimson and Marshall felt it necessary to issue a public denial. Second, professional armed forces journals, along with Marshall's colleagues on the JCS, objected to Marshall's going to OVER-LORD because they wanted him to retain his position in the Army and on the CCS. Roosevelt listened to the criticisms and kept his own counsel.[1]

Rumors of Marshall's prospective appointment arrived in North Africa during the critical week at Salerno. On September 16, after the crisis was passed, Eisenhower chatted with Butcher and Smith at breakfast about it. According to the American press, Eisenhower would replace Marshall as the Army Chief of Staff. The prospect made him unhappy. If it happened, he said, he would be forced to tell the President that it was a "tremendous mistake," for he was "not temperamentally fitted for the job." He feared it would destroy him. Eisenhower pointed out that he had no patience with politicians because he could not bear to continue an argument "after logic had made the opposition's position untenable, yet politicians persist against all logic."

Eisenhower's personal preference was to remain in the Mediterranean. If he had to leave, he said, there would immediately arise a problem of command in the Mediterranean. He thought his British deputies would insist on working under an American, since none of them would be willing to serve under a colleague. Each felt that because his service was represented by a ministry in the War Cabinet he should not be in an inferior position, yet each worked "superbly" under Eisenhower. The commander in chief thought the only American who could pick up the reins was Smith, but this would require promoting Smith to full general. Such a rapid advance "would throw out of joint the noses of other and more senior American generals," particularly Bradley and Patton. Smith said he did not want the job anyway, since his own desire was to serve out the war under Eisenhower.

Eisenhower offered a solution for the problem. Marshall could become the global field commander for all American forces and set up a staff in London to run his European Theater, with a field commander under him who would be responsible for the attack. When he had the European Theater properly organized, he could go to Hawaii to do the same thing in the Pacific. Back in Washington he could leave a deputy chief of staff, probably Somervell, to handle supply and administration problems. The proposal had little to recommend it beyond simplicity, since it involved no basic change in the existing structure. It did, however, open the way for Eisenhower to go to London and stay out of Washington. He could be the field commander of OVERLORD while Marshall would have the title of Supreme Commander. But with his continuing world-wide responsibilities, clearly Marshall would leave the conduct of operations to Eisenhower.

There was an even simpler solution. Butcher told Eisenhower that in his opinion "You are the logical and inevitable choice for the European command." Eisenhower liked the idea but thought it impossible. He felt the obvious choice for OVERLORD was either Brooke or Marshall, since they had been dealing on the highest level with the heads of government and would be less subject to harassment from officials in London. He thought the best he could realistically hope for was a solution which would allow him to remain in the Mediterranean, where he was relatively free from interference.[2]

In the first week of October, AFHQ began to fill with rumors on what was being decided and with stories about what had been done. Mountbatten paid a visit to Algiers and told Eisenhower that Brooke had been scheduled to take OVERLORD but Harry Hopkins had insisted on Marshall. Brooke had been working on the assault plans for three months, but since the Americans were going to make the larger contribution to the operation he had agreed to step aside. Churchill and the BCOS had also gone along, although Mountbatten reported that they felt "badly hurt." Cunningham confirmed Mountbatten's version. He also said that because Brooke had been "on the job it was impossible for anyone on a lesser level to be considered. This automatically threw out Ike."[3] Eisenhower meanwhile had no official word on his future, except that he had recognized that if Marshall took command of OVERLORD it was politically necessary to give the Mediterranean to a British officer in order to retain balance. A suitable post would then have to be found for Eisenhower. On October 1 a visiting VIP, Secretary of the Navy Frank Knox, covered that problem during lunch with Eisenhower at Amilcar. The Secretary reported that Marshall had been named to OVERLORD and it was "probable" that Eisenhower would be recalled to Washington to be Chief of Staff.[4]

Eisenhower was anxious to avoid such a fate. If he had to leave the Mediterranean, the job he wanted was command of an American group of armies under Marshall in OVERLORD. He had already decided to send Smith to Washington to confer with Marshall on AFHQ plans and future operations, and now he gave Smith the additional responsibility of finding out about his future. Under no circumstances, Eisenhower told Smith, was he to raise the subject, but if Marshall brought it up he wanted Smith to make clear to the Chief that his personal desire was to command in the field. Even if Marshall did not bring up Eisenhower's future, he "naturally hoped that Beetle would find the lay of the land."[5]

Before Smith left on October 5, Eisenhower gave him a detailed memorandum on points to take up with Marshall. Most of them concerned AFHQ problems, but Eisenhower did cover one that involved OVERLORD. He told Smith to discuss, "most secretly," the need Marshall would have in his new job for a top airman "who is thoroughly schooled in all the phases of strategic bombing and more particularly in the *job of supporting ground armies in the field.*" Eisenhower had experience in the field in World War II, and Marshall had not—thus Eisenhower felt qualified to give some advice, especially since, from that experience, he had "earnest convictions" on the matter. The great danger was getting an air commander who was totally wedded to the concept of strategic bombing or one without experience in the problem of air-ground co-ordination. Before and during the assault Marshall would need every plane he could get, but without the proper man at the top he would find that the airmen were scattering their effort on strategic raids inside Germany, making no direct contribution to the battle for the beachhead.

Eisenhower told Smith, "I seriously recommend he [Marshall] insist upon getting Air Chief Marshal Tedder" for his air commander. Eisenhower would hate to lose Tedder in the Mediterranean, but he thought the AFHQ team had developed to the point where he could afford to let Tedder go. Tedder was ideal for the OVERLORD job for two reasons. First, he was an expert in air-ground co-ordination. Second, he had the complete confidence of Chief of Air Staff Portal, which meant that "during critical junctures of the land campaign" Tedder could call on Portal for "every last airplane in England" for support. Tedder was a warm personal friend as well as an outstanding officer, Eisenhower said, "but I am ready to make this sacrifice in favor of a solution that I believe will be of the utmost advantage to the General."[6]

Eisenhower was anxious to share other lessons he had learned with Marshall. He did not presume to tell the Chief how to organize or train his forces, but he did feel that his comments on individuals would be helpful. Eisenhower knew that Marshall intended to have at least two American armies in the operation. Bradley had already been picked to lead one of them. Eisenhower suggested Patton for the other. "Many generals constantly think of battle in terms of, first, concentration, supply, maintenance, replacement, and, second, after all the above is arranged, a *conservative* advance," Eisenhower told Marshall, probably with Clark in mind. But he did add that "this type of person is necessary because he prevents one from courting disaster." Marshall's idea was to hit the beach with the untested divisions coming from the United States, holding back the experienced divisions until he was firmly ashore. The veterans would then lead the drive through the German defensive positions. Eisenhower recommended that he use Bradley to command the first wave, with Patton taking command of the veterans and leading the breakout.

"Patton's strength is that he thinks only in terms of attack as long as there is a single battalion that can keep advancing," Eisenhower declared. He would never consider Patton for an army group command, "but as an army commander under a man who is sound and solid, and who has sense enough to use Patton's good qualities without becoming blinded by his love of showmanship and histrionics, he should do as fine a job as he did in Sicily."[7] The implication was that Eisenhower was the army group commander who could handle Patton.

The pressure to get a commander for OVERLORD appointed, meanwhile, was mounting. The operation was scheduled for early May, only a half year away, and Lieutenant General Sir Frederick Morgan, head of the COSSAC planning group, insisted that a commander had to be named so that firm decisions could be made. On that main point, as far as AFHQ could tell from the stories told by visiting VIPs, Roosevelt's mind was made up. It would be Marshall. According to the reports, the President felt that Marshall should have the chance to command in the field the army he had created, for if he did not his name would be lost to history.

The repercussions of shifting Marshall, however, were far from settled. Averell Harriman, passing through Algiers on his way to Moscow, told Eisenhower that the President would insist on Eisenhower's coming back to Washington "to take over General Marshall's job." Secretary Stimson, it seemed, was a strong advocate of such a shift. Eisenhower still hoped for something better. He did not accept at face value the secondhand reports he was receiving and was anxious for Smith to return from Washington with the straight word from Marshall. On October 19 Butcher reported that they were still waiting for Smith and "sweating it out in big drops. This uncertainty takes the pep out of everyone. . . ."[8]

The opposition to removing Marshall from Washington, meanwhile, was growing. Admiral King told Roosevelt that the Chief was a great teammate and should stay where he was. The elder statesman of the Army, General John J. Pershing, warned the President in mid-September that the proposed transfer of the Chief would be a "fundamental and very grave error in our military policy." Marshall himself remained aloof from all the discussions. He never intimated to the President or to anyone else what his personal preference was.[9]

While Smith was gone and AFHQ marked time, another possibility for Eisenhower's future opened. With a presidential election a year away, Republicans and other opponents of Roosevelt had started casting about for a candidate. MacArthur was one obvious choice and a boom of sorts began to develop for him. Inevitably, Eisenhower's name also began to pop up. Arthur Eisenhower was bothered by this. He told his brother that MacArthur's reputation was suffering because he refused to deny that he had political ambitions, and urged Eisenhower to make an emphatic denial of his own ambitions. On October 20 Eisenhower told his brother he had seen some "careless and ill-considered items in the newspapers" about his supposed candidacy, but he felt this would happen to any man whose name "appears with some frequency in the public print." He felt no need to make "any statement whatsoever because to do so would, I think, merely be making myself ridiculous."

Eisenhower did admit, however, that it would be disastrous for him to have the idea spread that he was interested in politics. "I flatter myself that such a development would constitute also some small injury to our national war effort." He said he lived by one doctrine—to serve his country. The President had given him a responsible position, and "nothing could sway me from my purpose of carrying out faithfully his orders in whatever post he may assign me." In conclusion, Eisenhower declared he would "not tolerate the use of my name in connection with any political activity of any kind."[10]

Removing himself from the field was not that easy. In early October the World War Tank Corps Association passed a resolution supporting Eisenhower for the presidency. The members said they had no knowledge as to his political affiliations or beliefs but considered him presidential timber by virtue of his outstanding leadership qualities. A number of newspapers played up the story, and George Allen, an old friend, sent Eisenhower one clipping from the Washington *Post*. In a covering note, Allen asked, "How does it feel to be a presidential candidate?"

Eisenhower glanced at the clipping, grasped a pencil, and at the bottom of Allen's note scribbled, "Baloney! Why can't a simple soldier be left alone to carry out his orders? And I furiously object to the word 'candidate'—I ain't and won't."[11] Then Walter Winchell, in a radio broadcast, said that if the Republicans ran MacArthur, Roosevelt would take Eisenhower as his running mate on the Democratic ticket. Eisenhower's comment was short: "I can scarcely imagine anyone in the United States less qualified than I for any type of political work."[12] Lacking any encouragement at all from the prospective candidate, the Eisenhower boom quickly faded from the infinitesimal into total obscurity.

Smith, meanwhile, had returned from Washington, and Eisenhower could concentrate on the important matters at hand. He eagerly pumped his chief of staff for information, but the results were disappointing. Smith confirmed that Marshall was to go to OVERLORD, taking command on January 1. He had already called Morgan to Washington for planning conferences. Beyond that nothing had been settled. Eisenhower would be either the American army group commander for OVERLORD or Army Chief of Staff. Smith reported that Marshall was afraid that putting Eisenhower in charge of the army group would be a comedown and would look bad. Smith said he assured the Chief that no one at AFHQ, least of all Eisenhower, minded, but Marshall still felt that Eisenhower should become Chief of Staff. Smith had also had an interview with Roosevelt, who said he too wanted Eisenhower in Washington.[13]

That seemed to settle it. To console himself, Eisenhower said that he did not really want a command in OVERLORD anyway. He had studied Morgan's plans, which were based on a three-division assault. Morgan had been forced to limit the size of the attack because of the small number of landing craft the CCS had assigned to him. Under those circumstances, Eisenhower said, he was just as happy he would not be involved.[14]

But though the question of who would command OVERLORD was seemingly settled problems remained. One major remaining objection to Marshall's leaving Washington was that he would have to leave the CCS. This objection was later to prove a decisive one. It meant that the strongest advocate of OVERLORD would not be at the CCS meetings to force the British to keep their commitment to the cross-Channel attack. This appeared important because the British seemed to the Americans to be showing signs of wanting to back out. Their proposal to invade Rhodes and step up operations in the Balkans was only the most recent evidence of this desire. OPD and the War Department, therefore, wanted to give Marshall control of the operational forces in OVERLORD while allowing him to retain his seat on the CCS. This would give the Americans both ends of the stick, since they would have command of OVERLORD and still have the OVERLORD viewpoint fully represented in the CCS.[15] In one version of the plan, Marshall would command all United Nations forces in Europe and the Mediterranean and would sit as a voting member of the CCS whenever that body discussed European matters. The advantage of the proposal was that it would give Marshall a position commensurate with his rank and ability. For him to become a mere theater commander, albeit in charge of OVERLORD, would be a definite demotion.

From the start the British objected strenuously. The American scheme had the effect—probably unintended—of destroying the authority of the CCS. In the Pacific and in Asia the theater commanders were responsible to their respective chiefs of staff, not the CCS. Europe was the only theater in which the CCS had real authority. If Marshall took command of both Europe and the Mediterranean and in addition sat on the CCS, he would in fact make the CCS superfluous. The British pointed out that there were "immense political implications" in the American scheme and asked that the existing machinery for the high-level direction of the war be retained. Changes should be confined to improving the machinery rather than embarking "upon an entirely novel experiment, which merely makes a cumbrous and unnecessary link in the chain of command, and which will surely lead to disillusionment and disappointment."[16]

The implications were clear enough, although apparently neither Marshall, Roosevelt, nor the others involved saw them immediately. The Americans could not allow Marshall to step down to the level of theater commander, and the British could not allow him to stay on the CCS and in addition command in western Europe, Italy, North Africa, and the Middle East.[17] The only solution seemed to be to give command in western Europe to a man of lesser stature than Marshall.

At British insistence, the CCS and heads of government were about to meet again, first at Cairo and then with the Russians at Teheran. They would take up the vexing questions of command structure as well as a review of the strategy for 1944. The Americans were suspicious of British intentions, fearing that Churchill was trying to back out of OVERLORD. For Eisenhower and Smith these suspicions were increased as a result of a meeting with Churchill and the BCOS. On November 18 the AFHQ heads flew to Malta to confer with the British, who were en route to Cairo. Smith decided that the coming conference would be the "hottest one yet," as Churchill was still unconvinced about the wisdom of OVERLORD and persisted in his desire to strike Germany through the "soft underbelly." Churchill did say that if OVERLORD stayed on the agenda, with Eisenhower handing over the Mediterranean to a British theater commander and becoming Chief of Staff, he wanted Smith left with AFHQ to help the new boss there. Eisenhower said no—Smith would have to stay with him. He insisted that "this was one point on which I would not yield, except under directions from the President."[18]

Two days later, on Saturday, November 20, Eisenhower flew to Oran to meet the President and his party, also en route to Cairo. The American delegation had come via the battleship *Iowa*. After it docked, Eisenhower accompanied the President and his party to the airport and flew with them to Tunis, where Roosevelt was to spend two days. Eisenhower went on a motor trip with the President, inspecting battlefield sites, both recent and ancient, and had a long talk. Roosevelt shifted quickly from subject to subject and Eisenhower found him a fascinating conversationalist. At one point the President touched on OVERLORD. He said he dreaded the thought of losing Marshall in Washington, but added, "You and I know the name of the Chief of Staff in the Civil War, but few Americans outside the professional services do." Eisenhower confined his comments to saying he would do his best at whatever job Roosevelt gave him.[19]

Eisenhower had arranged for Marshall and Admiral King to stay at his cottage in Carthage, where he joined them before dinner. King began talking about OVERLORD. He said he had urgently and persistently advised Roosevelt to keep Marshall in Washington, but he had lost. "I hate to lose General Marshall as Chief of Staff," King told Eisenhower, "but my loss is consoled by the knowledge that I will have you to work in his job." Both Eisenhower and Marshall were embarrassed, but Eisenhower took King's statement as "almost official notice that I would soon be giving up field command to return to Washington."[20]

On the evening of November 21, Roosevelt, Marshall, King, and the remainder of the American delegation flew to Cairo. There they argued with the British about operations in 1944 and future command structure.

The Americans held out for the strongest cross-Channel attack possible, with an over-all commander for the forces of the Allies throughout Europe, the Mediterranean, and the Mideast. As had happened so often before, the British did not flatly reject OVERLORD; rather they wanted to center the discussion on increasing operations in the eastern Mediterranean. They did make it clear that they would never allow Marshall or any other American to have as much power as the JCS proposal envisioned.[21]

Eisenhower went to Cairo on November 24 to testify before the CCS on his theater. He talked briefly and to the point. The most important land objective in Italy, he contended, was the Po Valley, because land forces there threatened the Balkans, southern France, and even the Reich itself, while air forces in the Po were "closer to the vitals of the German industries." Eisenhower told the Chiefs that in order to get to the Po by spring he would need more assets than he had been given, but he warned that if the CCS were to provide the assets they would have to delay OVERLORD by sixty or ninety days. The CCS would have to make the decision. If the Chiefs gave him the material—especially landing craft—he could make a rapid descent upon the Dodecanese and destroy the German position in the Aegean Sea. This opened the question of Turkish entry into the war, a subject on which Eisenhower refused to make any statement "because I know nothing about it."

If the CCS decided that AFHQ would have to operate with its current assets, the Allies would have to content themselves with taking Rome and then establishing a defensive line in Italy. AFHQ could carry on active minor operations "but the general attitude would . . . be defensive." When Eisenhower concluded the Chiefs asked him a number of questions about the situation in Italy. His answers were straightforward. He again refused to be drawn into a discussion about Turkey, and especially would not comment on the political desirability of bringing Turkey into the war.

In response to a question from Brooke, Eisenhower stressed the vital importance of continuing the maximum possible operations in an established theater. Much valuable time was invariably lost, he said, when the scene of action was changed, for it necessitated the arduous task of building up from a fresh base. He also constantly emphasized that what AFHQ needed was landing craft, not more men. He could barely maintain the number of divisions he had now in Italy and there was no good port north of Naples until Leghorn was reached. But he did need landing craft, both to bring in supplies on open beaches and to mount amphibious operations.

Brooke also wanted to know what AFHQ was doing to support the Yugoslavian guerrillas. Eisenhower said he had put an officer in charge of supplying equipment to them, and arms captured in North Africa and Sicily were being sent in. He felt that all available equipment should go to Tito, leader of the Communist guerrillas, since he was doing so much more to fight the Germans than Mihailovic, leader of the government-sponsored guerrillas. Mihailovic, in fact, was only interested in fighting Tito.[22]

The Chiefs were impressed with Eisenhower's presentation. He had demonstrated a firm grasp of the military situation, shown himself to be realistic about the possibilities, and in general added to the good impression he had previously made because of his conduct of affairs in the Mediterranean. All four of the American Chiefs had a high opinion of him in any case. On the British side, Ismay remained the good friend he had been during the summer of 1942; Portal respected Eisenhower and, more important, respected Tedder, who himself had nothing but praise for Eisenhower; and Cunningham was, after Marshall, Eisenhower's strongest supporter. That left Brooke, who had his doubts about Eisenhower's strategic sense but who did appreciate the way Eisenhower had made the alliance work in the Mediterranean.

Following Eisenhower's appearance before them, the Chiefs broke up the Cairo meeting. They had been unable to reach agreement on the major points, but it was time to move on to Teheran to confer with the Russians. The night before they left Marshall gave a huge dinner party. The menu included turkey, cranberry, stuffing, and all the trimmings. When one of the guests was leaving he said to Marshall, "Thank you very much for a fine Thanksgiving dinner." Eisenhower, astonished, turned and said, "Well, that shows what war does to a man. I had no idea this was Thanksgiving Day."[23] Marshall decided he had been working too hard and suggested that he take some time off. Eisenhower said he had too much work to do. Marshall made the suggestion an order. "Just let someone else run that war up there for a couple of days," the Chief said. "If your subordinates can't do it for you, you haven't organized them properly." So Eisenhower traveled briefly to Luxor, site of the ancient city of Thebes, and to Jerusalem and Bethlehem.[24]

At Teheran, meanwhile, Stalin was putting the pressure on the British and Americans. He made it clear that he wanted OVERLORD to be the largest possible operation, which had the effect of being the deciding vote in the Allied split on what to emphasize in 1944. He then asked who was going to command OVERLORD. When told that no one had been appointed, Stalin said he could not believe the British and Americans were serious about the operation. Nothing would come of it, he believed, until a commander was appointed. Roosevelt whispered to Leahy, "That old Bolshevik is trying to force me to give him the name of our Supreme Commander. I just can't tell him because I have not yet made up my mind."[25] Churchill informed Stalin that the British had indicated their willingness to serve under an American, but the selection could not be made until other decisions had been reached. What the Prime Minister had in mind was the power of the OVERLORD commander—the British remained unwilling to allow him to sit on the CCS and have command of areas outside western Europe. Roosevelt told Stalin that he would make the selection in three or four days.[26] The Western Allies then returned to Cairo to continue their conference.

Sometime between the end of the Teheran meeting and the beginning of the second Cairo conference, the Americans dropped their proposal to appoint an over-all commander for all Allied forces fighting Germany. In so doing they were merely recognizing that they could never get British agreement to such a command arrangement. This put tremendous institutional pressure on Roosevelt to by-pass Marshall. Most accounts of the President's decision to deny Marshall the OVERLORD command emphasize the personal side, the most famous and frequently quoted statement being Roosevelt's remark that he could not sleep at night with George Marshall out of the country. The implication is that Marshall did not get OVERLORD because he was too valuable as Chief of Staff.

That, however, may have been only a part of Roosevelt's reasoning. It was true that the President felt Marshall could handle MacArthur better than Eisenhower could, and probably would have better relations with members of Congress. But the War Department was running smoothly, the Army had been created, and the key job now was to utilize it. A large part of the Chief of Staff's responsibilities had become administrative, and Eisenhower would have been satisfactory in the role. But if Marshall went to OVERLORD he would be taking a demotion. He would take his orders from the CCS, a body that would have two of his hand-picked subordinates on it (Arnold and Eisenhower). Marshall would have been senior in rank and experience—not to mention ability—to almost all his superiors. Most of all, Roosevelt realized, putting Marshall on OVERLORD would mean losing his services as the advocate of the American case in CCS sessions.

In short, when the Americans decided to drop their over-all commander proposal, Marshall dropped out of the running for OVERLORD. Roosevelt, however, shrank from the distasteful task of making the decision, and on December 4 he sent Hopkins to Marshall to ask if he would express a personal preference. Marshall replied that he would accept any decision the President might make. Not satisfied, the next day the President himself asked Marshall to make the decision. But Marshall refused to be the judge in his own case.[27]

If the commander were not going to be Marshall, it still had to be an American. This made Eisenhower the only choice. He had excellent relations with the CCS, and Churchill had already indicated to Roosevelt that Eisenhower was completely acceptable to him.

None of what was going on at Cairo was known to Eisenhower. He still assumed that he was about to return to Washington. The American officers at AFHQ had even asked him whom he was going to take home with him to serve on his staff at the War Department. Eisenhower laughed and said he thought he had better leave them all in the Mediterranean, as he would be carried up to Arlington Cemetery six months after assuming his responsibilities anyway. Nevertheless, he was resigned to going.

With the announcement expected any day, Eisenhower fell into a thoughtful mood. He hated to leave the Mediterranean, especially when his forces were still short of Rome. To keep his spirits up, he tried to concentrate on the bright side and reminded himself of how lucky he had been. At a meal with his staff on December 4, he expressed his gratitude to Marshall, Roosevelt, and the country for the opportunity he had been given. He thought of himself as a "fortunate beneficiary of circumstances." Looking back, he felt that the crucial day had come when he was still in OPD and told Marshall that he hated to serve in Washington but that he expected to be stuck there for the war, had no expectation of a promotion, and did not give a damn. He thought this outburst, as much as his day-to-day performance, led to Marshall's putting him in command of SLEDGEHAMMER and ROUNDUP. That brought him to Europe where, because of his familiarity with War Department thinking as well as his position as commander of ETO, he was immediately accepted as an equal by the top British leaders. When SLEDGEHAMMER gave way to TORCH, and an American was needed for Allied commander, Eisenhower was on the spot. He was thus the logical, yet "lucky," choice. Looking around at the familiar faces of his staff, Eisenhower said he had a lot to be thankful for.[28]

He was a soldier and he was prepared to do his duty. He expected that Marshall would want to take command of OVERLORD immediately, so he planned to depart for Washington in the near future. He thought he would go by a round-the-world route, stopping off to visit MacArthur and Mountbatten. Such a trip would give him firsthand information on conditions in their theaters, information he could use as Chief of Staff.[29]

While Eisenhower was making these plans Roosevelt, "against the almost impassioned advice of Hopkins and Stimson, against the known preference of both Stalin and Churchill, against his own proclaimed inclination to give to George Marshall the historic opportunity which he so greatly desired and so amply deserved," made his decision.[30] As the last meeting at Cairo was breaking up, Roosevelt asked Marshall to write a message to Stalin for him. As Roosevelt dictated, Marshall wrote. "From the President to Marshal Stalin," it began. "The immediate appointment of General Eisenhower to command of Overlord operation has been decided upon." Roosevelt then signed it.*

It was, perhaps, a thoughtless and cruel way to inform Marshall, but then there was no way the President could have done it easily. It put Marshall's Roman severity and sense of duty to the ultimate test. Of course he passed. Neither then nor later did he ever express the slightest disappointment, and he never complained. The next morning, in fact, after the message had been encoded and sent, he retrieved his original handwritten draft from the code room. At the bottom, Marshall scribbled, "Dear Eisenhower. I thought you might like to have this as a memento," and sent it to Eisenhower.[31]

An intimate associate of Roosevelt's felt it was "one of the most difficult and one of the loneliest decisions he [Roosevelt] ever had to make."[32] In the field of appointments, it was also one of his best.[33]**

Eisenhower got his first hint of the appointment on December 7, when he received a cryptic radiogram from Marshall. The Chief assumed that someone had already told Eisenhower of the decision, and merely said, "In view of the impending appointment of a British officer as your

---

* Roosevelt did tell Churchill beforehand. Churchill, *Closing the Ring*, p. 418. Roosevelt gave as his reason that he could not spare Marshall, and asked for Churchill's reaction to Eisenhower. Churchill said he would be delighted to have Eisenhower head OVERLORD.

** Brooke thought so. "The selection of Eisenhower instead of Marshall was a good one," he wrote. "Eisenhower had now had a certain amount of experience as a commander and was beginning to find his feet. The combination of Eisenhower and Bedell Smith had much to be said for it." Arthur Bryant, *Triumph in the West* (New York, 1959), p. 74.

successor . . . in the Mediterranean, please submit to me . . . your recommendations in brief as to the best arrangement for handling the administration, discipline, training and supply of American troops assigned to Allied Force under the new command."[34] It left Eisenhower puzzled, but he had little time to worry about it, as he had to fly to Tunis to meet Roosevelt, who was stopping there on his way back to Washington.

Roosevelt was taken off the plane and put in Eisenhower's car. Eisenhower joined him. As soon as the automobile began to drive off, the President turned to the general and said, "Well, Ike, you are going to command Overlord."[35]

CHAPTER 22

Preparing for OVERLORD

The news of Eisenhower's appointment electrified him and his AFHQ associates. They had not realized it, but their morale had declined as they prepared for Eisenhower's departure for Washington. They had all wanted to be in on the kill, where the action was, not in a secondary theater or in Washington where they would wither on the vine. No one had any spark. "We now feel," an aide wrote after the word of Eisenhower's appointment to OVERLORD, "that we have a definite and concrete mission. This adds zest to living and interest in pursuing the objective. It has already made a remarkable difference in Ike. Now he is back to his old system of incessant planning and thinking out loud of qualifications of this or that man for certain jobs."[1]

Eisenhower threw himself into the task of robbing the Mediterranean of key personnel for OVERLORD. Churchill wanted him to leave Smith to help his successor in Algiers, who would be Wilson, but from the first Eisenhower insisted that Smith had to come to England with him. He thought that during the assault there should be a single ground commander for OVERLORD, and he wanted Alexander for that job. After enough troops had gotten ashore to justify organizing two army groups, Alexander would take command of the British army group. Because of the narrow front on which the attack would be made, Eisenhower also wanted a single tactical air force, with the commander setting up his headquarters alongside Alexander's. Spaatz could take command of the American strategic air forces operating out of the United Kingdom. But Eisenhower wanted Tedder as his chief airman.

Bradley had already been selected to command the U. S. First Army, which of course delighted Eisenhower. He thought that when the forces increased Bradley should move up to army group command, with Patton taking one of the American armies. The other army commander could be either Lieutenant General Courtney H. Hodges of U. S. Third Army or Lieutenant General William H. Simpson of Fourth Army. Whichever of these two got the appointment should come to England immediately to serve as Bradley's deputy and familiarize himself with the plans. Eisenhower planned to deal personally with each of the army group commanders, which would put him in actual charge of operations, a shift from the practice in the Mediterranean, where Alexander ran the ground war. For his successor as American theater commander in the Mediterranean, Eisenhower recommended Devers, who "will be superfluous in the U.K." after Eisenhower took up his duties as the commander of ETO. At the appropriate moment, Clark could take command of Seventh Army, which would make the invasion of southern France, with Lucas replacing Clark at Fifth Army.[2]

Two things stood out. First, Eisenhower was taking the best men out of the Mediterranean, a policy which he had no difficulty justifying since Italy was now a secondary theater. Second, he was willing to keep Patton.

Eisenhower made his decision to retain Patton in the face of one of the most sensational press outbursts of the war. In late November radio commentator Drew Pearson had learned of the Patton slapping incident. Newsmen in the Mediterranean, at Eisenhower's request, had kept silent about the affair, but Pearson gave it full, if somewhat garbled and exaggerated, treatment. He made much of the fact that Eisenhower had not reprimanded Patton. Pearson delivered his broadcast at a time when there was a lull on the various battlefronts and it received front-page treatment everywhere. Eisenhower, the War Department, and the White House all received hundreds of letters, most demanding that any general who would strike a private in a hospital be summarily dismissed from the service. The correspondents were especially upset because Eisenhower apparently had done nothing to censor Patton. The pressure was so great that Marshall wired Eisenhower, demanding a full statement of the facts of the case with an account of what Eisenhower had done about the matter.[3]

Eisenhower's reply ran to four pages. He described what had happened, told Marshall that he had personally reprimanded Patton but had put nothing official in Patton's 201 file, had forced Patton to apologize to the privates, nurses, and doctors involved, and concluded: "I decided that the corrective action as described above was adequate and suitable in the circumstances. I still believe that this decision is sound."[4] Smith meanwhile held a press conference. Unfortunately, Smith confirmed Pearson's charge that Eisenhower had not reprimanded Patton, and the storm grew. Eisenhower decided the best thing to do now was remain silent. Smith, he thought, had made a "bad mistake" (Smith may not have known about Eisenhower's private letter to Patton), but, Eisenhower told Marshall, Smith was "my ablest and finest officer" and he had "no intention of throwing valuable men to the wolves merely because of one mistake." He thought the best thing to do was "to keep still and take the brunt of the affair myself."[5]

Eisenhower made no public defense of his actions. He did answer a number of the incoming letters of criticism, carefully pointing out that Patton was too important to lose. In each case he asked that the letter be regarded as strictly personal.[6] He advised Patton to keep quiet, since "it is my judgment that this storm will blow over." In the end partly because other events took news priority, it did.[7]

But meanwhile, Marshall was not as sure as Eisenhower about the wisdom of giving Patton command of an army in OVERLORD. It was not that the Chief of Staff was afraid of adverse publicity, but rather that he had made his own selections for the top positions and had not included Patton. Marshall's plan was to give Lieutenant General Lesley J. McNair the army group, with Bradley and Devers commanding the armies, or to put Devers in command of the army group, with Bradley and Hodges under him. McNair, he said, had the great advantages of "extreme firmness, expert knowledge of artillery and infantry combined action, perfect loyalty and dependability," while Hodges "is exactly same class of man as Bradley in practically every respect. Wonderful shot, great hunter, quiet, self-effacing. Thorough understanding of ground fighting, DSC, etc." McNair's only drawback was his deafness.[8]

Marshall not only disagreed with Eisenhower's personnel selections; he objected to Eisenhower's tendency to gut Mediterranean headquarters and the casual way in which he proposed to transfer to Algiers men who had been working in the United Kingdom, especially Eakers and Devers. Such wholesale shifting of personnel would create serious problems in AFHQ, and Marshall thought both Eakers and Devers should be left where they were, with Spaatz remaining in the Mediterranean. Marshall thought Smith too should stay in Algiers until at least February 1944, in order to help Wilson get oriented.[9]

Eisenhower disagreed with everything Marshall proposed. He thought it was logical to take Tedder and Spaatz to England with him because he was anxious to have for OVERLORD senior commanders who were experienced in the air support of ground troops. Eaker's experience had all been in the area of strategic bombing. The technique of air-ground co-operation "is one that is not widely understood and it takes men of some vision and broad understanding to do the job right. Otherwise a commander is forever fighting with those air officers who, regardless of the ground situation, want to send big bombers on missions that have nothing to do with the critical effort." If Spaatz and Tedder went to England, there would be nothing for Eaker to do there. He should, therefore, report to Algiers to head the air effort in the Mediterranean.[10]

With regard to Devers, Eisenhower said he had "nothing whatsoever" against him, a less than candid remark, "and thought I was recommending him for an important post." Eisenhower said he knew Marshall had great confidence in Devers and if the Chief wanted to leave Devers in England "I have no doubt that I will find a useful job for him." But Eisenhower did want experienced commanders leading the American armies in OVERLORD, or so he said, and Devers had no experience. Still, Eisenhower insisted on Gerow as a corps commander, and Gerow had no experience.

Nor would Eisenhower give up Smith. He wanted to send Smith on to London within the next few days so that he could check the present organization there. Smith could return to Algiers later and stay for a week or so after Eisenhower left in order to clear up details, but then Eisenhower wanted him to return to London to get to work. Eisenhower said he had conferred with Wilson, who was bringing his key staff people with him, and was sure he could handle all major problems without Smith. "I regret that you found anything disturbing in the recommendations I made," Eisenhower concluded, "but, frankly, they are the best I could evolve considering the jobs to be filled and the experience and qualifications of the several individuals that could be shuffled around."[11] He was, in short, gently reminding Marshall that OVERLORD was now his responsibility and that he wanted to hand-pick the team to carry it out.

At this point great confusion set in. The reason was that Eisenhower's messages were crossing Marshall's, and vice versa, because Marshall had gone on an extended trip to the Pacific.[12] Shortly after Christmas, Marshall got back to Washington. "Appears that we have gotten into complete confusion regarding future assignments . . . ," he wired Eisenhower. He said he had "followed a confused trail while traveling in the Pacific" and was just now catching up with some of Eisenhower's messages. He was willing to accept Eisenhower's proposals in toto.[13] "The message was like the sun breaking through the fog," Butcher recorded.

"When Ike received the good news . . . his whole demeanor changed."[14] Marshall even agreed to bringing Devers down to Algiers as American theater commander.

Eisenhower now had Bradley, Patton, Smith, Spaatz, and Tedder. Churchill had decided to leave Alexander in the Mediterranean, under Wilson, and had chosen Montgomery to command the British land contingent in OVERLORD, so most of the high command was now set. On the question of the second American army commander, Eisenhower preferred to wait. He did ask Marshall to send Hodges over to England early so that he could "live by Bradley's side during the . . . planning and preparation and . . . actually accompany him into the operation." Eisenhower would determine later whether to move Bradley or Hodges up to army group command. He promised Marshall that "in no repeat no event will I ever advance Patton beyond army command." As far as McNair was concerned, he was definitely out—his deafness was too big a handicap to overcome.[15]

With the personnel chosen, Eisenhower could turn to organization. Smith went to London right after Christmas to have a firsthand look at the setup there, and he was quite disturbed at one or two things that he learned. The CCS had made Air Chief Marshal Sir Trafford Leigh-Mallory the air commander in chief, which put him in command of the tactical air forces for OVERLORD. Tedder had been named deputy Allied commander without portfolio. Smith wired Eisenhower, "I personally believe that Tedder should be the real Air Commander and your advisor on air matters, which Mallory now considers himself." Smith was even more worried about a rumor he had heard that the BCOS intended to submit to the CCS for approval a directive to Eisenhower on the organization of his air forces. Smith urged Eisenhower to insist that no CCS directives be issued until Eisenhower and Tedder had arrived in England and become familiar with the entire situation there.[16]

Eisenhower sent a quick answer to Smith, saying he agreed entirely "on the necessity for preventing higher authority from dictating details of our organization," and telling Smith he could present this view to the BCOS as strongly as he wished.[17] He then wired Marshall, "I most earnestly request that you throw your full weight into opposing the tendency to organize in advance the sub-echelons of the OVERLORD operation in such a way as to tie the hands of the command." He believed that the AFHQ staff had learned some lessons about proper organization in the Mediterranean that might be of value in organizing OVERLORD. "I think it a tragedy to give us such rigid directives as to preclude the application of those lessons."[18] Marshall agreed, and the problem of air organization was left to be settled later.

There were, meanwhile, problems in the Mediterranean that needed wrapping up. The CCS had ordered Eisenhower to prepare an outline plan for Operation ANVIL, the invasion of southern France, which was to be staged simultaneously with OVERLORD. On December 24 his staff finished a draft. Eisenhower forwarded it to the CCS on the twenty-eighth, with the warning that he was not ready to give it his approval until he had examined OVERLORD plans in detail. He added that Wilson had not seen the ANVIL outline and as Eisenhower's successor he of course might wish to make changes in it. The plan itself called for a three-division assault under U. S. Seventh Army, with the initial assault in the Toulon area.[19]

Eisenhower's attitude toward operations within the Mediterranean, meanwhile, had undergone a marked shift. Whereas formerly he had repeatedly requested permission to retain landing craft and special units that had been marked for OVERLORD, now he looked with extreme disfavor on similar requests from Alexander. In late December, for example, Alexander asked to be allowed to retain the 504th Airborne Regimental Combat Team of the 82d Airborne Division for use in SHINGLE, an amphibious assault he planned to make at Anzio.[20] Eisenhower refused. "Our demands against OVERLORD resources have been so numerous and oft repeated," he declared, "that I am unwilling to put up another."[21] Alexander remonstrated and Eisenhower, perhaps beset by a guilty conscience, gave in. SHINGLE was scheduled for late January, and Eisenhower said Alexander could keep a paratrooper regiment until it was completed. Alexander had also wanted to keep some LSTs longer than scheduled, but on that point Eisenhower was adamant. "There can be no repeat no flexibility in the release date of all those destined for the U.K.," Eisenhower ordered.[22]

It was, somehow, fitting that the last problem Eisenhower had to deal with before leaving the Mediterranean concerned French politics and involved some of the same personalities who participated in the uproar over the Darlan affair. In the third week in December De Gaulle decided the time had come to settle accounts with some of the Vichy administrators who had opposed him. He placed Boisson, Peyrouton, and Flandin under arrest, and rumor had it that he intended to have them shot. Eisenhower heard of De Gaulle's action while he was at the front visiting troops. It came as a complete surprise and left him "profoundly disturbed," especially with regard to Boisson, who had acted for so long as a loyal subordinate. Eisenhower radioed Murphy in Algiers and told him to let the FCNL know that he was deeply concerned and hoped the matter would not be pushed to the point of holding a trial for treason, much less a firing squad. He also had Smith fly to Algiers to confer with Murphy and Macmillan.[23]

Eisenhower, who was improving all the time in dealing with the French, was most worried about a possible overreaction from the Prime Minister or the President. Events proved his fears justified. Churchill wanted to offer the three arrested Frenchmen political asylum and send a strong warning to De Gaulle. Roosevelt went farther. He cabled Eisenhower, "Please inform the French Committee as follows: In view of the assistance given the Allied armies during the campaign in Africa by Boisson, Peyrouton, and Flandin, you are directed to take no action against these individuals at the present time."[24]

Everyone in the Mediterranean thought the President's peremptory order went much too far. Eisenhower told Smith to see to it that it was softened. Smith talked with Churchill, who was in Algeria, then with Macmillan, and on his own decided to withhold delivery of the President's message. As Smith cabled Marshall, the President's directive would be regarded by the FCNL as an ultimatum. De Gaulle would certainly reject it, which would be "a direct slap at the President, which the United States could not accept." The only alternative then would be to withdraw recognition of the FCNL and stop French rearmament. That would be disastrous, since Eisenhower was counting on French manpower for ANVIL and for future operations in Italy, not to mention help from the Resistance in France itself.[25]

Roosevelt calmed down, took the advice, and on December 26 told Eisenhower to make a milder protest, saying merely that the United States "views with alarm" the reports of the arrests.[26] On the President's message Eisenhower penciled a heartfelt "good." On December 30 he called on De Gaulle, who wanted to discuss the liberation of Paris. The Frenchman wanted a guarantee from Eisenhower that the first troops into the capital would be French, and made it clear that if Eisenhower satisfied him on that point he would take good care of Boisson and the others. Eisenhower acquiesced, and De Gaulle then promised to delay the trial of the three Vichy administrators until after the FCNL had given way to a properly constituted national assembly in France. Eisenhower asked Marshall to "convey to the President my earnest recommendation that this assurance be accepted as satisfactory."

Marshall did so, Roosevelt agreed, and Eisenhower was able to leave the Mediterranean with the satisfaction of knowing that his policies toward the French had helped surmount another crisis.[27]

Through the second half of December Eisenhower and his staff were anxious to get to London and go to work on OVERLORD. They were losing interest in Mediterranean problems. They had to hang on, however, until the new year, when the shift would take place. (There had been some talk about waiting until Rome fell, as that would be a fitting climax to Eisenhower's career in the Mediterranean, but the Allied armies failed to make any progress and the proposal was quietly dropped). Eisenhower decided to spend the last few days of the old year in Italy, not only to say his good-bys but to have the satisfaction of having established an advance command post on the continent of Europe.[28]

The new headquarters were in the Caserta Palace north of Naples. Butcher found a palatial hunting lodge for Eisenhower's personal use and he was proud of his discovery. Eisenhower arrived on Sunday afternoon, December 19. Butcher had filled him with stories about the attractive features of the place. Eisenhower had hardly entered when an aide came running downstairs—there was a rat in the general's bathroom. Eisenhower took personal command. Pulling a revolver, he marched into the bathroom and fired four shots. All missed. Butcher finally killed the rat with a stick. They then got onto the elevator, where they became stuck and stood around for half an hour waiting to be freed. The fireplace in Eisenhower's bedroom did not work and there were lice in the beds. Butcher's laconic comment was, "It's a tough war."[29]

Two days later Eisenhower made an extended trip to the front. It rained most of the time and he was thoroughly miserable when he started back for Naples. A seven-hour drive through the rain and fog did not help his mood. Smith was with him, and Eisenhower asked Smith to join him for dinner. The chief of staff was just as disgruntled as his boss and he grumbled that he would rather not. Eisenhower had a violent reaction. He said Smith was discourteous. No subordinate, he shouted, not even the chief of staff, could abruptly decline his commanding officer's invitation to dinner. Smith threatened to quit. Eisenhower said that would be just fine. He added that he felt like telling Churchill that he had reconsidered the Prime Minister's request to leave Smith with AFHQ and that Smith could stay in the Mediterranean.

Both men were sullen for a while, but Smith finally calmed down and apologized. Eisenhower did also and said the incident would be forgotten.[30]

That Eisenhower could so completely lose his temper with Smith only illustrated how tired he was and how badly he needed a rest. Marshall had recognized this early in the month, and after he got back to Washington began urging Eisenhower to come to the States and take a furlough. Eisenhower begged off, saying there was too much work to be done. Marshall finally made it a direct order. "You will be under terrific strain from now on," he pointed out. "I am interested that you are fully prepared to bear the strain and I am not interested in the usual rejoinder that you can take it. It is of vast importance that you be fresh mentally and you certainly will not be if you go straight from one great problem to another. Now come on home and see your wife and trust somebody else for 20 minutes in England."[31]

Eisenhower capitulated. He decided to fly to the United States and take two weeks off. He left at noon on the last day of 1943. Just before departing the Mediterranean for the last time he told a friend, "I have put in a hard year here and I guess it is time to go."[32]

CHAPTER 23

Epilogue: Eisenhower on the Eve of OVERLORD

Eisenhower was occasionally given to reflecting on his good fortune. As he left Algiers for his furlough he may well have thought about his rapid rise in the Army. An obscure colonel two years earlier, his name was so little known that it appeared in the newspapers as "Lt. Col. D. D. Ersenbeing." Now he was preparing to command one of the greatest military operations in history. Luck had clearly played a large role in his success, but there were other factors, including his appearance, his personality, and most of all his abilities.

Physically, he gave the impression of being a big man. Although he was only a little over the average in height and weight, he dominated any gathering of which he was a member. People naturally looked at him. His hands and his facial muscles were always active. Through a gesture or a glance, as much as through the tone of his voice or what he was saying, he created a mood that imposed itself on others. A bald, shiny pate, with a prominent forehead and a broad, grinning mouth, made his head seem larger than it was. He had a wonderfully expressive face and it was impossible for him to conceal his feelings. His smiles, his grimaces, his anger, were all easily noticed. The whole face was always involved. It reddened when he was upset, lit up when he was happy. He could no more hide his emotions than he could his natural generosity and kindness.

His hands were large and knotty but well formed. They flashed through the air or jabbed at a listener. He would fold and unfold them, or thrust one into a coat pocket, then pull it out again. When he was making a series of points he would unconsciously hold up one hand, spread it, and then with the index finger of his other hand enumerate his points one by one, usually starting with the little finger and ending up with the climax on the index finger.

He was a man of extraordinary energy. He went to bed late, got up early, worked seven days a week, and had to be forced to relax. For four years he averaged five hours' sleep a night, but it never seemed to reduce his efficiency. He smoked incessantly. His fierce temper frightened him and he struggled to keep it under control, revealing it only to Butcher, Smith, and a few other intimates.

His language reflected his three decades in the Army. It was of the barracks room, filled with Anglo-Saxon phrases which he used as exclamation points and which he pronounced clearly and without embarrassment (although he was prudish about certain four-letter words). He talked rapidly and often was not a good listener, but he was not a nervous man, for he directed his energy toward obtainable objectives. He was a man of deep involvements, whether the issue at hand concerned strategic planning or the personal problem of an obscure member of his staff.

The overriding impression he gave was one of vitality. Dwight Eisenhower was an intensely alive human being.

At the end of the Mediterranean campaign he was fifty-three years old. He had a strong constitution, an absolute essential for a man about to embark on a long and arduous campaign, one which would make innumerable demands on his energy and his body. In his youth he had been an athlete and during his early career in the Army a football coach, and he had kept himself in good physical condition in middle age. Over the past two years, however, he had been so busy working in his office or traveling that he had neglected exercise. At Marshall's insistence he went horseback riding occasionally, or played a game of golf, but that was all. Still, his muscle tone remained firm and his health good. In the past two years he had lived in Texas, Washington, London, Gibraltar, and Algiers, with frequent trips to Tunisia, Sicily, and Italy. Despite all the changes in climate, water, food, and local diseases, he had lost only a few days to the flu or to colds.

It was not that he did not pay a price for all his activity, but rather that he did not let it show. In September 1943 a relative told him that he was pleased to see from some snapshots taken in Sicily that Eisenhower looked so healthy. In reply, Eisenhower said, "I must admit that sometimes I feel a thousand years old when I struggle to my bed at night."[1]

He had a sharp, orderly mind. No one ever thought to describe him as an intellectual giant, and outside of his professional field he was not well read. He was not liable to come up with brilliant insights. But he had the ability to look at a situation or a problem and analyze it, see what alternatives were available, and choose from among them. He might miss some nuances, but he seldom overlooked major points. When his superiors gave him a problem they could count on his taking all relevant factors into consideration.

Eisenhower had firm ideas on justice and fair play. He readily accepted the privileges of command but would not take more than he thought he had coming to him. On a cruise around the Isle of Capri on Christmas Eve, Eisenhower spotted a large villa. "Whose is that?" he asked. "Yours, sir," someone replied—Butcher had arranged it. Nodding at another, even larger villa, Eisenhower asked, "And that?" "That one belongs to General Spaatz." Eisenhower exploded. "Damn it, that's *not* my villa! And that's not General Spaatz' villa! None of those will belong to any general as long as I'm Boss around here. This is supposed to be a rest center—for combat men—not a playground for the Brass!"[2]

He was not just performing for the benefit of his aides. When he got back to shore he investigated, found that Spaatz had reserved Capri as a recreation facility for AAF officers, and exploded again. "This is directly contrary to my policies and must cease at once," he told Spaatz, and ordered him to see to it immediately that "all British and American personnel in this area, particularly from combat units, may be assured of proportionate opportunity in taking advantage of these facilities."[3]

The Capri story, and others similar to it, quickly got out to the troops and delighted them. Nothing pleased the foot slogger struggling in the mud of Italy more than hearing that Eisenhower had put Spaatz or some other general in his place. The fact that Eisenhower often referred to Churchill, Roosevelt, and the CCS as the "big shots," or that he swore like a sergeant, was much appreciated by the men. So were his frequent visits to the front lines, especially because he listened to the troops' complaints and, when he could, did something about them. His popularity with the men rested on his genuine concern for their welfare and on his common touch—they regarded him as one of them.

Eisenhower enjoyed his popularity but he did not always court it. He was a strict disciplinarian and constantly harped on the subject. As a result of his experiences in the Mediterranean, however, he was beginning to recognize that discipline alone was not enough to make men fight, or at least to fight well. Discipline and training "lie at the foundation of every success in war," he explained to a friend, but morale was just as important. In the prewar Army it was axiomatic that morale came from *esprit de corps.* Eisenhower still believed this, but he now realized that something more was needed. The battlefields of Tunisia and Sicily and Italy had made a deep impression upon him. So had talking with the men at the front and seeing the conditions under which they lived and fought. Eisenhower had decided that for an army to have morale "there must be a deep-seated conviction in every individual's mind that he is fighting for a cause worthy of any sacrifice he may make."

He seldom spoke about his deepest beliefs ("Professional soldiers do not like to get too sentimental about such things as the flag and love of country") but he felt, strongly, that the Allied cause was an inspiring one, and he thought that every commander had a responsibility to make the issues clear to the troops. The G.I. and the Tommy had to be made to realize that "the privileged life he has led . . . is under direct threat. His right to speak his own mind, to engage in any profession of his own choosing, to belong to any religious denomination, to live in any locality where he can support himself and his family, and to be sure of fair treatment when he might be accused of any crime—all these would disappear if the forces opposed to us should, through carelessness or overconfidence on our part, succeed in winning this war." The Allied cause was "completely bound up with the rights and welfare of the common man."[4]

Eisenhower's patriotism was simple and direct. As in his approach to many other things, it had few nuances or qualifications. In October his brother Milton sent him a recording of his inaugural speech as president of Kansas State College. He told Milton it was a masterpiece, but he wished his brother had referred to one other responsibility of the educator. "It is the necessity of teaching and inculcating good, old-fashioned patriotism—just that sense of loyalty and obligation to the community that is necessary to the preservation of all the privileges and rights that the community guarantees."[5] Two days later Eisenhower urged a boyhood friend, Swede Hazlett, who was on the staff at the Naval Academy, to teach the obligations as well as the privileges of American citizenship, the need for a clean, honest approach to life, and the necessity for "earnest devotion to duty." All these things were necessary "if we are to survive as a sturdy nation."[6]

Eisenhower's beliefs, and his expression of them, were those of Main Street. His personality was that of the outgoing, affable American writ large. It was, therefore, easy to dismiss him as a man of no depth, a general who had the common touch because he was common. But there was more to Eisenhower than that. His qualities may have been like those of the average American, but he had them in abundance.

Given his role, Eisenhower's lack of ruthlessness, at least in personal relations, was a source of strength. Although none of his immediate superiors or subordinates seemed to realize it, Eisenhower could not afford to be a table-thumper. With Montgomery's prestige, power, and personality, for example, had Eisenhower stormed into his headquarters, banged his fist on the table, and shouted out a series of demands, his actions could have been disastrous.

Precisely because of Eisenhower's personality, he was by all odds the best of the British or American officers available to deal with the French. De Gaulle liked, respected and counted on him heavily. Three days before Eisenhower left North Africa for the last time, De Gaulle paid him a great tribute: "I want to tell you that the French Committee of National Liberation has full confidence in you in the employment of the French forces that it is placing under your command for the next allied operations."[7] Eisenhower had come to have a certain grudging admiration for the tall, cranky, sensitive Frenchman who had given him so many problems. On December 30 he called on De Gaulle to say farewell; the meeting, according to Butcher, was "a love fest."[8] De Gaulle recognized that Eisenhower was his best friend in the Anglo-American camp, while Eisenhower realized that De Gaulle could be of great help in resolving the complex problems that would arise when France was liberated. The two generals looked forward to working together.[9]

All these relationships, and the many others involved in the position Eisenhower was assuming, had innumerable ramifications and complex interactions. Doing something to satisfy Montgomery might make Patton angry; a decision that pleased Marshall would leave Brooke unhappy; bowing to the President's wishes could mean opposing the Prime Minister. The Supreme Commander would have to be able to maintain a balance and still defeat the Germans.

Eisenhower was aware of the complexities. He had already been charged with bending over backward to please the British; Wedemeyer had said as much in September 1943. Eisenhower saw the report in which Wedemeyer made the charge and said it gave him a laugh. He told Wedemeyer that things were not quite so simple as they may have appeared from OPD. An allied command could work, he explained, "only if the Chief is truly self-effacing." He must have a fund of patience and good humor so that "when he necessarily drags out the big stick it is most effective." Eisenhower was well aware of the importance of personal relations. He thought that no man should be an allied commander in chief "unless he is rather well acquainted with the individuals comprising the Combined Chiefs of Staff, and unless he has the direct or indirect confidence of the two Heads of State." No man could achieve these results by pursuing a purely national policy.[10]

Good relations with those above him, and with the line officers in the field, were absolutely necessary to the Supreme Commander's success. Equally important was the way his staff operated. The manner in which Eisenhower put SHAEF together and into operation would be the cement that would hold the alliance together. For Eisenhower the ideal to be approached was AFHQ. He tried at SHAEF to gather a team of British and American staff officers who would match the performance of the AFHQ team. The most obvious first step was to rob AFHQ, and Eisenhower did so with skill. Most of his key staff personnel came out of Algiers. They worked well together. They knew each other's habits and those of their commander, shared a basic pattern of thought in dealing with alliance problems, and were imbued with the Allied approach. Eisenhower could count on them to continue and expand the teamwork concept of AFHQ.

The presence of men like Smith, Tedder, and the others gave Eisenhower confidence as he approached his new job.

The Germans summed up some of Eisenhower's qualities in an analysis the Luftwaffe made of him in February 1944. Eisenhower "is noted for his great energy, and his hatred of routine office work," the analysis said. "He . . . manages to inspire [his subordinates] to supreme efforts through kind understanding and easy discipline. His strongest point is said to be an ability for adjusting personalities to one another and smoothing over opposite viewpoints. Eisenhower enjoys the greatest popularity with Roosevelt and Churchill."[11]

As Eisenhower prepared to assume his duties at OVERLORD he had much to draw upon—his knowledge, based on his three decades of professional service and especially what he had learned in the Mediterranean; his personality; his skill in handling complex problems and relationships; his hand-picked and molded staff. Over and above these and the other factors that led to his success, however, one stood out. When associates described Eisenhower, be they superiors or subordinates, there was one word that almost all of them used. It was trust. From Churchill to the lowest Tommy, from Roosevelt to the buck private at a replacement depot, from De Gaulle to the Resistance fighter in southern France, people trusted Eisenhower.

They did so for the most obvious reason—he was trustworthy. His grin, his mannerisms, his approach to life all exuded sincerity. He wore his heart on his sleeve. There was nothing devious about him. It is, perhaps, a paradox that it was for this reason that he was such an outstanding diplomat, a profession in which the guarded phrase and the half-truth are supposed to count for much. Darlan and De Gaulle and Badoglio felt they could trust Eisenhower because they knew where he stood and that he said exactly what he meant. Montgomery never thought much of Eisenhower as a soldier ("I would not class Ike as a great soldier in the true sense of the word") but he did appreciate other qualities. While he thought Eisenhower intelligent, "his real strength lies in his human qualities. . . . He has the power of drawing the hearts of men towards him as a magnet attracts the bits of metal. He merely has to smile at you, and you trust him at once. He is the very incarnation of sincerity."[12]

Eisenhower once explained to Ismay the basis for his dealings with French politicians. "I immediately started a personal campaign to establish for myself a reputation for the most straightforward, brutal talk that could be imagined," he said. "I refused to put anything in diplomatic or suave terminology, and carefully cultivated the manner and reputation of complete bluntness and honesty—just a man too simple-minded to indulge in circumlocution."[13]

Eisenhower did all he could to make his word his bond. "I know only one method of operation," he once said. "To be as honest with others as I am with myself." In December 1942 he made some promises to Boisson about using his influence with Churchill to do some favors for French West Africa. For political reasons Churchill delayed. Eisenhower told the Prime Minister that Boisson had said to him, time and again, "As long as *you* tell me that, I believe it!" If it turned out that his word meant nothing, Eisenhower warned Churchill, his effectiveness in dealing with the French would come to an end. The Prime Minister did what the general wanted him to. Later, when Roosevelt tried to back out of American commitments to rearm the French, Eisenhower took the same line with the same results. With his staff and with his troops, with his superiors and with foreign governments, Eisenhower did what he said he was going to do. His reward was the trust they placed in him.

He had been successful at AFHQ because the people with whom he worked trusted him. If he could keep that trust, he would also be a success as Supreme Commander, Allied Expeditionary Force.

BOOK TWO

Supreme Commander,
Allied Expeditionary Force

Part I

THE PREPARATION

[*January 1944–June 1944*]

THE Western plan to insure German defeat centered on OVERLORD. The British and Americans were putting everything they had into the operation. Because they were holding nothing back, they were engaging in a tremendous gamble. If OVERLORD failed, it would take months to mount another assault, and by then weather on the Continent and on the coast would have deteriorated to the point that an expedition would have been impossible. But neither Eisenhower nor anyone else made any contingency plans about what to do in case the armies did not get ashore on D-Day, in part because they wanted to think positively, in part because if OVERLORD failed there was little else they could do in any case.

What the Eastern Ally would have done in the event of a disaster befalling the Western Allies is pure conjecture. There was a great fear in the West that the Russians, once they reached their historic borders, would stop their offensive and, possibly, negotiate a peace with the Germans. Stalin might have decided, had OVERLORD failed, that the West was less than serious about the war and made immediately the best peace with Hitler that he could. On the other hand, the Russians might have continued to drive forward into Europe, thus becoming the liberators —and therefore the occupiers—of Denmark, western Germany, the Low Countries, and France.

The point that stood out in January 1944 was that the Western Allies dared not fail, since the consequences were staggering. They therefore approached the task of making OVERLORD succeed with the gravest seriousness. A successful OVERLORD meant, in practice, getting ashore and staying. There was a good deal of talk at Allied headquarters about getting well inland on D-Day, and an over-all scheme for the campaign in Europe to follow, but in fact all recognized that if a bridgehead could be won Anglo-American superiority would sooner or later exploit it, and so planners and commanders concentrated on getting ashore. As Eisenhower put it, at Supreme Headquarters, Allied Expeditionary Force (SHAEF), there was "a very deep conviction, in all circles, that we are approaching a tremendous crisis with stakes incalculable,"[1] and everyone on the staff and in the field now prepared to use all his talents to meet and overcome that crisis.

CHAPTER 1

"We Cannot Afford to Fail"

The allied invasion of France in 1944 was one of the most complex operations in human history. The requirements and detailed plans involved were enormous. Although the number of men landing in the initial assault at Sicily was higher than the number that would hit the beaches at Normandy on D-Day, OVERLORD's over-all force of ships, planes, and divisions for the follow-up was vastly greater than at Sicily. OVERLORD was *the* military effort of the war for the British and Americans. A high percentage of everything done in the two countries for the preceding two years, from the refining of oil for airplane fuel to the training of infantry soldiers, had been aimed toward the operation. This was especially true of technological development.

As mentioned above, the main thrust of OVERLORD was to get ashore and stay. This goal affected every decision. In selecting the site of the landings, for example, the criterion was not proximity to the heart of German power in France, or to Berlin, or to the major Atlantic port of Antwerp for later build-up and exploitation purposes. The first question in site selection was, rather, Where are we most likely to succeed?

The requirements were complex. The site had to be within range of fighter planes based in Britain, and within an overnight sailing distance for ships in the southern ports of England. It was necessary to embark from the southern ports because the western ports were needed to unload men and goods coming from the U.S., and the eastern ports were too vulnerable to German observation and attack. The embarkation ports would be clogged for weeks before the invasion and would be a choice target for the Germans, whose much touted secret weapon, the rocket bomb, was about to become operational. The beach had to be firm enough to hold tanks rumbling inland with the invading troops. A high surf would be risky and had to be avoided. The ground inland had to be suitable for the construction of airfield landing strips. What was known about German defenses needed to be considered. The Allies had to be able to build up their invading force faster than the Germans could reinforce their defenders.

Calais seemed the obvious target. It was closest to Antwerp, Europe's best port, and to Germany. From it Allied forces might drive straight east and cut off the German divisions in France, thereby avoiding the political risk of making France a battlefield. It was within easy range of British-based fighters and was the closest port to England. But these and other factors were as obvious to the Germans as to the Allies, and German defenses were therefore strongest in the Calais area. As far as the Allies were concerned, that fact eliminated Calais as a landing site. To a lesser degree the same advantages and disadvantages were present at all the sites between Calais and Le Havre. North of Calais the potential sites were too close to Germany, and thus could be too easily reinforced by the enemy. These coast sites were also too inundated, too soft and liable to flood, had too many sand dunes, and were already too well defended. South of Normandy, the Brittany Peninsula was at the extreme edge of fighter range and was in any case too exposed to the extremes of Atlantic Ocean storms.

That left Normandy. The Cotentin Peninsula had at its tip a small but good port, Cherbourg, which was close to the British port of Portsmouth. The peninsula was fairly narrow, so that troops landing at its eastern base could push across it and seal it off, then capture the port. Near the Cotentin was the major communications network of Caen, from which highways and railroads led to Paris. The area inland from Caen was relatively flat and favorable to offensive maneuvers, which would allow the Allies to use their superiority in tanks and motor transport and to build airfields. The beaches were sufficiently firm, and the Cotentin extended far enough into the English Channel to protect the landing sites from the worst effects of Atlantic storms. Troops could be supplied over the beaches while Cherbourg was being captured and put into working order. There were good road nets behind the beaches. Finally, although Hitler personally believed that the attack would come at Normandy, the German defenses there were not as far advanced as they were to the north.

So Normandy would be the spot. The final choice of the site for history's greatest invasion was made by a process of elimination in which caution was the keynote.

As had been the case in all of Eisenhower's previous invasions, choosing the time of the assault was as complicated as choosing the place. It had to come at low tide, because the German defenses were built around steel obstacles that covered the area of the beach between the high- and low-water marks. The obstacles, often capped with Teller mines, would rip the belly out of any landing craft that passed over them. By landing at low tide, the Allies would have to cross an unprotected beach under German fire, but that was preferable to drowning in sinking landing craft. As the troops moved forward and the tide came in, Allied engineers could clear away the obstacles. The attack had to come at or near dawn, so that the invasion fleet could cross the Channel under cover of darkness and so that the troops would have a full day to get established on the beachhead. A full moon would make the operation too risky for the fleet, but there had to be some moon to facilitate a parachute drop, a maneuver needed to seize the exits from the beaches. The assault had to come late enough in the year to allow for final training of troops in the British Isles, but soon enough to give the Allies at least four months of good campaigning weather in France.

The conditions were met only three times in the spring of 1944—during the first few days of May and the first and third weeks of June. For planning purposes, the CCS had set May 1 as D-Day.

The technological innovations used in OVERLORD were bold and imaginative. There were, for example, more than a dozen devices developed by the British to put on the front of tanks to assist them in getting through mine fields. Since the Allies could not count on taking Cherbourg early, or on capturing it before the Germans destroyed it, and since there were not enough DUKWs to insure supply over the beaches, the British had developed artificial harbors and breakwaters. These monstrous gadgets would be towed across the Channel and sunk off the Normandy beaches. A pipeline under the ocean (PLUTO) would be laid from England to Normandy to supply the tanks and trucks with fuel, thereby saving on shipping. The only trouble with most of these devices was that they had never been used in combat before, so that despite the assurances of the inventors the soldiers could not be sure they would actually work. Still, the risk had to be taken.[1]

By the time Eisenhower became Supreme Commander many of the problems inherent in the OVERLORD operation had been settled. But many were not, such as selection of the time of day of the assault, the decision as to the proper use of air power, the cover plans and countless other details. Since the previous spring Lieutenant General Sir Frederick

E. Morgan, chief of staff to the Supreme Commander, Designate (COSSAC) and his staff had been working on OVERLORD. They had used as their starting point the plans Eisenhower had developed in the summer of 1942 for ROUNDUP, plans which, while not as detailed as Morgan's own, had come to some of the same conclusions about the site and timing of the assault. Morgan's role was to advise. Eisenhower's was to command. The Supreme Commander had to approve of everything COSSAC had done, to build on Morgan's base, while fully realizing that the responsibility for the major operation of the war was his, and his alone.

From the beginning, the high tension and drama of OVERLORD were obscured by the irritating, involved debate over ANVIL. Eisenhower had to spend more time and effort on the projected invasion of the south of France than he could on that of Normandy. One reason was that there was early agreement on OVERLORD's direct needs, so they did not have to be discussed once the basic decision to mount the operation had been made. But there was wide disagreement on subsidiary operations, both as to their requirements and their potential contribution to OVERLORD. Eisenhower wanted ANVIL, wanted it badly, and had strong support for this position from Marshall. In London, however, he stood almost alone—even Smith wanted to drop it for the present. The people with whom the Supreme Commander conversed daily all told him he was wrong, which increased the strain on him.

Fortunately, on the more important issues such as the Normandy invasion, Eisenhower and his principal superiors and subordinates were in agreement. They all accepted Morgan's ideas as to the place of the assault, they all were willing to depend on the untested artificial harbors and other gadgets the British had developed, and they all agreed that OVERLORD's needs came first. If this account emphasizes disagreements, it is not because disagreement dominated the coalition command —it did not—but because the leading actors did not need to discuss the matters they agreed on. They did have to argue, sometimes violently, about their disagreements.

From the time Eisenhower first began to work on OVERLORD his major concern was to widen the assault. COSSAC had prepared plans for a three-division landing near Caen in the Normandy area. Morgan had been forced to keep the size of the assault force low because of the limitations under which he worked, the most important of which were in the number of landing craft the CCS had allowed him for planning purposes. Eisenhower first saw the COSSAC plan in the fall of 1943, when one of Morgan's staff officers brought a copy of it to Algiers. His immediate reaction was that the assault frontage was too narrow and that the forces accordingly would not have enough punch. He thought that on every item, including airplanes, ships, landing craft, and assault divisions, COSSAC was being forced to skimp. After his experiences at Salerno, Eisenhower thought this was a bad, possibly disastrous, mistake.[2]

Eisenhower spent the first two weeks in January 1944 in the United States. He had a short vacation with his wife, saw his mother, and went to West Point to visit with his son, but he also managed to get some work done. Smith had stayed in Algiers, wrapping up AFHQ and making an intensive study of the COSSAC plans. His reaction to them was the same as Eisenhower's, and on January 5 he wired his superior (who was using Marshall's desk in the Pentagon) to say that it was imperative to widen the assault.

The first exchange between Eisenhower and Smith on OVERLORD set off a debate that would go on for months. Everyone involved agreed that more divisions were needed for D-Day, but to get them ashore SHAEF had to have more landing craft. There was a world-wide shortage of such vehicles, however, and production facilities were limited since landing craft had never been put at the top of the priority list. Thus, the major problem was where to obtain more of them.

On January 5 Smith proposed one obvious solution—cut down on operations elsewhere. Specifically, he wanted to cancel SHINGLE, the landing at Anzio, due to occur on January 21, and a simultaneous ANVIL. Smith thought SHINGLE should be dropped and forgotten (it had been Churchill's idea from the first and no one at AFHQ ever liked it), while ANVIL should come after OVERLORD or be reduced to merely a threat. The landing craft that would thereby be available could be used for OVERLORD.[3]

Eisenhower's initial point, which he maintained to the end of the debate, was that ANVIL was necessary to the success of OVERLORD and he did not want it abandoned. He was quite willing to give up SHINGLE (Churchill and Wilson were not, and it was mounted as scheduled), but he hoped that by improvising and cutting every other possible corner he could come up with the craft necessary for both ANVIL and OVERLORD. "We must develop the maximum in expedient and substitute to increase lift," he told Smith. "Only in event that OVERLORD cannot possibly be broadened without abandonment of ANVIL would I consider making such a recommendation to the Combined Chiefs."[4] The issue was clear. To Eisenhower, ANVIL was necessary to insure the success of OVERLORD, but to others it was not.

Montgomery, for example, agreed with Smith. He was already in London, preparing for the invasion in his role as general ground commander, and on January 10 wired Eisenhower to say that ANVIL should be reduced to a threat. He had already convinced the BCOS of the necessity of this, but no final decision could be made until Eisenhower expressed his opinion. Montgomery stressed the importance of arriving at a decision immediately and asked Eisenhower to hurl himself "into the contest and get us what we want."[5] Eisenhower said he too wanted a five- instead of a three-division OVERLORD, but he also explained to Montgomery some of the reasons for his hesitation about dropping a simultaneous ANVIL. An invasion of the south of France offered the only opportunity to engage the bulk of the forces already in the Mediterranean in support of OVERLORD. It would threaten the Germans in France in a way that the forces in Italy could never do. ANVIL would open additional ports in France, ports which the SHAEF forces would desperately need. With the additional ports, more U.S. divisions could be brought into the battle; without them, the size of SHAEF's forces would be limited by the capacity of the ports in northwestern France. There were also important political factors. Without ANVIL, the bulk of the French divisions could not participate in the liberation of France; Eisenhower thought it would be a mistake to deny to the French a significant role in the liberation of their nation. In addition, the Western Allies had promised Stalin at Teheran that they would mount ANVIL, and Stalin had been enthusiastic about the operation. To abandon it would appear underhanded.[6]

In the middle of January Eisenhower flew to London and returned to his old headquarters at 20 Grosvenor Square. He went over the original COSSAC plans with Morgan and Montgomery and immediately agreed with them that OVERLORD had to have more divisions in the initial assault. The landings had to be broadened to ensure initial success, to secure beaches for the build-up, and to have enough strength to get to Cherbourg quickly to capture and control a port. Eisenhower still thought, however, that he could increase OVERLORD without dropping ANVIL, and he had a number of expedients in mind to accomplish this. He was willing, for example, to take armored landing craft away from ANVIL and assign them to OVERLORD, substituting unarmored craft already in England. The British had planned on a seventy per cent serviceability rate for landing craft; that is, seventy per cent of the craft they had at any given date would be operationally available. Eisenhower thought this figure too low and was willing to plan on an eighty-five per cent serviceability rate. Through this kind of expediency, he hoped to mount a five-division OVERLORD and a simultaneous two-division ANVIL.[7]

"Every obstacle must be overcome," Eisenhower declared in his initial report on OVERLORD planning to the CCS, "every inconvenience suffered and every risk run to ensure that our blow is decisive. We cannot afford to fail." He emphasized that he was determined to have a five-division OVERLORD, since "nothing less will give us an adequate margin to ensure success." To get it, he was willing to make sacrifices with the forces allotted to him, such as cutting down on the number of tanks and trucks carried in the assault, but he would need 271 additional landing craft assigned to OVERLORD from resources outside the European Theater, and for training purposes they would have to be in the U.K. six weeks before D-Day.

Where could the additional vessels come from? As a start, Eisenhower was willing to put D-Day back a month, from May 1 to early June, in order to have available an extra month's production of landing craft (amounting to almost a hundred vessels). He would be willing in addition, he said, to reduce the simultaneous ANVIL to a threat, but "only as a last resort and after all other means and alternatives have failed to provide the necessary strength" for OVERLORD.[8]

Eisenhower's insistence on ANVIL, in view of his own feelings about the need to build up OVERLORD, was surprisingly strong. It came about, possibly, because of his belief, based on personal experience, that without ANVIL the Allies would never get a decent return on their investment in Italy. The only way the Mediterranean forces could help OVERLORD was through southern France. Eisenhower also believed that the French Resistance would be an important factor in the success of OVERLORD. Montgomery did not have to worry about the Maquis, but the Supreme Commander did. If French divisions did not participate in the liberation, De Gaulle would sulk. If De Gaulle sulked, the Resistance would not co-operate.

Beyond these diplomatic and important military considerations, Eisenhower's attitude reflected a certain cast of mind, perhaps peculiar to the American soldier and close to that of the American businessman. He sometimes referred to himself as chairman of the board and, like the corporate head, he thought it necessary to justify expenditures to the stockholders, in this case the American people. The U.S. had raised, armed, and trained eighty-nine divisions. Without ports in the south of France, many of these divisions, possibly as many as twenty, could never be brought into action. Also, as Eisenhower told Marshall, "we have put into the French Army a very considerable investment." Without ANVIL, the French could not be employed, and "all of our French investment will have been wasted.⁹

None of Eisenhower's arguments for ANVIL were original; they all came from Marshall. Eisenhower would sometimes stress different points than Marshall had emphasized, but there was no doubt that throughout the ANVIL debate he followed the Chief of Staff's lead. Breaking away from the verbiage and incidental arguments, Marshall insisted on mounting ANVIL primarily because of his determination to prevent the British from extending operations in Italy and to the east. Marshall's determination, a reflection of a complex set of factors outside the scope of this study, was so intense that he was willing to make ANVIL a test case in the alliance. Eisenhower had not given much thought to the strategic parameters involved, for they were not a part of his responsibilities, but during his two weeks in the United States he had talked about ANVIL with Marshall and learned how deeply the Chief felt about the operation. Thus although ANVIL was not Eisenhower's child, and although the military arguments in favor of it were weak, he fought for it to the bitter end. Marshall wanted ANVIL, and that was enough.

Eisenhower spent the first two months of 1944 trying to mount a simultaneous OVERLORD and ANVIL. Since there was nothing he could do to speed up production of landing craft in time for D-Day, or get the U. S. Navy to give up the craft it had in the Pacific, he had to find the resources within the European-Mediterranean theater. Much of the effort would involve narrow, specialized technical work, which could only be accomplished by the staff. To the problem of building up an efficient staff, therefore, Eisenhower turned his attention.

Shortly after arriving in London, Eisenhower wrote an old friend, "Right now we are busy getting settled and going through the business of ramming our feet in the stirrups."¹⁰ He had his first meeting with the SHAEF staff on January 19. Part of the staff came from COSSAC, while Smith had stolen the bulk from AFHQ. For the benefit of newcomers, Eisenhower began by covering familiar ground—he emphasized the need for Allied unity, and said that all problems should be approached from an objective, as opposed to a nationalistic, point of view. He said his door was always open and he preferred to do business informally rather than formally. If he failed to understand a given phase of operations, especially technical aspects, he begged their indulgence; their job, as the experts, was to explain and make the subject understandable. If he advanced an idea which had already been considered and accepted or rejected, he wanted to be told, not humored. Eisenhower pointed out that no commander could know everything; this was the very reason he had a staff.

On the more general subject of attitude, the Supreme Commander ordered his staff to exude confidence. He would not allow the officers even to consider failure. After the plan had been formulated, he wanted everyone to express faith in it, no matter what misgivings he had about it during its formative stages.[11] The speech, coupled with Eisenhower's own constant example, set the tone at SHAEF for the remainder of the war.

As at AFHQ, Eisenhower insisted that the SHAEF staff be a team. Officers had to be carefully selected to fit into such a staff; some highly capable men from COSSAC had to be transferred when it was found that they could not work closely with officers of a different nationality. As Tedder later testified, the task involved "getting the right people and being ruthless . . . and you must be ruthless. . . . If a man does not fit he will never learn the language and you will never make a team; that is the guts of the whole thing, the team. . . ."[12]

Smith did most of the dirty work in firing officers and finding their replacements. He had already raided AFHQ to what the British considered an alarming degree, but when he needed men he naturally turned to those he already knew and respected. Smith usually got on with the British quite well, especially with Brooke, who thought more of Smith than he did of Eisenhower, but Brooke and Smith did have a shouting argument over personnel for the SHAEF staff. In the middle of January Smith went to Brooke with a request for the services of Generals Gale, Whiteley, and Strong, respectively the chief administrative officer, the deputy chief of staff, and the G-2 at AFHQ. Brooke grumbled that Eisenhower was stealing AFHQ's best talent. Smith snapped that Brooke was not being "helpful" and started for the door. What Butcher later called "a bit of frank talk" ensued. Eisenhower apologized to Brooke for Smith and explained that Smith "fights for what he wants" but meant no disrespect.[13] At the same time Eisenhower made it clear to Smith that he still wanted the three British officers, and by April Smith had managed to pry them loose from AFHQ.

Eisenhower had no intention of cleaning house completely at COSSAC.

Morgan had been promised the position of chief of staff to the Supreme Commander, but when Eisenhower insisted on Smith for that job the British decided to offer Morgan a corps command. Morgan, however, asked to serve in some capacity in SHAEF, and Eisenhower made him Smith's deputy. His responsibilities in that post were great and his functions broad; after the war Smith described him as his British alter ego, "a man I wouldn't willingly have dispensed with."[14] Major General Ray W. Barker, an American and Morgan's deputy at COSSAC, became G-1 at SHAEF, and other key members of the COSSAC staff who proved able to work with the newcomers from AFHQ were retained in their positions.

Eisenhower commanded ETO as well as SHAEF, so he was primarily responsible for the selection of the American field commanders of OVER-LORD. Here, as with his staff, he wanted men he had worked with successfully in the past, which again meant taking them from AFHQ. When Smith set out to do this, however, Devers—now commanding the American forces in the Mediterranean—raised a storm. Like Brooke, he resented the raid and assigned an officer to investigate so that he could present the facts in a complaint to Marshall. Smith went over the list of proposed transfers in detail with one of Devers' representatives and convinced him that all were appropriate, but Devers himself was not satisfied and would not give in. For Eisenhower, the loss that hurt the most was Lucian Truscott. Eisenhower wanted him badly but Devers simply would not let him go. Eisenhower complained that Devers was "obstinate" and would not co-operate and later regretted that he had not ordered Truscott to England before December 1943, when he still commanded AFHQ.[15]

At one point Devers wired to say, "We have tried to meet your requests for personnel to the utmost possible limit. Sorry we could not do it 100 per cent." Referring to ANVIL, he added, "You may count on me to be in there pitching with one idea, to assist you." Smith sarcastically noted on the bottom of the cable form, "This is just swell. I love this 'One idea to assist you' stuff."[16]

Devers was difficult, but even had he been more co-operative the basic problems would have remained. Eisenhower needed one army group commander, three army commanders, over a dozen corps commanders and, eventually, nearly half a hundred division commanders. This made personnel selection much more involved, intricate and larger in scope than anything Eisenhower had faced in North Africa or Italy and meant that he had to spend much of his time exchanging cables with Devers and Marshall to get the men he wanted. Almost all the generals he picked, or took on Marshall's recommendation, were Regular Army soldiers, many of whom he had come to know during his prewar career. Old friendships counted for much. He insisted on having Gerow lead a corps in the invasion, even though Gerow had no combat experience. He had wanted Truscott, with whom he had served before the war, for the other assault corps; when Devers would not let Truscott go, Eisenhower took Major General J. Lawton Collins. Eisenhower and Collins had been together at West Point. The commander of one of the follow-up corps, Major General Troy H. Middleton, had been with Eisenhower in the Philippines. Even at the division level, Eisenhower was personally acquainted with most of the leaders. His usual practice was to talk with Bradley and Smith about any prospective commander; in every case one of the three generals knew the man in question well. In a letter to Marshall about a proposed infantry division commander, Eisenhower made a remark that illustrated the way he worked: "This happens to be one man that I don't know personally, but Bradley thinks he is tops. So does Smith."[17]

As far as possible, Eisenhower did want men with combat experience. Obtaining them was not easy, however, because the bulk of the American Army had not yet been engaged in battle. Most of those divisions and generals who had experience were still in the Mediterranean, and as Eisenhower reported to Marshall, "Devers has constantly reported it is impossible to let any of his people come up here." Eisenhower realized that because he and Smith had organized AFHQ and "tested and placed the field commanders, we are quite likely to feel an unjustified proprietary interest in them and therefore exhibit a natural tendency to think that we are entitled to anything for which we ask." Eisenhower lamely remarked that he knew this was wrong, but he continued to try to get his subordinates from the Mediterranean. His justification was that OVERLORD was so much more important than the Italian campaign that he should have the best men for it.[18]

The shifting of officers could become complex. In January the general idea was that if Lucas was successful at Anzio he could then move up to take command of Fifth Army, with Clark taking command of ANVIL. Eisenhower approved of this, but thought that if ANVIL had to be reduced to a threat Patton should be put in charge of the southern France operation because his reputation, which was respected by the Germans, would increase the value of the threat. One objection to this proposal was that Devers and Patton were not congenial. Another was that it might lead to Patton having no role in the final campaign. On that basis Eisenhower decided to bring Patton to England and give him command of the U. S. Third Army.[19] Then, on January 22, Lucas launched the attack on Anzio. It quickly bogged down. Alexander put the blame on Lucas and sent a stinging complaint about the American general to Brooke. Lucas, Alexander said, was depressed and negative. Alexander had a meeting with Wilson, Devers, and Clark to try to solve the problem, but was unsuccessful. He asked Eisenhower what the reaction would be if he replaced Lucas with a British officer. If Eisenhower thought that solution impossible, Alexander asked if he could send down an American to take Lucas' place.

Eisenhower was upset because Alexander had not consulted Clark, the American army commander, about his proposal, and even more by the implication that in the whole of the Mediterranean Theater Alexander could not find an American general capable of taking over at Anzio. An aide had awakened Eisenhower from a sound sleep to give him the message; "although I had to shake the sleep out of my head in order to make an answer," Eisenhower told Marshall, he thought his answer was correct. He told Alexander that all American matters in Italy were the exclusive business of Devers and Clark, and that he should not have been consulted. Since he was, however, he did comment that it was "absolutely impossible" in an Allied force to shift command of a unit from one nationality to another. Alexander had indicated that the man he wanted was Patton; Eisenhower said that if Devers would ask for Patton he would be willing to send him to Italy immediately, although he could only spare him for one month.[20] Expecting that this solution would be accepted, Eisenhower then started Patton on his way. Clark, however, solved the problem locally by offering Truscott to Alexander, and on February 17 Truscott took over from Lucas. This one illustration should suffice to describe the complexities involved in officer transfer that took place while OVERLORD was being planned.

Patton returned to his headquarters and resumed the training of Third Army. On April 25 he attended a meeting of some sixty people near his headquarters to inaugurate a club for American servicemen. Persuaded to say a few words, Patton spoke on Anglo-American unity. He thought it an important subject, "since it is the evident destiny of the British and Americans to rule the world, [and] the better we know each other the better job we will do." A reporter was present, the statement went out over the wire services, and the next morning the British press featured Patton's remark. Some editorial writers were indignant because Patton had omitted Russia from the list of ruling powers, others because of the implicit insult to smaller nations. By April 27 Patton's remarks were widely circulated in the United States, where he was denounced by both liberal and conservative congressmen.[21]

Patton, in short, had again put his foot in his mouth. Marshall, much upset, wired Eisenhower. The Chief had just sent a list of "permanent makes," that is, permanent Regular Army promotions, to the Senate, and Patton's name was on the list. Marshall sadly noted, "This I fear has killed them all." He asked Eisenhower to investigate.[22]

Eisenhower was out observing a training exercise; Smith got him on the telephone and read Marshall's message to him. Eisenhower dictated a reply. "Apparently he is unable to use reasonably good sense," he said of Patton. "I have grown so weary of the trouble he constantly causes you and the War Department to say nothing of myself, that I am seriously contemplating the most drastic action." Eisenhower asked Marshall to wait a few days and gauge the public reaction to the story. If it turned out that Patton's retention would diminish confidence in the War Department, Eisenhower was ready to relieve him.[23] Instead of waiting, Marshall replied the same day. After quoting an extremely hostile editorial from the Washington *Post,* he pointed out that Patton had actual experience in fighting Rommel, who commanded the German coastal defenses in Normandy. Marshall said this advantage had to be kept in mind and left the decision up to Eisenhower. "You carry the burden of responsibility as to the success of OVERLORD." If Eisenhower thought the operation would work without Patton, "all well and good." If Eisenhower thought not, "then between us we can bear the burden . . ." of keeping Patton on the job.[24]

Eisenhower meanwhile sent a stinging letter to Patton. He warned that the incident was filled with "drastic potentialities" and said he was not so upset at the press reaction as at "the implication that you simply will not guard your tongue. . . . I have warned you time and again against your impulsiveness in action and speech and have flatly instructed you to say nothing that could possibly be misinterpreted. . . ." Eisenhower said he was forced to doubt Patton's "all-round judgment, so essential in high military position." He was waiting for word from Marshall before acting, but warned that if Patton in the meantime did anything that in any way embarrassed the War Department or SHAEF, "I will relieve you instantly from command."[25]

On April 30 Smith called Patton and ordered him to report to Eisenhower the next day. Eisenhower had, in the meantime, received Marshall's cable giving him the responsibility, and had all but decided to send Patton home. "I will relieve him," Eisenhower told Marshall, "unless some new and unforseen information should be developed in the case." He thought Courtney Hodges would do as well commanding the Third Army, and Hodges had the great advantage of not getting his superiors in trouble. Like many soldiers, Eisenhower admired Patton's dash and daring, but he had about given up on Patton. "After a year and a half of working with him it appears hopeless to expect that he will ever completely overcome his lifelong habit of posing and of self-dramatization which causes him to break out in these extraordinary ways."[26]

Marshall told Eisenhower to do what he thought best. "The decision is exclusively yours," the Chief said. "Do not consider War Department position in the matter. Consider only OVERLORD and your own heavy burden of responsibility for its success. Everything else is of minor importance."[27]

At 11 A.M. on May 1, Eisenhower met with Patton. An old hand at getting out of a fix, Patton let out all the stops. He was plunged into despair, said he felt like death, but he would fight if "they" would let him. He dramatically offered to resign his commission to save his old friend from embarrassment. To Eisenhower, he seemed on the verge of tears. "His remorse was very great," Eisenhower later recalled, not only for the trouble he had caused but because, Patton abjectly confessed, he had criticized Eisenhower to his aides when he thought Eisenhower was going to relieve him. The outpouring of emotion made Eisenhower slightly uncomfortable, and he did not really want Patton on his knees begging. He ended the interview.

For the next two days Eisenhower mulled it over. As he cooled off, he found it more and more difficult to imagine going onto the Continent and engaging the German Army without George Patton at his side. He finally sent Patton a telegram informing him that he would stay on. Patton celebrated with a drink, then sent a sentimental letter to Eisenhower, assuring the Supreme Commander of his unflinching loyalty and eternal gratitude. To his diary he confessed that his retention "is not the result of an accident"; rather, it was "the work of God."[28]

Butcher, a more or less objective witness to the Eisenhower-Patton relationship, was never as taken in by Patton as Eisenhower was. He noted that Patton "is a master of flattery and succeeds in turning any difference of views with Ike into a deferential acquiescence to the views of the Supreme Commander."[29] But if Butcher saw something that Eisenhower missed, there was a reverse side to the coin. Patton bragged that he was tolerated as an erratic genius because he was considered indispensable, and he was right. The very qualities that made him a great actor also made him a great commander, and Eisenhower knew it. "You owe us some victories," Eisenhower told Patton when the incident was closed. "Pay off and the world will deem me a wise man."[30]

Throughout the period of planning OVERLORD, Eisenhower was constantly forced to turn his attention away from the more substantial issues to concentrate, however briefly, on smaller incidents like the Patton case. Just living in London caused constant interruptions, because the Prime Minister, the American ambassador, and other officials felt free to call him at any hour. He sent his British aide, Lieutenant Colonel James Gault, out into the countryside to find him a more suitable, remote home. Gault selected a large mansion in Kingston Hill that General Eaker had been using. But it was much too grand for Eisenhower, and when he discovered that Tedder and his wife were living in Telegraph Cottage, he persuaded Tedder to switch homes. The Supreme Commander thus had the least pretentious home of any general officer in the U.K., but Eisenhower was happy, for at Telegraph he could work, think, relax, play golf, and read Westerns without being interrupted.[31] Eisenhower also insisted on moving SHAEF out of 20 Grosvenor Square in London. The new site, in Bushey Park near Kingston, code name Widewing, was a tented, camouflaged area. Having all the staff together in one place helped build up the team concept on which Eisenhower insisted; a nice touch of international unity was added by serving coffee in the morning break and tea in the afternoon.[32]

Unity was, as always, a problem. In late January the First Sea Lord, Eisenhower's old friend Admiral Cunningham, was upset by the methods some American staff officers at SHAEF had used to get information from the Royal Navy. Both Eisenhower and Smith saw Cunningham and apologized, so that "everything is serene," but Eisenhower knew that such incidents were bound to happen again and feared their bad effects. To avoid this, he made it a policy to take the blame for them himself. He asked Marshall to "please make it appear . . . that the mistake was made by me since I am always in a position to go and make a personal explanation or apology, even when I and my Headquarters may have had nothing to do with the case." Eisenhower did not have to add that by taking the blame in all things he received a bonus—members of his staff could take a position without fear. Equally important was Eisenhower's belief that the best thing, by far, in such cases was to "apply salve instead of an irritant onto fancied hurts."[33]

The behavior of American troops in Britain, as had been the case in the summer of 1942, had a direct effect on the alliance. Eisenhower turned most ETO problems over to his deputy for the theater, Lieutenant General John C. H. Lee, who also commanded the Services of Supply, but from time to time he sent memoranda to the field commanders reminding them of their responsibilities. In a typical note, he told Lee to remind all officers to see to it that the troops did not drink excessively in public places, use loud or profane language, show any slovenliness in appearance, or be discourteous to British civilians. He stressed the need for road courtesy on the part of all drivers of U. S. Army cars.[34] In another memorandum he told Lee to be especially watchful to see that "extravagance does not characterize the American Army in this Theater," either in purchases in public places or in housing of officers.[35]

Lee himself, and SOS generally, posed some special problems. Lee was a martinet who had an overly exalted opinion of himself. It worked to his disadvantage both because he exhibited a strong religious fervor (Eisenhower compared him to Cromwell) and because as head of SOS he dispensed the material. Lee and his organization decided which division got the new rifles or machine guns, which general received a late-model luxury automobile for his personal use, etc. Since he had something akin to a supply sergeant's attitude and handed out the equipment as if it were a personal gift, he was cordially hated. Field officers and enlisted men gave him a nickname based on his initials, J. C. H.— "Jesus Christ Himself," they called him. Still, he was a man who got things done and was an effective administrator, so Eisenhower kept him on.

Lee was the cause of one of Eisenhower's rare outbursts of anger against Marshall. When Eisenhower was in the United States in early January, Somervell had suggested that Lee be promoted to lieutenant general. Eisenhower guessed that Somervell wanted the promotion so that he could then argue that as Lee's superior he, Somervell, ought to be promoted to full general. Eisenhower refused to make the recommendation, but in March he found that Lee had been promoted anyway. Eisenhower complained to Marshall, since there were supposed to be no promotions in ETO above the rank of lieutenant colonel without Eisenhower's recommendation. Marshall sent a warm apology, saying he had assumed a recommendation had come from Eisenhower. He explained that he had moved Lee up because when Smith had been promoted to lieutenant general, MacArthur insisted that his chief of staff, Richard K. Sutherland, also be promoted. Marshall wanted to promote others at the same level at the same time in order to dilute the effect of Sutherland's promotion, and had seized upon Lee's name. Lee had been the beneficiary of Army politics, and the situation represented no attempt on Marshall's part to cut into Eisenhower's authority as theater commander.[36]

Eisenhower often escaped the pettiness and politicking by going out into the field, where he would observe training exercises and afterward meet and talk with the troops. His ready grin, warm handshake, and sincere interest in the problems of the G.I.s and Tommies made him a popular figure. In the four months from February 1 to June 1 he visited twenty-six divisions, twenty-four airfields, five ships of war, and countless depots, shops, hospitals, and other installations.[37] Bradley, Montgomery, Tedder, Spaatz, Patton, and the other commanders made similar visits.

Montgomery was best at that sort of thing. He would roar up in his jeep and, amid a cloud of dust, climb up on the hood. The troops were usually ramrod straight in formation around the vehicle. Montgomery would shout, "Break ranks and come close," and the men would rush in upon the jeep. "Sit down," Montgomery would order to the men's great approval. "Take off your helmets so I can get a look at you." He would then tell them that they were a fine-looking bunch, that it would be an honor to command them, and that no one wanted to get the war over with and get home more quickly than he did.

All the visits paid off. On the eve of D-Day Smith reported that the confidence of the troops in the high command was without parallel. Montgomery had managed to visit every American division in the U.K., and Smith said the G.I.s idolized him. They thought he was a friendly, genuine person without any traces of pomposity.[38]

Eisenhower's own relations with his principal subordinates, men like Smith and Tedder, were excellent, and there was a warm friendliness in his relationship with the BCOS and Churchill. Indicative of the tone at SHAEF was a small dinner party Cunningham gave for Eisenhower in February. Only twelve Britishers, most of them senior officers at SHAEF, and Smith were present. They presented Eisenhower with a silver salver as a token of their esteem.

In making the presentation, Cunningham began by recalling the days of October 1942, when many of the men present first started to work under Eisenhower. They had all wondered what sort of a man he was. "It was not long before we discovered that our Commander was a man of outstanding integrity," Cunningham declared, "transparent honesty and frank almost to an embarrassing degree. . . . No one will dispute it when I say that no one man has done more to advance the Allied cause." Eisenhower mumbled a reply. The next day he apologized to Cunningham for not being more eloquent but said that the gift itself, plus the admiral's remarks, "came so nearly overwhelming me that my only recourse was to keep a very tight hold on myself."[39]

The attitudes that Eisenhower insisted upon at SHAEF, and which he helped to bring about through his own bearing, were those of friendship, honesty, and hard work. He did not always get them, but he never quit trying. He had everyone "working like dogs," he declared with some satisfaction in late March.[40] As always, he insisted upon a positive outlook. "Our problems are seemingly intricate and difficult beyond belief," he noted in April, but he refused to allow anyone even to hint that they would not be overcome.[41]

When Eisenhower visited Gerow, the corps commander began to complain that he could see no way to solve the problem of the underwater beach obstacles. After Gerow went on in a pessimistic vein for some time, Eisenhower stopped him and said he should be optimistic and cheerful. After all, he would have behind him the greatest fire power ever assembled on the face of the earth. On D-Day there would be six battleships, two monitors, twenty-one cruisers, and an untold number of destroyers pounding the German defenses. In addition there would be the greatest air force in history, plus rocket ships and army artillery firing from the landing craft. Gerow mumbled that he was just being realistic; Eisenhower grinned and told him to keep smiling.[42]

Eisenhower's emphasis on the positive was deliberate play-acting. Privately, he was more worried than anyone else, but he never let his subordinates or his superiors in London and Washington know it. Once he explained his reasoning to Somervell. "As the big day approaches," he wrote in early April, "tension grows and everybody gets more and more on edge. This time, because of the stakes involved, the atmosphere is probably more electric than ever before." Under the circumstances, "a sense of humor and a great faith, or else a complete lack of imagination, are essential to sanity."[43]

Eisenhower had a vivid imagination and he could conceive of all sorts of problems that might emerge. Unless they were situations over which he could exercise some kind of control, however, he never discussed them. It was in that spirit, with the emphasis on hard work and optimism, that Eisenhower and the SHAEF staff approached the great problems of OVERLORD.

CHAPTER 2

The ANVIL Debate

Both during and after the war, Eisenhower often complained that men who had limited responsibilities, like Montgomery and Patton, came to conclusions that were narrow, hidebound, and mistaken. They thought of their own armies as the only one that really counted, their own fronts as the decisive ones, and felt that they should have all the supplies and reinforcements AFHQ or SHAEF had available. They never took into account the Supreme Commander's greater over-all responsibilities or larger areas of interest. Much in the complaint was justified, as was the implication—that Eisenhower took the broader view.

But even the Supreme Commander in the European Theater had a limited outlook, as the ANVIL debate was to show. For just as Patton never understood why Eisenhower would not give him everything he wanted, so Eisenhower could not understand when the CCS would not give ETO all that SHAEF asked for. And just as Montgomery later would urge Eisenhower to gear the movements and operations of all other armies to help his, so would Eisenhower ask that the CCS arrange world-wide strategy to fit the needs of OVERLORD. This desire extended to resources; at one point in the ANVIL debate Eisenhower was asking that all surplus landing craft, along with vessels already scheduled for operations elsewhere, be transferred to ETO from the other two principal theaters, the Mediterranean and the Pacific. On his own level, in short, Eisenhower could be just as narrow as the men he criticized, he could fight just as hard for ETO as MacArthur did for Southwest Pacific.

In the particular case of the ANVIL debate, Eisenhower's attitude contributed to an already great strain on the alliance, a strain brought about for many reasons: because the resources were limited; because the Americans were suspicious of the British and their intentions; because the

British were irritated at what they regarded as the bullying attitude of the Americans; and most of all, because it did make a significant military difference where the major Allied forces in the Mediterranean operated, whether in southern France, Italy, or the Adriatic.

Eisenhower wanted the debate to center around the question of which operation would most help OVERLORD. Marshall wanted to retain world-wide balance and keep the British from dragging him into any more adventures in the Mediterranean, especially in Italy or even farther to the east. The British doubted that there was much the forces in the Mediterranean could do to help OVERLORD, felt that what they could do they were already doing in Italy, and sensed that operations in Italy or to the east could be pushed with great profit. And these differing positions were only the beginning of the complexities in the debate.

The world-wide shortage of landing craft colored the entire situation and made all events related. At one point Churchill growled that "the destinies of two great empires . . . seem to be tied up in some God-damned things called LSTs."[1] The shortage stemmed from these sources: a failure earlier in the war to put landing craft at the top of the production priority list; the U. S. Navy's (and MacArthur's) insistence on assuming the offensive in the Pacific; and the unexpectedly determined German resistance in Italy.

There was little Eisenhower could do about the U. S. Navy except complain, and he did a lot of that. On January 25 he said that Admiral King was keeping all information as to the number and location of landing craft in the Pacific a secret. Army planners were forever in the dark. No one but King and his immediate subordinates, Eisenhower moaned, knew how many craft there were in the Pacific. "He spoke of action in the Pacific as 'the Navy's private war.' "[2] Two weeks later Eisenhower wrote, in a memorandum for the diary, "The fighting in the Pacific is absorbing far too much of our limited resources in landing craft during this *critical* phase of the European war." To him this was a major error, for he thought OVERLORD should have every resource available until the invading force was firmly established on the Continent. "But we are fighting two wars at once—which is wrong—so far as I can see from my own limited viewpoint."

Eisenhower had no control over events in the Pacific, and he was equally helpless with regard to developments in Italy. In January the Allied forces in the Mediterranean had made an assault at Anzio, hoping to drive inland and cut off the German forces facing Clark's Fifth Army. Von Kesselring had decided to fight rather than retreat and nearly drove the Anzio forces back into the sea. By early February it was obvious that they were stymied. Since there was no good port at Anzio, the troops there had to be supplied over the beaches by landing craft, which tied up ships previously counted on for ANVIL. When ANVIL was planned, it had been thought that there would be no need for landing craft in Italy after the end of January. It was on that very basis that the British had agreed in principle to ANVIL. Eisenhower recognized that the requirements at Anzio (which would continue until May, although no one knew that at the time), could not be ignored, "no matter how much we shout 'principle and agreements.'" Even before the Anzio stalemate Smith and Montgomery had argued that ANVIL ought to be abandoned in order to free landing craft for OVERLORD; now the BCOS joined them. Eisenhower was being forced into that position. On February 7 he noted, "It looks like ANVIL is doomed. I hate this."[3]

Marshall disagreed. When Eisenhower hinted that he was ready to drop ANVIL, Marshall replied that he still strongly favored the operation and expressed a fear that the BCOS were influencing Eisenhower's views. "I merely wish," the Chief declared, "to be certain that localitis is not developing and that pressure on you has not warped your judgment." He also asked the British not to discuss strategic matters with Eisenhower before Eisenhower had had a chance to give Washington his opinion. Marshall pointed out that canceling ANVIL would have the effect of losing a number of divisions because they could not be employed either in Italy or northwestern France due to inadequate port facilities. He did admit that the whole question would become academic if Rome had not fallen by early April. If the Allies were still south of the city at that time, ANVIL could not go concurrently with OVERLORD. But if Alexander's armies were north of Rome, there would be many divisions available and ANVIL could be mounted. This conclusion was based on the assumption that the offensive in Italy would end when Rome was taken.[4]

In any debate, Eisenhower's practice was to seek agreement. Brooke, for one, felt that this often meant the Supreme Commander was susceptible to the influence of the last person to whom he talked. Marshall evidently agreed. But the Chief also realized that he was the single most influential person in Eisenhower's life, and was usually careful not to state his views too strongly, for fear of unduly swaying the Supreme Commander. But ANVIL fit in very closely with Marshall's over-all view of how to defeat Germany—through a power drive on the Continent. In addition the Chief had so determinedly set himself against any extension of the Mediterranean campaign that in this case he very definitely did want to influence Eisenhower.

He was successful. Eisenhower bristled at Marshall's charge that he was letting the British influence his views and on February 8 sent a long, defensive answer. After a discussion of the background, in which he emphasized his own insistence on beefing up OVERLORD to five assault divisions, Eisenhower pointed out, "I felt so strongly that ANVIL should be preserved while we were achieving the necessary strength for OVER-LORD that [when Smith and Montgomery advised dropping ANVIL and adhering to a May 1 date for OVERLORD] I replied we would accept a date of 31st May in order to get an additional month's production of every kind of landing craft from both countries" so as to make both operations possible. Eisenhower insisted that only after he had formed his conclusions about dropping a simultaneous ANVIL to make OVER-LORD strong enough did he learn that the BCOS themselves wanted to abandon ANVIL. Then, in a ringing defense of himself, Eisenhower declared, "In the various campaigns of this war I have occasionally had to modify slightly my own conceptions of campaign in order to achieve a unity of purpose and effort. I think this is inescapable in Allied operations but I assure you that I have never yet failed to give you my own clear personal convictions about every project and plan in prospect." He was not aware of being "affected by localitis," and protested that his over-riding concern was to make sure OVERLORD worked. He was, in short, responding to different pressures than Marshall. As commander of OVER-LORD, he saw it as his responsibility to fight for all possible support for it; beyond that, living in London made him more aware than Marshall of the requirements of the alliance.

Eisenhower then gave Marshall his thoughts, based on a month of intensive study of OVERLORD. First, the initial assault had to have five divisions heavily reinforced with armor. Second, it had to be preceded by two months of intensive air preparation. Third, at least one full airborne division would have to be dropped inland. Fourth, at least two reinforced divisions should land on the second tide of D-Day. Since landing craft would be needed to carry them, OVERLORD would in fact require enough craft for seven, not five, divisions. Last, "we must have the strongest possible support from the Mediterranean," which meant ANVIL. Eisenhower did warn Marshall, "From D day to D plus sixty this thing [OVERLORD] is going to absorb everything the United Nations can possibly pour into it," but the implication was that, having given Marshall a long defense of his proposal to drop ANVIL, he would bow to Marshall's wishes and continue to fight for the operation.[5]

Marshall was satisfied with Eisenhower's response, and on February 11 he got JCS permission to give Eisenhower authority to represent the JCS in ANVIL discussions with the BCOS. The British had been pressing for a conference of the CCS in London to settle ANVIL; the JCS did not want to come because the members were involved in an internal debate over strategy in the Pacific. Marshall's decision to make Eisenhower the JCS executive for ANVIL discussions meant that Eisenhower became in effect a member of the CCS when southern France came up. The British were amazed that the Americans would delegate so much authority to a commander in the field, but happily accepted the arrangement since dealing with Eisenhower was easier than dealing with Marshall. The JCS may not have realized it, but the grant of authority made Eisenhower's complex role even more difficult, for it gave him two responsibilities; as Supreme Commander, he had to fight for what he thought best for OVERLORD, while, as the JCS representative, he was obliged to present as strongly as possible the American strategic position.[6] It is also possible that Marshall's motives were not altogether pure, that he realized that by making Eisenhower the JCS executive he was forcing Eisenhower to take the JCS position on ANVIL.

At a meeting with Brooke on February 10, Eisenhower found that he had reached an impasse on the issues at hand. He finally accepted Brooke's contention that the only reasonable approach to the problem was to decide what resources were required for OVERLORD and allot them, then to consider how best to use the remaining forces so as to make the maximum contribution toward the success of OVERLORD.[7] Four days later Eisenhower attended a meeting with Rear Admiral Charles "Savvy" Cooke, Jr., Admiral King's chief war planner, and Major General John E. Hull of OPD. Both had come to London to discuss with Eisenhower the plans for allocation of landing craft to OVERLORD and ANVIL. The three Americans, together with members of the SHAEF staff, made a minute examination of OVERLORD's needs. Their conclusion was that not enough landing craft had been allotted and that neither current production nor overloading of the craft on hand would be sufficient to complete OVERLORD's requirements. More craft would have to come from the Mediterranean, Eisenhower warned Marshall on February 14, even though he added that "we have *not* reached final conclusion. . . ."[8]

With Cooke's and Hull's help, Eisenhower then prepared a memorandum to present to the BCOS, with whom he would be meeting on February 19. As the JCS representative, Eisenhower made a number of specific recommendations. The most important was a proposed trade; twenty Landing Ship, Tank (LSTs) and twenty-one Landing Craft, Infantry (Large) (LCI(L)s) from the Mediterranean for OVERLORD in exchange for six AKAs from England to ANVIL. The AKAs were large cargo ships that lacked tactical flexibility, and Eisenhower justified the exchange on the grounds that the cumbersome AKAs could more easily be used in the calmer southern waters, where there was much less tidal ebb and flow. If the BCOS agreed to the trade, Eisenhower wanted a directive sent to Field Marshal Wilson ordering him to prepare ANVIL. After making these proposals, Eisenhower put on his other hat and as Supreme Commander warned that the trade would still leave OVERLORD fifteen LSTs short. This could be made up by increasing loading and serviceability and by allocating seven additional LSTs to OVERLORD from current U.S. production. Still under these conditions, the operation would be risky.[9]

At the meeting on February 19 the British made it clear that they were not going to slow the offensive in Italy, for ANVIL or anything else. This was the crux of the disagreement, for as always Marshall and the JCS were ready to shut down offensive operations in Italy, while the British wanted to increase them and even extend them into the Adriatic. Brooke told Eisenhower that, since Hitler had decided to fight in full force south of Rome, the main objective of ANVIL had already been met—German troops were being tied down. The British view was that Wilson "requires all the resources on which he can lay hands" and they feared that "the shadow of ANVIL is already cramping General Wilson. . . ." Eisenhower's proposal, Brooke complained, meant that "both OVERLORD and ANVIL are skimped." Eisenhower replied that his personal view was that the landing in southern France "might no longer be practicable owing to the developments of the situation in Italy," but warned that if ANVIL were dropped he would expect to receive nearly all the landing craft in the Mediterranean. He felt that the British wanted to abandon ANVIL in order to expand operations in Italy and the Adriatic, rather than for the purpose of providing more landing craft for OVERLORD, and to this he would never agree.[10]

After the meeting Eisenhower sent a long cable to Marshall. He summarized what had happened, then warned that the British might now argue three points: first, that Eisenhower could get along with the minimum requirements he had outlined for OVERLORD; second, that this still did not leave enough for ANVIL; and third, that therefore the remaining craft in the Mediterranean should be used to step up operations in Italy. The fallacy was in thinking that OVERLORD could be mounted on a shoestring even without ANVIL. Eisenhower disagreed with Brooke's statement that Italy was already tying down as many German troops as ANVIL would. In the Supreme Commander's view, ANVIL would hold German troops in the south of France and make it possible for him to launch OVERLORD with a minimum of resources. But if there were no ANVIL, the Germans could swing troops in southern France to Normandy, and in that case OVERLORD had to be as strong as possible. This argument lacked force, for the German soldiers in southern France were almost exclusively garrison troops, incapable of rapid movement or active combat. Eisenhower nevertheless asked Marshall if ANVIL were to be called off to be immediately authorized to take from the Mediterranean whatever he needed. He also warned Marshall that his own feeling was that "ANVIL will probably not be possible."[11]

Despite the pressure from the British to make a clear-cut choice, Eisenhower did not want to make a final negative decision on a matter about which Marshall felt so strongly. On February 19 Montgomery told Eisenhower that he had learned that the divisions fighting in Italy had suffered heavy casualties, were tired, needed to be reinforced, and required rest. They were not in a position to get to and beyond Rome in the near future, and Montgomery did not see how any divisions could be withdrawn for ANVIL. "There is no point in cutting ourselves down and accepting a compromise solution for OVERLORD, if ANVIL can never come off," Montgomery said. "It would be far better to have a really good OVERLORD." Two days later he added that ANVIL should be canceled immediately, so that Wilson, Alexander, Clark, and the others in the Mediterranean could concentrate on Italy and put ANVIL out of their minds.[12] Eisenhower merely replied that he wished to retain flexibility in strategic plans as long as possible.

Agreement on priorities, however, could not be put off. At a meeting with the BCOS on February 22, Eisenhower accepted Brooke's suggestion that until Rome was taken Italy have priority over all present and future operations in the Mediterranean. Eisenhower did insist that, subject to that priority, alternative plans had to be prepared to assist OVERLORD. The first alternative was ANVIL. The participants then agreed to order Wilson to release, in April, the twenty LSTs and twenty-one LCI(L)s Eisenhower wanted, in exchange for six AKAs. All these arrangements would be reviewed on or about March 20, when the situation in Italy would be clearer. The President and Prime Minister accepted the proposal.[13]

The number of contingencies surrounding OVERLORD-ANVIL seemed to grow daily, making it exceedingly difficult for planners to get on with their work. Firm commitments were needed if frustration was to be avoided. The Germans, by fighting savagely in Italy, had forced Marshall and the President to retreat from their previous insistence on ANVIL and accept the proposal that everything be reviewed on March 20. Eisenhower now wanted to go beyond that and, once and for all call off ANVIL. On February 26 he told Smith he was considering cabling Marshall "his view that ANVIL was impossible" in order to force a decision to release ANVIL craft for OVERLORD. Smith talked him out of it, for he "feared that it would give the impression of changing our minds too quickly."[14]

Eisenhower wanted to act quickly because he realized that the British had their own ideas about how to use the ANVIL craft if ANVIL were canceled. Having gained a bit by getting the Americans to agree to review ANVIL on March 20, the British now prepared to go all out. At the end of February Alexander asked for additional craft for his troop movements in Italy. This meant that the British had now gone beyond merely suggesting that ANVIL be canceled in order to aid OVER- LORD to the point of proposing that craft be withheld from OVERLORD in order to insure success in Italy. The BCOS backed up Alexander, requesting that the LSTs and LCI(L)s not be transferred from the Mediterranean and that they be replaced by dispatching craft directly from the U.S. (which meant, in effect, at the expense of the Pacific war).[15]

This was exactly what Eisenhower had feared all along. To make sure he got the craft, he wanted to make the negative decision on ANVIL final and have the LSTs and LCI(L)s sent on their way to England. "It becomes daily more apparent that a two division ANVIL is out of the question," he told Marshall on March 3,[16] and he reiterated the point six days later. Marshall wanted him to preserve ANVIL, while the British wanted him to support the Italian offensive. He was caught in the middle. He had made his plans for OVERLORD fifteen LSTs short in order to leave them in the Mediterranean, which satisfied both the JCS and the BCOS so long as no decision on their final use had been made. In the process, however, OVERLORD suffered.

Asserting himself as Supreme Commander, Eisenhower told Marshall that "uncertainty is having a marked effect on everyone responsible for planning and executing operation OVERLORD." He was upset with both Marshall and the BCOS, since each seemed willing to skimp on OVER-LORD, even though they had different concepts of what ought to be done with the resources held in the Mediterranean. "It seems to me," Eisenhower said, referring to both his British and American superiors, "that all concerned except ourselves [SHAEF] take it for granted that the actual assault will be successful and relatively easy, whereas we feel that it will be extremely difficult and hazardous." The time had come to put first things first. The Marshall-BCOS debate about operations in the Mediterranean was now two years old, and it had to be suspended so that SHAEF could get on with OVERLORD. In an unusually direct and stern statement, Eisenhower told Marshall, "I think it is the gravest possible mistake to allow demands for ANVIL to militate against the main effort. . . ." As an example of what he meant, Eisenhower said that five LSTs had been torpedoed in the past week, which had the most serious possible effect on OVERLORD planning. It was ridiculous. Because the allotment of resources was so close to the bone, the loss of five comparatively small vessels threw the largest Anglo-American venture of the war into jeopardy.[17]

On the evening of March 17 Smith talked to General Handy, head of OPD, by transatlantic telephone. Smith said that the SHAEF planning estimate for OVERLORD was the "very lowest, skimpiest, measliest figure that we can possibly calculate to get by on in the assumption there would be a strong landing in the Mediterranean." He added that if Washington could guarantee ANVIL "we will stick by that measly figure, but time is getting short." Expressing Marshall's views, Handy replied that "we better hang on to that [ANVIL] as long as we can," for it was necessary to OVERLORD's success. "I thoroughly agree with you," Smith cut in, "but you can't imagine the difficulties here in planning. It is enough to drive you mad with this uncertainty and these changes."[18]

The same day Marshall wired Eisenhower. The Chief said it was unlikely that there would be enough of a break in German resistance in Italy to permit an advance to Rome in the near future, or even to allow Fifth Army to link up with the forces at Anzio. What he feared was that the Germans would take desperate measures to crush OVERLORD, including the transfer of troops from the Russian front, Italy, the Balkans, and southern France. He wanted to make firm decisions, but he realized that "the only clearcut decision would be to cancel ANVIL," which he did not want to do. Still, Marshall assured Eisenhower, he would support the Supreme Commander's desires as to ANVIL whatever they might be.[19]

Eisenhower had arranged to meet with the BCOS on March 22 to make the final decision. Two days before, he told Marshall he was going to recommend that a simultaneous ANVIL be canceled. In defense of his decision, he pointed out that all his LSTs were scheduled to be used on the first three tides of the invasion. It took the LSTs three days to return from France to England, reload, and return to Normandy. This meant that SHAEF would have no LSTs reaching the beaches after the morning of D plus one until the morning of D plus four. Eisenhower had to have more LSTs, and since they could only come from the Mediterranean, it meant the end of ANVIL. As far as Eisenhower was conerned, that was the inescapable conclusion.[20]

What would happen in the Mediterranean now? This was the first question the British posed after accepting Eisenhower's recommendation to cancel ANVIL. Eisenhower replied that he still wanted to operate offensively in the area, "initially in Italy and extending from there into France as rapidly as we can." He wanted Wilson to "constantly look for every expedient, including threat and feint, to contain the maximum possible enemy forces in that region."[21] In other words, Eisenhower only wanted to postpone ANVIL, not cancel it altogether. After OVERLORD was successful he would send LSTs back to the Mediterranean for a midsummer invasion of the south of France. Wilson, on the other hand, recommended stepping up operations in Italy itself, with end runs like Anzio whenever possible. This meant continuing operations in Italy after Rome fell, which could only be done at the expense of an ANVIL mounted later in the summer. The British felt the best strategy was to maintain a strong campaign in Italy and a threat to southern France; they feared that letting up in Italy would allow the Germans to send troops from Italy to northern France.

The JCS, upon learning the results of the Eisenhower-BCOS meeting of March 22, agreed that ANVIL could not be launched concurrently with OVERLORD and "must therefore be delayed." The Chiefs also agreed to Eisenhower's request for extra shipping from the Mediterranean. They insisted, however, that ANVIL be only delayed, not abandoned, and that it have priority over a continuing full offensive in Italy once Rome had been reached. They proposed a target date of July 10 for a two-division ANVIL assault. For this purpose, they were willing to divert landing craft earmarked for the Pacific, but only on the hard and fast condition that the British agree that the July 10 ANVIL would be "vigorously pressed."[22]

Marshall, in other words, felt so strongly about ANVIL that he had accomplished the seemingly impossible—he had been able to persuade Admiral King to divert some of the precious craft from the Navy's "private war" to the Mediterranean. Like Marshall, however, King was willing to do so only if he had a guarantee that the British were not going to take the extra resources and extend their operations in Italy and to the east. ANVIL would be the vehicle through which the Americans could force the bulk of the strength in the Mediterranean into France. In this sense the American insistence on ANVIL was just another of the long list of attempts to drop the peripheral strategy the British favored and concentrate on the bulk of the Wehrmacht. Only on that basis would King approve the diversion of landing craft.

Brooke complained to Eisenhower that the JCS were "pointing a pistol." Eisenhower met with him on March 27 and emphasized the importance of the reallocation of landing craft. This was the first time the JCS had ever offered to withdraw resources fully committed to Pacific operations, which was an indication of how Marshall and King felt about ANVIL. Eisenhower reminded Brooke that there was great pressure on Marshall within the United States to step up operations in the Pacific. Brooke merely replied that he, for one, was unwilling to give a firm commitment to an operation five months in the future. In replying to the JCS offer, the BCOS said they were willing to accept the offer of the landing craft, but they wanted to give priority to Italian operations over ANVIL.[23]

When the JCS heard the British position, Field Marshal Dill reported, the members were "shocked and pained to find out . . . how gaily we proposed to accept their legacy while disregarding the terms of their will."[24] The Americans told the British that they would never accept a diversion of landing craft from the Pacific unless the British agreed to a July 10 ANVIL.[25]

By now Eisenhower was growing exceedingly tired of the whole debate. His recommendation on the main point—canceling ANVIL as originally planned—had been accepted, and he had the landing craft he needed. Planning for OVERLORD was proceeding rapidly, new issues and problems came up every day, and he wanted to concentrate on them. He was becoming somewhat irritated with Marshall, whose insistence on "hard and fast" agreements, a reflection of his continuing suspicion of the British and their motives, seemed to Eisenhower rather hidebound.

"A present complete freezing of ideas as to where and in what ultimate strength an amphibious attack" in the Mediterranean should be launched, Eisenhower warned Marshall at one point, "might later cause much embarrassment."[26] Still, there was no way for Eisenhower to back out of the discussions in which he was already so deeply involved.

On April 4 the JCS told the British that a July ANVIL had to have priority after Fifth Army linked up with the Anzio beachhead. The British replied that this was unacceptable. The Americans then said they were withdrawing their offer to divert assault shipping from the Pacific to the Mediterranean. Churchill, growing somewhat frantic, entered the debate. Why not, he suggested, delay making a decision until the link-up? At that time the CCS could "survey the situation." The Allies could then decide whether to go "all out for ANVIL or exploit the results of victory in Italy."

Marshall remained stubborn. Referring to Churchill's proposal, he sarcastically commented to Eisenhower, "You can draw your own conclusions." The United States, he explained to Churchill, could not stop the momentum it had started in the Pacific "unless there was assurance that we are to have an operation in the effectiveness of which we have complete faith."[27]

Marshall's attitude distressed Eisenhower as much as it did Churchill. It seemed to Eisenhower so obvious that the European Theater was more important than the Pacific, and so clear that "additional lift is going to be badly needed in the European Theater this summer," that he could hardly understand why Marshall was acting as he was. As head of OPD in early 1942, Eisenhower had had a better instinct for world-wide strategy and would have had no difficulty then in understanding Marshall's position. Even now he was aware that it was "not in my province to attempt to intervene in Chief of Staff discussions and decisions, but the issues at stake are so great that I felt I should submit to you personally my earnest conviction. . . ."[28]

Like Eisenhower, Churchill would not give up without a fight. On April 16 he wired Marshall to plead for the additional landing craft. In the message he summarized everyone's feeling of frustration. "The whole of this difficult question arises out of the absurd shortage of LST's. How it is that the plans of . . . Britain and the United States should be so hamstrung and limited by a hundred or two of these particular vessels will never be understood by history."[29]

The next day Eisenhower and Smith met with Churchill, Brooke, and Alexander. They found themselves in agreement on a long list of propositions, the two most important of which were, first, that the JCS ought to divert landing craft from the Pacific to the Mediterranean and, second, that it was impossible to make any firm plans about future operations in the Mediterranean until there had been a link-up with the Anzio beachhead.[30] After the meeting Churchill proposed a compromise to Washington. He wanted to send a directive to Wilson that would mention neither a fixed target date for ANVIL nor additional landing craft. This amounted to no decision at all, and on that basis the JCS accepted it. Everything—a July ANVIL, the diversion of landing craft from the Pacific, operations in Italy—was left to be settled later.

The chief effect of the three-month debate, aside from the engendering of bad feelings all around, was to give OVERLORD some additional lift for the initial assault at the expense of postponing ANVIL. Neither side had given way. The Americans still hoped for ANVIL, the British for increased offensives in Italy. For Eisenhower, the stalemate meant that he would have the landing craft essential to the five-division OVERLORD, but it also meant that many more arguments with the British over Mediterranean strategy lay ahead.[31]

The U. S. Navy had never become actively involved in the debate. Nevertheless, Eisenhower held it chiefly responsible for all the trouble. If Admiral King had been willing to see OVERLORD for what it was, the crucial operation of the war, he could have provided the landing craft to make both a five-division OVERLORD and a simultaneous two-division ANVIL possible. A proper world-wide strategy, Eisenhower felt, dictated a slowing down of Pacific operations in order to support OVERLORD. But King was stubborn, more so even than Marshall, so ANVIL instead of the Pacific had to suffer. On April 17 Eisenhower told Butcher he "would like to fly home just to have an opportunity to put all the facts before General Marshall and the President." What was needed "above all else," Eisenhower said, was "for the President to order the U. S. Navy to allot enough landing craft so the Mediterranean can be kept boiling throughout the summer." In the fall of 1942 that was the way the inside-outside debate over landing sites for TORCH had been resolved— Roosevelt had forced King to turn over the necessary ships to make three landings possible. But in the spring of 1944 King would not give in. Butcher noted that "Ike put no stock in the glib phrase used with respect to the Pacific needs, i.e., 'To keep operations going so as not to lose the benefit of the momentum,'" but evidently Marshall and Roosevelt did.[32]

As long as Eisenhower was assigning blame, he might have looked to his own European operations. What made a simultaneous ANVIL impossible was not so much King's intransigence as it was the failure of the offensive in Italy. Had Rome fallen in the fall of 1943, or even in early 1944, there would never have been an ANVIL debate. Eisenhower knew, however, that he had done everything possible in Italy, and he was sure Wilson and Alexander had too. He just was not willing to give King the benefit of the same judgment in the Pacific.

In any event by mid-April, even though the decision on the transfer of craft from the Pacific had gone against them, Eisenhower and the SHAEF planners at least knew where they stood. The margin of strength in OVERLORD was still thin, but it was better than the "skimpiest, measliest figure" it had been. It was now possible to concentrate exclusively on the great invasion.

CHAPTER 3

The Transportation Plan

General Spaatz of the U. S. Strategic Air Forces and Air Chief Marshal Sir Arthur Harris of RAF Bomber Command, like Admiral King, had a private war to fight. The airmen verbally agreed that OVERLORD was important, even crucial, but in practice they held back from a total commitment. As early as September 1943 this had been apparent to Eisenhower's deputy chief of staff, General Whiteley, who had gone to the Quebec conference as an AFHQ representative. Whiteley reported that there was much discussion in the corridors about OVERLORD. He received the impression that within the RAF and U. S. Army Air Forces (AAF) there were powerful groups "who hoped OVERLORD would meet with every success, but who were sorry that they could not give direct assistance because, of course, they were more than fully occupied on the really important war against Germany."[1]

From the first Eisenhower agreed with Whiteley's estimate that "if OVERLORD is to be a success, we must put our entire resources into it." The airmen, wedded to Douhet's theories of independent bombing, believed that the farther behind the lines they operated the more good they did. Eisenhower, along with most ground soldiers, never accepted that proposition. Theory aside, Eisenhower's experiences at Sicily and Salerno convinced him that getting ashore and staying there would be extraordinarily difficult. He wanted all the help he could get, and this very definitely included close-in attacks by the big bombers beginning well before D-Day. As had been the case in the ANVIL debate, however, the trouble was that few commanders outside SHAEF took the problem of getting ashore as seriously as he did. Eisenhower and his SHAEF associates were filled with foreboding as they thought of the things that might go wrong; those not so directly involved almost casually assumed that OVERLORD would work.

This difference in perspective was crucial. By February–March 1944 the largest single advantage the Allies had over the Germans was command of the air. It was only a slight exaggeration to say that Spaatz' and Harris' bombers could fly where they wanted when they wanted, with only ground fire to worry about. The question was: how this advantage could be exploited most effectively. There was fundamental disagreement over the answer. Eisenhower and most members of SHAEF thought the bombers could best help the over-all war effort by participating directly in the OVERLORD campaign for some six weeks before D-Day. Spaatz, Harris, and most airmen argued instead for an independent strategic campaign aimed against oil targets and cities far inside Germany. In practice, disagreements were blurred because few commanders believed in simple dependence on one alternative and because doctrine was at the mercy of limited means, which meant that doctrines constantly changed in response to availability of resources. It is now therefore difficult to line up commanders on one side or the other, as there was much shifting and turning in positions taken. But if the sides were neither clear nor fixed, they were nonetheless real and significant. Their positions were crucial because a misuse of the air forces could spell disaster for the entire project.

The first requirement was a proper organization. But everything was well muddled. In North Africa Eisenhower had commanded all the military resources of the two nations in his theater, but this was not the case in Great Britain. Although he was the American theater commander, as far as the British were concerned he was in effect a task force commander, with authority only over those British forces assigned to OVERLORD. This meant that important parts of the British ground, naval and air forces in the British Isles were independent of Eisenhower's sphere of jurisdiction. Churchill and the BCOS could take forces away from Eisenhower and OVERLORD as they saw fit; by the same token, they could assign additional forces by a simple stroke of the pen. In only one area did this cause difficulty. Cunningham was willing to give Eisenhower everything he wanted from the Royal Navy for the invasion and Brooke had already assigned to Montgomery more army troops than there were landing craft to carry. But Bomber Command of RAF was another matter. It was independent of SHAEF and wished to remain so.

"I anticipate," Eisenhower told Smith on January 5, "that there will be some trouble in securing necessary approval for integration of all Air

Forces that will be essential to success of OVERLORD."[2] He had in mind not only Bomber Command but also Spaatz's Strategic Air Forces, because although in theory as ETO commander Eisenhower was in charge of Spaatz's activities, in practice Spaatz was independent. This latter situation came about because Spaatz was operating under a directive from the CCS, prepared at Casablanca in January 1943, which gave as his mission "to secure the progressive destruction and dislocation of the German military, industrial, and economic system. . . ." All through 1943 the U. S. Strategic Air Forces, as well as Bomber Command, which worked under the same directive, concentrated on this program, code name POINTBLANK. The trouble was that POINTBLANK was not making any direct contribution to OVERLORD. But until or unless the big bombers were reassigned to SHAEF, there was nothing Eisenhower could do about it.

When Eisenhower took over, the only air power SHAEF possessed was the British Tactical Air Force, which would work with Montgomery's group of armies, and the American Tactical Air Force (Ninth Air Force), which was scheduled to co-operate with the American group of armies. Air Chief Marshal Sir Trafford Leigh-Mallory would co-ordinate the whole. Leigh-Mallory's entire experience had been with fighters, he was the senior airman at SHAEF (Tedder, although Eisenhower's deputy supreme commander, was without portfolio), and it became obvious that the CCS did not intend to give Eisenhower control of the big bombers.

This bothered Eisenhower. While he was in Washington he discussed the situation with Marshall and indicated that he thought Harris and Spaatz should work under him for a period of several weeks before the invasion. Marshall agreed. Eisenhower also received support from an unexpected quarter. He told General Arnold that he had "strong views" on the subject, and Arnold said he agreed that the bombers "should be placed under your direct command for the impending operations." The chief of staff of the AAF promised to do all he could to help accomplish the transfer.[3]

Like Eisenhower, Tedder thought that the organization ought to be cleared up, and quickly. When he raised the question with Churchill, however, the Prime Minister insisted that "everything is . . . quite simple." He roundly declared that Spaatz could be told by Eisenhower to obey Tedder, and "there will be no difficulty in arranging between Tedder and Harris." He thought, in short, that Tedder would not be hampered by lacking legal authority and that he could, through persuasion, get what was needed from Spaatz and Harris. "As Tedder is only to be a sort of floating kidney," Churchill felt, he would be able to con-centrate on co-ordinating the strategic air blows against the enemy.[4]

Neither Eisenhower nor Tedder shared the Prime Minister's confidence. When Eisenhower arrived in London he had a series of conferences with Tedder, and time and again said that what worried him most was what his relations were going to be with Harris. According to Tedder, "Harris was by way of being something of a dictator who had very much the reputation of not taking kindly to directions from outside his own com-mand." Eisenhower, Tedder recalled, "saw rocks ahead."[5]

To avoid a breakup, Eisenhower moved cautiously. All through Jan-uary and the first weeks of February he conferred with Tedder about organization and possible targets for the bombing attacks. On February 9 he told Marshall that he expected to have a complete draft of the SHAEF air program ready in a day or so, a plan that "will not only lay out exactly what we have to do, with priorities, but will also fix our recom-mended dates for the passage of command over Strategical Air Forces to this Headquarters." Before he presented it to the CCS, however, he was going to have a full meeting of the senior SHAEF personnel on the program "so that thereafter it becomes 'doctrine,' so far as this Head-quarters is concerned."[6]

On February 12 the plan was ready. It proposed a simple organization—Harris and Spaatz should come under SHAEF. This proposal was neces-sary in order to carry out SHAEF's target program, but in itself it raised an even more complicated set of problems. The plan began by ac-knowledging those points on which everyone agreed. First and foremost, the German Air Force had to be destroyed before D-Day. Much of the POINTBLANK campaign had been directed to this end with great success, but it was a continuing effort. CROSSBOW targets, the V-weapons launch-ing sites on the European coastline, should be hit whenever weather per-mitted. The Allied leaders also agreed on the proper use of air in the invasion itself. On D-Day bombers should conduct a short but heavy attack on the beach defenses just before and during the time landing craft hit the beach. Meanwhile a vast umbrella of Allied fighters would protect the LSTs and the crowded beaches from enemy air forces. After the troops were ashore, the bombers could operate against hostile com-munications and airfields and delay and harass land reinforcements. But the question of what to do with the Allies' greatest asset, their Strategic Air Force, in the period before D-Day was open.

The SHAEF proposal was to concentrate on the railway system in France in order to make it difficult for the Germans to move reinforcements to the beachhead. As the official historian of SHAEF notes, "In getting the proposal adopted, Eisenhower, Tedder, and Leigh-Mallory were vigorously opposed, on both strategic and political grounds, by most of the bomber commanders, by members of the 21 Army Group staff, and by the Prime Minister and most of the War Cabinet."[7] Eisenhower bore the chief responsibility. The fact that he held firm to his position, even to the point of threatening to resign if defeated, was perhaps his greatest single contribution to the success of OVERLORD.

The Transportation Plan, as the railway target proposal came to be called, had its origin in the bombing of Rome's marshaling yards in July 1943. Solly Zuckerman, a professor of anatomy, was one of those thousands of British experts who during World War II devoted himself to the war effort. Tedder had put him to work studying the effect of the bombing of Rome, and Zuckerman had reached some definite conclusions. Tedder sent the professor back to London to work with Leigh-Mallory, and Zuckerman convinced Leigh-Mallory that planned assaults on only a limited number of railway centers could virtually paralyze an entire railroad system. Further, Zuckerman insisted that the bombing had to be strategic, not tactical—that is, a program had to be worked out in advance and extended over a period of time. Strafing and bombing a couple of days before the invasion would not do the trick. According to the professor, the Strategic Air Forces could best aid OVERLORD by knocking out the railroad network in France and the Low Countries before D-Day.[8]

Leigh-Mallory adopted the plan as his own. Zuckerman convinced Tedder of its validity, and he in turn convinced Eisenhower. But Harris and Spaatz protested vigorously. Harris argued that Bomber Command, built for night raids and area bombing, could not achieve the accuracy required to hit marshaling yards. Tedder even accused him of juggling figures to prove that his airplanes could not hit the proposed targets.[9] Spaatz insisted that the continuing success of operations against aircraft production facilities and oil refineries would assure great support for the objectives of both OVERLORD and POINTBLANK, while to turn from these targets to railways would allow German production to return to high output. He even convinced Arnold to change his mind and support him.[10] Spaatz realized, as one of his intelligence officers reminded him, that he would have to make "a quick and decisive effort . . . to prevent the Strategic Air Forces being engulfed in the Zuckerman program," that he would, in fact, have to come up with an alternative use of the bombers that would make a direct contribution to OVERLORD. Spaatz's solution was the "Oil Plan," which gave first priority to the German oil industry, with emphasis on gasoline. This, he announced, would in the long run immobilize the Germans much more effectively than the Transportation Plan.[11]

The difficulty with Spaatz's proposal was that it would have no immediate effect. The Germans had accumulated large stocks of oil in France and scattered them so that they were comparatively safe. Only when the stocks were used up—only, that is, after D-Day—would a stoppage of oil production affect Germany's military operations. Spaatz shrugged off this point by saying that the Transportation Plan would be only of slight help in isolating the battlefield by keeping German reinforcements out of Normandy, while the Oil Plan would be of major help later.[12] This was exactly the attitude to which Eisenhower objected and the crux of the matter: Spaatz assumed that it would be easy to get ashore and stay there, while Eisenhower did not. The Supreme Commander wanted any help he could get. The Transportation Plan promised some help for OVERLORD, while the Oil Plan offered none.

But it seemed that everyone's first reaction to Zuckerman's proposal was negative. Brooke doubted the effectiveness of the proposed attack. Doolittle pronounced it a waste of effort. More serious were Portal's objections. He reminded SHAEF of a 1940 War Cabinet ruling which forbade air attacks on occupied countries if there were risk of serious damage to the population. Since it was estimated that the Transportation Plan would cause 80,000–160,000 French casualties, of which one fourth might be deaths, political approval seemed unlikely. Churchill and Eden both indicated that they could never give their blessing to such a large-scale attack against French targets.[13]

While Tedder worked to convince Portal, Eisenhower concentrated on Churchill. But the Prime Minister was as much concerned with organization as with targets. He did not want to give Eisenhower command of all the RAF in Great Britain, especially Coastal Command, which was responsible for the defense of the home islands, and he was much disturbed at the thought of Leigh-Mallory commanding Harris' bombers. Eisenhower did some "long and patient explaining" to show that he had no interest in controlling Coastal Command. At a meeting with Churchill on February 28, Eisenhower said he was prepared to issue an order stating that he would exercise supervision of all air forces through Tedder, giving Tedder authority to use already existing air force headquarters to make his control effective. Under this system, Eisenhower emphasized, Leigh-Mallory's "position would not be changed so far as *assigned* forces are concerned but those *attached* for definite periods of definite jobs would not come under his *command.*"[14] In other words, Eisenhower promised that if the CCS gave him command of the Strategic Air Forces, he would see to it that Leigh-Mallory was in effect out of a position of control.

Chruchill seemed to like the idea. Tedder, he said, could be the "Aviation lobe" of Eisenhower's brain. Still, he ruled that "there can be no question of handing over the British Bomber, Fighter or Coastal Commands as a whole to the Supreme Commander and his Deputy." He was willing to assign forces from those commands to Eisenhower as the need arose, but maintained that SHAEF air plans should be subject to CCS approval. Eisenhower strongly objected to submitting his plans to the CCS and "demurred at anything short of complete operational control of the whole of Bomber Command and the American Strategic Forces." It seemed to Eisenhower that Churchill was reneging on what had been agreed upon as the supreme effort in Europe. If the British refused to make anything less than a full commitment to OVERLORD by holding back part of Bomber Command, Eisenhower told the Prime Minister, he would "simply have to go home."

In reporting these developments to Tedder, Eisenhower warned that Churchill was "very impatient," and he urged Tedder to "push conferences and planning. . . . Otherwise the P.M. will be in this thing with both feet."[15] Churchill, alarmed at Eisenhower's vehemence, conceded. He said he would accept whatever plan Portal and Eisenhower agreed upon.

Among them Eisenhower, Portal, and Tedder worked out a solution. They proposed that Tedder supervise all air operations for OVERLORD. Eisenhower, as Supreme Commander, and Portal, who was the CCS executive for POINTBLANK, would approve of the air program that Tedder developed. The key sentence in the draft directive the three men prepared read, "The responsibility for supervision of air operations out of England of all the forces engaged in the programme including U. S. Strategic and British Bomber Command together with any other air forces that might be available should pass through the Supreme Commander." After OVERLORD had been "established" on the Continent the directive for the employment of the Strategic Air Forces could be revised.[16] The BCOS accepted the proposal. Eisenhower was completely satisfied. He told Marshall, "I must say that the way it is now shaping up I am far happier than I was a week ago."[17]

Although Eisenhower described the new organization as "exactly what we want," and although everyone on the British side accepted it, opposition unexpectedly arose on the other side of the Atlantic. The JCS protested that the new proposal did not give Eisenhower "command" of the Strategic Air Forces. The British replied that Eisenhower had helped write and had already approved the proposal. They had objected to the word "command" and insisted that "supervision" was adequate. It suddenly struck Eisenhower that the British were going to back out, that he would not after all be given control of the bombers. He confessed himself "astonished" at the British reluctance to substitute the word "command" for "supervision," for in his talks with Portal it had always been clear that command was in fact what was meant. "The question of exact terms and phraseology did not arise at that time," Eisenhower reported to Marshall, "but it was clearly understood that authority for operational control of forces . . . should reside in me." He recommended that Marshall find some word "that leaves no doubt as to the right of the Supreme Commander to control these air forces. . . ."[18]

The morning of March 22 Eisenhower dictated a memorandum for the diary. He recounted the history of his air problems, and by the time he got to the end he was so upset that he declared, "If a satisfactory answer is not reached I am going to take drastic action and inform the Combined Chiefs of Staff that unless the matter is settled at once I will request relief from this Command." That same morning the British Chiefs were meeting. When Eisenhower heard the results of their deliberations he added a handwritten postscript to his memorandum: "I was told the word 'direction' was acceptable to both sides of the house. Amen!"[19]

"Whether strategic bombers work on oil or transportation is a question up to Ike for determination," Butcher noted on March 27.[20] But it was not quite that simple. Eisenhower was still responsible to the CCS and, beyond that body, to Churchill and Roosevelt. He still had to take the views of Harris and Spaatz into account. Superiors and subordinates alike had to be shown that the Transportation Plan was feasible, and the politicians had to be convinced that the damage done in France would not leave a heritage of hatred. Some proof was already available. Portal had ordered a test, and on the night of March 6 Bomber Command carried out a raid against the railway center at Trappes. No planes were lost and civilian casualties were far lighter than opponents of the plan had predicted. Trappes itself did not function properly for a month. Somewhat gloatingly, Tedder noted that Harris had "underestimated the skill of his crews."[21]

But Trappes was just a trial run that settled nothing definitely. Spaatz continued to argue against pulling his bombers off their targets inside Germany much before D-Day, since it would give the Germans too long to repair the damage at home. He grew almost frantic late in March, therefore, when Leigh-Mallory, exercising his jurisdiction over Ninth Air Force's P-47 fighters, transferred them from escort duty with Eighth Air Force to the strafing of railroad targets in France. Spaatz complained to Eisenhower that without the P-47s as escorts his "deep penetrations will result in greatly increased heavy bomber losses and we will be losing many opportunities to deal punishing blows. . . ."[22] Eisenhower called both Leigh-Mallory and Spaatz into his office, listened to both sides, and decided in favor of Spaatz. It was too early to begin the Transportation Plan, so "for the present" he gave Eighth Air Force first call on the fighters.[23] The dispute illustrated that much remained to be settled. To thrash it out, Eisenhower called a meeting for March 25 at his headquarters. Portal, Spaatz, Harris, Leigh-Mallory, and Tedder would attend.

It was a dramatic confrontation. Eisenhower acted as chairman, listening judiciously to both sides, then making the final decision. Leigh-Mallory spoke first. The Strategic Air Force advocates had offered to participate in an interdiction program that would begin shortly before D-Day and would concentrate on line-cutting, strafing, bridge-breaking, and the destruction of a few railroad focal points. Leigh-Mallory wanted instead a prolonged attack on rail yards, sidings, stations, sheds, repair shops, roundhouses, turntables, signal systems, switches, locomotives, and rolling stock. This, he claimed, would destroy the German's capacity to move reinforcements to the beachhead while interdiction would only prove to be a temporary irritant.

Tedder supported Leigh-Mallory. He emphasized the military maxim of concentration of effort. If the air forces had their way, Spaatz would have his bombers flying over Germany making precision attacks against oil targets, Harris would be engaged in area drops against cities, while Leigh-Mallory's fighters worked over the battlefield. This was to him unsatisfactory. The Allies could derive full value from their immense air power, Tedder argued, only by selecting "one common object towards which all the available air forces can be directed." He admitted that the Oil Plan would "ultimately produce grave effects on the whole German war effort," but he did not think it could be done in time to assist OVERLORD.

Tedder cited other advantages to the Transportation Plan. It would retard the movement of supplies to the V-weapons launching platforms in France, and it would force the Germans to move by road, where they would become targets for strafing. It offered a wide selection of targets. Since the Oil Plan had to be concentrated on a few sites, it often was hampered by bad weather, which would not be the case with the Transportation Plan. In sum, Tedder declared that the Transportation Plan "is the only one offering a reasonable prospect of disorganizing enemy movement and supply in the time available, and of preparing the ground for imposing the tactical delays which can be vital once the land battle is joined."[24]

Spaatz rose to speak. It was a crucial moment in his life. He had begun his combat flying career in 1916 with the First Aero Squadron of the Mexican Punitive Expedition. As much as Harris, he was wedded to the doctrine that strategic bombing could win the war alone. He believed, according to the official historians of the AAF, that "the effects of such bombings [oil] on German industry and troop mobility on all fronts would be so drastic that the enemy high command might consider whether or not to oppose OVERLORD, or even to continue the war."[25] Graying around the temples, with a rather distinguished mustache and a wide, hard-set mouth, Spaatz was a poker player who enjoyed the good life. Extraordinarily efficient, with a sharp, incisive mind, he had an air about him of a man who was willing to indulge those who had not yet realized the true potentialities of the new weapons of war. Now Spaatz was happy to instruct them.

The Transportation Plan would not work, he began. At best, the Allies could reduce by thirty per cent the present efficiency of the enemy railroads, which was hardly sufficient. The Germans could make up that loss by cutting down on the food carried for the civilian population. On the other hand, fourteen synthetic oil plants produced eighty per cent of all German petrol and oil; by concentrating on them, Eighth Air Force could practically dry up the German supply. He therefore recommended continuing the destruction of the German Air Force (all agreed to this), an all-out attack against Axis oil production, and finally tactical support of OVERLORD beginning shortly before D-Day. This last should include "attacks in great strength upon communications and military installations of all kinds to assist to the maximum the initial phases of OVERLORD." To cement his argument, Spaatz presented an order from a German quartermaster general of the high command which declared that since motor fuel was short every unit should economize whenever possible.

Portal began the questioning. He forced Spaatz to admit that, since the Germans had plenty of stocks in France, the Oil Plan would produce no noticeable effect until four or five months after it began. Harris then said he wanted no part of the oil program; rather he wished to continue attacking cities at night.

For the first time, Eisenhower entered the discussion. He cut right to the heart of the matter by reiterating that it was essential to take every possible step to ensure that the troops got ashore and stayed ashore. "The greatest contribution that he could imagine the air forces making to this aim was that they should hinder enemy movement." Even Spaatz admitted that the Transportation Plan would make a small contribution to that end. A British intelligence officer agreed with Eisenhower's diagnosis of the problem but said his prescription was wrong. Interdiction just before and during the battle would do as much as the Transportation Plan in hampering German movements. Eisenhower "weighed in to the effect that all he had read had convinced him that apart from the attack on the German Air Force, only the Transportation Plan offered the air forces a reasonable chance of making an important contribution to the land battle in the first vital weeks after the landing." He added that it was his view that it was only necessary "to show that there would be some reduction, however small, in military movement to justify adopting the plan, provided that there were no alternatives available."[26]

Eisenhower decided in favor of the Transportation Plan, and that ended the discussion. Spaatz could not complain, since he had received a fair hearing. There were others, however, who could. As the meeting broke up, Portal warned that political difficulties lay ahead. Eisenhower decided to meet them when they came; meanwhile he sent a directive to Tedder on "Preparation and Execution of OVERLORD Air Plan." The Supreme Commander made Tedder responsible for preparing an over-all outline plan "for the employment of Air Forces in OVERLORD." Tedder could call on Leigh-Mallory, Spaatz, Harris, and their staffs for help. Eisenhower enjoined him to keep in mind "the tremendous advantages accruing to OVERLORD through current POINTBLANK operations" and to try to integrate POINTBLANK and the Transportation Plan. This meant, in effect, that Spaatz and Harris should be allowed to continue bombing in Germany, although on a reduced scale. It was a necessary concession; without it the airmen might have grown sullen and done everything by half measures.[27]

Tedder prepared a list of more than seventy railway targets in France and Belgium. On April 3 it went before the War Cabinet for approval. The ministers were not convinced that the military advantages would outweigh the obvious political drawbacks. "The argument for concentration on these particular targets," Churchill wrote Eisenhower, "is very nicely balanced on military grounds." He added that the Cabinet took "rather a grave and on the whole an adverse view of the proposal."[28] Foreign Secretary Eden was especially adamant. He pointed out that after the war Britain would have to live in a Europe which was already looking to Russia "more than he would wish." He did not want the French people to regard the British and Americans with hatred. He was also concerned with the propaganda value of the raids to the Germans.[29] In theory, it was not necessary for Eisenhower to clear targets with the War Cabinet before undertaking the bombing of the transportation network in France. Under the terms of his directive from the CCS, he could have Tedder issue orders to Spaatz and Harris. As Tedder reported, however, "in practice, it was not easy to do so" in the face of War Cabinet opposition.[30]

Eisenhower consulted with Tedder in making his reply. He admitted to Churchill that the weight of the argument that had been brought against the Transportation Plan was "heavy indeed," but stated that he was convinced that it would increase the chances for success, "and unless this could be proved to be an erroneous conclusion, I do not see how we can fail to proceed with the program." The French people, Eisenhower reminded Churchill, were "slaves." They were the ones who would benefit most from success. "We must never forget," Eisenhower added in his strongest argument, "that one of the fundamental factors leading to the decision for undertaking OVERLORD was the conviction that our overpowering air force would make feasible an operation which might otherwise be considered extremely hazardous, if not foolhardy." He thought it would be "sheer folly" to refuse approval to the Transportation Plan.[31]

Churchill then met with Tedder and Portal. Tedder continued to support the plan while Portal, who had once been opposed to it, said that Tedder and Zuckerman had convinced him that it was a military necessity. Churchill said there was no need to make a firm decision as yet; the debate, therefore, continued over the next few weeks.

On April 29 Churchill, following a meeting with the War Cabinet, sent another protest to Eisenhower, repeating the familiar arguments and suggesting that the Transportation Plan be revised to include attacks only on railway centers where the casualties would not exceed 100 to 150 Frenchmen. Eisenhower asked Tedder to draft the reply, which also contained the familiar rejoinders.[32] On the evening of May 2 Churchill showed the document to the War Cabinet. The Prime Minister spoke eloquently of Eisenhower's onerous responsibilities. Care should be taken, he said, not to add unnecessarily to his burdens. Still, he said he had never realized that air power would assume so cruel and remorseless a form. The Transportation Plan, he feared, "will smear the good name of the Royal Air Forces across the world."[33]

Neither Eisenhower nor Tedder would give in. As Eisenhower reported to Marshall, the British were trying to make him change his mind, but "I have stuck to my guns because there is no other way in which this tremendous air force can help us."[34] Churchill thought the French themselves should be consulted, so Smith talked to Major General Pierre Joseph Koenig, head of the French forces in the United Kingdom. "To my surprise," Smith reported, "Koenig takes a much more cold-blooded view than we do. His remark was, 'This is War, and it must be expected that people will be killed. We would take the anticipated loss to be rid of the Germans.' "[35]

Eisenhower continued to press Churchill for approval of all targets. The Prime Minister, almost but not quite beaten down, decided to take the issue to the President and thus force the Americans to take their share of the responsibility for approval of the plan. He told Roosevelt of the War Cabinet anxiety about "these French slaughters" and of the British doubts "as to whether almost as good military results could not be produced by other methods." He then, in effect, left the matter up to the President. Roosevelt replied that military considerations must dominate, and his statement was decisive.[36]

The Transportation Plan had won. It could not have done so had it not been for Tedder, and for Portal standing behind him. If the two RAF leaders had joined with Spaatz and Harris to present a solid phalanx against the program, Churchill never would have accepted it. Tedder's contribution went beyond simple support. His charm and reasonableness, along with his indefatigable labors, were essential to the plan's acceptance. But Eisenhower had played the key role in his original choice of Tedder for his staff. He had wanted Tedder at SHAEF precisely because he knew that Tedder's views on the proper use of air power agreed with his, and he backed Tedder in every confrontation with the strategic bombing advocates and political opponents.

The bombings which began in April were extended in May. By D-Day the Allies had dropped 76,000 tons of bombs on rail centers, bridges, and open lines. The Seine bridges north of Paris were virtually destroyed and remained out of commission until late in June. Based on an index of 100 for January and February 1944, railway traffic dropped from 69 in mid-May to 38 by June 9. The French people accepted the necessity of the program and there were no serious political repercussions. Casualties were light, much less than the pessimists in the War Cabinet had feared. Partly to make it difficult for the Germans to repair damaged facilities, partly to force what remained of the German Air Force to fight, mainly to keep Harris and Spaatz happy, about one quarter of the total strategic air effort continued to concentrate on targets inside Germany.[37]

Estimates of the effectiveness of the Transportation Plan vary. The official U. S. Army Air Force historians declare, "Long after D-Day, there remained the sobering question as to whether the results of the plan were commensurate with the cost in air effort and the ruin inflicted on French and Belgian cities."[38] The SHAEF historian wrote, "As to the general effectiveness of the bombings, both tactical and strategic, there can be no doubt." He emphasized that the German generals were "strong in their belief that the various air attacks were ruinous to their counter-offensive plans" against the beachhead.[39] Gordon Harrison, the closest student of the cross-Channel attack, concluded that by D-Day the "transportation system was on the point of total collapse," and this was "to prove critical in the battle for Normandy."[40]

Eisenhower had made the Transporation Plan his own and had seen it through. It was a resounding success. The bombers sealed off Normandy and made it almost impossible for the Germans to move reinforcements to the beachhead. Strategic bombing was no panacea offering a short cut to victory but, used properly in close co-ordination with other arms, it proved to be invaluable. Eisenhower thought the Transportation Plan was the decisive factor in his victory at OVERLORD, and he was right.

CHAPTER 4

Le Grand Charles and Other Political Problems

For a year and a half Eisenhower had been trying to find a properly constituted French authority with whom he could deal on a straightforward, impersonal basis, one which would allow him to avoid as much as possible the political complexities inherent in working with a government without a country, authority, or recognition. By early 1944, having gone through various expedients, he felt that he had found it in the form of De Gaulle's French Committee of National Liberation. In every way that mattered De Gaulle had established the FCNL as sovereign in North Africa and clearly was going to do the same in France when it was liberated. Since the Supreme Commander was counting heavily on the Resistance for help once the Allies got ashore, he thought the time had come to shelve political delicacies and recognize the FCNL as the provisional government of France.

President Roosevelt took a different view. One could not, he roundly declared in the face of all the evidence, prejudge the political attitudes of the people of France. Still clinging to his tired old metaphor, he said he refused to help De Gaulle or anyone else ride into power on a white horse. As far as possible, he wanted to ignore the FCNL, maintain a military occupation in France until the prisoners of war returned, then hold free elections supervised by the American Army. On the surface it was a policy of idealism and justice, but it ignored many realities, of which De Gaulle's self-evident popularity was only one. Eisenhower did not want to occupy France because it would waste manpower. From a purely military standpoint, the French had fighting divisions to offer and the Supreme Commander had to have the Resistance with him. To have the Resistance he had to have De Gaulle. There was in addition a contradiction in Roosevelt's policy; time and again he told Churchill the

United States would not be responsible for France in the postwar world, while at the same time asserting that the American Army could hold the country in trust until the French people could create their own government.

The larger reality, obscured often by smaller considerations, was the question of who would control Europe when the German grip on the Continent ended. The United States had twice in a quarter century gone to war to prevent one-nation dominance of Europe. The unconditional-surrender policy guaranteed that when the war ended there would be a vacuum in central Europe. The Red Army, growing stronger every day, would certainly, it seemed, flow into that vacuum. The smaller European nations, all defeated by the Germans, could not resist. Italy was distraught and occupied. Few doubted at that time that the American people would certainly insist on bringing the boys home, so there seemed little possibility of America playing a leading role. Britain, strained to the limit, was incapable of matching Russian strength, even in western Europe. That left France. Churchill had insisted from the first that he wanted a strong and vigorous France after the war precisely because he wished to maintain some kind of balance of power in Europe and Britain would need help in offsetting the Russians. None of this had much, if anything, to do with ideology; it was simply traditional British diplomacy, a diplomacy to which the United States had in 1917 and again in 1941 lent its name and its great power. For innumerable reasons, the United States agreed with the United Kingdom that one-nation control of the Continent would be bad.

Roosevelt was aware of the many complex factors in the situation. He was not opposed to a strong, revived France, but he doubted that such a recovery was possible and certainly was opposed to a France dominated by De Gaulle. He seems to have genuinely felt that France's policy under De Gaulle would be anti-American. Churchill may have agreed with this analysis, but he could see no way of promoting the revival of France without De Gaulle. For Churchill, a weak France was a greater danger than a Gaullist France.

Eisenhower was caught in the middle. With all his great responsibilities and many worries, he found that the difficulties that arose between the Western Allies and De Gaulle created one of the "most acutely annoying" problems he had to face before D-Day.[1] He had to try to reconcile the conflicting policies and at the same time to emphasize his first concern, the defeat of Germany. France could render invaluable aid in this task, but only through De Gaulle. Eisenhower therefore gave first priority to convincing Roosevelt and the State Department that the Americans had no choice—they had to co-operate with *le grand Charles.*

Eisenhower began his campaign for a working relationship with De Gaulle in January when he was in Washington. He tried hard to persuade the President and the JCS that a close operating arrangement with the FCNL could be helpful, if not essential, to the success of the campaign in France. But Roosevelt was adamant. He insisted that the French people would not submit to the authority of the FCNL and that any attempt to impose De Gaulle on France could lead to civil war.[2] The State Department, meanwhile, made the American position clear to the British in a January 14 note from Hull to Eden. SHAEF should have complete control in liberated France, Hull declared. "The restoration of civil administration in France will be left to the French people in conformity with the traditional love of liberty and independence." Hull added that "it is the hope of the Allies that the French people, having as their primary objective the freeing of France from Nazi domination, will subordinate political activity to the necessity for unity in ejecting and destroying the enemy."[3]

Eisenhower knew better than to put much faith in Hull's hopes, and had in fact already taken steps to ensure the success of a policy based on more practical and predictable conditions. On December 27 Smith, acting as Eisenhower's representative, had met in Algiers with De Gaulle and produced a draft of an agreement with the FCNL. De Gaulle approved of putting French forces under Eisenhower's control and Smith in turn assured the French that they would play a major role in the return to their homeland, including a "presence" in northwestern France. Smith further agreed that when the Allied forces approached Paris, Eisenhower would ask the CCS "to insure the inclusion of a token French Force, preferably a Division,"[4] in the liberation of the capital.

But Hull's position knocked the pins from under the Smith-De Gaulle agreement. Eisenhower was disturbed by this and was even more upset to learn from Smith that there was no intention in the United States of dealing with the FCNL on civil affairs. Eisenhower agreed with Smith that the Committee was the only realistic "vehicle" with which to deal with the French on both military and civil matters, and felt that if the Committee was ignored on civil affairs De Gaulle surely would not co-operate on military matters. Shortly after arriving in London, therefore, Eisenhower sent a plea for a more realistic policy to Marshall and the CCS. In tightly constructed sentences, Eisenhower declared, "It is essential that immediate crystallization of plans relating to civil affairs in metropolitan France be accomplished. This requires conferences with properly accredited French authorities. I assume, of course, that such authorities will be representatives of the Committee of National Liberation." He requested that De Gaulle be invited to send an individual or a committee to London with whom he could enter into immediate negotiations. The need for prompt action could not be overemphasized, Eisenhower said, since he wanted to turn over to the French control of the countryside at the earliest possible date after the invasion.[5]

Marshall gave Eisenhower's cable to Assistant Secretary of War John McCloy, who took it to the President. When McCloy emphasized the importance of the Resistance to SHAEF's success, Roosevelt agreed to a slight shift in position. He authorized McCloy to cable Eisenhower, saying "informally" that he should "feel entirely free" to make decisions about the Resistance, even if it involved dealing with representatives of the FCNL. McCloy did so, and added his own belief that on civil administration real progress was being made. He hoped that the CCS would soon send Eisenhower a basic directive for dealing with the Committee.[6] Roosevelt, however, continued to hold back on any directive that might in any way imply a recognition of the FCNL as the provisional government of France.

Roosevelt delayed in acting for more than two months, as conversation went on in Washington and London. Finally, on March 15, the President sent Eisenhower a basic directive. He gave the Supreme Commander power to decide where, when, and how the civil administration of France should be exercised by French citizens, "remembering always that the military situation must govern." Eisenhower had permission to "consult" with the FCNL for local civil administration, subject to the distinct understanding that this action did not constitute recognition of the Committee as the government of France. If Eisenhower did choose to deal with the FCNL, he should require from it three guarantees: (1) it had no intention of exercising the powers of government indefinitely, (2) it favored the re-establishment of all French liberties, and (3) it would take no action to entrench itself pending the selection of a constitutional government by the free choice of the French people.[7]

De Gaulle, upon being informed of these requirements, commented, "The President's intentions seemed to me on the same order as Alice's Adventures in Wonderland." Giving Eisenhower a choice in deciding which French officials to deal with was ridiculous. The alternatives were Vichy or De Gaulle, and Vichy was too compromised by collaboration, and the reaction to the Darlan deal too fresh in everyone's minds, to make it a real alternative. De Gaulle felt that, "without any presumptuousness, I could defy General Eisenhower to deal lawfully with anyone I had not designated." De Gaulle professed himself not to be worried anyway, since, he said, Eisenhower had told him, "Now I can assure you that as far as I am concerned and whatever apparent attitudes are imposed upon me, I will recognize no French power in France other than your own in the practical sphere."[8]

In public, De Gaulle took a strong position. On March 27, referring to Roosevelt's requirement that he guarantee traditional liberties, he declared, "France, who brought freedom to the world and who has been, and still remains, its champion, does not need to consult outside opinions to reach a decision on how she will reconstitute liberty at home." A week later he added, "Wherever they may be and whatever may happen, Frenchmen must accept orders only from this Government [the FCNL] from the moment they are no longer personally subjected to enemy coercion. No authority is valid unless it acts in the name of this Government."[9]

The Roosevelt-De Gaulle clash distressed Eisenhower. While he agreed "that too great a concession to the French National Committee will result only in that body becoming even more arbitrary and high-handed than at present and will cause us acute embarrassment," he realized "we are going to need very badly the support of the Resistance Groups in France," and they could be brought to play their full role only with De Gaulle's help. Meanwhile Eisenhower had no one at all with whom he could deal on civil affairs in France.[10]

In April the French took one step forward and one backward. On the twenty-first the FCNL adopted an ordinance providing for the election of a Constituent Assembly by universal suffrage within one year of the liberation and promised to surrender its power to the new Assembly. This was reassuring, but the effects were lost a few days later when De Gaulle assumed final authority in all matters relating to French armed forces. General Giraud, angry at being reduced to a figurehead, resigned and went into retirement. This signaled the end of the original Roosevelt-Murphy French policy. The situation brightened again on April 25, when General Koenig, the senior French commander in the United Kingdom, began what was intended to be a series of informal discussions with the SHAEF staff. At the first session he pleased everyone by saying that questions involving the sovereignty of France could be put aside until later.[11]

Almost immediately, however, the FCNL instructed Koenig to end the discussions. De Gaulle was unhappy because the British had declared that all foreign diplomatic representatives, save those from the United States and the U.S.S.R., would be barred from sending or receiving uncensored communications. This diplomatic ban had come about as a result of a fervent plea from Eisenhower, who on April 9 had told Brooke that diplomatic communications had to be censored as a part of the over-all security measures for OVERLORD. Eisenhower explained, "I regard this source of leakage as the gravest risk to the security of our operations and to the lives of our sailors, soldiers and airmen." Although De Gaulle still carried the reputation of being unable to keep a secret, there is no evidence that Eisenhower had the French specifically in mind in propagating the ban, and when the War Cabinet imposed it, it applied the policy equally to all nations except its two major Allies.[12]

Every party except De Gaulle was agreeable, albeit with some grumbling. De Gaulle, rather than have his communications censored, decided to have no communications at all. No notes moved between London and Algiers, which made it impossible to secure any agreement between the FCNL and SHAEF, or even to have informal meetings with Koenig, since Koenig could not receive instructions. De Gaulle took his drastic action because he was sure a compromise would be reached. He based his belief on the assumption that he had a high-placed friend in London. General Eisenhower, he told an American correspondent, had "a friendly disposition toward France."[13]

Whatever the Supreme Commander's disposition, he had a battle to fight and was willing to make concessions to De Gaulle or anyone else in order to be in a position to fight it at full strength. He complained to the CCS that the limitations under which SHAEF had to operate with the French were "becoming very embarrassing and are producing a situation which is potentially dangerous." The President had told him to deal with any French body that could deliver the military forces needed for OVERLORD; in practice this meant the FCNL. Eisenhower suggested to the CCS that the best course would be to bring De Gaulle himself to London and tell him of the place and date of the invasion. SHAEF could then work out civil affairs agreements with the French.[14]

Eisenhower told Churchill of his request, and Churchill sent a cable to Roosevelt urging him to agree to it. The President approved of bringing De Gaulle to London but emphasized, "I do *not* desire that Eisenhower shall become involved with the Committee on a political level."[15] Roosevelt also insisted that if De Gaulle did come to London and was informed about OVERLORD, for security reasons he would have to stay in the city until after the invasion. Smith talked over the telephone to Churchill about this requirement; both agreed that De Gaulle would indignantly refuse an invitation that had strings attached. Nothing, therefore, was done.

This situation left Eisenhower unable to act. He had no formal directive from the CCS for carrying on French affairs, he had been warned by the President to avoid all political discussions with De Gaulle, an obvious impossibility, and he was acting on a unilateral directive from the President, which was difficult because he was an allied commander. Most of all, he still had no agreement with the French about either civil or military affairs. He decided to try for conciliation again. On May 16 he sent a message to Marshall for delivery to the President. Eisenhower promised to make no political agreements with De Gaulle but added, "I think I should tell you that so far as I am able to determine . . . there exists in France today only two major groups, of which one is the Vichy gang, and the other characterized by unreasoning admiration for de Gaulle." He expected that the Allies, once ashore, would find "a universal desire to adhere to the de Gaullist group." Having explained the realities, Eisenhower made a final plea: "Because this is an allied command, I hope that your desires on this subject of which I am aware, can eventually come to me as a joint directive of the two governments."[16]

The timing of Eisenhower's request for a saner French policy was unfortunate. The same day the FCNL passed a resolution stating that henceforth it would be known as the Provisional Government of the French Republic. Roosevelt was livid. He ordered OWI never to refer to the Committee as the Provisional Government, which gave the French an opportunity to have some fun at America's expense. The Committee delighted in issuing bulletins referring to itself as the Provisional Government. The BBC read the bulletins as issued, while American broadcasters had to substitute "the French Committee" for the forbidden words.

Pettiness aside, Roosevelt disagreed with Eisenhower's basic analysis of the situation. On June 2 he told Marshall that Eisenhower "does not quite get the point. He evidently believes the fool newspaper stories that I am anti-de Gaulle, even the kind of story that says I hate him, etc., etc. All this, of course, it utter nonsense. I am perfectly willing to have de Gaulle made President, or Emperor, or King or anything else so long as the action comes in an untrammeled and unforced way from the French people themselves." The President thought that when the

Allies got into France SHAEF should do what AFHQ had done in Italy—that is, send a team into each of the villages, talk to local leading citizens, and appoint a mayor. He should not let De Gaulle appoint one, Roosevelt said, as he already knew of one case in which De Gaulle had designated a mayor for a town, and the man was "an unsuccessful politician and, in all probability, a porch-climbing robber." Referring to Eisenhower's belief that France was split into two groups, Vichy and Gaullist, the President mused, "I wonder how he knows this because nobody else knows anything really about the internal situation in France." Roosevelt thought the largest group in France was the one that did not know what was happening. He knew it was "awfully easy to be for de Gaulle . . . but I have a moral duty that transcends 'an easy way.'" It was, he felt, his responsibility to see to it that the French did not have a government foisted on them by outside powers.[17]

Whatever motivated Roosevelt—he himself said it was idealism, a concern for "a very deep principle in human affairs," that of self-determination—his policy made for "friction and bad atmosphere," as Eisenhower put it. Still, Eisenhower would not give up. He thought that once OVERLORD started "I can secure from the French the cooperation that I need."[18]

He had help. In late May Koenig worked out the diplomatic ban impasse. He allowed Allied authorities to examine his cables going to Algiers, then sent them in French code. The Allies allowed him to do this because he gave his word he would make no changes before encoding the messages. Incoming cables from Algiers were of course not at issue.[19]

On June 1 Churchill made his contribution to conciliation by inviting De Gaulle to come to London to be briefed on the operation.[20] The Frenchman at first refused, but the other members of the Committee convinced him he had to go, and on June 4 he arrived in England. Immediately, he began to say *non* to every proposal SHAEF made. Churchill briefed him on OVERLORD and asked him to co-operate by broadcasting to the French people and to the Resistance the strong request that they follow Eisenhower's orders. De Gaulle refused. He was, Churchill noted, "bristling." De Gaulle said political and military matters went hand in hand and that he could do nothing until political recognition of some kind was accorded him. He asked for an absolutely free right to telegraph to Algiers in his own cipher, without anyone reading the messages beforehand. Churchill calmed him, then asked him to make a broadcast to the French people on the eve of the invasion.

De Gaulle agreed, or at least seemed to. The conversation turned to the American President. De Gaulle made no attempt to hide his bitterness, and finally Churchill shouted at him, "Each time we must choose between Europe and the open sea, we shall always choose the open sea. Each time I must choose between you and Roosevelt, I shall always choose Roosevelt." De Gaulle growled that he had expected as much and the interview ended.[21]

Churchill had arranged to bring Eisenhower and De Gaulle together on June 3. Eisenhower would come to the advanced command post at Portsmouth, where last-minute preparations for the invasion were under way. The Prime Minister arrived first and had a few quiet minutes with the Supreme Commander. De Gaulle then appeared, and Eisenhower took him on a grand tour of the war room, pointing to the maps that covered the walls and explaining the forthcoming operation. De Gaulle lectured on how it should be done. Eisenhower nodded gravely and said he regretted that he did not have time to make the changes De Gaulle suggested. Churchill then withdrew and Eisenhower and De Gaulle went for a stroll up a shady cinder path "where there was enough elbow room for de Gaulle to wave his arms and talk. Ike did some too."[22]

Eisenhower handed De Gaulle a copy of the speech he was going to make to the French people. He did so, according to De Gaulle, with some embarrassment, for in it the Supreme Commander urged Frenchmen to "carry out his orders," told them that local administration would continue, and promised that once France was liberated "the French themselves would choose their representatives and their government."

For De Gaulle this was all nonsense, dangerous nonsense. Eisenhower spoke of the French forces under his command, when in fact no agreement about the employment of French troops in OVERLORD had yet been signed. There was no mention at all of De Gaulle or the FCNL. Vichy administrators would stay in power. Worst of all, SHAEF, it seemed to De Gaulle, was obviously planning for a military occupation of France. De Gaulle told Eisenhower that the speech had to be changed. Eisenhower replied that it was too late—it had already been cleared with both governments and recorded. In that case, De Gaulle declared, he would not speak after Eisenhower, since that would give the impression that he approved of the SHAEF program. He had not asked to come to London but, since he was there, he would do what he could to save the sovereignty of France. If the Allies insisted on going ahead with their plans, there was nothing he could do to stop them, but he certainly was not going to help them.[23]

Another major issue that aroused De Gaulle was currency. SHAEF had printed occupation francs and wanted De Gaulle to issue a statement telling the French people he authorized their use and would guarantee them. De Gaulle refused. He pointed out with some intensity that France was being treated precisely like Italy and that he alone, as President of the Provisional Government, had the right to issue currency.[24]*

It was, Eisenhower sadly noted, "a rather sorry mess." He was most worried about the Resistance. SHAEF had lines to the Resistance through the British Special Operations Executive, and the Resistance was primed to carry out extensive railroad sabotaging which would help to deny the German strategic mobility. If the underground did not act, much would be lost. But, as Eisenhower reported, "all our information leads us to believe that the only authority these Resistance Groups desire to recognize is that of de Gaulle and his Committee."[25]

Because of the nature of Eisenhower's address and because of the currency issue, De Gaulle resisted all pressure and refused to make his own broadcast to the French people. A comic opera ensued with nearly every important American and Britisher in London arguing with De Gaulle. How would it look, they asked, if it became known that he was in London on the eve of the invasion and had refused to add his voice to those of the other heads of governments in exile? A series of cables to Washington charted the course of the discussion. "General de Gaulle will speak," "General de Gaulle will not speak," and "the General has changed his mind."[26]

The evening of June 5 Smith telephoned Eisenhower—who had other things on his mind—to report that De Gaulle would not speak. Giving in to his impulses, Eisenhower said, "To hell with him and if he doesn't come through, we'll deal with someone else."[27] There was, however, no one else to deal with and the efforts to convince De Gaulle to make the broadcast continued.

* In the end SHAEF had to go ahead and use the invasion francs without De Gaulle's support. On June 10 Eisenhower issued a proclamation about the currency; to soften its effect, he guaranteed representative government in France. De Gaulle called a press conference and said Eisenhower's proclamation ominously foreshadowed "a sort of taking over of power in France by the Allied military command." Churchill meanwhile told Roosevelt that the only alternative to having De Gaulle authorize and stand behind the notes (which would give him de facto recognition) was "to guarantee the money ourselves." Roosevelt stood firm. Eisenhower should use the invasion francs, and if De Gaulle wanted to issue something on his own individual responsibility, he could sign the currency "in any capacity that he desires, even to that of the King of Siam. Prima Donnas do not change their spots." The problem dragged on through the summer. EP, No. 1745.

But final victory was De Gaulle's. He spoke on the day of the invasion, from his own text. "The orders given by the French government and by the leaders which it has recognized must be followed precisely," he emphasized.[28] Another French crisis had been, if not met and overcome, at least passed over.

Eisenhower had been unable to avoid the complexities of French politics. He had been forced into the heart of them because of his position. On two other major political issues he became involved because of his own actions. He felt strongly about the form that the military occupation of Germany would take and about the policy of unconditional surrender. He believed the President was making serious errors. Ignoring his own oft-repeated comments about being apolitical, he initiated discussion with Roosevelt on the subjects. This irritated the President and, since Eisenhower did not get his way, the Supreme Commander was left unhappy.

Eisenhower raised his first political objection while he was in Washington in January. He called on the President, who was sick in bed with influenza. They had a long conversation on the occupation of Germany. COSSAC had prepared a plan, to be implemented in case of a sudden German collapse, which set up three zones, with the Russians in the east, the British in the northwest, and the Americans in the southwest. The European Advisory Commission, which had just been formed and which included representatives of each of the Big Three, had accepted the basic idea. So had Roosevelt, although he wanted to switch zones with the British. Eisenhower, who had been briefed on these developments, told the President that the policy was a mistake. Germany, he declared, should not be divided into zones. Rather, the military government ought to be conducted by a coalition of the Allied forces, including the Russians.

In a memorandum to Smith on May 20 Eisenhower said he realized the point was academic if the United States intended to withdraw all troops from Europe shortly after the conclusion of hostilities. But, he added, his conversation with Roosevelt convinced him that the President was beginning to realize that the Americans would have to leave occupation troops in Germany for some time to come. This in turn was a logical outgrowth of Roosevelt's over-all European policy and plans: with Britain exhausted, a vacuum in Germany, and France unlikely to recover, the Americans had to stay in Germany or perforce leave the Red Army as the sole power base in central Europe. But since it was not to be expected that Roosevelt could keep American boys in Germany indefinitely, there had to be some way to compel the Red Army to pull back when the Americans came home. Having a single supreme commander who took his orders from all three governments would solve the problem. Eisenhower told Smith that when the time came to turn Germany over to civilian authorities it would be easier to get the Red Army out if there were such a commander, as there would be in the kind of coalition military government Eisenhower had proposed.

Eisenhower expected the Russians would take some drastic action in Europe, but he did not feel that they would become points of disagreement, for he thought they were justified. Thus, he told Smith, the Russians "will undoubtedly demand the utilization of German labor in order to restore their own devastated districts," and predicted that the Soviets would keep a tight control on eastern Germany and the Balkans. Eisenhower did not believe these actions would put any strain on the alliance.

Years later, Eisenhower succumbed to the temptation to reconcile his World War II views with Cold War rhetoric, and the story he then told about his conference with Roosevelt differed significantly from what he had said to Smith in May 1944. When he wrote his memoirs Eisenhower recalled that he had told Roosevelt that a joint occupation was necessary to control the Soviets. If Germany were divided into zones, he feared administration would be difficult. Roosevelt, Eisenhower remembered, made light of his fear of the Russians, and when Eisenhower pressed the point the President grew impatient. Roosevelt said he could deal with the Russians, which conveniently put all the blame on the dead President. Eisenhower also later declared that he had opposed a "hard" policy toward postwar Germany, when in fact his record was at least ambivalent.[29]

In any case the President had set forth his policy and the general continued to question its wisdom. In February Eisenhower proposed to Marshall that the United States refuse to take specific responsibility for any area. Instead, he asked, "Why should we not place ourselves on record as saying we will retain responsibility . . . only so long as the Allied principle of unity of Command is observed . . . ?" Eisenhower thought this "simple formula" would help keep the United States out of "unnecessary difficulties and would still give our President a major voice in the establishing of policy." This was important, Eisenhower added, because the United States would be making the largest contribution to the rebuilding of Europe, and thus ought to have a say everywhere.[30]

Marshall sent the suggestion over to Roosevelt, who passed word back to Eisenhower to "sit tight."[31]

Eisenhower did, but he continued to discuss the idea. In mid-May Major General LeRoy Lutes, who was on an inspection tour for Somervell, stopped in at Widewing to talk with Eisenhower. The Supreme Commander went on at length about the future organization of Europe, "stating that in his opinion an Allied General Headquarters, or Mission, should be set up to handle Europe until such time as the United States Army withdrew." Eisenhower thought that if this were not done the Russians would play the British against the United States and the United States against the British. An Allied GHQ could settle such matters and could allocate resources to the best interests of all. Lutes liked the idea. His only fear was that since in his opinion the British already dominated SHAEF they might dominate an Allied GHQ.[32]

During the next two weeks, possibly as a result of conversations with traveling Americans, Eisenhower dropped the idea of Big Three cooperation throughout Germany. He still wanted to avoid an Anglo-American division into zones. On June 27 he wrote Marshall, "I have reason to believe that the President is still open-minded on the question which has given us all considerable thought, namely—a combined or separate British and American zones of occupation in Germany." His talks with Roosevelt convinced him that the President contemplated keeping a small American force on the Continent for a considerable period after the armistice, but he felt that Roosevelt had not distinguished in his own mind whether there should be a complete amalgamation of British and American units, or a complete segregation of them. Eisenhower favored keeping SHAEF in existence and treating West Germany as a common zone. One advantage was that the CCS would remain in existence as long as the war with Japan continued, and the Chiefs would look upon the Anglo-American forces remaining in Europe as a reservoir from which they could draw strength to pursue the Pacific war. But CCS orders were valid only when processed through an Allied commander in chief; thus it would be "convenient and desirable" to keep SHAEF.

What Eisenhower was most concerned about was "abandonment of the Allied principle." As always, his commitment to Anglo-American solidarity was complete. He thought it dangerous to set up special areas with special interests, since it might lead to a split. "Instead of presenting a solid front that has characterized all our operation . . . every problem arising would first have to be settled on a British versus American basis. . . ."[33]

Unfortunately for Eisenhower's position, the President was not still open-minded on the subject of zones. While Eisenhower's letter was en route, Roosevelt told Marshall to tell Eisenhower to proceed in his occupation planning on the assumption that the Americans would have their own zone. Eisenhower therefore let the subject rest, although in August he would raise it again.[34]

The second political question in which Eisenhower involved himself was the unconditional surrender policy. Eisenhower and Smith had privately agreed that it was an error, but no one had asked their opinions and they had not gone out of their way to make them known. In April, however, when Under Secretary of State Edward Stettinius was in London, the subject did come up. Stettinius told Eisenhower the President was far from well and "becoming increasingly difficult to deal with because he changes his mind so often."[35] After more discussion, both Smith and Eisenhower said there should be some clarification of the meaning of unconditional surrender "by announcing the principles on which the treatment of a defeated Germany would be based." Eisenhower said this was highly desirable "in view of the accumulated evidence that German propaganda is interpreting the words of 'Unconditional Surrender' to strengthen the morale of the German Army and people."

Specifically, the two generals wanted a tripartite statement to guarantee law, order and political justice, thus making it possible to create a mood in Germany that might lead to Hitler's overthrow. They proposed that as soon as SHAEF had won a beachhead in Normandy Eisenhower should issue a statement summarizing the terms of surrender and calling on the Germans to lay down their arms. Smith said that "from all available evidence, in default of such declarations, it would be impossible to exploit the crisis in the German Army which will undoubtedly arise immediately after a successful Allied landing."[36]

Hull brought up the matter with Roosevelt, who said first that he doubted that the Russians would agree with the proposal and second that SHAEF could certainly not deliver on promises made only by the British and Americans. On May 20 Eisenhower, in a memorandum to Smith, said that he recognized the force of Roosevelt's objections, but that he still maintained something could be done. He tried drafting a tripartite statement himself but was not satisfied with the results. In the end, he guessed that if this obstacle could not be surmounted "then we had better drop the whole matter and let it ride as it is."[37]

Although he never overcame the obstacle, Eisenhower did use his memorandum to Smith as the basis for a letter to Marshall, which the Chief passed on to Roosevelt.[38] The President had earlier said that "he did not want the subject to be further considered without his approval," but after looking at Eisenhower's message he made an attempt to compose a statement. The attempt failed, partly because Churchill and Stalin were opposed to it, partly because Roosevelt could not decide how to deal with the quandary of war criminals. Any pronouncement that did not include a declaration of intended punishment for war crimes would leave the Allies open to charges of deception, but any announcement which did mention the subject would terrify the Germans and lead to even more intense resistance. As a final decision, no statement was made.[39]

Thus, in the three major political areas in which he tried to exert an influence, Eisenhower had failed. Unconditional surrender remained the official policy, the occupation of Germany would be by zones, and the United States and United Kingdom would not formally recognize the FCNL as the Provisional Government of France, nor even give Eisenhower clear-cut permission to deal with De Gaulle. Important as all these matters were, however, they did not have priority among Eisenhower's concerns. His interest in politics was peripheral. His main concern was OVERLORD itself, and to it he continued to devote by far the great bulk of his time and energy.

CHAPTER 5

Worries of a Commander

All the problems of modern warfare generally, and of Operation OVER-
LORD specifically, fell on the Supreme Commander. Everyone else had
a single given role to play and could concentrate on one set of problems;
Eisenhower's worries were infinite. He and his headquarters were the
funnel through which everything passed, but even at SHAEF only Smith
worked from Eisenhower's point of view and shared the range and
scope of his problems, and Smith did not have the awesome burden of
command. All the others were experts struggling with their specialties.
They could study and analyze a problem and make recommendations,
but they could not decide and order. The bureaucracy did very well
what it was created to do, but its limitations were obvious. Someone had
to give it direction; someone had to be able to take all the information
the bureaucracy gathered, make sense out of it and impose order on it;
someone had to decide; someone had to take the responsibility. If the
operation failed, the CCS could not fire the bureaucracy.

It all came down to Eisenhower. This position put enormous pressure
on him, pressure that increased geometrically with each day that passed
in May. "Ike looks worn and tired," Butcher noted on May 12. "The
strain is telling on him. He looks older now than at any time since I have
been with him." It would get worse as D-Day got closer and innumerable
problems came up each day, many unsolved and some unsolvable. Still,
Butcher knew that all would turn out all right, that Eisenhower could
take it. "Fortunately he has the happy faculty of bouncing back after a
night of good sleep," Butcher recorded, "or a ride on a horse or some
exercise."[1]

On May 6 Eisenhower told Marshall of some of his principal worries.
"Our worst problems these days involve methods for removing under-

water obstacles," he began, "production of Mulberries and all the other special equipment pertaining to artificial harbors, accuracy in weather predictions and perfection of methods for getting a completely co-ordinate assault—including airborne." There were major concerns, but Eisenhower confessed that in the midst of all these great problems "some of my most intense irritations are caused" by trivial matters, such as Patton's latest indiscreet statement about the United States and the United Kingdom running the world. Despite the pressure, Eisenhower concluded, "most of us are staying in very good health" and a spirit of optimism prevailed.[2]

As with most major seaborne assaults, OVERLORD's overriding problem was that there were so many unknown factors. What would the weather be like on D-Day? If an Atlantic storm blew in, the air forces could not fly, the paratroopers could not drop, and the soldiers would at best be seasick and unable to fight. At worst, the landing craft would pile up on the beaches with the surf tossing them around like rubber balls. What was the state of the German defense? How effective was the Transportation Plan going to be? Could the Germans move reinforcements to the beachhead quickly? What about the artificial harbors, the mulberries and gooseberries? SHAEF had accepted the COSSAC plan of relying on them for supply until Cherbourg was captured and put in working order, but they were new implements of war and no one really knew whether or not they would work. Construction of them was behind schedule, and Admiral Cunningham told Eisenhower he was worried that he would not have enough tugs to tow the concrete barges from the places they were manufactured to the assembly points and thence across the Channel.[3]

The immediate task—getting ashore with troops—was going to be difficult. The Germans were feverishly working at improving their defenses, laying mines in the Channel, building up pillboxes and gun emplacements inland, clearing the local population from the coast and setting up observation posts, and trying to upgrade the quality of the troops themselves. Most of these measures, however, SHAEF officers had coped with before. They could be met and overcome. The serious unknown factor was the steel obstacles the Germans were placing all along the Atlantic coast. Some of the obstacles were multi-pointed at the top and would tear out the bottom of any landing craft passing over them. Others were simple steel stakes, made from I-beams or rails and sunk into the sand by water jet. They were capped with Teller mines. The Germans had started placing the obstacles at the high-water mark and by May 1944 had covered the area halfway to the low-water mark. This development was one of the reasons SHAEF had decided to land shortly after low tide, accepting the risk of passing troops over an exposed beach. Engineers could clear the obstacles as the tide came in. A further advantage of landing at low tide was that landing craft could run ashore, disgorge the troops, and then be floated free by the rising tide.

Eisenhower had to make an attempt to probe the mind of the enemy commander, Field Marshal Gerd von Rundstedt, a tight-cheeked old aristocratic professional officer who was something of a pessimist. Von Rundstedt had two army groups under him; the one Eisenhower would be attacking was under Rommel's command. What these men thought, and what their relationship to Hitler was, would make an enormous difference in the way the Germans fought the campaign. In trying to find out what the Germans intended to do, Eisenhower relied on SHAEF and Twenty-first Army Group intelligence for information. From his G-2 people, for example, Eisenhower learned many things: that the Germans thought there was a possibility that the Allies would invade Norway; that they expected the main attack at Pas de Calais; that they had fifty-eight divisions in France (but that the divisions had been cut in size from 17,000 to 13,000); that they had no general reserve of troops and if they wished to strengthen themselves in France would have to do so at the expense of the fighting fronts in Russia or Italy; and that Rommel wanted to meet the attack head on and drive the invaders back into the sea.[4] What G-2 could not supply Eisenhower with was detailed information on personality conflicts and strategic differences of opinion within the German high command. In these areas, he would have to rely on his intuition.

Eisenhower knew that traditional German tactics emphasized mobility, and Von Rundstedt was a traditional soldier. Rommel was not, and Eisenhower realized that Rommel, greatly impressed by American armor and mobility, would try to convince Von Rundstedt that he should meet the invaders on the beach, which meant a linear, static defense with the emphasis on holding ground and the primary dependence on concrete fortifications. After his experiences in the later stages of the Tunisian campaign, Rommel would probably view with skepticism any proposal that relied on moving large forces to the battlefield for a counterattack, since he would fear that Allied airplanes would strafe, bomb, and cut up the columns while they were on the road. But Rommel was the subordinate, Von Rundstedt the superior, and Von Rundstedt would probably want a defense in depth with large-scale counterattacks spearheaded by armored striking power. In contrast to Rommel's probable program, this would mean keeping the bulk of the German strength back from the coast. Beyond the Rommel-Von Rundstedt disagreement there was Hitler. Throughout the war Eisenhower counted on Hitler's "conqueror mentality," with its empahsis on holding every piece of ground, to make his task easier. Eisenhower's own guess was that the Germans would follow Rommel's ideas and try to force a decisive battle on the beachhead.

Eisenhower had experience in meeting either type of response. At Sicily the beach had been hard but the counterattack soft; at Salerno the troops had no trouble getting ashore but Von Kesselring's counterattack had almost driven the Allies back into the sea. Eisenhower decided that in Normandy the Germans would put the emphasis on static defense; OVERLORD planners therefore concentrated on getting ashore and staying.

One vexing problem was choosing the day to go ashore. Eisenhower had already moved the target date back from May 1 to June 1 in order to have the benefit of extra time for training and procuring landing craft; now he had to decide on the exact date. June 1 was Y-Day; that is, the assault would occur at the first favorable opportunity after June 1. Many factors went into Eisenhower's selection of D-Day, but a low tide shortly after dawn was the major requirement. The troops had to hit the beach at low tide and the commanders wanted a full day in order to get established. The navies wanted to cross the Channel under cover of darkness but wanted daylight to facilitate their bombardment of the coast. The air force needed a full moon the night before D-Day to make parachute and glider operations possible. What Eisenhower needed, then, was a day on which low tide came just about at dawn, with a moon the night before. In June this combination of conditions came only in two periods, early in the month and at the middle of the month. On May 8 Eisenhower made his decision. D-Day would be Y-Day plus 3, that is, June 4, when the conditions of the moon and tide would be the most favorable. And although the conditions would not be quite so good the following two days, they would be satisfactory, so by picking June 4 Eisenhower gave himself leeway.[5]

The plans for the air drops reflected Eisenhower's concern with getting ashore. The U.S. 82d and 101st Airborne would drop on the Cotentin Peninsula, with the British 6th Airborne coming in east of Caen. The paratroopers' task was to provide immediate tactical assistance to the landings through the seizure of bridges, road junctions, and the like. They would keep German forces at the front occupied, not attempt to engage or disrupt the enemy's strategic reserve.

The concept ran counter to Marshall's wishes. At the beginning of the war the Chief had had great hopes for the paratroopers as a new element in warfare, but his hopes had not been realized. Early in 1944 he told Eisenhower that this had been a disappointment to him and he thought SHAEF could do much more to exploit its command of the air with respect to the ground battle. Marshall thought there had been "a lack in conception," caused by a piecemeal approach, with "each commander grabbing at a piece to assist his particular phase of the operation." If he had been given command of OVERLORD, Marshall said, he would have insisted on a single, large paratroop operation, "even to the extent that should the British be in opposition I would carry it out exclusively with American troops." Marshall suggested to Eisenhower that he make his drop south of Evreux, nearly seventy-five miles inland from Caen, in the greatest strength possible. There were four good airfields near Evreux which could be quickly taken, with a resulting build-up of the force.

"This plan appeals to me," Marshall declared, "because I feel that it is a true vertical envelopment and would create such a strategic threat to the Germans that it would call for a major revision of their defensive plans." It would be a complete surprise, would directly threaten both the crossings of the Seine River and Paris, and would serve as a rallying point for the French underground. The only drawback Marshall could see was "that we have never done anything like this before, and frankly, that reaction makes me tired." The Chief concluded by saying that he did not want to put undue pressure on Eisenhower but did want to make sure that he at least considered the possibility.[6]

Eisenhower's reply was long and defensive. He said that for more than a year one of his favorite subjects for contemplation was getting ahead of the enemy in some important method of operation, and the strategic use of paratroopers was an obvious possibility. Marshall's suggestion, however, was impossible. First, Eisenhower had to have the airborne divisions to meet the first tactical crisis, the battle for the beachhead. Second, and even more important, a paratrooper force well inland would not be self-contained, would lack mobility, and would therefore be destroyed. The Germans had shown time and again that they did not fear a "strategic threat of envelopment." Using the road nets of western Europe, they could concentrate immense firepower against an isolated garrison and defeat it in detail. Anzio was an example. Eisenhower said that "any military man . . . required to analyze" the situation in Italy right after the landing there "would have said that the only hope of the German was to begin the instant and rapid withdrawal of his troops." Instead, the Germans attacked, and because the Anzio force did not have enough tanks and trucks to provide mobile striking power, the Allies barely held out. And they held out, Eisenhower emphasized, only because AFHQ commanded the sea and could provide support to the beachhead. An inland airborne force would be cut off from almost all supply, would not have tanks or trucks, and would thus be annihilated.

Eisenhower, in short, was unwilling to take the risk Marshall advocated. He insisted that an independent force had to be strong enough to operate alone, and to be strong enough to do that it had to have balance. Airborne divisions did not have the tanks or vehicles required for that balance. Far from being a strategic threat to the Germans, paratroopers dropped near Evreux would just be paratroopers wasted. "I instinctively dislike ever to uphold the conservative as opposed to the bold," Eisenhower concluded, but he refused to change his plans. Marshall did not raise the subject again.[7]

Even with the limited-objective drops there were problems. Eisenhower had originally thought that there would be "very little difficulty because of our tremendous preponderance in fighters," but the almost total coverage of the European continent by anti-aircraft meant that the paratroopers would have a "most sticky time of it." One answer was gliders, which could approach silently, but there were many areas in which gliders could not operate at night. To add to Eisenhower's worries, ten days before D-Day Bradley had to change the 82d Airborne's drop zones, as his G-2 discovered that the Germans were reinforcing the area originally scheduled for the drop.[8]

The assault plan for the lead divisions was Montgomery's and Bradley's responsibility. There would be five beachheads, with the British on the extreme left (Sword beach), then the Canadians (Juno), another British division (Gold), and on the right the Americans (Utah and Omaha beaches). Eisenhower had wanted to assault with new divisions, then pass his veterans over the beaches and let them force the breakthrough and overrun France. For the most part Bradley followed this policy (four of the first seven American divisions to enter the battle had never participated in combat before), but with the emphasis on getting ashore he did put a leavening of tested units into the first day's battle. Two of the best divisions from the Mediterranean, the 9th Infantry (at Utah) and the 2d Armored (at Omaha) were in the immediate follow-up, and leading the assault at Omaha was the most battle-tested infantry division in the Army, the Big Red One. All the assault divisions had essentially the same task—to get ashore, move inland, link up with the paratroopers, and expand the beachhead.

Eisenhower's responsibility was to oversee and approve of the planning and to set the basic goals. In practice this often came down to working smoothly with the three commanders in chief. On May 22 Eisenhower complained that while it had been easier to establish teamwork on the SHAEF staff than it had been at AFHQ, he was having trouble with his commanders. They would not accept the principle of unity of command as easily as had Cunningham, Tedder, and Alexander. One reason, Eisenhower thought, was that in the Mediterranean "we were engaged in desperate battling and everybody could see the sense of and necessity for complete unification." Another factor was that while the commanders in chief in the Mediterranean were men of "the broadest possible calibre," two of the commanders in OVERLORD were "somewhat ritualistic in outlook and require a great deal more of inoculation." Butcher asked Eisenhower if he meant Montgomery and Leigh-Mallory; Eisenhower said no, he was thinking of Leigh-Mallory and Admiral Bertram Ramsay, the naval commander in chief.[9]

Perhaps because of his negative feelings toward two of his three commanders in chief, Eisenhower met with them much less frequently than he had with Cunningham, Tedder, and Alexander. This threw responsibility for co-ordination of effort onto Smith and the SHAEF staff. All commanders did come together for reviews, the most notable being the great gathering at St. Paul's School on May 15 for the final run-through of the plans for OVERLORD. Formal invitations went out from SHAEF to the guests; among those who attended were the King, the Prime Minister, Field Marshal Jan Smuts, the BCOS, and other notables. Patton was there, resplendent in a new uniform and with his pistols on.[10]

Eisenhower made a brief speech of welcome, then introduced his commanders in chief, each of whom outlined his plans in some detail. Spaatz, Harris, Bradley, and other senior officers also spoke. Brooke, who was in a sour mood, was unimpressed. Spaatz, for example, bored him. In his diary Brooke complained that "Bert Harris told us how well he might have won the war if it had not been for the handicap imposed by the existence of the two other Services." The CIGS was especially worried about Eisenhower. "The main impression I gathered was that Eisenhower was no real director of thought, plans, energy or direction." Brooke feared that the Supreme Commander was "just a co-ordinator, a good mixer, a champion of inter-Allied co-operation."

He wondered if those abilities were sufficient for the task at hand and doubted it.*

Montgomery's presence gave Brooke confidence. In his presentation Montgomery exuded optimism. There was a relief map of Normandy the width of a city street on the floor and—as Bradley recalled—"with rare skill, Monty traced his 21st Group plan of maneuver as he trampled about like a giant through Lilliputian France."[11] In deference to Eisenhower and Churchill, Montgomery even broke his long-standing rule and allowed smoking in his presence. As he talked and explained, he grew expansive. Storming the beaches was the least of his problems. He wanted to get well inland on D-Day itself and *"crack about* and force the battle to swing our way." It was possible, he said, that he would get to Falaise, thirty-two miles inland, the first day. He intended to send armored columns quickly toward Caen, for "this will upset the enemy's plans and tend to hold him off while we build up strength. We must gain space rapidly and peg claims well inland." He said he intended to take Caen the first day, break through the German lines on that (left or eastern) flank, then drive along the coast toward the Seine River.[12] His exaggerated claims would later be the cause of much difficulty, since it proved impossible for his armies to move as far or as fast as he thought they could.

After Montgomery spoke, the King made a brief address. Then Churchill "let go with a slow-starting but fast-ending stemwinder. He preached bravery, ingenuity and persistence as human qualities of greater value than equipment." The King had to leave early; before he left, Eisenhower thanked him for his attendance and told him not to worry. There would be 11,000 planes overhead on D-Day, he said. The navies had "marshalled the greatest armada of transports, landing craft and warships the world had ever seen." All the ground troops had to do was land and capture some villas for the VIPs, "particularly one to accommodate the King who would be as welcome in France as he had been in North Africa."[13] At two-fifteen the meeting broke up, thus ending, the minutes noted, "the greatest assembly of military leadership the world has ever known."[14]

The meeting helped swing Churchill around to thorough belief in OVERLORD. At the beginning of 1944 he had still wondered about

---

* Years later, in looking over the diary entry, Brooke commented that he would repeat every word of it. Eisenhower was "a past-master in the handling of allies," he said, "entirely impartial and consequently trusted by all. A charming personality and good co-ordinator. But no real commander." Brooke thought it fortunate that Eisenhower had Smith to help him. Sir Arthur Bryant, *Triumph in the West* (New York, 1959), p. 139.

the wisdom of the operation, saying to Eisenhower on one occasion, "When I think of the beaches of Normandy choked with the flower of American and British youth, and when, in my mind's eye, I see the tides running red with their blood, I have my doubts . . . I have my doubts."[15] Early in May Eisenhower had lunched alone with the Prime Minister. When they were parting, the Prime Minister grew emotional. With tears in his eyes he said, "I am in this thing with you to the end, and if it fails we will go down together."[16] But after the St. Paul's briefing Churchill told Eisenhower, "I am hardening toward this enterprise." The Americans, meanwhile, were also growing in confidence; as Eisenhower put it, "the smell of victory was in the air."[17]

Eisenhower, SHAEF, the generals, and the admirals could plan, prepare the ground, provide covering support, ensure adequate supplies, and in countless other ways try to ensure victory. But in the end success rested with the footslogger carrying a rifle over the beaches of Normandy. If he were willing to drive forward in the face of German fire, OVERLORD would succeed. If he cowered behind the beached landing craft, it would fail. The operation all came down to that.

Because Eisenhower was aware of this simple fact, and not incidentally because it gave him an opportunity to escape the office and its problems, he spent much of his time before D-Day visiting troops in the field. He wanted to let as many men as possible see him, and he usually managed to talk to a number of individuals. On May 13, for example, he visited the British troops who would be making the initial assault. He attended eight parades, spoke to enlisted men before each one, and then addressed the formations. The British officers all had their men drawn up in formal parade ground fashion. Borrowing a technique from Montgomery, Eisenhower began his talk by telling them to break ranks and gather around informally in front of him.[18]

How effective his visits were with the troops cannot be judged. Eisenhower thought it important that the men get at least one look at the general who was sending them into battle, and perhaps it was important. Certainly the fortunate soldiers who got to talk to him personally got a kick out of the visit, for Eisenhower was informal, friendly, and sincerely interested in what they had to say.[19]

Success in OVERLORD depended in large measure on surprise. Eisenhower's greatest advantage over Von Rundstedt, aside from air superiority, was that he knew where and when the battle would be fought, while Von Rundstedt did not. If SHAEF could keep the Germans guessing, the Allies could tie down large numbers of enemy troops at relatively small expenditure. The Germans had to defend the entire coastline of France, and even after OVERLORD had been mounted they would not know whether it was the main assault or merely a diversion. If, on the other hand, they knew where and when Eisenhower was coming, they would unquestionably be able to concentrate enough strength to throw his forces back into the sea.

Surprise depended primarily on two points: the development of a cover plan that would make the Germans think the main attack was coming elsewhere, and guarding the secret of OVERLORD. Morgan and COSSAC had developed the cover plan, code name FORTITUDE, and Eisenhower stayed with it. FORTITUDE was designed to make the Germans think that the invasion would begin with an attack on southern Norway, launched from Scottish ports in mid-July, with the main assault coming later against Pas de Calais. The attack on Norway would be the responsibility of a non-existent British "Fourth Army," while Patton was supposed to lead an American army of twelve divisions against Pas de Calais. The notion of Patton's personal involvement was crucial in the deception, for the Germans had a high regard for his abilities and assumed that he would lead the main effort. His imaginary army had dummy troops, make-believe exercises, and contrived radio traffic conducted with deliberate indiscretion. FORTITUDE worked; a month after OVERLORD began the Germans still had an entire army waiting for Patton in the Pas de Calais area.[20]

FORTITUDE's success resulted in part from the tight security that surrounded OVERLORD. One aspect of this security was the ban on diplomatic correspondence imposed by the War Cabinet at Eisenhower's request. Eisenhower wanted to continue the ban after D-Day, for he feared that if it were lifted the Germans would realize that OVERLORD was the real thing and FORTITUDE would be compromised. Eden objected. The Foreign Secretary pointed out that all the Allied governments expected the ban to be lifted as soon as the invasion was announced, and that if it were not their anger at the British for imposing it in the first place would be all the greater. He asked Eisenhower to agree to lifting the ban on D plus one or two. Eisenhower replied that he realized that the British government had to carry the "entire burden" of responsibility for the ban, and the question of continuing it would be "influenced by factors of which I know very little." But, he added, if the ban were lifted the Germans would "deduce the fact that from that moment he is safe in concentrating his forces to repel the assault we have made." He therefore asked that it be continued well beyond D-Day.[21]

Churchill responded by saying that the War Cabinet could not agree to an indefinite diplomatic ban after D-Day because of the great inconveniences and frictions which the ban caused. He proposed that it be continued only to D plus 7.[22] Eisenhower said that would not be good enough, and in the end he had his way. The ban continued until June 19.[23]

In the interests of security, Eisenhower even became a speech writer, drafting a part of an address the Prime Minister made to the British people. The final rehearsal for OVERLORD took place on May 3–5; Eisenhower was worried about it, for if the Germans interpreted it correctly they would realize that FORTITUDE was a mere cover plan. Two months earlier, therefore, he asked Churchill to include in his next radio address a statement that ran, "It will be necessary to hold a series of exercises during the next few months which, being unprecedented in scale, will call for many restrictions on the public," and to ask the people to bear the restrictions with patience and refrain from speculation about them. Churchill redrafted the paragraph and used it in his next speech.[24]

The tremendous activity going on in the British Isles, the heavy concentration of troops, the schedules of aircraft—all were potential sources of security leaks regarding OVERLORD. This was especially true on the coastal areas, where the training exercises could provide much information to a German spy. COSSAC realized the danger and Morgan had tried to persuade the government to bar the entry of civilians into coastal areas. The government objected. Intimating that the reason for the government's objection was that the politicians were fearful of offending the civilian population, Morgan warned, "If we fail, there won't be any more politics." Still, the government had its way, and no action was taken to bar civilians. Then in March Montgomery urged Eisenhower to keep civilians out of his training areas. The Supreme Commander then insisted that the War Cabinet had to impose the ban. He warned that it "would go hard with our consciences if we were to feel, in later years, that by neglecting any security precaution we had compromised the success of these vital operations or needlessly squandered men's lives." Four days later the War Cabinet imposed the ban.[25]

With the British government co-operating so admirably, Eisenhower could not do less. His orders on security to his commanders and their units were clear, direct, and stern. He told all units under his command to maintain the highest standard of individual security discipline and to mete out the severest possible disciplinary action in cases of violations of security.[26]

Despite all precautions, there were more than 2,500,000 men under Eisenhower's command and thus inevitably there were scares. In late March there was great upset when documents relating to OVERLORD, including information on strength, places, equipment, and the tentative target date, were discovered loosely wrapped in the Chicago post office. A dozen postmen in Chicago had seen some or all of the documents. The package was intended for G-4 in the War Department but had been addressed to a girl in Chicago. What made everyone scared was the fact that the sergeant who had put the wrong address on the package, Richard E. Tymm, was of German extraction. He underwent a thorough grilling; it turned out that he was not a spy, just careless. He had been daydreaming about home when he addressed the package and wrote his sister's address on it.[27]

Eisenhower had ordered very harsh punishment for anyone who violated security, and he was as good as his word. In April Major General Henry J. Miller, commander of the Ninth Air Force Service Command, went to a cocktail party at Claridge's Hotel. He began talking freely, complaining about his difficulties in getting supplies from the States. But, he added, his problems would end after D-Day, which he declared would begin before June 15, 1944. When challenged on the date, he offered to take bets. Eisenhower learned of the indiscretion the next morning, went to see Spaatz, and then acted. Miller was a West Point classmate and an old friend, but Eisenhower ordered him reduced to his permanent rank of colonel and sent him back to the United States. Miller pleaded with Eisenhower just to send him home in his present rank, "there to await such action as the fates have in store for me," and protested his innocence. Eisenhower wrote back, "I know of nothing that causes me more real distress than to be faced with the necessity of sitting as a judge in cases involving military offenses by officers of character and of good record, particularly when they are old and warm friends," but said his decision stood. Miller retired shortly after returning to the States.[28]

There was another flap in May when it was reported to Eisenhower that a United States Navy officer got drunk at a party and revealed details of impending operations, including areas, lift, strength, and dates. Eisenhower had no administrative power with regard to the Navy, but he could appeal to Admiral Stark. The Supreme Commander asked Stark to look into the situation and do what he thought best. Sometimes, Eisenhower confessed to Marshall, "I get so angry at the occurrence of such needless and additional hazards that I could cheerfully shoot the offender myself. This following so closely upon the Miller case is almost enough to give one the shakes."[29] In the end all turned out all right. Stark investigated, found that the officer had not been drunk and that most of what had been said was common newspaper knowledge, but still decided to send the officer home for talking too loosely.[30]

Security for OVERLORD included keeping from the Germans information about the various new devices on which Eisenhower was depending for success, such as the artificial harbors and the swimming tanks. And these devices were but small aspects of the larger scene. World War II was, as the phrase has it, fought in large part on the drawing boards. All the nations involved were striving frantically to make technological breakthroughs. By far the most important of these was the development of the atomic bomb. In the United States the Manhattan Project, under the directorship of Major General Leslie R. Groves, was making progress, but Groves and several of the leading scientists on the project were worried about the possibility of the Germans using radioactive poisons against the cross-Channel attack. Groves talked with Marshall and warned him of the possibility, though a remote one, of having the "invading army subjected to the terrifying effects of radioactive materials." The War Department then sent Major Arthur V. Peterson of the Manhattan Project to London to see Eisenhower and explain the danger to him. Peterson emphasized the need for secrecy so strongly, however, that there was little Eisenhower could do to meet the possible threat. He did tell Stark, Spaatz, and Lee about it, but he did not brief any of the other commanders. He also informed the doctors of the symptoms which would occur if the Germans used radioactive materials.[31]

As the Peterson mission indicated, the Supreme Commander's concerns covered all possible situations connected with OVERLORD. It would take chapters, perhaps a full volume, to describe all the problems with which Eisenhower dealt, for he was the one, in the end, to whom everybody had to turn for help. For example, when the U. S. First Army made its estimates on ammunition expenditure on the Continent, the War Department rejected them and refused to send all the ammunition First Army wanted. Bradley appealed to Eisenhower, who broached the subject with Marshall. The Supreme Commander assumed that the War Department decision had been made by a lower-ranking member of the bureaucracy and asked the Chief to ask Somervell to "resurvey this problem from the very highest level." Marshall did, and in most cases the cuts were restored.[32]

There were other supply problems. A standard joke in Great Britain during the war was that the Americans were sending over so much material and so many men that only the barrage balloons kept the island from sinking into the sea. The amount of material coming into the island did create serious problems and bottlenecks. Congestion at the southern ports, where the landing craft and ships of war were preparing for D-Day, forced imports to enter at the northern ports. The food and material of war then had to be moved to London and to the troops in the south by railroad, placing a heavy strain on England's rail system. The northern ports, meanwhile, were working at full capacity.[33] During the third week in May shipping experts suddenly discovered that there were forty American ships on the Atlantic, sailing for Britain, for which no provision for discharge had been made. There were simply not enough berths. The ships were carrying material needed in OVERLORD.

Eisenhower turned to the Prime Minister. "I find myself facing a serious situation," the Supreme Commander said, and he begged Churchill for help. His own suggestion was to make an appeal to the longshoremen for "a superhuman effort during the ensuing weeks." He assured Churchill that the matter was one of grave importance and that it was imperative to get the ships unloaded.[34] For the Prime Minister, there were two problems. First, more supplies for OVERLORD would add to the already severe strain on the island's railroads, and, second, every ship that carried military material meant one less ship carrying food, and Britain was already stretched to the limit on food. Still, the Prime Minister wanted to help. Rejecting Eisenhower's suggestion of a "superhuman effort" out of hand (the longshoremen were already working to the limit), Churchill said he would reduce imports of food temporarily in order to get the OVERLORD material unloaded, if Eisenhower would get Marshall to make the President promise to make up the food losses later in the year.

Eisenhower explained the situation to Marshall, asked for his help, and concluded, "Everyone here has plunged into this problem with the greatest goodwill and I cannot see where anyone is to blame. We simply have developed one of those bottle necks incident to big operations and the only chance of breaking it is to cut further into the current import program."[35] Marshall asked the President to make the promise Churchill wanted, Roosevelt did, the arrangement was made and the crisis overcome.[36]

By the last week in May Eisenhower felt he had met and dealt with all the problems in his power to settle. The number of unknowns was still large, but there was nothing he could do about them. The most important remaining unknown factor was the weather. For the past month, every Monday morning he had picked a hypothetical D-Day and then asked his chief weather man, Group Captain J. M. Stagg, to predict what the weather would be. This procedure had given him a good indication as to the reliability of the predictions, and they had been generally accurate. Only one mistake, however, could be disastrous. Eisenhower arranged to have daily meetings, starting June 1, with his commanders in chief to discuss the weather reports; on June 3 he would have to make the final decision as to whether or not OVERLORD would go.[37]

The long-term forecasts were favorable. On May 29 Stagg drew up an optimistic forecast of the weather to be expected around Normandy during the first week of June. Each day Eisenhower discussed the weather reports with Stagg, to be sure he understood fully the value of the reports and the basis on which they were made.[38] "Everyone is in good heart," Eisenhower reported to Marshall on June 1, "and barring unsuitable meteorological conditions we will do the trick as scheduled."[39]

As D-Day loomed, the pressure increased and the tension mounted. Making last-minute adjustments was one way to relieve the strain, but it was not a thoroughly satisfactory one. For Eisenhower, the most complete momentary escape came in a game of bridge, especially when he held good cards.[40] Often he just walked or brooded. Butcher reported that on Sunday, May 28, after working at the office in the morning, he ate a late lunch, then "enjoyed lolling in the garden at Telegraph Cottage, which is now gloriously alive with azure, purple, and red rhododendron flowers, not to mention roses, poppies, violets, and what not. We even have cuckoos with echoes." Eisenhower tried sketching a big pine tree but it did not come out well and when he finished he wrote under it "baloney."[41]

He needed all the relaxation he could get, for he could not escape the last-minute problems and worries of others. On May 29 Leigh-Mallory wrote him to say that he was disturbed over intelligence information acquired during the past week that indicated the Germans were reinforcing the area where the 82d Airborne was going to drop. Bradley had agreed to a change in the drop zones, but the new areas east of Utah Beach were not suitable for the glider units. Leigh-Mallory told Eisenhower that it was probably that "at the most 30 per cent of the glider loads will become effective for use against the enemy." He concluded that the operation was likely "to yield results so far short of what the Army Commander in Chief expects and requires that if the success of the seaborne assault in this area depends on the airborne, it will be seriously prejudiced." He wanted the drop and the glider landings canceled.[42] Thinking the matter over, Leigh-Mallory then decided his letter about it was not alone sufficient to its importance, and on May 30 called on Eisenhower to present his case personally. He spoke of the "futile slaughter" of two fine divisions (he had decided the 101st Airborne was also doomed), warning that losses might run as high as seventy per cent.

As Eisenhower later put it, "It would be difficult to conceive of a more soul-racking problem." He knew that Bradley felt the landings would never work without the aid of the 82d and the 101st. If Leigh-Mallory was right, Utah Beach at least would end in bloody failure, and the effect of that disaster might spread to the entire force. Eisenhower went to his tent, alone, and thought about the alternatives. If he canceled the airborne operation he would have to cancel the landing at Utah, which would in turn disrupt all the plans. He decided the greater risk was in cancellation, went to the telephone, and told Leigh-Mallory that the operation would go ahead as scheduled. He followed up the call with a letter, telling Leigh-Mallory that there "is nothing for it" but for the commanders to "work out to the last detail every single thing that may diminish the hazards." The Supreme Commander also ordered him to see to it that the troops involved were not needlessly depressed. "Like all the rest of the soldiers, they must understand that they have a tough job to do but be fired with determination to get it done."[43]

Eisenhower planned to go to his advance headquarters at Portsmouth on June 1. Just before he left, Ramsay, who was already there, telephoned. Ramsay said that the Prime Minister insisted that he go along on the invasion, and Ramsay wanted Eisenhower to stop him. Eisenhower talked to Churchill, but with no luck. The Supreme Commander complained that if the ship Churchill was on got hit, four or five ships would drop out of line to help it, whereas if the Prime Minister were not on board the battle would go on while the ship would look after itself as best it could. The argument made no impression. Eisenhower then said that Churchill's presence would add to his worries. To this he got no response either. Finally Eisenhower simply became firm and said that as Supreme Commander of the Allied Expeditionary Force he was ordering Churchill not to go.

The Prime Minister replied that, whereas Eisenhower was indeed the sole commander of the operation, he had no administrative control over the forces of His Majesty's Government. "This being true," he continued, "by shipping myself as a bona fide member of a ship's complement it would be beyond your authority to prevent my going." Eisenhower admitted defeat, but then help came along. The King, learning of the Prime Minister's intention, said that if Churchill went he too would ship on at the head of his troops and participate in the invasion. The Prime Minister then backed down.[44]

After Eisenhower arrived at Portsmouth he tried to concentrate on the weather, but there were other problems he could not avoid, the chief one being Charles de Gaulle. Favorable weather helped the Supreme Commander remain cheerful. On the morning of June 3 he listened to the weather report, which was good. Sea conditions were acceptable, and although from the air force viewpoint the forecasts were poor, "we have almost an even chance of having pretty fair conditions." Eisenhower reported to Marshall that only a marked deterioration would disarrange the plans.[45]

After sending off the report, Eisenhower went into his tent and, as he had done on the eve of TORCH, dictated a memorandum for the diary. It gave him a chance to occupy his time and allowed him to put his worries into perspective. At the top of his list was De Gaulle, and he dictated three paragraphs on the difficulties of dealing with the French. Next came weather: "The weather in this country is practically unpredictable," he complained. If it turned worse, he knew he would be advised by at least some of his associates to call off the invasion and wait for better conditions. This might mean a delay of some weeks. "Probably no one that does not have to bear the specific and direct responsibility of making the final decision as to what to do," he declared, "can understand the intensity of these burdens. The Supreme Commander, much more than any of his subordinates, is kept informed of the political issues involved, particularly the anticipated effect of delay upon the Russians." Only the Supreme Commander could sort out conflicting weather reports and decide on which one to act. Only he could make the kind of judgment involved if, for example, the weather were suitable for all other plans, but unsuitable for the airborne operation. In that case should he risk the airborne movement anyway, or defer the whole operation in hopes of getting better weather?

He discussed his worries over the German defenses. The mines would have to be swept away, the underwater obstacles removed. The combination of the two created a serious problem, "but we believe we have it whipped." Turning to the Transportation Plan, Eisenhower wondered how effective it had been. Would the Germans be able to rush reinforcements to Normandy? Weather made a difference here, too, for the Transportation Plan would continue after D-Day, with the bombers trying to disrupt German movements. Good weather would greatly facilitate their task.

Eisenhower, Butcher once noted, was always racing ahead in his thoughts, for it was in the nature of his job to look ahead, to anticipate, in a sense to operate in the future. He discounted success before it happened and worried about what was going to happen. Sitting in his tent in Portsmouth on the morning of June 3, with the greatest sea armada in the world's history around him waiting for his word, for the decision that would make both OVERLORD and himself either monumental successes or tragic failures, Eisenhower's thoughts turned to the future organization of the Allied armies in Europe. Once the Allies were established and moving out of their Normandy beachhead, he planned to bring in dozens of additional American and British divisions. Montgomery could not handle them all, so Eisenhower intended to make Bradley an army group commander, co-equal with Montgomery, and have himself take control of the land battle, with both Bradley and Montgomery taking their orders from him.

But that was weeks, maybe even months in the future. Outside Eisenhower's tent the wind was coming up and the sky darkening. He would soon have to make the final decision. "My tentative thought," he recorded before going to meet with the weather men again, "is that the desirability for getting started on the next favorable tide is so great and the uncertainty of the weather is such that we could never anticipate really perfect weather coincident with proper tidal conditions, that we must go unless there is a real and very serious deterioration in the weather."[46]

Part II

THE INVASION

[*June 1944–September 1944*]

CERTAINLY it seems that the supreme direction of an Army (and the direction of every whole) must be greatly facilitated if there are only three or four subordinates to command, but the Commander-in-Chief must pay dearly for this convenience in a twofold manner. In the first place, an order loses in rapidity, force, and exactness if the gradation ladder down which it has to descend is long, and this must be the case if there are Corps-Commanders between the Division Leaders and the Chief; secondly, the Chief loses generally in his own proper power and efficiency the wider the spheres of action of his immediate subordinates become. A General commanding 100,000 men in eight Divisions exercises a power which is greater in intensity than if the 100,000 men were divided into only three Corps. . . . But on the other hand the number of parts must not be too great, otherwise disorder will ensue. . . . [Thus],

1. If a whole has too few members it is unwieldy.
2. If the parts of a whole body are too large, the power of the superior will is thereby weakened.

Clausewitz, *On War,*
Book 5, Chapter V

CHAPTER 6

The Sixth of June

Everything that could be done had been done. The Supreme Commander, SHAEF, 21st Army Group, the Allied armies, navies, air forces, and governments of the United States and United Kingdom had made every effort to insure that the men who crossed the Channel would have the greatest chance of success at as low a cost and risk as possible.

In mid-May Eisenhower had ordered a concentration of the assault force near the invasion ports in southern England. The enormous heaps of supplies that had been gathered and stored throughout the United Kingdom then began the final move, carried by unending convoys to the south. The supplies quickly filled all available warehouses; the overflow was stored alongside roads in carefully camouflaged positions. Hundreds of thousands of men meanwhile traveled to tented areas in the fields of Cornwall, Devon, and the southern counties, where they waited for their transfer to the landing craft floating in nearby coves and inlets. The craft, when loaded, would add to the great concentrations of ships at Portland, Plymouth, Portsmouth, Southampton, and the Isle of Wight.[1]

Simple housekeeping for the invasion forces required 54,000 men. Just to cook their meals, more than 4500 new cooks had been trained since January. More than 3800 trucks and drivers were needed to haul their supplies. They were completely sealed off from the rest of the world, with barbed-wire fences stretching around their camps, keeping all the troops in and all non-authorized personnel out. Some 2000 Counter Intelligence Corps men guarded the area.[2] Camouflage was everywhere, for this was the most tempting and profitable military target in the world, and the German Air Force, though weak, was still capable of launching damaging raids. In addition, the Allies knew that the Germans were almost ready to make their V-weapons operational. Fortunately, with one minor exception the Germans missed their chance to hit the gathering invasion force.

Within the encampments, the men received their final briefings. They pored over foam rubber models of the beaches and detailed maps and charts of their landing areas, examined photographs of fortifications and obstacles, and in units as small as platoons and squads studied their particular assignments. Each man was told of his responsibility and his relation to other men in his platoon and the units on his flanks. He became familiar with landmarks, exits from the beach, probable locations of mine fields and machine gun nests. He was assured of overwhelming naval and air support. In the end, he was given the over-all picture, the target date of the attack and the broad outline of what SHAEF intended to do.

By the end of May all was ready. The men had invasion money, gas masks (there was a last-minute scare that the Germans would use gas), vomit bags for the voyage across the Channel, cigarettes, toothbrushes, extra socks and food rations, and, most of all, additional rounds of ammunition. There was a brisk business in French phrase books.[3] Some 800,000 pints of plasma, 600,000 doses of penicillin, 100,000 pounds of sulfa, and other medical supplies were loaded onto fifteen hospital ships, with 8000 doctors ready to help the wounded.[4] By the first days of June, as loading began, there was almost unbearable tension. This was it. Everything that had gone before—TORCH, Sicily, Salerno—seemed unimportant, even insignificant. The Allies were about to come to grips with the Wehrmacht on the Continent.

Eisenhower's men were set to go, living on the edge of fearful anticipation. "The mighty host," in Eisenhower's words, "was tense as a coiled spring," ready for "the moment when its energy should be released and it would vault the English Channel. . . ."[5]

SHAEF had prepared for everything except the weather. It now became an obsession. It was the one thing for which no one could plan, and the one thing that no one could control. In the end, the most completely planned military operation in history was dependent on the caprice of winds and waves. Tides and moon conditions were predictable long in advance, but storms were not. From the beginning everyone had counted on at least acceptable weather. There had been no contingency planning, no preparation made to put the assault force ashore somewhere else if it was impossible to land at Normandy. No one even knew whether it would be possible to stop the forward motion of the invasion force once it started. If it were, and if it became necessary to call a halt because of adverse weather, the effects would be horrendous. Certainly there was at least one spy in all the thousands of troops who had been briefed, and clearly he would find a way to get word to Germany before mid-June, when tidal conditions would permit the invasion to go again.

The troops had been so totally primed to go during the first week of June that canceling the invasion at the last minute would have destroyed their morale. Living in suspended animation for two weeks, waiting for the next usable tide, deflated, unable to communicate with the outside world, the troops would become—at the least—tense and irritable. June 19 was not a good time to go anyway, not only because it would cost two weeks in the decent campaigning season in France but because there would be no moon to facilitate the air drop. Waiting would give the Germans more time to get the V-weapons into operation and more time to spot the concentration of troops in the south of England.

But if the Supreme Commander held to a rigid timetable and proceeded, ignoring the weather, the invasion might fail. Wind-tossed landing craft could flounder before reaching the shore, or the waves might throw them up on the beaches, making them easy targets for the German defenders. Seasick troops would not be able to fight effectively. The Allies would not be able to use their air superiority to cover the beaches. If OVERLORD failed, it would take months to plan and mount another operation, too late for 1944.

On Saturday, June 3, Eisenhower cabled Marshall to say he thought everything would go on schedule. He then talked with Churchill and De Gaulle, who still refused to broadcast to the French people. The British Prime Minister, accompanied by his old friend Field Marshal Smuts, was traveling all over the invasion encampment. He hoped to see troops loading, but kept arriving at sites a little too late or too early and had had no luck. He finally decided to go to the tented area that was SHAEF's advance command post and talk to Eisenhower. He had come down from London on a special train and had been met by a caravan of cars and a motorcycle escort, which he used for his touring. The entourage roared into Eisenhower's camp, filled its gas tanks, and had a drink or two. Churchill made one last unsuccessful plea to be allowed to go along on the invasion, then roared off again.[6]

That evening Eisenhower drove from his command post to Southwick House, Admiral Ramsay's headquarters north of Portsmouth. There he met in the mess room with his commanders and Group Captain Stagg. The weather man had bad news. The high pressure system that had prevailed over England the past few weeks, bringing perfect weather

with it, was moving out, and a low was coming in. The weather on June
5 would be overcast and stormy, with a cloud base of five hundred feet to
zero and Force 5 winds. Worse, the situation was deteriorating so
rapidly that forecasting more than twenty-four hours in advance was
highly undependable. It was too early to make a final decision, but word
had to go out to the American Navy carrying Bradley's troops to Omaha
and Utah beaches, since they had the farthest to travel. Eisenhower decided to let them start the voyage, subject to a possible last-minute cancellation. He would make the final decision at the regular weather
conference the next morning.[7]

At 4:30 A.M. on Sunday, June 4, Eisenhower, who had had a poor
night's sleep, met with his associates at Southwick House. Stagg said sea
conditions would be slightly better than anticipated, but the overcast
would not permit the use of the air force. The meteorologists added
that the sea conditions, although improved, would still render naval gunfire support inefficient and might interfere with the handling of small
boats. To Tedder's amazement, Montgomery said he wanted to go
ahead anyway. Tedder and Leigh-Mallory wanted a postponement. Ramsay said the navy could do its part of the job but remained neutral
when asked whether or not the whole operation should go. Eisenhower
remarked that OVERLORD was being launched with ground forces that
were not overwhelmingly powerful. The operation was feasible only because of the Allied air superiority. If he could not have that advantage,
the landings were too risky. He asked if anyone present disagreed, and
when no one did he declared for a twenty-four-hour postponement.[8]
The word went out to the American fleet by prearranged signal. Displaying superb seamanship, the fleet drove through the incoming storm,
regained its ports, refueled, and prepared to sail again the next day.

That evening, June 4, Eisenhower ate at Southwick House. After dinner
he moved into the mess room. Montgomery, Tedder, Smith, Ramsay,
Leigh-Mallory, and various high-ranking staff officers were already there.
The wind and the rain rattled the windowframes in staccato sounds. The
mess room was large, with a heavy table at one end and easy chairs
at the other. Three sides of the room were lined with bookcases, most of
which were empty and forlorn. The officers lounged in easy chairs. Coffee
was served and there was desultory conversation. Stagg came in about
nine-thirty with the weather report. Eisenhower called his associates to
order and they all sat up to listen intently.[9]

Stagg reported a break. The rain that was then pouring down would
stop in two or three hours, to be followed by thirty-six hours of more or

less clear weather. Winds would moderate. The bombers and fighters ought to be able to operate on Monday night, June 5–6, although they would be hampered by clouds. Leigh-Mallory remarked that it seemed to be only a moderately good night for air power. The heavy bombers would have great difficulty in getting their markers down and doing anything useful. Tedder, his pipe clenched between his teeth and forcibly blowing out smoke, agreed that the operations of heavies and mediums were going to be "chancy." Eisenhower countered by pointing out that the Allies could call on their large force of fighter-bombers.

The temptation to postpone again and meet the following morning for another conference was strong and growing, but Ramsay put a stop to that idea by pointing out that Admiral Alan G. Kirk, commanding the American task force, "must be told within the next half hour if 'Overlord' is to take place on Tuesday [June 6]. If he is told it is on, and his forces sail and are then recalled, they will not be ready again for Wednesday morning. Therefore, a further postponement would be for forty-eight hours."[10] A two-day delay would put everything back to June 8, and by that time the tidal conditions would not be right, so in fact postponement now meant postponement until June 19.

Still Eisenhower did not want to make the decision. He listened intently as someone asked Stagg, "What will the weather be on D-Day in the Channel and over the French coast?" Stagg hesitated for two dramatic minutes and finally said, "To answer that question would make me a guesser, not a meteorologist."[11]

Whatever Eisenhower decided would be risky. He looked at Smith. "It's a helluva gamble but it's the best possible gamble," Smith said, indicating that he wanted to go.[12] Turning to Montgomery, Eisenhower asked, "Do you see any reason for not going Tuesday?"

"I would say—Go!" Montgomery replied.

"The question," Eisenhower pointed out, was "just how long can you hang this operation on the end of a limb and let it hang there?"[13]

If there was going to be an invasion before June 19, Eisenhower had to decide now. Smith was struck by the "loneliness and isolation of a commander at a time when such a momentous decision was to be taken by him, with full knowledge that failure or success rests on his individual decision."[14] Looking out at the wind-driven rain, it hardly seemed possible that the operation could go ahead. Eisenhower calmly weighed the alternatives, and at 9:45 P.M. said, "I am quite positive that the order must be given."[15]

Ramsay rushed out and gave the order to the fleets. More than 5000 ships began moving toward France. Eisenhower drove back to his trailer and slept fitfully. He awoke at 3:30 A.M. A wind of almost hurricane proportions was shaking his trailer. The rain seemed to him to be traveling in horizontal streaks. He dressed and gloomily drove through a mile of mud to Southwick House for the last meeting. It was still not too late to call off the operation. In the now familiar mess room, steaming hot coffee helped shake the gray mood and unsteady feeling. Stagg began the conference by saying that the bad weather he had predicted for June 5 was here; this, Eisenhower supposed, was intended to inspire confidence in the weather man's abilities. Stagg then said that the break he had been looking for was on its way and that the weather would be clear within a matter of hours. The long-range prediction was not good, to be sure, he said, for the Channel might be rough again on June 7, raising the possibility that the Allies would get the first and second assault waves ashore and then be unable to reinforce them.[16] But even as Stagg talked the rain began to stop and the sky started to clear.

A short discussion followed. Montgomery still wanted to go, as did Smith and Ramsay. Smith was concerned about proper spotting for naval gunfire but thought the risk worth taking. Tedder was ready. Leigh-Mallory still thought air conditions were below the acceptable minimum but said he realized this applied equally to the enemy.[17]

Everyone had stated his opinion. Stagg had withdrawn to let the generals and admirals make the decision. No new weather reports would be available for hours. The ships were sailing into the Channel. If they were to be called back, it had to be done now. The Supreme Commander was the only man who could do it.

Eisenhower thought for a moment, then said quietly but clearly, "O.K., let's go."*

The commanders rushed from their chairs and dashed outside to get to their command posts. Within thirty seconds the mess room was empty, except for Eisenhower. The outflow of the others and his sudden isolation were symbolic. A minute earlier he had been the most powerful man in the world. Upon his word the fate of millions of men, not to mention great nations, depended. The moment he uttered the word,

---

* Pogue, *Supreme Command*, p. 170, is the most authoritative account. There are many versions of what Eisenhower actually said; Pogue, in despair, decided to use none of them, concluding that he could not positively settle on one or another, such as "O.K., we'll go," or "Well, let's go." De Guingand has Eisenhower saying, dramatically, "This is a decision which I must take alone. After all, that is what I am here for. We will sail to-morrow." I use "O.K., let's go," on the basis of an interview with Eisenhower on October 27, 1967. He was sure that was what he said.

however, he was powerless. For the next two or three days there was almost nothing he could do that would in any way change anything. The invasion could not be stopped, not by him, not by anyone. A captain leading his company onto Omaha, or even a platoon sergeant at Utah, would for the immediate future play a greater role than Eisenhower. He could now only sit and wait.

Eisenhower was improving at killing time. He visited South Parade Pier in Portsmouth to see some British soldiers climb aboard their landing craft, then returned to his trailer. He played a game of checkers on a crackerbox with Butcher, who was winning, two kings to one when Eisenhower jumped one of Butcher's kings and got a draw. At lunch they exchanged political yarns. After eating, Eisenhower went into a tent with representatives of the press and nonchalantly announced that the invasion was on. Smith called with more news about De Gaulle. After hanging up, Eisenhower looked out the tent flap, saw a quick flash of sunshine, and grinned.[18]

When the reporters left, Eisenhower sat at his portable table and scrawled a press release on a pad of paper, to be used if necessary. "Our landings in the Cherbourg-Havre area have failed to gain a satisfactory foothold and I have withdrawn the troops," he began. "My decision to attack at this time and place was based upon the best information available. The troops, the air and the Navy did all that Bravery and devotion to duty could do. If any blame or fault attaches to the attempt it is mine alone." He then stuffed the note in his wallet and forgot about it. Nearly a month later he happened to pull it out, chuckled over it, and showed it to Butcher, saying he had written a note in a similar vein for every amphibious operation in the war but had torn up the others.[19]

After writing the note, Eisenhower went to dinner. Then at 6 P.M. he and a group of aides drove to Newbury, where the 101st Airborne was loading up for the flight to Normandy. The 101st was one of the units Leigh-Mallory feared would suffer seventy per cent casualties. Eisenhower wandered around among the men, whose blackened faces gave them a grotesque look, stepping over packs, guns, and other equipment. He chatted with them easily. The men told him not to worry, that they were ready and would take care of everything. A Texan promised him a job after the war on his cattle ranch. He stayed until all the big C-47s were off the runway.[20]

As the last plane roared into the sky Eisenhower turned to his driver with a visible sagging in his shoulders. A reporter thought he saw tears in the Supreme Commander's eyes. He began to walk slowly toward his car. "Well," he said quietly, "it's on." It took nearly two hours to get back to camp. Eisenhower arrived at 1:15 A.M., June 6. He sat around and chatted with Butcher and some aides for a while, then finally went to bed. Shortly before 7 A.M. Ramsay called to tell him everything was going according to plan. Then Butcher came over to his trailer with good news from Leigh-Mallory—the air drop had been a success and casualties were light. Butcher found the Supreme Commander sitting up in bed, smoking a cigarette and reading a Western novel.[21]

A GI came up the path carrying the first edition of the Portsmouth morning paper. "Good morning, *good* morning," Eisenhower called out cheerfully. Grabbing the paper, he found that it had been published before the news of D-Day had been released and that the headlines belonged to Mark Clark—Fifth Army had scored a crushing victory and taken Rome. Eisenhower washed, shaved, and strolled over to the war tent. He found "Pinky" Bull, the SHAEF G-3, on the telephone arguing with Smith. Bull wanted to release a communiqué saying that the Allies had a beachhead, but Smith refused until Montgomery said it was all right, and Montgomery wished to be absolutely sure he was going to stay ashore before authorizing any such statement. News from the beachhead, as always in the first hours of an invasion, was spotty and often contradictory. General Morgan, Smith's deputy, came into the tent. Eisenhower grinned at him and congratulated him on the success of the plan, reminding him that COSSAC had done much of the hard work on OVERLORD. Morgan thanked Eisenhower and said, "Well, you finished it." Major General Kenneth Strong, the SHAEF G-2, was all smiles, telling everyone that the Allies had surprised the Germans.[22] Eisenhower sent a brief message to Marshall, informing him that everything seemed to be going well and adding that the British and American troops he had seen the previous day were enthusiastic, tough, and fit. "The light of battle was in their eyes."[23]

Eisenhower soon grew impatient with the incessant chatter in the war tent and decided to visit Montgomery at Twenty-first Army Group headquarters. He found the British general wearing a sweater and a grin. Montgomery was too busy to spend much time with the Supreme Commander, as he was preparing to cross the Channel to set up an advanced headquarters in Normandy, but they did have a brief talk. When Eisenhower invited him to see the world press representatives, Montgomery said he could spare a few minutes for that, and Eisenhower had Butcher call and arrange the interview. The Supreme Commander then went on to Southwick House to see Ramsay. "All was well with the Navy," Butcher noted, "and its smiles were as wide as or wider than any." Losses were unbelievably light—two destroyers and one LST had hit mines, and that seemed to be all. The German Navy and Air Force were nowhere in sight.[24]

The Germans had, in fact, as Strong emphasized, been completely surprised. Their reaction to the landing was confused and unco-ordinated. Partly this was due to luck—two of the three German division commanders in the Cotentin, along with some of their subordinates, were away attending a war game. The Allied naval and air bombardment had cut telephone and telegraph lines, making communication difficult. The weather had worked against the Germans; because they had no weather bases out in the Atlantic, they had not seen the break in the storm that Stagg had correctly predicted, so the troops were not on a full alert status, as they had been so many times in May. Even Rommel was not there. When the storm struck, he decided there would be no invasion in the immediate future and went to Germany to celebrate his wife's birthday and to see Hitler. The ploy of developing FORTITUDE played a major role; none of the German senior officers believed OVERLORD was the major invasion. They thought it a feint and braced themselves for the real thing at Pas de Calais.

But the Allies made some errors too. At Omaha Beach the landings nearly failed because the Big Red One ran directly into the German 352d Infantry Division. Neither the SHAEF nor the Twenty-first Army Group G-2 had spotted the 352d, even though it had been in place for almost three months. Thus, the troops at Omaha were pinned down and on the verge of being driven back into the sea. But the Germans never delivered the final blow, in part because of the lack of direction from the top, in part because the local commanders felt they had already repulsed the invasion. Still, for the whole of June 6, the Germans had an excellent opportunity to defeat OVERLORD. A concentrated attack at Omaha would have put the Germans between the American forces on Utah and the British and Canadian units to the east. But the Germans had been misled by the airborne landings the previous evening and they grossly overestimated the Allied strength. They were in any case centering their attention on Gold, Juno, and Sword beaches, because the Allies had gotten farther inland there and because the British and Canadians threatened Caen.[25]

By noon much of these situations were clear to Eisenhower. He had returned to the war tent where he anxiously watched the maps and listened to the disturbing news coming from Omaha. A messenger brought a note from Liegh-Mallory; the air commander said that it was sometimes difficult to admit that one was wrong, but he had never had a greater pleasure in doing so than on this occasion. He congratulated Eisenhower on the wisdom of his command decision in sending the airborne troops in, despite his own warnings, and apologized for having added to the Supreme Commander's worries.[26]

For the remainder of the day Eisenhower paced, his mood alternating between joy and worry as he received news of the situation on the British and Canadian beaches and on Omaha. After eating, he retired early to get a good night's sleep. At a cost of only 2500 casualties, his men had gained a striking victory. More than 23,000 airborne troops had entered Normandy the night of June 5–6, and 57,500 Americans and 75,215 British and Canadian troops had come ashore during the day. More than 156,000 Allied soldiers had breached Hitler's much-vaunted Atlantic Wall.[27]

After breakfast the next morning Eisenhower boarded the British mine layer *Apollo*, under Captain J. A. Grindle, to cross the Channel and visit the beachhead. Ramsay and other naval officers came along. The *Apollo* went in close to Omaha Beach and dropped the anchor; Bradley came aboard, along with Admiral Kirk, to discuss the situation. It was generally good, but there was cause for concern. All the five divisions ashore were seriously deficient in transport, tank support, artillery, and supplies generally. The worst situation was at Omaha where, of the 2400 tons of supplies planned to be unloaded during D-Day, only 100 tons had actually made it. The ammunition shortage was grave. The beach obstacles had cut holes in the bottoms of many landing craft, and fire from the Germans interfered with the unloading. Both Utah and Omaha were still under enemy artillery fire, and on Omaha pockets of enemy riflemen still held out at various points along the coast. Beach obstacles were only about a third cleared, beach exits had not been opened, and vehicle parks had not been established inland. The 101st and 82d Airborne Divisions had created havoc in the German lines, but they had not come together as fighting units. The 82d especially was scattered far and wide in enemy territory. Tanks were needed to spearhead the drive inland but at Omaha, of the thirty-two swimming tanks launched on D-Day, twenty-seven floundered at sea.

All these deficiencies could be overcome, given time. Thanks to the Transportation Plan, the Allies had time. The Germans were finding it increasingly difficult to move reinforcements to the battle zone because of bombed-out bridges and railroad centers, and the French Resistance, now unleashed, was adding seriously to their problems. Air power had not been effective in neutralizing the coastal fortifications, which continued to pour artillery shells into the beachhead, but naval gunfire support here was making an increasingly successful contribution.[28]

The most serious immediate problem was the gap between the forces at Utah and those at Omaha. Eisenhower discussed this situation with Bradley and decided to change the plan, which had called for both the 4th Infantry at Utah and the Big Red One at Omaha to drive inland. Instead, Eisenhower told Bradley to have them concentrate on moving toward each other, with Carentan as the immediate objective, in order to link up and provide a solid, continuous front. It was his only major command decision of the entire first week of the battle; all others he left to Montgomery and Bradley.[29]

After Bradley left to carry out his orders, Eisenhower's ship, the *Apollo,* moved east along the British beaches. Stopping alongside H.M.S. *Hilary,* the *Apollo* received the local British naval officers, who told Eisenhower that, over all, things were going well on their beaches. Heavy seas slowed the unloading but, looking through his binoculars, Eisenhower could see tanks and lorries moving inland. Montgomery came aboard, said he was happy, and indicated that he thought the battle was going well. After he left the *Apollo* began moving east again, with Eisenhower and Ramsay urging Captain Grindle to take them closer inland so they could see more. They watched the British unloading and saw some of the artificial breakwaters and harbors being towed toward their destinations. Aircraft were overhead all the time; the air forces had flown 10,500 sorties on June 6 and nearly as many the next day. Wherever Eisenhower looked he saw only Allied ships and Allied planes.

Suddenly there was a lurch—Grindle had gone too close and his ship was stuck on a sand bar. He tried to force his way across it, which set the entire ship to jerking, grinding, and bouncing, but with little success. The *Apollo* finally floated free, but the propellers were bent and Eisenhower and Ramsay had to transfer to H.M.S. *Undaunted* for the trip back to England. Eisenhower knew that Grindle would have to face a court of inquiry and was concerned about his fate. The Supreme Commander said the fault was his for urging Grindle to swing closer in. Ramsay reassured Eisenhower by saying Grindle would get off with a reprimand from the Admiralty and "most good naval officers have a reprimand or two on their records." Eisenhower got back to Portsmouth at 10 P.M. after what he regarded as a "most fruitful day."[30]

The next few days were spent in consolidating gains. Nowhere along the front had initial objectives been fully achieved on D-Day or even D plus one, but the Allies held the initiative by putting pressure on the Germans everywhere. Each day the Germans attacked at one point or another, but all the counterattacks were beaten off with loss. None of them were concentrated; the Germans could not move enough reinforcements into an area. The continuation of the Transportation Plan and the concentration of fighter bombers on French highways made it almost impossible for the enemy to move columns to the battle by day. Still Rommel rejected the idea of a static defense built along a solid line and continued to probe, without much luck. On June 12 the 101st Airborne took Carentan and the link-up between the American forces was solid; the British and Canadians, who took on the bulk of Rommel's armored counterattacks, also held firm. By the end of the first week of the invasion Eisenhower's forces had consolidated a bridgehead eight to twelve miles deep and fifty miles wide.[31]

The Supreme Commander kept busy, holding press conferences, answering messages of congratulation, dealing with De Gaulle, talking to Churchill, gathering incoming information, and urging all his subordinates to redouble their efforts. At Bradley's request he removed a division commander who had failed the test of combat. On June 9 he went to SHAEF Main at Widewing to catch up on all the business that had piled up during his absence, conferred with Eden about the diplomatic ban (it remained in effect), and had a long conference with Smith on the problem of the French invasion currency. He was delighted to learn that the Russians, as promised, had launched a major offensive in the Leningrad area, and he sent a message of congratulation to them.[32]

On June 10 Marshall, Arnold, and King arrived in London, ostensibly for a meeting of the CCS, in reality because they wanted to see the great invasion for themselves. They came to Widewing along with Churchill. Eisenhower gave them all a guided tour of the headquarters and especially of the war room, where the maps showed current unit positions. Churchill loved the set-up, and even Marshall was impressed. Eisenhower and Marshall discussed promotions, decorations, the need to speed the build-up, and the schedule of shipping divisions into France from the United States.[33] On June 12 Eisenhower, Marshall, King, Arnold, and members of their staffs crossed the Channel in a destroyer and went ashore on Omaha Beach. They lunched at Bradley's headquarters on C rations and discussed recent operations with some of the corps and division commanders. Ernie Pyle, the newspaper reporter, found them and complained that he could not get any news. Eisenhower said he himself depended on the reporters for his information, but Marshall satisfied Pyle's curiosity by telling him that the attack on the island of Guam in the Pacific was being launched that day.[34] Marshall also praised Eisenhower, although characteristically not to his face. "Eisenhower and his staff are cool and confident," the Chief reported to Roosevelt, "carrying out an affair of incredible magnitude and complication with superlative efficiency."[35]

The trip to Omaha symbolized the success of OVERLORD. If that much brass could safely go ashore in France, the beachhead was clearly secure. More than ten divisions were now engaged on the Allied side, with more coming in every week. There were still problems, but the great invasion had worked. The artificial harbors, on which so much depended, were in place and functioning. The threat of FORTITUDE was still tying down the German Fifteenth Army at Pas de Calais.

There had already been enough drama in Eisenhower's decision on the morning of June 5 to launch OVERLORD to satisfy anyone, but more was to come. On the morning of June 19 a severe storm struck the French coast, ripping up one of the artificial harbors and bringing unloading to a complete standstill. The Allies in fact suffered more from the storm than they had from the German resistance on D-Day. Group Captain Stagg wrote Eisenhower a note, reminding him that if he had decided on June 5 to delay until June 19 he would have run into the worst weather in twenty years. Eisenhower scribbled at the bottom of the message, "Thanks, and thank the gods of war we went when we did!" and sent it back to Stagg.[36]

Eisenhower's gamble on the weather had paid off. What Churchill rightly called "the most difficult and complicated operation that has ever taken place" had put the Allies back on the Continent. The liberation of Europe was at hand.

CHAPTER 7

Stalemate

On June 15 Butcher recorded, "last night Ike was concerned that Monty couldn't attack" until Saturday, the seventeenth. "Ike was anxious that the Germans be kept off balance and that our drive never stop. But apparently Monty wants to tidy up his 'administrative tail' and get plenty of supplies on hand before he makes a general attack. . . . Ike also said," Butcher added, "that yesterday we had made no gains, which he didn't like."[1]

Less than two weeks after the exultation over the success of D-Day, came the letdown. It was caused by a variety of factors, one of which was the relationship between the Supreme Commander and the commander of the Twenty-first Army Group. For the next seven months, many of Eisenhower's worries would center, one way or another, on Montgomery.

That the two men would have difficulty in dealing with one another was almost inevitable, given the contrasts between them. Eisenhower was gregarious, while Montgomery lived in isolation. Eisenhower mixed easily with his staff, discussing all decisions with his subordinates; Montgomery set himself up in a lonely camp, where he slept and ate in a wood-paneled trailer he had captured from Rommel.[2] Montgomery wrote his directives by hand and handed them down from on high, while Eisenhower waited for general agreement among his staff and often had his G-3 officer dictate the final directive. Montgomery once told his chief of staff what he thought of this practice. "You can't run a military operation with a committee of staff officers in command," he explained. "It would be nonsense!"[3]

Montgomery shunned the company of women after his wife's death and did not smoke or drink. He had never mixed easily with "the boys" or been an athlete, as Eisenhower had. Eisenhower was modest, Montgomery was conceited. "I became completely dedicated to my profession," Montgomery once said of himself, and claimed that he had developed the ability to concentrate so completely that it was a habit.[4] He had indeed made an intensive study of how to command. What he had not studied, unfortunately, was how to get his ideas across without irritating his listener. He always seemed to be talking down to people, and his condescension became more marked the more intensely he felt about a subject. He had no idea in the world about how to persuade. Eisenhower, on the other hand, always seemed to be open-minded and eager to seek out compromise.[5]

The personality differences between Eisenhower and Montgomery were significant factors in their often difficult relationship, but what mattered more was their fundamental disagreement over strategy and tactics. Eisenhower's military theory, reflecting that of Marshall and the traditions of the United States Army, was straightforward and aggressive. Like Grant in the Virginia Wilderness in 1864, he favored constant attack, and he became disturbed if any substantial part of his force was not gaining ground. He was an advocate of the direct approach and put his faith in the sheer smashing power of great armies. This was one reason he concentrated on logistics, on the orderly and efficient administration that would insure the flow of goods from America's factories to the battlefield. He was once accused of having a mass-production mentality, which was true but beside the point. He came from a mass-production society and, like any good general, wanted to use his nation's strengths on the battlefield.

To Montgomery, "it was always very clear . . . that Ike and I were poles apart when it came to the conduct of war." Montgomery was the senior British officer on the Continent, responsible for his nation's interests and responsive to her traditions. Except for the temporary aberration of 1914–17, the British Army had never acted as if it had unlimited resources, either human or material, and it had always tried to husband its strength. Montgomery believed in "unbalancing the enemy while keeping well-balanced myself." He tried to make the Germans commit their reserves on a wide front, after which he would make a counterattack on a narrow front. With one concentrated blow, he would cut through the German lines (not push them back everywhere) and dash on to his objective.[6]

The problem of executing a planned strategy in war involves command structure, communications, weather, enemy reaction, logistics, and scores of other unpredictable factors. In an alliance, another important concern is the strength of national commitment. When half the troops on the Continent were British, Montgomery was much more inclined to insist upon his own views than later, when the American forces heavily outnumbered the British. The problems involved in the different national outlooks effected not only Eisenhower and Montgomery but everyone in SHAEF and among the armies in the field. Getting senior officers from different countries to work together was as complex a problem as interpreting German intentions, and as Patton illustrated most dramatically, it was not simply a British-American problem. All the top commanders were strong personalities, successful men who were accustomed to having their own way. They expected people around them to pay deference to their views and adopt their programs enthusiastically.[7] Montgomery's great moments had come in the desert with Eighth Army, at a time when he was very much his own man. At the heart of the command problem, therefore, was the human factor. The relations between Eisenhower and his subordinate commanders, especially Montgomery, caused as much of an adjustment of strategy during the European campaign as did German action and reaction, weather, or logistical matters. The complications began at Normandy.

SHAEF's expectations about what would happen after D-Day had been set at the May 15 meeting at St. Paul's School, when Montgomery talked about capturing Caen on the first day and then driving inland. This plan had pleased Tedder and Leigh-Mallory, who counted on being able to build forward airfields for fighter bombers on the plains southwest of Caen, and had dovetailed with the original COSSAC plan, which called for a breakout through Caen. By mid-June both of these expectations had been dashed. The Allied troops were ashore, but barely, and they seemed to be getting nowhere. Hitler and Rommel, astutely realizing that if the Allies broke out of the beachhead they would use their overwhelming air and transport superiority to overrun all of France, bent every effort to containing them. The result was that, far from taking Caen and the airfield sites on the first day, and then racing on to the Seine, Montgomery was still outside the city weeks after D-Day.

That Caen would not be taken easily was apparent to Lieutenant General Miles Dempsey, commanding the British Second Army, as early as June 9. He abandoned the idea of capturing the city by a quick thrust and began the development of a plan to envelop Caen. On the morning of June 11, however, he was warned by his G-2 that the

Germans were preparing for a counterattack from Caen. Not realizing that the combination of the Transportation Plan and sabotage by the French Resistance had made it impossible for the Germans to concentrate their reserves, he expected it to come in great strength and braced his forces. Dempsey dropped his offensive plans and concentrated his armor to meet the Germans. "This bit of ground," he told a corps commander, "is the heart of the British Empire. Don't move your armour from there!"[8] When the attack came it was not in great force and was easily beaten back.

On June 11 Montgomery told Brooke, "My general policy is to pull the enemy on to Second Army so as to make it the easier for First Army to expand and extend the quicker."[9] The note was the beginning of what would become one of the great controversies of the war. In the specific circumstances, it meant that Montgomery was willing to subordinate Second Army activities in order to concentrate on helping First Army take Cherbourg (Eisenhower had been emphasizing to everyone the need to capture the port and make it operational). Priority went to Cherbourg, not Caen. Eisenhower agreed with that option, but he did not agree to the implications of Montgomery's plan. The British general was preparing to settle into what amounted to a siege of Caen, hoping to draw off German strength and thus make it possible for Bradley to break out on the right. Eisenhower had expected the breakout on the left, on the shortest road to Paris, and regarded Montgomery's program as a change in the basic plan, brought on by his unsuccessful attempt to get Caen.

Whether or not Montgomery changed his plan after failing to capture Caen will never be known for certain. His opponents, both British and American, claim that he did, while he maintained after the war that he always intended to hold with his left and break out on the right. Individual reaction to Montgomery's claims depended in large part on the reaction to Montgomery's personality. Thus one British officer at SHAEF who did not like Montgomery maintained vehemently that Montgomery was "a big cheat" in his claims. For Montgomery to say that he was holding the Germans so Bradley could break out was "absolute rubbish" and "a complete fabrication" that only developed after he was stopped outside Caen.[10]

Whatever Montgomery's plans were, he never communicated them clearly to SHAEF, and the battle he fought was not the one Eisenhower expected. Throughout the second half of June and into early July Eisenhower tried to get Montgomery moving against Caen. There was, however, a certain passivity in Eisenhower's own response to the situation. The Supreme Commander did not approve of Montgomery's handling of the battle and wanted some decisive results, but he never gave clear and forceful orders to achieve the desired ends. He refused to act partly because it was neither his nor SHAEF's battle, but Montgomery's. The Twenty-first Army Group commander's position was similar to that Alexander had held under Eisenhower in the Mediterranean, for as chief ground commander Montgomery had a large degree of independence. As Supreme Commander, Eisenhower could indicate broad policy to Montgomery, but it was difficult for him to take full control over the battle because he could not deal directly with Dempsey or Bradley. One of the strongest American military traditions was to grant a high degree of independence to tactical commanders, and Eisenhower was a firm supporter of that tradition. The difficulty was that Eisenhower at this time was not clear in his own mind about the point at which independence became license.

Two weeks after the invasion Montgomery's troops were still outside Caen, but he continued to build up his forces, make probing attacks, talk about keeping the Germans "off balance," declare himself satisfied with the results, and all the while blithely ignore the growing uneasiness about the situation at SHAEF. The Germans in the Cotentin Peninsula, meanwhile, who were supposed to have been outflanked by the drive out of Caen, were not. The enemy had been expected to withdraw from the area. Instead of doing so, the Germans put their major effort into sealing off the beachhead, fighting stubbornly in some of the best natural defensive terrain in the world.

Meanwhile, the Americans on Montgomery's right were in a country of small fields separated by hedges, banks, and sunken roads, where the hedgerows—fences of earth, hedge, and trees—varied in height from six to twenty-seven feet. By Montgomery's plan, the Americans had to cross over through this country to the west coast of the Cotentin, move on and take Cherbourg, get the port operating, turn around and break through the German lines, and finally make a wide turn, pivoting on Caen, to flow into the French interior. Under this plan British troops on the left flank would contain as many German divisions as possible. Montgomery's plan was reasonable and workable, and in the end it succeeded brilliantly, but it was not what SHAEF expected or Eisenhower wanted.

In addition, disappointment over the change in plan was all the greater because progress by the Americans on the right was discouragingly slow. This was mainly due to the terrain, the absence of good intelligence information on the hedgerow country of Normandy, and the resulting lack of proper equipment and weapons. No one had bothered to study the hedgerow country in any depth for the simple reason that no one expected to fight a major battle there.* Not until June 18 did Bradley's men reach the Gulf of St. Malo on the west coast of the Cotentin, and only after that could they turn north and drive all out for Cherbourg. Montgomery, meanwhile, launched spoiling attacks. His Second Army struck the Germans on June 13, but Montgomery called off the offensive when the resistance mounted. His failure to take Caen was balanced by his success in drawing off German strength, which came about both because the Germans feared above all else a breakout at Caen and because the city was indispensable to them for lateral communications.

Second Army faced seven armored and two infantry divisions, while Bradley faced only seven infantry divisions. The disparity in figures, which Montgomery later stressed heavily, was not as impressive as at first glance, since tanks could not be used effectively in the hedgerow country anyway. The shortest road to Paris was through Caen; the area around Caen was well suited to offensive operations; the hedgerows of Normandy were ideal for defensive deployment. No matter what Montgomery did, the Germans would have placed their strongest forces in the Caen area.

Even within the context of Montgomery's over-all plan, the passive role of holding the Germans around Caen represented an inadequate plan. With possession of the city, the Germans could move supplies and reinforcements to the troops facing Bradley. On June 18, therefore, Montgomery gave Bradley the immediate task of seizing Cherbourg and his Second Army the immediate task of capturing Caen. Eisenhower, who tended to find agreement where none existed, was pleased by these developments. He was convinced that Montgomery was at last going to launch an all-out attack. "I can well understand that you have needed to accumulate reasonable amounts of artillery ammunition," he told Montgomery, "but I am in high hopes that once the attack starts it will have a momentum that will carry it a long ways." Eisenhower said that Montgomery had every reason to be proud of his troops, and

---

* In an interview on October 27, 1967, Bradley said he expected to fight in the hedgerows but did not visualize the difficulties involved. The lack of information on the hedgerows seems to be decisive in determining the question, Did Montgomery change his plans? If he had really expected to fight the major battle on his right he would have ordered intensive studies of the terrain. Of course, the change in plans only showed how flexible he could be, a usually unnoticed virtue in Montgomery.

added, "I thoroughly believe you are going to crack the enemy a good one."[11]

The next day, June 19, the aforementioned severe storm struck the Normandy coast, halting unloading operations and severely damaging the two artificial harbors. The storm also delayed Montgomery's attack. Still, Eisenhower kept his hopes high. On June 24 he visited Bradley at his headquarters just as the American VII Corps opened the direct assault on Cherbourg. Eisenhower was satisfied that he would control the port in a few days. When he returned to England, Eisenhower learned that Montgomery's attack would begin the next morning. "All the luck in the world to you and Dempsey," he wired the Twenty-first Army Group commander. "Do not hesitate to make the maximum demands for any air assistance that can possibly be useful to you." Eisenhower promised to "blast the enemy with everything we have."[12] Obviously the Supreme Commander expected great success, and Montgomery did not dissuade him. In reply Montgomery said that the attack had started, initial objectives had been captured, and "blitz attack of VIII Corps goes in tomorrow at 0730 hours and once it starts I will continue battle on eastern flank till one of us cracks and it will not be us."[13]

But the brave words were not matched by deeds. The British advance was slow and cautious, especially where it met resistance, and after creating a salient five miles deep (but less than two miles wide), Montgomery called off the offensive. The reason for this was that the Germans were concentrating for a counterattack and all the enemy armor in Normandy faced the Second Army. As the official British historian notes, "General Montgomery's desire to fight the German armour on the British front had so far succeeded but it would only be justified if the armour were held and there was no setback. For the time being that was the most important consideration."[14]

Montgomery's real achievement was in preventing the Germans from regrouping their forces for a major counterattack. He had denied them the initiative. On June 12 Hitler had recalled an SS Panzer corps from the eastern front and dispatched it to the west. Five days later Von Rundstedt and Rommel conferred with Hitler. They agreed to launch a decisive counterattack toward Bayeux with a strengthened Panzer Group West, under Rommel's control. While tactical plans were being readied and troops and supplies assembled, however, Montgomery's attack caused the Germans to use their reinforcements piecemeal. Thus, the Germans never mounted the decisive counterattack.[15]

This was a clear gain, but it did not satisfy Eisenhower. "Ike is considerably less than exuberant these days," Butcher noted.[16] The reason for his dissatisfaction, Montgomery and Brooke agreed, was that he never understood the campaign. Montgomery's attitude did not help. On June 27 Bradley took Cherbourg, the first big victory since June 6. Montgomery discounted it. He thought Bradley should have done more. He explained to Brooke that he had tried to get Bradley to drive south toward Coutances at the same time as he was moving on Cherbourg, "but Bradley didn't want to take the risk."* Montgomery felt there was no risk involved: "Quick and skilful regrouping was all that was wanted." Taking a broader view, Montgomery explained, "I have to take the Americans along quietly and give them time to get ready; once they are really formed up, then they go like hell."[17] On Second Army's front, meanwhile, the situation was relatively calm. The British were stalled.

Eisenhower now put his hopes in Bradley. After taking Cherbourg, Bradley faced his troops south and prepared to force his way out of the Cotentin. "I am very anxious that when we hit the enemy . . . we will hit him with such power that we can keep going and cause him a major disaster," Bradley told Eisenhower on June 29. "I want to keep going without any appreciable halt until we turn the corner at the base of the peninsula."[18] This indicated that Bradley accepted Montgomery's view of the campaign—hold with the left, strike with the right—and for the time being, so did Eisenhower. On July 1 he told Bradley he agreed completely with his ideas, and added that he was coming over to Normandy, with "nothing but a bedroll, one aide and an orderly," to see the offensive for himself. He wanted "nothing but a slit trench with a piece of canvas over it."[19]

Montgomery had instructed Bradley to wheel First Army in a wide turn, upon completion of which it would face east along a north-south line from Caumount, through Vire and Mortain, to Fougères, with its right flank near the entrance into Brittany. At that point, Montgomery wanted Patton's Third Army made operational. The plan was that it would move south and west to seize Brittany, while First Army would advance east toward the Seine and Paris. Bradley planned to carry out the orders by attacking from right to left, with VIII Corps advancing first along the west coast of the Cotentin, through La Haye-du-Puits to

---

* In his memoirs, Bradley emphasizes that Montgomery's condescension, which caused so much irritation later, did not appear during the Normandy campaign, where Montgomery "exercised his Allied authority with wisdom, forbearance, and restraint." Bradley, *A Soldier's Story* (New York, 1951), pp. 319–20. Bradley also emphasized that he understood and agreed with Montgomery's over-all plan. *Ibid.*, p. 325.

Coutances; then the VII Corps would pick up the attack, moving along the Carentan—Périers axis; finally the XIX Corps would attack last, moving from Carentan toward St. Lô.

The plan hinged on Bradley's ability to break through the German defenses, and it imposed on the American troops a most difficult task. Montgomery evidently expected quick results, since all the German armor was on Second Army's front, but there are few places in the world more easily defended than the hedgerow country of the Cotentin. The advance was from field to field, hedgerow to hedgerow.[20] Progress was measured in yards. In a little less than a month First Army made a general advance of less than ten miles.

Eisenhower watched the start of the offensive. He went to Normandy on July 1 and stayed for five days. He visited with the troops, inspected the battlefield, and talked with Bradley and the American corps and division commanders. At one point, driving a jeep himself with his British aide, James Gault, and an orderly, he got behind the German lines. No startling events occurred, and he did not know he had been in danger until he reached 90th Division headquarters and was told where he had been. The GIs were delighted to see Eisenhower driving the jeep and shouted and whistled as he drove past. On July 4 he went to visit a fighter airfield of the Ninth Air Force; while there, he learned that a mission was about to be flown. Eisenhower said he wanted to go along in order to see the hedgerow country from the air. Bradley, who was with him, demurred, but Eisenhower insisted. His last words, as he climbed into a Mustang, were "All right, Brad, I am not going to fly to Berlin."[21]

He returned to England on July 5 and related his impressions to Marshall. He had been with VIII Corps on July 3 when it opened the attack, and with VII Corps the next day when it joined in. "The going is extremely tough," he said, for three reasons. First, the fighting quality of the German soldiers; second, the nature of the countryside; third, the rain, which reduced air operations. In the hedgerow country, however, the last factor was not as important as it would have been elsewhere, because with or without the rain "it is extraordinarily difficult to point out a target that is an appropriate one for either air or artillery." The only really cheerful news Eisenhower had was that the port of Cherbourg had not been demolished thoroughly and he expected it to be operating soon.[22]

Since there obviously would not be a quick breakout by Bradley on the right, Eisenhower turned his attention to Dempsey on the left. Nothing significant had happened there since the German counterattack late in June and, as Butcher put it, "Ike has been smoldering." On July 6 he met with Tedder and Smith, both of whom felt Montgomery was too cautious, and they urged him to act. Tedder said Montgomery was unjustly blaming the air forces for his lack of progress, and the deputy supreme commander thought "the Army did not seem prepared to fight its own battles." Eisenhower agreed to draft a letter to Montgomery telling him tactfully to get moving.[23]

The note was weak. Eisenhower made a statement of desired objectives rather than giving a firm order. He pointed out that the air power had done what had been asked of it—to gain superiority and delay the arrival of enemy reinforcements at the front. The problem now was that limited port facilities meant that the Allied build-up had about reached its maximum level while the Germans were increasing their strength daily. It was essential, therefore, to gain depth in the bridgehead and to get additional airfields. "It appears to me," Eisenhower said, "that we must use all possible energy in a determined effort to prevent a stalemate or of facing the necessity of fighting a major defensive battle with the slight depth we now have in the bridgehead." The Supreme Commander said he was familiar with Montgomery's plan of holding with his left and attacking with his right, but pointed out that "the advance on the right has been slow and laborious." He said that the arrival of German reinforcements on the St. Lô front had allowed the enemy to place some armored divisions in reserve, and suggested that the enemy ought to be more actively occupied. Since "a major full-dress attack on the left flank" had not yet been attempted, Eisenhower offered to send forward to Montgomery any unit he wanted. He would include an American armored division if Second Army needed it. Eisenhower promised Montgomery that everything humanly possible would be done "to assist you in any plan that promises to give us the elbow room we need. The air and everything else will be available." Eisenhower said he knew Montgomery was thinking every minute about these problems; "what I want you to know is that I will back you up to the limit in any effort you may decide upon to prevent a deadlock. . . ."[24]

Eisenhower's letter did not constitute an order and Montgomery did not interpret it as such. Still, the pressure on him was growing. "If we don't let go and avoid mistakes," he had told Brooke on July 6, "we ought to be in a very good position in another week or two." But he realized that, viewed from the English side of the Channel, the battle was flagging, and there was a growing fear of static trench warfare. There was also a growing tendency to attribute the slowness of the advance to Montgomery's caution and insistence on overpreparation, and, in the case of at least some Americans at SHAEF, to Britain's reluctance to expose her dwindling manpower to casualties.[25]

Eisenhower took some of these complaints to Churchill, telling the Prime Minister that Montgomery was bogged down and appealing to Churchill to "persuade Monty to get on his bicycle and start moving." Churchill was inclined to listen to the complaints, for, as Brooke recalled after the war, "Winston had never been very fond of Monty."[26] This led to a furious set-to between Churchill and Brooke that lasted from 10 P.M. until 2 A.M. on July 5–6. Churchill "began to abuse Monty because operations were not going faster," and Brooke "flared up and asked him if he could not trust his generals for five minutes instead of belittling them." Churchill said he had never done such a thing, and throughout the evening "kept shoving his chin out, looking at [Brooke] and fuming at the accusations that he ran down his generals." Brooke blamed Eisenhower for the trouble, since Eisenhower had taken the original complaints to Churchill.[27]

Although he did not know the details, Montgomery was aware of the growing criticisms of his handling of the battle. He determined, therefore, to attack, this time with a concentrated force instead of with one or two divisions. In his reply to Eisenhower's letter Montgomery roundly declared that he was "quite happy about the situation," then added that he was working on a "very definite plan." He was beginning to see daylight and had decided "to set my eastern flank alight, and to put the wind up the enemy by seizing Caen and getting bridgeheads over the Orne." He was beginning operations that day, promised that the Second Army attack would be a "big show," and said he intended to "put everything into it."[28] The next day, July 9, he wired Eisenhower, saying that operations on Second Army front were "going entirely according to plan and will continue without a halt."[29]

Eisenhower was delighted. The campaign was now going the way he wanted it to, with attacks on both flanks. Somewhere, he was sure, the enemy would crack. On his way from SHAEF Main in Bushey Park to SHAEF Forward in Portsmouth, he stopped off at Chequers to confer with Churchill. He told the Prime Minister, "We are going to the offensive all along the line and would gain room and would kill Germans."[30] While at SHAEF Main, Eisenhower had made good on his promise to give Montgomery everything he could for the attack by ordering the air forces to go all out. They proceeded to drop 2300 tons of bombs to open a path for Second Army.

But still the attack moved slowly. The biggest trouble was that there was a six-hour pause between the aerial bombardment and the ground attack, which gave the Germans a chance to recover. In addition the high-explosive bombs had created craters which slowed the advancing British troops. Not until July 10 did Second Army have that part of Caen which lay west of the Orne, and still the large suburban areas east of the river remained in German hands. Although Montgomery did not have his goal of a bridgehead over the Orne, he called off the operation.[31]

German losses were heavy, but there had been nothing approaching a breakthrough. On July 10 Montgomery talked with Bradley, who confessed that he was discouraged over the slowness of First Army's advance, and with Dempsey, who suggested that the British might do more than draw German troops onto their front. Dempsey said there was not much point to holding the Germans around Caen if Bradley could not break out of the hedgerows anyway. Montgomery agreed to another offensive, telling Dempsey to build up a corps of three armored divisions, then hold it in reserve for a "massive stroke" east of the Orne from Caen to Falaise. He would call it Operation GOODWOOD.[32]

In his operational instructions to his subordinates Montgomery made it clear that he did not regard GOODWOOD as a decisive battle for a breakout. The object, he said, was to "improve our positions on the eastern flank" and "generally to destroy German equipment and personnel." He did not mention a breakout but did say that "a victory on the eastern flank will help us to gain what we want on the western flank."[33] He was, in short, realistic and continued to operate on the same policy he had followed for a month or more. He was sure that if he could only keep SHAEF off his back he would in the end score a tremendous victory. He was right about the victory, but since he either could not or would not explain the master plan to SHAEF he caused much irritation and never got the credit he deserved for his eventual great success.

The word Montgomery sent up the chain of command was quite different from what he had sent down. He raised hopes at SHAEF about GOODWOOD to a very high level. On July 12 he told Eisenhower, "My whole Eastern flank will burst into flames. . . . The operation . . . may have far-reaching results." He wanted the full weight of the air force thrown into the battle, and asked that Eisenhower keep all visitors away from his headquarters so that he could concentrate on his work.[34] He repeated the same sentiments in a telegram later that day, and on July 14 wired Tedder to say that "Plan if successful promises to be decisive."[35]

Montgomery made his presentation in general terms and was careful never to mention specifically a breakthrough. But following so closely upon his statements of July 8 about his disappointment over the slowness of the advance on the right and the need to "put the wind up the enemy," Montgomery's presentation of GOODWOOD indicated to Eisenhower that the basic plan was to strike out from the left and achieve a significant breakthrough.

Acting on the assumption that GOODWOOD would be decisive, Eisenhower reported that all the senior airmen were enthusiastic because they felt it would be "a brilliant stroke which will knock loose our present shackles." Tedder assured Montgomery, "All the Air Forces will be full out to support your far-reaching and decisive plan to the utmost of their ability." The airmen were awed by the size of the bombardment Montgomery wanted (and got)—a drop of 7700 tons of bombs delivered by 1676 heavy bombers and 343 medium and light bombers, in what was "the heaviest and most concentrated air attack in support of ground troops ever attempted."[36]

Eisenhower, expecting great things from GOODWOOD, told Montgomery on July 14 he was "confident that it will reap a harvest from all the sowing you have been doing during the past weeks." The whole front would act aggressively, Eisenhower said, pinning down the Germans so that the British on the left could "plunge into his [the German's] vitals" in a "decisive" manner. Bradley, Eisenhower promised, would "keep his troops fighting like the very devil, twenty-four hours a day, to provide the opportunity your armored corps will need, and to make the victory complete." Eisenhower grew eloquent in his summary: "I would not be at all surprised to see you gaining a victory that will make some of the 'old classics' look like a skirmish between patrols."[37] Eisenhower was delighted that without having had to take drastic action he would be getting the offensive he wanted.

Montgomery had misled Eisenhower, but he now had an opportunity to rectify the misunderstanding. He received Eisenhower's message five days before GOODWOOD began, and there could have been no doubt in his mind that his superior had an entirely erroneous impression. Montgomery could have accepted Eisenhower's standing offer to come to Twenty-first Army Group headquarters, where he could have explained to the Supreme Commander what he did have in mind, but he did not, probably because he did not want interference with his battle. It is also possible that by this stage Montgomery was himself beginning to dream of a breakout through GOODWOOD, and of course he was ready to take advantage of it if his limited attack produced it.

On July 14 Montgomery told Brooke, "I have decided that the time has come to have a real 'show down' on the Eastern flank, and to loose a corps of three armoured divisions into the open country about the Caen–Falaise road." He then sent his military assistant to the British War Office to explain his intentions verbally. The military assistant declared, "All the activities on the eastern flank are designed to help the [American] forces in the west while ensuring that a firm bastion is kept in the east." That certainly was clear enough, but the next statement muddled the picture again: "At the same time all is ready to take advantage of any situation which gives reason to think that the enemy is disintegrating." To reinforce success was, obviously, sound military policy, and Montgomery would have been remiss had he not been ready to take advantage of a major victory. But he did not really expect one since GOODWOOD was not designed to gain one. He failed however to make this clear to Eisenhower.

Other factors may have influenced Montgomery in his exaggeration of the scope of GOODWOOD and in his refusal to inform Eisenhower of its exact aims. Montgomery knew that Eisenhower had been disappointed over results so far. Gossips at SHAEF were speculating on "who would succeed Monty if sacked," and this could have reached Montgomery's ears.[38] He knew that Tedder and others were urging Eisenhower to set up an advanced tactical headquarters in France and to take control of the land battle himself, or better yet relieve Montgomery.[39] Eisenhower said that removal was out of the question, in view of the adulation Montgomery enjoyed with the troops, Brooke, and the British population (the Supreme Commander seems to have been the only senior officer at SHAEF who recognized this obvious political truth).[40]

Montgomery was keenly aware that he had to buy time, not so much to protect his position, which was secure, as to keep Eisenhower in England so that he could run the land battle. Even Montgomery, however, did not realize the extent of the impatience at SHAEF. Supreme Headquarters was under constant pressure from the British and American press, which increasingly talked about stalemate and World War I. In France, Twenty-first Army Group did not feel and possibly was not fully aware of this pressure. SHAEF was the raw nerve end, Twenty-first Army Group the muscle. In any case, by exaggerating the scope of GOODWOOD, Montgomery was successful in buying time.

Another factor in Montgomery's exaggeration of the aims of GOOD-WOOD involved the airmen. Montgomery knew that they did not like to see their weapons diverted from the strategic bombing operations on which they banked so heavily and may have felt he could get them to make a full effort only by presenting GOODWOOD as a decisive operation.

GOODWOOD began on July 18. In its initial stages, helped by the tremendous air bombardment, the attack went well. The British 8 Corps was on the verge of achieving a clean penetration. The Germans committed their reserves at noon, four tank and four infantry battalions, in a counterattack that stopped the British but did not gain any ground. Hitler gave permission to rush in a Panzer division from Fifteenth Army north of the Seine, but the tanks could hardly arrive in time to save the situation. Nevertheless Montgomery did not press his advantage. He had lost 270 tanks and 1500 men. On the second day, as he tried to extend limited local gains, he lost 131 tanks and suffered 1100 casualties. Finally a heavy thunderstorm on the afternoon of July 20 brought an end to the offensive.[41]

Montgomery had captured the remainder of Caen and some of the plain to the southeast, gained a few square miles, and used up the bulk of the remaining German reserves. He announced he was satisfied with the results.[42]

Eisenhower was livid. He thundered that it had taken more than seven thousand tons of bombs to gain seven miles and that the Allies could hardly hope to go through France paying a price of a thousand tons of bombs per mile.[43] Tedder discussed "the Army's failure" with Portal, and they "agreed in regarding Montgomery as the cause."[44] Staff officers wondered whether Montgomery should be made a peer and sent into the House of Lords or given the governorship of Malta.[45] When General Dempsey asked what all the fuss was about—there had never been any intention of achieving a breakout, he pointed out—the reaction was even more intense.*

---

* Major Ellis' conclusions need to be considered here. He points out that Montgomery and Bradley regarded GOODWOOD as a preliminary to COBRA (Bradley's late July breakout), with the two operations so closely connected in fact that they could be considered one. Had Bradley been able to mount COBRA the day after GOODWOOD ended, Ellis feels, there would have been no confusion or displeasure with Montgomery. But bad weather held up COBRA, and it therefore seemed that the mighty expenditure of effort for GOODWOOD had been wasted. "The truth is that at this time the unaccommodating behaviour of the weather provided the only real grounds for complaint." *The Battle of Normandy* (London, 1962), p. 358. The trouble with this analysis is that no one at SHAEF suspected that GOODWOOD and COBRA were related.

Montgomery had set the stage for one of the great victories of modern military history, but no one knew that at the time. And meanwhile, he had failed to give Eisenhower the kind of operation the Supreme Commander expected, wanted, and thought he was getting. Had a senior British RAF or Navy officer done anything remotely similar, Eisenhower probably would have sacked him via the device of requesting action from the head of the service. In Montgomery's case this option was not open. The head of the British Army, Brooke, was a strong Montgomery supporter, had no real confidence in Eisenhower, understood the basic idea in GOODWOOD and agreed with it, and would have used his position and powers to prevent any change in leadership in Twenty-first Army Group.[46]

Eisenhower might have turned to Churchill, but the Prime Minister would have been reluctant to take action because of Montgomery's prestige. El Alamein was far from being one of the great battles in history, but it was the only major victory the British had had in the first three years of the war. The British public had desperately needed a hero and after El Alamein the government deliberately built up Montgomery so much that no other general in the war, including Rommel, enjoyed such high prestige. Churchill would have found it difficult to face the political repercussions of relieving him.

After the war Eisenhower said he felt the powers of a supreme commander should be greater. He thought the supreme commander of one nationality should be in a position to dismiss an inefficient or recalcitrant subordinate general of another.[47] As it was, however, there was nothing Eisenhower could do in 1944, and in any case the factors that prevented Churchill from acting came to bear just as strongly on Eisenhower. Sensitive to the morale factor, Eisenhower was unwilling even to consider asking for Montgomery's removal. Still, he did have a war to fight and felt he could not allow Montgomery to continue to act so independently. He needed to devise a system that would insure that Montgomery directed his operations toward the objectives SHAEF set for Twenty-first Army Group.

Tedder also felt this need strongly. Early on July 21 SHAEF learned of the attempt on Hitler's life the previous day by members of the German high command. Tedder told Eisenhower that "Montgomery's failure to take action earlier had lost us the opportunity offered by the attempt on Hitler's life" and asked Eisenhower to act at once. Tedder later recorded that he intended, if Eisenhower did not act firmly, "to put my views in writing to the British Chiefs of Staff. I told Eisenhower that his own people would be thinking that he had sold them to the British if he continued to support Montgomery without protest." Later, Tedder attended Smith's regular morning meeting and said it was imperative that the Allies get to Pas de Calais quickly to overrun the enemy's flying-bomb sites. Smith said the Allies were in fact not going to get there soon. Tedder commented, "Then we must change our leaders for men who will get us there."[48]

Eisenhower, meanwhile, had drafted and sent a letter to Montgomery. "I think that so far as we can foresee we are at this moment *relatively* stronger than we can probably hope to be at any time in the near future," the Supreme Commander said. *"Time is vital."* The Allies had to hit with all the force they had, and do it quickly. When GOODWOOD began, Eisenhower confessed, "I thought that at last we had him [the enemy] and were going to roll him up. That did not come about." He thought Montgomery ought to insist that Dempsey keep up the strength of his attack, that he put all his forces into action, since in the long run it would save lives. Eisenhower pointed out that eventually the Americans would have many more troops in Europe than the British, "but while we have equality in size we must go forward shoulder to shoulder, with honors and sacrifices equally shared."[49]

Tedder saw a copy of Eisenhower's letter that afternoon. He was upset because he had not seen it before dispatch, and told a member of his staff that it was "not strong enough. Montgomery can evade it. It contains no order."[50] For the immediate future, Montgomery's situation was not crucial, however, since, as Eisenhower had noted in his letter, "now we are pinning our . . . hopes on Bradley." More important was that the stalemate in Normandy was coloring the Supreme Commander's thinking about other problems, most particularly the German V-weapons and landings in southern France.

CHAPTER 8

CROSSBOW and ANVIL Again

On June 13 four flying bombs (V-1s) landed in southeast England. On June 15 the German attack began in earnest. It had an immediate effect. "Most of the people I know," Butcher declared four days after the attack started, "are semidazed from loss of sleep and have the jitters, which they show when a door bangs or the sounds of motors, from motorcycles to aircraft, are heard."[1]

The Allies had long known of the German experiments with flying bombs and their successors, rockets. In August 1943 COSSAC and Bomber Command had directed an attack on the German research station at Peenemuende on the Baltic Sea, and in December Bomber Command carried out a series of raids against the German launching sites in the Pas de Calais area. The results seemed impressive, and by March 1944 SHAEF felt that the direct effects of enemy V-weapons were among the "smaller hazards of war to which OVERLORD is liable." In April the air forces reported that of the 96 sites attacked, 65 were so badly damaged as to be unusable. By D-Day the number of neutralized sites was up to 86 (of a total of 97). Seemingly, CROSSBOW, code name for the operation, was a success and the challenge of the V-weapons had apparently been met and overcome.[2]

But unfortunately this was not to be the case. In the next two months the V-1s killed more than 5000 people, injured 35,000 more, and destroyed some 30,000 buildings.[3] For the war-weary English, this was a major disaster. The attacks were not especially damaging to actual military capabilities, but it was the moral effect that mattered. At first Churchill hoped to ignore them. On June 16 he talked with Tedder and said he would refuse to allow the flying bombs to upset Allied concentration on the battle in Normandy. Two days later he had changed his mind.

On June 18 he came to Widewing to meet with Eisenhower and Tedder. He had had to order a halt to all anti-aircraft fire in the London area and try to knock the V-1s down over non-populated areas, for when a flying bomb was hit it plummeted to earth and exploded. The program was not working well, however, and it was increasingly obvious that the only way to nullify the threat was to get the weapons at their source, either by bombing the sites or by actually overrunning them on the ground. Since the armies were still bottled up in Normandy, the latter policy was not feasible. Churchill therefore turned to Eisenhower, who controlled the air forces, and asked him to make the launching sites the first priority for Eighth Air Force and Bomber Command. Eisenhower agreed and told Tedder to see that it was done. That afternoon the Supreme Commander put the order in writing, instructing Tedder to keep CROSSBOW targets at the top of the priority list (except for the urgent requirements of the battle in Normandy), "until we can be certain that we have definitely gotten the upper hand of this particular menace."[4]

The attacks began in earnest, but results were not satisfactory. It developed that it was fairly easy for the Germans to repair damaged launching sites, so efforts were transferred over to hitting supply sites and storage dumps, which in turn meant that it would take some time before the effectiveness of the bombing could be judged.[5] Whatever the results, the pressure to do something, anything, was great, and Eisenhower continued to emphasize CROSSBOW. On June 23 he reminded Smith that the air forces had two, possibly three, months of good flying weather left in 1944, so "we should strive in every possible way to make the maximum use of our air" during that period. Spaatz and Harris had been complaining about ignoring strategic targets in Germany, but Eisenhower insisted that there were five operations that came before the strategic campaign—close support of ground forces, the Transportation Plan, airborne operations, supply of troops by air, and now most of all CROSSBOW.[6]

Spaatz and Harris had co-operated handsomely in CROSSBOW, putting forty per cent of the bomber effort into the program, but both were, in Tedder's words, "not unnaturally anxious to return to the kind of operation which seemed to them to offer the prospect of decisive, early triumph."[7] On June 28 Spaatz urged Eisenhower to make a basic policy decision. He thought that, on days when the weather made visual bombings over Germany possible, the bombers should concentrate on operations "designed to deny the German Armies the means to continue resistance." Spaatz agreed to two exceptions to strategic bombing: (1) a major emergency involving ground forces and (2) CROSSBOW. But on those few days when weather over Germany was suitable, Spaatz still felt the most useful operations were attacks on the Reich itself, for operations by bombers against CROSSBOW targets or for tactical ground support just were not as relatively effective. The bombers, in short, were, he felt, being misused, although Spaatz was willing to continue CROSSBOW for its moral effect—it did give the British public the feeling that something was being done.[8]

Spaatz' arguments brought to the fore the disagreement and even bitterness latent in the question of the proper use of air power. The airmen remained committed to the belief that their primary role was to destroy Germany's potential to make war. Ground commanders, while often agreeing with this view at least for conversational purposes, tended to call on the bombers for close-in support nearly every day. This was especially true during the discouraging period when the armies were penned up in Normandy. Eventually the air commanders began to mutter that the ground commanders were "too hesitant in spirit and too reluctant to take advantage of favorable situations which air effort had brought about."[9] The political need for CROSSBOW was obvious to all, and the airmen complained less about that program, but they still were not very pleased about the priority it received.

Eisenhower rejected Spaatz' arguments. The Supreme Commander told Tedder, "Instructions for continuing to make CROSSBOW targets our first priority must stand," and adding that CROSSBOW, the Transportation Plan, oil, and everything else "must give way . . . to emergencies in the land battle. . . ."[10]

Still the flying bombs came. By early July, with Montgomery as far from breaking out as ever, the Prime Minister began to grow desperate. He began to toy with the idea of reprisal, of warning the Germans that unless the V-weapons attacks ceased the Allies would wipe out certain named towns in Germany. Portal was opposed, for he felt it would be a mistake to enter into what amounted to negotiations with the enemy, since this would provide them with proof of the success of the flying-bomb campaign. He also thought that retaliation would not alter the German plan. In any case, for the Allies to bomb civilian population centers would merely divert effort from attacking targets directly connected with Germany's power to carry on the war. Cunningham felt the threat of retaliation might have some effect and that "we should not lightly discard anything which offered a chance of stopping the flying-bomb attacks." But Brooke agreed with Portal.[11]

The decision rested with Eisenhower, and at the bottom of the minutes of the BCOS meeting where the issue had been discussed, the Supreme Commander wrote a memorandum to Tedder. "As I have before indicated," Eisenhower declared, "I am opposed to retaliation as a method of stopping this business—at least until every other thing has been tried and failed. Please continue to oppose." On July 5th BCOS discussed the possibility of using gas against CROSSBOW installations. Eisenhower told Tedder that he would refuse to be a party to the use of gas: "Let's, for God's sake, keep our eyes on the ball and use some sense."[12]

That gas could even be considered revealed how badly Britain was being hurt and how poorly CROSSBOW was doing in eliminating the threat. It had become clear that the only way to stop the attacks was to overrun the V-1 launching sites. This in turn added to the pressure, already great, to break out of the beachhead. The problem, as SHAEF saw it, was Montgomery. Tedder complained that Montgomery could be "neither removed nor moved" to action.[13]

Intimately connected with CROSSBOW and the stalemate was the question of what to do in the Mediterranean. On June 5 Wilson's forces in Italy had liberated Rome, and it had long been assumed by the JCS that when the capital had been reached operations in Italy would shut down. This in turn meant that the Allies would have, potentially, a large strategic reserve in the Mediterranean. The proper use of this reserve now became a matter of hot dispute, forcing Eisenhower into "one of the longest-sustained arguments that I had with Prime Minister Churchill throughout . . . the war."[14]

When ANVIL was canceled in the spring, the Americans had thought of it as only being delayed and felt it would go ahead when the needed landing craft were available. Not so the British, who had never liked ANVIL. Consequently the CCS had considered four possibilities for the use of reserve forces in the Mediterranean, without reaching a decision: a descent on Bordeaux, for a thrust into central France; a landing near Sète in the Gulf of Lion, for a thrust northwest; a landing in the Marseilles–Toulon area, followed by a thrust northward up the Rhône Valley (ANVIL); and a landing at the head of the Adriatic, to turn the German flank in Italy and to aid the Yugoslav partisans. Alexander added another possibility. He proposed to keep all his forces in Italy, drive overland up the peninsula to the Lombard plain, and then a thrust either eastward into northern Yugoslavia and toward Austria, or westward into southern France.[15] A landing north of the Seine River was never considered, probably because the German defenses in the Pas de Calais were too strong.

Wilson's resources were limited, so only one of the proposed plans could be carried out. Each had something to recommend it. A landing at Bordeaux or Sète would set central France aflame, open a port through which U.S. divisions could enter the Continent, and improve the supply situation. ANVIL would accomplish the same objectives, although at higher cost, provide a better port, and threaten the German flank between Burgundy and Switzerland. An Allied force at the head of the Adriatic would help to contain and disrupt the German forces already pinned in Yugoslavia and threaten the southern flank of the German homeland. Driving north to the Lombard plain would hold German troops in the Italian Peninsula and give the Allies options when the goal was reached.

Much has been written, and much claimed, about the arguments that ensued. A great deal of what has been said has been colored by the Cold War that followed so quickly on the heels of the hot one. To generalize, the British have accused the Americans of being shortsighted, of having only one objective—to defeat Germany—and of having no idea at all as to what kind of Europe they wanted in place of one dominated by the Nazis. The British claim they recognized the threat of the Red Army and the dangers inherent in the vacuum that would be created upon the unconditional surrender of Germany. Some power had to flow into the Balkans, southern Germany and Austria, and even central Europe when the Wehrmacht retreated; better that it be the British and Americans than the Russians.[16]

Mark Clark agreed with the British position. In his memoirs he declared, "The weakening of the campaign in Italy in order to invade Southern France, instead of pushing on into the Balkans, was one of the outstanding political mistakes of the War." What Stalin wanted most, Clark felt, was to keep the Western Allies out of the Balkans, which was the reason he had been so enthusiastic about ANVIL. Had the Allied Mediterranean forces gone on to the Lombard plain and then into Austria, Clark later claimed, it would "have changed the whole history of relations between the Western world and the Soviet Union," drastically reducing the postwar influence of the Soviets.[17]

Marshall and Eisenhower were the two men most insistent on ANVIL. Because of their limited horizons, the argument goes, the military campaigns were run with no political objectives in view (this assumes that defeating the Nazis was not a political objective); as a result, the political fruits of victory fell to the Soviets instead of to the West. The great difficulty with this argument is that neither Clark nor Churchill nor anyone else mentioned the political imperatives *at the time*. Clark, for example, favored extending the campaign in Italy *only* because the Allied forces there had the Germans on the run and he did not want to see his army broken up.[18] Churchill too insisted that he had no political aims in the Adriatic and was only advocating the militarily correct course.

The debate in June–July 1944 over what to do with the strategic reserve in Italy never involved any political differences. It was initiated, discussed, and settled on military grounds. To choose among five possible courses of action, strategists must set priorities. In this instance general agreement was easily reached—the first and only priority was the defeat of Germany. What was done with the Allied forces in Italy should be done to bring about unconditional surrender. There was disagreement on the question that followed the setting of priorities. There were two ways of approaching the problem: was OVERLORD the key to victory, and if so could the forces in Italy help SHAEF; or should Wilson's troops make an independent contribution? Marshall and Eisenhower insisted that everything turned on OVERLORD and argued that the Italian forces could make a real contribution to it. Churchill felt that OVERLORD was going to be successful anyway, that the Allied forces in Italy could not help the armies in Normandy, and that Wilson and Alexander could help speed the victory through independent operations.

Churchill could point out that southern France was a long way from the main battlefield; the Americans could reply that Italy was too. Both sides were in fact proposing scattering the effort. Under the circumstances, it seems strange that no one discussed, much less advocated, a landing at the Pas de Calais, especially since the landing craft were already in England. That they did not only indicates how cautious everyone was, including Marshall. A landing in southern France made little sense, except as a method of preventing an extension of activities in the eastern Mediterranean, unless it were essential to opening ports. Even then, Marseilles was so far from northern France that much of what was unloaded there would be used up in transporting goods to the main SHAEF armies. An attack directed at Pas de Calais, if successful, would open Antwerp sooner, and Antwerp was the real key to the success of the campaign. Churchill was right in objecting to an operation that landed thousands of men hundreds of miles south of Normandy, but even he would not advocate the risk involved in an assault against the German defenses at Pas de Calais. The irony was that the Germans, who had always expected an attack at Pas de Calais for the very good reason that it offered great strategic advantages to the Allies, had finally decided there would be none and had pulled their troops out of the area.

More important by far to the debate than the then non-existent question of postwar control of central Europe was the fact that the Mediterranean was a British theater, while in practice northwestern Europe belonged to the Americans. Each side naturally emphasized operations in its own area. At the commanders' level, the ANVIL debate at times seemed almost to be a simple case of the two theater commanders, Eisenhower and Wilson, asking for everything they could get for themselves. Time and again the two generals presented long, detailed arguments, based on a thorough analysis of the world-wide situation as it changed from week to week, but they always came to the same conclusions—the strategic reserve should be used in their particular theaters.

The debate began on June 7, when Wilson informed the BCOS that he would be ready to launch an amphibious operation about August 15. SHAEF planners were delighted, and immediately argued that ANVIL would be the most fruitful operation for the Mediterranean forces. If there were a stalemate in Normandy, the planners said, ANVIL would draw enemy forces from the battlefield. If Montgomery broke out, ANVIL would open ports through which American divisions could enter the Continent. On June 11 Marshall, King, and Arnold met in London with the BCOS to discuss the future. Brooke favored continuing the campaign in Italy until the Lombard plain was reached. So did Portal. The JCS held firmly to their preference for ANVIL. Having reached an impasse, the CCS avoided a final decision. Instead, they told Wilson to prepare to mount a three-division assault by July 25, without specifying an objective.[19]

Marshall and Arnold then left London and went to the Mediterranean, where they discussed the future with Wilson. The Mediterranean commander was impressed by Marshall's argument, which "brought out clearly for the first time a point which seems to be of paramount importance . . . namely that there are between 40 and 50 divisions in the United States which cannot be introduced into France as rapidly as desired and maintained there through the ports of Northwest France. . . ." Marshall had emphasized that these divisions could not fight the Wehrmacht until the Allies had another major port.

Wilson then raised, for the first time, a crucial question. Within the context of assigning the first priority to defeating Germany, there was the question of timing. The CCS had to make a decision, Wilson declared, "as to whether our strategy in the coming months is to be aimed at the defeat of Germany this year, or, while making every endeavor to defeat him this year, at ensuring his defeat in the first half of 1945." If the Allies decided to try for victory in 1944, ANVIL would be a mistake, for it would take too long to make its effects felt. If they decided to go for a long range target date, ANVIL was strategically sound. Wilson had offered a reasonable basis on which to make a decision, but the Americans paid no attention to it, possibly because he was right—that is, if the CCS decided to try for victory in 1944, ANVIL was unsound.

This was so because the CCS had agreed to continue operations in Italy until the Pisa–Rimini line was reached, which could not be done before August 15; thus ANVIL could not be launched until mid-August. ANVIL had other disadvantages. It would break up the Allied force in Italy, "a force which has proved itself to be a first class fighting machine." Switching the offensive effort in the Mediterranean from Italy to ANVIL would involve a five-week pause in all operations in the Mediterranean, giving the Germans a breathing space. How then to defeat Germany in 1944? "The course that holds out the best chance of really decisive results in this Theater," Wilson maintained, "is to exploit the present success in Italy through the Pisa–Rimini line across the Po and then to advance towards Southern Hungary through the Ljubljana Gap."[20]

Wilson's suggested plan was based on his assumption that the OVER-LORD bridgehead was secure. His written formulation arrived in London on the same day as the great storm that wrecked the artificial harbors, at a time when SHAEF was growing increasingly worried about Montgomery's inability to break out. Under the circumstances it was inevitable that Eisenhower's reaction to Wilson's plan would be hostile. The Supreme Commander in Europe accused the Supreme Commander in the Mediterranean of ignoring the fact that the CCS had long ago decided to make western Europe the decisive theater. "To authorize any departure from this sound decision," Eisenhower said, "seems to me ill advised and potentially dangerous." He thought that even to contemplate "wandering off overland via Trieste to Ljubljana" was unsound, for it failed to meet the "overriding necessity for exploiting the early success of OVERLORD" and was simply another British tactical mistake of scattering instead of concentrating forces. He could not understand why it would take until August 15 to mount ANVIL, which after all had been under active consideration for a year. SHAEF was prepared to send landing craft to the Mediterranean to help. Time was the vital factor, Eisenhower said, even though he completely ignored Wilson's question regarding the date the Allies wished to aim for in the defeat of Germany. "To speculate on possible adventures in south central Europe in the coming autumn . . . has no repeat no reference to current operations in this theater." Eisenhower asked Marshall to see to it that the CCS send a directive to Wilson ordering him to mount ANVIL. He concluded his long cable, "We need big ports."[21] Marshall said he agreed completely.[22]

On June 23 representatives from AFHQ came to London to discuss future plans with Eisenhower. He insisted on ANVIL, but for reasons not directly connected to his earlier advocacy of the operation. In the first ANVIL debate Eisenhower followed Marshall's lead and at times seemed to want the invasion of southern France only because Marshall favored it. At that time he had hardly mentioned the additional port capacity ANVIL would provide. Now, with stalemate in Normandy, and with the lesson of the storm of June 19—that he could not rely on artificial harbors when winter weather set in—Eisenhower emphasized the importance of ports. Montgomery was still months away from Antwerp, and ANVIL would give SHAEF the port it needed.[23]

In addition, the Rhône Valley provided a direct route to northern France, and forces advancing up the valley would give direct assistance to OVERLORD, drawing enemy troops from Montgomery's front. He stressed that OVERLORD was the decisive campaign of 1944, and a stalemate in Normandy would be regarded by the world as a major defeat, with possibly far-reaching effects in Russia. An advance through Ljubljana would not divert any German divisions from France, nor would it give SHAEF any additional port capacity. In any case, France was the decisive theater, and the Allies could not afford to maintain two major theaters in the European war. Eisenhower therefore recommended that ANVIL be launched by August 15. If this was impossible, he wanted all French divisions in the Mediterranean, plus those American divisions previously allocated to ANVIL, to be brought to England for use in OVERLORD as soon as shipping and port capacity permitted.[24] Wilson's chief of staff put it more succinctly when, following his meeting with the Supreme Commander, he wired Wilson: "He [Eisenhower] said he wanted ANVIL and he wanted it quick."[25]

The JCS accepted Eisenhower's arguments, adding reasons of their own for preferring ANVIL and saying they hoped it could proceed by August 1.[26] The BCOS were not convinced. Feeling that a threat against the Marseilles–Toulon area would hold German troops in the south of France as surely as the real thing, they wanted to accept Eisenhower's second proposal—i.e., to send the French divisions in the Mediterranean to England as soon as shipping resources would permit.

This would be a long time in the future, however, and meanwhile they wanted Alexander to press the campaign in Italy north of the Pisa–Rimini line. The JCS reply to the BCOS proposal was, if hardly tactful, at least straightforward: "We wish you to know now, immediately, that we do not accept statements in your paper in general, with relation to the campaign in Italy as sound and as in keeping with the early termination of the war." The CCS, in short, had reached another impasse.[27]

Churchill now entered the fray, going over the heads of the CCS and appealing directly to Roosevelt. He told the President he was disturbed by the "arbitrary" tone the Americans were adopting. He asked Roosevelt to "consent to hear both sides" before making a decision. Churchill claimed that he was willing to help Eisenhower, but not at the expense of the complete ruin "of our great affairs in the Mediterranean and we take it hard that this should be demanded of us." In effect, he accused Eisenhower of being narrow-minded and pointed out that the selection of future operations should be based on the largest possible considerations, not just aid for OVERLORD. Specifically, he felt that the general strain on Germany and political considerations (the possible revolt of German satellites in central Europe) should play a dual role in future policy decisions. As for aid to OVERLORD, Churchill argued that this could best be achieved by landings in the Bay of Biscay. The Prime Minister called ANVIL "bleak and sterile" and said he found it difficult to believe that it could have any influence on OVERLORD in the coming summer or fall. He concluded, "Whether we should ruin all hopes of a major victory in Italy and all its fronts and condemn ourselves to a passive role in that theatre, after having broken up the fine Allied army which is advancing so rapidly through that Peninsula, for the sake of ANVIL with all its limitations, is indeed a grave question for His Majesty's Government and the President, with the Combined Chiefs of Staff, to decide."

The President refused to be swayed. He immediately cabled Churchill, "You and I must . . . support the views of the Supreme Allied Commander. He is definitely for ANVIL and wants action in the field by August 30th preferably earlier." In another message Roosevelt added, "For purely political reasons over here, I should never survive even a slight setback in OVERLORD if it were known that fairly large forces had been diverted to the Balkans."[28]

Because the Americans had twelve million men in arms, the British five million, Churchill was forced to give Roosevelt the deciding vote in disputes, which galled Brooke. What made it worse from the CIGS's point of view was the basis on which Roosevelt cast his vote. Brooke charged that the "basic reason" for Roosevelt's support for ANVIL was "the coming Presidential Election," which made it "impossible to contemplate any action with a Balkan flavour on its strategic merits." Brooke saw further trouble ahead, for "the Americans now begin to own the major strength on land, in the air and on the sea. They, therefore, consider that they are entitled to dictate how their forces are to be employed. We shall be forced into carrying out an invasion of Southern France. . . ."[29]

While the debate raged, Eisenhower and Marshall urged each other to stand firm. On June 29 Eisenhower told the Chief that although it was obvious Churchill and the BCOS were honestly convinced that greater results would flow from a drive toward Trieste than from ANVIL, his impression was that in the end they would agree to mount ANVIL. He warned that this view was conjecture, but said that it represented both his own and Smith's impressions gathered in separate conversations with Churchill.[30] In turn, in all his messages to Eisenhower, Marshall said that the JCS was holding and were continuing to inform the BCOS that an operation in the Balkans was unacceptable.

Alexander raised a controversy on June 29 when he asked for an immediate decision, at the same time informing Brooke that the Americans were already taking independent action by withdrawing small units from the front lines in Italy in preparation for ANVIL. Such action hardly helped solidify the alliance, but there was nothing the British could do about it. On June 30 the BCOS informed Churchill that although they remained "completely unshaken" in their unfavorable view of ANVIL they would defer to the Prime Minister's views "in the broadest interests of Anglo-American co-operation" if Churchill thought ANVIL necessary to hold the alliance together.

But the Prime Minister was not quite ready to give up. On July 1 he sent one last, long appeal to the President. In it, for the first and only time, he raised long-range political possibilities. Roosevelt had suggested that they lay their differences before Stalin. Churchill pointed out that the Russian leader "might prefer that the British and Americans should do their share in France in this very hard fighting that is to come, and that East, Middle and Southern Europe should fall naturally into his control. However, it is better to settle the matter for ourselves and between ourselves."

The Prime Minister quickly backed off from the political argument and returned to military considerations. Churchill concluded his note by saying it would be a dreadful mistake to break up the Italian offensive, "with all its dazzling possibilities," under the assumption that in several months' time ANVIL would be of some help to Eisenhower. Still, if the Americans insisted, there was nothing to do but to go ahead, and Churchill promised that the forces of the Empire would do their best.[31] He then called Eisenhower on the telephone and told him substantially the same thing. Eisenhower immediately wired Marshall, telling the Chief that, while the information was not verified and was extremely confidential, Churchill was ready to give in.[32] Marshall probably relayed this information to Roosevelt, and the next day, July 2, the President told the Prime Minister that he still wanted ANVIL. "I always think of my early geometry," Roosevelt concluded. "A straight line is the shortest distance between two points."[33] That afternoon the CCS sent a directive to Wilson, instructing him to launch a three-division ANVIL as early as possible.[34]

Arrangements now moved forward smoothly. After discussion, SHAEF agreed to shift landing craft to the Mediterranean on July 15, with warships to follow. As the commander in whose interests ANVIL was being undertaken, Eisenhower was given authority to outline the objectives of the operation. On July 6 he told Wilson that these should be: (1) containing forces that might otherwise oppose OVERLORD; (2) securing a port for the entry of additional forces; (3) advancing northward to threaten enemy flanks, and (4) developing lines of communication to support ANVIL and OVERLORD forces. Wilson would retain over-all command of ANVIL until such time as SHAEF assumed it (which would happen when the ANVIL forces linked up with those from OVERLORD). Lieutenant General Alexander M. Patch would command the Seventh Army in ANVIL; the American divisions involved would be organized into the VI Corps, under Truscott. The French forces, under General de Lattre de Tassigny, would be organized into an army as soon as the beachhead was secure, and at that time Devers would step in as commander of the Sixth Army Group.[35]

The operation and disagreements about it now seemed settled, but in fact were not. British anger and foreboding remained. Churchill had not accepted the final decision in good grace and he composed (but did not send) several protests to Washington. He told the BCOS "an intense impression must be made upon the Americans that we have been ill-treated and are furious."[36] On July 12 the BCOS cabled Washington that they did not consider ANVIL the "correct strategy" and had given way only to dispel the view that they were using delaying tactics to gain their point. Still, they assured the JCS, they would do their best to make it work. Churchill, meanwhile, told Hopkins on July 19, "We have submitted under protest to the decision of the United States Chiefs of Staff even in a theatre where we have been accorded the right to nominate the Supreme Commander. You can be sure we shall try our best to make the operation a success. I only hope it will not ruin greater projects."[37]

But ANVIL still had a long way to go before it reached the sunny shores of southern France. In August Churchill made one last effort to stop the operation, which he had by then renamed DRAGOON, on the grounds that he had been dragooned into it. The possibility, then feasible, of capturing the Brittany ports gave him his opportunity. On August 4 he held a staff conference and convinced the BCOS that DRAGOON should be shifted to Brest and other Brittany ports. Although no details had been worked out, the Prime Minister immediately telegraphed the President, "I beg you will consider the possibility of switching 'Dragoon' into the main and vital theatre where it can immediately play its part at close quarters. . . ." As Churchill saw it, the great advantage was not only that the DRAGOON forces could make their contribution in northwest France, but also that the drain on Alexander's armies in Italy would be relatively small and Alexander still might reach Trieste before winter.[38] The Prime Minister dispatched a telegram to Wilson asking him if he could bring the forces then assembling for DRAGOON north to a landing at Brest.

In ringing phrases that mince no words, John Ehrman, the official British historian, shows the absurdity of the proposal. "Now, eleven days before the operation was due to begin, they [the British] were playing with the idea of transferring it to an entirely new area where conditions were still largely unknown, some 1,600 miles from its initial base, beyond the reach of air cover from the Mediterranean, and involving an unknown commitment for shipping. Hitherto, all assaults from the sea had been prepared in considerable detail. But no proper plan existed in this case, and no assessment had been made of its effect on current operations or on the subsequent campaign. The British were in fact proposing, for the sake of a hypothetically easier line of supply, to jettison a carefully planned operation on the eve of its execution, to alter the balance of the whole campaign in western Europe, and to abandon a strategy which they had worked out originally in concert with the Russians and had only recently accepted with every appearance of finality."[39]

Eisenhower learned of the British proposal late on the evening of August 4, after returning to Portsmouth from Normandy. The next morning he cabled Marshall, assuring the Chief, "I will not repeat not

under any conditions agree at this moment to a cancellation of DRA-
GOON." The Supreme Commander admitted that he was anxious to
bring divisions in through Brittany ports but pointed out that no one
knew when Brest and Lorient would be available. Given all the unknown
factors in the situation, Eisenhower thought it only common sense that
DRAGOON as originally planned be pushed "energetically and speed-
ily."[40]

Churchill came to Portsmouth for lunch. After discussing the situation
in Normandy, he turned to the point at issue. He grandiloquently declared that history would show that Eisenhower had missed a great
opportunity if he did not shift DRAGOON from southern France to
Brest and Lorient. Eisenhower tried to mumble that it was too late to
make a change, which was just the sort of argument that made the
Prime Minister most impatient. He believed that anything in war was
possible if men just put their minds to it. Nothing was settled. After lunch
General Smith and Admirals Cunningham, Ramsay, and William G.
Tennant joined Churchill and Eisenhower in the war room at SHAEF
Forward. The argument continued for six hours. Eisenhower said no to
Churchill, continued to say no all afternoon, and "ended saying no in
every form of the English language at his command." Cunningham supported Churchill, while Tennant and Ramsay sided with Eisenhower
(Tennant thought Eisenhower "sound at every step of the argument and
thoroughly magnificent."). To Eisenhower's surprise, Smith agreed with
Churchill. A message came in from Wilson; he said that to switch the plan
at this late date would involve unloading and reloading the landing craft
and he thought the whole idea of a change most unwise. This message
had no effect on Churchill, nor did a message from the JCS registering
their complete disapproval of Churchill's proposal. By the end of the
session, Eisenhower was limp, but DRAGOON was still on. After
Churchill left, Eisenhower told Butcher that he expected the Prime
Minister "would return to the subject in two or three days and simply
regard the issue as unsettled."[41]

Eisenhower was right. On August 9, in a meeting at 10 Downing
Street that Eisenhower later described as one of the most difficult
sessions he had in the entire war, Churchill pressed his point. He
intimated that the United States was taking the role of "a big strong
and dominating partner" rather than attempting to understand the British
position. The Americans, he complained, were indifferent to British interests in the Italian campaign.

Two days later Eisenhower replied to this charge in a letter to

Churchill. He said he was disturbed over their differences but insisted that they were not nationalistic. "I do not, for one moment, believe that there is any desire on the part of any responsible person in the American war machine to disregard British views," Eisenhower said, "or cold-bloodedly to leave Britain holding an empty bag in any of our joint undertakings." He said he always examined such problems from a strictly military point of view, "and I am sorry that you seem to feel we use our great actual or potential strength as a bludgeon in conference." He reminded Churchill that he had sat in on many CCS conferences in which the British view had prevailed—which may have been exactly what Churchill had in mind. The British dominated the CCS when they were making the preponderant contribution to the war effort in Europe. Now that the Americans had the greater strength, all the decisions seemed to be dictated by what the JCS wanted. Nothing was being settled objectively, Churchill felt, and he did not like it now that the shoe was on the other foot.

The entire August 9 interview was painful for Eisenhower, who found Churchill "stirred, upset and even despondent." He wondered if Churchill's motives were political, if his aim were to get Allied troops into the Balkans ahead of the Russians. If that were so, he told the Prime Minister, then Churchill should lay the facts and his own conclusions before the President. Eisenhower said he well understood that military campaigns could be affected by political considerations, and if the head of government should decide that getting into the Balkans was worth prolonging the war, then he would "instantly and loyally adjust plans accordingly." But Eisenhower did insist that as long as Churchill argued the matter on military grounds alone he was wrong. "In this particular field I alone had to be the judge of my own responsibilities and decisions," the Supreme Commander commented later. "I refused to consider the change so long as it was urged upon military considerations."

Churchill then waved the political argument aside. He said he had no political objectives in the Balkans. The correct military policy as he saw it was to avoid the sterile campaign in the south of France, open Brest, and push on in Italy. Eisenhower answered him point by point, putting his strongest emphasis on the need for more port capacity. Even with Brest, Eisenhower argued, the Allies would not have enough ports to maintain their armies for the final conquest of Germany. They could move forward to the German border, but at that point they would outrun their supplies, just as the British Eighth Army had done so often in its westward drives in the North African desert, or as had happened to Rommel when he reached El Alamein. Eisenhower had to have either Antwerp, the best port in Europe, or Marseilles, the best port in France. He had no ideas as to when he would get Antwerp, but with DRAGOON he could have Marseilles soon.

Eisenhower also had a political argument on his side and, unlike the Prime Minister, he was willing to use it. He reminded Churchill that the American government had gone to great expense to equip and supply a number of French divisions, that De Gaulle was most anxious to have them fight in the struggle to liberate France, and that the only way they could be brought to the battlefield was through DRAGOON. Churchill was unimpressed. "So far as I can determine he attaches so much importance to the matter [of switching DRAGOON to Brittany]," Eisenhower told Marshall, "that failure in achieving this objective would represent a practical failure of his whole administration." At one point Churchill told Eisenhower that if DRAGOON went on schedule into southern France, "I might have to go to the King and lay down the mantle of my high office."[42]

But Churchill could not move Eisenhower, who took his orders from the CCS, not the heads of government, and the discussion finally ended. The next day Churchill left for a visit to Italy. While there, he took the opportunity of watching the assault he had hoped would never take place, and "adopted" it. When Eisenhower heard this, he told Marshall, and thought of "all the fighting and mental anguish I went through in order to preserve that operation, I don't know whether to sit down and laugh or to cry."[43]

Throughout the debate major points had obviously been raised. They were not, however, the points publicists later emphasized. The issue did not involve a campaign in the Balkans versus a campaign in southern France. Churchill flatly insisted, time and again, that he did *not* propose to send Alexander into the area east of Trieste and that he did not have political motives. Despite these facts, the invasion of southern France stands at or near the top of all the innumerable lists of "Great Mistakes of the War." The argument is too well known to bother to discuss it here (and is admirably summarized by Maurice Matloff elsewhere)[44]; suffice it to say that the critics have consistently missed the point. The argument at the time centered around military opportunities and necessity, and to judge it on its political implications for the Cold War is to engage in wishful, ahistorical thinking.

As a soldier, Eisenhower had to set priorities and make his decisions accordingly. He objective was to defeat Germany. To do that, he had to bring powerful armies, well supplied, to the German border for a final campaign against the enemy homeland. To do that, he needed ports. The question, then, is: Did DRAGOON give the Allies the extra port capacity necessary to support the armies in the European campaign or, could SHAEF's armies have done as well as they did without Marseilles?

Churchill's argument was that Brest and Lorient could have done as much for SHAEF as Marseilles. Since they were never used, no one will ever know whether he was right or not, but the figures on the contribution made by the ports in southern France are impressive. From September through December 1944 Marseilles and its allied southern French ports unloaded more tonnage than any of the other ports available to SHAEF. In the last three months of 1944 well over one third of the total supplies unloaded in Europe by the Allies came in through the south of France. Not until January 1945, when Antwerp was in full operation, was Marseilles superseded as SHAEF's major port.[45]

Even with the help of Marseilles, from September until Antwerp was operating in January 1945, the Allied armies in Europe suffered from supply shortages, caused by inadequate port capacity. It could be argued that SHAEF did not need such large ground forces, especially if there were another major campaign in the Balkans, but it should be recalled that in December 1944 SHAEF had *no* manpower reserves. The situation was bad enough as it was; it could have been hazardous in the extreme without Marseilles. Brest, as a substitute for Marseilles as Churchill proposed, could have helped, but it was not as big a port and since there were no thorough plans prepared there was no assurance that the operation Churchill proposed would have worked. DRAGOON, in Eisenhower's thinking, was the best available option to meet the objectives. The trouble was that, although ANVIL gave the Allies the port of Marseilles, it did nothing to help open Antwerp.

CHAPTER 9

Breakout

As July drew to a close Eisenhower and his associates at SHAEF were close to despair. Flying bombs continued to fall on London. GOODWOOD had failed. Bradley's progress in the hedgerows was agonizingly slow. After seven weeks of fighting, the deepest Allied penetrations were some twenty-five to thirty miles inland, on a front of only eighty miles. This was hardly enough room to maneuver or to bring in the forces waiting in England and the United States for deployment. The Germans continued to fight savagely, taking advantage of every piece of cover and laying mines with extraordinary skill. The July 20 attempt by the German generals on Hitler's life seemed to have had no effect at all on the battlefield.

The situation, however, was much better than SHAEF recognized. Montgomery's optimism was justified, for his policy had succeeded. The build-up, which Eisenhower had never wanted but which Montgomery insisted upon, was about to come to an end. The Germans had been set up for the final blow. Montgomery's left jab at GOODWOOD had them off balance, and Bradley's right hook would finish the campaign. Whether this came about as a result of accident or by design was, for the moment at least, unimportant.

On July 18 Bradley's First Army captured St. Lô. It had been a bitter, long, costly struggle. First Army suffered nearly 11,000 casualties in two weeks, but by taking St. Lô it opened an important road center to the south and east from the beachhead and provided maneuvering space for a drive to the south which Bradley was already planning. The Americans had a compact, powerful force with which to strike; although First Army had suffered 73,000 casualties, the losses had been replaced, and there were seventeen U.S. divisions in the field. By July 23 the Americans had landed a total of 770,000 troops in Normandy. The 101st and 82d

Airborne had been withdrawn from the Continent for refitting; together with three divisions moving from the United Kingdom to the Continent and two more ready divisions in the United Kingdom, they constituted a large, immediately available reserve force. The British and Canadians had suffered some 49,000 casualties but, like the Americans, had replaced most of them and by July 23 had landed 591,000 troops in France. The supply situation was basically good. Landing craft continued to bring material in over the beaches, and on July 19 the first supplies were brought in through Cherbourg.

The German situation, meanwhile, looked increasingly bad. Allied air superiority made it almost impossible for the enemy to move reinforcements and supplies to the battlefield. The FORTITUDE deception plan added to the enemy's problems, for throughout June and two thirds of July the German high command assumed that a second landing would be made north of the Seine and therefore held the Fifteenth Army in the Pas de Calais area. The initiative belonged to the Allies, and the Germans, attempting a holding action everywhere, were consequently strong nowhere. They had committed their reserves piecemeal and could not move any large force to the front for a major counterattack. German replacements had not come forward, so although their total casualties were no greater than those of the Allies (116,863 by July 23), all German divisions were under strength. On July 25 the Germans had at most thirteen weak divisions to oppose seventeen full-strength American divisions, with seven infantry and five or six Panzer divisions against the seventeen British and Canadian divisions.

Even more than the Allies, the Germans suffered from divided counsel. Hitler insisted that every unit stand and fight, which at the tactical level kept troops in untenable positions. Von Rundstedt wanted to abandon the present lines and establish a defense line running roughly from Caen to Caumont, which would allow him to shorten his line and give his Panzers some rest, but Hitler forbade it and soon replaced Von Rundstedt with Generalfeldmarschall Guenther von Kluge. Rommel had been wounded on July 17 when an Allied fighter strafed the staff car in which he was riding; he was then implicated in the plot against Hitler and eventually committed suicide to avoid the shame of a trial. Von Kluge assumed Rommel's duties in addition to his other responsibilities. Hitler, however, did not trust Von Kluge, the man he himself had chosen, and insisted on giving him only the minimum amount of information absolutely essential for carrying on the battle. Hitler feared that if Von

Kluge, or any of the field generals, knew about more than their own local situation, they would give the information to the Allies.[1]

The German defense was a shell. Hitler had gambled on pinning down the Allies, believing correctly that if they once broke out they would use their overwhelming air and transport superiority to launch a war of maneuver that would crush the Germans in France. In a sense the situation of 1940 had been reversed, with the Germans playing the role of the immobile French at the Maginot Line and the British and Americans ready to begin a blitzkrieg of their own. But the Allied blitzkrieg could not come until someone broke through the shell, as Eisenhower and his subordinates very well knew.

Eisenhower felt that his greatest single advantage over the Germans was the Allied air superiority, and he wanted to make sure that it was fully used in the breakout attempt. He had been harping on the theme of air-ground co-operation since the North African campaign, and he continued to do so in Normandy. The airmen were unhappy because of what they considered excessive demands on their planes by the ground generals, while the soldiers at the front complained both because the airmen were not doing enough and because when they did fly close support missions the bombs sometimes fell short, killing Allied soldiers on the battle line. The airmen countercharged that the soldiers did not set up clear bomb lines. Eisenhower deplored the growing antagonism, admitted that there had been errors on both sides, and said the mistakes should not "sour us or any of the Services." Rather, they should serve as incentives to promote greater efficiency. "I am particularly anxious," he told Smith, "that any such occurrences do not discourage ground forces from calling upon the air for maximum assistance, or the air from being ready to render such maximum assistance."[2]

Bradley, a ground general, was still willing to work with the air forces, and he had a plan. He proposed to penetrate the enemy defenses west of St. Lô with VII Corps, pushing armored and motorized troops deep into the German rear toward Coutances. Essentially the plan was Bradley's alone.[3] Montgomery had approved of it but played no role in its preparation, while Eisenhower, who was flying frequently to Normandy to confer with his field commanders, did little more than nod his head in approval of it. Eisenhower did make a contribution to the plan by phasing forward additional units to build up Bradley's strength, by speeding up deliveries of ammunition and equipment, and most of all, by co-ordinating the Allied air effort.

The plan, COBRA, hinged on air power. Bradley wanted a small area (2500 by 6000 yards) saturated by bombs. Eisenhower saw to it that 1887 heavy and medium bombers and 559 fighter bombers, carrying more than 4000 tons of explosives, were made available to meet Bradley's requirements. It was, in a way, a 1916-style operation, with bombers substituting for artillery. The big difference between it and a World War I operation, however, was not the presence of air forces, but rather the relative thinness of the German line in 1944 coupled with the presence of Allied tanks to exploit the hole blasted in the line.

One advantage artillery had over air was that the guns could fire in any weather. COBRA was due to start on July 21, and Eisenhower flew over to Normandy to witness the beginning. The sky was overcast and his B-25 was the only plane in the air. By the time he arrived it was raining hard. Bradley told him the attack had been called off and dressed him down for flying in such weather. Eisenhower tossed away his soggy cigarette, smiled, and said his only pleasure in being Supreme Commander was that no one could ground him. "When I die," he added, looked at the steady rain, "they ought to hold my body for a rainy day and then bury me out in the middle of a storm. This damned weather is going to be the death of me yet."[4]

Despite the disappointment, Eisenhower had great confidence in Bradley and felt little need to encourage him to greater efforts. In the only message he sent Bradley before COBRA, the Supreme Commander promised to take full personal responsibility for answering to the American people for the casualties that would necessarily be incurred. He reminded Bradley that "a break through at this juncture will minimize the total cost." He wanted the Americans to "pursue every advantage with an ardor verging on recklessness. . . ." If both armies broke through, "the results will be incalculable."[5]

The Supreme Commander did, however, feel that it was necessary to put pressure on Montgomery, and he did so in a variety of ways. In the end Montgomery reponded handsomely, showing that at least in this instance Eisenhower's methods—cajoling, gentle persuasion, and pressure via third parties—worked better than threats or direct orders.

Eisenhower wanted Second Army to attack when COBRA began—in fact had promised Bradley that he would see to it that it did—and he flew to Montgomery's headquarters to urge on the British general. What he wanted, as Smith noted, was "an all-out coordinated attack by the entire Allied line, which would at last put our forces in decisive motion. He was up and down the line like a football coach, exhorting everyone to aggressive action."[6] On July 24 Eisenhower talked to Montgomery's chief of staff, De Guingand, for an hour; the next day De Guingand phoned Eisenhower to assure him that Montgomery had strengthened his supporting attack. Eisenhower also talked to Churchill, who agreed to the necessity of "keeping the front aflame" and accepted Eisenhower's conclusion that the British forces could and should be doing more. Churchill visited Montgomery in Normandy and told him as much.[7]

All of this was highly irritating to Montgomery and Brooke. "It is quite clear that Ike considers that Dempsey should be doing more than he does," Brooke wrote to Montgomery. "It is equally clear that Ike has the very vaguest conception of war." The British officers agreed that Eisenhower had no notion of balance. If everybody was to attack, Montgomery argued, nobody would have the strength to make a decisive breakthrough or to exploit it. Eisenhower "evidently . . . has some conception of attacking on the whole front," Brooke complained, "which must be an American doctrine judging by Mark Clark with Fifth Army in Italy." Unfortunately, he continued, the idea of attack along the whole front appealed to Churchill too, so "Ike may . . . obtain some support in this direction."[8]

While Eisenhower did everything possible to get Montgomery to move, he had at the same time to stall off Tedder, who was becoming almost obsessed by his countryman's lack of action. Tedder called Eisenhower on the telephone the morning of July 25, the day COBRA began, demanding to know why Montgomery was not doing more and what Eisenhower was doing about it. Eisenhower said he had talked with Churchill and that they were satisfied that this time Montgomery's attack would be in earnest. Tedder "rather un-huhed, being not at all satisfied, and implying the PM must have sold Ike a bill of goods." Eisenhower told Butcher of the conversation and said he thought he could work things out satisfactorily, for "there's nothing so wrong a good victory won't cure."[9]

To get away from the carping, and hopefully to enjoy seeing the beginning of the "great victory," Eisenhower went to Normandy after talking to Tedder to watch the start of COBRA. The tremendous bombardment was impressive, but Eisenhower returned to London that evening glum, even depressed. There had been a series of bombardments from the American bombers that had fallen short, killing and wounding several hundred G.I.s. General Lesley McNair, commander of the Army Ground Forces, who had gone to the front lines to observe, had been killed. In addition the ground attack which began at 11 A.M. seemed to be going slowly. The only encouraging note came when Bradley, who accompanied Eisenhower to the airstrip for the flight back to London, said he was convinced that the next day his forces would make extraordinary advances. Eisenhower would not allow his hopes to rise—he had heard the same thing the first day of GOODWOOD. Worse than the slow progress on the ground were the short bombardments, which convinced Eisenhower that he could not use his air power to help the troops break out. He told Bradley he would no longer employ heavy bombers against tactical targets. "That's a job for artillery," he said to Bradley. "I gave them a green light this time. But I promise you it's the last."[10]

The next day news from the front filtered in slowly, and the over-all picture was unclear. Eisenhower dictated a letter to Marshall, telling him only that an offensive was under way on both flanks. If either went well, he added, "we will be in a much improved position."[11] He had lunch with Churchill, who said he would see to it that Montgomery launched a major attack. The Supreme Commander then dictated a note to Montgomery. Eisenhower said he had had no news at all about activities on Second Army's front, but "I know the troops are fighting for all they are worth and I am certain the enemy will somewhere crack under the pressure." Churchill, he added, thought so too.[12] Montgomery was irritated at the thought that Eisenhower had complained about him to the Prime Minister, but there was little he could do about it except try to remove the reason for the complaint.[13]

This he did in exemplary fashion. On the morning of July 25 his Canadian forces started southward toward Falaise, attacking an area strongly held by Panzers. The Canadians suffered 1000 casualties and took little territory, but they did effectively screen the major offensive and delayed a German shift of reserves to the United States front. Still, neither Montgomery nor Brooke was at all happy with the way things were going. To Brooke it was "clear that Ike knows nothing about strategy. Bedell Smith, on the other hand, has brains, but no military education in its true sense." Even Smith, however, failed to recognize Montgomery's strategic genius, and thus lent his voice to the demands for all-out attacks everywhere.[14] Whatever his own feelings, Montgomery could not ignore all this pressure, and on July 27 directed the Second Army to strike in the Caumont area and ordered all British and Canadian forces to attack to the greatest possible degree with the resources available. He declared that the enemy "must be worried, and shot up, and attacked, and raided, whenever and wherever possible."[15]

By the evening of the second day of COBRA, meanwhile, the situation on Bradley's front was beginning to clarify. Major General J. Lawton

Collins' VII Corps was breaking through. The air attack had stunned the enemy, destroying his communications and rendering many of his weapons ineffective.[16] The VII Corps was extremely strong, with two armored and four infantry divisions, and it began to overrun enemy positions. Gerow's V Corps, on Collins' left, and Troy Middleton's VIII Corps, to the right, were also making progress. Before going to bed an elated Eisenhower wrote Bradley, "You have got the stuff piled up and we must give the enemy no rest at all until we have achieved our objective. Then we will crush him."[17]

The Americans had achieved a penetration and were on the verge of scoring a complete breakthrough. Brooke continued to complain in his diary about Eisenhower's lack of strategic sense, but the Supreme Commander's insistence on attack everywhere had brought about the crisis of the war in the West. If the Germans could not hold the line, American troops would pour through the gap and be free in the enemy rear. Eisenhower was rushing divisions over to the Continent to prepare for the exploitation and was ready to activate the U. S. Third Army, with Patton commanding, to take advantage of the situation. Fresh divisions under Patton, unopposed behind German lines, with their flanks protected by Allied air forces and their mobility insured thanks to their tanks and trucks, would create havoc. Short of the West Wall, the Germans had nothing to stop them with.

Eisenhower was fully aware that the crisis had come and was desperately anxious to make sure the opportunity was not lost. The Supreme Commander continued to press Montgomery. "Never was time more vital to us," he told the British general on July 28, and "we should not wait on weather or on perfection of detail of preparation." He wanted Montgomery to speed up Second Army's main blow, telling him that "I feel very strongly that a three division attack now on 2nd Army's right flank will be worth more than a six division attack in five days' time." He urged Montgomery not to waste an hour. "I am counting on you and as always will back you to the uttermost limit."[18] Montgomery, beginning to share the spirit of urgency, ordered Dempsey to throw all caution overboard and "to accept any casualties and to step on the gas for Vire."[19]

Bradley needed no special urging. On July 28 his forces captured Coutances, completing Operation COBRA. He immediately began to exploit his victory, ordering four U.S. corps to press their attack southward. He told Eisenhower his men were feeling "pretty cocky" and refused to have their enthusiasm dampened by reports that the enemy was sending reinforcements. "I can assure you," Bradley said, "that we are taking every calculated risk and we believe we have the Germans out of the ditches and in complete demoralization and expect to take full advantage of them."[20]

The German high command was as aware of the crisis at hand as Eisenhower. On July 27 Von Kluge got Hitler's permission to transfer a Panzer corps from the British front to Bradley's side of the line, and to move two divisions to Normandy from Pas de Calais and a third there from the Atlantic coast of France. Hitler did turn down Von Kluge's request for the transfer of a division from southern France to Normandy. But otherwise, he put everything he had into stabilizing the front, telling Von Kluge to "keep his eyes riveted to the front and on the enemy without ever looking backward."[21]

The German reinforcements came too late. Montgomery's insistence on drawing the Germans to Second Army's front was about to pay huge dividends.

General Collins, "Lightning Joe" to the newspapers, a veteran of Guadalcanal, led the attack. Bradley had deliberately put him at the point because he thought Collins "nervy and ambitious." Collins had a secret weapon. In World War I enormous artillery barrages had often created a gap in the enemy's front lines, but there had been no exploitation of them because of the depth of the line and because infantrymen slogging through the craters were mowed down by machine guns. Eventually tanks made it possible to exploit these gaps. In Normandy the hedgerows substituted for the depth of the World War I trench system. Always before, when Bradley got his tanks loose behind the German lines, the hedgerows had stopped them, for when the Sherman tanks hit the hedgerows the vehicles rose up over the tops of the mounds, exposing their soft underbellies to the enemy while their own guns pointed helplessly toward the sky. One of Bradley's tank sergeants solved the problem. Taking scrap steel from an enemy roadblock, he welded four steel tusklike prongs to the front of a tank. When the Sherman hit a hedgerow, the tusks bore into the earth, pinned down the belly, and allowed the tank to break through. Thanks to this simple invention, Collins was able to keep up the momentum of his advance.[22]

He held nothing back, committing all his reserves on the second day of the battle. By July 27 he had reached Tessy-sur-Vire and Coutances; by the thirtieth the VIII Corps, to his right, had taken Granville and Avranches and were on the verge of breaking into Brittany.[23] The Germans, analyzing Collins' attack later, were impressed:

"Co-operation between reconnaissance aircraft, fighter-bombers, armour, and infantry was excellent," they admitted.[24]

Montgomery did all he could to help. As he saw the situation, the Germans were still so strong in the Caen area that operations there "are definitely unlikely to succeed; if we attempt them we would merely play into the enemy's hands, and we would not be helping on our operations on the western flank." He therefore told the Canadians to hold position across the Orne River and initiate only local attacks to keep the Germans off balance. On his own right, however, Montgomery wanted the Second Army to move out. He directed Dempsey to regroup his army and begin a major offensive, involving at least six divisions, toward Caumont. "The main blow of the whole Allied plan has now been struck on the western flank," he told Dempsey, and "that blow is the foundation of all our operations, and it has been well and truly struck." In this "critical and important time" he wanted Dempsey to hurl his forces full strength at the enemy.

Montgomery did not, however, realize the full implications of the situation. He pointed out that the summer was already partly gone and that there were not many more months of good campaigning weather left. There was still much to be done. What, then, did he expect to accomplish thanks to COBRA's success? "We must secure the Brittany ports before the winter is on us," Montgomery declared.[25]

Eisenhower's view was not so limited. In commenting on Montgomery's operational orders, the Supreme Commander told Montgomery that "it is easily possible that the most tremendous results will follow." He reminded Montgomery that the Twenty-first Army Group still had "plenty of strength" in the Caen area to take advantage of any opportunity that might arise there. With a few days of good weather, which "would be a Godsend," the Allies "would possibly find the enemy Divisions exhausted both of fuel and ammunition and could capture and destroy them in place." To encourage Montgomery, he added, "This . . . is what you have been aiming toward for a long time and I must say that you deserve the luck of having a bit of good weather at such a critical time."[26]

Eisenhower's wishes were sincere. On July 29 he flew to Normandy to see Bradley, who gave a glowing progress report, and Montgomery. The British commander had a complaint. Newspaper stories in the American press had been sharply critical of Montgomery, charging that he sat in front of Caen and did nothing while the Americans took all the risks and casualties. Eisenhower said he would see what he could do about the situation. When he returned to Portsmouth he wired the chief public relations officer in the War Department, General Surles, telling him that the reporters were ignoring "the fact that I am not only inescapably responsible for strategy and general missions but they seemingly also ignore the fact that it is my responsibility to determine the efficiency of my various subordinates. . . ." He asked Surles to hold some off-the-record press conferences and in them to emphasize that he, Eisenhower, was the responsible officer. "When criticism is believed to be necessary it should be directed toward me equally at least with any of my principal subordinates."[27]

On the Continent, meanwhile, organization changes that Eisenhower had arranged earlier were about to be put into effect. With American divisions pouring into Normandy, the Supreme Commander wanted two American armies gathered together in one group. Bradley would take command of the whole, to be called Twelfth Army Group, with Courtney Hodges taking over First Army and Patton assuming command of Third Army. Until SHAEF could establish a forward command post on the Continent and Eisenhower could take command of the 12th Army Group, Bradley would continue to receive his operational instructions from Montgomery. Acting on Eisenhower's orders, Bradley declared that the organizational change would take place on August 1.[28] Both Patton and Hodges went to the Continent early to familiarize themselves with their staffs and subordinates, and the positions and objectives of their divisions.

By July 31 organizations and operations were meshing beautifully. The Allied armies in Europe began to swing into the open. On the western flank, VIII Corps had moved beyond Avranches. Collins' VII Corps had captured Villedieu and Tessy-sur-Vire, and V Corps was advancing southward. Dempsey began his attack on July 30, broke through at Caumont, and the next day was quite close to Le Bény-Bocage. The Canadians were stepping up their local attacks. On August 1 Patton was unleashed and began his race through Brittany and down to the Loire River. The nightmare of a static front similar to that of World War I was over. "This is great news," Eisenhower exulted. "Bradley has plenty of infantry units to rush into forward areas to consolidate all gains and permit armor to continue thrusting and surrounding enemy."[29]

His optimism growing with each bit of incoming news from the front, Eisenhower was determined not to lose the opportunity at hand. He still felt Montgomery needed occasional prodding, and on August 2 sent a note of encouragement to the Twenty-first Army Group commander. Enemy resistance in the Avranches region had disintegrated and Patton was in the open. Eisenhower wanted him to push into Brittany as rapidly as possible, and asked Montgomery to make sure all commanders were aware "that in an emergency we can drop them supplies by airplane in considerable quantities." Whatever happened, Eisenhower insisted, the momentum should not be lost. "I know that you will keep hammering," the Supreme Commander added, "as long as you have a single shot in the locker."[30]

Just before lunch on August 2nd, Butcher met Eisenhower in the hall at SHAEF Main, Widewing. The Supreme Commander was all smiles. "If the intercepts are right," he said, "we are to hell and gone in Brittany and slicing 'em up in Normandy."[31] The situation was the culmination of a soldier's dreams. Eisenhower had strong forces loose in the enemy rear and they could go in any direction he wanted them to. The options, if not unlimited, were wide. Patton might be sent east, toward Paris, or northeast, toward the German rear at Caen, or south into central France, or west into Brittany. Each option had something to recommend it. The seemingly most advantageous route was east into Brittany, both because this fit into the over-all OVERLORD plan and because SHAEF desperately needed the Brittany ports. Because of Eisenhower's desire to beef up Bradley's forces, the Americans already had more divisions in France than had been scheduled, but the port capacity controlled was less than anticipated. Thus supply for the onrushing armies was Eisenhower's major concern. If he were to keep the essential material flowing forward to the front lines, he had to have more ports, and Brest and Lorient were the best immediately available.

Ruppenthal, the leading student of the logistical support of the armies has concluded, "The importance of Brittany in the OVERLORD plan can hardly be exaggerated." The very success of OVERLORD seemed to depend on getting Brest and Lorient, for without them the necessary divisions could not be supported on the Continent. This was true even if there was no, or practically no, German opposition at all.[32]

The great urgency of getting Brittany, however, had to be balanced against other possibilities. If Eisenhower sent Patton tearing into the peninsula toward Brest, the Third Army would be moving away from the bulk of the German forces. As Eisenhower explained to Marshall on August 2, he did not want to lose a golden opportunity. The German Army in Normandy had been defeated; it was now possible to destroy it. When the flank opened and the options increased, Eisenhower decided to send only one corps of Patton's army into Brittany, devoting the "great bulk of the forces to the task of completing the destruction of the German Army, at least that portion west of the Orne, and exploiting beyond that as far as we possibly can." Brittany remained important, indeed "the rapid occupation of Brittany is placed as a primary task," but with the Germans on the run everywhere Eisenhower thought the objective could be obtained at small cost. Once Brittany was secure, Eisenhower told Marshall, the War Department could send over the divisions piling up in the United States. Even divisions that had been scheduled to enter the Continent via ANVIL should be diverted to Brittany. In conclusion Eisenhower said, "I am very hopeful as to immediate results, and believe that within the next two or three days we will so manhandle the western flank of the enemy's forces that we will secure for ourselves freedom of action through destruction of a considerable portion of the forces facing us."[33]

On the basis of Eisenhower's decision, Patton sent one corps into Brittany while his other three corps sped southward from Avranches. Middleton led the drive into Brittany and in four days overran the peninsula. He did not, however, have enough strength to take Brest and Lorient, and he was forced to lay siege to the two ports. In the end Middleton had to be content to contain the German garrisons, and neither port contributed anything to the Allied port capacity. Brest did not fall until mid-September, and Lorient held out to the end of the war. Critics charged that the only reason Eisenhower sent any troops into Brittany was blind obedience to an outdated OVERLORD plan, but it was equally true that had he strengthened Middleton's attack Brest and Lorient might not have held out, and Twelfth Army Group could have used the ports for support in the drive to the Seine. On the other hand, if another of Patton's corps had joined Middleton in Brittany, Patton might not have been strong enough in the Falaise area. It is also possible that had Eisenhower ignored Brittany altogether and sent Middleton toward Falaise with Patton, he could have achieved a greater success there.

The arguments were nicely balanced. War is a matter of choices among limited options, for always, no matter how powerful the force a general commands, there are limits to what he can do. In this case Eisenhower decided to try to get away with deploying as few troops as possible in Brittany in order to achieve as much as possible elsewhere. In effect, he failed everywhere. Patton was too weak at Falaise, and Middleton was too weak in Brittany. The policy of scattering forces had nothing to recommend it, especially in view of Eisenhower's insistence on DRAGOON. If he needed the Brittany ports, he did not need Marseilles; since he had DRAGOON, he did not need the Brittany ports.

Marshall was intrigued by the possibilities inherent in the quick overrunning of the Brittany ports, and by Eisenhower's suggestion that new divisions should come into the Continent through Brest. On August 8 the Chief therefore asked Eisenhower if he wanted divisions sent forward ahead of schedule. Eisenhower replied that the advance shipment of two infantry divisions was "very desirable" and said he could handle them at Cherbourg or over the Normandy beaches if the Brittany ports were not usable when they arrived.[34] When it became clear that Brest and Lorient were not going to fall quickly, Eisenhower told Marshall he was still unwilling to detach troops from his main forces "merely in order to save a week or so in capturing the Brest Peninsula ports." He explained that he had a chance for a great victory which if successful "will allow us complete freedom of action in France and will have incalculable results."[35]*

Clausewitz had long ago insisted on the necessity of careful planning in managing a large organization, with the first requirement being the definition of an objective. He also emphasized that all decisions had to be based on probability. Managers, he declared, had to accept uncertainty and act on the basis of thorough analysis and planning designed to minimize the uncertainty as much as possible. He advocated decisions based on science rather than on hunch.[36] In the case at hand, the planners told Eisenhower that when SHAEF's armies reached the Seine they would have to pause to regroup and refit. Within that context, capture of the Brittany ports was essential. On the other hand, Eisenhower knew he would never have a better opportunity to crush the bulk of the German armed forces in France. To allow that opportunity to pass would have been indefensible caution.

In the end, what threw everything out of balance and made Eisenhower's decision to go into Brittany appear overly cautious was the success elsewhere. The German Army in France was, if not crushed, badly beaten, and was unable to man another defensive line in France. There was no pause by SHAEF's armies at the Seine. As a result, by the time Brest was taken the Allied armies were so far from it that there was no point in using it. Eisenhower's staff was a much more scientific bureaucracy than anything Clausewitz ever imagined possible, but in Eisen-

* A sidelight on Brest-Lorient and Eisenhower's and Marshall's desire to bring the American divisions into the battle through those ports was that, if this had been done, the major argument in favor of ANVIL would have been eliminated. ANVIL's biggest contribution, the one Eisenhower always emphasized, was that it would allow him to put more American divisions into the Continent. If he could do the same thing with Brest-Lorient, ANVIL was unnecessary. Eisenhower and Marshall seem to have ignored this, but as has been seen in Chapter 8 the Prime Minister did not.

hower's time, as in Clausewitz', chance, accident, and most of all the seizing of an opportunity at hand could combine to render all plans meaningless.

While Dempsey and Hodges continued to attack, contain, and destroy the Germans in Normandy, Patton's forces made a wide sweep around the German left flank. Third Army moved with amazing speed, taking Rennes on August 3 and Le Mans five days later. Tedder, Spaatz, Harris, and the air forces generally gave Third Army all possible support. Fighters and fighter bombers protected the. armored columns' flanks. The American tanks had direct ground-to-air radio communication, ensuring immediate tactical support and reconnaissance. The big bombers, meanwhile, continued to interdict behind the German lines. Attacks all along the Seine, the Loire, and in between isolated the battlefield by destroying bridges, roads, and railroads. The Germans were reduced to moving troops by night; their supply deficiencies were acute. French Resistance activities added further to the German woes.

On August 4, caught up in the excitement, Montgomery issued a directive that aimed at the total destruction of the enemy. He decided the time had come for the Canadians near Caen to do more than contain Germans and ordered them to drive for Falaise not later than August 8, thus hopefully cutting off the withdrawal of German forces facing Dempsey. Second Army should continue its move south and east toward Argentan, while Hodges would maintain his drive eastward. Patton was to attack due east from Rennes toward Laval and Angers. Summing up, Montgomery said the Allies had "unleashed the shackles that were holding us down and have knocked away the 'key rivets.'" He intended to force the enemy back on the Seine, where the bridges had been destroyed, and then elimate Von Kluge's divisions as a fighting force.[37]

Eisenhower was thinking of bigger things. On August 7 he told Marshall his three main objectives were to get the Brittany ports, to destroy as much of Von Kluge's forces as possible, and "to cross the Seine before the enemy has time to hold it in strength, destroy his forces between the Seine and Somme and secure the Seine ports."[38] Eisenhower, in short, was already considering leaping the Seine, rather than pausing for regrouping when the river was reached. He did not, however, reach the next logical conclusion of pulling Middleton's wasted troops out of Brittany.

Hitler, meanwhile, had plans of his own. As Patton's Third Army moved away from Avranches, Hitler saw an opportunity to reverse the situation, cut Patton off, recapture the Cotentin ports, and possibly even drive the Allies back into the sea. He proposed to do this by a counter-attack, moving out to Mortain and then the coast. If successful, the attack would at the least isolate Patton, leaving him without a supply line and in danger of being engulfed by the enemy. Hitler described the plan as "a unique, never recurring opportunity for a complete reversal of the situation."[39] To strengthen the attack, he sent units to Von Kluge from Pas de Calais—the Germans having finally seen through FORTI-TUDE—as well as troops from the Vire and Caen area.

Von Kluge launched the Mortain counterattack late in the evening of August 6. Six armored divisions, some of them drastically under strength, led the way. The 30th Division of First Army caught the entire blow, and elements of the division were encircled. They continued to fight, and Bradley sent two additional divisions into the battle to help.

On the map, the situation for the Allies looked serious. The main problem for Eisenhower was deciding how much strength to leave in the Mortain area to keep the Germans away from the sea, so that the supply lines to Patton could remain open. This problem, like that of the question of the commitment to Brittany, was compounded by the opportunity at hand, an opportunity that had ironically been suddenly increased by the counterattack. For Hitler was risking more than he knew. By attacking westward, he was pushing his best formations deeper into the potential Allied trap. For Eisenhower, the question of allocation of resources was crucial. If he agreed to a thin line at Mortain, Von Kluge might break through, with incalculable results. But if the Supreme Commander strengthened the line at Mortain by slowing Patton's advance and using Third Army troops on the defensive mission, he would lose the chance to encircle and destroy Von Kluge.

By coincidence, Eisenhower was on the scene. He had been anxious for a long time to set up an advance command post in Normandy, and on the evening of August 7 had done so. The next day he met with Bradley. Both generals responded to the challenge in the same way—to hold Mortain with as little as possible and rush every available division south. Tedder was with Eisenhower and Bradley as they talked; he later remembered that Eisenhower approved of Bradley's decision "there and then. He [Eisenhower] told Bradley that if the Germans should temporarily break through from Mortain to Avranches and thus cut off the southward thrust, we would give the advance forces two thousand tons of supply per day by air."[40] The following morning Eisenhower told Marshall, "The enemy's . . . counter attacks . . . make it appear that we have a good chance to encircle and destroy a lot of his forces."[41]

The gamble paid off. Von Kluge's attack gained only a little ground, at an enormous cost. Late on August 8 the German general discontinued his offensive and refused to renew it despite Hitler's orders. The Canadians were by then posing a threat he could not ignore, for they had struck with tanks, artillery, and air east of the Orne on the Caen–Falaise road. Concerned about his rear, Von Kluge had to divert troops intended for the Mortain counterattack to meet the threat. To his left, meanwhile, an ever stronger Patton was getting into position to drive toward Falaise with Third Army.[42]

The Allied offensive was in full swing. Except for Middleton's corps stranded in Brittany, all forces were meshing perfectly, aiming for the same objective—the destruction of Von Kluge's forces. "Ike keeps continually after both Montgomery and Bradley," Butcher noted, "to destroy the enemy now rather than to be content with mere gains of territory."[43]

At the end of the first week of August the bulk of two German armies, the Seventh and Fifth Panzer, were within a huge salient, with the tip at Mortain and the base on the Falaise–Argentan line. To the east, U. S. First Army blocked the German path to Avranches, while the British Second Army covered the enemy on the north side of the salient. The Canadian First Army, meanwhile, was preparing to move south from Caen to meet with Patton's Third Army, swinging to the north from Le Mans. Under the original plan following the breakout, Montgomery had wanted Patton to drive straight east, in the general direction of Paris, but following the Mortain counterattack Bradley had decided to try to encircle the German armies and changed Third Army's course. He convinced Montgomery of the merit of the new plan. Eisenhower, meanwhile, had come to the same conclusion, and on the afternoon of August 8 visited Bradley at his headquarters to suggest to him that Patton "should swing in closer in an effort to destroy the enemy by attacking him in the rear." He found that Bradley "had already acted on this idea . . ." which was a typical example of the similarity of strategic thought among the members of the high command at this stage of the battle.[44]

The Allied generals licked their lips at the prospect of devouring two entire German armies whole, but they could not ignore two very real dangers. First, as the Canadians from the north and the Yankees from the south moved toward each other through the haze of smoke, crashing shells, and dive-bombing fighter planes, the prospect of their clashing by accident grew with each step that they took. Few things in war are more demoralizing to a soldier than to be shot at by one of his allies.

Second, the Allies might effect the juncture and create a line across the base of the German salient, only to find that they did not have enough strength to hold it. For sooner or later the Germans would realize the desperate nature of their position, at which point they could be expected to make a dash for the safety of the west bank of the Seine. Two German armies would come full force against the American or Canadian corps holding the line; in the process the Allied troops might be trampled.

Montgomery, as the over-all ground commander, was responsible for averting both dangers. His solution was to draw the boundary between the Canadians and Americans at Argentan. When Patton reached that town he was to concentrate his forces there, creating a position of such strength that it could withstand any German onslaught. The Canadians, meanwhile, would move down the Caen road to Falaise, then on to Argentan to complete the encirclement. With a clearly drawn boundary, there would be no difficulty in recognizing each other's position.

Eisenhower's role in these tactical arrangements was limited. He set the general policy, but day-to-day operations were in the hands of his subordinates. As Supreme Commander he sometimes had to nod his head in approval of a proposed movement, but often he was not consulted on individual maneuvers. One thing he could do was encourage, and he did a great deal of it, more with Montgomery than with the American generals, since he felt that Montgomery needed it more. Thus after dinner on August 8 he drove to Montgomery's headquarters "to make certain that Monty would continue to press on the British-Canadian front. . . ."[45]

The Canadian attack nevertheless went slowly. Patton, facing much slimmer resistance, made a steady advance. By August 10 Von Kluge, much alarmed, realized that his only hope for escape lay in an immediate withdrawal to the east. Hitler, however, wanted him to continue the attacks to the west. After an exchange of messages and a telephone conversation, Hitler finally consented to allow Von Kluge to suspend the westward attack, shorten his lines, and turn the offensive toward Patton's lead corps (the American XV) in order to keep the supply lines open. It was already too late. The German Seventh Army had lost its rear installations and was depending on the Fifth Panzer Army for supplies, and Patton's men had cut off all but one of the German supply roads. The Germans were on the verge of an incredible debacle.[46]

On August 12 Patton's XV Corps reached Argentan. The Canadians were still eighteen miles to the north and making only slight progress. Patton, impatient, wanted to cross the army boundary line and close the gap. He called Bradley on the telephone and pleaded, "Let me go on to Falaise and we'll drive the British back into the sea for another Dunkirk." Bradley refused. He did not want to take the chance of violating the boundary and having Americans and Canadians fire at one another, and he did not believe Patton had enough strength to hold the line once the Germans started to rush to escape. Besides, he thought the Canadians were strong enough to complete the encirclement.*

By August 14 the Allies were on the verge of closing the trap. If successful, they would practically eliminate all German strength in France, leaving them with open country between the current lines and the German border. DRAGOON would begin the next day, August 15, opening another port and tying down remaining German forces in the south of France, most of which were immobile occupation units in any case. Eisenhower, sensing the possibilities of the situation, called on the Allied forces to make a maximum effort to seize the fleeting opportunity to destroy the Germans in France. On August 14, in a rare Order of the Day (he issued only ten in the course of the war), he exhorted the Allied soldiers, sailors, and airmen. "The opportunity may be grasped only through the utmost zeal, determination and speedy action," he declared, and asked every flier "to make it his direct responsibility that the enemy is blasted unceasingly by day and by night, and is denied safety either in fight or flight." He asked the sailors to see to it that the supplies kept coming in, and requested "every soldier to go forward to his assigned objective with the determination that the enemy can survive only through surrender; let no foot of ground once gained be relinquished nor a single German escape through a line once established." If everyone did his job, "we can make this week a momentous one in the history of this war—a brilliant and fruitful week for us, a fateful one for the ambitions of the Nazi tyrants." The Order of the Day was broadcast over BBC and the Allied radio network, and distributed to the troops in mimeographed form.[47]

* There was later much controversy about this decision. Bradley has given the authoritative last word: "Monty had never prohibited and I never proposed that U.S. forces close the gap from Argentan to Falaise." *A Soldier's Story*, p. 377. Chester Wilmot concludes that the fault lay with the Canadians; he feels they should have closed the gap and prevented the escape of the German troops. *Struggle for Europe* (London, 1952), pp. 424–35.

Butcher had a simple way of judging the progress of events. He always felt that the best indication of how the battle was going was Eisenhower's disposition; on August 14 he found it "sunny, if not almost jubilant."[48] Another indication of Allied success, unknown to them at the time, was a crisis in the enemy's high command. Hitler decided that Von Kluge was a defeatist, believed the rumor that his general was making arrangements to surrender to Eisenhower, and then lost all faith in Von Kluge when he learned that the general was involved in the July 20 plot against his life. On August 16 Hitler replaced Von Kluge with Generalfeldmarschall Walther von Model.[49]

The general sentiment in the West during mid-August was one of enormous optimism. Newspaper correspondents who had been overly pessimistic during the Normandy stalemate now went to the other extreme. Eisenhower held a press conference on August 15 and the reporters kept asking him how many weeks it would take to end the war. Furious, "Ike vehemently castigated those who think they can measure the end of the war 'in a matter of weeks.' He went on to say that 'such people are crazy.'" He reminded the press that Hitler could continue the war effort through the Gestapo and pointed out that the German leader knew he would hang when the war ended so had nothing to lose in continuing it. Eisenhower said that he expected that Hitler would end up hanging himself, but before he did he would "fight to the bitter end," and most of his troops would fight with him.[50]

Eisenhower was right. The Germans in the Falaise pocket rejected the easy way out—surrender—and fought to hold open the jaws of the trap that were slowly closing on them. They tried to make it a Dunkirk in reverse. Despite Eisenhower's plea in his Order of the Day, it was the Germans, not the Allies, who made the supreme effort at Falaise. The rigidity with which the field commanders held to the boundary lines aided the Germans (Eisenhower supported Bradley's decision to adhere to the established boundary), even though late on August 15 Montgomery agreed to change the boundary slightly to permit the U.S. troops to come farther north.[51] Those Germans not involved in holding the gap open, meanwhile, were fleeing as fast as they could; in the end, some 40,000 escaped. The gap was not closed until August 19.[52]

Eisenhower was disappointed but not downcast. "Due to the extraordinary defensive measures taken by the enemy," he explained to Marshall, "it is possible that our total bag of prisoners will not be so great as I first anticipated." Still, he felt that "the beating up of his formations along our whole front has been such that with the cleaning up of the pocket and a resumption of our advance east and northeastward, the opposition will be greatly weakened."[53]

Falaise was, in short, a victory, even if a somewhat limited one that left a taste of bitterness and led to recrimination between the British and Americans as to whose fault it was that any Germans escaped. Some 50,000 German troops were captured, another 10,000 killed. Those who did escape left their equipment behind. An officer who had observed the destruction of the Aisne-Marne, St. Mihiel, and Meuse-Argonne battlefields in World War I found that "none of these compared in the effect upon the imagination with what I saw [near Falaise]. . . . As far as my eye could reach . . . on every line of sight, there were . . . vehicles, wagons, tanks, guns, prime movers, sedans, rolling kitchens, etc., in various stages of destruction. . . . I stepped over hundreds of rifles in the mud and saw hundreds more stacked along sheds. . . . I saw probably 300 field pieces and tanks, mounting large caliber guns, that were apparently undamaged."[54] The extent of the destruction is best measured in the August 28 report of strength by the Fifth Panzer Army; it had 1300 men, 24 tanks, and 60 pieces of artillery.[55]

The Allied Expeditionary Force was now approaching the Seine, with no coherent German defenses standing between it and the West Wall. The problems at Falaise and the escape of some German soldiers could not disguise the fact that Montgomery had engineered one of the great victories of the war. He had planned and conducted the operation, however, without consultation with Eisenhower and, in some cases, against Eisenhower's known wishes. He had achieved a complete breakthrough, but unless he could also achieve better co-ordination with SHAEF, or unless Eisenhower could learn to work with Montgomery and accept his methods, the Allies might not be able to take full advantage of the new situation.

CHAPTER 10

The Liberation of Paris

During June and July 1944 Allied-French relations seemed to be stuck in the mud. De Gaulle was furious with the Allies because they had disregarded his protests and issued their own invasion currency, just as if France were an occupied country like Italy. No civil affairs agreements with the French had been signed, and no recognition had been extended to the FCNL. Roosevelt still believed "that de Gaulle will crumple and that the British supporters of de Gaulle will be confounded by the progress of events," this despite the reports of all the military men in Normandy that the average Frenchman looked to De Gaulle "as the natural and inevitable leader of Free France."[1] De Gaulle was trying to drive a wedge between the smaller Allies and the British and Americans in order to get FCNL recognized, and while he was in London after D-Day persuaded the governments of Czechoslovakia, Poland, Belgium, Luxembourg, Yugoslavia, and Norway to recognize the FCNL as the provisional government of the French Republic. They did so despite American protests. De Gaulle also tried to split the Americans. He told his bitterest enemy in the State Department, Robert Murphy, that Eisenhower had been "most apologetic with regard to the arrangements which had been made for handling of civilian administration in France," and remarked that he realized that Eisenhower "was a good soldier who was being made to do something he did not want to do."[2]

By mid-1944 Eisenhower had become adept at weighing his own military needs against the instructions he received from the White House with regard to the French. Without making any long-term political commitments, he was able to work out a *modus operandi* that gave SHAEF the benefit of the forces at the disposal of the FCNL. The key decision was to elevate Koenig to a status equal to that of any other

Allied commander serving under Eisenhower and to give him command of the French Forces of the Interior (FFI, the Resistance). Whiteley, in co-operation with Koenig, drew up the basic agreement three days before D-Day; SHAEF issued Koenig's directive as commander of the FFI on June 17; on June 23 Eisenhower announced Koenig's new status. Smith, who had been Eisenhower's expert on French affairs in North Africa, continued meanwhile to work behind the scenes. By July 4 he was able to announce that Koenig had agreed to accept the Allied invasion francs, even for taxes. Smith had also arranged to attach French military tactical liaison officers to Allied army groups, corps, and divisions, and French administrative officers to the SHAEF section dealing with French civil affairs. Smith was most pleased about the good relations SHAEF had with Koenig.[3]

De Gaulle took note of the steady inroads he had been making. In a speech on June 18, the fourth anniversary of his call to arms, he stressed French sovereignty, then praised the strategic understanding of General Eisenhower, "in whom the French Government had complete confidence for the victorious conduct of the common military operations."[4] This speech helped set the stage for De Gaulle's previously planned trip to Washington and contributed to a smooth meeting between De Gaulle and Roosevelt. De Gaulle arrived on July 6, and both he and the President made efforts to be affable. On July 11 Roosevelt told the press that he had decided to consider the committee the "dominant" political authority of France until elections could be held. De Gaulle expressed his satisfaction with this formula. He added that it would not only be an error but an impossibility to exclude France from her true place among the great nations of the world.[5]

The breakout from the Normandy beachhead accelerated the amiable developments. Everyone was smiling and in a generous mood. As the Allied armies began to overrun France, meanwhile, the need for a signed, regularized civil affairs agreement—as opposed to the ad hoc arrangements Smith had worked out with Koenig—became more obvious. The FFI meanwhile contributed significantly to Allied military progress. The Resistance was of assistance everywhere, most notably in the south of France, in Brittany, and by protecting Patton's open flank through interference with enemy railroad and highway movements. Eisenhower later paid tribute to the FFI: "As the Allied columns advanced, these French forces ambushed the retreating enemy, attacked isolated groups and strongpoints . . . [and] provided our troops with invaluable assistance in supplying information of the enemy's dispositions and intentions. Not least in importance, they had, by their ceaseless harassing activities, surrounded the Germans with a terrible atmosphere of danger and hatred which ate into the confidence of the leaders and the courage of the soldiers."[6]

De Gaulle returned to Algiers in late July. As the Allies began to sweep across France he grew impatient. Unwilling to wait for an invitation from SHAEF or the British and American governments, and determined to be in France for the liberation of Paris, he announced on August 14 that he was flying to Normandy in the next day or two. He added that he would fly in a French plane piloted by a Frenchman, that he would land only in France and that he would not stop in the United Kingdom. Officers at AFHQ tried to convince him to fly in an American plane, partly because the French Lockheed Lodestar did not have the range to make the non-stop flight, and partly because the French plane was unfamiliar to the men operating Allied anti-aircraft batteries and might get shot down. General Eaker, the senior U.S. air officer in the Mediterranean, even offered De Gaulle the use of his private B-17. De Gaulle said *non*.[7]

A flurry of messages followed. Koenig tried to convince De Gaulle that he should co-operate with SHAEF. Smith warned that if the French leader flew in the Lockheed Lodestar he "does so at his own risk and the Supreme Commander will not be responsible for the consequences. . . ."[8]

For Eisenhower, meanwhile, the more important problem—assuming De Gaulle landed safely—was what to do with him when he arrived. No civil affairs agreement had yet been signed, so Eisenhower was still working under the pre-D-Day directive that instructed him to work with whatever Frenchman he chose on an informal basis. Eisenhower told the CCS he had no objection from a military standpoint to De Gaulle's coming to France, but he did want to know if it would in any way embarrass the British or American governments. He said that if De Gaulle arrived before the civil affairs agreement was signed he would receive the Frenchman as simply "Commander of the French Army." If however De Gaulle came after the signing, Eisenhower added, "he presumably will arrive as head of the Provisional Government of France."[9]

Eisenhower's little concluding phrase was hardly as innocent as it appeared. It amounted to a recognition of the FCNL as the provisional government, for if Eisenhower, the Supreme Allied Commander, received

De Gaulle on French soil in the capacity of "head of the Provisional Government," it would have the effect of committing the British and American governments to this recognition. Eisenhower may have been aware of this; certainly he desperately wanted to regularize his relations with the French, and recognition was the easiest way to do it. It would be making policy, and high-level policy at that, by a soldier in the field, but if it accomplished its purpose Eisenhower was willing to do it.

The CCS, however, saw what was at stake and would not allow Eisenhower to make policy in the field. The Chiefs told Eisenhower the governments had no objection to De Gaulle's coming to France but added, ". . . the signing of the agreement will have no bearing on the reception arrangements." Whether the agreement was signed or not, "General de Gaulle should be received as the Commander of the French Army." Eisenhower should treat him as a soldier, not a head of government, and the basic policy of ad hoc arrangements without recognition would continue.[10]

De Gaulle arrived on August 19. Within less than a week Patton's Third Army and Hodges' First, driving north and east, were approaching Paris. The immediate question was, Should Paris be liberated? Eisenhower wished to avoid it, at least for the present. To attack Paris might involve the Allies in prolonged street fighting and lead to the destruction of some of the most hallowed cultural monuments in the West. Once the Allies took Paris, they would be responsible for supplying its 2,000,000 civilians; planners estimated that 4000 tons of supplies per day would be required, equivalent to the daily needs of seven reinforced divisions. It would be better, Eisenhower and his planners thought, to encircle Paris, let the Germans in the city retain responsibility for it, and drive on to the German border. Eisenhower realized that this would mean a week or so of extreme privation for the Parisians, since the city was already low on food, coal, gas, and electricity, but he felt they would gladly accept the suffering if it brought a quicker end to the war.

There was also a political problem. So far De Gaulle had been able to maintain himself as the symbol around which all patriotic Frenchmen could rally, and the Resistance had held together only because its members all shared the fundamental aim of ridding France of the Germans. The presence of the Nazis was the organization's cement, and the conflicting groups in the Resistance and the FCNL would fall apart as soon as the Germans left. The Communists had a strong position within the Resistance, especially in the cities, and although they could easily profess their loyalty to a De Gaulle in far-off Algiers, a De Gaulle in Paris would be another matter. This does not mean that political lines were sharply drawn within all areas of the Resistance, but a large, vociferous, and influential group within the Paris Resistance was already preparing to contest De Gaulle's leadership. Both De Gaulle and the Allies had long recognized this problem, and therefore material supplied to the FFI had been dropped in rural areas rather than near urban centers, only partly to escape German detection, more particularly to inhibit the development of the Communists within the cities. As a result, few of the FFI within Paris were armed.[11]

In July, nonetheless, rumors of unrest in Paris and thoughts of a possible uprising similar to that of the Poles in Warsaw, caused great concern at SHAEF. Koenig ordered the Resistance to cease immediately any activities that might cause social or political convulsion, or might lead to German reprisals. His orders were not obeyed. On August 19 small local FFI groups in Paris, without central direction or discipline, took possession of police stations, national ministries, newspaper buildings, and the seat of the municipal government in Paris. They issued a call for a general uprising. That evening the German commander of the city, General Dietrich von Choltitz, asked for an armistice. Together with some Resistance representatives, he arranged for a truce until noon, August 23.[12]

From De Gaulle's point of view this was the most serious possible development. He would have been willing to consent to Eisenhower's plan to by-pass Paris as long as the Germans controlled the city, but he would not allow Paris to fall into the hands of the local Resistance. Acutely conscious of the dictum that he who holds Paris holds France, keenly aware of the Parisian's revolutionary instincts and his readiness to respond to the cry, *"Aux barricades!"* De Gaulle was determined to get regular French troops into Paris immediately.

Thanks to his own foresight, and Eisenhower's co-operation, a force was at hand. Before Eisenhower left Algiers in late 1943 he had made an agreement with De Gaulle—a French division would participate in OVERLORD and, by implication at least, liberate Paris. The division selected was Brigadier General Jacques Philippe Leclerc's 2d French Armored Division, and it entered France in late July as a part of Patton's Third Army. It had since been switched to Hodges' First Army as a part of Gerow's V Corps. Although it was near Argentan, more than a hundred miles from Paris (American troops were within twenty-five miles of the capital), it could still be the first Allied division into Paris.

On August 21 De Gaulle, accompained by Koenig, called on Eisenhower. They asked him to liberate Paris at once, and to use Leclerc's unit for that purpose. Eisenhower replied that he would not change his plan to by-pass Paris, but when the time came to take the city he promised that he would give Leclerc the honor of entering Paris first. De Gaulle found this thoroughly unsatisfactory. Although Koenig had promised that French military forces would obey the Supreme Commander's orders De Gaulle, after leaving the meeting, wrote a letter to Eisenhower in which he politely threatened that if Eisenhower did not send troops to Paris at once he would have to do so himself. Leclerc, in other words, would follow the orders of his government, not those of the Supreme Commander.[13] Eisenhower scribbled a memorandum to Smith at the top of De Gaulle's letter: "I talked verbally to Koenig on this. It looks now as if we'd be compelled to go into Paris. Bradley and his G-2 think we can and *must* walk in."[14]

But Eisenhower was only beginning to change his mind and had not yet made a final decision. The French, meanwhile, were growing more excited by the minute. Representatives from the Resistance had come from Paris to beg of Eisenhower, Bradley, Leclerc, or anyone they could find in authority that the Allies enter Paris immediately. They implied, falsely, that they controlled the city, but they said the Germans could not be trusted, might break the tenuous armistice at any time, and were capable of destroying the city. Leclerc pleaded with Gerow for permission to strike out toward the city; when Gerow refused, Leclerc started units toward Paris anyway.

Eisenhower was under pressure for a decision from all sides, from De Gaulle, from Leclerc, from the Resistance representatives, even from his own commanders. Paris was a magnet, attracting everyone toward her. France, it was felt, would not be free until Paris was free. Combat soldiers, American and British as well as French, could hardly wait to get into the city and sample its pleasures. Every division, corps, and army commander in Europe wanted the honor of liberating the city.

For Eisenhower, however, there were other pressures. He had held the alliance together so far by stoutly refusing to make any decision on political grounds. He had worked long and hard to gain British trust and had succeeded only by convincing them that all his actions were based on the Allies' military needs, not American or any other political objectives. To violate that rule now for De Gaulle's sake would open a

Pandora's box. If the French could use their military formations independently of SHAEF for political purposes, so could the British, the Poles, and everyone else. Before he could allow Leclerc to dash for Paris he would have to find a military reason—really, a rationalization—for doing so.

By August 22 Eisenhower was beginning to formulate a satisfactory reason. He later told Marshall that, although it would be desirable to defer capture of the city for supply reasons, "I do not believe this is possible. If the enemy tries to hold Paris with any real strength he would be a constant menace to our flank. If he largely concedes the place, it falls into our hands whether we like it or not."[15] Eisenhower's inclination was reinforced when Resistance representatives convinced him that they held the city by a thread, that Von Choltitz would withdraw if regular troops appeared in Paris, and that guerrilla warfare would begin if they did not. Sending troops into Paris thus became a matter of military reinforcement of success, and Eisenhower was able to think of the liberation as a military, not a political, move. Late on August 22, therefore, he decided to send Leclerc, along with the American 4th Division and a British contingent, into Paris.* He also ordered 23,000 tons of food and 3000 tons of coal dispatched to the city immediately.[16] In his orders, Eisenhower emphasized that "no advance must be made into Paris until the expiration of the Armistice [noon, August 23] and that Paris was to be entered only in case the degree of the fighting was such as could be overcome by light forces." He did not "want a severe fight in Paris," nor did he "want any bombing or artillery fire on the city if it can possibly be avoided."[17]

Leclerc and the other Allied forces entered the city on August 25. De Gaulle was with them. There was only scattered German resistance in Paris. Von Choltitz surrendered to Leclerc and the commander of the Paris FFI, who accepted his surrender in the name of the provisional government of France, not as representatives of SHAEF. De Gaulle appointed Koenig the military governor of the city (Eisenhower gave an identical job to Gerow), and the Gaullists moved immediately to take control of the government buildings. De Gaulle also ordered Leclerc to hold a parade on August 26, a parade that De Gaulle intended to lead.

---

* For the sake of future relations, Eisenhower would have been better advised to allow the French to liberate Paris themselves. The decision to include British and American troops was his own; I have seen no evidence of any pressure on him from either Churchill or Roosevelt. He may have felt that Leclerc was not strong enough to do the job alone.

Gerow meanwhile had already ordered Leclerc to move his division in pursuit of the retreating Germans, and in addition was fearful of the possible bloodshed involved in a parade. This was not only because of the number of Resistance members who were now armed in Paris but also because there were pockets of German troops in the city who had not yet surrendered. Gerow told Leclerc to "disregard" De Gaulle's orders, but instead Leclerc ignored Gerow.[18]

On August 26, after relighting the flame at the Tomb of the Unknown Soldier, De Gaulle led the parade down the Champs Elysées. It was one of the great scenes of the war. Nearly two million people were there, on the streets, at the windows, on the roofs, hanging on flagpoles and lampposts. De Gaulle marched. Occasionally there were spurts of gunfire, but no one, least of all De Gaulle, paid any attention. Finally he stopped, turned, looked at the crowd, drew himself to his full height, and in a hoarse, off-key voice, with his tears soaking the sacred soil of France, began to sing "La Marseillaise."

The same day Eisenhower visited Bradley at his command post near Chartres. The lure of Paris had become too much for him to resist, and he suggested to Bradley that they enter the city the next morning. It would be a Sunday, Eisenhower reminded Bradley, and "everyone will be sleeping late. We can do it without any fuss." He radioed Montgomery to ask him to join the party, but Montgomery replied that he was too busy.[19]

Sunday brought a beautiful, sunny morning, adding to the general air of gaiety and the exultant feeling of liberation. No one, it turned out, had slept late. Bicycles crowded the road. Gay and cheering Parisians quickly recognized Eisenhower and Bradley and surrounded them, holding up their fingers in Churchill's V sign, waving enthusiastically, and occasionally grabbing and kissing the generals. One huge Frenchman slathered Eisenhower on both cheeks as the crowd squealed in delight. Bradley had better luck; he got caught by one of Paris' beautiful girls.[20]

The American generals called on De Gaulle at the Prefecture of Police. He had surrounded himself with the traditional Republican Guards, resplendent in their Napoleonic tunics and black patent leather hats. But despite the show, De Gaulle was worried. He told Eisenhower he had to have food and other supplies immediately. He also needed thousands of uniforms, for he wanted to bring the FFI into the regular army. He would require help in disarming unruly members of the FFI whom he expected, correctly as it turned out, to resist being incorporated into a disciplined establishment. He had to establish his own authority in order to preserve stability in the capital, and he asked Eisenhower for a show of force.

Eisenhower turned to Bradley to ask what could be done. Bradley was already planning to attack eastward out of Paris, and he said he could march his men straight through the city rather than around its outskirts. Eisenhower thereupon decided to have two American divisions march through the city on their way to battle. This not only gave De Gaulle his show of force, but it also reminded the Parisians that the city had been liberated by "the grace of God and the strength of Allied arms." The parade became, in Eisenhower's words, "possibly the only instance in history of troops marching in parade through the capital of a great country to participate in pitched battle on the same day."[21]

By August 28 Paris was militarily secure, and on that day Gerow called on Koenig to formally turn over the capital to him. Koenig flatly informed Gerow, "The French authorities alone have handled the administration of the city of Paris since its liberation. . . . Acting as the military governor of Paris since my arrival, I assumed the responsibilities . . . the 25th of August, 1944."[22] Eisenhower was inclined to be charitable about the situation. "I guess we should not blame the French for growing a bit hysterical under the conditions," he told Marshall, "and I must say that they seem now to be settling down in good order."[23]

Hardly had the front line troops moved out of Paris than the rear-echelon people began to move in. First, there were the French. De Gaulle asked Eisenhower for help in moving some three thousand administrative officers from Algiers to Paris. SHAEF officials bluntly informed him that such a "mass immigration" was impossible. Eisenhower asked De Gaulle to establish a priority for necessary personnel. The issue was soon worked out, and on September 11 Eisenhower ordered that the hundred most important officials be brought in by air. The total movement was not completed until November. British and American businessmen, especially newspaper publishers who wanted to reopen their Paris offices, meanwhile plagued Eisenhower with requests for permission to enter the city.[24]

Far more important, however, was the way in which Headquarters, Communications Zone (Com Z, under General Lee), moved into the city. Eisenhower had reserved the city and its hotels, at least in his own mind, for the use of combat troops on furlough. He had frequently expressed his view that no major headquarters should be located in or near the temptations of a large city. During the early days of September, nevertheless, without Eisenhower's knowledge, Lee moved his entire enormous headquarters into Paris. His advance parties requisitioned most of the hotels and buildings previously occupied by the Germans and also took schools and additional billets. Koenig, when he learned that 8000 officers and 21,000 men were settling in Paris, pointed out that they would require more hotels than the city possessed, and the French began to complain that U. S. Army demands were in excess of those made by the Germans.[25]

The GIs were also unhappy. "Field forces in combat have always begrudged the supply services their rear-echelon comforts," Bradley wrote after the war, "but when the infantry learned that Com Z's comforts had been multiplied by the charms of Paris, the injustice rankled all the deeper and festered there throughout the war." The field commanders were furious also because Lee's move took place just at a time when transportation was short.[26] Led by Patton, they charged that Lee had used up precious gasoline in order to enjoy the hotels of Paris, and that by moving when he did he was out of touch with the supply situation at a time when fuel conservation was critical. Eisenhower then reiterated that he prohibited the establishment of any Allied headquarters within the area of Paris without his specific approval, but it was already too late for that.[27]

And when Eisenhower learned that supply service troops were engaged in black market activities in Paris on a grand scale, his patience was exhausted. He sent a firm order to Lee to stop the entry into Paris of every individual not absolutely needed there and told him to remove from the city every man whose presence was not essential. He made it explicit that essential duties "will not include provision of additional facilities, services and recreation for Line of Communication troops or Headquarters." Eisenhower said the initial move had been made without his knowledge or consent. Presented with a *fait accompli,* however, he had to allow Lee to remain, if only because he did not want to waste more gasoline in moving his headquarters out. But he said the influx of supply personnel was "extremely unwise" and insisted that the situation be corrected as soon as possible. Lee and his headquarters nevertheless stayed in the hotels of Paris.[28]*

* Com Z continued to be a problem throughout the war. In March 1945, for example, Eisenhower made a visit to the front. While there he noticed that one of his army commanders was driving a Chevrolet. The next day he saw a brigadier general from Com Z "in a very fine looking Packard." The contrast, Eisenhower said, "struck me as being about as illogical as anything I have seen in this Theater," and he told Lee that until every field commander had the type of automobile he wanted Com Z officers would have to give up their luxury vehicles. Eisenhower to Lee, March 14, 1945, EP, No. 2340.

With De Gaulle safely established in Paris, the only remaining step in his accession to political power was formal recognition of his provisional government by the British and Americans. Roosevelt still hesitated on this question, even though the French had gained de facto recognition through the device of a formal civil affairs agreement, concluded on August 26. The agreement declared that there would be two zones in France, a forward zone and a zone of the interior. In the former, Eisenhower's powers would be practically complete, while in the zone of the interior the French authorities would have full power of administration, subject to Eisenhower's military requirements. The French guaranteed the Allies' rights to use ports, naval bases, and troop concentration points in the zone of the interior. There were two difficulties with this arrangement. First, it seemed too early to set up a zone of the interior, so that all of liberated France remained officially in the forward zone. Second, although the British ratified the agreement at the foreign minister level, the Americans did so only by an exchange of ratifications between Eisenhower and Koenig. The United States, in other words, held to its policy of dealing with the French at a military rather than a governmental level.[29]

Throughout September De Gaulle pressed Eisenhower on both issues. Eisenhower in turn told Roosevelt, through the American representative to the FCNL, Jefferson Caffery, that it was in the Allies' interest to have a strong French government in power and warned that, if an early recognition was not forthcoming, forces of disorder would take advantage of the situation to endeavor to break down governmental authority in France, thereby creating an intolerable behind-the-lines problem for SHAEF. He also remarked that it would be a long cold winter and that SHAEF could provide only one third the amount of coal for civilian purposes that the Germans had allotted; better that a French government than SHAEF be blamed for this.

Whatever might be said about De Gaulle, Eisenhower added, there was no opposition leader in sight who had the slightest chance of overthrowing him, and if he were by some miracle overthrown chaos would follow. Eisenhower concluded by pointing out that if France fell into the orbit of "any other country" the rest of western Europe would follow. He did not believe that it would be in America's interest to have the Continent dominated by any single power, since that would result in a super-powerful Europe, a shaken British Empire, and the United States as the only active forces at the end of the war. He asked if that were the case, would America "maintain the adequate military, naval, and air forces" which that situation would demand. Many of these difficulties could be avoided, Eisenhower maintained, by recognizing and working with De Gaulle's government.[30]

Even Secretary of State Hull had become convinced of the validity of this position, recommending to Roosevelt on September 17 and again on the twenty-first that the United States recognize De Gaulle's government as the provisional government of France.[31] On August 30 De Gaulle had proclaimed the establishment in Paris of the provisional government of the French Republic, and two weeks later he announced that elections would be held as soon as French sovereignty had been restored, her territories liberated, and—most important—the French prisoners of war and labor deportees returned to their homes.[32]

Still Roosevelt refused to commit himself. The United States made no decision in September. On October 14 Churchill suggested to Roosevelt that "we can now safely recognize General de Gaulle's administration," but the President would not co-operate. He said he preferred to wait until the French had set up a real zone of the interior and the Assembly had been made more representative.[33] De Gaulle, meanwhile, had been making steady progress in discussions with Eiisenhower's representatives about creating a zone of the interior, SHAEF being just as anxious to rid itself of political responsibility as the French were to assume it. On October 20 Eisenhower was able to tell the JCS he had reached a firm agreement on the boundaries of the zone of the interior and would announce it shortly.[34]

The announcement would leave Roosevelt's French policy in a total shambles. The President's own candidates for power in liberated France had long ago dropped by the wayside. Only De Gaulle was left, and Roosevelt could no longer ignore the reality. On October 23 the United States, the Soviet Union, Great Britain, and five other nations recognized the French provisional government headed by General de Gaulle. It had been a long, tortuous struggle for everyone involved, and it left a heritage of bitterness. De Gaulle had triumphed, partly with Churchill's help but primarily on his own, and his great obstacle had always been the United States. France had been liberated, thanks in large part to the Army and Navy of the United States, but few Frenchmen, least of all De Gaulle, were filled with love and appreciation of the Yankees.*

---

* When someone accused De Gaulle of having a bad character, he replied that if it was so they knew the reason for it at the White House. "Indeed few statesmen have been so continually thwarted by their Allies, so hampered in their actions, so insulted by being told they aimed only at personal power. Yet, on the other hand, few leaders dependent on their Allies have dared to criticize them so harshly and so suspiciously as has de Gaulle." Dorothy Shipley White, *Seeds of Discord: De Gaulle, Free France and the Allies* (Syracuse, 1964), p. 357.

But if the Franco-American relationship was cold, at least there was a relationship. The two sides talked to each other and could still cooperate on common objectives. More than any man on either side, Eisenhower could take the credit for this achievement. A man of fierce temper, he had, despite countless provocations, never lost it in De Gaulle's presence. In fact, he had come to have a grudging admiration and even liking for the haughty Frenchman. Smith had handled most of the day-to-day details, and he still occasionally exploded when dealing with the French, but Eisenhower, who always accepted the burden of having the final confrontation with De Gaulle and who had to take most of the insults, never did. In 1942 Eisenhower had thought of the French as "those damn Frogs"; by late 1944, although he still found them troublesome, he respected them.

Because he did, and because they knew that he did, America's French policy in World War II was not a total failure. Eisenhower had no training as a diplomat, and he hated to be in a position in which Churchill was pulling him one way, Roosevelt another, and the military requirements a third. But through a mixture of patience, common sense, and honesty he accomplished much. His dealings with the French marked one of his greatest achievements.

CHAPTER 11

Crossing the Seine and a New Command Structure

Winston Churchill once said that to govern is to choose. The dictum applies as well to a military commander. In mid-August 1944, after the victory at Falaise, Eisenhower had to make two fundamental, related choices. They were among the most fateful tactical decisions of the war. One, whether to attack the retreating Germans on a broad or a narrow front, is well known and has been thoroughly examined. It is, indeed, one of the most debated controversies of the entire war, attracting interest not only because of the nature of the issue involved but also because of the inherent drama in the conflict between the Supreme Commander and the senior British general on the Continent. The other, the decision whether or not to cross the Seine on the run, is less discussed, possibly because at the time no leader of any stature advocated anything else. It was, however, a decision with consequences that reverberated for the remainder of the campaign.

The original OVERLORD plan had assumed that the Germans would mount a defensive line at the Seine and that the AEF would pause when it reached the river to regroup, reinforce, and most of all to build up supply depots. But as early as August 7, while the Mortain counterattack was in progress, Eisenhower was already thinking more boldly. He told Marshall that one of his objectives was "to cross the Seine before the enemy has time to hold it in strength, destroy his forces between the Seine and Somme and secure the Seine ports."[1] Ten days later he reported to Marshall that the beating the Germans were taking at Falaise would enable the Allies to "dash across the Seine."[2]

On August 19 Eisenhower made the irrevocable decision. The AEF would cross the Seine in strength. The next objective would be the German border. Little soul-searching was involved in the decision and there were no critics of it. Pursuit of a defeated enemy was axiomatic.

Eisenhower was aware that crossing the Seine and driving through northwest France would bring problems in its wake. He was primarily concerned about the need for ports close to the front lines. "We are promised greatly accelerated shipments of American divisions directly from the U.S.," he told Montgomery in explaining his decision to cross the river, "and it is mandatory that we capture and prepare ports and communications to receive them. This has an importance second only to the destruction of the remaining enemy forces on our front." Eisenhower wanted Montgomery to move toward Pas de Calais so that he could capture the Channel ports for the AEF.[3]

Eisenhower's emphasis on ports is explained by the fact that the AEF currently had only one major port, Cherbourg. Its total August discharge, when it did not work at full capacity, was 266,644 long tons of material. In addition, minor ports in Normandy in August contributed 40,291 long tons. More significant contributions were made at the beaches at Omaha and Utah, where unloading was much greater than anyone had dared hope for. In August Omaha discharged 348,820 long tons, while Utah handled 187,955 long tons.[4] These figures would obviously decrease, however, with the coming of bad weather in late fall and winter. It was for this reason, not because of any current shortage in discharge facilities, that Eisenhower wanted more all-weather ports.

More important, he wanted ports nearer the front lines. Location was the crux of the problem. A division in active combat required 600 to 700 tons of supplies per day. The AEF had thirty-six divisions in action, so it needed 20,000 tons of supplies per day, or around 600,000 per month. Cherbourg alone could handle two thirds of the need (in November Cherbourg discharged 433,301 long tons), so Eisenhower's problem was not so much the number of ports per se as it was moving supplies forward. His decision to take the Seine in full stride would obviously aggravate the problem. Not until Antwerp was captured and functioning would this difficulty be solved.

Even as the AEF reached the Seine there were supply shortages. Retail lines and pipe lines could not be pushed forward rapidly enough to keep up, so motor transport had to carry the entire burden. As a result, "motor transport facilities were strained to the breaking point attempting to meet even the barest maintenance needs of the armies."[5] Com Z could not establish stocks in advance depots. Added to these troubles for Com Z was Eisenhower's decision to strengthen the attack south of the Ardennes along the axis Reims–Verdun–Metz. Pre-OVERLORD planning had called for only a minor effort in this area, designed to protect the right flank of the forces attacking north of the Ardennes. The change in plan forced Com Z to open another major supply route.[6]

The closest student of the unglamorous but crucial subject of logistics, Roland G. Ruppenthal, sums up the consequences of Eisenhower's decision thus: "From the point of view of logistics these decisions to cross the Seine and continue the pursuit, and to augment the forces employed south of the Ardennes, constituted a radical departure from earlier plans. They carried with them a supply task out of all proportion to planned capabilities. They were much more far-reaching in their effects than the alteration in plans of early August by which the bulk of the Third Army's forces had been directed eastward rather than into Brittany. With the supply structure already severely strained by the speed with which the last 200 miles had been covered, these decisions entailed the risk of a complete breakdown."[7]

The problem of supply transport increased as the lines of communication extended farther and farther eastward. The effectiveness of the Transportation Plan now began to work against the Allies, as they drove forward through precisely those parts of France where their bombers had previously destroyed the railroads. Repair facilities were unequal to the task of keeping pace with the advance. Air supply could help, but delivery never matched promises. And in any case, there was no consistent policy with regard to air transport. Half the time, it seemed, the cargo aircraft were being held in readiness for a paratrooper operation that never materialized while the rest of the time paratrooper operations could not be planned because the cargo planes were engaged in carrying supplies to the front.[8] The burden therefore fell on the trucks, and they were unable to deliver the daily maintenance requirements, let alone to stock advance supply depots.

Before D-Day, Com Z had planned to support twelve divisions in an offensive across the Seine on D plus 120; at D plus 90 (September 4), however, Com Z was already supporting sixteen divisions at a distance of a hundred and fifty miles beyond the Seine. Planners had not contemplated reaching the German border until D plus 330; the armies were actually there on D plus 100. Motor transport was not adequate to meet these unexpectedly early supply needs. Even on the basis of the conservative pre-OVERLORD plans, a motor transport deficiency had been predicted. And in addition, of course, Com Z had been forced to assume the job of bringing supplies into Paris.

To meet the immediate needs, expediency became the rule. Incoming divisions and other combat elements were immobilized because their trucks were needed to haul supplies from the ports to the front. Com Z ignored the armies' needs for replacement equipment and carried forward only immediately usable goods. "Right now we are operating on the basis of having today's supplies only with each division," Eisenhower told Marshall on August 24, "and are accumulating no fat."[9] For a while everyone could rob Peter to pay Paul, and combat units in Third Army gleefully hijacked supplies from First Army to keep moving. The trouble was that First Army units were doing the same thing. Entire truck companies were "diverted." These and other irregular practices, while they worked temporarily and provided vast amusement, "prevented an orderly and business like organization of the Communications Zone. They left deep scars and had a prolonged effect on its efficiency and on its ability to serve the armies."[10]

By mid-September the trucks were badly worn. So were combat vehicles. The AEF had entered the Continent with new equipment and during the battle in Normandy maintenance had been relatively simple. But in August and early September the troops made a grueling run across northern France without adequate maintenance. Forward reserves of spare parts were non-existent. There was no depot system outside of the Normandy base area. Even after the armies reached the German border and had to halt the offensive because of supply shortages, there was no time for Com Z to recover and establish an orderly system of supply lines based on forward depots because the daily needs of the combat forces, even in fairly fixed positions, remained constant and heavy.[11] Eisenhower's decision to drive on to the German border without a pause, in other words, carried with it some hidden costs. His hope was that the Germans would surrender before they became excessive. He was to be disappointed.

Some of the problems involved were clear at the time, others would only appear later. In a way, Eisenhower's decision to bound across the Seine was like his decision in November 1942 to dash into Tunisia with whatever he could scrape up rather than to wait and build a decent supply base and line of communication. In both cases the results were the same—he got his men far forward, but when they reached their uttermost lines and had to stop and wait for supplies, they had not succeeded in crushing the enemy. Now another major battle had to be fought first, and before the Allies were strong enough to fight they had to straighten out their supply situation. But, given the atmosphere in which Eisenhower made his choice, it is difficult to imagine any military man pausing for this reason. With practically no coherent enemy force between the Seine and the German border, Eisenhower would have been thought mad had he stopped at the river.

Almost everyone at SHAEF and in the AEF generally felt that if the Allies could keep the pressure on the Germans unconditional surrender was imminent. The overriding necessity was to prevent the enemy from regrouping or strengthening his defenses. The SHAEF G-2 summary of August 23 declared, "The August battles have done it and the enemy in the West has had it. Two and a half months of bitter fighting have brought the end of the war in Europe within sight, almost within reach." First Army G-2 reflected the same thoughts. The Combined Intelligence Committee was certain that the German strategic situation had deteriorated to the point "that no recovery is now possible." Patton believed that he could cross the German border in ten days, then drive on almost at will. Only Patton's G-2, Colonel Oscar W. Koch, saw things differently. He warned that "the enemy . . . has been able to maintain a sufficiently cohesive front to exercise an overall control of his tactical situation. . . . Barring internal upheaval in the homeland and the remoter possibility of insurrection within the Wehrmacht, it can be expected that the German armies will continue to fight until destroyed or captured." Koch pointed out that the German retreat, although continuing, "has not been a rout or mass collapse," and warned that the enemy had certain advantages. The weather would soon deteriorate, which would take away some of the sting of Allied air power. In addition, German supply lines were shortening while those of the Allies lengthened. Finally, the Allied advance into Germany would have to be through relatively narrow corridors, and poor terrain would join poor weather as a major German ally.[12]

Colonel Koch's realism was rarely seen those balmy August days. Eisenhower had shared it to a certain extent, as when he warned reporters on August 20 that his forces had advanced so rapidly and supply lines were so strained that "further movement in large parts of the front even against very weak opposition is almost impossible."[13] But over the next ten days the troops kept moving, and Eisenhower began to allow himself to think that expedients would suffice until the Germans collapsed. On August 31 he told Marshall one of his worries was a "suspicion that the fanatics of that country [Germany] may attempt to carry on a long and bitter guerrilla warfare. Such a prospect is a dark one and I think we should do everything possible to prevent its occurrence." He thought Alexander ought to be prepared to thrust his forces into Vienna and the surrounding mountains "to defeat any [German] hope . . . for making that country one of guerrilla action." Churchill and Roosevelt were due to meet soon at the Second Quebec Conference, and Eisenhower said he hoped sincerely that much good would come out of the conference, "because as signs of victory appear in the air, I note little instances that seem to indicate that Allies cannot hang together so effectively in prosperity as they can in adversity."[14]

One of the signs of friction among the Allies was a clamoring for the credit of victory. Eisenhower had long planned to set up a forward headquarters on the Continent, make it large enough to handle his communications needs, and take personal command of the land battle when Bradley had his own army group. In mid-August SHAEF Public Relations Division announced that the Twelfth Army Group had been activated and that Bradley was now equal to Montgomery. London newspapers deplored Montgomery's apparent demotion. SHAEF was upset as it was not true that Bradley was equal to Montgomery, for until Eisenhower assumed direct command in the field Montgomery would continue to direct the land battle, giving general directives to Bradley. SHAEF PR officials therefore denied that Bradley was equal to Montgomery, without bothering to explain that he would be shortly. At this point the American press began to grumble, some newspapers demanding an apology from their counterparts in London for saying that it was a "demotion" for Montgomery to be placed on an equal footing with Bradley. The Washington *Times-Herald* began to write about "British dominance" of the AEF, and other American papers complained that since the British held the principal air, sea, and ground commands Eisenhower was a mere figurehead.[15]

No one was more upset than Marshall. On August 17 he told Eisenhower that "The Secretary [Stimson] and I and apparently all Americans are strongly of the opinion that the time has come for you to assume direct exercise of command of the American Contingent." Marshall said the reaction to British criticism in the United States had been serious and would, he feared, be injected into congressional debate. "The astonishing success of the campaign up to the present moment has emphatic expressions of confidence in you and in Bradley," he explained. "The late announcement . . . has cast a damper on the public enthusiasm."[16]

Eisenhower was at Bradley's headquarters when Marshall's message arrived. Both generals were "somewhat taken aback" at the extreme reaction and at the apparent misunderstanding in the War Department of ultimate command arrangements. Eisenhower had no intention of taking command of "the American Contingent," for example. Far more serious was the bickering over credit. "It seems that so far as the press and the public are concerned," Eisenhower complained, "a resounding victory is not sufficient; the question of 'how' is equally important."

Since the question of how had been opened, however, Eisenhower decided to make his and Bradley's case (London papers were saying Montgomery was responsible for all ground operations and was the tactical genius who brought about the victory). "In the first place," Eisenhower explained, "I have always been directly responsible for approving major operational policies and principal features of all plans of every kind." Because of the extent of his responsibilities, Eisenhower always had to be close to a major communications network so that he could send and receive messages from all over the world, and therefore could not go to the Continent until such time as proper arrangements had been made. Meanwhile it was essential to have one man co-ordinate the land battle. Eisenhower had given that job to Montgomery because of his "experience and seniority," but the British general always operated "under plans of campaign approved by me."

Eisenhower had planned to give Bradley his own army group when there were enough American troops on the Continent to justify it. He also planned to take personal command of the land battle at such time as he could establish a headquarters in France. Between the time that the American army group was formed and SHAEF moved to the Continent, Montgomery would continue to co-ordinate activities. He did not actually command Bradley in the true sense of the word, and in any case Eisenhower himself kept a tight grip on developments by making frequent trips to France and establishing a small forward headquarters there. "There has been no major move made of which I have not been cognizant or which has been contrary to the general purposes I have outlined," he declared. He was "exceedingly sorry" if Bradley's reputation had suffered. "As for myself, I am indifferent to what the New York *Times* or any newspaper may say about my conduct of this operation."

In conclusion, Eisenhower asked Marshall to inform General Surles, head of public relations in the War Department, who could presumably inform the public, that "No major effort takes place in this theater by ground, sea, or air except with my approval and that no one in this Allied command presumes to question my supreme authority and responsibility for the whole campaign."[17]

SHAEF officers were meanwhile looking around in liberated France for a suitable site for a headquarters for Eisenhower. Toward the end of August they decided that Jullouville, just south of Granville at the Cotentin Peninsula, would be satisfactory. On September 1 SHAEF became operational on the Continent. SHAEF Main remained in Bushey Park. Four days later another American army, the Ninth, was activated under Lieutenant General William H. Simpson and assigned to Twelfth Army Group. Simpson took command of all forces in the Brittany Peninsula. Eisenhower, meanwhile, assumed command of the two army groups and Montgomery's co-ordination of the land battle terminated. To soften the blow to Montgomery and the British public, on September 1 Churchill promoted Montgomery to the rank of field marshal.

Two weeks later Eisenhower added another army group to his command. The DRAGOON forces contained one French and one American army, organized into Sixth Army Group. Once they made contact with Patton's right wing, they were scheduled to come under SHAEF's control. Devers commanded the group. Eisenhower had not been consulted on Devers' selection but he assured Marshall that the rumor that he was opposed to Devers was untrue. He did not know Devers well, he said, but all reports indicated that he was doing a fine job.[18] The DRAGOON forces made rapid progress after the initial landing, driving north along the Rhône Valley route, and on September 15, the link-up having been achieved, Eisenhower assumed command of Sixth Army Group.

The complexities of paratrooper organization brought about another command change. Parachute and glider troops used in airborne operations were part of the ground force organization, while the aircraft which carried the troops, furnished escorts, and resupplied the airborne units were under air force command. The problem was further complicated because both U.S. and British air and ground forces were involved.[19] After lengthy discussion the solution was to form the First Allied Airborne Army (August 16) and put it under the command of Lieutenant General Lewis H. Brereton. First Allied Airborne Army included the American and British airborne divisions plus the IX Troop Carrier Command. August was a frustrating month for Brereton, for whenever he planned a drop he found that the ground armies had overrun the objective before he could execute the operation. To add to his problems, Troop Carrier Command was involved in supplying the forward troops, so he could not count on having his planes ready when he needed them.[20]

The big bombers presented another problem. When Eisenhower took command of the Strategic Air Forces in April it had been clearly understood that once OVERLORD was a success they would revert to their previous independence. On September 2 Spaatz informed Eisenhower that the CCS, at their coming meeting in Quebec, would make the change, taking the bombers away from Eisenhower. The Supreme Commander immediately wired Marshall, saying he "would regard any such change as a serious mistake. . . ." He thought all the available forces should be kept under one command and pointed out that there had been no clashes of policy or even sharp differences of opinion on the proper use of the air forces since the April dispute. Both Spaatz and Harris were happy with the present arrangement.[21]

Eisenhower also asked Arnold for his help. "The basic conception underlying this campaign was that possession of an overpowering air force made feasible an invasion that would otherwise be completely impossible," he said, and he felt that argument still held. "The air has done everything we asked." It had destroyed the German Air Force, disrupted communications, neutralized beach defenses, and made the breakthrough possible. The Strategic Forces had meanwhile been committed "to the greatest extent possible" to destroying German industrial and oil targets. But the front lines had moved so far forward so rapidly that airfield construction had fallen behind. Only big bombers could now reach the forward areas. To separate them from SHAEF would make co-ordination difficult if not impossible. Spaatz, Eisenhower added, agreed completely.[22]

The CCS, however, decided otherwise. On September 14 they took command of the strategic air forces away from Eisenhower and gave it to Portal and Arnold, with Spaatz and the Deputy Chief of the Air Staff, RAF, Air Marshal Norman Bottomley, as the executive agents. Eisenhower would still have the right to call on the heavy bombers during an emergency in the land battle. The Supreme Commander decided the new arrangement would be satisfactory because of the "goodwill of the individuals concerned" and the assurances that his operations would be supported. He knew he could count on Spaatz, and he had been pleasantly surprised by Harris, who had helped enthusiastically and "become exceedingly proud of his membership in the 'Allied team.'" Harris wrote Eisenhower a warm letter, saying how delighted he had been to be of service, assuring the Supreme Commander of his future support, and concluding, "I wish personally and on behalf of my Command to proffer you my thanks and gratitude for your unvarying helpfulness, encouragement and support which has never failed us throughout the good fortunes and occasional emergencies of the campaign. . . ."

Remembering all the difficulty he had had in bringing Harris over in the first place, Eisenhower kept the letter as one of his most cherished mementos of the war.[23]

Even with the loss of the Strategic Air Forces, SHAEF continued to grow in size. Hardly had the tents and trailers been set up in Granville for the initial 1500 officers and men than the available space proved insufficient. In addition the fighting lines had gone far beyond the Seine and Eisenhower felt Granville was too far behind the front. He therefore ordered another forward move as soon as possible. He also wanted SHAEF Main brought over from London to the Continent, since the need to be at a major communications network was imperative. Still, he insisted that SHAEF Main avoid a large city, particularly Paris, where there were "too many temptations to go night clubbing." Versailles was chosen as the new site, and on September 6 Eisenhower, who had been keeping in touch with his commanders by jeep and plane, directed that SHAEF Main move there as soon as possible. On September 20 the new head-quarters opened. By then Eisenhower had already had built a small advance headquarters outside Reims, with the tents and trailers set up on the grounds of the Athletic Club of Reims, which had the advantage of putting him near a golf course.[24] SHAEF did not move again until February 1945.

The command structure was thus complete and it remained essentially the same to the end of the war. Eisenhower had gathered firmly into his hands control of the Allied land forces from Holland to the Mediterranean and from the German border westward to the Atlantic. He also commanded the U.S. air and ground forces in the United Kingdom. He had one British, one Canadian, one French, one Allied airborne, and 4 U.S. armies, plus the British and U.S. tactical air forces, under his direct command. He had first call on the Strategic Air Forces for support of his ground operations. The total force available to him for the final blow against the Nazi regime was, clearly, enormous. It was now the Supreme Commander's task to see to it that the AEF was used effectively to bring about this final blow.[25]

Part III

THE GERMAN RECOVERY

[September 1944–December 1944]

VERTICAL bargaining in the upper reaches of the American executive [or in the Allied Expeditionary Force] reflects what might be called the principle of the inverse strength of the chain of command. On the organization chart, the lines of authority fan out from the top executive down level by level to the lowest subordinate. Actually, however, the lines at the bottom of the chart usually should be darker than those at the top, which might well be dotted or light gray. As one moves up a hierarchy the lines in the chain of command weaken and even tend to dissolve. Hierarchical control becomes less important; bargaining relationships more important. The reasons include the greater difficulty in replacing top level personnel, the wider span of lateral associations possessed by top executives [generals], and their broader and more diversified fields of responsibility (which make it more difficult for the superior to enforce his will on any single issue). The President [Supreme Commander] may be the most powerful man in the country, but relatively speaking he has less control over his cabinet [or army and army group commanders] than a lowly VA section chief has over his clerks or a corporal over his squad. Consequently, at the higher levels of government, relationships, even among hierarchical superiors and subordinates, tend towards egalitarianism and usually involve substantial bargaining. A hierarchical superior can control his subordinate by determining the goals which the subordinate is to pursue, controlling the resources available to the subordinate, or doing both.

Samuel P. Huntington, *The Common Defense:*
Strategic Programs in National Politics
(London, 1961), pp. 148, 151.

CHAPTER 12

Arnhem and Antwerp

On August 19, 1944 Eisenhower decided to cross the Seine. At the same time he declared his intention to take personal command of the whole land battle soon and outlined a plan of campaign beyond the Seine that would send Montgomery to the northeast, toward Antwerp and eventually the Ruhr, with Bradley heading straight east from Paris toward Metz. Montgomery disagreed with the latter decision, and on August 22 sent his chief of staff, De Guingand, to see Eisenhower. De Guingand carried with him a note from Montgomery to Eisenhower in which Montgomery argued that the quickest way to end the war was to send the bulk of the AEF northward to clear the coast to Antwerp, establish a powerful air force in Belgium, and advance into the Ruhr. The force had to operate as a single unit under single control, which was "a WHOLE TIME job for one man." Montgomery warned that "to change the system of command now, after having won a great victory, would be to prolong the war."[1]

Montgomery's note called into question not only Eisenhower's recent orders but also the original pre-OVERLORD plan. SHAEF planners had set the ultimate objectives of the AEF in early May 1944 in accordance with the CCS directive to Eisenhower which ordered him to undertake operations "aimed at the heart of Germany and the destruction of her armed forces." The planners selected the Ruhr as the "heart of Germany." Berlin was "too far east to be the objective of a campaign in the West," and in addition, the German economy could not survive the loss of the industrial region of the Ruhr. But although the planners wanted to concentrate on the Ruhr, they considered it dangerous to attack by a single route and thus narrow the advance and open it to a concentrated enemy attack. SHAEF planners preferred "a broad front both north and south of the Ardennes," which would give the AEF the advantage of maneuver and thus the ability to shift the main weight of attack to exploit opportunities.[2] On the question of a single command the SHAEF staff had always assumed that Eisenhower would take personal charge as soon as there were two army groups operating in Europe.

For two hours De Guingand discussed the issues with Eisenhower, but the Supreme Commander would not change his mind. When De Guingand reported this result to Montgomery, the Twenty-first Army Group commander invited Eisenhower to come to his tactical headquarters at Condé-sur-Noireau for lunch the next day, August 23, to go over future operations. Eisenhower accepted.

Early on the morning of the twenty-third Montgomery flew to Laval to see Bradley, hoping to persuade the American general to support his plan so that the two army group commanders would present a solid front to the Supreme Commander. Montgomery thought that Bradley agreed with his conception. It called for giving U. S. First Army to Twenty-first Army Group for the drive to the Ruhr and stopping Patton's Third Army where it was. He was shocked to learn that in fact Bradley now proposed to make the major AEF effort south of the Ardennes. Bradley felt that the U. S. First and Third Armies together could march through the middle of France to the Saar and beyond that river to the Rhine in the vicinity of Frankfurt.[3] Taken aback by Bradley's responses, but not ready to give up, Montgomery returned to his own headquarters for his luncheon with Eisenhower. The Supreme Commander would have to choose between the views of his two principal subordinates, each of whom wanted a single thrust in his own area, or else insist on his own plan calling for a broad front advance that would involve them both equally.

Eisenhower drove to Condé for the meeting from his small advance headquarters in the Normandy apple orchard. Smith had come over from London to attend the meeting with him, but when they arrived Montgomery said that he wanted to see Eisenhower alone and that Smith had to stay outside. Montgomery then tried his best to be tactful, but he had already set Eisenhower on edge by locking Smith out and he now made matters worse by proceeding to give him a lecture, as if he were patronizing a student at a staff college. He outlined the situation, said the "immediate need [was] for a firm and sound plan," discussed logistics, outlined his own plan on a map, declared that if Eisenhower's plan were followed the result would be failure, and told Eisenhower that he

"should not descend into the land battle and become a ground C-in-C."
He explained that the Supreme Commander "must sit on a very lofty
perch in order to be able to take a detached view of the whole intricate
problem," and that someone must run the land battle for him.

Eisenhower told Montgomery of the reaction in the United States to the
original announcement about the command shift and of Marshall's insistence that because of American public opinion he, Eisenhower, had to
take control of the land battle. Montgomery said that he felt so strongly
about the need for unified control of the armies that if American public
opinion were the only stumbling block, he would be willing to serve
under Bradley. Eisenhower interrupted° to say that he had no intention of doing anything of the sort, but he also made it clear that he did
not intend to change the proposed command changes and would take
personal control on September 1.

Unable to change Eisenhower's mind on the question of command,
Montgomery shifted to the subject of plans. He wanted Patton stopped
where he was, with all his supplies cut off and given instead to forces
operating under the control of Twenty-first Army Group. He wanted the
First Allied Airborne Army and the U. S. First Army assigned to him for
the drive north and northeastward. He insisted that even to get Antwerp
he would need at least twelve American divisions. He explained that this
was partly because he would have to drop off Canadian divisions as he
moved along the coast to invest and capture ports and partly because
of the strength of the German resistance he faced.

The two generals argued for an hour. Eisenhower conceded a bit,
but he refused to give Montgomery everything he wanted. He agreed to
issue a directive giving Montgomery the objectives of destroying the
enemy forces in his front, seizing the Pas de Calais area and the
airfields in Belgium, and pushing forward to Antwerp. The eventual
mission of Twenty-first Army Group would be to advance eastward on
the Ruhr. Bradley, meanwhile, would be directed to thrust forward on
Twelfth Army Group's left, with his principal offensive mission to support Montgomery. At the same time, Twelfth Army Group would be
directed to clean up the Brittany Peninsula and "begin building up, out
of incoming forces, the necessary strength to advance eastward from
Paris toward Metz." Montgomery could have control of the Airborne
Army, and he would have the "authority to effect the necessary operational coordination between" his right and Bradley's left wing (U. S.
First Army).⁴

"It has been a very exhausting day," Montgomery wrote Brooke after the meeting, but he was satisfied. Although he felt Eisenhower should have dismissed from his mind completely the idea of advancing from Paris toward Metz with Third Army, he was pleased at getting "operational control" over First Army.[5] Brooke too was satisfied. The CIGS regarded Eisenhower as "essentially a staff officer with little knowledge of the realities of the battlefield," and had remarked when he heard that Eisenhower intended to take command in Europe that this was "likely to add another three to six months on to the war."[6] If Montgomery would now have First Army under him, however, Eisenhower's presence would not be so disastrous.

The following day, August 24, Eisenhower outlined his thinking to Marshall. "The decision as to exactly what to do at this moment has taken a lot of anxious thought," he explained, "because of the fact that we do not have sufficient strength and supply possibilities to do *everything* that we should like to do simultaneously." He was giving priority to Montgomery's attack on the left because of the importance of the objectives there—the V-weapon launching sites, the airfields in Belgium, and Antwerp. But he still wanted Bradley to complete the conquest of Brittany and keep enough strength in the Paris area to protect the supply lines originating in Cherbourg. "In addition to all the above," he added, "I want Bradley to build up quickly, from incoming divisions, a force in the area just east of Paris so as to be ready to advance straight eastward to Metz."

Eisenhower said he had hoped to be able to carry out both operations (toward Antwerp and Metz) simultaneously, but that the AEF was not strong enough to do it. "I cannot tell you how anxious I am to get the forces accumulated for starting the thrust eastward from Paris," he added. "I have no slightest doubt that we can quickly get to the former French-German boundary but there is no point in getting there until we are in position to do something about it."[7]

Eisenhower had lunched with Montgomery on August 23. On August 29 he issued the new directive. During that time he spent two days with Bradley, who protested vigorously at giving control of First Army to Montgomery. So did Eisenhower's G-3, Major General Harold R. Bull, and his G-2, the British Major General Kenneth Strong. As a result, when Eisenhower issued the directive, he bowed to this advice and did not give Montgomery operational control of First Army. Instead, Montgomery was "authorized to effect," through Bradley, "any necessary coordination between his own forces" and First Army.[8]

The plan that Montgomery thought Eisenhower had agreed to was further watered down by Bradley's actions. Eisenhower had made it clear in a letter of August 24 and again in his directive of August 29 that he wanted Bradley to build up his forces east of Paris and to *"prepare* to strike rapidly eastwards towards the Saar Valley. . . ."[9] Bradley nevertheless on August 25 told Patton to advance to Reims and "be prepared to continue the advance rapidly in order to seize crossings of the Rhine river from Mannheim to Koblenz."[10] The next day Patton began the race toward the Meuse, which he crossed on August 30. This put him more than a hundred miles east of Paris and not much more than that distance from the Rhine. He was, however, out of gas. Eisenhower had ordered that priority in supplies for Twelfth Army Group go to Hodges' First Army so that Hodges could support Montgomery's advance. On August 30 Patton received only 32,000 gallons of the 400,000 gallons of gasoline he had demanded. Still, he wanted to push on. When Major General Manton S. Eddy reported that his XII Corps had stopped because if it went any farther its tanks would be without fuel, Patton told him "to continue until the tanks stop and then get out and walk." Patton realized that when his tanks ran dry Bradley and Eisenhower would have to give him more gasoline—even at the expense of Hodges' First Army.[11]

On the left, meanwhile, the British were speeding across the old battlegrounds of World War I, covering in hours distances that had taken months and cost tens of thousands of lives to cross in 1915–18. Hodges struck across the Seine on August 27. In less than a week he had taken 25,000 prisoners at Mons. Montgomery, determined to show the Americans that his British and Canadian troops were just as good as they were in the pursuit, drove the Twenty-first Army Group forward in one of the most extraordinary campaigns of the war. Dempsey began his offensive on August 29. He left one corps behind in order to motorize his 30 Corps fully. In two days it captured Amiens and in six days liberated Brussels. On September 4 Dempsey took the city of Antwerp, although the water approaches remained in German hands, which meant that the Allies could not use the port. While the Canadians invested the ports of Boulogne, Calais, and Dunkirk, and prepared to open Antwerp, Twenty-first Army Group made an advance of two hundred miles in less than a week.

This was indeed great news. Montgomery's advance opened seemingly unlimited possibilities. On September 2, Eisenhower went to Versailles to meet with Bradley, Hodges, and Patton to discuss their exploitation. According to the office diary that one of the Supreme Commander's aides kept, "E. says that he is going to give Patton hell because he is stretching his line too far and therefore making supply difficulties."[12] But at the meeting Patton convinced Eisenhower that the opportunities on his front were too good to pass up, and the Supreme Commander agreed to allocate gasoline stocks to Third Army. He also gave Patton permission to attack toward Mannheim, Frankfurt, and Koblenz. Eisenhower changed Hodges' orders, too, shifting the direction of First Army's advance from northeast to straight east. This meant that Bradley had full control of his armies again, that the Americans (less elements of First Army that were to stay with Montgomery) were gathered together, and that they were advancing south of the Ardennes. It meant, in short, that the broad front advance had been resumed.[13]

Eisenhower was aware of the risk involved in pursuing this strategy. As he told Marshall on September 4, ". . . the closer we get to the Siegfried Line [the German West Wall, a prepared defensive position consisting of pillboxes and concrete anti-tank obstacles that ran along the Rhine from Basel to Karlsruhe, then west to Saarbruecken, then north along the Saar through Aachen to the Dutch border] the more we will be stretched administratively and eventually a period of relative inaction will be imposed upon us." The danger was that "while we are temporarily stalled the enemy will be able to pick up bits and pieces of forces everywhere and reorganize them swiftly for defending the Siegfried Line or the Rhine." The way to keep the Germans from building a firm defensive line, Eisenhower felt, was to keep them "stretched everywhere," and the way to do that, in his view, was to advance on a broad front.[14]

In other words, Eisenhower felt that it was possible for the AEF to go beyond the West Wall before the Germans had a chance to man it. His greatest difficulty, he told Marshall, was maintenance. "We have advanced so rapidly that further movement in large parts of the front even against very weak opposition is almost impossible." Still, in a directive of September 4 that gave Bradley the mission of seizing Frankfurt, Eisenhower said, ". . . enemy resistance on the entire front shows signs of collapse." The only way the Germans could stop the advance would be to withdraw troops from other fronts, and in both Russia and Italy the Germans were hard pressed already.[15]

The dash across France had been heady. Eisenhower had told Marshall on August 24 that the AEF could not do *everything* that we should like to do simultaneously," but by September 4 he was in fact trying to do it all. He had fallen victim to the same virus that had infected so many of his subordinates. The virus, in many ways more dangerous than the

German armies, was the "victory disease," a malady which caused the patient to believe anything was possible. The Japanese and Germans had suffered from it at various times in the 1940–42 period. It had hit Montgomery hard, causing him to believe that he could break right through the German defenses and march on into Berlin. SHAEF planners, and Eisenhower, suffered too, although their hallucination was different— they thought that all the armies could advance right up to and beyond the West Wall.

It was inevitable however that Eisenhower and his commanders should feel optimistic. The three weeks from August 15 to September 5 were among the most dramatic of the war, with great successes following one another in rapid succession. Rumania surrendered unconditionally to the Soviets, then declared war on Germany. Finland signed a truce with the Russians. Bulgaria tried to surrender. The Germans pulled out of Greece. The Allies landed in the south of France and drove to Lyons and beyond, while Alexander attacked with early success in Italy. The Russian offensive carried the Red Army to Yugoslavia, destroying twelve German divisions, inflicting 700,000 casualties. Both in the east and the west the Germans seemed to have crumbled. Memories of November 1918 were in everyone's mind.

On his own front, Eisenhower had seen his armies advance from Falaise to Antwerp, Namur, and Verdun, destroying eight German divisions and freeing two European capitals in the process. The AEF had had only sporadic contact with the retreating Germans, who had been unable to mount a coherent defense. Panic infected rear areas. Supply installations had been destroyed, fuel depots demolished, ammunition dumps abandoned, ration and supply installations looted by troops and civilians. Model told Hitler he needed twenty-five fresh infantry and six Panzer divisions to restore the line; Hitler replaced Model with Von Rundstedt.[16]

The optimism that Eisenhower felt because of these events extended back to Washington. On September 13 Marshall sent a message to all his commanders on the subject of redeployment of U. S. Army forces to the Pacific. The Chief began, "While cessation of hostilities in the war against Germany may occur at any time, it is assumed that in fact it will extend over a period commencing any time between September 1 and November 1, 1944."[17] Under these circumstances then, Eisenhower felt that by carefully allocating supplies among his advancing armies he could indeed go forward everywhere into Germany.

Like Eisenhower, Montgomery believed that the Germans in the west were on the verge of total collapse, but he disagreed sharply on how to deliver the final blow. Since the only limiting factor of Allied power was logistics, and since the AEF would be able to deliver only one more blow before it would have to stop and wait for supplies from Antwerp to resume the offensive, he wanted the last effort to be a strong one, strong enough to finish the war. "I consider we have now reached a stage where one really powerful and full-blooded thrust toward Berlin is likely to get there and thus end the German war," he told Eisenhower on September 4. Since there were not enough supplies for two offensives, the one selected "must have all the maintenance resources it needs without any qualifications." Eisenhower could choose to advance against either the Ruhr or the Saar; Montgomery said the Ruhr was "likely to give the best and quickest results." In any event, time was vital and a decision had to be made at once. "If we attempt a compromise solution and split our maintenance resources so that neither thrust is full-blooded we will prolong the war," he warned.

Eisenhower answered the next day, September 5. He said his policy was settled. "The bulk of the German Army that was in the west has now been destroyed," he pointed out, and the AEF had to exploit its success by "promptly breaching the Siegfried Line, crossing the Rhine on a wide front and seizing the Saar and the Ruhr." A broad advance would cut off forces currently retreating from southwest France and give the AEF freedom of action to strike in any direction while forcing the enemy to disperse. It would also allow the Allies to open Antwerp. Eisenhower felt that if the troops went all the way and took the Saar and the Ruhr, they would destroy Germany's capacity to wage war. He told Montgomery he still gave priority to the drive to the Ruhr, and was allocating supplies on this basis.[18]

On August 24 Montgomery had complained to Brooke that Eisenhower had decided against sending the two army groups north into Belgium and then east into the Ruhr, and was going to send the Americans directly east from Paris into Germany via the Saar. "I do not (repeat not) myself agree what he proposes to do and have said so quite plainly," Montgomery had said, but "I consider that directive which is being issued by Ike is the best that I can do myself in matter and I do not (repeat not) propose to continue argument with Ike."[19] Despite his declaration of intentions, Montgomery was by his nature incapable of remaining silent when he was sure a mistake was being made. It was in addition his responsibility to present his views, as he was the senior British officer on the Continent, the executive agent for His Majesty's Government and the man to whom all Britain looked for a proper use of the forces the Empire had raised at such sacrifice.

Some officers and politicians were awe-struck by Eisenhower's grant of power from the CCS and at the title he carried. Montgomery was not. Montgomery felt somewhat the same way about Eisenhower as Haig had about Foch twenty-six years earlier. Certainly in his mind their relative positions had nothing to do with ability. Eisenhower was not the Supreme Commander because he was an abler general than anyone else in the AEF, but rather because in view of the relative contribution of the two nations to the alliance the Americans were entitled to have the top position. Montgomery was sure that on strictly military grounds he was a much better general than Eisenhower. Brooke felt the same way. Montgomery therefore felt it necessary to keep Eisenhower "on the rails," to guide him to the proper course of action.

Montgomery, however, could never get Eisenhower to accept his policy, partly because he had no competence in the fine art of persuasion. He was accustomed to working on a problem alone, then handing down a solution. While Eisenhower talked things over at length with Bradley and other commanders, as well as his own staff, before reaching a decision, Montgomery brooded in voluntary, solitary confinement. He met with Dempsey, De Guingand, and his other subordinates only to tell them what to do. He had made a great study of how to command and how to break down the command problems to their essentials, but he never understood human relationships. He did not get along well with people, nor did he try to, and he could not get his ideas across without appearing either patronizing or offensive, or both.[20]

Another factor in Montgomery's failure to get his own way was that Eisenhower controlled logistics. As the operations around Arnhem and Antwerp would illustrate, Montgomery could take an extremely broad view of Eisenhower's orders and in essence follow his own inclinations. But he could not conjure up supplies out of thin air. He had to fight within a framework that was tightly constricted by the amount of material Eisenhower chose to give him. And this situation applied not only to logistics but to manpower as well. Montgomery's army group was not strong enough by itself to carry out his proposed offensive across the north German plain to Berlin. He had to have help from

U. S. First Army, and it was Eisenhower's prerogative to decide whether First Army fought under Montgomery or Bradley.

Most of all, however, Montgomery failed to win Eisenhower over because there never was the slightest chance that he would be able to persuade Eisenhower to stop the Third Army where it was and put First Army under a British commander. No matter how brilliant or logical Montgomery's plan for an advance to the Ruhr was, (and a good case can be made that it was both), and no matter what Montgomery's personality was, under no circumstances would Eisenhower agree to give all the glory to the British. The American people would not have stood for it, nor would Patton, Bradley, Marshall, or Roosevelt.

Had the troops of the AEF been composed of one nationality only, Eisenhower might have adopted Montgomery's plan. Eisenhower almost never admitted, even to himself, that the alliance created problems on the battle front, but once, in Italy, he confessed in a private memorandum, "I think we have made Allied command work here with reasonable efficiency, even though at times it lacks the drive that could be applied were the force entirely homogeneous with respect to nationality."[21] But as things stood Eisenhower could not make his decisions solely on military grounds. He could not halt Patton in his tracks, relegate Bradley to a minor administrative role, and in effect tell Marshall that the great army he had raised in the United States was not needed in Europe.

Montgomery sensed these political truths, but he was still anxious to try to change Eisenhower's mind. When he received Eisenhower's directive of September 4, which gave Patton permission to continue his offensive toward Metz, Montgomery was unhappy. It was not yet apparent, but there were already signs that his warnings about the price that would have to be paid for a broad-front advance were about to be proven valid. Tanks and other vehicles had gone so long and so far without maintenance that in one armored division less than a third of the authorized number of medium tanks were actually fit for combat. Another armored division had left so many tanks by the wayside, either because of mechanical failure or for lack of fuel, that its vehicles were spread over the country for more than a hundred miles. Worn-out tank engines could not be replaced, nor could tracks that were falling apart. Jeeps and armored cars had been driven without pause for days and were literally falling apart. Ammunition was short. Com Z was getting further and further behind on deliveries every day.

The German defense, meanwhile, fighting close to its homeland, was beginning to stiffen. German troops had formed a continuous, if not solid, defensive line from the North Sea to the Swiss border. In what they would later call the "Miracle of the West," they were preparing to stop the Allied drive. When Von Rundstedt took over on September 5 his problems were enormous. A glance at the casualty lists showed him that his armies had lost 500,000 troops in France. The Allies, meanwhile, had landed 2,100,000 men on the Continent and sustained less than half the German losses. In their retreat the Germans had left most of their equipment in France. Von Rundstedt had forty-eight infantry and fifteen Panzer divisions, but he estimated their true worth at twenty-six infantry and six or seven Panzer divisions at the most, as opposed to Eisenhower's total of forty-nine combat divisions. But although Von Rundstedt's divisions were not up to full strength, German organization was intact. The staffs of all higher headquarters had stayed together, re-established their communications, and were functioning. Discipline remained or was being restored. By early September the German divisions that had been battered, outflanked, encircled, and apparently destroyed had miraculously reappeared and were making an honest effort to protect the German border.[22]

Still, the officers and men of the AEF found it hard to believe that the pursuit was about to end. They were sure that the Germans would be unable to mount a defense of the West Wall or even the Rhine, and continued to believe that the only limiting factor on their own advance was logistics. Montgomery was no exception to this response, although to his mind time was already running out. He felt his supply situation was so stretched that only a dramatic reversal of policy on Eisenhower's part, one that would give him all the resources available to SHAEF, would allow him to exploit the victory in France to bring about the end of the war.

Accordingly, when on September 7 Montgomery learned that although Eisenhower was giving the northern thrust "priority" in supplies he still intended to support Bradley's drive to the east, he protested. The field marshal pointed out that he had been forced to cut his intake to 6000 tons a day, which "is half what I consume and I cannot go for long like this." He needed an air lift of 1000 tons a day and was getting only 750 tons. After reciting the facts and figures of more of his complaints, Montgomery added, ". . . it is very difficult to explain things in a message like this." He wondered if it would be possible for Eisenhower to come and see him.[23]

It was typical of Montgomery that he should make such a request.

It evidently did not occur to him that he, not Eisenhower, was the supplicant, neither then nor at any other time during the war. Not once during the entire campaign did he visit Eisenhower at SHAEF, even though he was frequently invited to attend conferences; he always insisted that Eisenhower come to him. When they did meet he often refused to allow anyone else to be present, even the chiefs of staff.

Montgomery's request of September 7 was particularly untactful, for Eisenhower had just suffered an accident and movement was painful for him.[24] Montgomery knew about the injury, which occurred during a plane landing, but still he decided it would be better for Eisenhower to come to Brussels than for him to fly to Granville. Eisenhower asked Montgomery to come to SHAEF, but Montgomery said he had to meet with Dempsey and could not do it.

Eisenhower therefore flew to Brussels on the afternoon of September 10. He could not get out of the airplane because of his wrenched knee, so Montgomery came aboard. Tedder and Lieutenant General Sir Humfrey Gale, Eisenhower's chief administrative officer and the man primarily responsible for liaison between SHAEF and Twenty-first Army Group, were also on the plane. Montgomery asked that Gale leave, although his own administrative officer was with him. Eisenhower agreed. Immediately upon Gale's departure, Montgomery pulled from his pocket Eisenhower's directive of September 4 and in extreme language damned Eisenhower's policy. As the tirade gathered in fury Eisenhower sat silent. At the first pause for breath, however, he leaned forward, put his hand on Montgomery's knee, and said, "Steady, Monty! You can't speak to me like that. I'm your boss." Montgomery mumbled that he was sorry.[25]

Montgomery then proposed that he make a single thrust through Arnhem to Berlin. Eisenhower, according to Tedder, thought "it was fantastic to talk of marching to Berlin with an army which was still drawing the great bulk of its supplies over beaches north of Bayeux."[26] Montgomery thought it could be done if he got all the supplies, but Eisenhower refused even to consider the possibility. As Eisenhower put it in the office diary later, "Monty's suggestion is simple, give him everything, which is crazy."[27]

Eisenhower finally agreed to a less ambitious plan, Operation MARKET, in which Montgomery would use the First Allied Airborne Army (three divisions) to get across the Lek River at Arnhem, outflanking the Rhine and the West Wall. There would be a companion operation,

GARDEN, an attack northward by British Second Army designed to link up with the paratroopers near Arnhem.[28]

It was a bold plan involving a high degree of risk, and only commanders who were convinced that the enemy was routed could have agreed to it. "Had the pious teetotaling Montgomery wobbled into SHAEF with a hangover," Bradley recalled after the war, "I could not have been more astonished than I was by the daring adventure he proposed. For in contrast to the conservative tactics Montgomery ordinarily chose, the Arnhem attack was to be made over a 60-mile carpet of airborne troops. . . . Monty's plan for Arnhem was one of the most imaginative of the war."[29] It did have obvious disadvantages. By concentrating on MARKET-GARDEN, Montgomery would not be able to give his attention to Antwerp, so there would be a delay in opening the port. By moving northward, Second Army would open a gap between its right flank and First Army's left. Hodges would have to slide his divisions to his left to cover the gap, which meant an even broader front than before, with more stretching by everyone. Finally, the direction of the attack would carry Montgomery away from the Ruhr and give him another river to cross.

Eisenhower nevertheless decided to let Montgomery mount MARKET-GARDEN. Patton and Hodges were already slowing down, and although it was felt that their pause was only temporary and would be halted once supplies caught up with them, Eisenhower did want to make sure of getting a bridgehead over the Rhine before the momentum of the offensive was lost. The use of the Airborne Army in a major strategic operation as a unified force appealed to him, especially since both Arnold and Marshall had been recommending just such a deployment of the paratroopers for months. An added advantage of the plan was that the airborne troops could be supplied without imposing a further strain on the overburdened transport lines. Montgomery liked the operation because he felt it would outflank the West Wall, hit the enemy at a place he could hardly expect an Allied offensive, and occur in an area within easy range of support from the airborne forces.[30]

The conference ended on a happy note of agreement. Tedder wired his superior in London, "I felt the discussion cleared the air, though Montgomery will, of course, be dissatisfied in not getting a blank cheque."[31] Eisenhower returned to Granville, where in order to rest his knee he spent the next few days in bed. The morning he got up, he received a wire from Montgomery, who said that because the Supreme Commander had failed to give him priority in supplies he would not be able to launch MARKET-GARDEN until September 26.[32] Bradley, Bull, Smith, and Strong joined Eisenhower for lunch at his small house, where from his bedroom window they could see Mont St. Michel; together they discussed the logistical situation and MARKET-GARDEN.

Bradley was opposed to the Arnhem operation, in part because he thought it too risky, in part because it would cost him elements of his First Army and meant therefore that Patton had lost the contest of supplies (Patton had just started across the Moselle River).[33] Montgomery later made the serious charge that Bradley opposed the operation for fear it "should open up possibilities on the northern flank and I might then ask for American troops to be placed under my command to exploit them."[34] Tedder rather agreed with this view, although he tended to think that Montgomery, not Bradley, was the villain. "The advance to Berlin was not discussed as a serious issue," he said in his report on the Brussels airport meeting, "nor do I think it was so intended. The real issue is the degree of priority given to the American Corps operating on Montgomery's right flank, and the extent to which Montgomery controls its operations."[35]

Eisenhower's view was less parochial than that of his army group commanders. He was more concerned with getting across the Rhine than he was with who commanded what units, and he decided to give Montgomery all the support he could within the over-all structure of the broad-front policy. He told Smith to go to Montgomery's headquarters and inform the British field marshal that he could count on 1000 additional tons of supply per day, to be delivered by Allied planes and U.S. truck companies. In return, Eisenhower wanted MARKET-GARDEN started much sooner than September 26. To get the trucks to deliver the goods, Eisenhower ordered three newly arrived U.S. infantry divisions stripped of their vehicles, which immobilized the units at their ports of debarkation. Their trucks were used to supply Montgomery. The field marshal responded handsomely; he pushed the target date of MARKET-GARDEN up to September 17 and wired Eisenhower, "Most grateful to you personally and to Beetle for all you are doing for us."[36]

MARKET-GARDEN was designed to exploit a favorable local situation and had a limited objective. If successful, it would bar the land exit of the German troops in western Holland, outflank the West Wall, and position Twenty-first Army Group troops for a subsequent drive into Germany along the north German plain. It was not strong enough to qualify as a single thrust and did not, therefore, provide a test of the feasibility of Montgomery's plan. What it did do was to slow Patton and, much more important, delay the opening of Antwerp. For although Montgomery captured the city in early September, the Germans had reinforced the Scheldt Estuary and Walcheren Island, and as long as they held these places they could deny the use of Antwerp as a port to the Allies. The Canadian First Army was in the process of attacking the Germans, but since the British Second Army was getting all available supplies, no great gains could be expected. On September 11 Eisenhower wrote in the office diary, "Monty seems unimpressed by necessity for taking Antwerp approaches," but in effect Eisenhower's decision for MARKET-GARDEN meant he was agreeing to slow Patton and ignore Antwerp to achieve a tactical—not a strategic—gain. All the AEF was now involved in half measures, or less.

Eisenhower made his decision knowing full well the importance of Antwerp. On September 13 he wrote Bradley and the other commanders to explain his position. He said he was "confirmed in my previously expressed conviction that the early winning of deep water ports and improved maintenance facilities in our rear are prerequisites to a final all-out assault on Germany proper."[37] SHAEF pre-invasion planning had declared, ". . . until after the development of Antwerp, the availability of port capacity will . . . limit the forces which can be maintained," and getting Antwerp operating was a major factor in Eisenhower's decision to strengthen Montgomery's northern thrust in the first place. Tedder later pointed out that both he and Eisenhower had "insisted from the start that without Antwerp we could not get to Berlin," and he also contended that Montgomery's basic mistake was his underestimation of the difficulties of opening the approaches to Antwerp. "He thought, wrongly, that the Canadian Army could do it while 21 Army Group was making for the Ruhr."[38] But since SHAEF approved of MARKET-GARDEN, it had to share in whatever blame was attached to this mistaken view.*

On September 14 Eisenhower explained his thinking to Marshall. He outlined Montgomery's proposal for a dash to Berlin, gave his reasons for rejecting it, and said, "The only profitable plan is to hustle all our

* General Eisenhower read a note to this effect in the manuscripts of the Eisenhower Papers in 1966 and commented in a handwritten note, "I not only approved Market-Garden, I insisted upon it. What we needed was a *bridgehead* over the Rhine. If that could be accomplished I was quite willing to wait on all other operations. What this action proved was that the idea of 'one full blooded thrust' to Berlin was silly."

forces up against the Rhine . . . build up our maintenance facilities and our reserves as rapidly as possible and then put on one sustained and unremitting advance against the heart of the enemy country." He said he had "sacrificed a lot" to give Montgomery the strength he needed to get across the Rhine, for "that is, after all, our main effort for the moment." As soon as MARKET-GARDEN was over, Eisenhower added, "it is absolutely imperative" that Montgomery take the approaches to Antwerp. The Supreme Commander admitted that he had previously been willing to "defer capture of ports in favor of bolder and more rapid movement to the front," but bad weather was coming and now he had to control Antwerp.

The key to Eisenhower's current thought came near the end of his letter to Marshall. After outlining all his reasons for wanting to capture Antwerp, he declared, "My own belief is that . . . we will have to fight one more major battle in the West. This will be to break through the German defenses on the border and to get started on the invasion." Once into Germany, he thought the advance would not be as rapid as it had been in France, "but I doubt that there will be another full-dress battle involved." The major battle would be MARKET-GARDEN. Once it was won, Montgomery could clear Antwerp, which would yield port capacity enough to support all the armies, and the drive through Germany could begin.[39]

Eisenhower seemed to have come close to accepting Montgomery's plan for directing all of SHAEF's efforts to help the major drive in the north, but there remained a sharp difference in their views. In order to win the last big battle, Eisenhower was doing all he could to help Twenty-first Army Group. "It is my concern so to shape our operations that we are concentrating for that purpose," he told Montgomery on September 16, referring to the coming battle at Arnhem, "and by concentrating I include all troops and supplies that can be efficiently employed. . . . So Bradley's left is striking hard to support you; Third Army is pushing north to support Hodges; and Sixth Army Group is being pushed up to give right flank support to the whole."[40] In a message to Lee the next day, however, Eisenhower said that Com Z's first priority was to maintain the United States units in forward areas. "Equal with this priority" was delivery of 500 tons daily to Twenty-first Army Group by truck.[41]

Eisenhower made clear the reason for his emphasis on keeping Bradley's troops well supplied in a note to Montgomery in which he discussed post MARKET-GARDEN operations. The note also emphasized the difference between Eisenhower's policy and Montgomery's plan. Clearly, Eisenhower began, "Berlin is the main prize," the place where the Germans would concentrate their defenses. There was no doubt in the Supreme Commander's mind, therefore, "that we should concentrate all our energies and resources on a rapid thrust to Berlin." But he did not really mean "all," as he indicated by pointing out that it was also important to get the northern German ports and seal off the Danish Peninsula, and in addition to seize the industrial area of Leipzig-Dresden and the political center at Munich. He wanted, that is, to send his forces eastward on two main lines, one in northern Germany and the other through the center toward Leipzig. If the Russians got to Berlin first, Eisenhower wanted to make sure of at least taking the northern ports plus Leipzig-Dresden.[42]

Eisenhower's program was based on the assumption that Antwerp would soon be opened and would provide all the necessary supplies for the two-pronged drive into Germany. But he had not mentioned this in his letter. This was dangerous, for Montgomery's attention was already centered on Berlin, and to get him to look back at Antwerp, an immediate need, was difficult.

The letter kept Montgomery's mind on the east. Accordingly, Montgomery did not discuss Antwerp in his reply. Instead he said that a concentrated operation "in which all the available land armies move forward into Germany is not possible," since it could not be done *"quickly."* He again advocated that Twenty-first Army Group, reinforced by First Army, drive on to Berlin over the northern route and that these forces be given all the supply they needed. The other armies would do their best with what remained. "In brief," Montgomery concluded, "I consider that as *time* is so very important, we have got to decide what is necessary to go to Berlin and finish the war; the remainder must play a secondary role." He evidently included Antwerp among "the remainder."[43]

On September 17, on schedule, MARKET-GARDEN began. Good weather and excellent detailed planning combined to make the drop successful. The Germans were surprised and allied losses on the first day were slight. The U. S. 101st Airborne captured its assigned bridges, while the 82d Airborne, farther north, began its attack against the vital Nijmegen bridges. The British 1st Airborne landed seven miles west of Arnhem and secured the north end of the Arnhem bridge. The paratroopers were on the verge of opening the corridor to the German rear. An elated Eisenhower told Marshall that "the Team is working well. Without exception all concerned have now fully accepted my conception of our problem and are carrying it out intelligently and with energy." This was wishful thinking—neither Bradley nor Montgomery approved of Eisenhower's policy, as each thought the other was getting too much support. "I believe we can establish a firm bridgehead over the Rhine at Arnhem," Eisenhower added, and the next job on the northern flank would be to open Antwerp. "Meantime Hodges is going well. His operations are coordinated with those of Montgomery. Hodges is driving straight on to Cologne and Bonn for the eventual purpose of attacking the Ruhr from the south as Montgomery swings into it from the north."[44]

By September 20 prospects were not so bright, for bad weather had set in and it was impossible to reinforce the paratroopers. Contact with the airborne troops was limited, but it was known that the Germans were counterattacking fiercely, especially against the British around Arnhem. There was still hope, however, for on that day the 82d Airborne took the Nijmegen bridges. That day, also, SHAEF Main moved to Versailles. Weather forced Eisenhower's plane to circle the airfield for half an hour, but he finally landed and moved into his new headquarters in the Trianon Palace, where he held a conference with Bradley, Lee, Smith, and Tedder. He emphasized that Hodges had to be supplied so that he could keep his left wing up close to Montgomery's right, where the British Second Army was driving north in Operation GARDEN.

After the conference Eisenhower dictated a letter to Montgomery. As usual, he stressed the views they had in common. "Generally speaking I find myself so completely in agreement" with Montgomery's latest letter, Eisenhower began, "that I cannot believe there is any great difference in our concepts." The Supreme Commander declared that never at any time had he implied that he was going to advance into Germany with all armies moving abreast, and he intended to continue to give priority to the northern thrust. He refused, however, to consider stopping in place all divisions not involved in the "single knife-like drive toward Berlin." Eisenhower knew that Montgomery felt it was a waste of effort to give Patton any supplies, for a Third Army offensive had no connection with the main blow. The Supreme Commander therefore pointed out that the Germans were concentrating against Patton and that in the past four days the Third Army had captured 9000 prisoners and knocked out 270 tanks.[45] This had happened because, prior to the opening of MARKET-GARDEN, Hitler had feared above all else a breakthrough by Third Army into southern Germany. Against Von Rundstedt's wishes, therefore, he had assigned nearly all the 400 new Panthers and Mark VI tanks available for the western front to a counterstroke against Patton.[46]

Montgomery replied on September 21. His tendency in the letter was as usual to emphasize differences. "I can not agree that our concepts are the same and I am sure you would wish me to be quite frank and open in the matter," he declared. He definitely did want to stop the right flank of Twelfth Army Group, by binding orders, and "put every single thing into the left hook and stop everything else. It is my opinion that if this is not done you will not get the Ruhr."[47] To clear the air, Eisenhower called for a conference at Versailles on September 22. Before the meeting he told Marshall his hopes for a quick breakthrough were still high. British Second Army had linked up with the American airborne divisions and, although the ground troops had not 'yet gotten through to Arnhem, "we should get through . . . quickly." His major problem remained maintenance. The entire line was in bad shape, "reminiscent of the early days in Tunisia—but if we can only get to using Antwerp it will have the effect of a blood transfusion."[48]

The Versailles conference was the most important since D-Day. There were twenty-three generals, admirals, and air marshals there, including all the senior officers at SHAEF. Everyone of importance in the AEF, in fact, attended, except for the man whose name was uppermost in the minds of those present. For Montgomery had decided not to attend, and sent De Guingand to represent him. The field marshal had good reason for not coming. He knew he was not particularly good at persuasion, especially before a hostile audience, and the group at Versailles was almost uniformly hostile toward him. De Guingand, on the other hand, was popular at SHAEF, even with Bradley and Patton.[49]

Eisenhower was disappointed by Montgomery's absence for he felt that the best way to work out differences was in a face-to-face confrontation.* Before he left his office to go to the conference room, he dictated a letter to Montgomery, saying he still wanted to make the main drive in the north, with Twelfth Army Group in support. "It is because I am anxious to organize that final drive quickly upon the capture of the Ruhr," he added, "that I insist upon the importance of Antwerp." He said he would give Montgomery whatever he needed to open Antwerp, "including all the air forces and anything else that you can support."[50]

He then moved over to the conference room, where he began the meeting by asking for "general acceptance of the fact that the possession of an additional major deep-water port on our north flank [is] an indis-

---

* Two days later Eisenhower wrote Montgomery, "I regard it as a great pity that all of us cannot keep in closer touch with each other because I find, without exception, when all of us can get together and look the various features of our problems squarely in the face, the answers usually become obvious." Eisenhower to Montgomery, September 24, 1944, EP, No. 1993.

pensable prerequisite for the final drive into Germany." He also asked for an understanding of the clear distinction between logistical requirements for operations to breach the West Wall and the requirements for a drive to Berlin. He said that the main operations for the present were those of Twenty-first Army Group, which would both free Antwerp and attack the Ruhr from the north. De Guingand then presented Montgomery's views and persuaded Eisenhower to agree that "the envelopment of the Ruhr from the north by 21st Army Group, supported by the First Army, is the main effort of the present phase of operations." By contrast, opening Antwerp was "a matter of urgency." Spelling out the details of Montgomery's position for Bradley, Eisenhower said he should support Montgomery's operations by taking over a part of the Second Army's line and continuing the First Army attack toward Cologne and Bonn. Bradley could take whatever opportunities that presented themselves to attack the Ruhr from the south, but Third Army should take no more aggressive actions until the full requirements of the main effort had been met.

De Guingand was much encouraged by the conference. He wired Montgomery that his plan had been given "100 per cent support." This was not entirely true. Eisenhower's apparent change of heart was verbal only; he said Montgomery should have priority but he refused to implement the decision. Montgomery had wanted control of First Army; all he got was permission, limited largely to emergencies, to communicate directly with Hodges. And Patton, the source of so much of Montgomery's discomfort, believed that since Eisenhower was too closely committed to Montgomery's plan, it was up to him to make the greatest possible use of any loopholes in Eisenhower's orders to spur on his own battle. In order to avoid having to stop his offensive, he declared, "it was evident that the Third Army should get deeply involved at once. . . ."[51]

Patton had expected that the decision at Versailles would favor Montgomery's plan, and thus had already seen to it that his troops would be deeply committed. "In order to attack," he explained later, "we had first to pretend to reconnoiter, then reinforce the reconnaissance, and finally put on an attack—all depending on what gasoline and ammunition we could secure." His ordnance officers "passed themselves off as members of the First Army" and secured gasoline from one of Hodges' dumps.*

* Patton talked to Bradley on September 19, and Bradley warned him that "Monty wanted all the American troops to stop. . . . In order to avoid such an eventuality, it was evident that the Third Army should get deeply involved at once, so I asked Bradley not to call me until after dark on the nineteenth." *War as I Knew It* (Boston, 1947), pp. 125, 133.

Eisenhower probably knew what Patton was doing, and may have expected it. This fact was a source of enormous frustration for Montgomery. The Supreme Commander seemed to be constantly agreeing to Twenty-first Army Group plans, then reneging by allowing Patton and Bradley to go their own way. Thus Montgomery's policies, not to mention the announced wishes of the Supreme Commander, were not fully implemented.

While Patton was forcing Eisenhower to continue the flow of supplies to Third Army, Bradley was making adjustments in Twelfth Army Group designed to ease that burden. After taking over a section of Montgomery's front, Bradley transferred his two southernmost divisions to Devers' Sixth Army Group, which received its supplies through Marseilles. He also brought Lieutenant General William H. Simpson's Ninth Army into the line in the Ardennes, between Hodges and Patton. This allowed Hodges to concentrate more of his effort in support of Montgomery.

On the main front, meanwhile, the primary objective in Eisenhower's over-all plan had failed. The British 1st Airborne had been unable to secure the Arnhem bridge and was subject to increasingly severe counterattacks from two SS Panzer divisions. British ground forces could not get through to Arnhem until September 22, by which time the element of the British airborne division at the Arnhem bridge had disintegrated. Meanwhile the Second Army was unable to get across the river to the remnants of the division, and on the twenty-fifth the paratroopers withdrew from their advanced positions. MARKET-GARDEN had failed.[52]

Montgomery continued his attacks toward Arnhem in a futile effort to salvage the situation, giving priority to Second Army while the Canadians at Antwerp got what was left of men and supplies, which was very little. One difficulty was that Eisenhower continued to think both ends could be achieved and urged Montgomery to get as far east as possible; he never took a firm stand with Montgomery regarding Antwerp. The enemy, desperately afraid of being outflanked at Arnhem, reinforced themselves on Montgomery's front. Eisenhower, recognizing that this development meant that Twenty-first Army Group needed help, told Bradley to take over an additional section of Montgomery's line and declared on October 8 that the Allies "must retain as first mission the gaining of the line of the Rhine north of Bonn as quickly as humanly possible."[53]

The next day, October 9, British naval officers reported to Eisenhower that the Canadians would be unable to move until November 1 because of ammunition shortages. A furious Eisenhower wired Montgomery, "Unless we have Antwerp producing by the middle of November our entire operations will come to a standstill. I must emphasize that, of all our operations on our entire front from Switzerland to the Channel, I consider Antwerp of first importance, and I believe that the operations designed to clear up the entrance require your personal attention." He took all the sting out of the message, however, by adding, "You know best where the emphasis lies within your Army Group. . . ."[54]

Montgomery assumed that Admiral Ramsay had given Eisenhower the report on ammunition shortages, and he fired back a cable the same day. "Request you will ask Ramsay from me by what authority he makes wild statements to you concerning my operations about which he can know nothing rpt nothing." The Canadians, Montgomery said, were already attacking, and there "is *no* rpt *no* shortage of ammunition. . . ." He reminded Eisenhower that at the Versailles conference the Supreme Commander had made the attack against the Ruhr the "main effort." Montgomery promised to open Antwerp as early as possible, and concluded, "The operations are receiving my personal attention."[55] Eisenhower replied that he had not gotten the information from Ramsay and was glad to hear that the report was false. He reminded Montgomery that "the possession of the approaches to Antwerp remains with us an objective of vital importance," and added, "Let me assure you that nothing I may ever say or write with respect to future plans in our advance eastward is meant to indicate any lessening of the need for Antwerp. . . ."[56]

Shortly thereafter Smith called Montgomery on the telephone and demanded to know when SHAEF could expect some action around Antwerp. Heated words followed. Finally Smith, "purple with rage," turned to Morgan and thrust the telephone into his hand. "Here," Smith said, "you tell your countryman what to do." Morgan, sure that Montgomery would be CIGS after the war, thought to himself, "Well, that's the end of my career." He then told Montgomery that unless Antwerp was opened soon his supplies would be cut off.[57]

Despite this exchange, Montgomery continued to emphasize Second Army's attack. According to the most careful student of the campaign, Charles B. MacDonald, it was October 16 before Montgomery gave up on operations against the Ruhr and "blessed it [Antwerp] with unequivocal priority." Nearly a month had been lost.[58]

Taking the approaches to Antwerp was an extraordinarily difficult tactical problem, one that required a major use of resources and the full-time attention of the commander. To clear the Scheldt the Canadians had to drive across a narrow peninsula, the neck of the South Beveland, and then launch an amphibious operation against Walcheren Island. In September the Germans had been unprepared to defend their positions.

But they had used the time available to them in a frantic effort to strengthen the line, and by October they had laid mines, built fortifications, and established a formidable barrier. General Gustav von Zangen, commanding the German Fifteenth Army, was determined to make the Canadians pay a high price for opening Antwerp, and he was successful. The fighting was bitter. Some 50,000 Germans held the South Beveland, while another 7000 defended Walcheren Island. The Canadians sustained nearly 13,000 casualties during the campaign, but by October 30 they had taken the South Beveland. British commandos led the assault against Walcheren Island; by November 8 it had fallen. Then the mines were cleared out of the Scheldt. Finally, on November 28, the first Allied convoy reached Antwerp's docks.[59]

By the time the Allies finally opened Antwerp bad weather had set in and the opportunity of ending the war in 1944 was gone. Capturing Antwerp early had represented SHAEF's best chance to end the war early, a much better chance than a successful MARKET-GARDEN offered. As Brooke declared on October 5, "I feel that Monty's strategy for once is at fault. Instead of carrying out the advance on Arnhem he ought to have made certain of Antwerp in the first place." Brooke continued, "Ike nobly took all the blame on himself as he had approved Monty's suggestion to operate on Arnhem."[60]

The rosy expectations of September were now gone. No one wasted time any longer in arguing whether the AEF should aim toward Berlin or Dresden in its drive through Germany. The enemy had a firm defensive line from which he could not be moved until SHAEF had the supplies it needed and the weather cleared in the spring.

Who had failed? Montgomery blamed Eisenhower. In his view the Supreme Commander's vacillation had caused the frustration. Eisenhower always said he was giving priority to the north, but in practice, Montgomery felt, he let Patton get away with far too much. Eisenhower was a co-ordinator, not a commander, and his policy of "Have a go, Joe," instead of bringing victory all across the line, had brought stalemate everywhere.[61] Bradley and Patton, as well as many of the higher officers at SHAEF, thought on the other hand that Eisenhower had been much too easy with Montgomery. They accused Montgomery of refusing to obey direct orders and Eisenhower of refusing to make his orders strong enough. Eisenhower, in this view, was lax in issuing final orders and stopping further debate on Antwerp and the single thrust.[62] But Eisenhower's decision, and the factors he weighed in making it, were never as simple as the field generals liked to think.

CHAPTER 13

Single Thrust vs. Broad Front in Retrospect

A great opportunity had been lost, and Montgomery's postwar conclusion was bitter: "What cannot be disputed is that when a certain strategy, right or wrong, was decided upon, it wasn't directed. We did not advance to the Rhine on a *broad* front; we advanced to the Rhine on *several* fronts, which were un-coordinated."[1] Eisenhower had not taken a firm grip on the battle and he had vacillated. He felt that pleasing others and keeping them reasonably happy was the only way an alliance could be held together, but this necessity prevented him from stepping forward with clear orders, from forcing Bradley, Montgomery or Patton to do something they did not want to do. Even two and a half decades later it is impossible to read Eisenhower's letters and telegrams to Montgomery without a feeling of frustration because of their vagueness. Any one taken by itself seems clear enough, but following a rejoinder by Montgomery the next message from Eisenhower changed the priority again. The simple question as to whether Eisenhower wanted Arnhem or Antwerp most cannot be answered.

One difficulty in this situation was that Eisenhower and Montgomery tried to communicate with each other via the written word. Eisenhower had no trouble understanding Bradley, nor did Bradley experience any uncertainty in dealing with Eisenhower, in large part because they were together much of the time and could talk everything out. This in turn came about because they enjoyed each other's company. But it is not at all certain that if Eisenhower and Montgomery had spent more time together they could have reconciled their differences, or at least understood each other. The basis for mutual respect and understanding, so prominent in the Eisenhower-Bradley relationship, was simply not present.

Montgomery was a loner. He studied policies in solitude and proposed his own solutions. Often they were brilliant, reaching far beyond the self-imposed limits of the bureaucracy. But they were also often subject to well-founded objections, since by himself Montgomery was incapable of taking everything into account. Patton was like Montgomery in this regard, which was a factor in Eisenhower's favoring Bradley over Patton. —Bradley was a good committeeman. This is not to say, however, that Eisenhower opposed the imaginative approach. He had insisted on having Patton with him in OVERLORD precisely because he recognized that the Third Army commander brought to the operation qualities lacking in himself, in Bradley, and in SHAEF generally. But he also insisted on limiting the scope of Patton's influence and made sure Bradley kept a tight check on Patton. The difficulties in the Eisenhower-Montgomery relationship, in contrast to the Eisenhower-Patton relationship, were that Eisenhower did not have a Bradley to control Montgomery, and he did not count Montgomery as a personal friend, as he did Patton.

Given the difference in personality, national background, and position, it was inevitable that Eisenhower and Montgomery would disagree, and that they would find it difficult to agree on what they were disagreeing about. Eisenhower's vagueness contributed to this result, as did Montgomery's tendency to seize on a phrase Eisenhower had used and regard it as settled policy. When it turned out that Eisenhower had not meant it the way Montgomery thought, Montgomery grew furious. He accused Eisenhower of changing his mind and agreed with Brooke that the Supreme Commander was always shifting, "inclining first one way, then the other," according to the views of the last man with whom he had talked. Brooke thought Eisenhower was a man without backbone who acted as "an arbiter balancing the requirements of competing allies and subordinates rather than a master of the field making a decisive choice. . . ."[2]

But although it was true that in September and October Eisenhower never took a tight grip on the battle or gave clear, forceful orders, he had not allowed Bradley to change his mind. Eisenhower never came close to putting all his chips in Montgomery's hands and allowing the Twenty-first Army Group commander to gamble everything on the one shot. But he did give Montgomery priority in supply, since the objectives in the north were more important than those in front of Bradley, and he did give Montgomery verbal support whenever possible in an effort to keep the British general happy. Eisenhower's habit of seizing upon any agreement he had with Montgomery and emphasizing it while trying to ignore the more frequent and more serious disagreements may have led Montgomery and Brooke astray in their analysis of Eisenhower's thinking.

On the question of a broad front, Eisenhower had always made it clear that he intended to adhere to the original pre-OVERLORD plan and advance on both sides of the Ardennes. As he pointed out in an office memorandum of September 5, the broad-front approach "takes advantage of all existing lines of communication in the advance towards Germany and brings the southern force [Bradley's] on to the Rhine at Coblentz, practically on the flank" of Montgomery's forces. He said he could see no reason to change this conception, for "the defeat of the German armies is complete, and the only thing now needed to realize the whole conception is speed."

But if Eisenhower did not waver, a more important question remains. Was his insistence on a broad front wise? Was he right or was Montgomery? Since the AEF did not deliver the final blow in the fall of 1944, it is clear that Eisenhower's way did not work. The situation that Eisenhower had been afraid of but had been willing to ignore came about—his armies got overextended and became immobilized because of a lack of supplies. There was no point in reaching the German border unless the armies could exploit that position when they got there, Eisenhower had told Marshall, but that is exactly what happened. When the AEF reached the West Wall it was immobilized. But to say that Eisenhower's policy was unsuccessful does not say that Montgomery's would have succeeded. Since the single thrust strategy was not tried, it is impossible to judge.

Eisenhower's reasons for rejecting the single thrust were manifold. On military grounds, he doubted that Montgomery could deliver it, since SHAEF still had only the inadequate Channel ports available and they were insufficient to supply a thrust beyond the Rhine, even if Eisenhower followed Montgomery's advice and immobilized everyone outside of Twenty-first Army Group. Further, despite Montgomery's spectacular advance beyond the Seine, Eisenhower had doubts about his abilities. The failure of GOODWOOD still lingered in his mind. Had Bradley and Patton been on the left, Eisenhower might have given greater consideration to the single-thrust concept, but handling Montgomery was another matter. Eisenhower's thinking was reinforced because of the people around him, the officers he saw every day and to whom he looked for information and advice; none had confidence in Montgomery.

Even Montgomery's chief of staff disliked the single thrust concept. De Guingand saw Eisenhower on a number of occasions in late August and early September, and he made it clear he did not think the plan would work. As a competent staff officer, he had thought about some of the problems that would arise if it were used and he thought they were numerous. When (and if) Twenty-first Army Group reached the Rhine, for example, the bridges would almost surely be blown. To bring forward the necessary bridging material would have been a large and lengthy task and would have meant going short on other needed supplies. Also, there was no guarantee that the Germans would surrender once Montgomery was over the Rhine, and they would have been fighting there close to their supply bases with their homes at stake. De Guingand did not know that the Germans would fight to the bitter end, but he suspected they would, and we now know that it took 160 Russian divisions, seven armies from the west, plus eight additional months of devastating air attack, to force the Germans to capitulate. After the war De Guingand said he found it hard to believe that Montgomery could have brought about the same result with Twenty-first Army Group alone, even if reinforced by First Army, especially since it would have been fighting during a period of increasingly bad weather, which would have meant fewer supporting air sorties and less air lift support. "My conclusion is, therefore," De Guingand wrote, "that Eisenhower was right."[3]

If the disadvantages of Montgomery's proposal were obvious, so were the advantages. Montgomery believed, both at the time and afterward, that he could get to Berlin before winter. In a way, he could turn around De Guingand's argument about fanatical German resistance to fit his own. If De Guingand was right, Eisenhower's policy made no sense at all, since even Eisenhower admitted that, once he had reached the German border (or the West Wall, or some point slightly beyond there), his armies would be forced to pause and wait for Antwerp to become operational. The Germans meanwhile, if they were really determined to fight to the bitter end, would recover and patch up a defensive line. What Eisenhower was unconsciously counting on was a repetition of November 1918, when the Germans signed the armistice while their armies were still well west of the border. Eisenhower had chosen the safe, cautious route. Under his directives no army would take heavy casualties, no general would lose his reputation, credit for the victory could be shared by all, and there was no chance of the Germans reversing the situation by surrounding and destroying an advanced force. Eisenhower's policy would surely lead to victory. The only trouble was that if the Germans decided to fight on it would take time.

Time was what Montgomery wanted to save. The British economy and manpower situation were stretched to the limit. Every day that the war continued meant it would take Great Britain that much longer to recover from victory. The only chance of winning the war in 1944 was to take risks, and to take them right away, in the first week of September.

The AEF would never again have such an opportunity. The only problem was logistical, and the way to solve it was to immobilize Patton and those elements of First Army not supporting the single thrust.

The logistical argument could work both ways. The problems Com Z faced when Eisenhower decided to leap the Seine were multiplied many time over as the AEF raced across northwest France. The armies required a million gallons of gasoline daily. Each division ate thirty-five tons of field rations per day. Every man in the AEF wore out shoes and clothes, expended ammunition and other material, and lost or wore out equipment. Port capacity was minimal, transport ability stretched to the absolute limit. The situation was made worse because transport airplanes were called off supply missions to get ready for air drops, which in turn were canceled because the armies overran the ground objectives before the paratroopers were ready to jump. Paris required 1500 tons of supplies per day. Com Z did what it could, with the famous Red Ball Express truck line, the construction of as much as forty miles a day of pipe lines for carrying fuel, and the reconstruction of railway lines, but all of this was insufficient to meet the constantly pressing supply needs.

Every mile that the advancing troops moved away from the Normandy ports added to the problems. For example, forward airfields had to be constructed if the armies were to have air support from short-range fighters. But to construct them it was necessary to move men and materials forward, at the expense of other supplies. After the war the chief of staff of IX Engineer Command pointed out that if Patton had gone across the Rhine in September he would have done so without any logistical or air support at all. "A good task force of Panzerfaust, manned by Hitler youth, could have finished them off before they reached Kassel," he said in analyzing Third Army's chances.[4]

Montgomery, with the Belgian airfields for support, could have done better. He might have crossed the Rhine while the Germans were still unprepared and the shock of that event might possibly have caused a general German collapse. But if it had not, it is doubtful that Montgomery could have been maintained either, since he would have been forced to operate without Antwerp, and even had Patton stayed in Paris the transportation system was inadequate to the task.

Forrest Pogue points out that a real failure on the part of SHAEF was the lack of optimism on the part of the pre-OVERLORD planners. They had built Com Z with a slow, ponderous advance in mind. No one was prepared for what happened, and largely for that reason Eisenhower could not take advantage of the AEF's great victory.[5]

The situation was not unlike that which had faced the Germans in the summer of 1940. The Allies had achieved something tremendous, but the results turned out to be disappointing, largely because they had not expected to score such an overwhelming success. In 1940 the Germans defeated the French Army, but they did not win the war because they were not prepared to invade Britain, and they were not prepared because they had not dreamed they would win in France so quickly. Similarly, in 1944 the AEF defeated the German Army in France but it did not win the war, for the Allies were not primed for their own victory.

"In hardly any respect were the Allies prepared to take advantage of the great opportunity offered them to destroy the German forces before winter," Pogue writes. "Virtually the ·whole intricate military machine was geared to a slower rate of advance than that required in late August." If Com Z was behind in performance of its tasks, so was the civil affairs division. Not until three weeks after the Allies crossed the German frontier did SHAEF have occupation money for Germany to issue. Eisenhower spent much of his time in the first week in September desperately working on a handbook for occupation policy in Germany.[6] There was a great deal of preparation for the problems that victory would bring, but meanwhile that victory itself was slipping away. "There was not sufficient time," Pogue concludes, "however vast the effort, to make the necessary readjustments in the logistical machinery which would insure speedy victory."[7]

The CCS never entered the dispute, for by its nature it was not a matter for the Chiefs' intervention. At issue were two alternatives of a campaign whose object and shape they had already set and involved forces already within the theater. They were not called upon to provide reinforcements to support either the single thrust or the broad front; indeed, they had already provided more troops than Eisenhower could currently use because of supply. The individual members of the CCS followed the argument closely but did not interfere.[8]

Up to a point it is difficult to see how anyone could have acted any differently. In approving MARKET-GARDEN, Eisenhower was reinforcing success, and it was not only a risk worth taking, it was almost imperative that he take it. Montgomery felt that once Eisenhower had agreed to the Arnhem operation he should have stopped Patton cold, but Montgomery should have known better than to think that Eisenhower could just cut off all Patton's supplies. Aside from the political implications, Patton's men had to eat, had to have replacements, had to have ammunition to defend themselves from the German counterattacks, had to have gasoline for local battlefield maneuver. It would have been impossible to decide at exactly what point Patton was receiving more supplies than he needed for a defensive mission, and in any case the percentage of supplies that Patton did receive over his minimum needs was small.

The situation after MARKET-GARDEN was another matter. Almost all Eisenhower's associates, British and American, agreed that the Supreme Commander was more tolerant of strong dissent from Montgomery than he should have been. In its way it was a repeat performance of GOODWOOD, when the feeling at SHAEF and among the American field commanders was that Montgomery should have been relieved. On both occasions, Eisenhower would not consider it. Eisenhower felt he had to listen to his British allies and he believed he had to grant Montgomery the right to give full expression to his views.[9]

The political factors were crucial, in spite of Eisenhower's oft-repeated assertions that he made all his decisions on military grounds. Whether or not he was technically right in insisting on a broad front, it was simply inconceivable that he should accept Montgomery's proposition and stop U.S. troops where they were while allowing the British to make the kill. The Americans felt they had contributed at least as much to final victory as their British cousins, and they insisted on getting some of the glory. If Eisenhower had agreed to a single thrust by Twenty-first Army Group, General Marshall would have been furious. Montgomery showed no appreciation of the pressures on Eisenhower when he argued as long and as persistently as he did, but then Eisenhower's worries were not his responsibility. Montgomery did what he had to do. So did Eisenhower.

But if Eisenhower was firm in his views he was hardly decisive in the way he communicated them to Montgomery. His patience with the field marshal was enormous and he allowed Montgomery to carry every argument to its bitter end. Even Eisenhower had a limit to his tolerance, however, and Montgomery reached it on October 10, when he wrote Smith to suggest that the trouble with MARKET-GARDEN was lack of coordination between his forces and Bradley's. Montgomery said he should take over command of Twelfth Army Group.*

* Montgomery could irritate even his great friend Brooke. After a meeting on November 9 Brooke noted that Montgomery "still goes on harping over the system of command in France and the fact that the war is being prolonged." The CIGS agreed with the field marshal, but he felt that enough was enough. He realized that "the Americans naturally consider they should have a major say," and thought that Montgomery should not go too far in opposition. Bryant, *Triumph in the West*, p. 244.

It was obvious that a crisis had been reached and the time had come to have it out with Montgomery. The reply to his suggestion, therefore, had to be just right. Eisenhower asked Whiteley to draft it, since Whiteley knew Montgomery so well; Smith then went over the letter. The result was a stronger letter than Eisenhower would have drafted himself, but after some hesitation Eisenhower approved of it and it went out over his signature. It was the beginning of Eisenhower's assertion of his authority as Supreme Commander.

Eisenhower declared that the issue in question was not one of command but of taking Antwerp. It was essential, he felt, that it be done immediately. He said this view was shared by both Brooke and Marshall. "The Antwerp operation does not involve the question of command in any slightest degree," Eisenhower declared to Montgomery. He hoped that the "same close and friendly association" between them that had characterized their work in the past would continue, but if that were to be accomplished there would have to be agreement on logical command arrangements. Eisenhower then presented his own views. "If, having read these," he said, "you feel that you must still class them as 'unsatisfactory,' then indeed we have an issue that must be settled soon in the interests of future efficiency." He said he was well aware of his own powers and limitations, "and if you, as the senior Commander in this Theater of one of the great Allies, feel that my conceptions and directives are such as to endanger the success of operations, it is our duty to refer the matter to higher authority for any action they may choose to take, however drastic."

Eisenhower agreed that for any one major task on a battlefield "a single *battlefield* commander" was needed. This was the reason for creating armies and army groups. But when the battle front stretched from Switzerland to the North Sea, Eisenhower could not agree "that one man can stay so close to the day by day movement of divisions and corps that he can keep a 'battle grip' upon the overall situation and direct it intelligently." The campaign over such an extended front was broken up into more or less clearly outlined areas of operations, of which only one could be the principal and the others by necessity of secondary nature. The Supreme Commander had the task of adjusting the larger boundaries, assigning support by air or by ground and airborne troops, and shifting the emphasis in supply arrangements. A general who was involved in the detailed direction of a principal battle could not make such broad decisions.

Eisenhower then turned to the question of nationalism versus military considerations. Montgomery felt that Eisenhower had been trying to act for political reasons at the expense of military operations. Eisenhower said he had never hesitated to put U.S. forces under British command when necessary, and added: "It would be quite futile to deny that questions of nationalism often enter our problems. It is nations that make war, and when they find themselves associated as Allies, it is quite often necessary to make concessions that recognize the existence of inescapable national differences. . . . It is the job of soldiers, as I see it, to meet their military problems sanely, sensibly, and logically, and, while not shutting our eyes to the fact that we are two different nations, produce solutions that permit effective cooperation, mutual support and effective results. Good will and mutual confidence are, of course, mandatory."[10]

Montgomery took the lecture well. He had already concluded that the First Army could not reach the Rhine and had therefore dispatched part of Second Army to help the Canadian forces fighting to open Antwerp. "I have given you my views and you have given your answer," Montgomery replied to Eisenhower's letter. "I and all of us will weigh in one hundred percent to do what you want and we will pull it through without a doubt." He said he had given Antwerp top priority and would terminate the discussion on command arrangements. "You will hear no more on the subject of command from me," he said, and signed off, "Your very devoted and loyal subordinate."[11] That was that, or so at least it seemed.

In January 1945 other British officials, led by Brooke and Churchill, raised the question of over-all command again, and the nature of the advance through Germany remained a subject of dispute almost until the final surrender. The story of these controversies is long and complex; the point that stood out was that Eisenhower continued to make the decisions and continued to enforce his will. He had the strongest possible support, from his own staff and from Marshall, Roosevelt, and the War Department generally, but he also had to stand up against heavy pressure, including frequent personal visits and messages from Churchill. In the end the greatest support he had, the support that was really decisive, was his own self-confidence. He was sure he took everything into account, gathered all relevant information, and had considered all possible consequences. Then he acted. This is the essence of command.

CHAPTER 14

A Dreary Autumn

Fall was never Eisenhower's best season. In 1942 he had been stuck in the mud of Tunisia, in 1943 bogged down on the Italian Peninsula, and in 1944 the rains came again to turn the fields of northwest Europe into quagmires. His airplanes could not fly, his tanks were unable to maneuver, and his soldiers marched only with difficulty. He was still short on supplies and was beginning to have replacement problems. In mid-November he told Marshall, "I am getting exceedingly tired of weather."[1] But he was at his best in adversity. His optimism and his grin helped convince the troops and their commanders that there were sunny days ahead, and he managed to keep morale high.

During late October and all of November 1944 Eisenhower traveled incessantly. He tried to visit every division in the AEF, talk with as many men as possible, and spend at least some time with their officers. The trips involved a great deal more than simply showing himself to the front-line troops, for Eisenhower picked up much valuable information during his visits and used it later to improve or keep up morale. While on a trip in early November he noticed that ETO policies on recreation, rest, and comfort for the men were not being applied. "This applies to such matters as billets for resting of troops," he told his American subordinates, "to conditions of sanitation and convenience while travelling by motor, train or ship, and, *above all, it applies to equality of treatment as between officers and enlisted men.*" He pointed out that G.I.s had complained to him that officers had whiskey rations while enlisted men did not, that unit commanders disapproved leave for enlisted men but granted it freely to officers, that when units were out of line the men had to stay in their usually uncomfortable billets while the officers had the use of a car, that on the trip over to the Continent the

G.I.s were jammed into the holds while the officers had ample deck space, and the PX supplies were frequently reserved for officers. Eisenhower admitted that some of the complaints were probably unjustified, but that he had personally noted troops making bivouacs along the roads when, "with a bit of care and foresight," shelter could have been found for the night. He had also seen truckloads of men driving in the rain without top covers on the trucks.

The Supreme Commander wanted all these conditions changed. He laid it down as a rule that "care must be taken that privileges given to officers in any unit must be available in proper proportion to enlisted men." If, for example, a unit could provide a jeep or a car for its officers when out of the line, that vehicle should never be used for recreational trips unless the unit could provide a similar privilege to the men. Leave and furlough policies had to be applied with absolute fairness. All captured wine should be issued "on a basis where the enlisted man receives exactly as much as any officers." (Hard liquor was to be reserved for medical use.) General officers should make the trip to France by ship with their divisions, instead of flying on ahead, so that they could see what conditions actually were on board.

Acting on a suggestion from Marshall, Eisenhower said he wanted his general officers to make frequent trips by road, with the stars on their cars covered so that they did not receive preferential treatment in passing on a road. The generals could then "find out for themselves what conditions actually are and take proper steps for correction of defects." Finally, just in case anyone missed the overriding point, Eisenhower concluded, "Officers must invariably place the care and welfare of their men above their own comfort and convenience."[2]

The responses to Eisenhower's orders were neither instantaneous nor uniform, but they were significant. In early December following a trip which took him to every division in First and Ninth Armies, Eisenhower reported with some pride that "the morale and condition of our troops stay remarkably high. It is noticeable that each division, after it has been out of the line three or four days and has absorbed its replacements, is fit and ready to go back again into the line."[3]

Checking on the men's condition and welfare was not the only purpose of Eisenhower's travels. He also wanted to see for himself how his division and corps commanders were holding up. Only by personal inspection could he decide who needed a rest, who should be relieved, and who was adequately performing the tasks at hand. After his early December trip he sent three division and one corps commander home on sixty days' detached service so that they could get some rest and recreation. "In certain instances these officers themselves do not realize that they are momentarily exhausted," Eisenhower explained to General Handy in the War Department, and he asked Handy to make sure that before they started back they were fit to resume their duties.[4]

Eisenhower knew most of his division commanders personally and was able to obtain the information he desired in short chats with them. He told Marshall that he had sent two generals home because they had both lost their only sons in the war, "and this shock and distress, coupled with the abnormal strains always borne by an active Division Commander, are really more than any one man should be called upon to bear." He had learned, he added, that commanding a division was a much more exacting task than heading a corps, army, or army group. It was also easier to be in Bradley's or Patton's position than his own; "they are in that more fortunate middle area where their problems involve tactics and local maintenance, without on the one hand having to burden themselves with politics, priorities, shipping and Maquis, while they are also spared the more direct battle strains of a Division Commander."[5]

Eisenhower did not limit his efforts to improve operating procedure and morale to the front lines. He was also concerned with what was going on Stateside, especially after he discovered that a serious ammunition shortage in the AEF was the result not only of insufficient port capacity but also because of a manufacturing slowdown back home. When General Surles reported to him that public opinion in the United States regarded the war as good as won, Eisenhower did all he could to disabuse the American people of that notion. In a series of letters and cables to manufacturing organizations and labor unions he tried to convince the home front that there was a great deal of hard fighting left and that it was imperative for them to maintain high production.[6] When in December a group of manufacturers and another of labor leaders came to Europe, Eisenhower took time to have a long talk with each. He convinced them that ETO's demands for goods were not excessive and that it was necessary for labor to work overtime and for manufacturers to use their plants to full capacity.[7]

In his private letters, as well as in his public pronouncements, Eisenhower emphasized that the war was far from over. To his brothers and to family friends he pointed out that there was no basis for believing that the end was near. "One thing that puzzles me is where anyone finds any factual ground upon which to base a conviction that this battle is over, or nearly over," he wrote on October 20. "We have chased the Hun out of France, but he is fighting bitterly on his own frontiers and there is a lot of suffering and sacrificing for thousands of Americans and their Allies before the thing is finally over."[8]

He purposely tempered his optimism with realism for the very good reason that it was overwhelmingly obvious that bloody battles remained to be fought. The AEF was still on the general offensive, but its daily gains were measured in yards instead of tens of miles. There were three basic causes for the showdown: the German recovery, weather, and supply shortages. Hitler had scraped up a hundred fortress infantry battalions, formerly used in rear areas, and sent eighty of them to the western front. He had also organized twenty-five new Volks Grenadier divisions, which began to come into the lines at the beginning of October. He ordered every inch of ground held and counterattacks at the slightest opportunity. His generals skillfully moved armored units from one end of the front to the other to patch up holes in the line, and with these and other desperate measures the Germans were able to hold on. They paid a price, as vehicles and men became more worn out with each passing day and new operation, but the only hope the Nazis had left was a falling out between their Eastern and Western enemies, and Hitler would do anything to buy time in case that falling out took place. From SHAEF's point of view this reinforcement was irritating for the moment but promising for the future. General Strong believed that the Germans were getting themselves into the same dangerous situation that had prevailed in Normandy. "The dwindling fire brigade is switched with increasing rapidity and increasing wear and tear from one fire to another."[9] As had been the case in Normandy, this development increased Eisenhower's desire to attack all along the line.

The fanatic German resistance and the foul weather were hard on the men of the AEF. Somehow they managed to advance a little, despite freezing rain, driving snow, record floods, mile after mile of mud, and numbing cold. Trench foot and respiratory diseases took a heavy toll. The situation was not as bad as fighting on the eastern front, but it was bad enough. Needless to say, the weather also prevented the AEF from using its Tactical Air Force effectively.[10]

Since Antwerp was not functioning until the end of November, supplies remained inadequate until early 1945. On his visits to the front Eisenhower heard a constant complaint from division commanders—they had neither enough ammunition nor riflemen. In reporting the ammunition shortage to Marshall, Eisenhower said he hoped production of it in the States could be increased, but pointed out that a part of the problem was that the War Department allowances to divisions in combat did not meet minimum requirements.[11] In order to persuade Marshall to increase the allowance, he sent a team of staff officers to Washington to present all the facts and figures. "I have tried," Eisenhower told the Chief, "all through this war, to avoid presenting any problems in such a way as to appear to be whining or weeping, thus adding needlessly to your own burdens," but he did want to make sure Marshall clearly understood the problem.[12] Marshall increased the allowance, and by January 1945 imports through Antwerp had almost set things right.

The shortage in riflemen was a more difficult problem. It stemmed from many factors, but the chief was the decision early in the war to hold down the total size of the U.S. armed forces in order to have labor on hand at home to increase U.S. wartime production. Coupled with this was an attitude in the War Department that the coming conflict was going to be one of specialists. Thus, too many recruits had been put into branches other than the infantry—armored or airborne or mountain divisions, Services of Supply, the AAF, technical corps, and so on. The result was that when operations involved primarily the kind of hard, footslogging war that characterized the battles of October and November 1944 the American Army was not prepared. When the needs for infantrymen were immediate, all SHAEF could do was comb out men from Com Z and the Zone of the Interior and try to hire French civilians to do much of the work that military supply troops had been performing. This procedure was not very satisfactory, but it worked as a stopgap measure.[13]

Under the circumstances the battles that took place resulted in little beyond heavy casualties on both sides. On October 1 First Army launched an offensive designed to take Cologne, but it ran into German units brought down from the Arnhem front. Not until October 21 did the Germans, who were encouraged by Hitler's pleas for a final effort, pull out of Aachen, and even then, Hodges was still far from Cologne. To the south, Third Army tried unsuccessfully to take the fortress town of Metz. Sixth Army Group, meanwhile, made some gains, but General de Lattre's First French Army, hampered by the task of integrating the FFI into the Regular Army, was unable to drive the Germans out of Colmar.

The temptation at the end of October was to abandon the offensive, create an easily defended line, wait for the supply situation to improve, and prepare to attack when good weather came in the spring. But Eisenhower gave little serious consideration to such an alternative. There was still a feeling in SHAEF that somewhere the German lines *had* to crack. The German "Miracle of the West" was hardly believable, especially in view of the pressure on them from the Russians and the Allied forces in Italy, and it was obvious that the German line was thin. By attacking everywhere, Eisenhower hoped to find a weak spot through which he could roll up the German flanks and then send his armies in a dash across Germany that would not be unlike the dash across France. The emphasis in his plans was, therefore, not so much on a probe here or a skirmish there as it was on a general attack, designed to make sure the Germans suffered heavy casualties which in turn would mean a further stretching of their line. "During this period," he wrote after the war, "we took as a general guide the principle that operations . . . were profitable to us only where the daily calculations showed that enemy losses were double our own." It had become a war of attrition. Like Grant in 1864–65, Eisenhower could afford to adopt it only because his over-all resources were vastly superior to those available to the enemy and, like Grant, Eisenhower justified what many commentators considered a sterile, cold-blooded strategy on the grounds that in the long run "this policy would result in shortening the war and therefore in the saving of thousands of Allied lives."[14]

The comparison of Eisenhower with Grant can be extended. Among other things, Grant's Wilderness campaign of 1864 indicated his accept-ance of the fact that the Confederates were not going to crack, that they would never surrender as long as they could maintain an army in the field, and that there was no short cut to victory. In the fall of 1944 the German Miracle in the West proved that the Wehrmacht was not going to crack either. Montgomery at times likened his single thrust to the German offensive in 1940 in reverse, but what was obvious, and had been since D-Day, was that the Wehrmacht was not the French Army. The Russians had already recognized this fact, and their campaigns were designed to kill Germans, not force a breakthrough to be followed by a dramatic drive to Berlin. In deciding to engage in a campaign of at-trition, Eisenhower may have been cautious and unimaginative, but it appeared to him that the only way to defeat the Wehrmacht was to destroy it. In a general sense, this was the policy Montgomery adopted at Caen, and at that time Eisenhower was the one who grew impatient. But Montgomery's actions before Caen paid handsome dividends; so would Eisenhower's policy of attrition. As Eisenhower told Steve Early, Roosevelt's press secretary, "People of the strength and war-like tendencies of the Germans do not give in; they must be beaten to the ground."[15]

Another factor in Eisenhower's decision to continue the offensive in the fall and winter was internal. MacArthur and Nimitz were on the offensive in the Pacific, and every week they asked for more men, planes, ships, and guns. The resources of the United States were limited. The War Department had taken a deliberate gamble early in the war and decided to raise only ninety combat divisions; almost all of them were already committed, and in the end all but two saw combat. There was, in other words, no strategic reserve available. There were also, as noted earlier, ammunition shortages. Admiral King, one of the most powerful and intelligent of the leaders who believed the Pacific Theater should be the Allies' primary concern, had gone along with the Europe-first policy only because he expected the war against Germany to end quickly so that he could turn the full fury of the United States against Japan. Had Eisenhower gone over to a defensive strategy, a cry would have gone up from the Pacific Theater to send the excess troops (excess because it takes less men to man a defensive line than to mount an offensive) there, especially the divisions scheduled to go to Europe but not yet sent over. If this had happened, Eisenhower, when spring came, would have found himself with insufficient forces for the final blow.

One trouble with the strategy of attrition was that Great Britain could no more afford it than Germany could. Another was that, at least in Montgomery's eyes, it took a lot of time which meant a delay in the end of the war. This bothered the War Department, too, for it meant in turn a delay before redeployment of troops to the Pacific could take place. Marshall, always under great pressure from the Asia-first group in the United States, was especially concerned about this. He did not think the single thrust could bring a quick victory but did feel there might be other more favorable alternatives available. On October 23 he wired Eisenhower to say that the CCS were considering issuing at an early date a directive for an all-out effort to end the war in Europe before 1945. If the CCS did so, it would require extraordinary measures to carry out the directive, including "the use of Strategic Air Forces to get maximum immediate tactical advantage from use of our air power, expedited movement and employment of units and the use of the proximity fuze," a secret weapon that exploded as a shell reached the vicinity of the target. There was no point, however, in speeding up the flow of replacements to ETO, or in changing once again the targets of the heavy bombers, unless Eisenhower thought that these measures would bring a quicker end to the war. "Be frank with me," Marshall concluded his message. "I will accept your decision."

Eisenhower assured Marshall that he was just as anxious to "wind this thing up quickly" as anyone else, but he did have serious problems. For example, he could use more infantry replacements but until Antwerp was operating he could not support additional full divisions in the line. "This . . . is another of those gambles that we are forever faced with in war," he explained, for if he took the riflemen only, he could keep his front-line units fresh and might "produce the desired break," but when Antwerp was open he would want more full divisions in the line. He thought the best compromise was to send the infantry directly to northwest Europe, with the heavy elements of the divisions coming through Marseilles.

The problem of how to make proper use of air power was even more complicated. Ground force leaders felt strategic bombing took too long to have an effect and were pressing the air forces to undertake in Germany something similar to the Transportation Plan that had been so successful in France. Marshall's message indicated that he shared this sentiment. Eisenhower talked to Tedder about it and found that this time Tedder disagreed with the U. S. Army Chief of Staff. "As you are aware," Tedder told Portal on October 25, "the British Army have for months now been allowed to feel that they can, at any time, call on heavy bomber effort, and it will be laid on practically without question. . . . I am doing my best to get things straight, but I am sure you will realize that, the Army having been drugged with bombs, it is going to be a difficult process to cure the drug addicts. . . ." To Eisenhower, Tedder explained that, while the Transportation Plan had certainly been a success in France, the lesson could not literally be applied to Germany. He thought that the bombers should concentrate against the Ruhr and its rail centers, oil targets, canal system, and centers of population. The oil targets would be especially important, for the German stocks were low, but if the enemy had an opportunity to recover he could do so quickly.

Eisenhower told Marshall that using the bombers in direct tactical support work to help achieve another COBRA was out of the question. Such an operation was difficult enough in balmy July weather; with the overcast sky and almost constant rain of the autumn it was impossible. He felt that the only thing to do was keep the bombers on strategic targets inside Germany, with perhaps a slight increase in effort on the rail centers in the Ruhr.

The whole idea of ending the war in 1944 was, in fact, wishful thinking. Marshall's proposal came too late. As Eisenhower explained to him, ". . . our logistical problem has become so acute that all our plans have made Antwerp a *sine qua non* to the waging of our final all-out battle. . . ." Until Antwerp was open, using new weapons and shifting bombing priorities would be of little use.[16]

In November 16 Marshall tried again to restate his position. He said he had been talking to a scientist employed by the AAF who "has pictured to me a concept of aerial war this winter, which seems to me to have very great possibilities. He firmly believes that if the effort were put into it, fighter bombers almost unaided could win the war in Germany this winter." The idea was to move Eighth Fighter Command forward to Belgium or Holland, then fly fighter-bomber missions in all weather. The planes could fly low under the overcast, because of their speed and ability they could take care of themselves in combat, and they could drop their bombs on the first target of consequence that they saw. Fighter-bombers might attack 2500 targets a day "rather than the few which we now hit."[17] Eisenhower replied that the fighter-bombers were already carrying out low-flying attacks on their way back from escorting heavy bomber penetrations, and that he did not think it would be wise to stop the strategic air campaign for an unproven panacea.[18]

The search for some cheap method to end the war, one that would make the gruesome battles on the ground unnecessary, continued. Eisenhower himself, willing to try anything, took part in it. By November 20 he was becoming discouraged, as attrition had brought no noticeable decline in the strength of the German defense. German morale, he confessed, showed no sign of cracking, and the "enemy's continued solid resistance is a main factor postponing final victory. . . ." The average German soldier continued to fight because of the iron discipline of the Wehrmacht and because of successful Nazi propaganda, "which is convincing every German that unconditional surrender means the complete devastation of Germany and her elimination as a nation." Eisenhower thought something should be done to lower the German resistance, and one obvious method was to announce that unconditional surrender would not in fact lead to national destruction.[19]

Marshall agreed, and he reported to Eisenhower that Roosevelt had sent a message to Churchill asking him to join in a statement to the German people, one that stressed that the Allies did not seek to punish the people or to devastate Germany, but only to eliminate the Nazi Party. Churchill refused. He "thought it would be wrong at this juncture to show that we were anxious for them to ease off their desperate opposition. Goebbels would certainly be able to point to the alteration of our tone as an encouragement for further resistance, and the morale of the German fighting troops would be proportionately raised."[20] Churchill thus convinced Eisenhower that a propaganda statement would achieve just the opposite of its desired result. The Supreme Commander then told Marshall he had decided that "a statement at this moment would probably be interpreted as a sign of weakness rather than of an honest statement of intention," and said the Allies should wait for a major victory to make one.[21]

There was to be no short cut to victory—it would have to be won on the ground. On October 18 Eisenhower met in Brussels with Montgomery and Bradley to discuss future operations. Since Montgomery was occupied with the opening of Antwerp, Eisenhower decided to put the main offensive in November under Bradley. The Twelfth Army Group commander, fearful of losing one of his armies to Montgomery, had shifted his relatively untried Ninth Army northward, between Twenty-first Army Group and First Army. Eisenhower told Bradley to have Ninth Army drive east in support of Hodges, whose task was to establish a bridgehead south of Cologne. Patton should attack in a northeasterly direction in support of Hodges, while Sixth Army Group attempted to cross the Rhine. For the first time since early August, therefore, the main effort would be by the U.S. forces, although Montgomery did get Eisenhower to agree that once Antwerp fell the main effort would switch back to his army group and the offensive toward the Ruhr.[22]

The campaign that followed was the least glamorous, and the hardest, of all the actions in Europe. Hodges fought against bitter opposition, especially in the Huertgen Forest, where roads were nothing more than forest trails. Rain and snow added to the difficulties of mines, artillery, and the German infantry. By a supreme effort at the end of October, First Army reached the Roer, but it was still far from crossing the Rhine. Patton, meanwhile, did little better. Eisenhower eloquently described his difficulties to Marshall: "Every day we have some report of weather that has broken records existing anywhere from twenty-five to fifty years. The latest case is that of the floods in Patton's area. His attack [launched on November 8] got off exactly as planned. . . . Then the floods came down the river and not only washed out two fixed bridges, but destroyed his principal floating bridge and made others almost unusable. It was so bad that in one case where we had installed a fixed bridge, the approaches to it were under three feet of water. At one point the Moselle is more than one mile wide, with a current of from seven to ten feet a second." Still, Eisenhower remained an optimist. He hoped that "some little spell will come along in which we can have a bit of relief from mud, rain, and fog" so that the tanks, infantry, and air could do their job.[23] But the better weather did not come, and although Patton was able to take Metz on November 23 and, on his right, reach the Saar, his offensive soon ground to a halt.

By this time Montgomery and Brooke, who felt that Britain desperately needed an early end to the war and relief from the strains of full mobilization, were almost frantic about the way the battle was being fought. Eisenhower "has never commanded anything before in his whole career," Montgomery complained to Brooke on November 17. "Now, for the first time, he has elected to take direct command of very large-scale operations and he does not know how to do it."[24] On November 24 Brooke wrote in his diary that he was upset about "the very unsatisfactory state of affairs in France, with no one running the land battle. Eisenhower, though supposed to be doing so, *is on the golf links at Rheims* —entirely detached and taking practically no part in the running of the war."[25] Three days later the CIGS added, "Ike is incapable of running a land battle and it is all dependent on how well Monty can handle him. . . ."[26] Brooke thought Bradley much more capable than Eisenhower, for as he reminded Montgomery, "You have always told me, and I have agreed with you, that Ike was no commander, that he had no strategic vision, was incapable of making a plan or of running operations when started."[27]

On November 26 Montgomery flew to England to consult with Brooke about what positions to take with Eisenhower. They decided there were three fundamental needs: to "counter the pernicious American strategy of attacking all along the line," to change from three army groups to two, with one north of the Ardennes and the other south, and to get Bradley appointed as commander of the ground forces, with Montgomery taking the northern group (which would include Patton) and Devers the southern (Simpson's Ninth Army would trade place with Patton's Third). "Without some such change," Brooke thought, "we shall just drift on and God knows when the war will end!" He did not explain how two armies, both deeply committed in battle, could suddenly trade places.[28]

Eisenhower then, at Montgomery's request, went to Twenty-first Army Group Headquarters on November 28 to discuss future operations. The atmosphere was unpleasant, for Montgomery, reinforced by Brooke's sentiments, could barely conceal his contempt for Eisenhower. The field marshal did most of the talking. Eisenhower, patient as always, let him speak on without interruption, which unfortunately created the impression that Eisenhower agreed with what Montgomery was advocating, which was not at all the case. Montgomery reported to Brooke that Eisenhower had agreed that his plan had failed and "we had, in fact, suffered a strategic reverse," and had further agreed to abandon "the doctrine of attack all along front and concentrate our resources on selected vital thrust." Montgomery realized that he had not persuaded Eisenhower to appoint a single ground commander but did think he had convinced Eisenhower of the need to divide the theater into two parts, separated by the Ardennes, with Montgomery commanding in the north and Bradley in the south.

After reporting all this to Brooke, with some satisfaction, Montgomery began to have doubts about Eisenhower's acceptance of his arguments. He wondered if Eisenhower had really agreed to all his proposals and on November 30 wrote Eisenhower "to confirm the main points that were agreed on during the conversations. . . ." He opened by saying, "We have . . . failed; and we have suffered a strategic reverse. We require a new plan. And this time *we must not fail.*" Montgomery repeated that he felt the Allies had to "get away from the doctrine of attacking" everywhere and concentrate on the main selected thrust, and that they had to divide the front into two parts, separated by the Ardennes. He then said that he and Bradley made a "good team," and that things had not gone well "since you separated us. I believe to be certain of success you want to bring us together again; and one of us should have the full operational control north of the Ardennes; and if you decide that I should do that work—that is O.K. by me. . . ."[29]

By this time, Eisenhower was furious. On December 1 he wrote Montgomery to tell him that he did not at all concur with what the field marshal had said, nor had he agreed upon those points at their recent meetings. The only thing Montgomery's letter contained, he said, was "your conception and opinions as presented to me the other evening." Eisenhower said he did not know what Montgomery meant by strategic reverse. "We gained a great victory in Normandy," he pointed out, and "Bradley's brilliant break through made possible the great exploitation by all forces, which blasted France and Belgium and almost carried us across the Rhine." Had the AEF not gone forward on a broad front, "we would now have the spectacle of a long narrow line of communication, constantly threatened on the right flank and weakened by detachments of large fighting formations." Just in case Montgomery did not get the point as to where Eisenhower gave credit for the Normandy victory, the Supreme Commander added, ". . . if we had advanced from the beginning [i.e., at Caen] *as we had hoped,* our maintenance services would have been in a position to supply us during the critical September days, when we actually reached the limit of our resources."

Eisenhower said he did agree with Montgomery that it would be easier to have the battle front divided into two general sectors, but he thought the dividing line should be based on the natural lines of advance into Germany, rather than on the basis of rear areas. It should be divided, that is, by the Ruhr, not the Ardennes. Eisenhower said he had "no intention" of stopping Devers' and Patton's operations.

Montgomery had asked for a meeting between himself, Tedder, Bradley, and Eisenhower, and had asked that if the various chiefs of staff attended they "should not speak." Eisenhower pointed out that "Bedell is my Chief of Staff because I trust him and respect his judgment. I will not by any means insult him by telling him that he should remain mute at any conference he and I both attend."

He concluded, "I most definitely appreciate the frankness of your statements, and usual friendly way in which they are stated, but I beg of you not to continue to look upon the past performances of this great fighting force as a failure merely because we have not achieved all that we could have hoped. I am quite sure that you, Bradley, and I can remain masters of the situation and the victory we want will certainly be achieved."[30]

It was by far the toughest letter Montgomery had received from Eisenhower to date, and the field marshal hastened to reply that he had given the Supreme Commander a false impression. He had not wanted to imply that he looked upon all of the past performances of the Allies in Europe as a failure, he declared, but only the November battles, which anyone would admit had not been successful. After receiving Montgomery's note Eisenhower had a long talk with Smith and finally decided to be generous in his answer. "You have my prompt and abject apologies for misreading your letter," he said on December 2. He blamed his misunderstanding on his haste in answering, and was sorry if he had given any offense, since he would never do anything "that upsets our close relationship." He enclosed a report from General Strong, the SHAEF G-2, that pointed out the Germans were most upset by the offensives of the U. S. First and Ninth Armies, and told Montgomery, "You will find it most interesting indeed. . . ." A day earlier Eisenhower had wired Montgomery the information that since November 8 the Third

Army had captured more than 25,000 prisoners while First and Ninth Armies had captured 15,000 each. "I thought you would like to know this," Eisenhower said.[31]

The Supreme Commander remained convinced that his policy was sound. On December 5 he told Marshall, "There can be no question of the value of our present operations." The Germans were using divisions with only six weeks' training which contributed to their high casualty rate and indicated an eventual if not immediate crack in the line. Eisenhower saw his problem as one of continuing the attacks as long as attrition worked in the Allies' favor, "while at the same time preparing for a full-out, heavy offensive when weather conditions become favorable." He was not overly optimistic about the immediate future, for he realized that "unless some trouble develops from within Germany, a possibility of which there is now no real evidence, he should be able to maintain a strong defensive front for some time, assisted by weather, floods and muddy ground."[32]

On December 7 Eisenhower met with Bradley, Tedder, Smith, and Montgomery, at Maastricht. Montgomery felt he was an outsider, that SHAEF and Bradley were ganging up on him, as "they all arrived . . . and went away together." Eisenhower began the meeting by reviewing operations since September. He thought the battle was going as well as could be expected and emphasized that the Germans were taking heavy losses. The enemy could not stand this for long, especially as a Russian winter offensive was expected, and therefore the AEF should continue to attack as long as dividends were being collected. As for crossing the Rhine, he reported that his staff informed him that owing to floods it might not be possible to get over the river in major force until May. He then asked Montgomery for his views.

Montgomery said there were two requirements for the immediate future, and neither of them centered on killing Germans. First, the Allies had to cut off the Ruhr from Germany, and then second, force the Germans into mobile warfare. The only place where mobile warfare could be waged, because of terrain, was north of the Ruhr. It was therefore necessary, Montgomery said, to put everything into a concentrated attack across the Rhine north of the Ruhr.

It was like the September disagreement all over again. Eisenhower agreed that the "main" object was to cut off the Ruhr and impose mobile warfare but said that the area on the line Frankfurt–Kassel, in central Germany, was well suited to armored vehicles. He therefore refused to halt Patton, as Montgomery wanted, and said that if Third Army reached the Rhine he felt there would be great advantage in making a strong supporting thrust on the line Frankfurt–Kassel. By launching two attacks from widely separate points, the Allies would exploit the Germans' greatest weakness, immobility.

Montgomery interrupted to say that he could not agree that a thrust from Frankfurt had any prospect of success. If it were mounted, he warned, it would only mean that neither his drive north of the Ruhr nor Patton's to the south would be strong enough to succeed. He insisted that there was a fundamental difference between the way they looked at future operations.

Eisenhower would not agree that there were "fundamental differences." He argued that the basic concepts were the same, with the main drive taking place north of the Ruhr. Their only difference, which could not be called fundamental, was on the strength of the secondary attack in the south.

Montgomery rejoined that this *was* a fundamental disagreement, then turned to the question of command. He repeated what he had been saying for a week—he should have command of all armies north of the Ardennes. Eisenhower said again that the dividing point should be the Ruhr, especially since the Allies did not intend to operate in the industrial jungle of the Ruhr itself. Montgomery insisted, with great intensity, that this was a second fundamental difference of view, and reiterated his demands for command of all operations north of the Ardennes. Eisenhower refused.

Tedder, Bradley, and Smith said little, but it was clear where their support lay. After the meeting Montgomery blamed the lack of support for his policies on them. "It is therefore fairly clear that any points I made which caused Eisenhower to wobble will have been put right by Bradley and Tedder on the three-hour drive back to Luxembourg," he complained. He told Brooke that Eisenhower "has obviously been 'got at'" by the three officers and added, "I personally regard the whole thing as quite dreadful."

The relationship between Eisenhower and Montgomery seemed to have reached a breaking point, but neither of the two men was willing to carry things to that extreme. Eisenhower did not need to do so in any case, for the power was his, and after listening to Montgomery he was free to do what he wanted. Montgomery did not want a break either, in part because he kept hoping he could persuade Eisenhower to follow what he viewed as a proper course, in part because he realized that Roosevelt and Marshall would never allow the CCS to fire Eisenhower.

In a showdown it would be the field marshal, not the Supreme Commander, who would be relieved.

After the Maastricht meeting Eisenhower and Montgomery had, according to Montgomery, "a very cheery lunch." Montgomery continued, "Before he left I made it clear to Eisenhower that it was for him to command and for me to obey; but I was the Commander of the armed forces of one of the principal allies, and as such he must know what I thought about things. I said that in this case we differed widely and on fundamental issues. He said he quite understood and we parted great friends."[33]

Montgomery had decided that he had done all he could, and it now was up to Brooke. The CIGS invited Eisenhower to London, and on December 12 Eisenhower and Tedder had dinner with Churchill and the BCOS. At Brooke's urging Eisenhower presented his plan. "I disagreed flatly with it," Brooke recorded in his diary later, "accused Ike of violating principles of concentration of force, which had resulted in his present failures." Brooke became highly critical, and extremely loud, and then Churchill interrupted to say that he agreed with Eisenhower. Brooke sadly realized that he had failed "in getting either Winston or Ike to see that their strategy is fundamentally wrong. Amongst other things discovered that Ike now does not hope to cross the Rhine before May!" The last point was untrue; what Eisenhower had said was that his staff felt because of floods a *major* crossing might not be *possible* until May.[34]

In reporting on the same meeting to Marshall, Eisenhower said that Brooke had been "disturbed," but after he, Eisenhower, explained everything Brooke "seemed to understand the situation better than he had before." Eisenhower had misread Brooke's reaction, but more important was his assurance to Marshall that in the face of all the pressure from Brooke and Montgomery he still felt it was "most vitally important when the time comes that . . . we should be on the Rhine at Frankfurt." In other words, Marshall did not need to worry—Eisenhower would see to it that in the final campaign the Americans played a significant role.[35]

By mid-December SHAEF's plans were clear. There would be an all-out offensive north of the Ardennes early in 1945, with subsidiary attacks elsewhere. Eisenhower told Bradley to let Third Army make another attempt against the Saar, beginning on December 19, but warned him that unless the operation made great progress it would have to be stopped after a week so that supplies could be shifted to the main effort in the north. First Army, meanwhile, began on December 13 an attack against the Roer dams, which Hodges had to have before he could fully commit his men. Without their capture the Germans could stop an offensive through controlled flooding. Sixth Army Group attacked both toward the north to support Patton and directly east, against the Germans in Colmar.[36]

The only place the Allies were not on the attack was in the Ardennes itself, which was thinly held by one corps. On his way to Maastricht on December 7 Eisenhower had noticed how spread out the troops in the Ardennes were, and he questioned Bradley about the vulnerability of this sector of Twelfth Army Group's front, where four divisions held seventy-five miles. Bradley said he could not strengthen the Ardennes area without weakening Patton's and Hodges' offensives, and that if the Germans counterattacked in the Ardennes they could be hit on either flank and stopped long before they reached the Meuse. Although he did not expect a counterattack, he had taken the precaution of not placing any supply installations of major importance in the Ardennes. Eisenhower was satisfied by this explanation.[37]

On December 15 Montgomery wrote Eisenhower to say he would "like to hop over to England" for Christmas in order to spend the holiday with his son. Eisenhower said he had no objection and added, "I envy you." Montgomery also asked for .payment on a bet he and Eisenhower had made on October 11, 1943. Eisenhower had wagered five pounds that the war would end before Christmas 1944. He refused to pay, since he still had nine days to go, "and while it seems almost certain that you will have an extra five pounds for Christmas, you will not get it until that day."[38] Both the British and Americans began to anticipate the holidays—they both felt they would deliver a really crushing blow to the enemy with the beginning of the New Year.

CHAPTER 15

The Bulge

On December 16, at dawn, two German Panzer armies of twenty-four divisions struck an American corps of three divisions in the Ardennes. The attack was a complete surprise. Two divisions were trampled, and all along the front the Americans retreated in great confusion. Communications were so badly disrupted that as long as four hours after the attack began Twelfth Army Group still had no report of the German counter-offensive.[1]

Eisenhower, when he learned of the attack, was as surprised as everyone else. No one had expected a German offensive in the Ardennes, nor had any of the intelligence units realized that the Germans had such a sizable reserve available for such an attack. After the event the G-2s from divisions, corps, army, army group, and even SHAEF could point to this or that sentence or paragraph in an early December analysis and say, "You see, if that had been read correctly, you would have realized the attack was coming." This was probably true, but it was beside the point. What the intelligence reports revealed was that the Germans had pulled a number of armored units out of the front lines, that they were building up a reserve (which was consistently underestimated), and that they had the capability to attack somewhere. None of the G-2s had predicted where the attack would come, or when, or in what strength.

Strong, SHAEF's G-2, came closest in anticipating what eventually happened. He told Smith that the German reserve might be transferred to the eastern front, or that it might strike in the Ardennes or east of the Vosges, whenever the Germans had a prediction of six days of bad weather. Smith sent Strong to warn Bradley of this possibility, and Bradley said, "Let them come."[2] Eisenhower had also been worried about the Ardennes, where four divisions held a seventy-five-mile front, and had queried Bradley about this relatively weak position, but the Supreme Commander did not think the risk there sufficiently serious to justify moving additional units into the area.

In retrospect, critics of SHAEF have found it difficult to understand how such a momentous error could have been made but, on the day it happened, it was difficult to see how the attack could have been expected. True, the Germans had used the Ardennes as an invasion route in 1870 and again in 1940, but the terrain was not suited for mobile warfare, especially in the winter months when weather made the poor road net even more impassable than usual. And in the end, of course, the Germans paid heavily for this absence of mobility. Assembling two armies and secretly preparing them for an offensive was an arduous but not impossible task. German thoroughness never revealed itself to better advantage. The deception plans were so elaborate that some of the units earmarked for the attack were left off situation maps, even at the highest headquarters, so that only a very few high-ranking officers knew the details of the plan. The tanks were gathered together on German territory, so Allied intelligence did not have the benefit of local information that had been so helpful in France and Belgium.[3] The various G-2s did notice considerable activity in the area opposite the Ardennes, but the arrival of new units on the German front there seemed to be balanced by the withdrawal of others. The Twelfth Army Group concluded that the enemy was using the Ardennes as a training ground, putting replacements into the line there in order to give them experience. First Army G-2 reported, "During the past month there has been a definite pattern for the seasoning of newly-formed divisions in the comparatively quiet sector opposite VIII Corps prior to their dispatch to more active front." And VIII Corps, which took the full force of the initial attack, reported on December 9: "The enemy's present practice of bringing new divisions to this sector to receive front line experience and then relieving them out for commitment elsewhere indicates his desire to have this sector of the front remain quiet and inactive."[4]

Forrest Pogue, who has written a comprehensive analysis of the intelligence failure, concludes that there were four major reasons for it. First, although Eisenhower and Bradley realized the Germans were capable of striking, they did not know where an attack would come, or even if the Germans were building up a reserve to use in case of an Allied breakthrough. They were reluctant to move their troops from point to point to meet every possible threat, not only because it was impractical but because it would disrupt their own offensive plans. The second reason for the intelligence failure was SHAEF's emphasis on an offensive strategy. The third was the erroneous belief that Von Rundstedt, a cautious soldier, was controlling strategy and would not put his troops into the open where the Allied air force could destroy them. The fourth was the belief that the German fuel shortage would preclude any counterattack.

The most important factor of all was Eisenhower's emphasis on the offensive, coupled with the obvious fact that if the Germans used up their forces in a counterattack they would only be inviting a quicker defeat. Von Rundstedt's best hope for holding the line once spring came was to have all his forces at full strength. To use them up in a German offensive that could achieve nothing more than a slight tactical success made no sense. In any case the mood at SHAEF and among all the senior field commanders mitigated against any expectation of a major German thrust. In the AEF, and in the Allied world generally, the spirit was offense-minded. The U.S., U.K., and U.S.S.R. had held the initiative since the spring of 1943. The last time the Germans had decided where and when to fight had been in their disastrous offensive at Kursk. Not since Kasserine had Eisenhower been forced to think and act defensively. What SHAEF, the army groups, and the armies were concerned with then was not what the Germans might do but what they would do to the Germans. Thus, the total surprise at the counteroffensive.

Eisenhower accepted all the blame for it, and in the largest sense he was right in doing so, for he had failed to read correctly the mind of the enemy commander. He failed to see that Hitler, not Von Rundstedt, was directing the strategy; he failed to see that Hitler would try anything. The Supreme Commander was the man responsible for the weakness of the line in the Ardennes, the one who had insisted on continuing the offensives north and south of the area. As a result of his policies there was no general SHAEF reserve available.

On December 23 Eisenhower dictated an office memorandum. The Allied world had been shocked by Von Rundstedt's attack; after the drive through France and the lingering expectation of another breakthrough to be followed by a quick end to the war, the reporters and commentators could hardly believe what had happened. Obviously the Allies had been badly fooled, and the newspapers were full of criticism. In his memorandum Eisenhower confessed that although he had been aware of the building German reserve, that although he knew tank units had been pulled out of the line, and that although he had been told that "a counterattack through the Ardennes was a *possibility*," he did not think it probable that the enemy would try it. "Nevertheless," he admitted, "this is exactly what he did."[5]

But despite his mistakes Eisenhower was the first important Allied general to grasp the full import of the attack, the first to be able to readjust his thinking, the first to realize that, although the surprise German counteroffensive and the initial Allied losses were painful, in fact Hitler had given the AEF a magnificent opportunity. Eisenhower was at Versailles on the day of the attack, conferring with Bradley on the replacement problem in ETO. Scattered reports began to come in, indicating that some penetrations had been made with tanks. Bradley was inclined to think it was a local attack that could be stopped without difficulty. Eisenhower believed a larger movement was involved, and he urged Bradley to send the 10th Armored Division from the south and the 7th Armored Division from the north toward the flanks of the attack. He also told Bradley to order his army commanders to alert any division they had which was free for employment in the Ardennes area.[6]

Bradley stayed overnight at Versailles; the following morning, December 17, he returned to his own headquarters to take control of the situation. Not much was then known at SHAEF as to the strength of the attack, but each bit of news that came in indicated that it was a big one. Eisenhower's reaction was crucial. If he had panicked, shouting orders on the telephone and pulling units from various sectors to throw them piecemeal into the battle, he would have spread the panic all down the line. But he was calm, optimistic, even delighted at this seemingly ominous development. In the morning he dictated a letter to General Somervell about his munitions problems. In the last paragraph he said that the enemy had "launched a rather ambitious counterattack east of the Luxembourg area where we have been holding very thinly." He said he was bringing some armor in from the north and south to hit the German flanks, and concluded, "If things go well we should not only stop the thrust but should be able to profit from it."[7]

Eisenhower's biggest problem was the lack of a strategic reserve. He had already committed the two armored divisions that had been out of the line on a regular rest and rotation basis, with the 10th holding the southern shoulder of the penetration and the 7th occupying the important road junction of St. Vith. Beyond those two, the only additional reserve forces SHAEF had were the 101st and 82d Airborne Divisions, still refitting from the battles around Arnhem. After sending orders to the commanders of the paratroopers to prepare to move, Eisenhower conferred with Smith, Strong, and Whiteley. Together they studied the map and tried to estimate the enemy's intentions. They did not realize it, but Hitler was thinking on a grand scale—his ultimate objective was to destroy the Allied forces north of the Ardennes and take Antwerp, thus bringing about a decisive change in the over-all situation. SHAEF found it difficult to credit the Germans with such ambitions, and thought instead that Von Rundstedt's sole aim was to get across the Meuse River, which would have the effect of splitting Twelfth and Twenty-first Army Groups. This was, of course, a more realistic estimate of German capabilities and did in fact represent Von Rundstedt's thinking.

Whiteley, looking at the map, declared that Bastogne was the key point. It had an excellent road net, and without it the Germans would hardly be able to drive through the Ardennes toward Namur and the Meuse River. When Smith and Strong agreed, Eisenhower decided to concentrate his reserves at Bastogne. A combat command of the 10th Armored went to the city immediately, while the 101st Airborne was ordered to get there as soon as possible. Eisenhower sent the 82d to the north to join Ridgway's XVIII Corps, where it could participate in a counterattack against the German's right flank. The Supreme Commander also ordered the cessation of all attacks by the AEF "and the gathering up of every possible reserve to strike the penetration in both flanks."[8]

By December 18 Eisenhower had completed his plans and was ready to institute them. He told Bradley, Devers, and Patton to meet him the next day at Verdun, then outlined the action he wanted. Because Bradley still tended to think the offensive might be nothing more than an effort to pull forces away from the Allied offensives, Eisenhower began his message by saying that the enemy "is making a major. thrust . . . and still has reserves uncommitted. . . . It appears that he will be prepared to employ the whole of his armored reserve to achieve success." He said he intended to "take immediate action to check the enemy advance," and then to "launch a counteroffensive without delay with all forces north of the Moselle." He wanted Devers to eliminate the Colmar pocket, but that otherwise Sixth Army Group should abandon its offensive and slide to its left, relieving Patton on much of his front, including Metz, so that Patton could attack the German left flank. (This major boundary change was not made, because Patton had stuffed his supply dumps with bridging equipment to be used in spanning the Rhine and he was afraid that Devers would ransack the hoard. He insisted that the area remain within the jurisdiction of Third Army, and Eisenhower agreed.) Eisenhower told Bradley his first mission was to insure the security of the line Namur–Liége–Aachen, then to launch an attack north of the Moselle with Third

Army. The Supreme Commander wanted Twenty-first Army Group to attack southeastward in the area between the Rhine and the Meuse.[9]

By the time the conference at Verdun got under way the next morning, December 19, there was increasing German strength on the attack in the Ardennes. Von Rundstedt had hoped to be across the Meuse by the end of the second day of the attack (December 17), but his forces were nowhere close to achieving that objective. General Middleton's VIII Corps, although badly battered and overrun, had not been destroyed. Small units continued to fight, often without any direction from above or any idea at all about what was happening around them. Individual acts of heroism abounded. As a result the German timetable was badly off schedule. Adding to Von Rundstedt's problems, the Sixth Panzer Army on his right wing was under the command of Obergruppenfuehrer "Sepp" Dietrich, who had been hand-picked by Hitler because of his bravery and personal loyalty. These virtues, unfortunately for Von Rundstedt, did not solve the complex problems involved in handling a Panzer army on the attack. Dietrich's traffic jammed, forces moved in the wrong direction, and confusion reigned. As a result Sixth Panzer Army made only small gains. Seventh Army, on the southern end of the attack, was doing only slightly better. The really spectacular gains had been made by General der Panzertruppen Hasso von Manteuffel's Fifth Panzer Army, but even it was being delayed on its left by the 101st at Bastogne and on its right by the 7th Armored at St. Vith.

Hitler had wanted to pick up the attack in the north, with Fifteenth Army attacking U. S. Ninth Army. He decided on December 18, however, to reinforce Von Manteuffel's success and destroy the road blocks at Bastogne and St. Vith. He ordered Von Rundstedt to send all available reinforcements through the gaps created by Von Manteuffel. It was thus clear to Eisenhower, when he opened the conference at Verdun, that the Germans were going to make their supreme effort to reach the Meuse around Namur.[10]

The Allied high command met in a cold, damp squad room in a Verdun barracks, with only a lone potbellied stove to ease the chill. Eisenhower opened the meeting by declaring, "The present situation is to be regarded as one of opportunity for us and not of disaster. There will be only cheerful faces at this conference table." Patton quickly picked up the theme. "Hell, let's have the guts to let the ——— —— ——— go all the way to Paris," he said, grinning. "Then we'll really cut 'em off and chew 'em up."[11]

But brave words and grinning faces could not stop German Panzers.

As more news on Von Manteuffel's advance came in, it was obvious that the Allies faced a serious, potentially disastrous situation. If the 101st Airborne at Bastogne and the 7th Armored at St. Vith could not hold out, Von Manteuffel would have full use of the limited roads in the Ardennes. No Allied force of consequence stood between his Fifth Panzer Army and Namur. Acting on Eisenhower's orders, Bradley and Montgomery were rushing what troops they could to the front, but it would take time to get them there and in any case they did not have many divisions available. Most of the AEF was deeply involved in the various offensives along the front.

Eisenhower's first priority was to hold the line Namur–Liége–Aachen. He had studied the map with Whiteley, Strong, and Smith to determine how far back the Allies could afford to go, and each time they reviewed the situation the answer became more obvious—the Meuse had to be held. A major reason for this decision was the existence of huge supply dumps across the river at Liége, dumps that contained everything the Germans needed, most importantly gasoline. From the beginning SHAEF had correctly assumed that Von Rundstedt's key weakness was a shortage of fuel and had rightly guessed that he counted on capturing Allied stocks. Eisenhower was determined that he would not get any gasoline from the Allies.[12]

Holding at the Meuse was the *sine qua non* of Eisenhower's plan, but equally important was the other side of the coin—his own counterattack. He was not going to let the Germans get away with emerging from their holes without punishing them. He therefore told Patton to cancel his offensive in the Saar, change directions, take command of VIII Corps, and organize a major counterblow against the German southern flank with a target date of December 23 or 24. Patton protested, but Eisenhower insisted on that plan.

To enable the men to carry out his twin objectives of holding at the Meuse and attacking from the south, Eisenhower decided to convert to a strict defensive policy everywhere except in the Ardennes. He wanted Patton to retreat from his bridgeheads over the Saar and Devers to prepare to shorten his line. His general purpose, he explained, was "to yield ground in order to insure the security of essential areas and to add strength" to Patton's attack. He also wanted Montgomery to prepare to attack in the north.[13]

What Eisenhower needed most desperately to insure the success of his plans was men, especially rifle-carrying infantrymen. To obtain them, he sent personal representatives to Com Z units to pick out men who could fight and start them on their way to the front. He also made an offer to criminals who were under court-martial sentences. Any man who would pick up a rifle and go into the battle could have a pardon and a clean slate. All those who had fifteen years or more at hard labor ahead of them volunteered.[14] This helped, but there was still an over-all deficiency of 23,000 riflemen in ETO. Eisenhower talked to Lee, who pointed out that one untapped resource was black troops, most of whom were in Com Z and none of whom were infantrymen. Lee thought they would respond handsomely to an invitation from Eisenhower to volunteer for infantry service, especially if they could fight on an integrated basis. Eisenhower agreed and issued a circular offering the blacks an opportunity to serve in infantry units and promising that they would be assigned "without regard to color or race."

When Smith saw the circular he blew up. In a stern note to Eisenhower he pointed out that this ran directly against War Department policy. He said it was inevitable that "every negro organization, pressure group and newspaper will take the attitude that, while the War Department segregates colored troops . . . the Army is perfectly willing to put them in front lines mixed in units with white soldiers, and have them do battle when an emergency arises." Smith added that "two years ago I would have considered the . . . statement the most dangerous thing that I had ever seen in regard to negro relations."

By then the crisis had passed, and Eisenhower—no more ready to promote a social revolution than Smith—gave in. He said he did not want to "run counter to regs in a time like this" and personally rewrote the circular. The upshot was that the blacks who did volunteer—and non-coms had to give up their stripes to do so—were segregated into all-Negro platoons, with white non-coms and officers.[15]

Since the blacks had to be trained before they could fight, they could offer no immediate help in the Ardennes anyway. Neither could the reserves who were available in the United States, but Eisenhower wanted to use the crisis to get as many men sent over as he could, in order to be at full strength for the final offensive into Germany. On December 19, therefore, he informed Handy that he was sending the G-1s from SHAEF, Twelfth Army Group, and Com Z to Washington to "present an accurate and comprehensive picture of our critical replacement situation." He hoped they could bring about "a better mutual understanding of the problem. . . ."[16] But the War Department would not change its position. When the G-1s arrived Handy asked a number of pointed questions and made it clear that there was a great contrast between the drastic steps taken in the United States to recover manpower and the relatively poor performance of ETO in this regard, where Com Z had an exorbitant number of troops.[17]

The British were more sympathetic to Eisenhower's cause. Churchill immediately decided to have a new call-up of civilians, one which reached deeply into Britain's remaining industrial force, to provide Eisenhower with 250,000 more men.[18] Smith, contrasting the War Department and the British Ministry of Defence, told a Chief of Staffs' meeting, "When I was tossing on my bed last night, the thought came to me, 'Should we not go on record to our Masters in Washington that if they want us to win the war over here they must find us another ten Divisions.' Look at Britain, about to produce another 250,000 men. If she can do that we should produce another 2,500,000."[19]

The search for long-term replacements went on simultaneously with the effort to find men to plug the present gaps. On December 19, late in the evening, Eisenhower told Bradley and Lee to remember "the vital importance of insuring that no repeat no Meuse bridges fall into enemy hands intact." He wanted Lee to organize service units to protect them.[20] The order to protect the bridges was a matter of routine, but to Bradley it seemed to indicate that Eisenhower was getting "an acute case of the shakes." The Twelfth Army Group chief of staff, Major General Leven C. Allen, read the message and asked, "What the devil do they think we're doing, starting back for the beaches?"[21]

Evidence indeed seemed to be mounting that Eisenhower had gone into a panic. There was the frantic effort to find replacements, the most shocking aspect of which, given the era's social climate, was Eisenhower's willingness to use black troops alongside whites. In addition, there was his concern about the Meuse bridges. Adding to the impression of panic were the elaborate security precautions taken at SHAEF to protect Eisenhower. But these could quite legitimately be explained. As a part of their over-all plan for the Ardennes offensive, the Germans had organized a special group of English-speaking German soldiers, dressed them in American uniforms, given them American jeeps to drive, and spread them behind the American lines. Their mission was to issue false orders, spread defeatism, and capture bridges and road junctions. Rumor quickly spread, however, that their main intention was to assassinate the Supreme Commander.

Thus everyone at SHAEF became extra conscious of security. Eisenhower was sealed into the Trianon Palace. Guards with machine guns were placed all around the Palace and when Eisenhower went to Verdun or elsewhere for a meeting, he was led and followed by armed guards in jeeps. Butcher noted that "he is a prisoner of our security police and is thoroughly but helplessly irritated by the restriction on his moves."[22] After two days of being so confined, he came out of his office, grumbled, "Hell's fire, I'm going out for a walk. If anyone wants to shoot me, he can go right ahead. I've got to get out!" Slipping out a back door, he walked around the yard in the deep snow.[23]

Throughout France and Belgium, the presence of a great number of M.P.s added to the impression of panic. Understandably nervous at the idea of thousands of German soldiers running around in American uniforms, they stopped every passing car and—ignoring rank and credentials—quizzed the occupants on American slang or customs. Who is Minnie Mouse's husband? was one favorite, while baseball questions in general were popular. Bradley once had to identify the capital of Illinois (the M.P. was dubious, for he thought it was Chicago), the position of the guard in football, and Betty Grable's spouse.[24] Perhaps most serious of all, SHAEF public relations ordered a news blackout, which gave the impression in the United States that the Allies were taking a terrific beating and that Eisenhower did not want to let the American people know about it.[25]

But Eisenhower had not panicked. Although he was under pressure from all sides, especially from De Gaulle, not to give up any ground, he insisted on following his own plans. The Supreme Commander was not going to lose his chance to beat the exposed Germans by holding to a sterile policy of rigid defense. Late in the evening of December 19, for example, in his first message to Montgomery since the attack began (no British troops were yet engaged), he expressed his offensive approach. Eisenhower asked Montgomery's appreciation of the situation on the north flank of the penetration, "particularly with reference to the possibility of giving up, if necessary, some ground on the front of the First Army and to the north thereof in order to shorten our line and collect a strong reserve for the purpose of destroying the enemy in Belgium." Montgomery replied that the 7th Armored Division was holding at St. Vith and he saw "no need at present to give up any of the ground that has been gained in the last few weeks by such hard fighting."[26] On Twenty-first Army Group's particular front, it turned out, Montgomery was right, and Eisenhower went along with him.

While Eisenhower was dispatching his message to Montgomery, Strong was reporting to Whiteley that the Germans would soon drive a wedge between Bradley's two forces, making it impossible for Bradley to com-

municate with First Army. Whiteley thought that under the circumstances the best thing to do would be to give Montgomery command of
all forces north of the Ardennes, with Bradley retaining those to the
south. This meant Bradley would keep Third Army, while Montgomery
got U. S. First and Ninth Armies. Such a plan was exactly what Montgomery had all along been proposing and Eisenhower refusing, but
Whiteley felt the communications problem so serious that this stop had to
be taken. He took the proposal to Smith, who called Bradley on the
telephone to discuss the proposed shift with him. Bradley said he doubted
that it was necessary, and indicated that he feared "coordination between
both Army Groups would have to be directed from SHAEF." (SHAEF
thought it had always been co-ordinating the army groups.) Bradley's
strange comment pointed out one long-range significant result of the
Bulge. Both Twelfth and Twenty-first Army Groups had come to think
of themselves as independent agencies; the Bulge gave Eisenhower the
opportunity to assert himself and take full control. Smith brushed aside
Bradley's objection and said, "It seems the logical thing to do. Monty
can take care of everything north of the Bulge and you'll have everything
south." Bradley was concerned that such a move would discredit the
American command. "Bedell," he said, "it's hard for me to object. Certainly if Monty's were an American command, I would agree with you
entirely."[27]

No decision was made that night. The next morning, December 20,
Eisenhower met with Tedder, Smith, Strong, and Whiteley in the Trianon
Palace. Smith brought up Whiteley's proposal. It was obvious that
giving Montgomery command of two American armies at the height of
the battle would be a blow to American pride. The German penetration,
on the other hand, was getting deeper every minute, and Bradley's communication lines to Hodges, which ran through the Ardennes, had been
cut. Bradley still had auxiliary circuits available, but it was not certain
that they would suffice, and in any case his major preoccupation was
Patton's attack. Eisenhower decided that national pride would have to
suffer and declared that he would make the command shift.

He called Bradley on the telephone and told him what he was going
to do. Bradley accepted it. The Supreme Commander then told Bradley
that he could fall all the way back to the Meuse if that was the line he
could "hold the best and cheapest," but that when Patton attacked it
should be in great strength. After hanging up, Eisenhower placed a call
to Montgomery to inform him of the command switch.

The telephone connection with Montgomery was unfortunately indistinct. After failing to make himself understood, Eisenhower gave up and sent the orders by wireless.[28] Montgomery, however, anxious to step forward and take control, heard what he wanted to hear and attached his own meaning to the garbled conversation. He told Brooke that Eisenhower had called. "He was very excited," Montgomery said, "and it was difficult to understand what he was talking about; he roared into the telephone, speaking very fast." The only thing that Montgomery understood was that Eisenhower was giving him command of everything north of the Ardennes. "This was all I wanted to know. He then went on talking wildly about other things. . . ."[29]

That both Montgomery and Bradley felt Eisenhower had a bad case of nerves strongly indicates that the Supreme Commander was probably indeed unsure of himself. But aside from the contrary evidence—no one at SHAEF thought so—Montgomery's and Bradley's reactions could be viewed more accurately as a reflection of their own nervousness. Bradley was upset, for obvious reasons. He had lost practically two divisions, one of his corps had been badly surprised, and the Germans had made a deep penetration into his line. It was difficult to keep up a brave or calm exterior in the face of such calamities. Eisenhower seemed to be blaming him for these developments when he took two armies away from Twelfth Army Group and gave them to Montgomery, and a number of staff officers at Bradley's headquarters were furious. Under the circumstances, Bradley was not entirely objective in his estimate of Eisenhower. And Montgomery, though of course worried about a serious situation, could not totally repress a feeling akin to glee— everything he had predicted had come true, and now Eisenhower had to turn to him to set things right. He was inclined to exaggerate any slightly excited tone in Eisenhower's voice, or even a rise in voice level on a poor telephone connection, and he thus interpreted it as panic. There was of course tension in the air; coupled with the previous relations between Montgomery and Eisenhower, sharp or loud words spoken in heat during moments of stress led to misunderstanding, not so much of what was said but of the emotion involved.

Within two hours of his conversation with Eisenhower, Montgomery had visited with Hodges and Simpson. A British officer who accompanied him said he strode into Hodges' headquarters "like Christ come to cleanse the temple." Montgomery reported to Brooke that neither Simpson nor Hodges had seen Bradley or any of his staff since the battle had begun and there were no reserves anywhere. Morale was low, and Simpson and Hodges "seemed delighted to have someone to give them firm orders."[30]

While Montgomery scurried about acting as though to retrieve the situation and rescue the Americans from their mistakes, Eisenhower continued to shape the battle. He informed the CCS of his command changes and added that he had instructed Montgomery and Bradley "to hold their flanks securely but with minimum forces, to gather all available reserves and to thrust with great force against the flanks of the penetration." Weather had completely shut down air operations, so the Allied air forces were unable to do anything to help, but for once Eisenhower was thankful for bad weather—it prevented the Germans from flying reconnaissance missions and he thought that because of it the concentrations on their flanks could be carried out secretly.[31]

Eisenhower had set the forces in motion for his counterattack; now he had to wait for them to get in place, and not incidentally for the Germans to lose their momentum and slow down. Meanwhile he worked to smooth relations between his commanders. He realized that staff officers, especially junior ones, at Twelfth Army Group and Third Army had a strong antipathy toward SHAEF, a feeling based on the belief that Montgomery had too great an influence with Eisenhower. The situation was so bad that even before the German attack, the War Department had sent an observer to ETO to make a report. Montgomery, of course, felt Bradley and Patton had the inside track to Eisenhower.[32] That both army groups were suspicious may only have indicated how well SHAEF was doing what it was supposed to do, but the situation was hardly helped when Bradley and Montgomery would barely speak to each other. More serious were the attitudes of Simpson and Hodges, who did not like Montgomery either but who would now have to take orders from him.

To cheer Bradley, and to make certain that no one interpreted the command shift as a criticism of his abilities, Eisenhower cabled Marshall on December 21, asking the Chief of Staff to promote Bradley to four-star rank. "While there was undoubtedly a failure, in the current operations to evaluate correctly the power that the enemy could thrust through the Ardennes," he said, weather was a factor in the inability to see what was coming, and anyway "all of us, without exception, were astonished at the ability of the volksturm [sic] division to act offensively." Bradley had "kept his head magnificently" and had proceeded "methodically and energetically." Eisenhower said he retained his confidence in Bradley and that there was no tendency in any quarter to blame him for the counteroffensive.[33]

Eisenhower then sent a cable to both Hodges and Simpson, congratulating them for what they had done so far and pointing out that "your good work is helping create a situation from which we may profit materially." He asked them to remain calm, determined, and optimistic. Getting to the point, he added, ". . . now that you have been placed under the field marshal's operational command I know that you will respond cheerfully and efficiently to every instruction he gives."[34] Montgomery had not been impressed with Hodges, and the field marshal called on the telephone to tell Smith that some changes in command might become necessary because of physical exhaustion. As a British soldier, however, he was unwilling to relieve U.S. commanders personally. Smith told Montgomery that if such a step had to be taken, Eisenhower would take it. Eisenhower then sent a message to Montgomery, pointing out that "Hodges is the quiet reticent type and does not appear as aggressive as he really is. Unless he becomes exhausted he will always wage a good fight." Montgomery replied that Hodges was improving.[35]

Eisenhower wanted to encourage the men of the AEF as well as their commanders. On December 21 he told his staff to draft an Order of the Day, a brief one, not more than twenty-five words if possible. He said he did not want an order on a pessimistic note but one of encouragement that would point out the opportunity now available to the AEF. After making a number of changes in the draft, Eisenhower issued it on December 22. "We cannot be content with his mere repulse," he said of the enemy. "By rushing out from his fixed defenses the enemy may give us the chance to turn his great gamble into his worst defeat. . . . Let everyone hold before him a single thought—to destroy the enemy on the ground, in the air, everywhere—destroy him!"[36]

The strategic situation was rapidly becoming more and more favorable to the Allies, but on the map, based on territory overrun, it still looked as if the Germans might win a great victory. Von Manteuffel's forces continued to grind forward in the Ardennes. Because of this Eisenhower welcomed the moral support he received from the United States. On December 20 he learned that he had been promoted again, this time to the newly created rank of General of the Army (Marshall, MacArthur, and Arnold were the only other Army officers who received the right to wear five stars). Then, on December 22, Eisenhower received a warm Christmas letter from Marshall. Marshall said that Eisenhower, through his leadership, wisdom, patience, and tolerance, had "made possible Allied cooperation and teamwork in the greatest military operation in the history of the world, complicated by social, economic and political problems almost without precedent." Marshall concluded, "You have my complete confidence." Eisenhower told Marshall that the letter "was the brightest spot in my existence" since the AEF reached the West Wall. "Short of a major defeat inflicted upon the enemy, I could not have had a better personal present."[37]

By this time the spirit at SHAEF was almost buoyant. On December 23 St. Vith finally fell to the Germans, removing an important block on their right flank, but the 7th Armored made a successful withdrawal and soon returned to the battle. It had stalled an entire German corps that was flushed with earlier easy victories, choked one of the main enemy lines of communication, forced days of delay on the westward movement of troops and supplies, and given Montgomery and Bradley time to organize an effective defense.[38] Bastogne, meanwhile, held. On December 19 Middleton had given Brigadier General Anthony C. McAuliffe command of the Bastogne forces, mainly consisting of the 101st Airborne. Middleton gave McAuliffe one standing order: "Hold Bastogne." Despite intensive attack from three and sometimes more German divisions, the 101st held on, even after being encircled on December 21. The men were short of all supplies; the Germans were launching concentric attacks; the weather was bitterly cold. The attacks reached their peak on December 22. At noon on that day the Germans issued an ultimatum calling for "the honorable surrender of the encircled town." McAuliffe sent back a one-word answer: "Nuts."[39]

The leading German divisions, foremost of which was the 2d Panzer, which reached Celles some ten miles from the Meuse, had been immobilized since December 21. Von Manteuffel's vague hopes of reaching Allied supply dumps and getting desperately needed fuel had not been realized. On December 22 Tedder, infected by the spirit of the ground soldiers around him, commented, "The fact that the Hun has stuck his neck out is, from the point of view of shortening the whole business, the best thing that could happen. It may make months of difference. But he might have waited until after Xmas!"[40]

The Bulge could be compared to a gigantic Kasserine. As in February of 1943, the Germans had made a bold bid to reverse the strategic situation. The daring of their attack caused some anxious moments, but they were never really strong enough to succeed. The key problem was timing. At what point would the Germans decide they had had enough and start to pull back? At Kasserine the Allies had let an opportunity slip by because they delayed a day too long in starting the counterattack. Eisenhower realized the danger of piecemeal assault, of throwing divisions against the German flanks as soon as they were ready. If Bradley and Montgomery did that, each individual division would be destroyed by the powerful German Panzer armies and nothing would be accomplished.

At a meeting with his senior assistants at SHAEF on December 21, Eisenhower said he wanted Bradley informed that Patton's attack should be limited in scope. He wanted Patton to break through to Bastogne and relieve the encircled troops there, but otherwise the Supreme Commander declared that Bradley should hold the attack in check and not let it spread, because "it was for the purpose of establishing a firm stepping off point for the main counter-offensive." Eisenhower said that what he feared was having the impetuous Patton talk Bradley into allowing him to attack at once without waiting for a fully co-ordinated counteroffensive.[41] Eisenhower was pleased to learn that Montgomery was gathering two corps, one British and one American, on the German's northern flank. That would give him the force he wanted for a two-pronged attack.

The following day the defensive phase of the battle ended. The morning of December 23 broke clear and cold, with virtually unlimited visibility. For the first time since the counterattack had begun, SHAEF could get its planes into the air. That morning 241 C-47s, each carrying 1200 pounds of supplies, made air drops to the 101st in Bastogne, bringing mostly artillery ammunition, which had almost run out. At the same time fighter planes escorting the C-47s strafed the Germans in the Bastogne ring, while 82 P-47s hit them with fragmentation bombs, napalm, and machine gun fire. The German attacks continued until December 26, when Patton forced his way through to Bastogne and broke the encirclement, but for the 101st the crucial day was December 23. Eisenhower had sent the 11th Armored Division, which had just reached Europe and had been assigned to Sixth Army Group, on a forced march to the Meuse. On December 23 it took its place in the line.[42]

To the north, Montgomery was tidying up the battle front. He told Eisenhower he had reorganized First Army and it was "in good trim. . . . We will fight a good battle up here." Actually First Army had not been reorganized so much as it had re-established communications with its units, many of which had been cut off. Through great effort, Hodges had been able to direct a coherent defense that, at least as much as the more publicized struggle at Bastogne, had been responsible for stopping the Germans. Still, Montgomery was worried that he would not get enough support from Twelfth Army Group. Patton's attack, he declared, would probably not be strong enough to "do what is needed . . . [and] I will have to deal unaided with both Fifth and Sixth Panzer Armies." On Christmas Day he decided to shorten his own front and asked Eisenhower to send him some reserves from Sixth Army Group. Bradley met with Montgomery on Christmas Day. The field marshal, it seemed to Bradley, had adopted a highly defensive attitude. Montgomery rubbed salt into the wounds, making no attempt to disguise his view that the American command had deserved the German counteroffensive. He told Bradley that if there had been a single thrust none of this would have happened, and "now we are in a proper muddle." Montgomery reported that Bradley "looked thin, and worn and ill at ease" and said the American general agreed with everything he said. Montgomery noted of Bradley: "Poor chap; he is such a decent fellow and the whole thing is a bitter pill for him."[43] After the meeting Bradley wrote Hodges—who had already expressed his displeasure at the idea of giving up more ground—to outline his views. Bradley made it clear that as he had no control over First Army his letter should not be considered a directive. He then said he viewed with misgivings any plan to give up terrain which might be favorable for future operations, especially since he felt the Germans had suffered more than First Army and since Hodges had the greater strength in the area. Bradley then told SHAEF that he wanted First and Ninth Armies back.[44]

Eisenhower met with his assistants in the Trianon on December 26 to discuss the situation. He did not want to restore First and Ninth Armies to Bradley yet, for he thought it still logical that Montgomery control the forces on the northern flank of the penetration. What he was most concerned with was building up a strategic reserve. The way to do it was to have Devers shorten his line by withdrawing to the Vosges, thus freeing two or three divisions. Eisenhower went to the map, pointed, and—according to the minutes of the meeting—told his G-3, "Pinky" Bull: " 'Pink,' you'd better go and see Devers today. I think the best line is this." Eisenhower outlined the withdrawal on the map. "I'll tell you, boys," he continued, "what should be done. See Devers and give him this line. It will be a disappointment giving up ground, but this area is not where I told Devers to put his weight."[45]

Eisenhower's confidence in himself had grown tremendously during the crisis. He was laying down the line, telling the boys how it should be done. Two of his bitterest critics have recognized this change: "In all his career as Supreme Commander there was perhaps no other time when Eisenhower revealed so clearly the greatness of his qualities," Chester Wilmot has said. He points out that it was Eisenhower who on the first day overruled Bradley, decided the German attack was a major one, and acted accordingly. Eisenhower was the one who took Whiteley's suggestion and made Bastogne the concentration point for the 101st Airborne. It was the Supreme Commander who recognized the logic of the situation and, overriding national considerations and Bradley's protests, gave Montgomery the command of the forces north of the Ardennes. When the American commanders argued for a rigid defense with no abandonment of ground, Eisenhower saw to it that the front was shortened and reserves accumulated. Finally, Eisenhower was the one who insisted that Bradley and Patton restrain their enthusiasm to penetrate quickly and make the Allied counterattack "methodical and sure."[46]

Sir Arthur Bryant, who quoted with approval every criticism of Eisenhower by Brooke that he could find in Brooke's diary, also recognized Eisenhower's achievement at the Bulge. "Calamity acted on Eisenhower like a restorative and brought out all the greatness in his character," Bryant wrote.[47]

But Eisenhower still had the supreme test to face. Giving firm orders to Bradley, Patton, and Devers was one thing, giving them to Field Marshal Montgomery quite another. Eisenhower was beginning to share Bradley's worry that, as at Kasserine, the Allies would be too late in their counterattack. Montgomery, it appeared, was going to insist that every condition was optimum before he moved forward. Two days after Christmas, at a SHAEF meeting, the discussion centered upon the need to begin soon. Tedder emphasized that the good weather would not last much longer and that it was important to hit the Germans while the airplanes could still fly. At this point word arrived that Montgomery had a new plan for attack, one that involved two corps. "Praise God from whom all blessings flow," Eisenhower remarked.[48] The Supreme Commander decided he would go to Montgomery's headquarters the next day to see what could be done about moving up the date of the attack and strengthening it.

CHAPTER 16

Showdown with Montgomery, De Gaulle, and Brooke

"There is only one thing worse than fighting with allies, and that is fighting without them!"

—Sir Winston Churchill

"Give me allies to fight against!"

—Napoleon

Ferdinand Foch, Eisenhower's predecessor, once summed up his views on the subject of alliance command after reading a paper by a young French officer, Charles de Gaulle, in which De Gaulle had been critical of the Allied leadership in World War I. "There will never be an interallied command in a true sense," Foch declared, "unless you can make it a coalition of disinterested parties."[1]

When Eisenhower met with Montgomery on December 28 there was a temporary lull on the battle front. The Germans had been met and stopped. To the north, Twenty-first Army Group's line ran along the Maas River to Sittard, then turned directly east and, crossing the West Wall, reached the Roer River at Linnich. Simpson's Ninth Army occupied the west bank of the Roer from Linnich to Monschau (Simpson had taken over part of Hodges' front on December 20). Neither Simpson nor Dempsey had been much involved in the Battle of the Bulge. At Butgenbach, near the Eisenborn Ridge, the First Army line bent backward—this was the beginning of the German salient. One key factor in the Allied success at holding the German offensive had been Hodges' ability to hold Eisenborn Ridge. From Butgenbach, Hodges' line ran almost straight west to Celles, the tip of the salient. At this point Montgomery had positioned the British 29th Armored Division and there also, held the British 30 Corps in reserve. Below Celles, Bradley's Twelfth Army Group took over. On the southern flank of the salient the German line went east-southeast back to Trier and the West Wall, with an American salient into the German line at Bastogne. Devers was east of the Vosges. He had made some limited withdrawals and U. S. Seventh Army was occupying a part of the old Maginot Line.

Von Rundstedt wanted to pull out of the exposed tip of the salient, re-establishing a defensive line along the base from St. Vith to Wiltz. He was concerned about his tanks and wished to put them in reserve, both to preserve them and to have them available later to meet Allied counterthrusts. Hitler refused him. He said they should continue the offensive to the Meuse and that Von Rundstedt should concentrate on taking Bastogne. Hitler also decided to launch an offensive, beginning January 1, against Devers in the Vosges. He thought Sixth Army Group had been so weakened by stretching its front that the Germans could force a breakthrough there. None of these plans were very realistic, for all German divisions were under strength and badly battered. Supplies were, in many cases, non-existent.

Eisenhower sensed this and wanted to hit the salient as quickly as possible. Montgomery hesitated. He told the Supreme Commander that he was sure the Germans would make one last great attack in the north, against First Army. He thought the best thing to do would be to receive that attack, then launch his counterattack when the Germans were stopped. Eisenhower insisted that Von Rundstedt would either start to pull out of the salient or put infantry divisions into the line and his tanks in reserve. The latter, Eisenhower said, "we must not allow to happen." He repeated that he wanted Montgomery to attack quickly. Montgomery replied that first he must meet and stop the attack he expected against First Army. Eisenhower responded that if no attack came Montgomery should strike on January 1. He thought Montgomery agreed.[2]

When Eisenhower got back to Versailles he felt he had things well in hand. Tedder was going to Moscow to confer with Red Army leaders in an attempt to co-ordinate future operations and find out when the Russian winter offensive would begin (it started on January 12 and the Russians have since claimed that it saved the Western Allies from disaster in the Bulge). Eisenhower told Tedder to inform Stalin that his intentions were to eliminate the salient, pin down the Panzers committed to the battle and destroy them, and then start a strong drive toward Bonn. "The basic thing," Eisenhower said, "is to defeat the

German armies west of the Rhine. For this, everything must be concentrated to get to the Rhine from Bonn northwards." Eisenhower was holding to his pre-December plan of making a major effort in the north with a secondary one in the south, and the key to its success lay in destroying Von Rundstedt's tanks in the Bulge.[3]

The next day, December 30, De Guingand came to SHAEF with the bad news that Montgomery would not attack until January 3. Montgomery had been wise to send De Guingand instead of coming himself, for De Guingand was popular at SHAEF—he had a sense of balance and humor. Still, the blow was more than any of the SHAEF senior officers could take. "What makes me so Goddam mad," Smith exploded, "is that Monty won't talk in the presence of anyone else."[4] Montgomery claimed that Eisenhower had misunderstood him at their recent meeting, and De Guingand said there had been no agreement on a January 1 attack. Eisenhower muttered that Montgomery was wrong. Montgomery was holding the 30 Corps out of the line, waiting for an attack that Eisenhower was sure would never come. Eisenhower wanted the corps committed. The Supreme Commander dictated a blistering letter to the field marshal demanding that he live up to his promises, but De Guingand talked Eisenhower out of sending it.*

The next day, New Year's Eve, De Guingand returned to Versailles after a conference with Montgomery. He insisted that a delay in the attack was necessary, for it was impossible to switch suddenly from defensive positions to the offensive without careful preparation. Montgomery, he reported, felt the Allies had the enemy "on the run like a wet hen from one side of the salient to the other," that time was on the Allied side, and that Eisenhower should let the Germans exhaust themselves before attacking, since nothing could be worse than an ill-prepared offensive. Eisenhower was disturbed. He said Montgomery had definitely promised him he would attack on January 1. De Guingand said Eisenhower must have misunderstood. Eisenhower sent some staff officers to the files to see if they could find a message from Montgomery confirming the arrangements, but De Guingand warned that the mission was fruitless. "Knowing Monty," he said, "the last thing he would do is to commit himself on paper."[5] Bradley, meanwhile, had already attacked, believing that Montgomery would begin his offensive on January 1.

---

* Interview with Eisenhower, July 8, 1966. Eisenhower recalled that in his letter he "sacked Montgomery," but this is unlikely, for he intended to ask Brooke or Churchill to relieve the field marshal. Eisenhower's letter of December 29 to Montgomery was also not sent.

But Montgomery did not, and the Panzer divisions in the north were switched to the south to stop Bradley.

Eisenhower thought Montgomery's sense of timing in military operations deficient. That point may be open to question, but there can be none about Montgomery's total lack of a sense of timing in personal relations, or his complete inability to see things from someone else's point of view. At the height of the debate over what Montgomery had or had not promised, the field marshal sent a letter to Eisenhower, damning the Supreme Commander's policies and demanding that he, Montgomery, be given full control of the land battle. He did not mention the date of his attack.

Montgomery urged Eisenhower to write a directive setting tasks and objectives for the two army groups. After it was sent out, "one commander must have powers to direct and control the operations; you cannot possibly do it yourself, and so you would have to nominate someone else." He suggested that Eisenhower put into his directive a statement that would read, "From now onwards full operational direction, control, and coordination of these operations is vested in the C.-in-C. 21 Army Group. . . ." Montgomery said Eisenhower should assign all available offensive power to the northern line of advance to the Ruhr; otherwise there would be another failure.[6]

Because Eisenhower had given him command of two American armies, Montgomery felt the Supreme Commander was in his power now, disagreements over dates of attack notwithstanding. Marshall feared Montgomery was right. On December 30, after reading in the London papers that Eisenhower intended to leave First and Ninth Armies with Montgomery, the Chief of Staff cabled the Supreme Commander: "My feeling is this: under no circumstances make any concessions of any kind whatsoever. You not only have our complete confidence but there would be a terrific resentment in this country following such action. . . . You are doing a fine job and go on and give them hell."[7] Eisenhower's advisers at SHAEF also thought he needed bucking up, and several counseled him to have a showdown with Montgomery. Smith had a frank discussion with De Guingand and let him know that if someone had to go it would not be Eisenhower.

Montgomery, Marshall, Smith, and the others had all misjudged Eisenhower. He was not Montgomery's man, he had no intention of leaving both American armies with Montgomery, and he needed no encouragement to settle matters with the field marshal. The Bulge had given Eisenhower complete confidence in himself. On New Year's Eve he sent to Bradley and Montgomery a directive covering future operations. His plan remained what it had always been—a major thrust by Montgomery, a secondary one by Bradley. Because Montgomery needed the extra help, Eisenhower allowed him to retain U. S. Ninth Army but returned First Army to Bradley's control. "The one thing that must now be prevented," he emphasized, "is the stabilization of the enemy salient with infantry, permitting him opportunity to use his Panzers at will on any part of the front. We must regain the initiative, and speed and energy are essential."[8]

Eisenhower dictated a short covering note to Bradley to accompany the directive, then dictated a letter to Montgomery. It was simple and direct. "I do not agree," Eisenhower said, referring to Montgomery's contention that there should be a single ground commander. "My plan," the Supreme Commander added, put a complete U.S. army under Montgomery; this he had done only because "I consider [it] militarily necessary. . . ." He said he had done all he could for Montgomery and did not want to hear again about placing Bradley under Twenty-first Army Group: "I assure you that in this matter I can go no further. . . . I have planned" to advance on a broad front, he said, and instructed Montgomery to read his directive carefully. All the vagueness of earlier letters and directives to Montgomery was now gone.

In conclusion, Eisenhower told Montgomery that he would no longer tolerate any debate on the subject. "I would deplore the development of such an unbridgeable gulf of convictions between us that we would have to present our differences" to the CCS, he said, but made it clear that if Montgomery went any further that was exactly what he would do. "The confusion and debate that would follow would certainly damage the good will and devotion to a common cause that have made this Allied Force unique in history," Eisenhower added, but he could do nothing else if Montgomery persisted.[9]

Even before receiving Eisenhower's letter, Montgomery had begun to concede. De Guingand informed him of the depth of feeling on the matter at SHAEF, reporting that Smith "was more worried than I had ever seen him." De Guingand also had told Montgomery of Eisenhower's intention to turn the matter over to the CCS if necessary.[10] Montgomery had seen Marshall's message to Eisenhower (De Guingand had brought a copy), so he knew there was no possibility of Eisenhower's giving in to his demands. He thereupon sent a note to the Supreme Commander saying he realized there were many factors Eisenhower had to consider "beyond anything I realize." He asked Eisenhower to tear up his letter requesting sole control of the ground forces.[11]

On January 1 Montgomery received Eisenhower's stern letter of December 31. "Dear Ike," he began his handwritten reply. "I have no comments on the outline plan and details can be worked out later on. You can rely on me and all under my command to go all out one hundred per cent to implement your plan."[12] He began his attack with 30 Corps on January 3. For over a month the Allies battered away at the salient. The Germans, schooled in winter warfare from the Russian front, waged a fighting retreat, and not until February 7 had the original line been restored. Eisenhower had hoped for better results, but these were satisfactory, for most of the German armor was destroyed in the process. The enemy had practically no mobility left, and once Eisenhower's forces gained a breakthrough they would be able to dash through Germany at will. In that dash their commanding general would be Eisenhower.

Having dealt with Montgomery, Eisenhower next had to take on De Gaulle. The French President was upset about the situation on Sixth Army front. When Devers had begun his operations in Alsace-Lorraine in November, Eisenhower had told him to get and hold an easily defended flank on the Rhine River.[13] After Devers broke through the Vosges Mountains he reasoned that the French First Army could quickly finish off the German forces in the Colmar pocket and had consequently sent the bulk of his forces north to assist Patton. He expected that as soon as the French eliminated the Colmar pocket he could leave all of Alsace-Lorraine to the French and employ the entire U. S. Seventh Army on and west of the Vosges. But the French were incapable of driving the Germans out of Colmar and when the Bulge began, as Eisenhower later explained to Marshall, "we had on our extreme right flank, instead of the strong, easily defended line we expected, a situation that was inherently weak from a defensive standpoint." The U. S. VI Corps was east of the Vosges, while an American division had to be retained with the French First Army to hold the Germans at Colmar. The two northernmost corps of Seventh Army had not reached the Rhine—they were still in the Vosges. The danger was that the Germans would hit VI Corps's exposed left flank and, at the same time, launch a secondary attack from the Colmar pocket. Eisenhower had sent a message of encouragement to General Jean de Lattre de Tassigny, commanding the French First Army. "I request that you strike swiftly with your full might in the cause of France and the United Nations," Eisenhower said. It did little good—the Colmar pocket remained.[14]

Eisenhower wanted to pull some divisions out of Sixth Army Group in order to create a SHAEF reserve, and he decided that the way to do it was to fall back to the Vosges. He had instructed Devers to bring the bulk of VI Corps west, but Devers had been slow in carrying out the orders, and even asked for reinforcements himself. On New Year's Day Eisenhower met with Smith and told him, "You must call up Devers and tell him he is not doing what he was told, that is, to get VI Corps back and to hold the Alsace Plain with rec and observational elements." Eisenhower felt that the German divisions in that area were weak, and although they had started an attack that day against VI Corps, he thought it would be possible to hold the area with light elements. Smith did not agree with this view; he thought Devers should either try to hold where he was or fall back completely. "The bulk of VI Corps must come back," Eisenhower explained, "but from this force mobile elements must be sent out to give warning of the enemy advance. The first principle when taking a defensive position is to reconnoitre as far as possible to your front."[15]

The French were unhappy at the idea of withdrawing from the sacred soil of Alsace. On January 1 De Gaulle sent telegrams to Churchill and Roosevelt, protesting Eisenhower's intentions, and wrote a letter to the Supreme Commander. De Gaulle said Eisenhower's strategic reasons for retreating escaped him. "The French Government, for its part," he continued, "obviously cannot let Strasbourg fall into enemy hands again without first doing everything possible to prevent it." He declared he was ready to "push all French forces that were being mustered in this direction."[16]

Eisenhower had General Bull, the SHAEF G-3, draft a reply to De Gaulle's letter; in Eisenhower's name, Bull said he too was concerned about the fate of the French citizens in Alsace if the Germans returned to the area, and was grateful to De Gaulle "for indicating that you share my views from the military point of view."[17]

"Nothing of what you have been told from me and nothing I have written can make you think that from the military point of view 'I approve of your views,'" De Gaulle replied. "I should tell you frankly that the truth is just the opposite."[18]

French agitation grew. On January 2 General Juin, now Chief of Staff in the Ministry of Defense, had a stormy session with Smith. The next day Smith walked into Eisenhower's office and exclaimed, "Juin said things to me last night which, if he had been an American, I would have socked him on the jaw."[19] The French threatened to withdraw their forces from Eisenhower's control. On the third, when Lieutenant General Alexander M. Patch, commanding the U. S. Seventh Army, issued the orders for the withdrawal from Strasbourg, the French military governor of the city said he would not undertake such action without direct orders from De Gaulle.

The morning of January 3 Eisenhower met with his staff to discuss the situation. He was willing to leave light mobile elements north and west of Strasbourg, but he still wanted the bulk of the VI Corps withdrawn. Churchill flew to Versailles that day, accompanied by Brooke, to discuss Eisenhower's problems with Montgomery. After lunch the Prime Minister and CIGS sat in on a meeting attended by Eisenhower, Smith, Whiteley, and Strong. De Gaulle had asked to see Eisenhower and was expected shortly. Brooke and the SHAEF officers approved of Eisenhower's policy. When the meeting broke up Churchill stayed, and was present when De Gaulle stormed into the office.[20]

It would be fatal, De Gaulle immediately informed Eisenhower, to withdraw from Strasbourg without a fight. French public opinion would not stand for it. Eisenhower began to show De Gaulle on the map why it was necessary. "If we were at Kriegspiel I should say you were right," De Gaulle cut in. "But I must consider the matter from another point of view. Retreat in Alsace . . . would be a national disaster." Each man then threatened the other. De Gaulle said he would have to assume control of the French Army, removing it from SHAEF's command. Eisenhower countered by saying that if the French Army did not obey his orders he would stop its flow of supplies.

Eisenhower slowly began to realize that De Gaulle's real fear was that if Strasbourg were abandoned the French government "would lose control of the entire French situation and we would have a state bordering upon anarchy in the whole country." He had wanted to handle the problem on a military basis only, but "when I found that execution of the original plan would have such grave consequences in France that all my lines of communication and my vast rear areas might become badly involved through loss of service troops and through unrest," it became a matter of military necessity to hold Strasbourg. Having thus satisfied himself that he was making a military, not a political, decision, Eisenhower told De Gaulle he would hold Strasbourg, and immediately telephoned Devers to cancel the orders for the withdrawal.

When De Gaulle left, pleased with the result, Churchill—who according to De Gaulle's later account supported him, but who according to Eisenhower had merely watched the whole exchange—told Eisenhower, "I think you've done the wise and proper thing."[21]

Strasbourg was held and, although VI Corps fell back almost twenty-five miles from the Rhine, the German attack failed. Later in January the French, after considerable urging from Eisenhower and with the substantial help of an American corps, began operations to eliminate the Colmar pocket. By February 9 they had done so and closed to the Rhine.

Following his confrontation with De Gaulle, Eisenhower may have hoped for a little quiet and a belated chance to enjoy the holiday season, but he was not to have it. On January 7 Montgomery held a press conference to explain the Battle of the Bulge. Eisenhower later recalled that it caused him "more distress and worry" than anything else that happened during the war.[22] De Guingand saw a copy of what Montgomery was going to say in his prepared statement and asked him to call the conference off, or at least to tone down his remarks, but Montgomery said the British press had been critical of Eisenhower and Bradley and he had to set the record straight. In his statement Montgomery said that Von Rundstedt had sprung a tactical surprise and was heading for the Meuse. "As soon as I saw what was happening I took certain steps myself to ensure that if the Germans got to the Meuse they would certainly not get over the river. And I carried out certain movements so as to provide balanced dispositions to meet the threatened danger; these were, at the time, merely precautions, i.e., I was thinking ahead." But, he said, despite his best efforts the situation was deteriorating. Then Eisenhower "placed me in command of the whole Northern front." He brought the British forces into action and set them to fighting hard on the right flank of Hodges' First Army. "You have thus the picture of British troops fighting on both sides of American forces who have suffered a hard blow. This is a fine Allied picture." He then praised the fighting quality and spirit of the American G.I. and said the battle bore some similarity to El Alamein. It had been interesting, he said, "I think possibly one of the most interesting and tricky battles I have ever handled."[23]

Montgomery's statement, coupled with the fact that at the crucial moment Eisenhower had given command of two American armies to the field marshal, gave a totally false impression of how the battle had been fought. Bradley felt SHAEF was at fault for not having made clear the reason for the command shift and for not emphasizing that it was temporary. He issued a statement of his own, in which he declared—with justice—that Von Rundstedt had been stopped *before* Montgomery took control of the northern flank. Patton made his feelings, which were strong, known to American reporters too, and a debate began in the British and American press over who had really won the battle.

The amity of the command was about to be destroyed; if it were, much of what Eisenhower had worked for over the past three years would go down the drain. The British press began to urge that Montgomery be made sole ground commander; when Bradley read a story to that effect he called on Eisenhower and demanded to know how the Supreme Commander intended to respond. Eisenhower impatiently indicated that he had no intention of doing anything, but Bradley was not satisfied with his brusque reply. "You must know," Bradley declared, "after what has happened I cannot serve under Montgomery. If he is to be put in command of all ground forces, you must send me home, for if Montgomery goes in over me, I will have lost the confidence of my command." Eisenhower sat up. "Well," he said to Bradley, "I thought you were the one person I could count on for doing anything I asked you to." Bradley would not be put off. "You can, Ike," he replied. "I've enjoyed every bit of my service with you. But this is one thing I cannot take." He would ask to be sent home rather than subordinate himself to Montgomery's command.[24]

Bradley may have been wise in making his position so plain, for the storm was not yet over. The BCOS (not Montgomery) still wanted to prod Eisenhower on the question of a single ground commander, as well as on the nature of the spring offensive. The British Chiefs told Marshall, who passed it on to Eisenhower, that at the forthcoming CCS conferences, to be held at the end of January in Malta and Yalta, they wished to review the strategic situation in Europe. They indicated that they thought the AEF did not have enough strength to mount two major attacks; "hence, it is important to decide on one major thrust and to allocate overwhelming strength to this thrust to keep up the momentum." They also insisted that "one man should be directly responsible" for the ground campaign, and argued that Eisenhower had too many responsibilities to do the job himself.

Eisenhower had been over both points innumerable times with Montgomery, and he was able to dispatch two long cables to Marshall on these points the day he received Marshall's message, January 10. After covering all the familiar ground, he said if the CCS decided that his secondary attack should be launched farther north than he had planned, so that it would give more support to Montgomery, he would "accept such a decision loyally and as always do my utmost to carry it out." But he also made it clear he thought it would be a mistake. On command, he again pointed out that the Ruhr was the logical dividing point, "and in reaching this obvious conclusion I have submerged my own nationalistic tendencies [meaning he had left Simpson under Montgomery's command] just as I have ignored the personal ambitions of any individual."[25]

Using for support the experiences of recent weeks, and especially the German attack against Sixth Army Group, Eisenhower emphasized by underscoring that it was his conviction *"that in order to concentrate north of the Ruhr all the forces needed for a successful invasion of Germany, we must have throughout the rest of the front a very firm defensive line which can be held with minimum forces."* That line was the Rhine, and Eisenhower intended to continue attacking on a broad front until the AEF was up to the Rhine everywhere.

In his second cable of January 10, which was eight pages long, Eisenhower raised a new possibility: what if the ground commander were someone other than Montgomery? Eisenhower still thought having a ground commander in chief a poor idea, for all he could do would be to duplicate work SHAEF and Eisenhower were already doing. He would have to exercise his command through Bradley, Montgomery, and Devers, who were "already in such high position that for their respective sections at the front they are, each, a ground commander in chief." Besides, given "the personalities involved," Eisenhower did not think it would work out. He thought that the command system as it already existed was logical and did not see how anyone could exercise more control than SHAEF and the Supreme Commander already were. He did admit that, because of the great size of the land forces under his command, it would be "more convenient" for him if his deputy supreme commander were an experienced ground officer, rather than an airman. If he could have someone whom both Bradley and Montgomery would respect, he would be glad to have him, but "I am afraid it would be impossible to find such a deputy as I describe." The only general he could think of was Alexander, who had just become Supreme Commander in the Mediterranean and thus was unavailable.[26]

The almost casual way Eisenhower raised Alexander's name was a probing, an attempt to see how Marshall would react. Churchill and Brooke had raised the possible transfer of Alexander from the Mediterranean to northwestern Europe at their meeting with Eisenhower on January 3. They desperately wanted the British to play a greater role in the development of strategy, thought Tedder and Whiteley and the other British officers at SHAEF too much under Eisenhower's influence, and realized that Montgomery would never do. It was not just a case of national pride, although that played a part. They, or at least Brooke, sincerely believed that Eisenhower's strategy was faulty. Since Montgomery could not influence him, it was time to try someone else. Eisenhower liked Alexander personally, and said that if the CCS assigned him to SHAEF he would be glad to have him. He almost welcomed the idea, for with Alexander at SHAEF the British could no longer complain. He did not however intend to give Alexander sole ground control.

Marshall suspected Churchill and Brooke had gotten to Eisenhower, and he was fearful that Eisenhower was weakening under the intense British pressure to put one of their officers in charge of the ground forces. Knowing that the British would gladly pull Alexander out of the Mediterranean if his new assignment were land command in Europe, he wired Eisenhower to warn him that Alexander's appointment would mean two things: "First, that the British had won a major point in getting control of the ground operations in which their divisions of necessity will play such a minor part and, for the same reason, we are bound to suffer very heavy casualties; and second, the man being who he is and our experience being what it has been, you would have great difficulty in offsetting the direct influence of the P.M." In the face of Marshall's feelings, Eisenhower backed down. He admitted to Marshall that he had not thought of these disadvantages, but assured the Chief of Staff that he would seriously object to having any officer named "deputy for ground operations." Eisenhower had thought that Alexander might serve as deputy without portfolio; he was not willing to go back to the committee system that had prevailed in AFHQ. He said he had made that clear to Churchill.[27]

Since Montgomery could not move Eisenhower, and since Eisenhower —with Marshall's backing—had stood firm against Brooke, it was now up to Brooke to convince Marshall. The dispute had moved to higher levels. Within the AEF, relations between the British and Americans were improving. Montgomery helped matters greatly when, just prior to First Army's return to Bradley's command on January 17, he wrote Bradley a warm letter. He said it had been a great honor to command such fine troops, praised Simpson and Hodges for their good work, said the corps commanders (Gerow, Collins, and Ridgway) had been "quite magnificent," and—most important—said he greatly admired the way Bradley had conducted operations on the southern flank of the salient. "If you had not held on firmly to Bastogne the whole situation might have become very awkward."[28] It was difficult to remain angry with such a man.

But if Montgomery was ready to play by Eisenhower's rules, the CIGS was not. As Brooke prepared for the Malta meeting, however, he realized how weak his position was. The point at issue went beyond the relatively simple problem of choosing a ground commander, and even beyond the nature of the final offensive. Certainly the issue was also much more important than Montgomery's ambition and bad manners. In their related demands for a single offensive north of the Ruhr and a single ground commander, the British were trying to assert themselves. They were, they felt, being ignored.

There was a good reason for British feelings of relative inferiority. The United States had replaced Great Britain as the dominant power bordering on the Atlantic Ocean. By 1945 American production was reaching levels that were scarcely believable. The United States was producing forty-five per cent of the world's armaments and nearly fifty per cent of the world's total goods. Some two thirds of all the ships afloat in the world were American-made. Under the circumstances, what the Americans wanted, if they wanted it badly enough, they got. Montgomery knew that, if Eisenhower threw before the CCS the mutually exclusive choice of himself or Montgomery, Eisenhower would win because the JCS dominated the CCS, just as Eisenhower dominated the AEF. This American domination reflected a newly arrived era in the world's history.

Brooke knew that, for good or ill, the Americans were determined to claim their rightful position. In 1942 and even in 1943 he had been able to shape CCS decisions, but now that power had slipped away. It was galling but, more important, the strategy the Americans insisted upon was hurting Britain more each day because it delayed the final victory. The War Department's refusal to give Eisenhower any more replacements during the Bulge illustrated this point. The Americans had made, in 1942, a basic priority decision—the United States would concentrate on industrial production as her chief contribution to victory. The implementation of this decision involved holding the number of U.S. combat divisions to ninety. In denying Eisenhower his replacements, the War Department was holding firm to the original priority.[29] Churchill, meanwhile, had impulsively called up another quarter of a million men, so that while American production and wealth increased, Britain's, due to the resultant decrease in the industrial work force, decreased. A number of high-ranking British officials were critical of Churchill for overtaxing his country by putting too much of a strain on the economy in order to win the war.[30] No one accused Roosevelt or the Americans of making that mistake.

Even though the British strained to the limit of their power, American strength in the AEF at this time was so great that Eisenhower could do almost as he wished. That he had such great patience with Montgomery was, in fact, as much a mark of human courtesy as of need. The British contributed only about one quarter of his troops. Churchill, realizing this, and realizing that Britain would no longer be able to play a lone, powerful hand in world politics, but could exert an influence only through association with the United States, was much more inclined to tread lightly with the Americans than Brooke. It was the Prime Minister, for example, who told the British press that in the Ardennes the Americans engaged thirty or forty men for every British soldier in the battle, and had suffered sixty to eighty casualties for every British soldier killed or wounded. Churchill told the British press to be careful not to give too much credit to the British Army for victory in the Bulge, for he did not want to irritate the Americans.[31] Still, of course, the Prime Minister did want his nation to have a voice in making strategic decisions, and he was also concerned about British prestige. At a meeting with Brooke on January 2, Brooke noted that "Winston . . . then propounded strategies based on ensuring that British troops were retained in the limelight, if necessary, at the expense of the Americans"; that is, that Twenty-first Army Group make the drive across Germany alone.[32]

As Forrest Pogue points out, the British realized that they were no longer full partners in the alliance. "Their only hope for controlling the course of events . . . was to gain over-all ground command or to get a substantial portion of the Allied resources allocated to offensives led by British commanders. It was difficult under these circumstances to determine whether the British were advocating a course of action because they believed in it or because it would best serve British interests."[33]

Brooke and Churchill wanted to get Alexander transferred to Eisenhower's headquarters so that he could have an influence on Eisenhower's thinking. Brooke also wanted the CCS to send Eisenhower a directive that would force him to concentrate north of the Ruhr, where as he saw it lay the only hope of a quick victory. He was disturbed at what he felt to be an absence of a sense of urgency on the part of the Americans, especially Eisenhower, and was shocked at Eisenhower's statement before the Bulge that the Rhine might not be crossed before May. The British were dipping deeper and deeper into their human and material resources and it was imperative for them, if they were to have any position at all in the postwar world, to end the war as soon as possible. As Arthur Bryant puts it, "With their manpower and resources all but exhausted after five years of war and with no possibility of making good further losses, they [the British] had staked everything on an early victory in the West and had seen it, as they felt, thrown away by the inexperience of the American High Command. The war, instead of ending in 1944, had been prolonged into another year and, unless a very different method of conducting it was now to be adopted, seemed likely to continue until, not only their own position, but that of Europe was desperate."[34]

But the real point at issue was not what Brooke sometimes thought it was. Eisenhower was just as anxious to end the war as the British, and was willing to take any reasonable risk to do it. The disagreement was over strategy. All through January 1945 Montgomery protested to Brooke that Eisenhower was up to his old tricks, promising to make the major effort in the north but meanwhile allowing Bradley and Patton to operate as they wished. "The real trouble is that there is no control and the three Army Groups are each intent on their own affairs," Montgomery complained on January 22. "Patton to-day issued a stirring order to Third Army, saying the next step would be Cologne. . . . One has to preserve a sense of humour these days, otherwise one would go mad."[35] Eisenhower continued to insist on closing to the Rhine all along his front before crossing the river north of the Ruhr. He felt that if he could destroy the Germans west of the Rhine he could walk across the rest of Germany. Brooke thought that closing everywhere would take strength from Montgomery's drive and thus delay the victory. That was the real issue.

The CCS meeting at Malta began on January 30, 1945. Two days earlier Eisenhower had flown to Marseilles to meet with Marshall. After discussing ETO problems they turned to the British demands for a single ground commander and a directive forcing Eisenhower to turn over all his offensive power to Montgomery. Marshall said he would never agree to any proposal to set up a single ground command. If it were done, he added, he would resign as Chief of Staff. He told Eisenhower he was right to want to fight a major battle west of the Rhine and to close to the river everywhere before crossing in the north. Eisenhower flew back to Versailles knowing that, with the support Marshall was giving him, he would have his way.[36]

Brooke arrived in Malta with the air of a man who has one last, desperate chance. Eisenhower sent Smith to represent him, giving Smith two objectives—to retain the SHAEF plan for the campaign, and to hold the alliance together. The Americans might be dominant, but Eisenhower did not want to play the bully. All considerations of friendship and fair play aside, he still needed the British. He also believed, with Churchill, that Anglo-American co-operation was essential to a peaceful postwar world.

Smith got the job done. Brooke knew that the Americans were all against him, so he could not press matters too far. He did insist that it would be foolish to pass up an opportunity to cross the Rhine in the north if one presented itself, and Smith said that obviously Eisenhower would take advantage of any such opportunity. Brooke wanted it in writing, so Smith and Eisenhower exchanged cables in an attempt to find a satisfactory wording. The upshot was a cable from Eisenhower to Smith that Brooke accepted: "You may assure the Combined Chiefs of Staff that I will seize the Rhine crossings in the North immediately this is a feasible operation and without waiting to close the Rhine throughout its length." Then Eisenhower added, "I will advance across the Rhine in the North with maximum strength and complete determination as soon as the situation in the South allows me to collect the necessary forces and do this without incurring unnecessary risks."[37]

Reassured, although still suspicious because of Eisenhower's last sentence, Brooke then talked privately with Smith. The CIGS said he doubted that Eisenhower was "strong enough" to do his job. "Goddam it," Smith replied, "let's have it out here and now." He suggested that the two of them speak bluntly, off the record. He asked what Brooke meant. Brooke replied that Eisenhower paid too much attention to the desires of his field commanders, that he was too likely to be swayed by the last man to whom he talked. Going straight to the heart of the matter, Smith retorted by stressing Eisenhower's cordial contacts with his commanders and pointed out that the Supreme Commander could hold the Allied team together only by a combination of diplomacy and sternness. He added that if the BCOS doubted Eisenhower's ability they should put their cards on the table before the CCS. Brooke knew that would be hopeless. He lamely responded that Eisenhower had many abilities and conceded that there was no one else available and acceptable to Marshall who could hold down the Supreme Commander's job.[38]

Brooke made one more effort. When the CCS moved on to Yalta for the conference with the Russians, he proposed a switch—Tedder to go to the Mediterranean and become Supreme Commander there, with Alexander replacing him at SHAEF. On February 2 Brooke, Churchill, Marshall, and Roosevelt discussed the proposal. The Americans thought that "politically such a move might have repercussions in America if carried out just now. . . . They were, however, quite prepared to accept this change in about six weeks' time after further offensive operations will have been started and the Ardennes operation more forgotten."[39]

Word of the proposal reached SHAEF in mid-February. Eisenhower discussed it with Montgomery, who assured the Supreme Commander that he wanted no change and could see no good coming out of Alexander's moving to SHAEF. Tedder told Eisenhower the same thing.[40]

On February 16 Eisenhower wrote a long letter to Brooke on the subject. He said that any change in the working team would be deplorable, but if the CCS insisted upon it he wanted to make sure Brooke understood what Alexander's position would be. "There can be no question whatsoever of placing between me and my Army Group Commanders any intermediary headquarters, either official or unofficial in character." Montgomery agreed with this point, Eisenhower said, and indeed the field marshal had declared that "the command arrangements I have made are as nearly perfect as circumstances, including diverse nationalities, will permit."

Eisenhower was candid with Brooke. He pointed out that the Americans in the AEF, especially the senior commander, "feel themselves aggrieved" because of Montgomery's press conference on the Bulge and the treatment of the battle on BBC and in the London newspapers. "The upshot is that should there be any attempt on the part of any newspaper to interpret Alexander's appointment here as the establishment of a ground headquarters or the interposition of any kind of intermediate control between myself and my Army Group Commanders, I would find it immediately necessary to make a formal announcement setting forth the facts." This would be quite embarrassing to Alexander. Eisenhower said that he liked Alexander enormously and would be delighted to work with him again, "but it is one of my principal jobs to see that nothing occurs that may tend to create misunderstandings within my own command, or to mar the generally splendid British-American relationships that we try to promote."[41]

Brooke showed Eisenhower's letter to Churchill, who was upset at the implication that Eisenhower's British deputy had nothing to do. Eisenhower then wrote Churchill to set him straight. Tedder was an intimate member of the SHAEF family, the Supreme Commander pointed out, and Alexander would be too if he were transferred. Turning to the main point, Eisenhower added, "Far from regarding this problem from a British versus American viewpoint, my whole effort is to exercise the authority of my office so as to weld and preserve the sense of partnership that to my mind is absolutely essential to the winning of the war and to our common welfare."[42]

Montgomery added his voice in support of Eisenhower's position. On March 4 he declared that the command arrangement should be left as it was and warned that a change would merely raise a storm and cause an organizational setback. The next day Churchill met with Eisenhower and Tedder and agreed that the decision regarding command arrangements belonged entirely to Eisenhower. The Supreme Commander made no changes.[43]

Eisenhower had won, but that was not the most significant result of the long and often bitter dispute over command. Given the difference in the size of the contribution of the two nations to the AEF, Marshall's attitude, Eisenhower's support from the British members of SHAEF, and Roosevelt's inclination to follow Marshall's lead in military matters, it was inevitable that Eisenhower would have his way. His real achievement was that he had won without alienating the British. They felt strongly about the issues, and pressed their points as hard as they dared, giving Eisenhower's patience a thorough testing. He kept turning them down, but only after giving them the opportunity to fully state their views, and he never let himself be provoked into losing his temper. At the end of the war his reputation with the British remained extraordinarily high, a unique achievement for an allied commander.

Montgomery summed up Eisenhower's achievement in a letter he wrote the Supreme Commander shortly after the surrender. "Dear Ike," he began, ". . . I suppose we shall soon begin to run our own affairs." Before the AEF split up, he wanted to say "what a privilege and an honor it has been to serve under you. I owe much to your wise guidance and kindly forbearance." Montgomery said he knew his own faults very well "and I do not suppose I am an easy subordinate; I like to go my own way. But you have kept me on the rails in difficult and stormy times, and have taught me much." Montgomery thanked Eisenhower for all he had done for him and signed off, "Your very devoted friend, Monty."[44]

Eisenhower himself put things in perspective in a February 20 letter to Marshall. The Supreme Commander said he had just had two con-

ferences with Montgomery, who was "emphatic in his statement that
everything is developing soundly, and he has been especially vehement
in protesting his complete loyalty and his belief in the efficacy of our
command system." Eisenhower said he had told Montgomery that he
hoped the field marshal would have an opportunity to tell that to the
Prime Minister. Rumors about Alexander replacing Tedder continued
to crop up from time to time, but they no longer worried Eisenhower.
"The vague rumors and statements that tend to create . . . uneasiness
are largely froth," he said. Meanwhile, ironically, Americans had been
protesting that Churchill had a veto on all United States officers serving on SHAEF, and it was sometimes said that SHAEF was a British
operation. Eisenhower felt that "the trouble often is that to gain a
particular end, people, even in high places, are sometimes not above
using gossip and misinterpretation." But, he added, "all these things
I ignore as long as they have no important effect upon this Command."[45]

CHAPTER 17

Duties and Responsibilities

In January 1939 Eisenhower wrote a letter to his brother Milton, who had been offered a position as a dean at Pennsylvania State University. Milton wanted his brother's advice: should he continue his work at the Department of Agriculture, where he was head of a bureau, or should he go to Penn State? Lieutenant Colonel Eisenhower said that Milton's happiness was the most important consideration, then went on to warn his brother about overwork. "The human machine wears out," he declared, "although none of us ever applies this inescapable law to his own case. Deterioration and destruction are familiar phenomena, but the mind recoils from personal application of the logical conclusion." If Milton decided to stay in Washington, Eisenhower continued, he should be aware of the danger. "Men of ability in the government service see so much to be done, they create or have created for them so many jobs that lazier men like to shunt from their own shoulders (except of course when it comes to collecting the glory for recognized accomplishment) that gradually the victim . . . loses his sense of values, and with this needful governor failing him, he applies his mind, consciously and unconsciously, day and night, to important and intricate problems that march up ceaselessly, one after the other, for consideration." Do not, in other words, Eisenhower wrote his brother, get bogged down in detail. Save your time and energy for the really important matters. Be willing to delegate responsibility.[1] Eisenhower was not just handing out "trite but nevertheless sound truisms," as he put it—these were the rules he later followed himself as Supreme Commander.

At the height of the European campaign the total strength of SHAEF was 16,312. Nearly 1600 of those serving at SHAEF were U.S. officers; another 1229 were British officers. The remainder were British or American enlisted men.[2] In theory all matters moved up the chain of command to the Supreme Commander, his deputy, and his chief of staff, but in practice Tedder's role was usually advisory and he seldom served as an executive agent. The principal sections included the deputies to the chief of staff, the Allied naval commander, the air commander in chief (a position that disappeared in late 1944 when Leigh-Mallory left), the secretary, General Staff (the record-keeping agency), and the five G-divisions. Most of the men Eisenhower relied upon for advice and information could be found in one of these sections, officers like Humfrey Gale, the chief administrative officer (a deputy chief of staff), Morgan (also one of Smith's deputies), Whiteley (G-2 and later G-3), Bull (G-3), and Strong (G-2). SHAEF had twelve additional divisions and five "missions" (to France, the Netherlands, Belgium, Denmark, and Norway).

In order to administer the bureaucracy effectively, Eisenhower had to make firm decisions about those matters to which he would give his personal attention and those problems which he would leave to the various divisions. Smith's role was crucial. The chief of staff had to see to it that the divisions did their work, that SHAEF functioned efficiently, that the Supreme Commander did not waste his time, and that Eisenhower did deal with those matters on which only the Supreme Commander could make the decision. General rules often did not apply, and Smith frequently had to make fast, intuitive judgments as to whether to make a decision himself or to present it to Eisenhower.[3]

The process of bringing an issue before Eisenhower began at nine-thirty in the morning, when Smith held his regular conference. The heads of the G-divisions attended, along with Smith's deputies, other officers who had business to bring up, and, in the most important role of co-ordinator, the SGS (Secretary, General Staff). SGS decided upon the daily meeting's agenda. As in Algiers, Smith rode SGS hard, and in seventeen months three SGS heads resigned because they could not endure his browbeating. SGS kept a copy of all incoming and outgoing messages which were originated, seen by, or sent to Eisenhower, Smith, or the deputies, and a copy of all reports from the divisions. These logs and records, plus a daily summary of decisions made, gave Smith and Eisenhower a means of checking on the SHAEF divisions. Smith also had SGS bring into the meetings the relevant files, so that if he wanted to check back on an issue he could do so right there. After discussion, Smith would either bring the matter to Eisenhower, act himself, or send the problem back to the SHAEF divisions concerned with it. In the case of a matter requiring the Supreme Commander's attention, since Eisenhower was out of the office, visiting the front lines, almost as much as he was there, Smith—who ordinarily stayed behind to mind the store—often just had to delay. One of the first things Eisenhower would do when he returned from a trip was go over the log of incoming and outgoing cables.

After his own conference adjourned and if Eisenhower was in, Smith would go to the Supreme Commander's office (he was the only SHAEF officer who had the right to walk in without knocking) and lay before Eisenhower the problems that required the Supreme Commander's attention. Smith also brought along those officers he thought Eisenhower would want present to help deal with a given matter. Ordinarily Eisenhower dealt personally with all operational matters involving the army groups, so Bull, the G-3, usually attended. If the issue involved De Gaulle the head of the SHAEF Mission to France would be there; if it concerned supplies G-4 would attend. After discussion Eisenhower would make his decision. If the matter were important enough, or if he were so inclined, Eisenhower himself would dictate the outgoing message that initiated action, but more often the officer concerned prepared the message for Eisenhower's signature.

Every message that went out from SHAEF carried Eisenhower's signature, but obviously he did not see more than a fraction of the enormous number of cables and telegrams that bore his name. SHAEF had strict rules to govern the procedure so that Smith, SGS, and Eisenhower himself could quickly check back to find out whether or not Eisenhower had been aware of a given message. The SHAEF message form had a space for the name of the originating division or drafter. In addition, personal pronouns were used only when a message was prepared by the Supreme Commander, when it was prepared at his specific direction (Bull, for example, drafted most of the directives as well as the sitreps to CCS, but only after full discussion with Eisenhower), or when Eisenhower had personal knowledge of the matter at hand and approved of the context of the message.

SHAEF had the strengths and weaknesses common to most bureaucracies. It helped organize the Anglo-American military effort, provided order, system, and predictability, gave Eisenhower the information he had to have in order to make decisions, and made it possible for him to check on how well his decisions had been implemented. At the same time, however, it discouraged initiative and encouraged caution. Ideas and suggestions generated within SHAEF moved slowly up the chain of command, subject to protests all along the way. The tendency was to find consensus, which meant compromise, which in turn usually meant caution. SHAEF seldom presented split position papers to Eisenhower; rather, all protests were first taken into account and disposed of, so that by the time Eisenhower saw a proposal it had nearly universal support from his staff. But the support, more often than not, was negative rather than positive—if it made few men happy, it left almost no one unhappy.

The formal administrative arrangements worked well. The system that Smith devised insured that Eisenhower did not waste his time on trivia but enabled him to be involved in all important decisions. For the most part, Eisenhower knew what was going on, or if he did not Smith did. By checking with SGS they could both quickly find out what work had been done or needed doing. Eisenhower made mistakes, but except in rare instances it was not because he was unaware of what was happening.

A long message to Marshall in mid-January, 1945 illustrated the way the office worked. Marshall wanted to know Eisenhower's future plans and needs so that he could be prepared for his meetings with the British Chiefs at Malta and Yalta. Eisenhower met with Smith and Brigadier General Arthur Nevins (the brother of historian Allan Nevins), chief of the Operations Section, G-3. After Eisenhower presented his thoughts Nevins drafted a message to Marshall. Eisenhower reviewed it, making a number of stylistic changes and several of substance. He then sent it back to Nevins with a covering memorandum, explaining why he had made the changes and adding, "Don't hesitate in criticizing anything I have said."[4]

Much of this kind of work was done informally. Here again Smith's role was crucial. Eisenhower would send him a memorandum and expect him to follow up on it. On September 30, 1944, for example, the Supreme Commander reminded Smith that he was "terribly anxious about Antwerp. . . . Please have both G-3 and General Gale keep in the closest possible touch with all the planning on this affair so that we may always be in a position to do whatever we can to help."[5] Smith saw to it that SHAEF got in touch with Twenty-first Army Group about the situation, getting plans from Montgomery's staff officers and talking to De Guingand himself on the telephone.

Eisenhower often made decisions and took action when he was visiting commanders in the field. Upon returning to his office he would send a memorandum to Smith to inform him of what he had done and to insure that the action was made a part of the record. On December 15, 1944, for example, he told Smith he had just talked with General Lee of Com Z and ordered him to use civilians instead of soldiers in all static messes, barracks, and so on. He wanted Spaatz and Bradley to do the same thing, and asked Smith to see to it that SHAEF followed the same policy with regard to its orderlies and cooks.[6]

Like his Commander, Smith wore two hats. In addition to his SHAEF duties he was chief of staff to the Commanding General, European Theater of Operations. Eisenhower used Smith as his executive agent for ETO business, consulted with him (as well as with the field commanders) on recommended promotions for the American Army, and apart from the supply responsibilities exercised by Lee, left much of the detail of running the theater to Smith. "Where a combat commander requests an officer by name for a key position," Eisenhower instructed Smith in late September, "we will normally make a special effort to obtain this officer whether he is here or in the United States."[7] The same day Eisenhower told Smith that "when officers are relieved from duty because of failure in combat, all concerned . . . will be very careful not to hound tactical commanders for a mass of detail." Smith should see to it, Eisenhower said, that the commanding officer give a written statement about the reasons for the removal and make a recommendation as to what type of work the officer in question could handle. That was all. "I do not want to appear too arbitrary or unjust," Eisenhower said, "but we cannot have combat commanders working hours at a time to prepare long lists and detailed affidavits and reports. . . ."[8]

Some ETO matters, although detailed and often petty, Eisenhower could not escape. The American Army jealously guards the lines of responsibility, and on some issues the commanding general, and only the commanding general, must make the final decision. This especially applied to court-martial sentences. Eisenhower had to approve every sentence handed down by the military courts in ETO, from the firing squad (death was imposed once on a deserter) to a short prison sentence. Eisenhower ordinarily spent his Sunday mornings going over court-martial records with Brigadier General Edward C. Betts, the theater judge advocate. Betts had been professor of law at West Point, and Eisenhower relied heavily on his judgment in deciding whether or not to be lenient.

Eisenhower delegated much of the routine ETO administration to

General Lee but retained control over key problems that required War Department action, such as the ammunition shortage and the replacement problem. The latter was not something that suddenly arose during the Battle of the Bulge; two days before the German attack, for example, Eisenhower told Handy, "We are doing every possible thing to help strengthen our position in manpower. . . . You may be perfectly certain that we understand the seriousness of the problem at home, yet our replacement situation is exceedingly dark."[9] Eisenhower also used his influence when Lee could not get what ETO needed. In late October the War Department ordered the return to New York of ten tugs that were being used for unloading in ETO. Lee's staff sent a routine message back asking for permission to retain the tugs for a month or so. Marshall turned down the request, saying that it appeared unwarranted because of the urgent requirements in the Southwest Pacific.

Eisenhower then met with Lee and his staff; after the meeting he sent a long cable to Somervell, asking him to intercede with Marshall. Eisenhower said the tugs were essential to improvement in SHAEF's supply position and Lee had demonstrated an "undeniable need" for them. "I want to assure you personally of my sympathy with your gigantic problems and my earnest desire so to conduct our own logistical activities as to minimize wastefulness in the use of ships," Eisenhower told Somervell, but "we have here a problem that has never before been met in warfare and therefore cannot be solved by mere application of rules applicable where conditions have not been so difficult nor the battle problem so gigantic." The Supreme Commander promised that "this is the final message I will send on the subject of these tugs," and he hoped Somervell would meet his "earnest request." In this case even Eisenhower's personal intervention was not enough; Somervell turned him down.[10]

One responsibility Eisenhower never delegated was promotions. He insisted that any time ETO sent to the War Department a recommendation for promotion to colonel or above it be cleared with him first, and he handled promotions with as much care as he did his relations with Montgomery. He took the problem seriously partly because it was difficult to retain balance between staff and line, partly because he realized Marshall had to depend on him for information on ETO officers, partly because as an old career soldier himself he felt promotion was a serious matter to be treated carefully, but chiefly because promotions—which are in effect assignments of greater responsibility—involve a judgment on and prediction of leadership ability. To leave promotions to others, Eisenhower felt, would be to abdicate command responsibility.

Throughout the war Eisenhower kept a personal list of the officers he thought were doing well and deserved to be promoted. Before making a recommendation to Marshall, however, he checked his opinion of an officer with his senior subordinates. A memorandum he sent to Bradley, Smith, and Spaatz in late October was typical. He asked them to rate and then list in order of priority the twenty-five or thirty-five lieutenant generals and major generals they had observed during the war, both in France and the Mediterranean. He wanted the list so that when the time came, at the end of the war, to decide who should keep his stars in the Regular Army and who should be reduced to his permanent rank, he would be ready to present a validated opinion to Marshall.[11]

Eisenhower worked closely with Marshall on promotions. At the conclusion of the Bulge, for example, the Supreme Commander said he wanted to get more young men into command of the divisions and corps of ETO. Some of the older men currently in command would be retiring as soon as the shooting stopped; Eisenhower thought that, by putting generals in their early thirties in charge now, the men who would be senior in the Army after the war could gain valuable experience.[12] Marshall agreed and complied. The Chief of Staff also asked Eisenhower's opinion on promotions to three- and four-star rank. He was preparing a list to submit to Congress but he did not want the Army to appear greedy. Eisenhower argued that the Navy already had four full admirals and was going to nominate more; "in these circumstances you could make six or seven on your first list and be well on the conservative side considering the size of the Army." He thought Bradley, Spaatz, Somervell, Handy, McNarney, and a senior officer from the Pacific ought to get four stars immediately, with other four-star rank promotions to follow.[13]

On February 1 Eisenhower made a list of the commanders he had worked with during the war. He intended to use it as a basis for either recommending promotions to Marshall or making promotions himself after the war. The list was based on value of service and qualifications for future usefulness. Bradley and Spaatz stood at the top, followed in order by Smith, Patton, Clark, Truscott, Doolittle, Gerow, Collins, Patch, Hodges, and Simpson. Eisenhower made comments on each officer (the list extended to thirty-eight generals). Bradley was "quiet but magnetic leader; able, rounded field commander; determined and resourceful; modest." Patton was a "dashing fighter, shrewd, courageous," while Eisenhower thought Smith was "outstanding as C/S of Superior Hqs. Firm, loyal, highly intelligent." Nearly all the comments were positive; some were just more enthusiastic than others.[14]

Eisenhower also evaluated every division commander coming into ETO. If he did not know the man he would discuss him with Bradley or Smith, and if any one of the three generals disapproved, Eisenhower would so inform Marshall and a new commander for the division would be appointed. Eisenhower made every decision on moving generals up from division to corps, or from corps to army, command.

The surest way for an American general in ETO to make a poor impression on Eisenhower was to try to boost or glorify himself. A flagrant example came during the Battle of the Bulge. A division commander wrote Eisenhower to ask that he be given command of a corps. He said his division had done well and he had proved himself capable of handling a corps, and added that he made his request to satisfy his "personal and professional pride." On the day after Christmas Eisenhower dictated his reply. He began by saying he did not need to be reminded of the division's record: "I make it my business to keep in as close contact with such things as is possible, for the reason that the positioning of higher commanders is one of my chief preoccupations and responsibilities." Eisenhower confessed that he was "astonished" that anyone would feel it necessary to write to him on the subject.

"I would be truly disturbed," Eisenhower continued, "if I should interpret literally your statement that personal and professional pride prompted your request." The Supreme Commander felt that any man who had his country's trust to the extent that he had fifteen thousand young Americans under his command had already received full acknowledgment of his abilities. He also thought that in a well-run division the relationship between the commander and his subordinates should be so close that "any thought of separation should arouse disappointment rather than anticipation." Eisenhower concluded, "I assure you that no soldier can come out of this war with greater professional stature or personal reputation than that of a truly successful division commander." The general did not get command of a corps.[15]

Another personal responsibility the Supreme Commander had was to keep in close touch with the Chief of Staff and his problems. Eisenhower met it through voluminous correspondence and through Marshall's fairly frequent trips to Europe. One thing the Chief was determined to accomplish after the war, before America settled into her anticipated postwar complacency, was a program of universal military training. He had officers in the War Department working on the project, but he wanted Eisenhower's help too. In October he wrote Eisenhower to report on a survey that had been conducted with military personnel returned from overseas. The men had been invited to express freely any complaints they had. Marshall said the complaints were "too numerous and too serious to be considered as typical of the normal soldier's discontent," and added that he took them seriously. He realized that these enlisted men were also voters, and that a universal military training program would need strong support among veterans in order to get it through Congress. "A great deal of this is paralleled by the reaction of the enlisted men in the rear areas of the old AEF," he said, referring to his World War I experience, "and which had something to do with the failure to establish universal military training at that time. . . ." Eisenhower sent a copy of Marshall's letter on to Smith, with instructions to set up a staff under a brigadier general "responsible to me," and put it to work improving conditions for enlisted men in ETO.[16]

The second major part of Marshall's desired postwar program was the integration of the armed forces under a single Chief of Staff, with a single Secretary of Defense. The JCS, on Marshall's urging, had set up in May 1944 a special board to study the reorganization of national defense and to make recommendations for a peacetime military establishment. Marshall talked to Eisenhower about the subject on one of his visits to Europe. Eisenhower accepted Marshall's argument, and when the board came to ETO to interview senior officers, Eisenhower said he favored a single Department of Defense. The board made such a recommendation, but Admiral King would not accept it. King argued that centralized control was not necessary and that better results could be expected from friendly co-operation. Marshall replied that such co-operation "has been difficult and incomplete even in war, and will be infinitely more difficult in peace," but he could not convince the admiral, and the problem had to be faced anew after the war.[17]

Universal military training and a single Department of Defense were as much political issues as they were military. Eisenhower needed no reminder of his political responsibilities, and when congressmen came visiting in his theater he saw to it that they received VIP treatment. When seventeen members of the House Military Affairs Committee came to Paris in December, Eisenhower entertained them in the Trianon Palace.

One of the congressmen presented Eisenhower with a bottle of good bourbon whiskey. A few days later *Stars and Stripes* reported that Eisenhower had sent the whiskey to a nearby field hospital. When Eisenhower read the story he berated Butcher (who had taken a position with SHAEF Public Relations Division), saying that every congressman in the party would know that the story was a lie. Butcher replied that the congressmen, being politicians, would not mind, and asked what had happened to the bourbon. "Why, dammit," Eisenhower replied, "the Congressmen drank it before lunch."[18]

As Montgomery never tired of pointing out, Eisenhower had world-wide responsibilities. These included not only relations with Churchill, De Gaulle, and the heads of the occupied countries in Europe, but also the touchy problem of establishing and maintaining contact with the Soviets. Not until the end of 1943 had Stalin allowed the Western Allies to send a military mission to Moscow, and even then the only information the mission received was advance copies of the Red Army communiqués that were published in the press. In late October the SHAEF staff sent a message to the CCS, pointing out that liaison with the Red Army would soon be required to insure co-ordination of action by the air forces and full co-operation on other matters.[19] The CCS replied that the Soviets should be approached cautiously. Eisenhower then suggested that a SHAEF liaison group be sent to Red Army headquarters, one that would "be very small with the idea of avoiding suspicion on the part of the Russians." The prime need was to co-ordinate air action in order to avoid the bombing of each other's forces. Once the air group was established in Moscow and information on front lines and proposed movements was flowing freely, other groups could be established.[20] But the Russians held back, and nothing came of the attempted liaison.

When the Bulge began, Eisenhower's G-2 officers reported to him that a number of the German divisions involved in the Ardennes attack had come from the eastern front. On December 21 Eisenhower informed the CCS of this development and pointed out that "if this trend continues it will affect the decisions which I have to make regarding future strategy in the west." It was essential, therefore, that SHAEF learn from the Russians what their intentions were. If the Red Army was about to launch a major offensive, "I would condition my plans accordingly." Could the CCS help him get the information from the Russians?[21]

The CCS turned to Churchill and Roosevelt, who between them were able to convince Stalin to receive representatives from SHAEF. The heads of government were able to make the arrangements, and Eisenhower decided to send Tedder, Bull, and a G-2 officer. The SHAEF party was delayed by weather and did not arrive in Moscow until January 14. Tedder saw Stalin the next evening; the Russian leader informed him that the Red Army offensive had already begun (January 12) and said he had wanted to wait for better weather but had advanced the date of the operation in order to help SHAEF's embattled forces (the German offensive in the Ardennes had, in fact, been stopped two weeks earlier).[22]

Tedder then explained to Stalin Eisenhower's plans for the spring campaign. Stalin approved of them and promised to keep the enemy busy so that there would be no more transfers by the Germans from the eastern to the western front. The Russian leader commented that the Germans had more stubbornness than brains, as their stupid attack in the Ardennes demonstrated. In parting, he told Tedder that he considered it proper, sound, and selfish policy for all the Allies to help one another. It would be as foolish for him to stand aside while the Germans annihilated the British and Americans, he said, as it would be for them to allow Hitler to crush the Red Army.

The members of the Allied Military Mission in Moscow thought the talks between Tedder and Stalin had done much to clear the air and improve relations in the Alliance, and they credited Tedder's blunt, direct approach for this achievement. This approach reflected a slight shift in the expression of Allied attitudes toward the Russians. In January Eisenhower had sent an eloquent telegram of congratulations to the Russians on the opening of their offensive. Marshall saw a copy and told Eisenhower, "In future I suggest that you approach them [the Russians] in simple Main Street Abilene style. They are rather cynically disposed toward the diplomatic phrasing of our compliments and seem almost to appreciate downright rough talk of which I give a full measure."[23]

Although Eisenhower commanded one of the greatest fighting machines in the world, had at his disposal a bureaucracy larger than many governments, and controlled more raw power than most nations had, he was still only an agent, not a policy maker. However wide the range of his duties and responsibilities, he could not decide where or against whom the Anglo-American forces would fight, or the shape of postwar Europe, nor treatment of the country he was struggling to defeat. He did not question these limitations, but he did feel that he had a right—indeed, a duty—to try to influence the decisions. He believed that he knew as much about the situation in Europe as anyone within the State Department or the White House, and he thought he should be heard on the subject.

There were practical factors that in any case forced him to raise the question of the postwar organization of Europe. In September 1944 De Gaulle informed Eisenhower that he wanted some French troops to participate in the war on German soil. Eisenhower agreed to see to it that at least one French corps crossed the border. As Eisenhower told the CCS, this brought up "the question of what area of Germany, if any, is to be occupied by the French after the defeat of Germany." The position of the French First Army on the battle line meant that it would go into Germany in the neighborhood of the Swiss and Austrian frontiers, but De Gaulle might want to occupy a different area of Germany. Eisenhower reported that if the French President asked him about it "I intend to say that during the period of my command the occupation of Germany will be on a strictly military and Allied basis." He would run the occupation in accordance with military requirements "and regardless of any political considerations. . . ."[24]

On the face of it, Eisenhower's statement represented a complete commitment on his part to the deeply held American tradition that soldiers do not mix in politics. But in fact he was making an attempt to influence policy. The European Advisory Commission (EAC), composed of representatives from the Big Three, had been working on an occupation policy for Germany since the beginning of 1944. It had decided— over Eisenhower's protests—to divide Germany into three zones, with each of the Allies responsible for one area only. No decision on French participation had yet been made, nor had the heads of government ratified the EAC program.

Eisenhower was aware of this and, although he had discarded his original idea of three-power co-operation in Germany (that is, no division into zones), he still felt that the West should stick together, keep SHAEF intact, and run the British and American zones as if they were one. He realized that the trend of thought in Washington on the subject was against him, for it was feared that the Russians would see Anglo-American co-operation as an attempt to gang up on the U.S.S.R. Eisenhower told Marshall this had not been his intention; "my thoughts were restricted to the military problem; that is, the use of armed forces for carrying out the decisions of the Governments." He wanted to continue the military system that had brought about the victory. The decision, however, went against Eisenhower, and he accepted it. On September 25 he told Marshall that he was satisfied that his views had been fully considered by his superiors "and since they have decided otherwise, this is the last time that my own ideas on the subject will be expressed."[25]

Within the context of national zones, however, problems remained. The War Department was working on deciding the size of the American occupation force, and in October Eisenhower told Marshall that although he felt the ground forces allotted were sufficient he wanted a larger air force. His reasons again, while partly military, were primarily political. Once the Americans went into their own zone, he said, "there would probably ensue a period in which frequent and prompt demonstrations of real strength might be a most economical way of enforcing our policies and regulations." The mobility of a large number of bombers would be of great help in such situations. Eisenhower said he had talked to Spaatz about the problem, and "we felt that as long as Europe was in a state of almost violent unrest, any American contingent left here should be a powerful one and capable of instantaneous and effective action in any direction, possibly even outside our own area."

Finally, there were the Russians with which to contend. Eisenhower had no inkling of the size of the force Stalin intended to leave in eastern Germany, but he did know that America was far ahead of the Soviet Union in air strength. "Consqeuently, we felt that no matter how strong the Russian occupational force might be, the possession of a quite powerful bomber force would place the U.S. contingent on a substantial basis of equality and this might conceivably be a most desirable state of affairs."[26] The problem was left to be settled later, but for the most part the bombers were not retained on the Continent.

Sometimes Eisenhower got involved in political issues because high officials wanted his opinion. In late October the Assistant Secretary of War, John J. McCloy, wrote Eisenhower a long letter on American occupation policy. McCloy said the War Department was advising the President "that the government of Germany should be instituted on a military basis . . . [with] single, undivided responsibility in the military commander." Eisenhower would be that commander, and McCloy wanted to protect him from a mass of civilian agencies and advisers. He proposed, therefore, to appoint a single civilian, with a title of High Commissioner, who would be directly under Eisenhower and who would handle all the civilian agencies. McCloy wanted to know what Eisenhower thought of the idea and how he reacted to having Judge Robert P. Patterson, the Under Secretary of War, take the position.

Eisenhower was delighted. As had been the case in North Africa and Italy, he was finding it difficult to co-ordinate the action of the maze of agencies that had dealings with SHAEF one way or another. There were nearly a dozen of them, including the Civil Affairs Division of the War Department and a similar U.S.-British agency, the Combined Civil Affairs Committee, his own civil affairs advisers on the SHAEF staff, and committees and councils set up by the U. S. War, State, and Treasury departments. Eisenhower said he very much appreciated McCloy's efforts "to protect us from a complex system of advisers which would only add to the difficulties of a straightforward problem of military government." Patterson was quite acceptable, although "I always had you yourself in mind for this particular assignment."[27]

One reason McCloy had wanted to settle the administrative arrangements early was that he was disturbed at the tendency of various and diverse governmental officials to advance "plans" for the American sector, such as the "so called 'Morgenthau Plan,'" which, supported by the Secretary of the Treasury, called for dismemberment of German industry. At Quebec in the fall of 1944 both Churchill and Roosevelt had given tentative approval to the idea of making Germany a pastoral state, evidently without giving much thought to the matter; both later changed their minds. Stimson, McCloy reported, had objected to certain aspects of the "Morgenthau Plan," and the press had oversimplified the issue into "hard" and "soft" schools. Speculation was going on over the identity of the High Commissioner, with each school advancing a candidate.

Eisenhower was very much involved in the discussion of how to treat a defeated Germany. Morgenthau had been in London in August 1944 and spent an afternoon with Eisenhower. Two years later he claimed that it was during this discussion that the idea of destroying German industry came to him, and he credited Eisenhower with first suggesting it. Eisenhower's own memory of the conversation was different. Replying to Morgenthau's postwar statement, he recalled that the views he had advanced were: the German people should be made to feel a sense of guilt for the terrible tragedy; Germany's warmaking power should be eliminated; leading Nazis, Gestapo, and S.S. members, along with soldiers who had engaged in criminal acts, should be punished, and the German General Staff destroyed. "In eliminating German warmaking ability," he added, "care should be taken to see that the Germans could make a living," so that they did not become a charity burden on the American taxpayer. He thought the Ruhr should be worked by Germans under direct Allied supervision and control.[28] Eisenhower may have been trying to fit his wartime views into an acceptable Cold War mold, but in April 1945 he did what he could to avoid useless or unnecessary damage to existing industrial facilities in the Ruhr, and virtually called to a halt air attacks against Germany's major industrial region.[29] This came, of course, rather late in the war.

But at the beginning of 1945 his task was not to set occupation policy or pass judgment on the treatment of the German nation. Before these questions could be met, he first had to bring about a German defeat.

Part IV

THE LAST CAMPAIGN

[*January 1945–May 1945*]

T HE great question after the Battle of the Bulge was how long it would take to end the war. The great controversy remaining was where the AEF should put the bulk of its strength in order to hasten the final victory. Brooke and Montgomery, supported by Churchill, continued to advocate what amounted to a single thrust in the north. They thought Eisenhower's plan of closing to the Rhine all along his front before crossing the river north of the Ruhr would be disastrously slow, extending the European battle into the late summer or even the fall of 1945.

Eisenhower continually rejected the British arguments. He did not want to take the risk of stopping Twelfth and Sixth Army Groups where they were while giving priority to Twenty-first Army Group, because he feared that the Germans might launch another major counterattack. The armies assigned to Bradley and Devers did not have good defensive positions and were therefore vulnerable; but once they had reached the Rhine they could hold the line with far less troops than were needed to maintain their current positions. Eisenhower could then put more men into the offensives across the Rhine. Although he consistently denied that he had any political motives, he remained unwilling to give all the glory to Montgomery. Most important by far was his belief that his plan would lead to the destruction of the bulk of the Wehrmacht west of the Rhine and thus bring about an earlier victory.

CHAPTER 18

The Rhineland Battles

At the end of the first week of 1945 pessimism was widespread in the Allied high command. The Bulge was being eliminated, but because of the deep snows, overcast skies, and freezing weather the AEF was unable to cut off any major German units in the Ardennes. Ground soldiers were deeply disappointed. The Germans, Eisenhower noted in a review he sent to the army group commanders, were "fighting with great stubbornness," even the newly raised divisions composed of boys and old men who were "only vaguely acquainted with their tasks." There were many instances of men who, "although wounded for two days, refuse to give up the fight." There was a new fanaticism on the part of the enemy and Eisenhower had "no doubt that the Germans are making a supreme and all-out effort. . . ." He said that in his opinion the Ardennes and Alsace battles were "only episodes" and that the Allies must expect further action in other areas.[1]

Airmen were glum. Their theories about the effectiveness of bombing, based on Douhet, had proven unsound. The Germans, far from having their morale shattered as Douhet had predicted, were more determined than ever. Some fliers insisted this was because strategic bombing had not been given a real opportunity to show what it could do, but others were beginning to have their doubts. On January 7 Arnold wrote Spaatz, "We have a superiority of at least 5 to 1 now against Germany and yet, in spite of all our hopes, anticipations, dreams and plans, we have as yet not been able to capitalize to the extent which we should. We may not be able to force capitulation of the Germans by air attacks, but on the other hand, with this tremendous striking power, it would seem to me that we should get much better and much more decisive results than we are getting now." Arnold said he was not criticizing, "because frankly I don't know the answer and what I am now doing is letting my thoughts run wild with the hope that out of this you may get a glimmer, a light, a new thought, or something which will help us to bring this war to a close sooner."[2]

Marshall, who had not had any pet theories shattered and was consequently not as upset as Arnold, nevertheless was sufficiently concerned to query Eisenhower as to his plans. On January 8 he told Eisenhower that although he had given strict orders that no one should add to Eisenhower's burdens by asking him questions, "it may be . . . that we now face a situation requiring major decisions in order to prevent this war from dragging on for some time." He wanted Eisenhower's broad estimate of the resources the AEF would require and the steps that needed to be taken "to bring this war in Europe to a quick conclusion."

Eisenhower's reply of January 15 was long and complex. He had studied the problem minutely and he too was concerned, although not as pessimistic as some of his superiors. The key to the situation, he felt, was what happened on the Russian front. If the Red Army offensive was weak and ineffective, the Germans could safely keep a hundred full-strength divisions on the AEF front; if the Russian offensive "really gets to rolling" the Germans would be hard put to maintain eighty under-strength divisions in the West. "I do not even mention a lack of Russian offensive," Eisenhower added, "for without this a quick decision cannot be obtained. We would have to mobilize much French manpower and additional U.S. divisions."

Eisenhower's present strength was seventy-one divisions, but many of the U.S. divisions were seriously under strength in infantry. The French divisions had a low combat value. If schedules were met the AEF would have eighty-five divisions by May, of which eight would be French, but "French divisions are always a questionable asset." It was because of these figures, which indicated that Eisenhower could never expect, no matter what happened in the East, to have overwhelming ground superiority, that he insisted on closing to the Rhine before crossing the river.

"Unless we get a good natural line for the defensive portions of our long front," Eisenhower emphasized by underscoring, *"we will use up a lot of divisions in defense."* If his forces were up to the Rhine by spring, he said he would need to keep only twenty-five divisions on defense and in reserve, thus freeing sixty divisions for the offensive. But if the line were maintained as it currently existed, he would need to hold forty-five

on defense and in reserve, leaving only forty for the offensive. The reason for this was that the current line had few good natural defensive barriers, and nothing to compare with the Rhine as an obstacle. As things stood, the Germans could safely concentrate for counterattack behind the West Wall, then strike out against the AEF almost anywhere.

Eisenhower wanted to send thirty-five divisions on the major offensive north of the Ruhr. He also wanted to maintain flexibility and be able to reinforce success. If Bradley's crossing in the Frankfurt area showed promise, Eisenhower was determined to give him more troops. In order to do this he needed a reserve of at least twenty divisions. There were two ways to get the reserve: by closing to the Rhine and then pulling units out of the line, or by raising more divisions in the United States and stepping up the program of rearming the French. For a variety of reasons, neither of the latter alternatives was feasible. "This fact brings up again the great desirability of destroying German forces west of the Rhine, and closing up to that river throughout our front."

Throughout his review Eisenhower stressed the need for flexibility. "If we jam our head up against a concentrated defense at a selected spot," he declared, "we must be able to go forward elsewhere. Flexibility requires reserves." Flexibility was Eisenhower's outstanding tactical quality. He never allowed his mind to become set or rigid, and he was usually successful at creating tactical situations that presented him with a number of alternatives. This in turn allowed him to exploit any lucky break. Flexibility was what set him apart from most planners, including his own G-3. One never knew what to expect in war, except that the unexpected was likely. Only those who were ready could take advantage of the breaks, and to be ready it was imperative to have reserves.[3]

On January 17 Eisenhower told Montgomery that he had finally made Brooke understand "what I have been talking about in saying we must secure a decent line on which to station defensive forces so as to permit the greatest possible concentration for our offensives." Referring to Brooke's and Montgomery's desire to cross the Rhine north of the Ruhr as soon as Twenty-first Army Group reached the river, no matter where the line was elsewhere, Eisenhower added, "I like to be as bold as anyone else, but I know that we cannot go into a full blooded offensive and worry constantly about security." A major aspect of Eisenhower's operating strategy was his belief that Hitler would never willingly give up ground. Once the AEF was through the West Wall, the logical course for Von Rundstedt to follow would be to fall back across the Rhine, the last great defensive barrier between Eisenhower's armies and Berlin. But Eisenhower was certain that Hitler would force Von Rundstedt to fight in the area between the West Wall and the Rhine. This would give the AEF an opportunity to destroy the remaining German armored units, to kill or capture large numbers of German infantry, and, most important, to make the actual crossing of the Rhine easier. "We must substantially defeat the German forces west of the Rhine if we are to make a truly successful invasion with all forces available," Eisenhower explained to Montgomery.[4]

The first step in the program was to eliminate the Colmar pocket. Eisenhower had a number of conferences with the French in a vain attempt to inspire them to action. They resulted in an argument with De Gaulle, who charged that Eisenhower had made unfair accusations against the French forces. Eisenhower denied the charge but he also decided that the French could never do the job by themselves. In mid-January, therefore, he sent five U.S. divisions and 12,000 service troops from SHAEF reserve to Sixth Army Group and placed a U.S. corps under General de Lattre to help him reduce the pocket. The attack began on January 20; by early February the pocket was gone.[5]

From January 14 to 20 Eisenhower was in his office every day, and each morning he met with Smith, Spaatz, Strong, and Whiteley. The result of these discussions was the final SHAEF plan to implement Eisenhower's general concept of how the last campaign should proceed. Eisenhower himself dictated a seven-page cable on January 20 to the CCS outlining his intentions.

He said his operations would fall into three phases: first, the destruction of enemy forces west of the Rhine; second, crossing the river; third, the destruction of enemy forces east of the Rhine and an advance into Germany. He intended to put all the force he could into the crossing north of the Ruhr, then with what was left over launch a supporting attack in the south, but he wanted to retain enough flexibility to switch the main effort elsewhere if Montgomery encountered strong resistance.

Because he wanted to cross the Rhine where it would do the most good, at points from which his troops could overrun Germany, Eisenhower took up the three phases of his over-all plan in reverse order, starting with phase three. There were two main avenues of approach into Germany: north of the Ruhr across the plains of north Germany and on to Berlin; and from Mainz on the Rhine to Frankfurt on the Main River, then north to Kassel. An advance north of the Ruhr had the great advantage of denying to the Germans the manufactured goods coming from the cluster of industrial cities in the area. Montgomery's troops could cut the eastern exits from the Ruhr by enveloping the area, and the southern exits could be blocked by air action. A further advantage was that the area north of the Ruhr offered the most suitable terrain in Germany for mobile operations, and it was in this type of operation that the Allies had their greatest superiority.

The importance of the Ruhr could not be overemphasized. Eisenhower's original directive had instructed him to undertake operations aimed at the heart of Germany, and SHAEF had always considered the Ruhr to be that heart. As Smith put it after the war, the factories and blast furnaces of the Ruhr "pumped lifeblood into the [German] military system. Once the Ruhr was sealed off, the heart would cease to beat."[6] Because this was true, one trouble with an approach north of the Ruhr was that it was predictable to the Germans, and thus Eisenhower could expect Von Rundstedt to bend every effort to hold the Rhine north of the area. In order to meet and overcome the anticipated strong resistance Eisenhower needed to put powerful forces into the attack. The trouble was that the transportation network could only support thirty-five divisions across the Rhine on Montgomery's front. This meant that Eisenhower could not be as strong at the crucial point as he would have liked, but it also meant that he would have a reserve to use elsewhere (assuming he had closed to the Rhine).*

Then Eisenhower turned his attention to consideration of operations from Frankfurt. He felt that once Bradley's men had reached that city they could move almost at will straight north toward Kassel. There were valuable airfields around Frankfurt that could provide support for both Bradley and Montgomery, and Frankfurt was itself an industrial center, making it all in all a prize worth having. Eisenhower admitted that the advance from Frankfurt to Kassel would be over terrain less suitable for mobile warfare than the north German plain, "but once we reached the Kassel area there would be several possibilities of further developments," such as a thrust northward to link up with Montgomery and seal off the Ruhr. Eisenhower had discussed, with Smith, Hannibal's encirclement of the Romans at Cannae, and they had that historic operation in mind when they drew up this plan.[7] From Kassel, Bradley could also move northeastward toward Berlin or straight east toward Leipzig. Getting to Kassel, in short, would give Eisenhower the flexibility he wanted.

---

* The logistical limitation was the fallacy in Brooke's thinking about putting all available force into Montgomery's attack. Even had Eisenhower wanted to do so, he could not have supported more than thirty-five divisions in the area. The thirty-five-division figure, incidentally, was Twenty-first Army Group's, not SHAEF's.

In the back of Eisenhower's mind, perhaps if only in his subconscious, was a desire to give Bradley the leading role in the campaign if the opportunity presented itself. An indication of this was his comment about the importance of Frankfurt. He said it ranked next to the Ruhr in the Germans' minds, so they would put large forces in the area to defend it. This would give Bradley "an opportunity of destroying considerable German Forces" around Frankfurt. There would be even more German forces facing Montgomery, but Eisenhower never thought of this as an advantage. The Supreme Commander, in short, welcomed an enemy concentration against Bradley, for he felt that Bradley would do a good job of both killing Germans and exploiting a victory. "Bradley," Eisenhower once said, "has never held back and never has 'paused to regroup' when he saw an opportunity to advance." The officers at SHAEF who had influence with Eisenhower shared this view; as Whiteley put it after the war, "The feeling was that if anything was to be done quickly, don't give it to Monty." He continued, "Monty was the last person Ike would have chosen for a drive on Berlin—Monty would have needed at least six months to prepare."[8] Aside from the military necessity of gaining an easily defended line across the Rhine, in other words, Eisenhower was thinking of using Bradley for the last campaign, and he could only do so if Bradley were across the Rhine.*

Turning back to phase two, Eisenhower judged that there were three sites suitable for crossing the Rhine: north of the Ruhr, around Cologne, and south of Mainz. Since troops in a bridgehead at Cologne would have no place to go, Eisenhower eliminated that possibility. In the north, the assault would have to be on a narrow front and would be opposed by the heaviest concentrations of German troop strength. "To effect a crossing in the north it may, therefore, be necessary to divert enemy forces by closing and perhaps crossing the Rhine in the Frankfurt sector. . . ."

In analyzing phase one, closing to the Rhine, Eisenhower repeated his arguments in favor of bringing all his forces up to the river before crossing. "My superiority on land . . . is not . . . so very great," he explained, and only by getting up to the Rhine "shall I be able to concentrate in great strength east of the river." In order to bring this about, he in-

* It should be noted that this is *not* saying Eisenhower was telling the British one thing while planning another. He did intend to make the major crossing on Twenty-first Army Group's front, and in fact did do so. But he also wanted flexibility, a point he made to the British time and again. There is, however, the subconscious attitude. To use the football jargon American officers were so fond of employing, Eisenhower was the quarterback. When he got down near the goal line, the back he relied upon was Bradley and, everything else being equal, he wanted Bradley to carry the ball.

tended to begin immediately an offensive west of the Rhine. First he would destroy the enemy north of the Moselle and close to the Rhine north of Duesseldorf, staying on the defensive south of the Moselle until this was accomplished. He would then take up the attack in the south. Finally he would cross the Rhine in the north and the south, then deploy thirty-five divisions north of the Ruhr and as many divisions as were left over in the Frankfurt area.[9]

That was the plan. It was a staff product, but throughout it bore Eisenhower's personal touch. Marshall and the JCS agreed with it, but Brooke was opposed and most of Eisenhower's field subordinates had objections—Bradley did not want to go on the defensive while Montgomery closed to the Rhine; Montgomery did not want to wait for Bradley before crossing the river himself, nor did he think Bradley should drive on Frankfurt, much less Kassel. But Eisenhower held firm. He would see to it that all aspects of his plan were implemented. Smith in an April press conference, when the operation had been successfully completed, said "Of all the campaigns I have known this one has followed most exactly the pattern of the commander who planned it. With but one small exception, it proceeded exactly as General Eisenhower originally worked it out."[10]

The first phase of the Rhineland campaign was Operation VERITABLE, an attack southeast from the Nijmegen area by the Canadian First Army along the east bank of the Rhine. While this operation was progressing Bradley's First Army was to seize the Roer River dams in order to stop the Germans from flooding the region. Next would come Operation GRENADE, an attack to the northeast by U. S. Ninth Army, designed to link up with the Canadians near Wesel and cut off the Germans facing the British Second Army. The second phase would be Operation LUMBERJACK, an advance to the Rhine north and south of Cologne by First Army, and farther south by Patton's Third Army in the Koblenz area. Finally, Sixth Army Group would begin Operation UNDERTONE, advancing to the Rhine south of the Moselle. When Devers' mission was accomplished, Montgomery would launch Operation PLUNDER, the main crossing of the Rhine.

Eisenhower had assigned Simpson's Ninth Army to Twenty-first Army Group for the campaign, but he made careful preparations to insure that the kind of bitterness that broke out during the Bulge because of command arrangements would not emerge again. Bradley kept pestering him to return Ninth Army to Twelfth Army Group; Eisenhower continued to point out that Montgomery would need help and turned down the request. Bradley was also upset because Eisenhower ordered him to cease his attacks in the Ardennes and to concentrate on getting the Roer dams. To make sure that Montgomery did not anger Bradley even further by making public statements about how well the G.I.s fought when given British leadership, on January 31 Eisenhower had Whiteley call Montgomery (who was in London on a short leave) and tell him that if any member of the Twenty-first Army Group talked to the press Ninth Army would return to Bradley's control.[11]

On February 2 Bradley began the attack toward the Roer dams. Progress, against determined German resistance, was slow but steady. By February 10, V Corps of Hodges' army had control of the dams, but the Germans had wrecked the discharge valves the previous evening, thereby creating a steady flooding that left the ground in front of Ninth Army, to the north, covered with water. It would take two weeks for the water to recede enough to allow Simpson to attack. The Canadians, meanwhile, began VERITABLE on February 8. The previous evening, Bomber Command had pounded the area in front of the Canadians, and at dawn British artillery put down a five-and-a-half-hour bombardment. The attack moved forward until late on February 9, when the Canadians got to Cleves. There they found that Bomber Command had used high-explosive bombs against the town, rather than the incendiaries requested, and a wilderness of craters and debris halted their progress. To make matters worse, the next two days the Germans, relying on the floods to hold up Simpson, shifted reinforcements into the area. Fanatical young Nazis in parachute units fought literally to the last man. Continuous rains poured down; the Canadians were forced to use amphibious vehicles to resupply the troops and evacuate the wounded. Still they pressed on; by February 23 they had overrun the first two of the three prepared German defensive positions.[12]

For Eisenhower, things were looking up. He was moving his Forward Headquarters to Reims in order to keep a closer watch on the battle. On February 20 he told Marshall, ". . . all our preparations are made, the troops are in fine fettle and there is no question in my mind that if we get off to a good start . . . the operations will be a complete success." Simpson was using the enforced delay on his movements to complete his preparations for crossing the Roer River and had reported that he would be able to start Operation GRENADE in three days. This would bring pressure to bear on the rear of the Germans facing the Canadian First Army and would eventually clear or destroy all German forces west of the Rhine on Twenty-first Army Group's front. "If the weather improves with the advancing spring," Eisenhower told Marshall, "I feel that matters will work out almost exactly as projected." Eisenhower confessed that the weather made him "terribly impatient . . . but I never forget the situation of the German and consequently never lose my basic optimism."[13]

The optimism was justified. Simpson's attack got across the Roer on the morning of February 23, and his armored units drove rapidly eastward. By March 2 Simpson had reached the Rhine, and three days later had cleared the river from Duesseldorf to Moers. He wanted then to make a surprise crossing of the Rhine, but Montgomery told him to stay where he was—Montgomery wished to avoid a battle in the industrial jungle of the Ruhr. More important, Ninth Army had already achieved Eisenhower's basic purpose in the Rhineland battle, for it had killed 6000 Germans and had taken 30,000 prisoners. General Henry Crerar, commanding the Canadian First Army, later declared that Simpson's "attack led to the strategic defeat of the enemy."[14]

Patton, meanwhile, was growing impatient. Bradley had told him to undertake an "active defense." He interpreted the orders liberally and fought his way through the West Wall, then began a drive east along the north bank of the Moselle to open a path to the Rhine. Patton wanted to repeat his August 1944 breakout. On February 20 he asked Bradley for additional divisions so that he could broaden his attack. Patton pointed out that the great proportion of U.S. troops in Europe were not fighting and warned that "all of us in high position will surely be held accountable for the failure to take offensive action when offensive action is possible." Bradley told him to remain calm. Eisenhower had decided to concentrate north of the Ruhr, and "regardless of what you and I think of this decision, we are good enough soldiers to carry out these orders." Bradley added that Eisenhower had given First and Third Armies the mission of crossing the Rhine in the Frankfurt area and suggested that Patton should refit and retrain his troops so that they could deliver a decisive blow when the proper moment came.[15]

Patton was a problem, but Eisenhower had Bradley to control him and did not need to worry too much about what Third Army would do next. The situation with De Gaulle was different. In mid-February, just when Eisenhower was beginning to make progress in building up a strong reserve, the French President told the Supreme Commander he wanted to pull three French divisions back into the interior of France. De Gaulle felt that since the Colmar pocket was gone and the French First Army had a defensive mission in Alsace, this could safely be done. He said he wanted to use the troops to help train the new units the French were raising, and confessed that an additional reason for pulling back into France was the need "to assure contact between certain regions of the country and its organized Army." He was, in other words, having trouble with the Communists in the FFI again.

Eisenhower scribbled by hand at the bottom of De Gaulle's written request, "Does this mean French are ready to assume full responsibility for Alsace with only 5 divisions?" Smith discussed the matter with General Juin and worked out a compromise—only two divisions were pulled back, and they did not go as far into the interior as De Gaulle had wanted.[16]

Still Eisenhower was angered by De Gaulle's action. His own analysis was that the French President was showing a bit of pique at not having been invited to attend the Big Three conference at Yalta. Eisenhower told Marshall that "as usual we will work out something," but he noted that the most popular theme in the French press was an expression of dissatisfaction with the Allies, especially SHAEF, for failing to bring more food into France "and lack of political deference to their government." Remembering all the way back to TORCH, Eisenhower summarized the frustration and irritation to which he had been subjected in dealings with the French for nearly two and a half years. "The French continue to be difficult," he declared. "I must say that next to the weather I think they have caused me more trouble in this war than any other single factor." To emphasize the point, he added, "They even rank above landing craft."[17]

But with the AEF rolling forward, even the French could not break Eisenhower's spirits. During the first week in March the men of Twelfth and Sixth Army Groups took up the attack. Elements of Hodges' First Army reached the Rhine on March 5, his armored units roaring into Cologne, which they cleared of the enemy by March 7. From Cologne northward the Allies had closed to the Rhine; by March 10, as Patton pushed forward, they were up to the Rhine from Koblenz northward. The Germans had taken a terrible beating. In the Rhineland campaign (which in the south continued through March), they lost 250,000 prisoners and untold killed and wounded. More than twenty full divisions had been destroyed, and the total German strength in the West was no more than twenty-six complete divisions. Spaatz's oil campaign, now going at full force, had virtually eliminated the German fuel reserves. The Allied air forces were blasting virtually every German who moved during daylight hours, flying as many as 11,000 sorties in one day.[18]

Eisenhower's plan had worked. Late in March he met Brooke on the banks of the Rhine. The CIGS had come to observe Montgomery's crossing. "He was gracious enough," Eisenhower reported to Marshall the next day, "to say that I was right, and that my current plans and operations are well calculated to meet the current situation."* Eisenhower added that he did not want to sound boastful, "but I must admit to a great satisfaction that the things that Bradley and I have believed in from the beginning and have carried out in face of some opposition from within and without, have matured so splendidly."[19]

The situation that Eisenhower's plan had brought about was not dissimilar from that Montgomery had created in Normandy. By attacking on the left, with Twenty-first Army Group, Eisenhower had forced the Germans to concentrate in that area. As he explained to Churchill, this increased "the vulnerability of the enemy to the devastating later attacks of the 9th, 1st and 3rd Armies. With perfect teamplay every allied unit of every service has performed its part to its own further distinction and to the dismay of the enemy."[20] On the eve of an attack by Seventh Army, Eisenhower told Marshall, ". . . so far as we can determine there is not a single reserve division in this whole area. If we can get a quick breakthrough, the advance should go very rapidly." He realized that breaking through would be difficult, "but once this is accomplished losses should not be great and we should capture another big bag of prisoners."[21]

At the conclusion of the Rhineland campaign Eisenhower held a press conference. A reporter asked him if he thought it was Hitler or the German General Staff that had made the decision to fight west of the Rhine. Eisenhower answered, "I think it was Hitler. I am guessing because I must confess that many times in this war I have been wrong in trying to evaluate that German mind, if it is a mind. When it looks logical for him to do something he does something else." Later in the conference the Supreme Commander added, "When we once demonstrated with the attack of 21st Army Group and the Ninth Army that we could break through the defense west of the Rhine and he was exposed, any sensible soldier would have gone back to the Rhine and given us the Saar and

---

* In his memoirs Eisenhower gave a much fuller account of what Brooke told him. When Brooke saw Eisenhower's claim, he denied that he had ever said Eisenhower was right in insisting on the Rhineland battle. (Bryant, *Triumph in the West*, p. 333.) That Eisenhower made the claim the day after the event is strong evidence that Brooke did in fact say so. The CIGS may have later changed his mind.

stood there and said, 'Now try to come across.' They simply seem to want to stand and fight where they are. Starting on March 1, if they had gotten out the bulk of their force they would have been better off."[22]

Eisenhower spent most of the first week in March visiting his commanders in the field. He did not interfere with their conduct of operations but he was anxious to see how operations were proceeding and wanted to be where the action was. He usually contented himself with giving Simpson or Hodges or Patton a pat on the back and telling him to keep up the good work. On March 7 he was back at Reims and caught up on his work. After reviewing all the reports and attending a conference in the War Room, he dictated some personal letters. That evening he planned to relax and asked a few of his corps commanders to dinner. They had just sat down to eat when the telephone rang. Bradley wanted to talk to Eisenhower. When the Supreme Commander got on the phone Bradley said that one of Hodges' divisions had taken intact a bridge over the Rhine at Remagen.[23]

CHAPTER 19

Crossing the Rhine and a Change in Plan

While Eisenhower sat down to dinner with his corps commanders on March 7, Bradley had been talking with Bull about a SHAEF proposal to shift four divisions from Twelfth Army Group to Sixth Army Group in the south. Bull wanted to give the divisions to Patch to assist his attack south of the Moselle, on Patton's right flank. Bradley was furious. He told Bull the proposal was "larcenous." Bull shouted back, "By gosh, but you people are difficult to get along with, and I might add that you are getting more difficult every day."

"But SHAEF has had experience," Bradley replied, "in getting along with difficult people." Bull glared, then snapped, "The Twelfth Army Group is no harder to get along with than Twenty-first Group. But you can take it from me, it's no easier either."

It was at that point that Hodges called to tell Bradley that one of First Army's divisions had captured the Ludendorff Railroad Bridge, at Remagen, intact. "Hot dog, Courtney," Bradley shouted, and told him to get as much material over the river as he could. After hanging up, Bradley turned on Bull, grinned, thumped him on the back, and laughed. "There goes your ball game, Pink. Courtney's gotten across the Rhine on a bridge." Bull shrugged and said that did not make any difference, because nobody was going anywhere from Remagen. "It just doesn't fit into *the* plan." Bull explained to Bradley, "Ike's heart is in your sector, but right now his mind is up north."[1]

Bradley would not be put off. He could not believe that Eisenhower was so rigid that he would ignore a bridgehead over the Rhine, even though it did not fit into previous plans and was in an area ill suited to offensive operations. It was then that he decided to call the Supreme Commander on the telephone.

Eisenhower left the dining room to go into an adjacent office to take the call. Bradley told him about Remagen. "Brad, that's wonderful," Eisenhower replied. Bradley said he wanted to push all the force he had in the vicinity over to the east bank of the Rhine. "Sure," Eisenhower responded, "get right on across with everything you've got. It's the best break we've had. . . ." Bradley, grinning at Bull, then said that Eisenhower's own G-3 was opposed to such a move because Remagen did not fit into the over-all accepted plan. "To hell with the planners," Eisenhower replied. "Sure, go on, Brad, and I'll give you everything we got to hold that bridgehead. We'll make good use of it even if the terrain isn't too good."[2]

Over the next two weeks Hodges fought to extend his bridgehead. On March 11 he installed pontoon bridges and had ferries and landing craft bringing material across the river. The Germans made determined efforts to wreck the bridge, using air attacks, artillery fire, V-2 missiles, floating mines, and frogmen, but Hodges' elaborate defenses thwarted their efforts. By the time the big railroad bridge finally collapsed, the bridgehead was twenty miles long and eight miles deep, with six pontoon bridges across the river. It constituted a threat to the entire German defense of the Rhine, and the Wehrmacht—as in Normandy—counterattacked with whatever units were handy. All that the piecemeal attacks accomplished, however, was to use up the remaining German armor and to weaken the Germans defending the Rhine north and south of Remagen. Eisenhower had recognized these possibilities immediately; the morning after his telephone conversation with Bradley he informed the CCS that he was rushing troops to Remagen "with the idea that this will constitute greatest possible threat" to the enemy.[3]

To the south of Remagen, meanwhile, Patton had launched Operation LUMBERJACK, an attack toward the Rhine along the north bank of the Moselle. Once he broke through the initial defenses (March 6–8), his Third Army raced forward, closing to the Rhine on March 10. LUMBERJACK had been designed as a preliminary action to UNDERTONE, the advance to the Rhine by Sixth Army Group, but because of Patton's unexpected success Eisenhower changed the plan slightly and Patton now crossed the Moselle to attack south in support of Patch's Seventh Army. With Patch attacking from the front and Patton from the right flank, the German First and Seventh Armies were surrounded. By March 21 most of the German Seventh Army had been destroyed, the German First Army was caught in a salient along a short stretch of the Rhine, and Patton had closed to the river from Mannheim to Koblenz.[4]

Eisenhower now prepared to set his whole front in motion. On March 13 he told Montgomery to begin Operation PLUNDER, the crossing of the Rhine north of the Ruhr, on March 24. To assist Montgomery, Eisenhower assigned the First Allied Airborne Army to participate in the operation and directed the air forces to give PLUNDER highest priority. In the center, he directed Hodges to be ready to launch a thrust from Remagen toward Frankfurt, which meant that Remagen had now become more than a threat—it could act as a springboard for a major advance to the east. The advance from Remagen would take place after Devers closed to the Rhine and Patton got across the river, and would be designed to link up with Patton for the drive into Germany. In order to keep his options open, however, Eisenhower also told Hodges to be prepared to send as many as ten divisions to Montgomery to be used north of the Ruhr. If Montgomery got across without undue difficulty, and if he could get a railroad bridge built and operating over the Rhine, SHAEF would be able to support more than the thirty-five divisions allotted to Montgomery in the advance along the north German plain. If the railroad bridge was completed in time, Eisenhower wanted to be able to send Hodges to join Simpson in support of Montgomery. The use of First Army east of the Rhine, in other words, depended on forthcoming developments—Eisenhower was keeping an open mind and was prepared to reinforce success.[5]

Eisenhower's spirits were soaring. He felt so good that for practically the only time in the war he engaged in a little banter with the Chief of Staff. Marshall had told the Supreme Commander that he was having an argument with Senator Robert A. Taft, who objected to the use of eighteen-year-olds in combat. "I was impressed yesterday with the difficulties of my position," Marshall said, because he had simultaneously to answer attacks on the use of the young men and demands from MacArthur for more replacements. In addition, field commanders were protesting against the conversion of their specialists to infantry replacements. "The combined circumstances could hardly present a more illogical pressure." Eisenhower said Marshall's complaints gave him the "pleasant feeling of 'misery loves company.'" He explained that "sometimes when I get tired of trying to arrange the blankets smoothly over the several prima donnas in the same bed I think no one person in the world can have so many illogical problems." But after he read of Marshall's troubles, Eisenhower said, he "went right back to work with a grin."[6]

The smell of victory was in the air, and Marshall began to be concerned about how the credit for it should be apportioned. He thought it only just that the Army divisions that spearheaded the AEF attacks should receive the honor due them, and he was also concerned about the postwar situation, when the services would have to present their case for appropriations to congressmen anxious to cut the budget. A little publicity for the Army would help its financial cause. Many American divisions had done outstanding work in the Rhineland campaign, but practically none of them were known in the United States. "What I am interested in," Marshall told Eisenhower, referring to the 3d Division at the Colmar pocket, "is the result and I go back to my usual comparison, that had it been a Marine Division every phase of a rather dramatic incident would have been spread throughout the United States. They get the result, we do not. Our technique therefore must be faulty."

On March 12 Eisenhower explained to Marshall that he was doing the best he could, but the problem of getting publicity for any one division was almost impossible because there were so many American divisions in Europe and because so many of them were doing well. He named ten that could match the achievements of any Marine division, but obviously, he said, once publicity was spread that widely it lost its impact. Eisenhower threw the problem back to Marshall by saying that the Army might get more attention with the fact that it had fifty divisions engaged in combat in Europe: "I believe the War Department . . . might emphasize the number of divisions the Army has deployed and fighting all over the world," Eisenhower said.[7]

In his own theater, Eisenhower told Devers and Bradley to do what they could to publicize their divisions. "These matters may not seem very weighty," he admitted, and he did not want his subordinates to think "that we are fighting this war for headlines," but proper publicity did improve troop morale. "Moreover, it will have an enduring effect on the future of American defense forces and I hope that you and your staffs . . . will give to the matter some imaginative thought."[8]

Eisenhower's involvement with publicity continued. Marshall had sent Roosevelt's press secretary, Steve Early, to ETO to help the public relations experts, and SHAEF got a number of suggestions from Early that Eisenhower implemented. He loosened censorship controls so that more information could be released about individual divisions and their commanders.[9] He was also concerned about his more senior commanders. On March 30 he sent Marshall a long and glowing description of Hodges' achievements to date, made it clear that he thought Hodges had done more to bring about the victory than any other army commander, and declared, "I should like very much to see Hodges get credit in the

United States for his great work." Eisenhower could do little to achieve this within ETO, because if he singled out one commander for praise the others would be miffed, "but it occurs to me that as a purely United States proposition" the War Department could promote Hodges in the press.

Eisenhower also thought Bradley should get additional credit for his role throughout the European campaign. "Never once has he held back in attempting any maneuver, no matter how bold in conception. . . ." Bradley's handling of his army commanders had been "superb. . . . His energy, common sense, tactical skill and complete loyalty have made him a great lieutenant on whom I always rely with the greatest confidence." In trying to get either Hodges or Bradley publicized, however, Eisenhower was fighting a losing battle. Headlines in the United States continued to refer to First Army or Twelfth Army Group. Only Patton was identified by name; when Third Army took a town, the headlines inevitably proclaimed "Patton captures . . ."[10]

Marshall too was worried about the publicity individual commanders were receiving, although he liked Patton and had no objection in that specific case. What did bother him was all the attention Montgomery was getting, and he urged Eisenhower to praise Hodges and Bradley in a press conference "as a possible antidote for an overdose of Montgomery which is now coming into the country." Eisenhower, in reply, said he could not understand why Montgomery should be "getting a big play at this time," and added that he suspected "there is some influence at work that insists on giving Montgomery credit that belongs to other field commanders." He would, he promised, try to set the newsmen straight.[11]

The scramble for publicity and Eisenhower's readiness to take a bantering tone with Marshall illustrated only one side of the mood at SHAEF in early March. The Allies could hardly suppress the feeling that they had finished the war, but—and it was an important qualification— they recalled that they had felt the same way in September 1944. The Germans at that time had recovered. The Wehrmacht was still an impressively efficient machine and the individual German soldier still commanded respect. In addition to general worries, there was the specific, hard fact that the great Russian winter offensive had faltered badly. On February 15 the Red Army reached the Oder–Neisse line, some thirty-five miles from Berlin. Then it stopped. For the next month there was little activity on the Oder–Neisse front. The Russians did make further gains in Hungary, to the south, but all eyes were centered on Berlin, where no progress was being made. Perhaps, just perhaps, the Germans might achieve another miracle.

There was also the possibility of extensive enemy guerrilla activity. In September Eisenhower had been concerned about how he would handle the situation if the organized German resistance collapsed, the AEF moved into Germany, and then guerrilla warfare began. Guerrilla warfare was not a new phenomenon, but it had reached impressive new heights of efficiency during World War II. SHAEF believed that the Germans were organizing an underground army of "Werewolves," youngsters who were being trained for murder and terrorism. The SS provided them with leadership, weapons, and fanaticism. If the Germans had time enough to perfect the organization and training of these forces, they might make the occupation so costly that the conquerers would be glad to get out. "The evidence was clear that the Nazi intended to make the attempt and I decided to give him no opportunity to carry it out," Eisenhower later declared. "The way to stop this project . . . was to overrun the entire national territory before its organization could be effected."[12]

Connected to this fear of guerrilla activity was the idea, widespread in the Allied camp, that the Nazis intended to set up a mountain retreat in the Bavarian Alps, from which Hitler would direct the continued resistance. This area was easily the best natural defensive region the Germans could occupy, and from his mountain stronghold around Berchtesgaden Hitler could—it was feared—combine what remained of the fighting forces in Germany and Italy and hold out indefinitely. SHAEF intelligence reported that Germany's best SS divisions were moving toward Berchtesgaden, and stories were circulating about prepared positions. The natural defensive strength of the area was excellent. The persistently bad weather, the mountainous terrain, and the altitude would cut down on or eliminate the use of Allied air forces; the Germans had convincingly demonstrated in Italy how well they could fight in mountains; the Allies' most potent weapon, their mobility, would count for little in the area.

On March 11 SHAEF G-2 reported that the main trend of German defense policy was to safeguard the Bavarian Alps. "This area is, by the very nature of the terrain, practically impenetrable. . . ." The reporter, carried away with his own verbiage, continued, "Here, defended by nature and by the most efficient secret weapons yet invented, the powers that have hitherto guided Germany will survive to reorganize her resurrection; here armaments will be manufactured in bombproof factories, food and equipment will be stored in vast underground caverns and a specially selected corps of young men will be trained in guerrilla warfare, so that a whole underground army can be fitted and directed to liberate Germany from the occupying forces." This must rank as one of the worst intelligence reports of all time, but no one knew that in March of 1945, and few even suspected it.[13]

Even Churchill was afraid of these possible developments. On March 17 he asked Ismay to comment on Hitler's strategy, which puzzled him. The resistance Hitler was offering in Hungary to the Russians, Churchill felt, made sense only if the Nazis were planning to retire into southern Germany in an attempt to prolong the fighting there. To American (and Russian) intelligence, this was the only explanation for the transfer of Sixth Panzer Army to the Danube Valley *after* the Russians had arrived at the Oder River.[14]

For Eisenhower, the way to stop the build-up in the Alpine region and to stifle any attempt at guerrilla war appeared simple—overrun Germany as quickly and completely as possible. Bringing the war to a rapid conclusion therefore took on a new urgency for him, an urgency that went even beyond Brooke's. He was determined to push his forces forward wherever possible, and he tried to get more men for the final offensive. He began planning for a large-scale airborne drop in the Kassel area, well back from the Rhine, and at a place which offered numerous tactical opportunities. Paratroopers at Kassel could help Montgomery seal off the Ruhr, and to the east of Kassel there was an open plain that led directly to Dresden, which could be taken. Eisenhower was thinking of using seven to ten divisions, four or five of which would be normal infantry divisions to be flown into the area after the paratroopers secured it. Eisenhower's biggest problem was lack of manpower because he could not afford to take men from the other offensives. On March 12, therefore, he asked Marshall if he could possibly have one of Clark's divisions in Italy, and also asked Brooke if the British 1st Airborne Division, then refitting, could be sent to the Continent soon. Brooke was agreeable, but Marshall refused Eisenhower's request. "It would be asking a good deal to take one of Clark's six dependable American divisions at this particular moment," Marshall explained, "especially when he knows you have nearly ninety already available. . . ."[15]

Eisenhower accepted Marshall's decision, although not with good grace. He said he only asked "because this is presumably a vital front," and he was "merely seeking every possible soldier to apply at what might be a decisive moment so as to give us the greatest possible certainty of complete victory."[16] A little later, on March 27, he admitted that the Allied ground armies had advanced so rapidly that—as had happened scores of times—they would be overrunning the drop zone before the paratroopers could have been ready for the operation. Eisenhower explained that the only thing he feared was that "the German may still find enough strength to oppose our penetrations along some line fairly deep in his own country . . . [and] I was looking forward to an airborne operation . . . which would have made it impossible for the German to do this."[17]

So Eisenhower was thrown back on his own resources, which were in any case sufficient. Before beginning the final thrust he took a short vacation. Smith had been urging him for quite a while to take a brief rest cure, but he had insisted that he did not need one. When an American citizen offered the use of his villa in Cannes, Smith became more insistent. It took him four days, but he finally convinced the Supreme Commander that he had to get some relaxation or face a nervous breakdown. Eisenhower finally said he would go if Bradley came along. On March 19 a small party accompanied the generals to the Riviera, where Eisenhower spent five quiet days.[18]

While at Cannes Eisenhower had an opportunity to talk quietly with Bradley and to think through once again the plans for the drive through Germany. Since January, and especially after Remagen, his inclination had been to keep increasing the strength of the attack on Bradley's front. At first it had been intended as a diversion, then as a secondary effort to help Montgomery, or—a little later—as an alternative major thrust if Montgomery was halted. By the third week in March Bradley's operation had become, in Eisenhower's mind, equal in scope and importance to Montgomery's. On March 21 he finalized this conclusion by making it a part of his operational orders. He had left instructions with the SHAEF staff to prepare a directive on the subject, and while at Cannes talked over the telephone with Bull about it. The upshot was a directive that instructed Bradley to establish a firm bridgehead over the Rhine in the Frankfurt area, then make "an advance in strength" toward Kassel. This would lead to a link-up between Hodges' forces moving east from Remagen and Patton's coming up from Frankfurt. It would also, not incidentally, give Eisenhower a force south of the Ruhr equal in strength to Twenty-first Army Group north of the area.[19]

On March 22 Patton made a surprise crossing of the Rhine. He took the river "on the run," moving across as soon as he reached it, which contrasted sharply with Montgomery's operations. His preparations for

PLUNDER were meticulous. The next day, March 23, Eisenhower flew from Cannes to XVI Corps headquarters, where he stayed up all night to watch elements of the Ninth Army begin their crossing of the Rhine as part of PLUNDER. There was a big air drop on the east bank, so the sky was full of airplanes. Simpson pushed across quickly and strongly, thereby cutting his casualties, which were minimal—only fifteen killed in one assault division and sixteen in the other. More than 1200 artillery pieces delivered the preliminary bombardment, which Eisenhower told Marshall "was an especially interesting sight because of the fact that all the guns were spread out on a plain so that the flashes from one end of the line to the other were all plainly visible. It was real drum-fire."[20] To the north, meanwhile, British Second Army got across against heavy opposition, while Hodges and Patton to the south extended their bridgeheads. The offensive was rolling.

On March 24 Eisenhower and Bradley went to Montgomery's headquarters. Eisenhower carried with him a report to the CCS prepared by Morgan and Whiteley. In it the SHAEF officers argued that operations north of the Ruhr had only limited possibilities, as Montgomery's forces could not be deployed in strength until railroad bridges had been built over the Rhine, which would take two months. "I shall therefore be enabled," the draft read, "to widen the base of the operations to isolate the Ruhr, by advancing also in force from the south. This will greatly increase the speed of deployment of offensive forces against the enemy." The argument implicit in the draft corresponded nicely with Eisenhower's own thoughts, but before issuing it he wanted to get Montgomery's reactions.

Montgomery did not like the tone of the message. He wanted to retain U. S. Ninth Army in his army group, and he wanted the Allied emphasis placed on his offensive toward Berlin. To mollify him, Eisenhower changed the draft somewhat, making it more general, but he did not tamper with its substance. After pointing out that the Rhineland battles had destroyed a large proportion of the enemy forces on the western front, and adding that he did not want to seem overoptimistic, Eisenhower said it was his "conviction that the situation today presents opportunities for which we have struggled and which must be seized boldly." Hodges and Patton had secured bridgeheads "which can be consolidated and expanded rapidly to support a major thrust which will assist the northern operation and make our exploitation more effective." This still could be read to mean that Montgomery's attack would be the major one, with Bradley playing a supporting role, but that was not Eisenhower's intention, as his next sentence revealed. "It is my personal belief that the enemy strength on the Western Front is becoming so stretched that penetrations and advances will soon be limited only by our own maintenance." Montgomery already had all the forces he could maintain; the unmistakable implication was that Bradley, whose maintenance situation was much better, would be turned loose with all the men and supplies available. Eisenhower emphasized the point in his concluding remark: "I intend to reinforce every success with the utmost speed."[21]

Eisenhower spent the next two nights at Bradley's headquarters, where Bradley presumably urged him to concentrate his efforts in the center of the offensive. One result of the discussion was a directive that formalized the concept of attacks in equal strength north and south of the Ruhr. Earlier Eisenhower had spoken of Montgomery sealing off the Ruhr in the north and east while the air forces completed the job in the south. Now he definitely committed his troops to a gigantic encirclement, ordering both Montgomery and Bradley to advance toward Kassel–Paderborn, where they would link up. "Having effected junction," he continued, they should "mop up and occupy the whole area east of the Rhine enclosed by their advances and prepare for a further advance into Germany." Who would direct that "further advance" was still an open question.[22]

On March 25 Eisenhower went to Montgomery's headquarters for a quick visit. Churchill and Brooke were already there. The Prime Minister showed Eisenhower a note he had received three days earlier from Molotov. The Russian accused the West of dealing "behind the backs of the Soviet Union, which is bearing the brunt of the war against Germany," by conducting surrender negotiations with the German military command in Italy. Eisenhower, according to Churchill's later account, "was much upset, and seemed deeply stirred with anger at what he considered most unjust and unfounded charges about our good faith." The Supreme Commander said he would accept surrenders in the field whenever offered; if political matters arose he would consult the heads of governments. What Churchill said to Eisenhower is not known, but he implies strongly in his memoirs that his objective was to beat the Russians to Berlin and hold as much of eastern Germany as possible "until my doubts about Russia's intention have been cleared away."[23]

Thus was raised what would become one of the great controversies of World War II. Once the AEF was over the Rhine, and given the Russian position on the Oder–Neisse, the fate of Germany was sealed. Under the circumstances, critics have said, especially taking into account the clear evidence of Russian intentions, Eisenhower should have directed his forces in a pell-mell race for Berlin. In this context, the question of whether or not he could have beaten the Red Army to the capital is beside the point—he should have tried. What the Allies would have gained had Eisenhower, instead of the Red Army, taken Berlin, no one has ever made explicit. In any case, whatever Churchill said to Eisenhower on March 25 as they stood in a small house looking down on the Rhine, he did not convince the Supreme Commander of the need to drive to Berlin. SHAEF planners had already decided the AEF could not get there before the Russians. Eisenhower's basic purpose remained what it had always been—the rapid and thorough defeat of Germany. If advancing on Berlin would help achieve that purpose, Eisenhower would do so; if it would not, he would direct his forces elsewhere.

Eisenhower's planning for a final offensive by the Americans continued. He spent March 26 with Patton, Hodges, and Bradley at First Army headquarters. Together they went across the Rhine at Remagen, visited troops on the other side, had lunch in a German hotel, and talked. On the twenty-seventh Eisenhower went to Paris for a press conference; he spent the next day in the office clearing up a backlog of work ("Eisenhower did not have a minute to himself all day," the office diary reads. "Some member of his staff was in his office most of the afternoon.") Smith was ill, which did not help Eisenhower in his administrative endeavors.[24]

At the top of the pile · on Eisenhower's desk was a cable from Marshall. The Chief of Staff, like Bradley, had more of an American than an Allied orientation to his strategy, and he suggested that with the imminent breakup of German defenses Eisenhower might want to push heavy columns southeastward on a broad front, aiming for either Linz or Munich. Such a push would be a purely American operation. It would also avoid a head-on clash with the Russians, for to the south of Berlin Red Army lines bowed eastward. A possible clash was a problem Marshall took seriously. He asked Eisenhower what preparations he had made for "control and coordination to prevent unfortunate instances and to sort out the two advancing forces," and suggested an "agreed line of demarcation. The arrangements we now have with the Russians appear quite inadequate for the situation you may face and it seems that steps ought to be initiated without delay to provide for the communication and liaison you will need with them. . . ."[25] There was also a cable from Montgomery on Eisenhower's desk. The field marshal said that when the encirclement of the Ruhr was complete he intended to drive to the Elbe River (and thus toward Berlin). He assumed U. S. Ninth Army would remain under his command.

Montgomery's assumption was unfounded. Eisenhower had made his policy, and in a series of messages he dictated on March 28 he set in motion the final campaign. He had decided to make the main thrust in the center, under Bradley, with Dresden as the objective. He explained to Marshall that he rejected the idea of moving toward Munich or Linz because the advance toward Dresden offered the shortest route to the Russians and would divide the remaining German forces roughly in half. To provide Bradley with sufficient force, Eisenhower announced his intention of taking Ninth Army away from Montgomery and giving it to Bradley. To ensure co-ordination with the Russians, he wired Stalin to tell the Russians of his plans, suggest that the Red Army meet the AEF around Dresden, and to ask for information as to Russian intentions. The change in plans was complete.[26]

In making his decision Eisenhower had indicated that he was determined to direct his operations toward the quickest possible defeat of Germany. The negative aspect of the plan was that he left Berlin to the Russians. The Supreme Commander was still fighting World War II. According to his critics, this meant that he had ignored the obvious—that the Cold War was already under way—and in the process had thus thrown away the fruits of victory. The assumption of Eisenhower's critics has been that he could have taken Berlin and that had he done so it would have made an enormous difference in the Cold War. Both assumptions remain unproven.

But even if postwar events would not have been much changed by anything Eisenhower did at the late date of April 1945, the nagging question remains: Why didn't he try to take Berlin? The capture of the capital was the obvious culmination of the offensive that began in 1942 in North Africa. The Western press, and the American and British people, assumed that SHAEF was directing its armies toward Berlin. The SHAEF planning staff had in fact planned for that end. In September 1944, when it seemed that the AEF would soon be advancing into Germany, the planners drew up a proposal for the final offensive. "Our main object must be the early capture of Berlin," it began, "the most important objective in Germany." The way to accomplish this, according to the proposal, was to make the major advance north of the Ruhr, with a secondary advance coming from Frankfurt. In the two-pronged thrust, Montgomery's forces should be twice as powerful as Bradley's.[27] Eisenhower himself had told Montgomery on a number of occasions, "Clearly Berlin is the main prize."

But the military situation in late March 1945 was far different from that prevailing in September 1944. In September the Red Army was still outside Warsaw, more than three hundred miles from Berlin; the AEF was about the same distance from the German capital. In March 1945 the AEF remained more than two hundred miles away from Berlin, while the Red Army was thirty-five miles from the capital. At Eisenhower's press conference on March 27 a reporter asked him, "Who do you think will be into Berlin first, the Russians or us?" "Well," Eisenhower replied, "I think mileage alone ought to make them do it. After all they are thirty-three miles and we are two hundred and fifty. I wouldn't want to make any prediction. They have a shorter race to run, although they are faced by the bulk of the German forces."[28]

A second factor in Eisenhower's decision to forgo initial entry into Berlin was Bradley's advice. His influence on Eisenhower's thinking was always great. Sometime during the week before March 28, either at Cannes or while Eisenhower was at his headquarters, Bradley had a long talk with the Supreme Commander about Berlin. Bradley pointed out that, even if Montgomery reached the Elbe River before the Red Army crossed the Oder, fifty miles of lowlands separated the Elbe from Berlin. To get to the capital, Montgomery would have to advance through an area studded with lakes, crisscrossed with streams, and interlaced with occasional canals. Eisenhower asked Bradley for an estimate on the cost of taking Berlin. About 100,000 casualties, Bradley replied. "A pretty stiff price to pay for a prestige objective, especially when we've got to fall back and let the other fellow take over"[29] (Berlin was well within the occupation zone assigned to the Russians).

Marshall's message of March 27, in which the Chief of Staff suggested Linz or Munich as an objective, helped turn Eisenhower's thinking away from Berlin. So did the fact that Montgomery would lead the drive to Berlin, while Bradley would be in charge of an offensive directed into central Germany. The fear of a prolonged guerrilla campaign in Germany, directed from an alpine fortress, also played a role.

Finally, there was the political factor. The critics are right in saying that Eisenhower was still fighting World War II, but the implication involved—that he should have so directed his operations as to forestall the Russians in central Europe—carries with it the idea that soldiers in the field, rather than the President, should make national policy. In March 1945 the Cold War had not started, and Roosevelt appeared to be determined to prevent it. His policy was to defeat Germany, redeploy to the Pacific as soon as possible, and get along with the Russians. Eisenhower did not question the policy; he did do his best to carry it out. Later, writing at the height of the Cold War, Bradley could say, "As soldiers we looked naively on this British inclination to complicate the war with political foresight and non-military objectives,"[30] which was in effect a confession that the British had remarkable political skill and that the Americans were hopelessly unsophisticated. But the truth is that *at the time* Montgomery and the British advocated an attempt to take Berlin as a military move and Eisenhower rejected it on those grounds. The British had a different postwar policy than the Americans, which was just then taking its final form, but they did not urge it on Eisenhower until later. To SHAEF it seemed that the principal British concern was to make a hero out of Montgomery. "Monty wanted to ride into Berlin on a white charger wearing two hats,"[31] as Whiteley put it; Eisenhower wanted to finish the war.

CHAPTER 20

Controversy with the British

Eisenhower's March 28 cable to Stalin, informing him that the AEF would head for Dresden–Leipzig, set off a flurry of activity in the capitals of the Big Three. The Soviets moved first. Stalin replied with "altogether unusual alacrity" to Eisenhower's message, agreeing that the Allied and Soviet forces should meet as Eisenhower proposed in the Dresden area, and adding that Berlin had lost its former strategic significance. Stalin said the Soviet Supreme Command planned to allot only secondary forces to the capture of the German capital. In fact, however, the Red Army had already begun a major redeployment, carried out "in almost frantic haste," designed to make Berlin its primary objective.[1]

By early April Marshal Zhukov, on the Oder River, had 768,100 men and 11,000 artillery pieces, not counting smaller-caliber mortars. Marshal Koniev, on the Neisse River, had five field and two tank armies with artillery equal to Zhukov's. The total strength of the Red Army around Berlin was 1,250,000 men and 22,000 guns.[2] Zhukov and Koniev had what must be reckoned as the greatest armed force in so small an area in the whole of military history. To oppose them, the Germans had two armies. Clearly the Russians were determined to take Berlin themselves, as the only appropriate climax to their war with Germany. Stalin was delighted to learn of Eisenhower's plans, to see that the AEF would not engage in a race for Berlin, and to learn that the glory of taking Berlin would go to his armies. To ensure that Eisenhower did not change his mind, Stalin said he agreed about Berlin's insignificance and added that the Red Army, too, would concentrate on Dresden.

If Stalin feared that the British would try to get Eisenhower to alter his plans, he was right. The British did object to Eisenhower's proposed operation and to his opening direct communications with Stalin, because they were fearful that Stalin would make a dupe of Eisenhower. Their objections, however, were of a military, not a political, nature. The BCOS met on March 29; Brooke recorded their reaction in his diary. "A very long C.O.S. meeting with a series of annoying telegrams. The worst of all was one from Eisenhower direct to Stalin trying to coordinate his offensive with the Russians. To start with, he has no business to address Stalin direct, his communications should be through the Combined Chiefs of Staff; secondly, he produced a telegram which was unintelligible; and finally, what was implied in it appeared to be entirely adrift and a change from all that had been previously agreed on."[3] Montgomery was also unhappy. "I consider we are about to make a terrible mistake," he wired Brooke. "It seems doctrine that public opinion wins wars is coming to the fore again."[4]

The British made their feelings known to Field Marshal Wilson, the head of the Joint Staff Mission in Washington, who passed them on to Marshall. The message, considering the depth of British emotions upon learning that Montgomery would not lead the last offensive and that Berlin was not the objective, was softly worded. The BCOS said they were concerned at Eisenhower's "implied change of plan" in taking Ninth Army away from Montgomery and giving it to Bradley, and they objected to Eisenhower's getting into direct communication with Stalin. On the military side, they said that the original plan should remain in effect because: (1) it would open German ports in the north; (2) it would annul the U-boat war; (3) it would free AEF forces to move into Denmark. Nothing was said about political factors involved in taking Berlin.

The JCS were just as upset by the British cable as the BCOS had been by Eisenhower's message to Stalin. The American Chiefs resented the almost casual way their British counterparts called into question the strategy of the most successful field commander of the war, and they thought it unseemly for the British—of all people—to object to Eisenhower's direct approach to Stalin, since Churchill had always felt free to by-pass the CCS and go directly to Eisenhower. Most important, the JCS—especially Marshall—thought Eisenhower was right. The line from Kassel to Dresden offered the shortest distance to the Russians and thus to the division of Germany into two parts. It was a route that avoided the waterways of the northern plains and it provided a central axis from which the AEF could turn north or south as required. Finally, it led directly to the second greatest industrial area of Germany, the Silesian basin. As John Ehrman points out, "This was a reasoned case. But, as on previous occasions, the Supreme Commander's first telegram unfortunately failed to cover all of its aspects, and thus suggested that he had not in fact considered it as a whole."[5]

The BCOS had implied that Eisenhower had not thought about what he was doing or given full consideration to the consequences of his plans. Instead of treating him as an experienced commander who had proved his worth, they appeared to regard him as a beginner who needed guidance on every point from his superiors. That after all this time, and after the Rhineland battle, the British should display such a lack of trust in Eisenhower seemed to Marshall incredible. In replying to the British, the JCS got in a dig at British strategical insights by pointing out that Eisenhower's plan to fight the major battle west of the Rhine had been proved sound. As to the future, the JCS stated flatly that Eisenhower was "the best judge of the measures which offer the earliest prospect of destroying the German Armies or their power to resist," and added that the Supreme Commander's ideas were "sound from the overall viewpoint of crushing Germany as expeditiously as possible and should receive full support." The British had wanted to censure Eisenhower for contacting Stalin; Marshall emphatically rejected the proposal. He also sent the substance of the British objections on to Eisenhower so that Eisenhower would know what was going on.[6]

Eisenhower, unaware of how Marshall had responded to the British criticisms, sent a defense of his action to the Chief of Staff. He had Whiteley prepare it; while Whiteley was working, Eisenhower sent a short message of his own to Marshall. He said that "the charge that I have changed plans has no possible basis in fact." He had always planned, once the Ruhr was isolated, to launch "one main attack calculated to accomplish, in conjunction with the Russians, the destruction of the enemy armed forces. To disperse strong forces along the northern coast before the primary object is accomplished will leave me too weak to launch a powerful thrust straight through the center."[7] What he meant was that the objective of the plan—the German Army—had not changed, and he regarded a change in the direction of the advance as minor. With this the British could not agree.

Whiteley, meanwhile, had prepared a long justification for Eisenhower to send to Marshall. After reading it over, Eisenhower signed it and sent it off. It was strongly worded. The CCS had instructed Eisenhower to deal directly with the Russians concerning military co-ordination, it began,

so the British had no right to object.* "Even cursory examination of the
decisive direction" for the final thrust, the cable continued, "shows that
the principal effort should . . . be toward the Leipzig region. . . ." The
area of northern Germany across which Montgomery would have to
march, the "so-called 'good ground,'" was "not really good at this time of
year," for it was badly cut up by waterways and the ground was marshy.
"Merely following the principle that Field Marshal Brooke has always
shouted to me, I am determined to concentrate on one major thrust and
all that my plan does is to place the Ninth U. S. Army back under
Bradley" for that thrust.

Brooke wanted concentration; Eisenhower was finally willing to give
it to him. It should go for a significant military target, which Berlin
was not. "May I point out," the message continued, "that Berlin itself
is no longer a particularly important objective. Its usefulness to the German has been largely destroyed and even his government is preparing
to move to another area." Going straight eastward would send the AEF
toward the heart of what remained of German power.

In one paragraph Whiteley, a British officer, allowed himself to show
at least some of the irritation within SHAEF at the BCOS for the
constant interference and criticism they had provided from Normandy to
the Elbe. "The Prime Minister and his Chiefs of Staff," the paragraph began, "opposed 'ANVIL'; they opposed my idea that the German should be
destroyed west of the Rhine before we made our major effort across
that river; and they insisted that the route leading northeastward from
Frankfurt would involve us merely in slow, rough-country fighting. Now
they apparently want me to turn aside on operations in which would be
involved many thousands of troops before the German forces are fully
defeated. I submit that these things are studied daily and hourly by me
and my advisors and that we are animated by one single thought which is
the early winning of this war."[8] Eisenhower indicated that he shared
Whiteley's irritation by signing the cable. The JCS, with this confirmation
of Eisenhower's views, continued to give him the strongest possible
backing. The only concession they made was to agree that hereafter
Eisenhower should clear his messages to Stalin with the CCS before sending them on, but that made little difference since it was now perfectly
obvious that the Americans dominated the CCS.

* The British had assumed, when they agreed to this policy, that Eisenhower would
deal with the Red Army staff, not Stalin; Eisenhower had decided to contact Stalin
directly, since everything had to be decided by him anyway, and Eisenhower wanted
to save time.

But if the BCOS challenge had been met and overcome, there were still other British sources of power that could challenge Eisenhower's plans. Both Montgomery and Churchill were angry, and both made their views known. On March 29 Montgomery cabled Eisenhower, "I note that you intend to change the command set up. If you feel this is necessary I pray you do not do so until we reach the Elbe as such action would not help the great movement which is now beginning to develop." Eisenhower told Whiteley to prepare an answer. It went out on March 31. "My plan is simple and aims at dividing and destroying the German forces and joining hands with the Red Army," it began. The best way to do that was to drive through central Germany on the Kassel–Leipzig axis. Before this thrust could begin, however, it was necessary to destroy the German forces encircled in the Ruhr (Generalfeldmarschall Walther von Model's Army Group B), a task that would involve elements of both U. S. First and Ninth Armies. "A mopping task of this nature," Whiteley explained, "in a densely populated area, should clearly be controlled by one commander." Thus Bradley had to have Ninth Army under him. "Moreover, it is Bradley who will be straining to release his thrust to the east and it is clearly very desirable that he should be in the position to judge when the situation in the Ruhr warrants it." Eisenhower therefore would not change his decision, and Ninth Army would go to Bradley.

"You will note that in none of this do I mention Berlin," Whiteley's draft continued. "That place has become, so far as I am concerned, nothing but a geographical location, and I have never been interested in these. My purpose is to destroy the enemy's forces and his powers to resist." In conclusion, the message said that after the AEF-Red Army link-up and the division of Germany, Eisenhower intended to push across the Elbe near its mouth, take Luebeck, and seal off the Danish Peninsula. This was the first mention of Lubeck; later, Eisenhower would explain that he wanted to control the land approaches to Denmark in order to prevent the Russians from liberating the area (Denmark, of course, had not been assigned to any of the Big Three for occupation purposes, as presumably it would have its sovereignty restored).[9]

Montgomery had objected to Eisenhower's plan on the narrow basis that it upset his own calculations. Churchill broadened the discussion. A firm believer in civilian control of the military, he did not want his own soldiers raising political issues. He had already called down the BCOS for using a phrase in reference to Berlin that read, "issues which have a wider import than the destruction of the main enemy forces in

Germany." Churchill commented this was "a very odd phrase to be used in a staff communication. I should have thought it laid itself open to a charge of extreme unorthodoxy."[10]

Churchill did not hesitate to take up the theme himself. On March 30 he called Eisenhower on the telephone to ask why SHAEF had changed the plan. Eisenhower had Bull send a brief explanation. The next morning the Prime Minister wired the Supreme Commander. On both military and political grounds, he made clear, he felt serious errors were about to be made. "If the enemy's resistance should weaken," Churchill said, "as you evidently expect and which may well be accorded, why should we not cross the Elbe and advance as far eastward as possible? This has an important political bearing, as the Russian Army of the south seems certain to enter Vienna and overrun Austria. If we deliberately leave Berlin to them, even if it should be in our grasp, the double event may strengthen their conviction, already apparent, that they have done everything." Aside from the effect on the Russians, who to Churchill seemed already to be displaying a bullying attitude with regard to such issues as the German surrender in Italy and the future Polish government and borders, the Prime Minister thought the fall of Berlin would have a "profound psychological effect on German resistance in every part of the Reich." He felt that "whilst Berlin remains under the German flag, it cannot in my opinion fail to be the most decisive point in Germany." The difficulty with this argument was that presumably the effect of the fall of Berlin on the Germans would be the same whatever the nationality of the army that took the city. What really stood out in Churchill's message was his suggestion that Ninth Army remain under Montgomery, since this "only shifts the weight of one Army to the northernmost flank and this avoids the relegation of His Majesty's Forces to an unexpected restricted sphere."[11]

Churchill's message, according to the SHAEF office diary, "upset Eisenhower quite a bit." He dictated the reply himself. "In the first place," he began, "I repeat that I have not changed any plan." The furthest he had ever gone in approving or formulating specific strategic plans, he declared, was to the encirclement of the Ruhr and the elimination of the German armies there. Beyond that, he had always insisted on flexibility. The first phase was almost completed and it created new situations "requiring study and analysis before the next broad pattern of effort could be accurately sketched." The problem was to "determine the direction of the blow that would create maximum disorganization of the remaining German forces and the German power to resist."

Eisenhower continued to insist that he had not changed his plans. He did admit that Churchill had introduced "a new idea respecting the political importance of the early attainment of particular objectives." He said he could "clearly see your point in this matter," but insisted that the only difference between the SHAEF plan and Churchill's suggestion was one of timing. After he had linked up with the Red Army near Dresden, Eisenhower said, he would give American troops to Montgomery for a drive over the Elbe to Luebeck. Although Eisenhower did not say so, this policy would not meet Churchill's demands for the capture of Berlin, but it would give the British a leading role in the last act. "I am disturbed, if not hurt," Eisenhower declared, "that you should suggest any thought on my part to 'relegate His Majesty's Forces to an unexpected restricted sphere.' Nothing is further from my mind and I think my record over two and a half years of commanding Allied forces should eliminate any such idea."[12]

Eisenhower was not being totally candid with Churchill, a reflection perhaps of his irritation at having had his every move called into question. Like Marshall, he felt he had proven he should be trusted. Probably more important was the fact that he would not give in. Marshall had informed him of the backing the JCS was giving him, and Eisenhower knew how strong his position was. He did not want to hurt or disturb the British, but neither would he allow them to set the objectives of his last campaign. Determined to hold to his own plan, he still hoped to satisfy the British; thus his refusal to take up a discussion with Churchill on Berlin, which could only have led to recrimination and bad feeling, or to admit that he had made any change in plan. If he were forced, however, he would speak out. "So earnestly did I believe in the military soundness of what we were doing," Eisenhower later declared, "that my intimates on the staff knew I was prepared to make an issue of it."[13]

One way to avoid placing a strain on the alliance, and the one Eisenhower usually tried to adopt, was to act as if there were only objective military considerations at stake. This would work, however, only if the British agreed to limit the discussion to military objectives. Eisenhower tried to get them to do so, and at the same time to feel that British interests were well protected in SHAEF, by emphasizing the number and importance of the British officers on his staff. "I hope it will not be forgotten that some of the ablest members of my staff are from the British Army," he said in one cable to Marshall. "Such men as Tedder, Morgan, Whiteley and Strong possess great ability and are absolutely unimpeachable in their objective approach to every question." He said Tedder had been consulted at every step of the way.[14] To Churchill, Brooke, and Montgomery, this was hardly satisfactory, however, as they considered that the British officers at SHAEF were too much under Eisenhower's influence.

Still, the BCOS quickly recognized that, unlike the 1942–43 period, they could no longer control CCS decisions. To save face, they decided to accept Eisenhower's formula, which held that there had been no change in plans. At an April 1 meeting at Chequers, the Chiefs discussed the entire problem. Brooke said he was mollified because "it is quite clear that there is no very great change," but he was still irritated because "most of the changes are due to national aspirations and to ensure that the U.S. effort will not be lost under British command. It is all a pity and straightforward strategy is being affected by the nationalistic outlook of allies."[15]

There was a court of last resort. If the British contribution to the AEF was not sufficient to allow the BCOS to dominate or even have an equal voice in the CCS, Churchill still might be able to persuade the President of the soundness of British policy and thereby bring about a switch in the plans. His appeals to Roosevelt, however, were unsuccessful. Marshall, whose influence with the President had grown steadily throughout the war, convinced Roosevelt that all matters of military importance should be left to Eisenhower.

The storm now began to subside. Neither side wanted a split. The British agreed in practice to the relegation of Montgomery to a secondary role. Churchill, deeply impressed by the need for Anglo-American solidarity in the postwar world, took the lead in calming the waters. In a message to Roosevelt he said, "I wish to place on record the complete confidence felt by His Majesty's Government in General Eisenhower, our pleasure that our armies are serving under his command and our admiration of his great and shining quality, character and personality. . . ." Churchill passed the statement on to Eisenhower, saying in addition that it would "be a grief to me" if anything he had said "pains you." The Prime Minister took the opportunity, however, to add that he still felt the AEF should take Berlin. "I deem it highly important that we should shake hands with the Russians as far to the east as possible." Thus, though the British had accepted the transfer of Ninth Army from Montgomery to Bradley, they still wanted the question of Berlin left open.

Eisenhower was fulsome in his reply. "I feel an immense satisfaction that up to this point our strategic plans formulated more than a year ago have successfully developed so closely according to conception," he declared. "The generosity of your language is equalled only by my continued determination that every action of mine shall be governed by the single purpose of winning this campaign at the earliest possible moment. In doing so I shall likewise devote myself toward sustaining among the forces of the United States and Great Britain those feelings of mutual respect and unification that have been the mainspring of effectiveness in this command." He promised that the G.I. and the Tommy would march forward shoulder to shoulder, and "if Berlin can be brought into the orbit of our success the honors will be equitably shared."[16]

Three days later Brooke sent Eisenhower his best wishes on the occasion of the U. S. Army Day. The CIGS offered his "warmest congratulations" on Eisenhower's "super-leadership" and said the overwhelming victories which Eisenhower was winning would "go down in history as among the greatest military achievements of all time."[17] Eisenhower told Marshall of Brooke's message, said it was especially pleasing because of all the arguments he had had with the CIGS, and added that it showed "that there is a bigness about him that I have found lacking in a few people I have run into on this side of the water."[18]

On April 5 Churchill put the seal on the controversy by wiring the President: "The changes in the main plan have now turned out to be very much less than we at first supposed. My personal relations with General Eisenhower are of the most friendly character. I regard the matter as closed, and to prove my sincerity I will use one of my very few Latin quotations: *Amantium irae amoris integratio est,"* which the War Department translated to read, "Lovers' quarrels are a part of love."[19]

Eisenhower had not waited for the BCOS or Churchill to approve of his plans; he had already acted. On April 2 he sent out the directive that implemented his program. The Ruhr had been isolated, and so Eisenhower declared it was his intention to divide and destroy the enemy forces by launching a powerful thrust on the axis Kassel–Leipzig. He gave Montgomery the objective of advancing on Bremen, then going on to the Elbe, where he should "seize any opportunity" to capture a bridgehead "and be prepared" to conduct operations east of the river. Bradley's task was to mop up the encircled German forces in the Ruhr, drive from Kassel to Leipzig, and take bridgeheads over the Elbe if possible. Devers was to protect Bradley's right flank and, after that was secured, advance on the axis Nuremberg–Linz.[20]

The British did not approve. Having surrendered on the point of command of Ninth Army, they still wanted the advance from Kassel to head for Berlin. Again, however, the BCOS were rebuffed by the JCS.

On April 6 the JCS told their British counterparts, "Only Eisenhower is in a position to know how to fight his battle, and to exploit to the full the changing situation." Even if the JCS wanted to interfere they would not in this case, because they agreed with the Supreme Commander's assessment of the situation. On Berlin, the JCS declared that such "psychological and political advantages as would result from the possible capture of Berlin ahead of the Russians should not override the imperative military consideration, which in our opinion is the destruction and dismemberment of the German armed forces."[21]

The next day Eisenhower told Marshall that once he reached the Elbe River he planned to clear out his northern and southern flanks. If after these operations were concluded he could still take Berlin, he would do so. He insisted that his judgments were made purely on military grounds, and declared that he would need a new directive if the CCS wished him to operate on political grounds. He said he regarded a drive to Berlin as militarily unsound and added, "I am the first to admit that a war is waged in pursuance of political aims, and if the Combined Chiefs of Staff should decide that the Allied effort to take Berlin outweighs purely military considerations in this theater, I would cheerfully readjust my plans and my thinking so as to carry out such an operation."[22] If, in other words, Churchill was prepared to make Russia instead of Germany the enemy, and if he could get Roosevelt to agree, Eisenhower would willingly change his plans, for then the military considerations would be much different. But the CCS did not even discuss Eisenhower's cable or the question of Berlin, and the final decision was left to Eisenhower.[23] His directive remained unchanged, Germany remained the enemy, and Russia continued to be an ally.

On April 6 Montgomery made another effort to persuade Eisenhower to try to take Berlin. He said that after the British Second Army captured Hamburg and reached the Elbe it should advance both toward Luebeck and to the southeast toward Berlin. Montgomery felt this would hit the Germans from an unexpected direction "and should be comparatively easy." Montgomery knew that Eisenhower did not feel Berlin had much value as an objective but said, "I would personally not agree with this; I consider that Berlin has definite value as an objective and I have no doubt whatever that the Russians think the same; but they may well pretend that this is not the case!!"

Eisenhower told Montgomery that his proposal for a double thrust from the Elbe was currently unfeasible, for it implied that Bradley would protect the right flank of Second Army. This was not what Eisenhower wanted; Twenty-first Army Group's responsibility was, on the contrary, to give security to Bradley's left flank. "It is not his [Bradley's] role to protect your southern flank," Eisenhower said. "My directive is quite clear on this point." Eisenhower admitted that Berlin had "political and psychological significance but of far greater importance will be the location of the remaining German forces. . . . It is on them that I am going to concentrate my attention." He added that if he had a chance to take Berlin cheaply he would do so.[24]

With the Berlin question settled for the time being, it was imperative for Eisenhower to get some co-operation with the Russians under way. The danger was real and apparent—troops of the Red Army might bump into American or British soldiers and start shooting. The chances were great because of the unfamiliar uniforms and the language differences. Further, Bradley and Eisenhower had been given to understand that the Russians "had grown increasingly cocky and rash with each mile they advanced toward the west." They were shooting everything in sight.

Early in February Eisenhower had discussed with Bradley the problem of avoiding an accidental clash in closing head on with the Russians. The two Americans agreed that prearranged recognition signals were not likely to work; they had even less faith in the use of radio contact because of the language barrier. What they needed was a visible geographic line of demarcation. At the time of the conversation the Russians had closed to the Oder–Neisse, SHAEF forces to the Rhine. The only major river between them was the Elbe, which ran north and south to Magdeburg, where it bent to the east. South of Magdeburg the Mulde River ran on nearly straight south to the Czech border. It could be used to continue the boundary. Eisenhower, from then on, had the Elbe–Mulde in mind as a demarcation line. It was an optimistic thought, for his forces were two hundred and fifty miles or more from the Elbe while the Russians were within a hundred miles; in Bradley's words, "The Elbe River line looked almost hopelessly beyond the reach of our Allied forces."[25]

Reaching agreement on a line of demarcation proved extraordinarily complex. Soviet, British, and United States airmen had been trying to work out solutions to the problems of bomb lines since June 1944, with little success. On the ground the matter was even more difficult because, in addition to such problems as language barriers and the absence of direct wire communication, there were the questions of the nature of lines of demarcation, procedure to follow when contact was imminent, withdrawal of various troops to their proper zones of occupation, and the probable necessity of having to advance beyond an agreed line of demarcation for emergency military purposes. There was no effective liaison between the advancing forces, for although the Russians had some political contact with the Western Allies the Soviet government had consistently refused to allow the British and Americans to gain any significant knowledge of the Red Army's military plans and operations. The United States and Great Britain maintained military missions in Moscow, but until Eisenhower began his direct communication with Stalin the military missions merely passed on general information of SHAEF's operations; the amount of information the West received through the missions was infinitesimal.

In view of all these problems and, more important, in view of the rapidly changing military situation, Eisenhower knew it was obviously impractical to make any definite proposals on boundaries until he had a better idea as to where the two sides would actually meet. General agreements were, however, imperative. On April 5, therefore, he proposed that "both fronts should be free to advance until contact is imminent." Stop lines might then be worked out by local commanders on the spot. Since this might bring the Western armies into the Russian Zone, he further proposed that, subject to operational necessity, either side would withdraw into its own zone at the request of the other.[26]

The British, just recovering from their shock over Montgomery's secondary role, were furious. Churchill felt that Eisenhower's proposal would throw away the best bargaining point the West would hold at the end of the war. He most definitely wanted Allied troops within the Russian Zone when the Germans surrendered, and he did not want them pulled out until he was certain Stalin would give something in return.* He insisted that questions of withdrawal from the Russian Zone were governmental, not military matters, and had the British Chiefs of Staff suggest to the Joint Chiefs of Staff that Eisenhower be directed that "On cessation of operations our respective armies will stand fast until they receive orders from their Governments."[27]

The business of holding the other side's territory for trading purposes, however, could work two ways, as the State Department was quick

* What Churchill wanted to trade was the Western-occupied areas of the Russian Zone for American and British entry into Berlin. In addition, the Red Army was probably going to overrun Austria, which had not been divided; Churchill wanted to make sure the West got into Austria and the best way to do so, he felt, was by trading. He also wanted food from eastern Germany for the Ruhr.

to see. Officials of the European and Russian Affairs Divisions declared "that for governments to direct movement of troops definitely indicated political action and that such movements should remain a military consideration at least until SHAEF is dissolved and the ACC [Allied Control Commission] is set up." The State Department feared that the British proposal might send the Russians racing over Germany in an attempt to acquire as many square miles as possible before the war ended. Officials of the War Department were thankful for this interpretation of the British proposal because it indicated that the Department of State preferred "a straight military solution to the problem"[28]

The BCOS and the JCS directed Eisenhower to get an agreement with the Russians that would allow both sides to advance until contact was imminent. Division of responsibility would then be settled by army group commanders. The Russians were suspicious of the proposal, fearing that the West was trying to redraw the zonal boundaries, and demanded that Eisenhower clarify that point. He assured the Red Army leaders that these arrangements were tactical only, and on April 15 agreement was reached. The Combined Chiefs of Staff then instructed Eisenhower to make no major withdrawals without consulting his superiors. The policy was finally clear.[29]

The question of where to stop was not. Even with agreement reached, Eisenhower could not simply have his troops rushing forward until they bumped into the Russians. He attempted to work out a system of signals and markings through which the two sides could identify themselves and avoid firing on each other, but no one had much faith in them. On April 21, therefore, Eisenhower told the military missions to Moscow to tell the Soviets that he intended to stop on the Elbe–Mulde line. Thereafter he would turn his forces north and south.* The Russians almost immediately agreed.[30]

Thus Eisenhower had turned down both Montgomery, who wanted his army group to have the leading role in the last campaign, and Churchill, who no longer argued about who was to do it but still wanted the AEF to get as far into the Russian Zone as possible, and certainly into Berlin. The differences in views were caused, in large part, by different perspectives. Montgomery was a field commander whose forces had won great victories in Africa, Italy, France, and Germany. He was proud of what his men had done and was convinced that they could achieve almost

---

* The first link-up came on April 25 at Torgau on the Elbe River; others followed rapidly along the entire front. The line did not apply in the north, where Twenty-first Army Group did cross the Elbe. There were no major incidents.

anything he asked of them. They wanted to deliver the final blow, he wanted to see them do it, and he thought they could. Berlin was before them, the obvious objective. The Germans defending the capital were facing east, awaiting the Russian onslaught. Montgomery was confident he could take Berlin with one lightning thrust, and it seemed to him madness to hold his armies back.

Churchill's concerns were wider. If Eisenhower's responsibility was to defeat Germany, the Prime Minister's was the security of Great Britain. This was a continuing problem and he had to take into account what Europe would be like once German military might had been eliminated. The most obvious fact then would be the presence in central Europe of a triumphant Red Army, backed by a state that had the sharpest possible ideological differences with the West and had already indicated deep suspicions of Western motives. Roosevelt had told Churchill that the Americans would not leave their troops in Europe for more than two years, and Britain was exhausted.

Under the circumstances Churchill wanted the West to emerge from the war in a strong position. The Americans were already preparing to redeploy forces to the Pacific; April 1945 marked the high-water mark of Anglo-American power in Europe. Churchill thought it should be used to secure the West's postwar position. As John Ehrman puts it: "Disappointed, distrustful and sometimes deeply alarmed [by the Soviets] as they were, [British] hopes, and British policy, rested on a continuing partnership of the three Powers expressed in and operating through the instrument of the United Nations to which it was complementary. The strategy they wished to adopt in Germany was designed, not for reasons of defence or attack against Russia . . . but with the object, which they recognized must remain subsidiary to the immediate military task, of negotiating from strength. In the atmosphere of the time, this seemed to them a useful—possibly an essential—contribution to the tripartite alliance, guarding it from that threat of excessive Soviet ambition which Soviet conquests appeared to foster. The British in fact had not abandoned the objects, or even entirely the hopes, of the Yalta Conference. . . . They did not despair of a solution with the Russians: indeed they expected it. But they expected it as a result of firm and timely measures which would remind their ally of his obligations, and whose inception depended on the movements of the Western armies in the few weeks that remained."[31]

Ehrman's argument is, of course, friendly to British policy. New Left historians in the United States would never accept Ehrman's analysis. By April 1945, they argue, it was abundantly clear that Churchill's intention was to somehow deny the Soviets the fruits of victory, specifically in eastern Europe. Churchill could not bear the thought of a Soviet domination of the old *cordon sanitaire* or of Soviet support for the political left in Rumania, Poland, and the other eastern European nations. American policy makers also wanted to keep the Soviet Union hemmed into its prewar boundaries. But even if this is a correct analysis of the policy, and even if it is a logical, rational policy, it is difficult to see where Berlin fit into the pattern. Unless the West was willing and able to hold the city, up to and beyond the point of resisting a Red Army attack, taking Berlin made little sense. Eisenhower's suspicion of the time remains—Churchill wanted Berlin for prestige purposes that had little or nothing to do with the defeat of Germany and could hardly fit into a logical pattern of resisting Soviet encroachment in Europe. The Red Army had paid the price in blood, and the West was fortunate that the Soviets did not come further into central Europe than they did. To think that a Western capture of Berlin would have reversed the process and changed the situation in eastern Europe is absurd.

In any event, whatever Churchill's (and Montgomery's) motives, Eisenhower's concerns were different. The shape of postwar Europe was up to the heads of government; his task remained the rapid defeat of Germany. This was not yet an accomplished fact, and he felt there was reason to believe that it might take a great deal more time. On April 13 the CCS asked him for his views on declaring Victory in Europe Day. The Chiefs thought he should not wait until all isolated centers of resistance had been mopped up, and they doubted that any German government would sign a formal document of surrender. Eisenhower said he expected continued German resistance in the Alpine redoubt, the north German ports, western Holland, Denmark, Norway, the Channel Islands, and the German pockets left in France. He feared that operations against Norway and the Alpine redoubt "may involve considerable forces and also may last for some time." He thought, therefore, that the declaration of VE-Day should wait until it was evident "that further months of hostilities on a fairly considerable scale do not lie before us." Nothing so far had indicated that German morale had cracked, and "it must be remembered that the storming of the final citadels of Nazi resistance may well call for acts of endurance and heroism on the part of the forces engaged. . . ." He recommended that VE-Day not be announced until the AEF and the Red Army had joined hands, the Allies had occupied the key positions in the alpine redoubt, and the AEF was in Denmark and able to mount an assault on Norway.[32]

On April 15 Eisenhower explained his thinking on the political aspects to Marshall. "Frankly, if I should have forces in the Russian occupational zone and be faced with an order or 'request' to retire so that they may advance to the points they choose, I see no recourse except to comply. To do otherwise would probably provoke an incident, with the logic of the situation all on the side of the Soviets. I cannot see exactly what the British have in mind for me to do, under such circumstances. It is a bridge that I will have to cross when I come to it but I must say that I feel a bit lost in trying to give sensible instructions to my various commanders in the field." This represented the key to both this particular question and the broader one of Churchill's policy vis-à-vis the Russians. Eisenhower simply could not "see exactly what the British have in mind" because he continued to center his attention on the defeat of Germany, while Churchill looked to the shape of postwar Europe. What Churchill had in mind certainly was for Eisenhower to refuse a request to pull back, meanwhile referring it to the heads of government, who could then use it as a bargaining point to get concessions from the Russians. This had little or nothing to do with the defeat of Germany. It had everything to do with Britain's postwar security.[33]

The picture that Montgomery saw was open ground between Twenty-first Army Group and Berlin. Churchill looked at the situation maps, saw the link-up of Twenty-first Army Group and Twelfth Army Group east of the Ruhr and the relative weakness of the German forces standing between the AEF and Berlin, concluded that the war was won, and advocated policies designed to strengthen the postwar position of the West. Eisenhower saw something altogether different. His forces were advancing almost at will, but not into those areas in which the Germans might mount a prolonged defense. Until he had taken the alpine redoubt and Denmark and secured a broad link-up with the Red Army, he could not be sure of a quick, decisive end to the war. In one message to the CCS, Eisenhower warned that if the Germans in Norway decided to fight on he would not be able to mount an offensive there until winter, when because of the terrain and weather conditions it would be "almost impracticable." As long as the Germans held Norway they could continue the submarine war and if the continued German resistance in isolated parts in France was any guide, the enemy in Norway could hold out for a long time. The same was true of the Alpine redoubt, so "it must be our aim to break into it rapidly before the enemy has an opportunity to man it and organize its defense fully."

The final decision was the Supreme Commander's, and he based it on the situation as he saw it. On April 14 he informed the CCS that when the AEF had a firm front in central Germany on the line of the Elbe he would then concentrate on taking Lubeck and driving into the Alpine area. "Since the thrust on Berlin must await the successful outcome" of those operations, he declared, "I do not include it as part of my present plan."[34] He sent out the orders to the field commanders the next day.[35] The last campaign had taken shape.

CHAPTER 21

Victory

By late April 1945 the Germans were finished. SHAEF G-2 reported that all but the most fanatic Nazis had given up hope, and even the Nazis were beginning to wonder. They could see only three dim possibilities that could reverse their situation: (1) a falling out between the Western Allies and the Russians when they met in central Germany; (2) a holding action in the Alpine redoubt through the winter; (3) large-scale guerrilla warfare throughout Germany.[1] Eisenhower, aware of these German hopes, shaped his operations to prevent any of the three possibilities from coming to fruition. Specifically, this meant that he fanned out the AEF in order to overrun Germany and at the same time did everything he could to avoid a clash with the Russians. He did not race them to Berlin but instead arranged for the easily recognized stop lines on the Elbe–Mulde line.

All through April the AEF rolled forward. Superiority in quality of troops, mobility, air power, material, and morale was enormous. Commanders chose objectives for units that, more often than not, were reached and captured before the time set by the commander. Regiments, companies, squads, sometimes even three men in a jeep dashed on ahead, leaving their supply bases far behind, ignoring wide gaps on their flanks and enemy units in the rear that sometimes were superior in numbers, roaming far and wide with only sketchy knowledge of the enemy's positions—all the time certain that there was little or nothing the Germans could do about it. The German high command was, for all practical purposes, non-existent; even regimental commanders did not know where their troops were. Most German units were immobilized because of the lack of fuel. There was no coherent defense.[2]

Eisenhower felt a deep sense of pride as he watched the Americans drive forward. He wanted Marshall, the man who built the Army that was doing so well, to share the feeling. "If you could see your way clear to do it," he wrote the Chief on April 15, "I think you should make a visit here . . . while we are still conducting a general offensive." Eisenhower was sure Marshall "would be proud of the Army you have produced." The U.S. air and ground forces were operating as a unit "all the way down the line from me to the lowest private." Eisenhower could see no evidence of any jealousy, suspicion, or lack of understanding. Marshall would also be impressed by the veteran quality of the organization. "Commanders, staffs, and troops, both air and ground, go about their business in a perfectly calm and sure manner that gets results." Eisenhower was sure that no organization had ever existed that could reshuffle and regroup on a large scale as well as the American Army in Europe could. This, in turn, was a reflection of the "high average of ability in our higher command team." The corps commanders were without exception outstanding, and the only weakness among the army commanders he could single out was Patton's unpredictability. Bradley "remains the one whose tactical and strategical judgment I consider almost unimpeachable."

Eisenhower concluded with another plea to Marshall to come to Germany so "you could see, in visible form, the fruits of much of your work over the past five years. In a matter of three or four days I am sure you would see things that would be of great satisfaction to you from now on." Eisenhower did not need to add that, since redeployment would soon begin, this would be Marshall's last opportunity to see the greatest armed force the United States had ever put together. Unfortunately Marshall's commitments at home, compounded by Roosevelt's death, prevented him from making the trip.[3]

The AEF, meanwhile, spread out in all directions. Its dispersion soon became so great that army and corps commanders did not know where their units were at any particular time of the day. Under the circumstances, Eisenhower played a small role in the direction of the battle. He intervened only when army group shifts were required, or where a major change in the direction of an army was called for, or when a command question with political overtones was involved.

During the first two weeks of April, while spearheads of Twelfth and Sixth Army Groups moved into central Germany, Bradley undertook the systematic reduction of the Ruhr pocket. By April 18 resistance there came to an end as 317,000 German soldiers surrendered—the largest mass surrender of German troops in the war. To the north, Montgomery's

Canadian and British troops made good progress, while at the other end of the front Devers' French and American soldiers overran the area between Frankfurt and the Czech border. Patton and Hodges were closing to the Elbe while Simpson, skirting the northern edge of the Harz Mountains, drove forward. On April 11 spearheads of Simpson's Ninth Army reached the Elbe at Magdeburg. Simpson got two bridgeheads over the Elbe, one north of Magdeburg on April 12 and another to the south on April 13. The one to the north was wiped out by a German counterattack on April 14, but the one to the south held.

Suddenly it seemed that the Americans had an opportunity to take Berlin. The Russian drive for the capital had not yet started and Simpson was within fifty miles of the city. He thought he could get to Berlin before the Russians and asked Bradley's permission to try. Bradley checked with Eisenhower, who said no, and Simpson was stopped where he was.[4]

On April 15 Eisenhower explained his thinking to Marshall. He felt that getting to Lubeck and clearing up the Alpine redoubt area were tasks "vastly more important than the capture of Berlin." He also thought that Simpson could not get to the capital before the Russians and so it was foolish to try. "We'd get all coiled up for something that in all probability would never come off." While it was true that Simpson had a bridgehead over the Elbe, "it must be remembered that only our spearheads are up to that river; our center of gravity is well back of there."[5]

When Simpson reached the Elbe the Russians were still thirty-five miles from the city, but the Red Army had had two months in which to build up its strength, while Simpson had just covered more than two hundred miles in two weeks. The American center of gravity was indeed far back. No one, on either side, could have sustained- an offensive of this scope and magnitude beyond the Elbe. Modern armies are unable to live off the countryside, and their means of transportation cannot forage for themselves. The armies of World War II were dependent on gasoline, a new phenomenon in the history of war. Offensives ordinarily reached their limit after a 200 to 250-mile advance. This was true of the German campaign in Russia in 1941, of the Russians in their 1944–45 winter offensive, and of the AEF in September 1944. It happened to the AEF again in April 1945. As one example of the problems involved in a headlong advance, Eisenhower's armies had left the fighter strips so far behind that airplanes had to carry reserve gasoline tanks on their wings just to keep up with the troops. They left their bombs behind.

The Americans reached the Elbe on April 11. They had one small bridgehead, were faced by one weak German army, and had a number of water barriers between them and Berlin. American strength in the area was not much more than 50,000 men, with little artillery. There were a few reinforcements available in the area, but to supply a drive beyond the Elbe Eisenhower would have had to devote to it nearly his entire air transport. The Russians, fifteen miles closer to Berlin, had two solid bridgeheads, 1,250,000 men, and 22,000 pieces of artillery. They were faced by two weak German armies and had flat, dry land between them and Berlin. The only way, under the circumstances, for the Americans to beat the Red Army to Berlin would have been with German help. Had the Germans decided that it was in their interest to have an American occupation of their capital, they might have fought fiercely against the Russians to the east while welcoming the Americans coming in from the west. They might have so decided, but Eisenhower could not be sure of it at the time, and thus far the Germans had shown no inclination to surrender on their western front while continuing to fight in the east. As long as Hitler lived and continued to direct the Battle of Berlin from his bunker in the city, it could be expected that the Germans would put up a fight against all comers.

Simpson was not alone in thinking that Berlin was worth a try. On April 16, after learning of Eisenhower's plans, the BCOS suggested to the JCS that they jointly direct Eisenhower to take any opportunity to advance to Berlin. Churchill agreed with the position his Chiefs took. The next day, April 17, Eisenhower flew to London and had a conference with the Prime Minister. The Supreme Commander convinced Churchill of the soundness of his views, and shortly after the meeting Churchill wired his Foreign Minister, who was in the United States. "It would seem that the Western Allies are not immediately in a position to force their way into Berlin," Churchill declared. "The Russians have two and a half million troops [*sic*] on the section of the front opposite that city. The Americans have only their spearheads . . . which are covering an immense front and are at many points engaged with the Germans."[6]

Eisenhower also convinced Churchill of the significance of Lubeck. The Supreme Commander emphasized the importance of Montgomery's taking the city in order to keep the Russians out of the Danish Peninsula. To British eyes Denmark, in comparison to Berlin and eastern Germany, was relatively unimportant, but Eisenhower concentrated on it for three reasons. First, he had to have Denmark if he was later forced to undertake a campaign into Norway. Second, he was not willing to give the Russians anything the EAC had not already assigned to the Soviet sphere. Third, by stressing Lubeck he gave Twenty-first Army Group a significant role to play, which hopefully would mollify the British. One of the things Eisenhower and Churchill discussed at their April 17 meeting was Eisenhower's position with respect to Russian requests that he withdraw the AEF from areas assigned to the Russian Zone. Churchill insisted that Eisenhower should move his men as far forward as possible and keep them inside the Russian Zone until the heads of government had worked out withdrawal procedures. After the meeting Eisenhower wrote Marshall, "I do not quite understand why the Prime Minsiter has been so determined to intermingle political and military considerations. . . ." He added that he had proposed that each side withdraw from the zone of another upon request because of "the possibility that the Russians might arrive in the Danish peninsula before we could fight our way across the Elbe and I wanted a formula that would take them out of that region on my request."[7]

To give Montgomery enough strength to get to Lubeck first, Eisenhower assigned the U.S. airborne corps to Twenty-first Army Group and told his staff to give Montgomery all necessary logistical support. He sent a series of messages to Montgomery, urging him to press on, and a letter for the record to Brooke, recording all that he had done with respect to Lubeck.[8] Churchill, unable to get Eisenhower to change his mind on Berlin, decided that Lubeck was the best he could get, both in relation to the role British forces would play and on political objectives. He told Eden, "Our arrival at Lubeck before our Russian friends from Stettin would save a lot of argument later on. There is no reason why the Russians should occupy Denmark, which is a country to be liberated and to have its sovereignty restored. Our position at Lubeck, if we get it, would be decisive in this matter." As indeed it was. Churchill also agreed with Eisenhower's decision to push on south of Stuttgart to capture the German atomic research facilities in the area.[9]

There was one more controversy with the British. By April 25 (the day Germany was split in half by an American-Russian link-up at Torgau, northeast of Leipzig), Patton's Third Army had reached the Czech border. There was open ground between his tanks and Prague. The BCOS felt there would be "remarkable political advantages derived from liberation of Prague and as much as possible of Czechoslovakia by U.S.-U.K. forces." The British Chiefs thought Eisenhower should be directed "to take advantage of any improvement in his logistical situation or any weakening of enemy resistance to advance into Czechoslovakia provided such action does not hamper or delay final German defeat." In passing this on to Eisenhower, Marshall declared: "Personally and aside from all logistic, tactical or strategical implications I would be loath to hazard American lives for purely political purposes."

Forrest Pogue has pointed out that Marshall's statement, startling as it appears in retrospect, was in accord with current American policy.[10] The aim throughout the war had been the quick defeat of Germany, and it remained the aim at the end. Marshall was trying to make a political-military division that was not there, for the decision to concentrate single-mindedly on defeating Germany was, at bottom, a political decision. There were other political factors that affected Marshall's position, most importantly the need to redeploy and the necessity of getting the Soviets to help crush the Japanese enemy.

Eisenhower understood Marshall's meaning. In his reply the Supreme Commander said his first priority would be Lubeck and the Alpine redoubt. These operations were "straining our resources" and were all that could be currently undertaken. If additional forces became available he intended to attack the Germans wherever they were located, which meant that if they were still holding out in Czechoslovakia he would go there. The Red Army was in position to clean out Czechoslovakia and it appeared to Eisenhower that they could certainly reach Prague before Patton could. In conclusion, he assured Marshall that "I shall *not* attempt any move I deem militarily unwise merely to gain a political prize unless I receive specific orders from the Combined Chiefs of Staff."[11]

This then became the policy; it remained only to implement it. On April 30 Eisenhower told the Russians of his plans. He explained that he would launch an operation across the lower Elbe, south of Dresden, to establish a firm operational east flank. The exact position could be adjusted locally by the commanders on the spot. From the headwaters of the Mulde southward he intended to hold to a line approximately along the 1937 Czech border. To the south, he would advance to Linz, which would put the AEF in position to clear out any resistance in the Alpine redoubt. If at any time the situation required his forces to advance farther to the east, he would take such action as the situation allowed.

The Red Army leaders quickly indicated their full agreement with Eisenhower's proposals. "Please inform General Eisenhower," they told the Allied military missions, "that the immediate plan of the Soviet Command contemplates both the occupation of Berlin, and also cleaning out of the German forces from the eastern shore of the Elbe River north and south of Berlin, and the Mulde River Valley [which included Prague], where according to information we have, the Germans are concentrating considerable forces."[12]

On May 4, with Patton straining to go forward, Lubeck taken, and the Alpine redoubt no longer a threat, Eisenhower informed General Antonov of the Red Army that he now proposed to send the Third Army east to the Moldau and the outskirts of Prague. Antonov expressed strong dissent. To avoid "a possible confusion of forces," he asked Eisenhower "not to move the Allied forces in Czechoslovakia east of the originally intended line," which was generally Pilsen–Karlsbad. Antonov pointed out that the Soviet forces had stopped their advance north of Berlin well short of the Elbe, leaving Lubeck to Montgomery, and said he hoped Eisenhower would comply with Russian wishes in Czechoslovakia. Eisenhower thereupon assured Antonov that he would not move beyond Pilsen–Karlsbad, thus leaving Prague and most of Czechoslovakia to the Soviet forces. He held to his position even when the Czechs in Prague rose up against the Germans and, over captured radios, specifically asked the AEF for help.[13] This was a bitter pill for Churchill.

Churchill was a romantic who believed that the fate of great empires could be decided through the skill or luck of one man on one day, that sweeping historical movements or the development of a people or nation could be turned decisively by success or failure at one battle. Marlborough, the Prime Minister once told Montgomery, "sat on his horse and directed by word of mouth a battle on a five- or six-mile front, which ended in a day and settled the fortunes of great nations, sometimes for years or generations to come."[14] He felt this intuition about the taking of Berlin. If Eisenhower took the capital, he felt, it would put a crimp in Russian ambitions in central Europe. Thus also his anxiety about Prague. Aside from the prestige value involved, (and for Churchill this was of incalculable value), it was to him true that if the West took Prague, Czechoslovakia would be safe. But, at least after the event, it is hard to see what all the excitement was about. The Russians kept troops in Czechoslovakia, to be sure, but so did the United States. Both sides pulled out at the same time. It is true that Soviet troops were on the Czech border when the Communist coup delivered that unhappy land to the Communists, but so were American soldiers. That there were more Red Army than U. S. Army men in the area was a result of postwar policy, not anything that had been done or decided during the war. There is no hard, or even any circumstantial, evidence to support the view that if Eisenhower had liberated Prague Czechoslovakia would be free today. Churchill's views to the contrary, single battles do not decide the fate of great nations. Nothing Eisenhower could have done at the late date of April 1945 could have made any significant difference.

But there can be no doubt that there was a certain lack of precision in Eisenhower's statements and actions. He wished to make all decisions on military grounds, and did not see anything to fear from the Russians—yet he sent Montgomery toward Lubeck, away from the remaining German armies, for an indisputably political objective. Even taking into account the need to give the British some satisfaction, Lubeck contrasted strangely with Prague. The policy was inconsistent, perhaps a result of the confusion at headquarters in the rush of events, perhaps caused by general exhaustion, perhaps a result of the failure of the CCS to provide clear objectives, which in turn may have been a consequence of Roosevelt's illness and death. But the inconsistency may also have been a result of conflicting demands. The general American policy, at least while Roosevelt lived and in the early days of Truman's presidency, was to try to retain Soviet friendship, while Churchill wanted to take a firm stand. Eisenhower could never satisfy both his masters.

The end of the war brought with it one last dispute with the French. At the beginning of the third week in April Patch's Seventh Army had enveloped Stuttgart. On April 23 General de Lattre's First French Army took the city. The day before, however, Devers had redrawn the boundary lines, putting Stuttgart within Patch's sector. Devers wanted to prevent U.S. and French units from becoming entangled and to provide proper lines of communications for his armies—his new boundary, in other words, was drawn as a matter of military routine. De Gaulle, however, thought the United States had ulterior political motives. The French President believed that Devers was more interested in getting the French out of an important German city than in the logistics of Seventh Army's supply lines. This came at a time when the French had no assigned zone of occupation in Germany and there was still some question as to whether they would get one at all.

De Gaulle therefore told De Lattre that establishing boundaries was a political and not a military matter, and that therefore the French forces were not answerable to Eisenhower or Devers but only to their own government. As a result, when Patch moved forces into Stuttgart on April 24 to relieve the French units in the city, De Lattre was polite but firm—

the French would not leave. Patch could use the city for communications purposes, but the French would hold it. Devers again issued orders to De Lattre to get out; De Gaulle responded with orders of his own to the French general: "I require you to maintain a French garrison at Stuttgart and to institute immediately a military government." De Gaulle told De Lattre to tell Patch that his orders were to hold "the territory conquered by our troops until the French zone of occupation has been fixed between the interested Governments. . . ." Patch passed this on to Devers, who appealed to Eisenhower, saying his authority was being flouted.[15]

This was the most direct challenge to his position that Eisenhower had yet had to face. For all the British criticism of his strategy, they had never refused to carry out an order. De Lattre did. Eisenhower, knowing that it would do no good to continue the argument with De Lattre, dictated an official protest to De Gaulle.

Eisenhower began by saying he had learned with "regret" of De Gaulle's orders to De Lattre. The question of a French Zone of Occupation, Eisenhower pointed out, "is a matter entirely outside the scope of my responsibility, which is limited to the military defeat of our common enemy, Germany." Under the circumstances, Eisenhower said, "I must of course accept the situation, as I myself am unwilling to take any action which would reduce the effectiveness of the military effort against Germany, either by withholding supplies from the First French Army or by any other measures which would affect their fighting strength." Nor, he added, would he ever be a party to starting any struggle or quarrel between the French government and the troops under his command, "which could result only in weakening bonds of national friendship as well as the exemplary spirit of cooperation that has characterized the actions of French and American forces in the battle line."

Eisenhower told De Gaulle that he believed the issuance of orders to De Lattre based on political considerations "violates the understanding with the United States Government under which French divisions, armed and equipped by the United States, were to be placed under the Combined Chiefs of Staff whose orders I am carrying out in this Theater of Operations." Eisenhower had had complete faith in De Gaulle's willingness to abide by the spirit of the agreement when he placed French troops under SHAEF's control. As it was, "I can do nothing else than fully to inform the Combined Chiefs of Staff of this development, and to point out that I can no longer count with certainty upon the operational use of any French forces they may contemplate equipping in the future."

De Gaulle, in reply, admitted that the difficulty was not of Eisenhower's doing, but rather was due to the lack of agreement and liaison between France and the Allied governments "on that which relates to the war policy in general and in particular to the occupation of German territory." Since the French had no representative on the CCS, there was no way for De Gaulle to put French interests before the Chiefs. Regretfully, therefore, he had to push French views separately. This situation had forced De Gaulle, to his "very great regret," to step in "either with respect to plans or their execution." He added that Eisenhower surely was aware that in placing French forces under SHAEF "I have always reserved the right of the French Government eventually to take the necessary steps in order that French Forces should be employed in accordance with the national interest of France which is the only interest that they should serve." He reminded Eisenhower that the United States had not fulfilled its commitments to rearm the French and ended by expressing his appreciation for the efforts Eisenhower personally had made. He hoped that good will would continue between American and French forces in the field.[16]

Eisenhower may have had some sympathy for De Gaulle, both because the French were contributing two corps to the offensive but had no voice on the CCS, and because of De Gaulle's efforts to re-establish the French position in Europe, first of all through obtaining an occupation zone in Germany. In any case there was nothing Eisenhower could do about De Gaulle's orders to De Lattre, and with the war so near its end he decided the time had come for the politicians to handle De Gaulle. The Supreme Commander thanked the French President for the courtesy of his full explanation, said he understood De Gaulle's position, and concluded, "while I regret that you find it necessary to inject political considerations into a campaign in which my functions are purely military, I am gratified to know that you understand my situation and attitude."[17] Soon after De Gaulle got the occupation zone he wanted, plus a seat on the Allied Control Council.

The last weeks of the war were full ones for the Supreme Commander. Much of his time, and even more of that of his staff, went into the effort to reach an agreement with the Germans in Holland that would allow the Allies to feed the starving population there. There was also redeployment to worry about. On April 25 Marshall told Eisenhower that he had offered Hodges and his First Army headquarters to MacArthur, "who has accepted . . . gladly." MacArthur did not plan to have an army group command for the final invasion of the Japanese home islands, Marshall added, but he would accept Bradley as an army commander. The Chief of Staff wondered if Bradley would like to go to the Pacific in that role.

Eisenhower blistered. He was ready to send Hodges immediately, but under no circumstances would he agree to what amounted to a demotion for Bradley. "While MacArthur's failure to form an army group command is of course his own business," Eisenhower said, "I personally recommend urgently against Bradley going to the Pacific as an army commander. . . ." Bradley had been commanding more than 1,000,000 men in Europe, fighting against the "most highly prepared and skillful army that existed." To give him merely an army command would diminish Bradley's stature, which was unfair and unwise. Bradley's "brains, selflessness, and outstanding ability as a battleline commander are unexcelled anywhere in the world today." He would be needed in the postwar Army, and to be effective there he had to preserve his reputation. In addition, Eisenhower would need him to help solve the great problems of occupation. Anyway, there were nearly a dozen other generals in ETO who were competent enough to lead an army into Japan.

"After dictating the above," Eisenhower concluded, "I called Bradley in person to determine his own feelings in the matter. His only answer was: 'I will serve anywhere in any position that General Marshall assigns me.'" Still, Eisenhower thought it would be a mistake. So did Marshall, and Bradley remained in Europe.[18]

As his armies rolled forward Eisenhower inspected some of the concentration camps they uncovered. "The things I saw beggar description," he told Marshall. "The visual evidence and the verbal testimony of starvation, cruelty and bestiality were so overpowering as to leave me a bit sick." In one room he saw naked men piled to the ceiling, dead by starvation. "I made the visit deliberately," Eisenhower said, "in order to be in position to give *first-hand* evidence of these things if ever, in the future, there develops a tendency to charge these allegations merely to 'propaganda.'" He saw to it that British M.P.s and American congressmen visited the camps to see for themselves, and sent photographs of the camps to Churchill.[19] The experience deepened his already great hatred for the Nazis and led him to take a stern attitude when the time came for them to surrender.

Two major obstacles stood in the way of a quick, sharp end to the war. First, most Germans believed that the 1918 armistice had come at a time when their armies were still winning and they were determined to avoid another unnecessary capitulation. All German leaders, not just the Nazis, wanted to avoid a postwar charge of having stabbed the armed forces in the back. Nazi ideology, with its doctrine that defeat was impossible, reinforced this tendency, and as long as Hitler lived it was unlikely that the Germans would quit. The unconditional surrender policy, with its implication that the German government would not survive, also played a role, since any government that signed an unconditional surrender document was simultaneously signing its own death warrant. Second, the Germans hoped for—indeed expected—a falling out between East and West. If they could hold firm until it occurred, they would survive as a nation, possibly even joining the West in an anti-Communist crusade.

The first obstacle was removed, or at least partly overcome, when the Russian Army took Berlin and when Hitler, on April 30, committed suicide. The second now loomed larger, however, as the new German government and the remaining military leaders felt that with Hitler gone the West would be more inclined to see Germany as a bulwark against Communism in Europe. Specifically, the way Admiral Karl Doenitz, Hitler's successor, tried to speed up the East-West split and salvage something for Germany was through piecemeal surrender to the Western Allies only. This process had begun even before Hitler's death; on April 26 Marshall informed Eisenhower that Reichsfuehrer SS Heinrich Himmler had sent an agent to Sweden to try to arrange for a surrender of German forces in the West. President Truman had replied that the only terms acceptable were unconditional surrender of all German armies to the U.S.S.R., the U.K., and the U.S. Stalin, informed of these developments, had said Truman's attitude was "absolutely correct." Churchill told Eisenhower that "the offer looked like a last desperate attempt to create a schism between ourselves and the Russians," and the Supreme Commander himself was in complete agreement with Truman's policy. "In every move we make these days," Eisenhower assured Marshall, "we are trying to be meticulously careful in this regard."[20]

Given the determination of both Truman and Churchill to maintain good relations with the Russians, and Eisenhower's eagerness to get the war over, being meticulously careful was highly important. By both word and act the Germans continued their effort to split the alliance. Soldiers on the eastern front, rightfully fearing above all else capture by the Red Army, which they knew would demand revenge for German atrocities in Russia, fought desperately. On the western front, soldiers surrendered at the first sight of an AEF unit. German civilians tried to flee to the West so that they would be inside the Anglo-American lines when the end came. And on May 1 Doenitz, in a radio address to the nation in which he announced Hitler's death, said the Wehrmacht would "continue the struggle against Bolshevism until the fighting troops and the hundreds of thousands of families in Eastern Germany gave been preserved from destruction."[21] But by May 2 or 3 Doenitz realized that the British and Americans would not accept any general surrender in the West only; he thereafter tried to achieve the same end by surrendering armies and army groups to SHAEF while fighting on in the East.

The first important offer came from the Germans facing Montgomery, who indicated that they wanted to surrender to the British the army group in northern Germany facing the Red Army. There were hints that they would also be willing to surrender all of northwest Germany, Denmark, and even Norway to Montgomery. Eisenhower immediately informed General Susloparoff, the Russian liaison officer at SHAEF, and laid down instructions that if the more general surrender did occur he would arrange "for a more formal and ceremonial surrender with Russian representatives present."[22] Eisenhower also told Montgomery to refuse to accept the surrender of German armies facing the Russians, but he did allow Montgomery to tell the Germans that "individual soldiers of these Armies surrendering would be accepted as prisoners of war." Montgomery, in discussing the matter with the German officers who came to negotiate with him, added that he personally would not turn over to the Russians any individual soldiers who surrendered.[23] Doenitz then agreed to the smaller surrender—that is, of those German forces facing Montgomery—and on the afternoon of May 4 German representatives came to Twenty-first Army Group headquarters to capitulate unconditionally on the British front. The terms they signed, which went into effect on the morning of May 5, stipulated that the capitulation was independent of and would be superseded by any general instrument of surrender imposed by the Allies and applicable to German armed forces as a whole.

Farther south, German generals appeared at Hodges' headquarters and offered to surrender the remaining elements of two German armies still facing the Russians east of the Elbe. The U. S. Ninth Army representatives refused to accept and forbade German civilians to cross the

Elbe and surrender to the American troops. The surrender of individual soldiers would be accepted. In fact, no real effort was made to prevent civilians from crossing the river, and thousands did so. In southern Germany and western Austria Von Kesselring was also ready to give up, but hopefully only to the West. On May 4 he notified SHAEF of his readiness to discuss terms. Eisenhower replied that unless Von Kesselring was willing to surrender all the forces under his command, and especially those facing the Red Army, he should go to Sixth Army Group headquarters, not SHAEF. Von Kesselring thereupon sent his representatives to Devers' headquarters and on May 5 signed an instrument of surrender for only those German troops opposing Sixth Army Group.[24]

Doenitz, meanwhile, had sent Admiral Hans von Friedeburg to SHAEF with instructions to arrange for the surrender of the remaining German forces in the West. Eisenhower insisted that any general surrender take place on the eastern and western fronts simultaneously, and he invited Susloparoff to attend the negotiations.[25] Smith and Strong, who had handled the Italian surrender negotiations, carried on the discussion with Von Friedeburg, as Eisenhower refused to see any German officers until the document of surrender had been signed. When Smith told Von Friedeburg that there could be no bargaining and showed him a short surrender document drawn up by the SHAEF staff, the German admiral said he had no power to sign. Smith then showed Von Friedeburg SHAEF situation maps to illustrate the hopelessness of the enemy situation, and even brought out some special maps on which imaginary attacks had been projected. The admiral was impressed, and he cabled Doenitz asking for permission to sign an unconditional and simultaneous surrender.[26]

Doenitz, shocked, decided to send Generaloberst Alfred Jodl, chief of OKW, to Eisenhower's headquarters in Reims to explain why a simultaneous surrender on both fronts was impossible. Jodl arrived on Sunday evening, May 6. After conferring with Von Friedeburg, he went into Smith's office to talk with Smith and Strong. Jodl emphasized that the Germans were willing, indeed anxious, to surrender to the West, but not to the Red Army. The Germans, he said, would order all their troops remaining on the western front to cease firing no matter what SHAEF did about their offer to surrender. When Smith replied that the surrender had to be a general one, Jodl asked for forty-eight hours "in order to get the necessary instructions to all their outlying units." Smith replied that such a course was impossible, and Jodl again asked to surrender to the West only. After the talks had dragged on for over an hour, Smith decided that Jodl was stalling and put the problem before Eisenhower.

Eisenhower felt that all Jodl was trying to do was gain time so that more German soldiers and civilians could get across the Elbe and escape the Russians. He told Smith to inform Jodl that "he would break off all negotiations and seal the western front preventing by force any further westward movement of German soldiers and civilians" unless Jodl signed the surrender document immediately.

Jodl then sent a cable to Doenitz, who replied, enraged, that Eisenhower's demands were "sheer extortion." He nevertheless felt impelled to accept them because Jodl, who was the strongest opponent of surrender in the East, now insisted that there was no choice. Doenitz was consoled somewhat by the thought that he could still save many troops from the Russians during the forty-eight-hour period Eisenhower had granted before the capitulation went into effect. Early on Monday morning, May 7, therefore, he telegraphed Jodl: "Full power to sign in accordance with conditions as given has been granted by Grand Admiral Doenitz."[27]

At 2 A.M. Jodl, accompanied by Von Friedeburg and an aide, marched into the small recreation hall of the Ecole Professionelle et Technique de Garçons. It served as the SHAEF War Room. Generals Smith, Morgan, Bull, Spaatz, Strong, Susloparoff, and a half dozen others were already there.

While the somewhat elaborate procedures for the signing went on, Eisenhower waited in his office, pacing and smoking. The signing took more than a half hour, so he had time to think. In the War Room Jodl was delivering the German nation into the hands of the Allies and officially acknowledging that Nazi Germany was dead; outside, spring was bursting forth, promising new life.

Eisenhower had a wealth of accomplishments to think about, as well as the long path he had followed to reach this office at this momentous time. Smith's call that brought him to Washington in December 1941 and the work under Marshall in OPD, for example, or the disappointment he felt at not being able to do anything to save the Philippines, or the moment he always considered the critical one in his career, the day he told Marshall that he was willing to spend the war working as a staff officer and did not give a damn about promotions. The moment was dramatic, as many had been throughout the war, such as the dripping cave that served as an office in the bowels of Gibraltar, the

Mess Room at Portsmouth and the decision to launch OVERLORD, or the barracks room with the old potbellied stove in Verdun during the crisis of the Bulge.

He had dealt with a remarkable group of people throughout the war. Henri Giraud, the ponderous old soldier who never seemed to understand what was going on. Charles de Gaulle, with his preposterous, haughty manner and his deep, indomitable patriotism. Churchill, clamping his teeth down on his cigar and sticking out his chin, frowning, growling, fighting to preserve the Empire he loved and to destroy the guttersnipe Hitler he hated. Roosevelt, almost casually telling Eisenhower he would command OVERLORD. Montgomery, always lecturing, always condescending, and Brooke, forever critical.

Eisenhower liked to emphasize his Abilene childhood and was constantly amazed at his good fortune. He had established friendships with a widely disparate group of strong-willed men. He had worked side by side with the great and the near great. It had been, by any standard, a challenge to live in close association with such a body of men, powerful in their own right, accustomed to having their own way, and responsible for the fate of their nations. The issues were always critical, so when men like De Gaulle, Churchill, Brooke, Montgomery, Bradley, and the others discussed a subject with Eisenhower, they did everything they could to swing him to their point of view. Eisenhower could not afford to insult any of them, and he had to give each an opportunity to state his case fully. The Supreme Commander had a legendary temper, but he had even greater self-control, and he drew on his enormous fund of patience to hold things together.

He was able to do so because it was his deepest conviction that victory depended upon making the alliance work and he would do anything to achieve that purpose. His basic method was to approach all problems objectively himself, and to convince others that he *was* objective. Equally important, he had the ability to see matters from other peoples' point of view. He did not dismiss De Gaulle as an egotist who wanted to become a dictator; had he done so, he could never have achieved the successes he did in dealing with the French. Some American officers were darkly suspicious of Churchill, seeing him as a meddlesome old man whose only aim was to promote the interests of the British Empire. Eisenhower did not make that mistake, nor did he assume, as others did, that Montgomery was motivated by considerations of personal advancement. Rather, Eisenhower believed these men to be honest. This attitude made it possible for him to base his decisions on the issues, not on personalities.

But he did not ignore the personalities. No one could have. People like Patton, Churchill, De Gaulle, Montgomery, and scores of others all had habits, mannerisms, and idiosyncrasies that set them apart and demanded attention. But, in a way, dealing with such men, responding to them at different levels, helped Eisenhower get through the war. He looked upon the relationships as challenges and found them intensely interesting. He had been given an opportunity to work with some of the most fascinating men of the century, and he made the most of it. No matter how bitter the struggle over an issue, Eisenhower always maintained good personal relations. He was able to do so because he enjoyed being with such men.

Eisenhower was by nature a modest man. He knew he had been decisive when he had to be, that he had been able to build an effective organization and hold the alliance together, that he was an accomplished diplomat, that he had proven himself as a soldier, especially during the Bulge and the Rhineland battles. But he had been heard to say that these were the tasks he had been trained for, as had all other senior officers in the U. S. Army, and it was to be expected that he would do them well.

When Eisenhower talked about the root causes of his personal success, he usually spoke immediately not of himself but of three men, Walter B. Smith, Omar N. Bradley, and George C. Marshall. Smith had been at his side since the late summer of 1942, the driving force behind AFHQ and SHAEF, the man who made the staff function. Smith did more than build and run the staff, too, although God knew that was essential. It was Smith, not the civilian representatives at AFHQ and SHAEF, to whom Eisenhower turned for guidance through the tortuous maze of French and Italian politics, for advice in dealing with field subordinates, for help in composing an answer to a Churchill demand. Eisenhower thought him the perfect chief of staff.[28]

Bradley had joined up in the spring of 1943. In Tunisia, Sicily, Normandy, at the Bulge, crossing the Rhine, overrunning Germany, he had always been the man Eisenhower could turn to, the one he trusted implicitly, the general who never let him down. Eisenhower thought Bradley was the best field soldier America produced, a man without whom the plans, no matter how good, would not have worked.

Most of all, there was Marshall. The Chief of Staff had stood like a rock through crisis after crisis. When criticism of the Darlan deal mounted, it was Marshall who had protected Eisenhower. During the long, disappointing Tunisian winter, Marshall was the one who gave Eisenhower the encouragement he needed, sent him the generals he wanted, saw that AFHQ got the trucks and reinforcements it had to have. When the Patton slapping incident threatened to deprive Eisenhower of one of his best tactical commanders, Marshall arranged matters so that Eisenhower could keep Patton. During the struggle with the airmen over the Transportation Plan, Marshall was the CCS member most responsible for Eisenhower's success in getting the plan adopted. During the long, arduous argument with Churchill over the invasion of the south of France, Marshall was the one who made it possible for Eisenhower to stand firm by letting him know that he had total support from the JCS.

During the last few months Marshall's support had, if possible, been even greater. The pressure on Eisenhower to give in to Churchill and make Alexander the single ground commander in Europe was enormous; Marshall, realizing this, did everything in his power to help the Supreme Commander, even to the point of saying he would resign if the organization did not remain as Eisenhower wanted it. Eisenhower had made the plans for fighting the Rhineland battles, for crossing the river, and for overrunning Germany, but he could not have held to them had it not been for Marshall, who protected Eisenhower from Brooke and gave SHAEF all possible support.

Always, when Eisenhower needed him, Marshall was there, giving him everything he needed, by both word and deed. Marshall had been the sustaining force.

A day or so after the war ended, Eisenhower tried to sum up his feelings in a cable to Marshall. "I feel a compulsion to attempt to tell you some things personally that have been very real with me during this war," Eisenhower began. "Since the day I first went to England, indeed since I first reported to you in the War Department, the strongest weapon that I have always had in my hand was a confident feeling that you trusted my judgment, believed in the objectivity of my approach to any problem and were ready to sustain to the full limit of your resources and your tremendous moral support, anything that we found necessary to undertake." The knowledge that Marshall stood behind them, Eisenhower said, "had a tremendous effect on my staffs and principal subordinate commanders."

The conviction that Marshall "had basic faith in this headquarters and would invariably resist interference from any outside sources, has done far more to strengthen my personal position throughout the war than is realized even by those people who were affected by this circumstance." Eisenhower said Marshall had an unparalleled place among the leaders and peoples of the alliance, as well as with the American Army. "Our army and our people have never been so deeply indebted to any other soldier."

As Eisenhower finished dictating, a cable came in from Marshall. "You have completed your mission with the greatest victory in the history of warfare," Marshall began. "You have commanded with outstanding success the most powerful military force that has ever been assembled. You have met and successfully disposed of every conceivable difficulty incident to varied national interests and international political problems of unprecedented complications." Eisenhower, Marshall said, had triumphed over inconceivable logistical problems and military obstacles. "Through all of this, since the day of your arrival in England three years ago, you have been selfless in your actions, always sound and tolerant in your judgments and altogether admirable in the courage and wisdom of your military decisions.

"You have made history, great history for the good of mankind and you have stood for all we hope for and admire in an officer of the United States Army. These are my tributes and my personal thanks."[29]

It was the highest possible praise from the best possible source, and it had been earned.

Whatever Eisenhower thought of as he waited for notification that the surrender document had been signed, his mood was broken at two forty-one when Smith led Jodl into Eisenhower's office and announced that the war was over. Eisenhower sternly asked Jodl if he understood the terms and was ready to execute them. Jodl said yes. Eisenhower then warned him that he would be held accountable officially if the terms were violated. Jodl bowed stiffly and left.

Eisenhower gathered the SHAEF officers around him and some photographers took pictures. The Supreme Commander then made a short newsreel and radio recording. When all the newsmen had left, Smith said it was time to send a message to the CCS. Everyone had a try at drafting an appropriate document. "I tried one myself," Smith later recalled, "and like all my associates, groped for resounding phrases as fitting accolades to the Great Crusade and indicative of our dedication to the great task just completed." Eisenhower quietly watched and listened. Each draft was more grandiloquent than the last. The Supreme

Commander finally thanked everyone for his efforts, rejected all the proposals, and dictated the message himself.

"The mission of this Allied force was fulfilled at 0241 local time, May 7, 1945."[30]

Glossary

AAF	Army Air Forces
ABDA	Australian-British-Dutch-American Command
ACC	Allied Control Commission
ACCOLADE	Planned operations in the Aegean, 1943
AEF	Allied Expeditionary Force
AFHQ	Allied Force Headquarters
AKA	Cargo ship, attack
ANVIL	Invasion of south of France, 1944
ARCADIA	Chiefs of Staff meeting, Washington, 1941
AVALANCHE	Invasion of Italy at Salerno, 1943
BCOS	British Chiefs of Staff
BOLERO	Build-up of U.S. forces in U.K., 1942
BUTTRESS	Planned operations against Italian toe, 1943
CCS	Combined Chiefs of Staff
CIGS	Chief of the Imperial General Staff
COBRA	U. S. First Army breakout in Normandy, 1944
COM Z	Communications Zone
CORKSCREW	Invasion of Pantelleria, 1943
COSSAC	Chief of Staff to the Supreme Allied Commander (Designate) and his staff
CROSSBOW	Operations against German rockets and pilotless aircraft, 1944
DRAGOON	Invasion of south of France, 1944
DUKW	Amphibious truck (duck)
EAC	European Advisory Commission
ECLIPSE	Posthostility plans for Germany, 1944–45
EM	Eisenhower Manuscripts
EP	*The Papers of Dwight David Eisenhower*
ETO	European Theater of Operations
ETOUSA	European Theater of Operations, United States Army
FCNL	French Committee of National Liberation
FORTITUDE	Cover and deception plan for OVERLORD, 1944
G-1	Personnel section of divisional or higher staff

G-2	Intelligence section
G-3	Operations and training section
G-4	Logistics section
G-5	Civil affairs section
GIANT II	Plan to drop 82d Airborne Division near Rome, 1943
GOODWOOD	Offensive across the Orne River south of Caen, by 21st Army Group, 1944
GRENADE	Ninth Army supporting attack for VERITABLE, 1945
GYMNAST	Proposed invasion of French North Africa, 1942
HUSKY	Invasion of Sicily, 1943
JCS	Joint Chiefs of Staff
KINGPIN	Code name for Henri Giraud
LCA	Landing craft, assault
LCI	Landing craft, infantry
LCI (L)	Landing craft, infantry (large)
LCT	Landing craft, tank
LSD	Landing ship, dock
LSI	Landing ship, infantry
LST	Landing ship, tank
LUMBERJACK	Offensive to close the Rhine north of the Moselle, 1945
MARKET-GARDEN	Airborne operation in Nijmegen–Arnhem area, with a ground operation to open a corridor from Eindhoven northward
MTO	Mediterranean Theater of Operations
MULBERRY	Artificial harbor off Normandy
NATO	North African Theater of Operations
NEI	Netherlands East Indies
OPD	Operations Division, War Department General Staff
OVERLORD	Invasion of France at Normandy, 1944
PLUNDER	21st Army Group crossing of the Rhine, 1945
POINTBLANK	Combined strategic bombing assault on Germany
QUADRANT	CCS meeting, Quebec, 1943
ROUNDUP	Proposed 1943 invasion of France
SCAEF	Supreme Commander, Allied Expeditionary Force
SGS	Secretary General Staff
SHAEF	Supreme Headquarters, Allied Expeditionary Force
SHINGLE	Invasion of Italy at Anzio, 1944
SITREPS	Situation reports
SLEDGE-HAMMER	Proposed suicide invasion of France, 1942

SOS	Services of Supply
TIDALWAVE	Air attack at oil refineries at Ploesti, Rumania, 1943
TRIDENT	CCS meeting, Washington, 1943
TORCH	Invasion of North Africa, 1942
UNDERTONE	6th Army Group offensive to breach West Wall and cross the Rhine, 1945
V-1	Flying bombs; pilotless aircraft
V-2	Supersonic rocket
VERITABLE	Canadian First Army attack between the Maas and the Rhine, 1945
WPD	War Plans Division, War Department General Staff

Notes

BOOK ONE

PART 1

1. Dwight D. Eisenhower, *Crusade in Europe* (New York, 1948), pp. 14–15; Forrest C. Pogue, *George C. Marshall*, 2 vols. (New York, 1963–66), Vol. II, *Ordeal and Hope 1939–1942*, p. 238.
2. Pogue, *Ordeal and Hope*, p. 237.
3. Ibid., pp. 238–39; Eisenhower, *Crusade in Europe*, pp. 16–18.
4. "Steps to Be Taken," in Alfred P. Chandler (ed.), *The Papers of Dwight David Eisenhower* (5 vols., Baltimore, 1970), No. 1, hereinafter cited as EP. See also Louis Morton, *Strategy and Command: The First Two Years*, in Kent Roberts Greenfield (ed.), *The United States Army in World War II* (Washington, 1962), pp. 90–91, and Maurice Matloff and Edwin M. Snell, *Strategic Planning for Coalition Warfare, 1941–1942*, in Greenfield (ed.), *U. S. Army in World War II* (Washington, 1953), pp. 87–88. On Eisenhower's typing the document himself, my source is an interview with Eisenhower on October 11, 1967.
5. Pogue, *Ordeal and Hope*, p. 239; Eisenhower, *Crusade in Europe*, pp. 21–22; interview with Eisenhower, October 11, 1967.

CHAPTER 1

1. Dwight D. Eisenhower, *At Ease, Stories I Tell to Friends* (New York, 1967), pp. 185–89, 195; interview with Eisenhower, October 11, 1967.
2. MacArthur's comments are in Eisenhower's 201 file in the Pentagon; the best biography is Kenneth S. Davis, *Soldier of Democracy: A Biography of Dwight Eisenhower* (New York, 1945); see also Eisenhower, *At Ease*, pp. 1–233.
3. There are many competent accounts of WPD. Especially good are Pogue, *Ordeal and Hope*, pp. 289–301, and Ray S. Cline, *Washington Command Post: The Operations Division*, in Greenfield (ed.), *U. S. Army in World War II* (Washington, 1951), pp. 90–106.
4. Cline, *Washington Command Post*, p. 28.
5. Eisenhower to Krueger, December 20, 1941, EP, No. 13.

6. Interview with Eisenhower, December 14, 1964.
7. See Eisenhower's speech in *Addresses Delivered at the Dedication Ceremonies of the George C. Marshall Research Library* (Lexington, Virginia, 1964), pp. 14–15.
8. Morton, *Strategy and Command*, pp. 148–53; Matloff and Snell, *Strategic Planning*, pp. 72–73, 82–84.
9. Marshall to Brett, December 17, 1941, EP, No. 6. On War Department outgoing messages, the drafter's initials appear in the top right-hand corner.
10. Morton, *Strategy and Command*, pp. 152–53.
11. Marshall to MacArthur, December 24, 1941, EP, No. 24 fn. 1. Morton, *Strategy and Command*, p. 153.
12. Eisenhower to Marshall, September 25, 1944, EP, No. 1994.
13. Marshall to MacArthur, February 8, 1942, EP, No. 120.
14. Louis Morton, *The Fall of the Philippines*, in Greenfield (ed.), *U. S. Army in World War II* (Washington, 1953), pp. 240–42; Matloff and Snell, *Strategic Planning*, pp. 114–19; Pogue, *Ordeal and Hope*, p. 244.
15. Eisenhower's desk pad entry of January 17, 1942, EP, No. 66.
16. Desk pad entry of January 30, 1942, EP, No. 97; Wesley Frank Craven and James Lea Cate (eds.), *Plans and Early Operations, January 1939–August 1942*, in *The Army Air Forces in World War II*, Vol. I (Chicago, 1948) p. 375.
17. Matloff and Snell, *Strategic Planning*, p. 108.
18. Eisenhower desk pad entry of January 12, 1942, EP, No. 53.
19. Matloff and Snell, *Strategic Planning*, pp. 137–38.
20. Eisenhower desk pad entries of January 4 and January 24, 1942, EP, Nos. 36 and 79.
21. Eisenhower desk pad entry of January 22, 1942, EP, No. 73.
22. Ibid.
23. Eisenhower to Edgar Eisenhower, March 30, 1942, EP, No. 216.
24. Eisenhower desk pad entry of January 17, 1942, EP, No. 66; Marshall to Brett, January 17, 1942, EP, No. 67; Pogue, *Ordeal and Hope*, pp. 244–46.
25. Pogue, *Ordeal and Hope*, p. 246.
26. MacArthur to Marshall, ⋕226 and ⋕227, February 8, 1942, quoted in EP, No. 120, fn. 1.
27. Pogue, *Ordeal and Hope*, p. 247.
28. Roosevelt to MacArthur, ⋕1029, February 9, 1942, EP, No. 122.
29. MacArthur to Marshall, ⋕252, February 11, 1942, quoted in EP, No. 123, fn. 2.
30. Pogue, *Ordeal and Hope*, pp. 249–51; Morton, *Strategy and Command*, pp. 194–95.
31. Eisenhower desk pad entry of March 31, 1942, EP, No. 219.

CHAPTER 2

1. Forrest C. Pogue, *George C. Marshall*, 2 vols. (New York, 1963–66), Vol. I, *Education of a General, 1880–1939;* Pogue, *Ordeal and Hope*, pp. 95–98.
2. Interview with Eisenhower, December 14, 1964.
3. Eisenhower, *At Ease*, pp. 248–50.
4. Pogue, *Ordeal and Hope*, p. 338.
5. On ARCADIA, see ibid., pp. 261–88, and Matloff and Snell, *Strategic Planning*, pp. 97–118.
6. Matloff and Snell, *Strategic Planning*, pp. 99–102. The quotation is from Maurice

Matloff, "The American Approach to War," in Michael Howard, (ed.), *The Theory and Practice of War* (London, 1965), p. 234.

7. Pogue, *Ordeal and Hope,* p. 288.
8. Matloff and Snell, *Strategic Planning,* p. 101.
9. Undated paper [December 25, 1941], "Methods of Cooperation between U. S. Air and Allied Forces in the Southwestern Pacific," EP, No. 22.
10. Quoted in EP, No. 23.
11. EP, No. 24; see also Matloff and Snell, *Strategic Planning,* pp. 123–25.
12. Pogue, *Ordeal and Hope,* pp. 277–79.
13. Ibid., pp. 282–85; Matloff and Snell, *Strategic Planning,* pp. 125–26.
14. The JCS operated on an informal basis, never receiving formal approval.
15. Eisenhower desk pad entries of January 4 and 24, 1942, and February 28, 1942, EP, Nos. 36, 80, and 161. Eisenhower to Lutes, December 31, 1941, in Lutes Scrapbook; interview with Milton Eisenhower, March 13, 1965. Eisenhower was also involved in numerous conferences and meetings, as the Stimson diary entry of December 24, 1941, Yale University Library, indicates.
16. Eisenhower's notes of March 11, 1942, EP, No. 189.
17. Eisenhower desk pad entry of February 6, 1942, EP, No. 119.
18. The best account is Cline, *Washington Command Post,* pp. 90–141.
19. Eisenhower desk pad entry of February 23, 1942, EP, No. 145.
20. Eisenhower desk pad entry of January 27, 1942, EP, No. 89.
21. Eisenhower's undated paper is in EP, No. 160.
22. EP, No. 162.
23. Cline, *Washington Command Post,* pp. 147–49.

CHAPTER 3

1. Cline, *Washington Command Post,* p. 153.
2. Ibid., p. 151.
3. Ibid., pp. 149–50.
4. Eisenhower's desk pad entry of March 10, 1942, EP, No. 185, indicated that he agreed with Handy.
5. "Critical Points in the Development of Coordinated Viewpoint as to Major Tasks of the War," March 25, 1942, EP, No. 207.
6. Pogue, *Ordeal and Hope,* pp. 305–6; Cline, *Washington Command Post,* p. 155.
7. See Gordon A. Harrison, *Cross-channel attack,* in Greenfield, ed., *U. S. Army in World War II,* (Washington, 1951), pp. 12–19.
8. Pogue, *Ordeal and Hope,* pp. 306–20; Cline, *Washington Command Post,* pp. 156–60.
9. Cline, *Washington Command Post,* p. 160.
10. Eisenhower desk pad entry of April 20, 1942, EP, No. 254.
11. Memo for Record, April 20, 1942, EP, No. 255.
12. Marshall to Roosevelt, May 4, 1942, EP, No. 276.
13. See ibid., espc. fn. 1.
14. Eisenhower desk pad entries of May 5 and 6, 1942, EP, Nos. 278 and 280.
15. See EP, No. 292, fn. 2.
16. "Notes on Bolero organization charts attached hereto," May 11, 1942, EP, No. 292.
17. Eisenhower desk pad entry of May 21, 1942, EP, No. 314.
18. Eisenhower kept a diary of his BOLERO trip; see EP, No. 318. See also Kay Summersby, *Eisenhower Was My Boss* (New York, 1948), pp. 5–9.

19. Mark W. Clark, *Calculated Risk* (New York, 1950), p. 19; Eisenhower's diary, EP, No. 318.
20. Sir Arthur Bryant, *The Turn of the Tide: Study Based on the Diaries and Autobiographical Notes of Field Marshal the Viscount Alanbrooke* (London, 1957), p. 285.
21. Eisenhower desk pad entry of June 4, 1942, EP, No. 320.
22. "Command Arrangements for Bolero," June 3, 1942, EP, No. 319.
23. "Command in England," June 6, 1942, EP, No. 325.
24. "Establishment of Western Theater of Operations," May 12, 1942, EP, No. 293; Eisenhower, *Crusade in Europe*, p. 50.
25. Eisenhower, *Crusade in Europe*, p. 50.
26. Pogue, *Ordeal and Hope*, pp. 338–39.
27. Eisenhower desk pad entry of June 8, 1942, EP, No. 328.
28. Eisenhower, *Crusade in Europe*, p. 51.
29. Pogue, *Ordeal and Hope*, pp. 330–35.
30. Eisenhower kept the minutes of the meeting; see EP, No. 344.
31. Winston S. Churchill, *The Second World War*, 6 vols. (Boston, 1948–53), Vol. IV, *The Hinge of Fate*, p. 383.
32. Eisenhower to Akin, June 19, 1942, EP, No. 341.

CHAPTER 4

1. Summersby, *Eisenhower Was My Boss*, p. 24.
2. Captain Harry C. Butcher, *My Three Years with Eisenhower* (New York, 1946), p. 7.
3. Eisenhower to Marshall, June 26, 1942, EP, No. 353.
4. Interview with Eisenhower, October 11, 1967; Butcher, *My Three Years*, p. 7.
5. Interview with Eisenhower, October 11, 1967.
6. Butcher, *My Three Years*, pp. 25–26.
7. Eisenhower, *Crusade in Europe*, pp. 55–56.
8. Eisenhower to Somervell, July 27, 1942, EP, No. 398.
9. Same to same, June 26, 1942, EP, No. 355.
10. Same to same, July 27, 1942, EP, No. 398.
11. Butcher, *My Three Years*, pp. 35–36; Eisenhower to Handy, July 16, 1942, EP, No. 378.
12. John Gunther, *Eisenhower, the Man and the Symbol* (New York, 1951), p. 75.
13. Summersby, *Eisenhower Was My Boss*, pp. 25–26.
14. Ibid., p. 28.
15. Eisenhower to Russell Hartle and others, July 19, 1942, EP, No. 382.
16. Eisenhower, *Crusade in Europe*, pp. 58–59; Eisenhower to Hartle and others, July 19, 1942, No. 382. Eisenhower often put into his personal letters to members of his family or old friends a paragraph or two on the need for discipline.
17. Eisenhower to Prichard, August 27, 1942, EP, No. 457.
18. *Life*, July 27, 1942.
19. Butcher, *My Three Years*, p. 23.

CHAPTER 5

1. Eisenhower to Marshall, June 30, 1942, EP, No. 358.
2. Eisenhower, *Crusade in Europe*, p. 67.

3. Churchill, *The Hinge of Fate,* p. 433.
4. Ibid., pp. 345–46.
5. Ibid., pp. 381–82.
6. Ibid., pp. 344–45.
7. Eisenhower to Marshall, July 11, 1942, EP, No. 370.
8. Matloff and Snell, *Strategic Planning,* p. 276.
9. Marshall to Eisenhower, ⋕2135, July 13, EP, No. 371, fn. 1.
10. Richard M. Leighton and Robert W. Coakley, *Global Logistics and Strategy,* 1940–43, in Greenfield, (ed.), *U. S. Army in World War II,* (Washington, 1955), pp. 385–86.
11. Pogue, *Ordeal and Hope,* pp. 342–43.
12. Eisenhower reported making this statement in a cable to Marshall, July 14, 1942, EP, No. 371.
13. Eisenhower, *Crusade in Europe,* pp. 70–71.
14. See Harry Hopkins' remarks, quoted by J. M. A. Gwyer, *Grand Strategy,* in J. R. M. Butler (ed.), *History of the Second World War,* (London, 1964), Vol. III, Pt. 1, pp. 125–26.
15. Sir Ian Jacob, "A Year Late?" *The Economist,* September 28, 1946.
16. Bryant, *Turn of the Tide,* p. 341.
17. Churchill, *The Hinge of Fate,* p. 439.
18. Ibid., pp. 434–38.
19. EP, No. 379.
20. Ibid., No. 381.
21. Eisenhower memo for record, July 21, 1942, EP, No. 386.
22. Eisenhower note of July 20, 1942, EP, No. 384.
23. Eisenhower to Somervell, July 27, 1942, EP, No. 398.
24. Eisenhower note of July 22, 1942, EP, No. 387.
25. Matloff and Snell, *Strategy Planning,* pp. 276–78; Leighton and Coakley, *Global Logistics and Strategy,* p. 387.
26. Robert E. Sherwood, *Roosevelt and Hopkins: An Intimate History* (New York, 1948), p. 610.
27. Butcher, *My Three Years,* pp. 29–30.
28. Eisenhower memo for Marshall, July 23, 1942, EP, No. 389.
29. Pogue, *Ordeal and Hope,* p. 347; Matloff and Snell, *Strategic Planning,* pp. 272–81; George F. Howe, *Northwest Africa: Seizing the Initiative in the West,* in Greenfield (ed.), *U. S. Army in World War II* (Washington, 1957), pp. 7–10.
30. Butcher, *My Three Years,* p. 23.

CHAPTER 6

1. Eisenhower, *At Ease,* p. 252.
2. Pogue, *Ordeal and Hope,* p. 348; E. Dwight Salmon, *et al, History of AFHQ,* lithograph copy in author's possession, p. 2; Eisenhower, *Crusade in Europe,* p. 71; interview with Eisenhower, December 7, 1965.
3. Salmon, *History of AFHQ,* p. 6.
4. Ibid., p. 8.
5. Ibid., p. 17.
6. Interview with Eisenhower, October 11, 1967.
7. Hastings L. Ismay, *The Memoirs of General Lord Ismay* (New York, 1960), pp. 258–59, 263.
8. Butcher, *My Three Years,* p. 49.

9. Eisenhower, *Crusade in Europe*, pp. 54–55; interview with Eisenhower, October 11, 1967; interview with Sir Frederick Morgan, July 17, 1965; interview with Sir Ian Jacob, July 21, 1965.
10. Interview with Dr. Forrest Pogue, September 11, 1967.
11. Eisenhower to Gailey, September 19, 1942, EP, No. 510; interview with Eisenhower, October 11, 1967.
12. Quoted in Salmon, *History of AFHQ*, p. 13.
13. Howe, *Northwest Africa*, p. 16.
14. Eisenhower to Ismay, October 10, 1942, EP, No. 541.
15. Eisenhower, *Crusade in Europe*, p. 82; the best biography is Ladislas Farago, *Patton: Ordeal and Triumph* (New York, 1964).
16. Interview with Eisenhower, October 11, 1967; see Eisenhower's tribute to Cunningham in *Crusade in Europe*, p. 89.
17. Eisenhower, *Crusade in Europe*, p. 77.
18. Butcher, *My Three Years*, p. 47.
19. This discussion is based on Leo J. Meyer, "The Decision to Invade North Africa (TORCH)," in Kent Roberts Greenfield (ed.), *Command Decisions* (Washington, 1960), pp. 188–89.
20. Eisenhower to Marshall, July 31, 1942, EP, No. 403, fn. 1.
21. Marshall to Eisenhower, and Eisenhower to Marshall, both August 1, 1942, EP, No. 403.
22. See Matloff and Snell, *Strategic Planning*, pp. 286–89, for a discussion.
23. Eisenhower to Marshall, August 9, 1942, EP, No. 418.
24. Quoted in Pogue, *Ordeal and Hope*, p. 403.
25. EP, No. 424, n. 1.
26. Eisenhower to Handy for Marshall, August 13, 1942, EP, No. 424.
27. Eisenhower, *At Ease*, p. 253.
28. Butcher, *My Three Years*, p. 54.
29. Eisenhower to Marshall, August 15, 1942, EP, No. 430.
30. Butcher, *My Three Years*, p. 59.
31. Eisenhower to Marshall, August 17, 1942, EP, No. 435.
32. EP, No. 444, n. 1.
33. Matloff and Snell, *Strategic Planning*, p. 289.
34. Eisenhower to Ismay, August 22, 1942, EP, No. 444.
35. Butcher, *My Three Years*, p. 68.
36. Eisenhower to CCS through Ismay, August 23, 1942, EP, No. 445.
37. Eisenhower to Marshall, August 24, 1942, EP, No. 447.
38. Same to same, August 25, 1942, EP, No. 448.
39. Butcher, *My Three Years*, p. 74.
40. Eisenhower to Marshall, August 26, 1942, EP, No. 453.
41. Eisenhower, *Crusade in Europe*, p. 62; interview with Eisenhower, October 11, 1967.
42. Interview with Eisenhower, October 11, 1967.
43. Eisenhower to Marshall, August 26, 1942, EP, No. 453.
44. Same to same, August 29, 1942, EP, No. 463.
45. Butcher, *My Three Years*, p. 79.
46. Eisenhower to Handy, August 31, 1942, EP, No. 467.
47. Eisenhower to Patton, August 31, 1942, EP, No. 468.
48. Butcher, *My Three Years*, p. 80.
49. Ibid., p. 85.
50. Churchill, *The Hinge of Fate*, pp. 534–35.

51. Ibid., p. 537.
52. Eisenhower to Handy, September 5, 1942, EP, No. 483.
53. Churchill, *The Hinge of Fate*, pp. 542–43.

CHAPTER 7

1. Quoted in Oliver Warner, *Cunningham of Hyndhope: Admiral of the Fleet* (London, 1967), p. 185.
2. The subject of Roosevelt's relationship with De Gaulle is enormously complex; see Arthur L. Funk, *Charles De Gaulle–The Crucial Years, 1943–1944* (Norman, Okla., 1960) and William L. Langer, *Our Vichy Gamble* (New York, 1947).
3. Murphy tells his own story in *Diplomat Among Warriors* (New York, 1964); see also Funk, *De Gaulle*, pp. 31–32, and Langer, *Our Vichy Gamble*, pp. 310–14.
4. Murphy, *Diplomat Among Warriors*, pp. 104–5.
5. Murphy to Atherton, July 6, 1942, U. S. Department of State, *Foreign Relations of the United States, Diplomatic Papers, 1942*, 7 vols. (Washington, 1960–63), Vol. II, *Europe*, pp. 331–32.
6. Howe, *Northwest Africa*, p. 21.
7. Funk, *De Gaulle*, pp. 34–35.
8. Murphy made no attempt to contact General Alphonse Juin, commander in chief of the French Army in North Africa. Howe, *Northwest Africa*, p. 78; Funk, *De Gaulle*, pp. 34–35.
9. Murphy, *Diplomat Among Warriors*, pp. 103–7.
10. Eisenhower to Marshall, September 19, 1942, EP, No. 506.
11. U. S. Dept. of State, *Foreign Relations, 1942*, Vol. II, p. 379.
12. Eisenhower to Somervell, September 13, 1942, EP, No. 501.
13. Eisenhower, *Crusade in Europe*, p. 195.
14. Eisenhower to Marshall, September 10, 1942, EP, No. 491.
15. Butcher, *My Three Years*, pp. 95–97.
16. Eisenhower note of September 13, 1942, EP, No. 499.
17. Eisenhower to Marshall, September 12, 1942, EP, No. 498.
18. Same to same, September 21, 1942, EP, No. 513.
19. Samuel Eliot Morison, *The Battle of the Atlantic, 1939–1943*, in *History of United States Naval Operations in World War II* (Boston, 1947), pp. 360–67.
20. Eisenhower to Marshall, September 19, 1942, EP, No. 509; Butcher, *My Three Years*, pp. 90–93.
21. Eisenhower to Marshall, October 12, 1942, EP, No. 943.
22. Butcher, *My Three Years*, pp. 93–97.
23. Eisenhower Office Diary, October 5, 1942.
24. Murphy to War Department, October 15, 1942, and Murphy to Leahy, October 14, 1942, in U. S. Dept. of State, *Foreign Relations, 1942*, Vol. II, pp. 394–95.
25. Eisenhower to Marshall, October 17, 1942, EP, No. 557.
26. Same to same, October 17, 1942, EP, No. 558.
27. Churchill, *The Hinge of Fate*, p. 630.
28. Charles de Gaulle, *The War Memoirs of Charles de Gaulle*, Vol. II, *Unity 1942–1944* (trans. Richard Howard, New York, 1959), pp. 412–14.
29. Eisenhower to Gailey, September 19, 1942, EP, No. 510.
30. Eisenhower to Marshall, October 20, 1942, EP, No. 559.
31. Butcher, *My Three Years*, p. 152.
32. Eisenhower to Marshall, October 27, 1942, EP, No. 567; Howe, *Northwest*

Africa, pp. 77–82; Murphy (who was at the Clark-Mast meeting), *Diplomat Among Warriors,* pp. 118–19.

33. Eisenhower to Marshall, October 29, 1942, EP, No. 569.

CHAPTER 8

1. Eisenhower, *Crusade in Europe,* p. 95.
2. See note 1, Eisenhower to Giraud, November 4, 1942, EP, No. 582.
3. Butcher, *My Three Years,* pp. 162–64.
4. Ibid., pp. 170–72.
5. Eisenhower to Marshall, November 7, 1942, EP, No. 585.
6. Eisenhower to CCS, November 8, 1942, EP, No. 586; Butcher, *My Three Years,* pp. 165–70.
7. Eisenhower to Marshall, November 7, 1942, EP, No. 585.
8. Butcher, *My Three Years,* pp. 171–72.
9. Eisenhower, *Crusade in Europe,* p. 101.
10. Butcher, *My Three Years,* p. 188a.
11. Eisenhower to Smith, November 9, 1942, EP, No. 592.
12. Butcher, *My Three Years,* pp. 173–76.
13. Eisenhower to CCS, November 8, 1942, EP, No. 590.
14. Butcher, *My Three Years,* p. 177.
15. Eisenhower note of November 8, 1942, EP, No. 589.
16. Howe, *Northwest Africa,* pp. 249–53.
17. Butcher, *My Three Years,* p. 178a.
18. Eisenhower to Smith, November 9, 1942, EP, No. 592.
19. Eisenhower to Marshall, November 9, 1942, EP, No. 594.
20. Eisenhower, *Crusade in Europe,* p. 87.
21. Eisenhower to Clark, November 10, 1942, EP, No. 599.
22. Same to same, November 11, 1942, EP, No. 608; Howe, *Northwest Africa,* p. 258.
23. Eisenhower to Smith, November 11, 1942, EP, No. 609.
24. Milton Viorst, *Hostile Allies, FDR and Charles de Gaulle* (New York, 1965), pp. 119–21.
25. Smith to Eisenhower, November 12, 1942, in EP, No. 615, fn. 1.
26. Eisenhower to Smith, November 12, 1942, EP, No. 615.
27. Same to same, November 12, 1942, EP, No. 616.

CHAPTER 9

1. The full text of the agreement is in Harry L. Coles and Albert K. Weinberg, *Civil Affairs: Soldiers Become Governors,* in Stetson Conn (ed.), *U. S. Army in World War II* (Washington, 1964), p. 36; Eisenhower, *Crusade in Europe,* pp. 107–8.
2. Butcher, *My Three Years,* pp. 190–93.
3. Eisenhower to Smith, November 13, 1942, EP, No. 621.
4. Churchill, *The Hinge of Fate,* p. 637.
5. Langer, *Our Vichy Gamble,* p. 369; Funk, *De Gaulle,* p. 44.
6. Eisenhower to CCS, November 14, 1942, EP, No. 622.
7. Sherwood, *Roosevelt and Hopkins,* pp. 648–55.

8. Eisenhower to Churchill, November 14, 1942, EP, No. 623.
9. Eisenhower to Smith, November 14, 1942, EP, No. 625.
10. Milton Eisenhower visited Algiers in December and wrote a brief account of the American reaction, in author's possession.
11. Funk, *De Gaulle,* p. 42.
12. U. S. Dept. of State, *Foreign Relations, 1942,* Vol. II, p. 445.
13. Ibid., p. 446.
14. Coles and Weinberg, *Civil Affairs: Soldiers Become Governors,* p. 35.
15. U. S. Dept. of State, *Foreign Relations, 1942,* Vol. II, pp. 442–43.
16. Cordell Hull, *The Memoirs of Cordell Hull,* 2 vols. (New York, 1948), Vol. II, p. 1197.
17. See Milton Eisenhower's memorandum cited in n. 10 above.
18. Sherwood, *Roosevelt and Hopkins,* pp. 648–55.
19. Darlan to Clark, November 21, 1942, EP, No. 644, fn. 4.
20. Viorst, *Hostile Allies,* pp. 122–23.
21. Eisenhower to Marshall, November 17, 1942, EP, No. 640.
22. Eisenhower to Smith, November 18, 1942, EP, No. 641.
23. Eisenhower to Smith, November 18, 1942, EP, No. 642.
24. Eisenhower to Marshall, November 19, 1942, EP, No. 644.
25. Eisenhower to Clark, November 19, 1942, EP, No. 645.
26. Herbert Feis, *Churchill-Roosevelt-Stalin: The War They Waged and the Peace They Sought* (Princeton, 1957), p. 91.
27. Eisenhower to John Eisenhower, April 8, 1943, EP, No. 939.
28. Eisenhower to CCS, November 24, 1942, EP, No. 663.
29. Eisenhower, *Crusade in Europe,* pp. 112–14.
30. Viorst, *Hostile Allies,* p. 126.

CHAPTER 10

1. Butcher, *My Three Years,* pp. 198–99.
2. Sir Ian Jacob diary (loaned to the author), entry of December 30, 1942.
3. Eisenhower to Ismay, November 30, 1942, EP, No. 675.
4. Tedder related his thoughts to Sir Frederick Morgan. Interview with Morgan, July 17, 1965.
5. Eisenhower to Ismay, November 30, 1942, EP, No. 675.
6. Butcher, *My Three Years,* pp. 202–3.
7. Howe, *Northwest Africa,* pp. 299–310.
8. Eisenhower to Marshall, November 30, 1942, EP, No. 673.
9. Anderson to Eisenhower, December 2 and 4, 1942, EP, No. 685, fn. 1.
10. Eisenhower to CCS, December 3, 1942, EP, No. 685.
11. Eisenhower to Handy, December 7, 1942, EP, No. 698.
12. Eisenhower Office Diary, December 9, 1942.
13. U. S. Dept. of State, *Foreign Relations, 1942,* Vol. II, p. 473.
14. Eisenhower to Marshall, December 3, 1942, EP, No. 683.
15. Eisenhower to CCS, December 4, 1942, EP, No. 689.
16. Eisenhower to P. A. Hodgson, December 4, 1942, EP, No. 687.
17. Butcher, *My Three Years,* pp. 222–23; U. S. Dept. of State, *Foreign Relations, 1942,* Vol. II, p. 483.
18. Marshall to Eisenhower December 8, 1942, and Eisenhower to Marshall, December 9, 1942, EP, No. 701.

19. Eisenhower notes of December 10, 1942, EP, No. 705.
20. Interview with Sir Ian Jacob, July 21, 1965. Jacob was no exception. "The U. S. Army is a mutual admiration society," he declared on December 30, 1942, "and any failings in this theater can be comfortably blamed on the British." Jacob diary.
21. Butcher, *My Three Years*, pp. 225–26.
22. Eisenhower to Churchill, December 16, 1942, EP, No. 724.
23. Eisenhower, *Crusade in Europe*, p. 124.
24. Eisenhower to CCS, December 24 (sent December 26), 1942, EP, No. 738.
25. Eisenhower, *Crusade in Europe*, pp. 129–30.
26. Michael R. D. Foot, *SOE in France: An Account of the Work of the British Special Operations Executive in France, 1940–1944* (London, 1966), p. 221.
27. Butcher, *My Three Years*, pp. 227–29; Eisenhower to Churchill, December 28, 1942, EP, No. 741.
28. Clark, *Calculated Risk*, pp. 128–31.
29. Coles and Weinberg, *Civil Affairs: Soldiers Become Governors*, p. 47.

CHAPTER 11

1. Eisenhower to CCS, December 29, 1942, EP, No. 742; Eisenhower, *Crusade in Europe*, pp. 125–37. Fredenhall's force was redesignated II Corps.
2. Eisenhower to CCS, January 4, 1943, EP, No. 756.
3. Eisenhower to Gailey, January 1, 1943, EP, No. 751.
4. Eisenhower to Hartle and others, Jamuary 15, 1943, EP, No. 770.
4. Eisenhower to Hartle and others, January 15, 1943, EP, No. 770.
6. Churchill to Eisenhower, January 1, 1943, EP, No. 745, fn. 2.
7. See note 1, Eisenhower to BCOS, December 31, 1942, EP, No. 747.
8. Macmillan, *The Blast of War, 1939–1945* (New York, 1968), p. 173.
9. Churchill to Eisenhower, January 2, 1943, EP, No. 750, fn. 4. A good discussion is Funk, *De Gaulle*, pp. 89–91; see also Murphy, *Diplomat Among Warriors*, pp. 115–21.
10. U. S. Dept. of State, *Foreign Relations of the United States, Diplomatic Papers, 1943*, 6 vols. (Washington, 1963–65), Vol. II, *Europe*, p. 24.
11. Eisenhower to Smith, January 3, 1943, EP, No. 755.
12. Eisenhower to Gailey, January 1, 1943, EP, No. 751.
13. Bryant, *Turn of the Tide*, pp. 442–43; interview with Sir Ian Jacob, May 8, 1968.
14. Albert N. Garland and Howard M. Smyth, *Sicily and the Surrender of Italy*, in Conn (ed.), *U. S. Army in World War II* (Washington, 1965), p. 11; Albert C. Wedemeyer (New York, 1958), *Wedemeyer Reports!*, p. 192.
15. Eisenhower to Handy, January 28, 1943, EP, No. 796.
16. Bryant, *Turn of the Tide*, p. 448; Sir Ian Jacob diary.
17. Bryant, *Turn of the Tide*, pp. 452–55.
18. Ibid., p. 447.
19. See EP, No. 811, fn. 2.
20. Eisenhower to Marshall, February 8, 1943, EP, No. 811.
21. Howe, *Northwest Africa*, pp. 376–83.
22. Eisenhower memo for G-3, January 19, 1943, EP, No. 781.
23. Eisenhower memorandum of January 21, 1943, EP, No. 787.
24. Eisenhower to King, January 25, 1943, EP, No. 789; Eisenhower, *Crusade in Europe*, p. 149.

25. Butcher, *My Three Years,* pp. 246–48.
26. Summersby, *Eisenhower Was My Boss,* p. 59.
27. Butcher, *My Three Years,* pp. 254–58.

CHAPTER 12

1. Eisenhower to CCS, February 3, 1943, EP, No. 805.
2. Eisenhower to Fredendall, February 4, 1943, EP, No. 808.
3. Martin Blumenson, *Kasserine Pass* (Boston, 1967), pp. 86–87.
4. Eisenhower, *Crusade in Europe,* p. 141.
5. Eisenhower to Fredendall, February 4, 1943, EP, No. 808.
6. Eisenhower, *Crusade in Europe,* p. 146.
7. Ibid., pp. 141, 147.
8. Blumenson, *Kasserine Pass,* pp. 94–95.
9. Eisenhower, *Crusade in Europe,* p. 142.
10. Blumenson, *Kasserine Pass,* pp. 128–29; Eisenhower to Marshall, February 15, 1943, EP, No. 819.
11. Eisenhower to Marshall, February 15, 1943, EP, No. 819.
12. Blumenson, *Kasserine Pass,* p. 163.
13. Ibid., pp. 175–76; Eisenhower to CCS, February 15, 1943, EP, No. 818. Howe, *Northwest Africa,* pp. 423–24.
14. Blumenson, *Kasserine Pass,* pp. 71–112; Eisenhower to CCS, February 15, 1943, EP, No. 818.
15. Eisenhower to Marshall, February 15, 1943, EP, No. 819.
16. Same to same, February 21, 1943, EP, No. 832.
17. Same to same, February 17, 1943, EP, No. 821; Blumenson, *Kasserine Pass,* p. 273.
18. Eisenhower to Truscott, February 16, 1943, EP, No. 820.
19. Blumenson, *Kasserine Pass,* pp. 278–79.
20. Fredendall to Eisenhower, February 19, 1943, EP, No. 830, fn. 1.
21. Eisenhower to Fredendall, February 20, 1943, EP, No. 830.
22. Eisenhower to Marshall, February 21, 1943, EP, No. 832.
23. Blumenson, *Kasserine Pass,* pp. 282–83; Eisenhower, *Crusade in Europe,* pp. 145–46.
24. Blumenson, *Kasserine Pass,* pp. 289–90.
25. Blumenson, *Kasserine Pass,* pp. 297, 306.
26. Eisenhower to Patton, March 6, 1943, EP, No. 865.
27. Eisenhower to Gerow, February 24, 1943, EP, No. 841.

CHAPTER 13

1. Eisenhower to Prichard, March 1, 1943, EP, No. 854.
2. Eisenhower to Marshall, April 5, 1943, EP, No. 927.
3. Eisenhower to Patton, March 6, 1943, EP, No. 865.
4. Farago, *Patton,* p. 253; Arthur Tedder (London, 1966), *With Prejudice,* p. 410.
5. Tedder, *With Prejudice,* p. 411.
6. Eisenhower to Patton, April 5, 1943, EP, No. 928.
7. Tedder, *With Prejudice,* p. 411.
8. Howe, *Northwest Africa,* pp. 590–92.

9. Butcher, *My Three Years,* pp. 285–88.
10. Marshall to Eisenhower, April 14, 1943, EP, No. 945, fn. 1.
11. Eisenhower to Marshall, March 29, 1943, EP, No. 910.
12. Eisenhower to Marshall, April 16, 1943, EP, No. 946.
13. Eisenhower to Marshall, April 15, 1943, EP, No. 945; and same to same, March 15, 1943, EP, No. 889.
14. Eisenhower to Marshall, March 8, 1943, EP, No. 870.
15. Eisenhower to Bradley, April 16, 1943, EP, No. 947.
16. Butcher, *My Three Years,* p. 289.
17. Eisenhower to Marshall, April 30, 1943, EP, No. 959.
18. Eisenhower to Alexander, April 30, 1943, EP, No. 960.
19. Bradley to Eisenhower, May 7, 1943, quoted in EP, No. 978, fn. 1.
20. Eisenhower to Arthur Eisenhower, May 18, 1943, EP, No. 1013; Eisenhower to John Eisenhower, May 22, 1943, EP, No. 1016.
21. Eisenhower to Marshall, May 8, 1943, EP, No. 973.
22. Eisenhower memorandum of June 11, 1943.
23. Marshall to Surles, May 8, 1943, COS Decimal File 1942–43, 000.7 Publicity, Modern Military Records, National Archives.
24. Eisenhower to Marshall, May 13, 1943, EP, No. 992.
25. Same to same, May 10, 1943, EP, No. 979.

CHAPTER 14

1. Macmillan, *The Blast of War,* pp. 241–43.
2. Murphy, *Diplomat Among Warriors,* p. 180.
3. Macmillan, *The Blast of War,* p. 265.
4. Ibid., p. 250.
5. De Gaulle, *Unity,* p. 95.
6. Macmillan, *The Blast of War,* pp. 250–54.
7. U. S. Dept. of State, *Foreign Relations, 1943,* Vol. II, pp. 111–13.
8. Ibid., p. 113; Viorst, *Hostile Allies,* p. 54; Macmillan, *The Blast of War,* p. 205.
9. Butcher, *My Three Years,* p. 318.
10. Ibid., pp. 320–22.
11. De Gaulle, *Unity,* pp. 120–21; Feis, *Churchill-Roosevelt-Stalin,* p. 138; U. S. Dept. of State, *Foreign Relations, 1943,* Vol. II, p. 134.
12. Eisenhower to Churchill, June 7, 1943, EP, No. 1043.
13. De Gaulle, *Unity,* pp. 125–27; Eisenhower to CCS, June 10, 1943, EP, No. 1050.
14. U. S. Dept. of State, *Foreign Relations, 1943,* Vol. II, p. 146.
15. Butcher, *My Three Years,* pp. 331–34.
16. Eisenhower to Roosevelt, June 12, 1943, EP, No. 1054.
17. U. S. Dept. of State, *Foreign Relations, 1943,* Vol. II, pp. 152–55.
18. Ibid., pp. 156–57.
19. Ibid., p. 155.
20. Eisenhower to Roosevelt, June 18, 1943, EP, No. 1057; Eisenhower to Marshall, June 18, 1943, EP, No. 1058.
21. Eisenhower to Marshall, June 19, 1943, EP, No. 1064, and De Gaulle, *Unity,* pp. 129–31, are in essential agreement on what happened at the meeting.
22. Eisenhower to Marshall, June 19, 1943, EP, No. 1064.
23. Roosevelt to Eisenhower, June 22, 1943, EP, No. 1058, fn. 5.

24. Eisenhower to Marshall, June 22, 1943, EP, No. 1069.
25. Same to same, June 22, 1943, EP, No. 1070.
26. EP, No. 1070, fn. 5.
27. Eisenhower to Marshall, June 26, 1943, EP, No. 1075.
28. Same to same, June 24, 1943, EP, No. 1073.
29. Macmillan, *The Blast of War,* p. 287.
30. Funk, *De Gaulle,* pp. 148–50.
31. Macmillan, *The Blast of War,* p. 282.
32. Winston S. Churchill, *The Second World War,* 6 vols. (Boston, 1948–53), Vol. V, *Closing the Ring,* pp. 177–79.
33. Ibid., p. 179.
34. Roosevelt to Eisenhower, July 8, 1943, EP, No. 1130, fn. 1.
35. Eisenhower to Marshall, July 22, 1943, EP, No. 1130.
36. Funk, *De Gaulle,* pp. 158–60; Churchill, *Closing the Ring,* pp. 182–83.

CHAPTER 15

1. Eisenhower to Somervell, March 19, 1943, EP, No. 896.
2. Eisenhower to Handy, March 20, 1943, EP, No. 899.
3. Eisenhower to Marshall, March 15, 1943, EP, No. 889.
4. Eisenhower, *Crusade in Europe,* pp. 162–64; Bernard L. Montgomery, *The Memoirs of Field-Marshal the Viscount Montgomery of Alamein, K.G.* (Cleveland and New York, 1958), pp. 153–65; Tedder, *With Prejudice,* pp. 426–29.
5. Patton's force remained under the administrative wing of Fifth Army until the night of the invasion, when it was activated as Seventh Army.
6. Eisenhower to CCS, March 20, 1943, EP, No. 898.
7. Garland and Smyth, *Sicily,* pp. 57–59; Omar N. Bradley, *A Soldier's Story,* (New York, 1951), pp. 102–21.
8. Eisenhower to Marshall, April 5, 1943, EP, No. 927.
9. Eisenhower to CCS, April 7, 1943, EP, No. 942, fn. 1.
10. Tedder, *With Prejudice,* pp. 429–30.
11. JCS to Eisenhower, April 9, 1943, and Eisenhower to CCS, April 12, 1943, EP, No. 942.
12. Montgomery, *Memoirs,* pp. 60–62.
13. Tedder, *With Prejudice,* p. 433.
14. Garland and Smyth, *Sicily,* pp. 419–20; Farago, *Patton,* p. 279.
15. Eisenhower, *Crusade in Europe,* p. 163; interview with Eisenhower, October 7, 1965.
16. Eisenhower to Marshall, April 19, 1943, EP, No. 949.
17. Marshall to Eisenhower, April 30, 1943, EP, No. 949, fn. 2.
18. Garland and Smyth, *Sicily,* pp. 22–23.
19. Maurice Matloff, *Strategic Planning for Coalition Warfare, 1943–1944,* U. S. Army in World War II, ed. Kent Roberts Greenfield (Washington, 1959), pp. 152–62.
20. Garland and Smyth, *Sicily,* p. 24.
21. Ibid., p. 24; Matloff, *Strategic Planning,* pp. 152–62.
22. Butcher, *My Three Years,* pp. 319–20.
23. Bryant, *Turn of the Tide,* p. 637.
24. Bradley, *A Soldier's Story,* pp. 118–19.
25. Garland and Smyth, *Sicily,* p. 24; Matloff, *Strategic Planning,* pp. 152–54.
26. Eisenhower to Patton, June 4, 1943, EP, No. 1038.

27. Butcher, *My Three Years,* pp. 322–23.
28. Tedder, *With Prejudice,* p. 439.
29. Eisenhower to John Eisenhower, June 19, 1943, EP, No. 1062.
30. Sir Andrew B. Cunningham, *A Sailor's Odyssey* (New York, 1951), p. 540.
31. Eisenhower, *Crusade in Europe,* pp. 165–66; Hanson Baldwin, *Battles Lost and Won* (New York, 1966), p. 204.
32. Eisenhower to Marshall, June 11, 1943, EP, No. 1057.
33. Interview with Eisenhower, November 7, 1967.
34. Eisenhower to Marshall, July 1, 1943, EP, No. 1092.
35. Garland and Smyth, *Sicily,* p. 88.
36. Eisenhower to Marshall, June 26, 1943, EP, No. 1077.
37. Butcher, *My Three Years,* p. 343.
38. Eisenhower, *Crusade in Europe,* p. 172; Garland and Smyth, *Sicily,* pp. 108–9.
39. Eisenhower to Marshall, July 9, 1943, EP, No. 1104.
40. Interview with Lord Louis Mountbatten, July 9, 1965.

CHAPTER 16

1. Butcher, *My Three Years,* pp. 351–54.
2. Eisenhower to CCS, July 10, 1943, EP, Nos. 1106 and 1107.
3. Butcher, *My Three Years,* pp. 351–54.
4. Eisenhower to CCS, July 11, 1943, EP, No. 1112.
5. Bradley, *A Soldier's Story,* pp. 130–31.
6. Garland and Smyth, *Sicily,* p. 206.
7. Baldwin, *Battles Lost and Won,* pp. 227–31.
8. Garland and Smyth, *Sicily,* p. 206.
9. Montgomery, *Memoirs,* pp. 166–67.
10. Eisenhower to Marshall, July 17, 1943, EP, No. 1118.
11. Garland and Smyth, *Sicily,* pp. 234–35.
12. Bradley, *A Soldier's Story,* pp. 138–39.
13. Garland and Smyth, *Sicily,* pp. 89, 235–36.
14. Bradley, *A Soldier's Story,* pp. 134–38; Farago, *Patton,* pp. 303–17.
15. Mountbatten to Eisenhower, September 2, 1943, EP, No. 1256, fn. 1.
16. Eisenhower to Mountbatten, September 14, 1943, EP, No. 1256.
17. Eisenhower, *Crusade in Europe,* p. 176.
18. Baldwin, *Battles Lost and Won,* p. 230.
19. Farago, *Patton,* pp. 314–16, has an excellent discussion.
20. Butcher, *My Three Years,* pp. 371–73.
21. Ibid., pp. 383–84.
22. Eisenhower to CCS, August 5, 1943, EP, No. 1168.
23. Same to same, August 16, 1943, EP, No. 1185.
24. Eisenhower to Patton, August 17, 1943, EP, No. 1190.
25. Farago, *Patton,* pp. 318–43; see especially the Patton folder in EM which contains all the reports and correspondence concerning the incidents.
26. Eisenhower to Patton, August 17, 1943, EP, No. 1190.
27. Farago, *Patton,* pp. 343–44.
28. Ibid., pp. 344–45; Eisenhower to Marshall, November 24, 1943, EP, No. 1396.
29. See the Patton file in EM, and Farago, *Patton,* pp. 345–46.
30. Patton to Eisenhower, August 29, 1943, quoted in EP, No. 1193.
31. Baldwin, *Battles Lost and Won,* pp. 227–31.
32. Eisenhower to Marshall, August 18, 1943, EP, No. 1191.

33. Eisenhower to Marshall, August 24, 1943, EP, No. 1205.
34. Marshall to Eisenhower, August 25, 1943, EP, No. 1209, fn. 1.
35. Eisenhower to Marshall, August 27, 1943, EP, No. 1209.
36. Same to same, August 28, 1943, EP, No. 1214; Bradley, *A Soldier's Story*, pp. 171–73.

CHAPTER 17

1. Eisenhower to CCS, July 18, 1943, EP, No. 1111.
2. Same to same, June 29, 1943, EP, No. 1088.
3. Churchill to Eisenhower, July 18, 1943, EP, No. 1120, fn. 1.
4. Eisenhower to Churchill, July 18, 1943, EP, No. 1120.'
5. Eisenhower to CCS, June 30, 1943, EP, No. 1089.
6. Same to same, July 15, 1943, EP, No. 1117.
7. Craven and Cate, *Europe—Torch to Pointblank*, pp. 463–65, in *Army Air Forces in World War II*.
8. Churchill, *Closing the Ring*, p. 47.
9. Garland and Smyth, *Sicily*, p. 281; Feis, *Churchill-Roosevelt-Stalin*, Chapter 17.
10. Churchill, *Closing the Ring*, pp. 55–65; Feis, *Churchill-Roosevelt-Stalin*, Chapter 17.
11. Macmillan, *The Blast of War*, p. 305.
12. Ibid., p. 307.
13. Murphy, *Diplomat Among Warriors*, p. 186.
14. Eisenhower to CCS, July 26, 1943, EP, No. 1138.
15. Marshall to Eisenhower, quoting Churchill, July 28, 1943, and Churchill to Eisenhower, July 28, 1943, EP, No. 1138, fn. 1.
16. Eisenhower to CCS, July 27, 1943, EP, No. 1139.
17. Churchill to Eisenhower, July 27, 1943, EP, No. 1140, fn. 1.
18. Eisenhower to Churchill, July 27, 1943, EP, No. 1140.
19. Marshall to Eisenhower, July 29, 1943, EP, No. 1147, fn. 1.
20. Eisenhower to Marshall, July 29, 1943, EP, No. 1147.
21. Macmillan, *The Blast of War*, pp. 308–9.
22. Garland and Smyth, *Sicily*, pp. 283–88.
23. Churchill to Eisenhower, July 29, 1943, EP, No. 1148, fn. 2.
24. Eisenhower to Churchill, July 29, 1943, No. 1148.
25. Eisenhower to Marshall, August 4, 1943, EP, No. 1165.
26. Same to same, August 4, 1943, EP, No. 1164.
27. Marshall sent Eisenhower a copy of Churchill's protest; see Marshall to Eisenhower, August 3, 1943, EP, No. 1159, fn. 1.
28. Macmillan, *The Blast of War*, p. 309.
29. Eisenhower to Marshall, August 4, 1943, EP, No. 1164.
30. Butcher, *My Three Years*, pp. 371–73.
31. Eisenhower to CCS, July 27, 1943, EP, No. 1141.
32. Craven and Cate, *Europe—Torch to Pointblank*, p. 477.
33. Marshall to Eisenhower, July 19, 1943, EP, No. 1126, fn. 1.
34. Eisenhower to Marshall, July 20, 1943, EP, No. 1126.
35. Craven and Cate, *Europe—Torch to Pointblank*, pp. 477–85.
36. Eisenhower to CCS, July 28, 1943, EP, No. 1145.
37. Devers to CCS, July 29, 1943, EP, No. 1145, fn. 2.

38. Eisenhower to Marshall, July 30, 1943, EP, No. 1154; Eisenhower Office Diary, July 30, 1943.
39. Marshall to Eisenhower and Devers, July 31, 1943, EP, No. 1154, fn. 1.
40. Eisenhower to Marshall, August 3, 1943, EP, No. 1161.
41. Eisenhower to CCS, August 12, 1943, EP, No. 1180.
42. Eisenhower to Marshall, August 12, 1943, EP, No. 1181.
43. Arnold to Eisenhower, August 19, 1943, EP, No. 1181, fn. 1.
44. Eisenhower to Marshall, July 7, 1942, EP, No. 367.
45. Eisenhower to CCS, August 19, 1943, EP, No. 1198.

CHAPTER 18

1. Garland and Smyth, *Sicily*, p. 444.
2. Sherwood, *Roosevelt and Hopkins*, pp. 742–43.
3. There is a good discussion in Paul Kecskemeti, *Strategic Surrender, the Politics of Victory and Defeat* (Stanford, 1958), pp. 88–89.
4. Devers to Eisenhower, August 17, 1943, EP, No. 1189, fns. 1 and 2; Garland and Smyth, *Sicily*, pp. 435–60; Macmillan, *The Blast of War*, pp. 290–337.
5. Eisenhower to CCS, August 17, 1943, EP, No. 1189.
6. CCS to Eisenhower, August 18, 1943, EP, No. 1189, fns. 1 and 2.
7. Eisenhower to CCS, August 20, 1943, EP, No. 1200; Garland and Smyth, *Sicily*, pp. 455–58.
8. Reprinted in Garland and Smyth, *Sicily*, pp. 559–64; Macmillan, *The Blast of War*, p. 308.
9. Garland and Smyth, *Sicily*, p. 449.
10. Eisenhower to CCS, August 28, 1943, EP, No. 1213.
11. Garland and Smyth, *Sicily*, pp. 460–64.
12. Eisenhower to CCS, August 28. 1943, EP, No. 1213.
13. CCS to Eisenhower, August, 29, 1943, EP, No. 1213, fn. 1.
14. Eisenhower and Murphy to Marshall and Hull, August 30, 1943, EP, No. 1217.
15. Macmillan, *The Blast of War*, p. 322.
16. Eisenhower and Murphy to Marshall and Hull, August 30, 1943, EP, No. 1217; Macmillan, *The Blast of War*, p. 322.
17. Garland and Smyth, *Sicily*, pp. 474–79. The number of citations to Garland and Smyth is, I hope, eloquent testimony to my debt to their work in helping me through the maze of the Italian surrender negotiations. A good concise discussion is Feis, *Churchill-Roosevelt-Stalin*, pp. 160–82.
18. Eisenhower to CCS, September 1, 1943, EP, No. 1221.
19. Garland and Smyth, *Sicily*, pp. 476–80.
20. Eisenhower to Smith, September 2, 1943, EP, No. 1228.
21. Eisenhower to Whiteley for CCS, September 3, 1943, EP, No. 1229.
22. Garland and Smyth, *Sicily*, p. 484.
23. Eisenhower to CCS, September 6, 1943, EP, No. 1232.
24. Eisenhower to Marshall, September 6, 1943, EP, No. 1233.
25. Eisenhower to Smith for CCS. September 8, 1943, EP, No. 1243.
26. Garland and Smyth, *Sicily*, pp. 498–501.
27. Kecskemeti, *Strategic Surrender*, pp. 91–97.
28. Garland and Smyth, *Sicily*, pp. 501–5.
29. Eisenhower to CCS, September 8, 1943, EP, No. 1245.

30. Eisenhower to Badoglio, September 8, 1943, EP, No. 1244. Garland and Smyth, *Sicily*. pp. 506–7.
31. Garland and Smyth, *Sicily*, pp. 508–9.
32. Garland and Smyth, *Sicily*, p. 509.
33. Kecskemeti, *Strategic Surrender*, p. 95.

CHAPTER 19

1. Butcher, *My Three Years*, pp. 411–17.
2. Eisenhower to CCS, September 9, 1943, EP, No. 1246.
3. Garland and Smyth, *Sicily*, pp. 515–20.
4. Eisenhower to CCS, September 9, 1943, EP, No. 1246.
5. Same to same, September 13, 1943, EP, No. 1251.
6. Eisenhower to Wedemeyer, September 13, 1943, EP, No. 1248.
7. Butcher, *My Three Years*, pp. 417–19; Eisenhower, *Crusade in Europe*, p. 187.
8. Eisenhower to Wedemeyer, September 13, 1943, EP, No. 1248.
9. Eisenhower to CCS, September 16, 1943, EP, No. 1260.
10. Eisenhower to Marshall, September 13, 1943, EP, No. 1249.
11. Eisenhower, *Crusade in Europe*, p. 188; Clark, *Calculated Risk*, p. 199.
12. Memorandum of September 14, 1943, EP, No. 1255.
13. Samuel Eliot Morison, *Sicily-Salerno-Anzio, January 1943–June 1944*, in *History of United States Naval Operations in World War II* (Boston, 1964), p. 280.
14. CCS to Eisenhower, September 15, 1943, EP, No. 1257, fn. 2.
15. Churchill to Alexander, September 15, 1943, EP, No. 1258, fn. 1.
16. Eisenhower to Churchill, September 15, 1943, EP, No. 1258.
17. Eisenhower to CCS, September 15, 1943, EP, No. 1257.
18. Craven and Cate, *Europe—Torch to Pointblank*, p. 536.
19. Eisenhower to Marshall, September 18, 1943, EP, No. 1265.
20. Eisenhower to Marshall, September 20, 1943, contained similar but broader arguments. EP, No. 1271.
21. Marshall to Eisenhower, September 24, 1943, EP, No. 1286, fn. 2.
22. Butcher, *My Three Years*, p. 424.
23. Marshall to Eisenhower, September 23, 1943, EP, No. 1284, fns. 1 and 5.
24. Eisenhower to Handy, September 26, 1943, EP, No. 1291.
25. Butcher, *My Three Years*, pp. 423–26.
26. Eisenhower to Marshall, September 25, 1943, EP, No. 1287; Churchill to Eisenhower, September 22, 1943, EP, No. 1283, fn. 1.
27. Eisenhower to CCS, September 26, 1943, EP, No. 1290.
28. Viorst, *Hostile Allies*, pp. 180–81; De Gaulle, *Unity*, pp. 158–64.
29. Viorst, *Hostile Allies*, p. 181.
30. Eisenhower to Badoglio, September 10, 1943, EP, No. 1247; Garland and Smyth, *Sicily*, p. 535.
31. Garland and Smyth, *Sicily*, p. 540.
32. Eisenhower to Badoglio, September 13, 1943, EP, No. 1250.
33. Eisenhower to Marshall, September 13, 1943, EP, No. 1249.
34. Garland and Smyth, *Sicily*, pp. 542–43.
35. Eisenhower to CCS, September 18, 1943, EP, No. 1264.
36. Eisenhower to Smith, September 19, 1943, EP, No. 1266.
37. Eisenhower to Mason-MacFarlane, September 23, 1943, EP, No. 1282. Churchill, *Closing the Ring*, p. 194.

38. Mason-MacFarlane reported this in a cable to Smith of September 26, 1943, EP, No. 1287, fn. 1.
39. Garland and Smyth, *Sicily*, p. 548.
40. Press conference of September 30, 1943.
41. Garland and Smyth, *Sicily*, pp. 538–49.
42. Eisenhower to Badoglio, September 29, 1943, EP, No. 1298.
43. Eisenhower to CCS, September 30, 1943, EP, No. 1299.
44. Garland and Smyth, *Sicily*, pp. 551–52.
45. Eisenhower to Dill, September 30, 1943, EP, No. 1301.

CHAPTER 20

1. J. F. C. Fuller, *The Second World War, 1939–45, A Strategical and Tactical History* (New York, 1962), p. 268.
2. Colonel Vincent J. Esposito (ed.), *The West Point Atlas of American Wars,* 2 vols. (New York, 1959), Vol. II, Map 98.
3. Churchill to Eisenhower, September 26, 1943, EP, No. 1289 fn. 1; Matloff, *Strategic Planning*, p. 254; John Ehrman, *Grand Strategy*, in J. R. M. Butler (ed.), *History of the Second World War* (London, 1956), Vol. V, pp. 88–94.
4. Eisenhower to Churchill, September 26, 1943, EP, No. 1289.
5. Churchill to Eisenhower, October 3, 1943, EP, No. 1313, fn. 1.
6. Eisenhower to CCS, October 3, 1943, EP, No. 1314.
7. Tedder to Eisenhower, October 4, 1943, EP, No. 1318, fn. 1; Tedder, *With Prejudice*, p. 476.
8. Eisenhower to Tedder, October 5, 1943, EP, No. 1318.
9. Wilson to Eisenhower, October 5, 1943, EP, No. 1319, fn. 1.
10. Eisenhower to Wilson and CCS, October 5, 1943, EP, No. 1319.
11. Churchill to Eisenhower, October 7, 1943, EP, No. 1323, fn. 1.
12. Eisenhower, *Crusade in Europe*, p. 194.
13. Butcher, *My Three Years*, pp. 429–30.
14. Eisenhower to Marshall, October 7, 1943, EP, No. 1323.
15. Marshall to Eisenhower, October 7, 1943, EP, No. 1323, fn. 3.
16. Matloff, *Strategic Planning*, pp. 258–59; Tedder, *With Prejudice*, p. 482.
17. Eisenhower to CCS, October 8, 1943, EP, No. 1326.
18. Eisenhower, *Crusade in Europe*, p. 191.
19. Eisenhower to CCS, October 9, 1943, EP, No. 1328.
20. Eisenhower to Churchill, October 9, 1943, EP, No. 1329.
21. Churchill, *Closing the Ring*, pp. 219–20.
22. Butcher, *My Three Years*, pp. 429–30, 433–36; Eisenhower, *Crusade in Europe*, pp. 202–3.
23. Eisenhower to Smith, October 13, 1943, EP, No. 1337; Eisenhower to CCS, October 8, 1943, EP, No. 1327; Eisenhower to Alexander. October 14, 1943, EP, No. 1338.
24. Smith to Eisenhower, October 13, 1943, EP, No. 1333, fn. 2.
25. Eisenhower to CCS, October 25, 1943, EP, No. 1360.
26. Eisenhower to CCS, October 31, 1943, EP, No. 1370.
27. Ehrman, *Grand Strategy*, p. 74.
28. Eisenhower to CCS, November 4, 1943, EP, No. 1373.
29. Eisenhower to Alexander, November 9, 1943, EP, No. 1380.
30. Eisenhower to Alexander, November 10, 1943, EP, No. 1381.
31. Esposito (ed.), *The West Point Atlas*, Vol. II, Map 99.

32. Butcher, *My Three Years,* pp. 426–29; Summersby, *Eisenhower Was My Boss,* p. 83.

33. Butcher, *My Three Years,* pp. 443–44; Summersby, *Eisenhower Was My Boss,* p. 108.

34. Eisenhower to Cunningham, October 16, 1943, EP, No. 1340.

35. Cunningham to Eisenhower, October 10 and October 21, 1943, EP, No. 1340, fns. 1 and 2.

CHAPTER 21

1. Forrest C. Pogue, *The Supreme Command,* in Greenfield (ed.), *U. S. Army in World War II* (Washington, 1954), p. 25; Sherwood, *Roosevelt and Hopkins,* pp. 759–64.

2. Butcher, *My Three Years,* pp. 419–21.

3. Ibid., pp. 428, 430–31.

4. Ibid., p. 428.

5. Ibid., p. 428.

6. Memorandum to Smith, October 2, 1943, EP, No. 1310.

7. Eisenhower to Marshall, September 20, 1943, EP, No. 1271.

8. Eisenhower memorandum of December 6, 1943, EP, No. 1408; Eisenhower Office Diary, October 19, 1943.

9. Pogue, *Supreme Command,* p. 27.

10. Eisenhower to Arthur Eisenhower, October 20, 1943, EP, No. 1352.

11. Butcher, *My Three Years,* p. 434; Eisenhower's comment of October 28, 1943, EP, No. 1366.

12. Eisenhower to Van Horn Moseley, October 7, 1943, EP, No. 1324.

13. Butcher, *My Three Years,* pp. 433–36.

14. He told Butcher there was "not enough wallop in the initial attack." Ibid., p. 434.

15. If made Chief of Staff, Eisenhower would be on the CCS to represent the OVERLORD viewpoint, but OPD feared he would not be as effective in dealing with the British as Marshall.

16. Pogue, *Supreme Command,* pp. 29–30; Ehrman, *Grand Strategy,* Vol. V, pp. 170–71.

17. Mideast and AFHQ had, after the Cos disaster, been combined into one theater. Eisenhower's authority in Mideast, however, was vague.

18. Eisenhower memo of December 6, 1943, EP, No. 1408; Eisenhower, *Crusade in Europe,* p. 194.

19. Eisenhower, *Crusade in Europe,* p. 197; Eisenhower memo of December 6, 1943, EP, No. 1408.

20. Butcher, *My Three Years,* pp. 451–52; Eisenhower, *Crusade in Europe,* p. 196.

21. Matloff, *Strategic Planning,* pp. 334–58; Ehrman, *Grand Strategy,* Vol. V, Chapters 4 and 5; U. S. Department of State, *Foreign Relations of the United States, Diplomatic Papers, The Conferences at Cairo and Tehran 1943* (Washington, 1961), pp. 203–9, 248, 424, 481.

22. U. S. Dept. of State, *Foreign Relations, Cairo,* pp. 360–61; Eisenhower memo of December 6, EP, No. 1408. Here, on Tito, as elsewhere in the second half of 1943, Eisenhower was in agreement with the British and rejected the American view.

23. Eisenhower, *Crusade in Europe,* p. 200.

24. Ibid., Eisenhower, *At Ease,* p. 266.

25. William D. Leahy, *I Was There* (New York, 1950), p. 208.

26. Pogue, *Supreme Command,* pp. 30–31.
27. Ibid., pp. 31–32.
28. Butcher, *My Three Years,* pp. 452–53.
29. Ibid., pp. 453–55.
30. Sherwood, *Roosevelt and Hopkins,* pp. 802–3.
31. Eisenhower, *Crusade in Europe,* p. 208. The original is framed and hangs in Eisenhower's Gettysburg office.
32. Sherwood, *Roosevelt and Hopkins,* p. 801.
33. Ehrman, *Grand Strategy,* Vol. V, p. 201.
34. Marshall to Eisenhower, December 10, 1943, EP, No. 1423.
35. Eisenhower, *Crusade in Europe,* pp. 206–7.

CHAPTER 22

1. Butcher, *My Three Years,* 454–57.
2. Eisenhower to Marshall, December 17, 1943, and December 23, 1943, EP, No. 1423 and No. 1426.
3. Marshall to Eisenhower, November 23, 1943, EP, No. 1396, fn. 1.
4. Eisenhower to Marshall, November 24, 1943, EP, No. 1396.
5. Same to same, December 17, 1943, EP, No. 1423.
6. See EP, No. 1414.
7. Eisenhower to Patton, November 24, 1943, EP, No. 1397.
8. Marshall to Eisenhower, December 21, 1943, and December 28, 1943, EP, No. 1440, fns. 1 and 3.
9. Marshall to Eisenhower, December 24, 1943, EP, No. 1428, fn. 1.
10. Eaker himself protested in a message to Eisenhower of December 18 (in Smith Coll. EOC). The same day he told Arnold it was "heartbreaking to leave just before the climax." Craven and Cate, *Europe—Torch to Pointblank,* p. 749.
11. Eisenhower to Marshall, December 25, 1943, EP, No. 1428.
12. Butcher, *My Three Years,* pp. 454–57.
13. Marshall to Eisenhower, December 28, 1943, EP, No. 1440, fn. 3.
14. Butcher, *My Three Years,* pp. 463–64.
15. Eisenhower to Marshall, December 29, 1943, EP, No. 1449.
16. Smith to Eisenhower, December 30, 1943, EP, No. 1469, fn. 1.
17. Eisenhower to Smith, December 31, 1943, EP, No. 1469.
18. Eisenhower to Marshall, December 31, 1943, EP, No. 1470.
19. Eisenhower to CCS, December 28, 1943, EP, No. 1446.
20. Alexander to Eisenhower, December 27, 1943, EP, No. 1453, fn. 1.
21. Eisenhower to Alexander, December 29, 1943, No. 1453.
22. Same to same, December 31, 1943, EP, No. 1487. Eisenhower played no role in SHINGLE planning. He felt that as he was leaving the theater he should leave it up to Alexander.
23. Eisenhower to Roosevelt, December 22, 1943, EP, No. 1425.
24. Roosevelt to Eisenhower, December 23, 1943, EP, No. 1425, fn. 2; U. S. Dept. of State, *Foreign Relations, 1943,* Vol. II, p. 195.
25. EP, No. 1425.
26. Roosevelt to Eisenhower, December 26, 1943, EP, fn. 4.
27. Eisenhower to Marshall, December 31, 1943, EP, No. 1466. De Gaulle, *Unity,* p. 241.

28. Butcher, *My Three Years,* pp. 454–57.
29. Ibid., pp. 460–61.
30. Interview with Eisenhower, October 11, 1967.
31. Marshall to Eisenhower, December 29, 1943, EP, No. 1450, fn. 8.
32. Eisenhower to Mrs. Kincaid, December 28, 1943, Eisenhower's possession.

CHAPTER 23

1. Eisenhower to Aksel Nielsen, September 6, 1943, EP, No. 1238.
2. Summersby, *Eisenhower Was My Boss,* p. 114.
3. Eisenhower to Spaatz, December 24, 1943, EP, No. 1427.
4. Eisenhower to Colonel William Lee, October 29, 1943; EP, No. 1368.
5. Eisenhower to Mrs. Milton Eisenhower, October 18, 1943, EP, No. 1347.
6. Eisenhower to Hazlett, October 20, 1943, Ep, No. 1353.
7. De Gaulle to Eisenhower, December 28, 1943, EP, No. 1457, fn. 1.
8. Butcher, *My Three Years,* p. 464.
9. Viorst, *Hostile Allies,* p. 189.
10. Eisenhower to Wedemeyer, September 13, 1943, EP, No. 1248.
11. Quoted in Pogue, *Supreme Command,* p. 34.
12. Montgomery, *Memoirs,* p. 484.
13. Eisenhower to Ismay, December 16, 1942, EP, No. 723.

BOOK TWO

PART I

1. Eisenhower to Marshall, January 22, 1944, EP, No. 1496.

CHAPTER 1

1. The best over-all discussion of OVERLORD is Gordon A. Harrison, *Cross-Channel Attack,* in Greenfield (ed.), *U. S. Army in World War II* (Washington, 1951), pp. 46–82.
2. Interview with Eisenhower, October 5, 1967, and memo, February 7, 1944, EP, No. 1536.
3. Smith to Eisenhower, January 5, 1944, EP, No. 1473, fn. 2.
4. Eisenhower to Smith, January 5, 1944, EP, No. 1473.
5. Montgomery to Eisenhower, January 10, 1944, EP, No. 1475, fn. 1.
6. Eisenhower to Montgomery, January 13, 1944, EP, No. 1475; see also Eisenhower to Smith, January 13, 1944, EP, No. 1476.
7. Eisenhower to Marshall, January 17 and January 22, 1944, EP, Nos. 1483 and 1496.
8. Eisenhower to CCS, January 23, 1944, EP, No. 1497.
9. Eisenhower to Marshall, January 17, 1944, EP, No. 1483.
10. Eisenhower to Haislip, January 24, 1944, EP, No. 1504.
11. Butcher, *My Three Years,* pp. 472–74.
12. Quoted in Pogue, *Supreme Command,* p. 56.
13. Butcher, *My Three Years,* pp. 472–74.
14. Quoted in Pogue, *Supreme Command,* p. 64.
15. Butcher, *My Three Years,* pp. 472–74; Eisenhower to Marshall, April 30, 1944, EP, No. 1660.
16. Butcher, *My Three Years,* p. 488.
17. Eisenhower to Marshall, January 29, 1944, EP, No. 1520.
18. Same to same, February 9, 1944, EP, No. 1539.
19. Same to same, January 18, 1944, EP, No. 1486.
20. Same to same, February 16, 1944, EP, No. 1553.
21. Farago, *Patton,* pp. 417–18.
22. Marshall to Eisenhower, April 26, 1944, EP, No. 1657, fn. 1.
23. Eisenhower to Marshall, April 29, 1944, EP, No. 1657.
24. Marshall to Eisenhower, April 29, 1944, EP, No. 1657, fn. 2.
25. Eisenhower to Patton, April 29, 1944, EP, No. 1659.
26. Eisenhower to Marshall, April 30, 1944, EP, No. 1660.
27. Marshall to Eisenhower, May 2, 1944, EP, No. 1660, fn. 2.
28. Farago, *Patton,* pp. 421–23; Eisenhower to Marshall, May 3, 1944, EP, No. 1666.

29. Butcher, *My Three Years*, pp. 480–82.

30. Eisenhower, *Crusade in Europe*, p. 225.

31. Butcher, *My Three Years*, pp. 475–78.

32. Summersby, *Eisenhower Was My Boss*, p. 129.

33. Eisenhower to Marshall, January 28, 1944, EP, No. 1517.

34. Eisenhower to Lee, February 19, 1944, EP, No. 1559.

35. Same to same, March 22, 1944, EP, No. 1602.

36. Butcher, *My Three Years*, pp. 499–500.

37. Eisenhower, *Crusade in Europe*, p. 238.

38. Montgomery, *Memoirs*, p. 201, quoting a letter from Smith.

39. Eisenhower to Cunningham, February 23, 1944, EP, No. 1564.

40. Eisenhower to John Eisenhower, March 31, 1944, EP, No. 1617.

41. Eisenhower to Marshall, April 17, 1944, EP, No. 1645.

42 Butcher, *My Three Years*, pp. 527–33.

43. Eisenhower to Somervell, April 4, 1944, EP, No. 1627.

CHAPTER 2

1. Harrison, *Cross-Channel Attack*, p. 68.

2. Butcher, *My Three Years*, p. 479.

3. Memo, February 7, 1944, EP, No. 1536. What he meant, of course, was a simultaneous ANVIL. Throughout this chapter, when I use ANVIL, I mean one going concurrently with OVERLORD.

4. Marshall to Eisenhower, February 7, 1944, EP, No. 1531, fn. 3.

5. Eisenhower to Marshall, February 8, 1944, EP, No. 1538.

6. Pogue, *Supreme Command*, pp. 113–15; Harrison, *Cross-Channel Attack*, pp. 168–70.

7. EP, No. 1547, fn. 1.

8. Eisenhower to Marshall, February 14, 1944, EP, No. 1547.

9. Memorandum, February 18, 1944, EP, No. 1555.

10. BCOS to JSM, COS (W), February 19, 1944, EP, No. 1556, fn. 1.

11. Eisenhower to Marshall, February 19, 1944, EP, No. 1556.

12. Montgomery to Eisenhower, February 19 and 21, 1944, EP, No. 1561, fn. 1.

13. Eisenhower to Marshall, February 22, 1944, EP, No. 1562; Harrison, *Cross-Channel Attack*, pp. 171–72.

14. Pogue, *Supreme Command*, pp. 114–15; Harrison, *Cross-Channel Attack*, p. 172.

15. Pogue, *Supreme Command*, p. 115.

16. Eisenhower to Marshall, March 3, 1944, EP, No. 1577.

17. Same to same, March 9, 1944, EP, No. 1582.

18. Quoted in Matloff, *Strategic Planning*, p. 422.

19. Marshall to Eisenhower, March 17, 1944, EP, No. 1591, fn. 1.

20. Eisenhower to Marshall, March 20, 1944, EP, No. 1593.

21. Same to same, March 21, 1944, EP, No. 1595.

22. Pogue, *Supreme Command*, p. 116.

23. Eisenhower to Marshall, March 27, 1944, EP, No. 1608; Pogue, *Supreme Command*, pp. 116–17; Ehrman, *Grand Strategy*, Vol. V, pp. 249–54.

24. Matloff, *Strategic Planning*, p. 425.

25. Marshall to Eisenhower, March 31, 1944, EP, No. 1621, fn. 1.

26. Eisenhower to Marshall, March 27, 1944, EP, No. 1608.

27. The texts of these messages are given in full in Marshall to Eisenhower. April 13, 1944, EP, No. 1641, fn. 2.
28. Eisenhower to Marshall, April 12, 1944, EP, No. 1641.
29. Matloff, *Strategic Planning*, p. 426.
30. See draft of an Eisenhower to Marshall cable, not sent, April 17, 1944, EP No. 1645.
31. Pogue, *Supreme Command*, p. 117; Ehrman, *Grand Strategy*, Vol. V, pp. 252–58.
32. Eisenhower Office Diary, April 18, 1944.

CHAPTER 3

1. Whiteley to John Kennedy, September 23, 1943, EP, No. 1539, fn. 2, covers the issue. Senior officers at U. S. Eighth Air Force had been heard to say that they only wanted twenty or thirty clear operation days and they would finish the war on their own.
2. Eisenhower to Smith, January 5, 1944, EP, No. 1473.
3. Arnold to Eisenhower, no date, EP, No. 1539, fn. 2.
4. Tedder, *With Prejudice*, pp. 499–501.
5. Ibid., p. 502.
6. Eisenhower to Marshall, February 9, 1944, EP, No. 1539.
7. Pogue, *Supreme Command*, p. 127.
8. Harrison, *Cross-Channel Attack*, p. 217; Tedder, *With Prejudice*, pp. 503–4; Pogue, *Supreme Command*, pp. 127–29.
9. Tedder, *With Prejudice*, p. 508.
10. EP, No. 1539, fn. 2.
11. Harrison, *Cross-Channel Attack*, p. 219.
12. Ellis, *Victory in the West*, pp. 99–100. Lionel F. Ellis, *Victory in the West*, in *History of the Second World War* (London, 1962), pp. 99–100.
13. Pogue, *Supreme Command*, p. 128.
14. Eisenhower to Tedder, February 29, 1944, EP, No. 1575.
15. Tedder, *With Prejudice*, pp. 510–12; Pogue, *Supreme Command*, p. 124; Harrison, *Cross-Channel Attack*, pp. 219–20.
16. Pogue, *Supreme Command*, p. 125.
17. Eisenhower to Marshall, March 3, 1944, EP, No. 1577.
18. Same to same, March 21, 1944, EP, No. 1599.
19. Memorandum, March 22, 1944, EP, No. 1600.
20. Butcher, *My Three Years*, p. 507.
21. Tedder, *With Prejudice*, p. 513; Ellis, *Victory in the West*, p. 98.
22. Butcher, *My Three Years*, pp. 503–4.
23. See Eisenhower memorandum for the record, March 22, 1944, EP, No. 1600.
24. Pogue, *Supreme Command*, p. 129; Tedder, *With Prejudice*, pp. 520–22; Harrison, *Cross-Channel Attack*, pp. 221–22; Ellis, *Victory in the West*, p. 99.
25. Wesley Frank Craven and James Lea Cate (eds.), *Argument to VE Day*, in *The Army Air Forces in World War II*, Vol. III (Chicago, 1951), p. 73.
26. Tedder, *With Prejudice*, p. 520; Harrison, *Cross-Channel Attack*, pp. 221–22; Pogue, *Supreme Command*, p. 129.
27. Eisenhower to Tedder, March 9, 1944, EP, No. 1584.
28. Churchill to Eisenhower, April 3, 1944, EP, No. 1630, fn. 1; Tedder, *With Prejudice*, p. 521.
29. Tedder, *With Prejudice*, p. 524.
30. Ibid., p. 526.

31. Eisenhower to Churchill, April 5, 1944, EP, No. 1630.

32. Churchill to Eisenhower, April 29, 1944, and Eisenhower to Churchill, May 2, 1944, EP, No. 1662.

33. Tedder, *With Prejudice*, pp. 528–30.

34. Eisenhower to Marshall, April 29, 1944, EP, No. 1658.

35. Tedder, *With Prejudice*, pp. 531–33.

36. Churchill, *Closing the Ring*, pp. 529–30.

37. Pogue, *Supreme Command*, p. 132; Harrison, *Cross-Channel Attack*, pp. 224–30; Ellis, *Victory in the West*, p. 96.

38. Craven and Cate, *Argument to VE Day*, p. 73.

39. Pogue, *Supreme Command*, p. 132.

40. Harrison, *Cross-Channel Attack*, pp. 224, 230.

CHAPTER 4

1. Pogue, *Supreme Command*, p. 140.

2. Feis, *Churchill-Roosevelt-Stalin*, p. 318.

3. U. S. Dept. of State, *Foreign Relations, 1944*, Vol. III, pp. 641–42.

4. Eisenhower to CCS, January 4, 1944, EP, No. 1489, fn. 1.

5. Eisenhower to Marshall for CCS, January 19, 1944, EP, No. 1489.

6. McCloy to Eisenhower, January 25, 1944, EP, No. 1489, fn. 2.

7. Roosevelt to Eisenhower, March 15, 1944, in U. S. Dept. of State, *Foreign Relations, 1944*, Vol. III, pp. 675–76.

8. De Gaulle, *Unity*, pp. 240–41.

9. Pogue, *Supreme Command*, pp. 145–46.

10. Memorandum for diary, March 22, 1944, EP, No. 1601.

11. Pogue, *Supreme Command*, pp. 146–47.

12. Eisenhower to Brooke, April 9, 1944, EP, No. 1636; Pogue, *Supreme Command*, p. 163.

13. Pogue, *Supreme Command*, p. 147.

14. Eisenhower to CCS, May 11, 1944, EP, No. 1681.

15. Summarized in Marshall to Eisenhower, May 13, 1944, EP, No. 1691, fn. 1.

16. Eisenhower to Marshall, May 16, 1944, EP, No. 1691.

17. Roosevelt to Marshall, June 2, 1944, FDR Library, Hyde Park.

18. Memorandum for diary, May 23, 1944, EP, No. 1708.

19. Pogue, *Supreme Command*, p. 147.

20. The Americans did not know the Prime Minister was going to act; see Hull to Chapin, June 2, 1944, U. S. Dept. of State, *Foreign Relations, 1944*, Vol. III, p. 698.

21. Churchill, *Closing the Ring*, pp. 629–30; De Gaulle, *Unity*, p. 253.

22. Eisenhower Office Diary, June 4, 1944.

23. De Gaulle, *Unity*, pp. 255–56, Funk, *De Gaulle*, pp. 257–59.

24. U. S. Dept. of State, *Foreign Relations, 1944*, Vol. III, p. 701.

25. Eisenhower to CCS, June 4, 1944, EP, No. 1733; memorandum for diary, June 3, 1944, EP, No. 1732.

26. Pogue, *Supreme Command*, p. 149.

27. Interview with Eisenhower, October 21, 1967.

28. De Gaulle, *Unity*, p. 256.

29. This account is based on interviews with Eisenhower, on *At Ease*, pp. 267–68,

on *Crusade in Europe*, p. 431, and on an Eisenhower memorandum to Smith, May 20, 1944, EP, No. 1696.
30. Eisenhower to Marshall, February 15, 1944, EP, No. 1550.
31. Handy to Eisenhower, February 21, 1944, EP, No. 1550, fn. 3.
32. Lutes personal diary, June 16, 1944, Lutes Coll. Personal File.
33. Eisenhower to Marshall, June 27, 1944, EP, No. 1781.
34. Feis. *Churchill-Roosevelt-Stalin*, p. 351–54.
35. Butcher, *My Three Years*, p. 518.
36. Stettinius to Marshall for Hull, April 13, 1944, EP, No. 1696, fn. 2.
37. Eisenhower to Smith, May 20, 1944, EP, No. 1696.
38. Eisenhower to Marshall, May 27, 1944, EP, No. 1719.
39. Feis, *Churchill-Roosevelt-Stalin*, p. 355.

CHAPTER 5

1. Butcher, *My Three Years*, pp. 538–39.
2. Eisenhower to Marshall, May 6, 1944, EP, No. 1672.
3. Butcher, *My Three Years*, pp. 519–24.
4. Ibid., pp. 544–45.
5. Ibid., pp. 533–35; Harrison, *Cross-Channel Attack*, pp. 148–57, 258–69.
6. Marshall to Eisenhower, February 10, 1944, EP, No. 1558, fn. 1.
7. Eisenhower to Marshall, February 19, 1944, EP, No. 1558.
8. Memorandum, May 22, 1944, EP, No. 1701; Harrison, *Cross-Channel Attack*, p. 289.
9. Butcher, *My Three Years*, p. 545.
10. Ibid., pp. 539–42.
11. Bradley, *A Soldier's Story*, p. 239.
12. Sir Arthur Bryant, *Triumph in the West* (New York, 1959), p. 149; Sir Francis de Guingand, *Operation Victory* (New York, 1947), p. 317; Bradley, *A Soldier's Story*, pp. 240–42.
13. Butcher, *My Three Years*, pp. 539–42.
14. Jacob diary, May 15, 1944.
15. Eisenhower, *At Ease*, p. 273.
16. Butcher, *My Three Years*, pp. 533–37.
17. Eisenhower, *At Ease*, p. 275.
18. See various entries in Eisenhower Office Diary for the spring of 1944.
19. Butcher, *My Three Years*, pp. 545–48.
20. Farago, *Patton*, p. 400.
21. Eisenhower to Churchill, May 29, 1944, EP, No. 1718.
22. Churchill to Eisenhower, May 30, 1944, EP, No. 1718, fn. 2.
23. Eisenhower to Churchill, June 1, 1944, and to Hollis, June 28, 1944, EP, Nos. 1726 and 1784.
24. Same to same, March 25, 1944, EP, No. 1604; New York *Times*, March 27, 1944.
25. Pogue, *Supreme Command*, pp. 162–63; Eisenhower to BCOS, March 6, 1944, EP, No. 1580.
26. Eisenhower to commanders, February 23, 1944, EP, No. 1561.
27. Butcher, *My Three Years*, p. 505.
28. Pogue, *Supreme Command*, pp. 163–64.
29. Eisenhower to Marshall, May 21, 1944, EP, No. 1699.

30. Eisenhower to Stark, May 21, 1944, and Stark to Eisenhower, May 23, 1944, EP, No. 1699, fn. 1.
31. Leslie R. Groves, *Now It Can Be Told—The Story of the Manhattan Project* (New York, 1962), pp. 199–206; Eisenhower to Marshall, May 11, 1944, EP, No. 1683.
32. Eisenhower to Marshall, May 26, 1944, EP, No. 1699; Roland G. Ruppenthal, *Logistical Support of the Armies*, in Greenfield (ed.), *U. S. Army in World War II*, 2 vols. (Washington, 1953), Vol. I, pp. 537–38. Still, there was a shortage of ammunition in ETO later in the war.
33. Ruppenthal, *Logistical Support of the Armies*, Vol. I, pp. 231–40.
34. Eisenhower to Churchill, May 20, 1944, EP, No. 1698.
35. Eisenhower to Marshall, May 23, 1944, EP, No. 1707.
36. JCS to Eisenhower, June 2, 1944, EP, No. 1707, fn. 2.
37. Butcher, *My Three Years*, pp. 543–49.
38. Harrison, *Cross-Channel Attack*, p. 272; Pogue, *Supreme Command*, p. 168.
39. Eisenhower to Marshall, June 1, 1944, EP, No. 1728.
40. Butcher, *My Three Years*, pp. 543–49.
41. Ibid., pp. 549–51.
42. Leigh-Mallory to Eisenhower, May 29, 1944, EP, No. 1720.
43. Eisenhower to Leigh-Mallory, May 30, 1944, EP, No. 1720, fn. 1; Eisenhower, *Crusade in Europe*, pp. 246–47.
44. Eisenhower, *Crusade in Europe*, p. 251.
45. Eisenhower to Marshall, June 3, 1944, EP, No. 1731.
46. Memorandum for diary, June 3, 1944, EP, No. 1732.

CHAPTER 6

1. Pogue, *Supreme Command*, pp. 166–67.
2. Harrison, *Cross-Channel Attack*, pp. 268–70.
3. Pogue, *Supreme Command*, pp. 167–68.
4. De Witt MacKenzie, *Men without Guns* (Philadelphia, 1945), p. 97.
5. Eisenhower, *Crusade in Europe*, p. 249.
6. Butcher, *My Three Years*, pp. 559–61.
7. Pogue, *Supreme Command*, p. 169; Harrison, *Cross-Channel Attack*, p. 272.
8. Tedder, *With Prejudice*, p. 545; Eisenhower, *Crusade in Europe*, p. 249.
9. De Guingand, *Operation Victory*, p. 302.
10. Tedder, *With Prejudice*, p. 545.
11. Butcher, *My Three Years*, pp. 560–63.
12. John Frayn Turner, *Invasion '44* (New York, 1959), p. 82.
13. Harrison, *Cross-Channel Attack*, p. 274.
14. Pogue, *Supreme Command*, p. 170.
15. Tedder, *With Prejudice*, p. 546.
16. Eisenhower, *Crusade in Europe*, p. 250.
17. Turner, *Invasion '44*, p. 84; Pogue, *Supreme Command*, p. 170.
18. Butcher, *My Three Years*, pp. 560–63.
19. Ibid., front matter.
20. Ibid., pp. 560–63; Eisenhower, *Crusade in Europe*, p. 252.
21. Butcher, *My Three Years*, pp. 565–70.
22. Ibid.
23. Eisenhower to Marshall, June 6, 1944, EP, No. 1737.
24. Butcher, *My Three Years*, pp. 565–70.

25. Harrison, *Cross-Channel Attack,* pp. 317–20; Esposito (ed.), *The West Point Atlas,* Vol. II, Map 49.

26. Butcher, *My Three Years,* pp. 565–70.

27. Ellis, *Victory in the West,* p. 223; Chester Wilmot, *The Struggle for Europe* (London, 1952), p. 293.

28. Harrison, *Cross-Channel Attack,* pp. 302, 336.

29. Eisenhower to CCS, June 8, 1944, EP, No. 1739.

30. Butcher, *My Three Years,* pp. 571–75.

31. Pogue, *Supreme Command,* p. 173; Ellis, *Victory in the West,* pp. 226–27.

32. Eisenhower to CCS, June 9, 1944, EP, No. 1745 n. 2; memoranda to Smith, June 11 and June 16, 1944, EP, Nos. 1747 and 1754.

33. Memorandum to Smith, June 16, 1944, EP, No. 1754.

34. Butcher, *My Three Years,* pp. 578–81.

35. Marshall to Roosevelt, S-53824, June 14, 1944, Smith Coll. EOC.

36. Stagg to Eisenhower, June 22, 1944, EP, No. 1772.

CHAPTER 7

1. Butcher, *My Three Years,* p. 581.

2. Bradley, *A Soldier's Story,* p. 321.

3. Wilmot, *Struggle for Europe,* p. 465.

4. Montgomery, *Memoirs,* p. 43.

5. A good discussion of the differences is in Wilmot, *Struggle for Europe,* pp. 463–68.

6. Ibid., pp. 338–39; Montgomery, *Memoirs,* p. 235.

7. Sir Ian Jacob stressed this point in an interview of July 21, 1965.

8. Wilmot, *Struggle for Europe,* p. 302.

9. Ibid., p. 311.

10. Interview with Brigadier Kenneth G. McLean, July 17, 1965.

11. Eisenhower to Montgomery, June 18, 1944, EP, No. 1759.

12. Same to same, June 25, 1944, EP, No. 1774.

13. Montgomery to Eisenhower, June 25, 1944, EP, No. 1774, n. 2.

14. Ellis, *Victory in the West,* p. 283.

15. Martin Blumenson, *Breakout and Pursuit,* in Conn (ed.), *U. S. Army in World War II* (Washington, 1961), p. 188; Ellis, *Victory in the West,* pp. 283–85.

16. Butcher, *My Three Years,* pp. 593–95.

17. Montgomery to Brooke, June 27, in Bryant, *Triumph in the West,* p. 178.

18. Bradley to Eisenhower, June 29, 1944, EP, No. 1794, n. 1.

19. Eisenhower to Bradley, July 1, 1944, EP, No. 1794.

20. Blumenson, *Breakout and Pursuit,* pp. 36–43.

21. See Gault's account of the trip in Eisenhower's Office Diary, July 5, 1944.

22. Eisenhower to Marshall, July 5, 1944, EP, No. 1797.

23. Tedder, *With Prejudice,* pp. 557–59.

24. Eisenhower to Montgomery, July 7, 1944, EP, No. 1807.

25. Bryant, *Triumph in the West,* p. 170.

26. Ibid., p. 175.

27. Ibid., p. 171.

28. Montgomery to Eisenhower, July 8, 1944, EP, No. 1813, n. 1.

29. Same to same, July 9, 1944, ibid.

30. Eisenhower to Montgomery, July 10, 1944, EP, No. 1813.

31. Blumenson, *Breakout and Pursuit,* p. 189; Pogue, *Supreme Command,* p. 185.

32. Blumenson, *Breakout and Pursuit,* p. 188.

33. Wilmot, *Struggle for Europe,* p. 354.
34. Montgomery to Eisenhower, July 7, 1944, EP, No. 1826, n. **1.**
35. Montgomery to Tedder, July 14, 1944, EP, No. 1826, n. 2.
36. Pogue, *Supreme Command,* pp. 188–89.
37. Eisenhower to Montgomery, July 14, 1944, EP, No. 1827.
38. Bryant, *Triumph in the West,* p. 170.
39. Tedder, *With Prejudice,* pp. 558–61.
40. Interview with Eisenhower, July 8, 1966.
41. Blumenson, *Breakout and Pursuit,* p. 193.
42. Ibid., p. 194.
43. Butcher, *My Three Years,* pp. 617–19.
44. Tedder, *With Prejudice,* p. 562.
45. Butcher, *My Three Years,* pp. 617–19.
46. Bryant, *Triumph in the West,* pp. 170–79.
47. Interview with Eisenhower, April 15, 1946, by Wing Commander Alan Campbell-Johnson, copy in my possession.
48. Tedder, *With Prejudice,* pp. 565–67.
49. Eisenhower to Montgomery, July 21, 1944, EP, No. 1844.
50. Tedder, *With Prejudice,* p. 567.

CHAPTER 8

1. Butcher, *My Three Years,* pp. 585–89.
2. Pogue, *Supreme Command,* pp. 134–36.
3. Tedder, *With Prejudice,* p. 584.
4. Tedder, *With Prejudice,* p. 580; Eisenhower to Tedder, June 18, 1944, EP, No. 1758.
5. Tedder, *With Prejudice,* p. 582.
6. Eisenhower to Smith, June 23, 1944, EP, No. 1771.
7. Tedder, *With Prejudice,* p. 580.
8. Spaatz to Eisenhower, June 28, 1944, EP, No. 1786, n. 1.
9. Craven and Cate (eds.), *Argument to VE Day,* pp. 278–323.
10. Eisenhower to Tedder, June 29, 1944, EP, No. 1786.
11. EP, No. 1800, n. 1.
12. Tedder, *With Prejudice,* p. 582.
13. Ibid., p. 559.
14. Eisenhower, *Crusade in Europe,* p. 281.
15. Ehrman, *Grand Strategy,* p. 345.
16. For an expression of this view, see Wilmot, *Struggle for Europe,* pp. 454–57.
17. Clark, *Calculated Risk,* pp. 348–51.
18. Ibid., p. 358.
19. Pogue, *Supreme Command,* pp. 218–19.
20. See Eisenhower to Wilson, June 16, 1944, and Wilson to Eisenhower, June 19, 1944, EP, No. 1775.
21. Eisenhower to Marshall, June 20, 1944, EP, No. 1765.
22. Marshall to Eisenhower, June 22, 1944, EP, No. 1765, n. 3.
23. Eisenhower to Somervell, June 25, 1944, EP, No. 1777.
24. Eisenhower to CCS, June 23, 1944, EP, No. 1770; Eisenhower to Marshall, June 23, 1944, EP, No. 1769.
25. Gammell to Wilson, June 22, 1944, EP, No. 1770, n. 3.
26. Pogue, *Supreme Command,* p. 221.

27. Ehrman, *Grand Strategy*, pp. 350–52.
28. The Churchill-Roosevelt correspondence is summarized in Marshall to Eisenhower, three cables of June 29, 1944, EP, No. 1785, n. 1; see also Pogue, *Supreme Command*, pp. 218–33; Ehrman, *Grand Strategy;* pp. 352–58; Churchill, *The Second World War*, 6 vols. (Boston, 1948–53), Vol. VI, *Triumph and Tragedy*, pp. 716–23.
29. Bryant, *Triumph in the West*, pp. 167–68.
30. Eisenhower to Marshall, June 29, 1944, EP, No. 1785.
31. Ehrman, *Grand Strategy*, pp. 355–57.
32. Eisenhower to Marshall, July 1, 1944, EP, No. 1792.
33. Ehrman, *Grand Strategy*, p. 357.
34. Pogue, *Supreme Command*, pp. 222–23.
35. Ibid., pp. 223–24; Eisenhower to Marshall, July 8, 12, and 15, 1944, EP, Nos. 1812, 1822, and 1835.
36. Ehrman, *Grand Strategy*, p. 361.
37. Pogue, *Supreme Command*, p. 224.
38. Ehrman, *Grand Strategy*, p. 363.
39. Ibid., pp. 363–64.
40. Eisenhower to Marshall, August 5, 1944, EP, No. 1883.
41. Pogue, *Supreme Command*, p. 225.
42. Eisenhower to Marshall, August 11, 1944, EP, No. 1892; Pogue, *Supreme Command*, p. 225; Eisenhower, *Crusade in Europe*, pp. 281–83; Eisenhower to Churchill, August 11, 1944, EP, No. 1891.
43. Eisenhower to Marshall, August 24, 1944, EP, No. 1910.
44. In his "The ANVIL Decision: Crossroads of Strategy," in Kent Roberts Greenfield (ed.), *Command Decisions* (Washington, 1960), pp. 383–400, Matloff concludes that Eisenhower was right.
45. Ruppenthal, *Logistical Support of the Armies*, Vol. I, p. 124.

CHAPTER 9

1. Pogue, *Supreme Command*, pp. 192–96; Ellis, *Victory in the West*, pp. 373–76; Blumenson, *Breakout and Pursuit*, pp. 175–84.
2. Eisenhower to Smith, June 25, 1944, EP, No. 1773.
3. Interview with Bradley, October 27, 1967.
4. Bradley, *A Soldier's Story*, p. 343.
5. Eisenhower to Bradley, July 24, 1944, EP, No. 1853.
6. Wilmot, *Struggle for Europe*, p. 362.
7. Eisenhower to Montgomery, July 26, 1944, EP, No. 1854; Montgomery, *Memoirs*, p. 233.
8. Bryant, *Triumph In the West*, pp. 181–82; Wilmot, *Struggle for Europe*, p. 363.
9. Eisenhower Office Diary, July 25, 1944.
10. Eisenhower, *Crusade in Europe*, p. 272; Bradley, *A Soldier's Story*, p. 349.
11. Eisenhower to Marshall, July 26, 1944, EP, No. 1857.
12. Eisenhower to Montgomery, July 26, 1944, EP, No. 1854.
13. Montgomery, *Memoirs*, p. 233.
14. Bryant, *Triumph in the West*, p. 181.
15. Pogue, *Supreme Command*, p. 200.
16. Collins later concluded that "the bombing was the decisive factor in the initial success of the breakthrough." Pogue, *Supreme Command*, p. 199.
17. Eisenhower to Bradley, July 26, 1944, EP, No. 1855.

18. Eisenhower to Montgomery, July 28, 1944, EP, No. 1866.
19. Pogue, *Supreme Command,* p. 201.
20. Bradley, *A Soldier's Story,* pp. 340–41.
21. Pogue, *Supreme Command,* pp. 201–3.
22. Bradley, *A Soldier's Story,* p. 342.
23. This action can be followed in detail in Esposito (ed.), *West Point Atlas,* Vol. II, Map. 53.
24. H. A. Jacobsen and J. Rohwer, *Decisive Battles of World War II: The German View* (New York, 1965), p. 345.
25. Montgomery to commanders, M.515, July 27, 1944, EP, No. 1866, n. 5.
26. Eisenhower to Montgomery, July 29, 1944, EP, No. 1867.
27. Eisenhower to Surles, July 30, 1944, EP, No. 1870.
28. Eisenhower to Marshall, July 30, 1944, EP, No. 1869; Pogue, *Supreme Command,* p. 262.
29. Eisenhower to Montgomery, July 31, 1944, EP, No. 1873.
30. Same to same, August 2, 1944, EP, No. 1875.
31. Butcher, *My Three Years,* pp. 630–32.
32. Ruppenthal, *Logistical Support of the Armies,* Vol. I, p. 467.
33. Eisenhower to Marshall, August 2, 1944, EP, No. 1876.
34. Marshall to Eisenhower, August 8, 1944, and Eisenhower to Marshall, August 9, 1944, EP, No. 1889.
35. Eisenhower to Marshall, August 9, 1944, EP, No. 1889.
36. For a discussion, see Claude S. George, Jr., *The History of Management Thought* (Englewood Cliffs, New Jersey, 1968), p. 71.
37. Pogue, *Supreme Command,* p. 206.
38. Eisenhower to Marshall, August 7, 1944, EP, No. 1886.
39. Pogue, *Supreme Command,* p. 207.
40. Tedder, *With Prejudice,* p. 575.
41. Eisenhower to Marshall, August 9, 1944, EP, No. 1889.
42. Esposito (ed.), *West Point Atlas,* Vol. II, Map 54; Pogue, *Supreme Command,* pp. 208–10; Blumenson, *Breakout and Pursuit,* pp. 457–58; Bradley, *A Soldier's Story,* pp. 369–72.
43. Pogue, *Supreme Command,* p. 209; Farago, *Patton,* pp. 514–42.
44. Memorandum of August 8, 1944, EP, No. 1890.
45. Butcher, *My Three Years,* p. 636.
46. Pogue, *Supreme Command,* pp. 210–11.
47. Pogue, *Supreme Command,* p. 546.
48. Butcher, *My Three Years,* pp. 640–43.
49. Pogue, *Supreme Command,* pp. 121–31; Von Kluge committed suicide on August 19.
50. Butcher, *My Three Years,* pp. 644–46.
51. Pogue, *Supreme Command,* p. 214.
52. Blumenson, *Breakout and Pursuit,* pp. 506–58.
53. Eisenhower to Marshall, August 17, 1944, EP, No. 1898.
54. Blumenson, *Breakout and Pursuit,* p. 558.
55. Esposito (ed.), *West Point Atlas,* Vol. II, Map 55.

CHAPTER 10

1. Henry L. Stimson and McGeorge Bundy, *On Active Service in Peace and War* (New York, 1947), p. 551; Feis, *Churchill-Roosevelt-Stalin,* p. 321.

2. De Gaulle, *Unity*, p. 258; U. S. Dept. of State, *Foreign Relations, 1944*, Vol. III, p. 705.

3. Smith to John Hilldring, July 4, 1944, SHAEF Civil Affairs CCS Dirs., Modern Military Records, National Archives.

4. Pogue, *Supreme Command*, p. 234.

5. Feis, *Churchill-Roosevelt-Stalin*, pp. 321–22; De Gaulle, *Unity*, pp. 270–71; U. S. Dept. of State, *Foreign Relations, 1944*, Vol. III, p. 723; Pogue, *Supreme Command*, pp. 234–35.

6. Pogue, *Supreme Command*, p. 238.

7. Wilson to SHAEF, August 14, 1944, and Eisenhower to AGWAR, August 15, 1944, EP, No. 1896.

8. Smith to NADIST, August 18, 1944, EP, No. 1896, n. 2.

9. Eisenhower to CCS, August 15, 1944, EP, No. 1896.

10. CCS to Eisenhower, August 16, 1944, EP, No. 1896, n. 2.

11. This account is based heavily on Blumenson's chapter, "The Liberation of Paris," *Breakout and Pursuit*, pp. 590–628.

12. Ibid., pp. 595–98; Pogue, *Supreme Command*, p. 240.

13. De Gaulle to Eisenhower, August 21, 1944, EP, No. 1908, n. 1; Blumenson, *Breakout and Pursuit*, pp. 598–99.

14. EP, No. 1908.

15. Eisenhower to Marshall, August 24, 1944, EP, No. 1910.

16. Blumenson, *Breakout and Pursuit*, pp. 604–05.

17. Ibid., p. 607.

18. Ibid., pp. 618–20.

19. Bradley, *A Soldier's Story*, p. 394.

20. Bradley, *A Soldier's Story*, p. 395.

21. Blumenson, *Breakout and Pursuit*, p. 622; Pogue, *Supreme Command*, p. 242; Eisenhower, *Crusade in Europe*, pp. 297–98; Bradley, *A Soldier's Story*, pp. 394–95.

22. Blumenson, *Breakout and Pursuit*, p. 625.

23. Eisenhower to Marshall, August 31, 1944, EP, No. 1925.

24. Pogue, *Supreme Command*, p. 321.

25. Ibid., pp. 322–23.

26. Bradley, *A Soldier's Story*, pp. 405–6.

27. Pogue, *Supreme Command*, pp. 322–23.

28. Eisenhower to Lee, September 16, 1944, EP, No. 1963.

29. Pogue, *Supreme Command*, pp. 319–20.

30. Caffery to Hull, reporting conversation with Eisenhower, October 20, 1944, in U. S. Dept. of State, *Foreign Relations, 1944*, Vol. III, pp. 742–43.

31. U. S. Dept. of State, *Foreign Relations, 1944*, Vol. III, pp. 735–37.

32. Pogue, *Supreme Command*, p. 325.

33. Churchill, *Triumph and Tragedy*, pp. 246–49.

34. Eisenhower to JCS, October 20, 1944, EP, No. 2049.

CHAPTER 11

1. Eisenhower to Marshall, August 7, 1944, EP, No. 1886.

2. Same to same, August 17, 1944, EP, No. 1898.

3. Eisenhower to Montgomery, August 19, 1944, EP, No. 1901.

4. Ruppenthal, *Logistical Support of the Armies*, Vol. II, p. 124.

5. Ibid., p. 5.

6. Ibid., p. 6.
7. Ibid.
8. Eisenhower to Tedder, August 16, and to Brereton, August 22, 1944, EP, Nos. 1897 and 1906.
9. Eisenhower to Marshall, August 24, 1944, EP, No. 1910.
10. Ruppenthal, *Logistical Support of the Armies,* Vol. II, p. 8.
11. Ibid.
12. All these reports are quoted in Pogue, *Supreme Command,* pp. 244–45.
13. Ibid., p. 245.
14. Eisenhower to Marshall, August 31, 1944, EP, No. 1925.
15. Pogue, *Supreme Command,* pp. 263–64.
16. Marshall to Eisenhower, August 17, 1944, EP, No. 1900, n. 1.
17. Eisenhower to Marshall, August 19, 1944, EP, No. 1900.
18. Same to same, July 12, 1944, EP, No. 1822.
19. Pogue, *Supreme Command,* p. 269.
20. Brereton to Eisenhower, August 20, and Eisenhower to Brereton, August 22, 1944, EP, No. 1906.
21. Eisenhower to Marshall, September 2, 1944, EP, No. 1930.
22. Eisenhower to Arnold, September 3, 1944, EP, No. 1931.
23. Eisenhower, *Crusade in Europe,* p. 308; Pogue, *Supreme Command,* pp. 272–74; Eisenhower to Marshall, September 25, 1944, EP, No. 1994.
24. Pogue, *Supreme Command,* p. 277.
25. This account of command structure in Europe is heavily based on Pogue's Chapter XV, "Command Reorganization, June–October 1944," *Supreme Command,* pp. 261–78.

CHAPTER 12

1. Montgomery, *Memoirs,* p. 240.
2. Pogue, *Supreme Command,* pp. 249–50.
3. Montgomery, *Memoirs,* p. 240; Bradley, *A Soldier's Story,* p. 398.
4. Montgomery, *Memoirs,* pp. 241–42; Eisenhower to Montgomery, August 24, 1944, EP, No. 1909.
5. Ellis, *Victory in the West,* p. 461.
6. Bryant, *Triumph in the West,* pp. 195–96.
7. Eisenhower to Marshall, August 24, 1944, EP, No. 1910.
8. Eisenhower to commanders, August 29, 1944, EP, No. 1920.
9. Italics mine. Eisenhower sent Bradley a copy of his August 24 letter to Montgomery.
10. Ellis, *Victory in the West,* p. 464.
11. George S. Patton, Jr., *War as I Knew It* (Boston, 1947), p. 120; Wilmot, *Struggle for Europe,* p. 469.
12. Eisenhower Office Diary, September 2, 1944.
13. Pogue, *Supreme Command,* p. 253.
14. Eisenhower to Marshall, September 4, 1944, EP, No. 1934.
15. Directive of September 4, 1944, EP, No. 1933.
16. Blumenson, *Breakout and Pursuit,* pp. 688–701.
17. Marshall to Eisenhower, W-29970, September 13, 1944, Lutes Papers.
18. Eisenhower to Montgomery, September 5, 1944, EP, No. 1935.
19. Ellis, *Victory in the West,* p. 463.
20. Interview with Sir Ian Jacob, May 8, 1968.

21. Memorandum, December 6, 1943, EP, No. 1408.
22. Blumenson, *Breakout and Pursuit*, pp. 696–701.
23. Montgomery, *Memoirs,* pp. 243–46.
24. Eisenhower, *Crusade in Europe*, pp. 305–6.
25. Wilmot, *Struggle for Europe*, pp. 488–89.
26. Tedder, *With Prejudice*, pp. 590–91.
27. Summersby, *Eisenhower Was My Boss,* p. 170.
28. Montgomery, *Memoirs,* pp. 246–47; Eisenhower, *Crusade in Europe*, pp. 306–7.
29. Bradley, *A Soldier's Story,* p. 416.
30. Pogue, *Supreme Command,* pp. 281–82.
31. Tedder, *With Prejudice*, pp. 590–91.
32. Montgomery, *Memoirs,* pp. 247–48.
33. Bradley, *A Soldier's Story,* pp. 416–18.
34. Montgomery, *Memoirs,* p. 259.
35. Tedder, *With Prejudice*, p. 591.
36. Pogue, *Supreme Command,* pp. 283–84. The logistical movement is discussed in detail in Charles B. MacDonald, *The Siegfried Line Campaign,* in Conn (ed.), *U. S. Army in World War II* (Washington, 1963), pp. 199–239.
37. Eisenhower to Bradley and others, September 13, 1944, EP, No. 1946.
38. Tedder, *With Prejudice*, p. 596.
39. Eisenhower to Marshall, September 14, 1944, EP, No. 1953.
40. Eisenhower to Montgomery, September 16, 1944, EP, No. 1962.
41. Eisenhower to Lee, September 17, 1944, EP, No. 1963.
42. Eisenhower to Montgomery, September 15, 1944, EP, No. 1957.
43. Montgomery, *Memoirs,* pp. 250–51.
44. Eisenhower to Marshall, September 18, 1944, EP, No. 1968.
45. Eisenhower to Montgomery, September 20, 1944, EP, No. 1975.
46. Wilmot, *Struggle for Europe*, p. 536.
47. Montgomery, *Memoirs,* pp. 250–51.
48. Eisenhower to Marshall, September 21, 1944, EP, No. 1978.
49. Wilmot, *Struggle for Europe*, pp. 533–34.
50. Eisenhower to Montgomery, September 22, 1944, EP, No. 1979.
51. Bradley, *A Soldier's Story,* pp. 422–23; Pogue, *Supreme Command,* pp. 293–94; Wilmot, *Struggle for Europe,* pp. 533–34; Patton, *War as I Knew It,* p. 120.
52. The best account is MacDonald, *Siegfried Line Campaign,* pp. 119–206.
53. Eisenhower to Bradley and Montgomery, October 8, 1944, EP, No. 2028.
54. Eisenhower to Montgomery, October 9, 1944, EP, No. 2031.
55. Pogue, *Supreme Command,* p. 296.
56. Eisenhower to Montgomery, October 10, 1944, EP, No. 2032.
57. Interview with Sir Frederick Morgan, July 17, 1965.
58. MacDonald., *Siegfried Line Campaign,* p. 220.
59. Pogue, *Supreme Command,* pp. 299–301.
60. Bryant, *Triumph in the West,* p. 219.
61. Wilmot, *Struggle for Europe*, p. 670.
62. Pogue, *Supreme Command,* p. 289.

CHAPTER 13

1. Montgomery, *Memoirs,* p. 257.
2. Bryant, *Triumph in the West,* p. 213.

3. De Guingand, *Operation Victory,* pp. 329–30.
4. Pogue, *Supreme Command,* p. 259.
5. Ibid., p. 260.
6. Eisenhower to CCS, September 5, 1944, EP, No. 1937.
7. Pogue, *Supreme Command,* p. 260.
8. Ehrman, *Grand Strategy,* p. 380.
9. Pogue, *Supreme Command,* pp. 289–90.
10. Eisenhower to Montgomery, October 13, 1944, EP, No. 2038.
11. Pogue, *Supreme Command,* p. 298.

CHAPTER 14

1. Eisenhower to Marshall, November 11, 1944, EP, No. 2114.
2. Eisenhower to Bradley, Lee, and others, November 6, 1944, EP, No. 2106.
3. Eisenhower to CCS, December 3, 1944, EP, No. 2148.
4. Eisenhower to Handy, December 3, 1944, EP, No. 2150.
5. Eisenhower to Marshall, November 27, 1944, EP, No. 2143.
6. Eisenhower to Surles, October 6, 1944, EP, No. 2027, and EP for October and November generally.
7. Eisenhower to Marshall, December 3, 1944, EP, No. 2149.
8. Eisenhower to Aksel Nielsen, October 20, 1944, EP, No. 2051.
9. Pogue, *Supreme Command,* pp. 305–6.
10. Ibid., p. 306.
11. Eisenhower to Marshall, October 20, 1944, EP, No. 2049.
12. Same to same, November 27, 1944, EP, No. 2142.
13. Robert R. Palmer, Bell I. Wiley, and William R. Keast, *The Procurement and Training of Ground Combat Troops,* in Greenfield (ed.), *U. S. Army in World War II,* (Washington, 1948), pp. 165–240.
14. Eisenhower, *Crusade in Europe,* p. 323.
15. Eisenhower to Early, December 26, 1944, EP, No. 2203.
16. Tedder, *With Prejudice,* pp. 605–15; Eisenhower to Marshall, October 23, 1944, EP, No. 2063; Pogue, *Supreme Command,* pp. 307–9.
17. Marshall to Eisenhower, November 16, 1944, EP, No. 2136, n. 1.
18. Eisenhower to Marshall, November 22, 1944, EP, No. 2136.
19. Eisenhower to CCS, November 20, 1944, EP, No. 2131.
20. Same to same, November 20, 1944, and Eisenhower to Churchill, November 26, 1944, EP, Nos. 2131 and 2140.
21. Eisenhower to Marshall, November 27, 1944, EP, No. 2142.
22. Eisenhower's directive of October 28, 1944, EP, No. 2074.
23. Eisenhower to Marshall, November 11, 1944, EP, No. 2114.
24. Bryant, *Triumph in the West,* p. 252.
25. Ibid., p. 255.
26. Ibid., p. 259.
27. Ibid., p. 254.
28. Ibid., p. 256.
29. Ibid., pp. 258–60.
30. Eisenhower to Montgomery, December 1, 1944, EP, No. 2145.
31. Same to same, December 2, 1944, EP, No. 2146.
32. Eisenhower to Marshall, December 5, 1944, EP, No. 2154.
33. Tedder, *With Prejudice,* pp. 620–23; Montgomery, *Memoirs,* pp. 270–74; Pogue, *Supreme Command,* pp. 316–17; Bryant, *Triumph in the West,* pp. 264–65.

34. Bryant, *Triumph in the West*, p. 266.
35. Eisenhower to Marshall, December 13, 1944, EP, No. 2163.
36. Pogue, *Supreme Command*, pp. 317–18.
37. Wilmot, *Struggle for Europe*, pp. 573–74.
38. Eisenhower to Montgomery, December 16, 1944, EP, No. 2173.

CHAPTER 15

1. Pogue, *Supreme Command*, p. 373.
2. Ibid., p. 365.
3. Ibid., p. 361.
4. Ibid., p. 365.
5. Memo of December 23, 1944, EP, No. 2198.
6. Pogue, *Supreme Command*, p. 374.
7. Eisenhower to Somervell, December 17, 1944, EP, No. 2177.
8. Memo of December 23, 1944, EP, No. 2198; Pogue, *Supreme Command*, p. 374.
9. Eisenhower to Bradley and Devers, December 18, 1944, EP, No. 2178; Bradley, *A Soldier's Story*, p. 469–70.
10. Pogue, *Supreme Command*, pp. 375–77.
11. Bradley, *A Soldier's Story*, p. 470; Eisenhower, *Crusade in Europe*, p. 350.
12. Eisenhower, *Crusade in Europe*, pp. 348–49.
13. Eisenhower to CCS, December 19, 1944, EP, No. 2180; Eisenhower to army group commanders, December 20, 1944, EP, No. 2187; Pogue, *Supreme Command*, pp. 376–77.
14. Eisenhower, *At Ease*, p. 292.
15. Ulysses Lee, *The Employment of Negro Troops*, in Conn (ed.), *U. S. Army in World War II* (Washington, 1966–) pp. 688–98.
16. Eisenhower to Handy, December 19, 1944, EP, No. 2182.
17. Ruppenthal, *Logistical Support of the Armies*, Vol. II, pp. 323–25.
18. Eisenhower to Churchill, December 23, 1944, EP, No. 2196.
19. James Robb's notes of meeting, December 27, 1944, EM.
20. Eisenhower to Bradley and Lee, December 19, 1944, EP, No. 2183.
21. Bradley, *A Soldier's Story*, pp. 475–76.
22. Butcher, *My Three Years*, pp. 727–28.
23. Ibid., p. 728; Summersby, *Eisenhower Was My Boss*, p. 205.
24. Bradley, *A Soldier's Story*, pp. 468–69.
25. Butcher, *My Three Years*, p. 728.
26. Eisenhower to Montgomery, December 20, 1944, EP, No. 2184.
27. Bradley, *A Soldier's Story*, p. 476.
28. Robb's notes on December 20, 1944 meeting, EM.
29. Bryant, *Triumph in the West*, p. 272.
30. Ibid., p. 273.
31. Eisenhower to CCS, December 20, 1944, EP, No. 2186.
32. Pogue, *Supreme Command*, pp. 379–80.
33. Eisenhower to Marshall, December 21, 1944, EP, No. 2191. Bradley did not get the promotion because Congress had adjourned.
34. Eisenhower to Simpson, December 22, 1944, EP, No. 2193.
35. Pogue, *Supreme Command*, p. 381; Eisenhower to Montgomery, December 22, 1944, EP, No. 2194.
36. Order of the Day, December 22, 1944, EP, No. 2194; Robb's notes on December 21, 1944 meeting, EM.

37. Eisenhower to Marshall, December 23, 1944, EP, No. 2200.
38. Hugh M. Cole, *The Ardennes: Battle of the Bulge*, in Conn (ed.), *U. S. Army in World War II* (Washington, 1965), p. 422.
39. Cole, *The Ardennes*, Ch. XIX.
40. Tedder, *With Prejudice*, p. 629.
41. Robb's notes on December 21, 1944 meeting, EM.
42. Eisenhower's memo of December 23, 1944, EP, No. 2198.
43. Bryant, *Triumph in the West*, p. 278.
44. Robb's notes on December 26, 1944 meeting, EM; Pogue, *Supreme Command*, pp. 382–83.
45. Robb's notes on December 26, 1944 meeting, EM.
46. Wilmot, *Struggle for Europe*, p. 614.
47. Bryant, *Triumph in the West*, p. 274.
48. Robb's notes on December 27, 1944 meeting, EM; Tedder, *With Prejudice*, p. 629.

CHAPTER 16

1. Forrest C. Pogue, "Political Problems of a Coalition Command," in Harry L. Coles (ed.), *Total War and Cold War* (Columbus, Ohio, 1962), p. 108.
2. Eisenhower to Montgomery, December 29, 1944, EP, No. 2206; Eisenhower, *Crusade in Europe*, pp. 360–61; Montgomery, *Memoirs*, p. 284.
3. Tedder, *With Prejudice*, p. 631.
4. Ibid.
5. Tedder, *With Prejudice*, pp. 632–33.
6. Montgomery, *Memoirs*, pp. 284–85.
7. Pogue, *Supreme Command*, p. 386.
8. Eisenhower to Bradley and Montgomery, December 31, 1944, EP, No. 2211.
9. Eisenhower to Montgomery, December 31, 1944, EP, No. 2210.
10. De Guingand, *Operation Victory*, p. 348.
11. Montgomery, *Memoirs*, p. 286.
12. Ibid., p. 289.
13. The section that follows is based on Eisenhower's cable to Marshall of January 6, 1945, EP, No. 2224.
14. Eisenhower to Devers for Le Clerc and de Tassigny, December 20, 1944, EP, No. 2185.
15. Robb's notes on meetings, January 1 and January 3, 1945, EM.
16. *The War Memoirs of Charles de Gaulle*, Vol. III, *Salvation*, p. 166.
17. Eisenhower to De Gaulle, January 2, 1945, EP, No. 2216.
18. De Gaulle, *Salvation*, pp. 169–70.
19. Robb's notes on meeting of January 3, 1945, EM.
20. Pogue, *Supreme Command*, pp. 400–1.
21. Eisenhower to Marshall, January 6, 1945, EP, No. 2224; Eisenhower to De Gaulle, January 5, 1945, EP, No. 2221; De Gaulle, *Salvation*, pp. 169–70; Eisenhower, *Crusade in Europe*, pp. 362–63.
22. Eisenhower, *Crusade in Europe*, p. 356.
23. Pogue, *Supreme Command*, pp. 387–88; Bradley, *A Soldier's Story*, pp. 484–85.
24. Bradley, *A Soldier's Story*, pp. 486–88.
25. Eisenhower to Marshall, January 10, 1945, EP, No. 2232.
26. Same to same, January 10, 1945, EP, No. 2233.
27. Same to same, January 12, 1945, EP, No. 2235.

28. Pogue, *Supreme Command*, p. 395.
29. Maurice Matloff, "90 Division Gamble," in Greenfield (ed.), *Command Decisions*.
30. Interview with Sir Ian Jacob, June 27, 1968.
31. Pogue, *Supreme Command*, p. 389.
32. Bryant, *Triumph in the West*, pp. 282–83.
33. Pogue, "Political Problems of a Coalition Command," p. 124.
34. Bryant, *Triumph in the West*, pp. 277–81.
35. Ibid., p. 294.
36. Eisenhower's notes on conference with Marshall, January 28, 1945, EP, No. 2264.
37. Eisenhower to Smith, January 31, 1945, EP, No. 2268.
38. Summersby, *Eisenhower Was My Boss*, pp. 218–19; interview with Sir Ian Jacob, June 27, 1968.
39. Bryant, *Triumph in the West*, p. 305.
40. Tedder, *With Prejudice*, p. 663.
41. Eisenhower to Brooke, February 16, 1945, EP, No. 2284.
42. Eisenhower to Churchill, February 25, 1945, EP, No. 2294.
43. Pogue, *Supreme Command*, p. 391.
44. Eisenhower, *Crusade in Europe*, p. 286.
45. Eisenhower to Marshall, February 20, 1945, EP, No. 2292.

CHAPTER 17

1. Eisenhower to Milton Eisenhower, January 3, 1939, quoted in introduction to EP.
2. Pogue, *Supreme Command*, p. 534.
3. Much of this chapter—indeed a large part of this book—is based on information given by Joseph P. Hobbs, the assistant editor of the Eisenhower Papers. For three years Hobbs has been working on a study of Smith's wartime career, and during all of that time he has generously shared with me his great knowledge of Smith's activities. This book certainly could not have been written without Hobbs's help; I hope the introduction has adequately indicated how deep my debt is to him.
4. Eisenhower to Nevins, January 14, 1945, EP, No. 2241.
5. Eisenhower to Smith, September 30, 1944, EP, No. 2012.
6. Same to same, December 15, 1944, EP, No. 2171.
7. Same to same, September 30, 1944, EP, No. 2014.
8. Same to same, September 30, 1944, EP, No. 2013.
9. Eisenhower to Handy, December 14, 1944, EP, No. 2169.
10. Eisenhower to Somervell, November 5, 1944, EP, No. 2100.
11. Eisenhower to Bradley and others, October 25, 1944, EP, No. 2068.
12. Eisenhower to Marshall, January 19, 1945, EP, No. 2251.
13. Same to same, January 14, 1945, EP, No. 2238.
14. Memo, February 1, 1945, EP, No. 2271.
15. Eisenhower memo, December 26, 1944, EM.
16. Eisenhower to Smith, October 30, 1944, EP, No. 2083; Marshall discussed the problem with Eisenhower at Marseilles in late January 1945; Eisenhower to Lear, January 30, 1945, EP, No. 2266.
17. Eisenhower to Marshall, October 31, 1944, EP, No. 2084, notes 1 and 2.
18. Butcher, *My Three Years*, pp. 716–17.
19. Eisenhower to CCS, October 29, 1944, EP, No. 2079.

20. Same to same, December 14, 1944, EP, No. 2168.
21. Same to same, December 21, 1944, EP, No. 2190.
22. Eisenhower to Marshall, December 26, 1944, EP, No. 2201; Pogue, *Supreme Command*, pp. 406–7.
23. Pogue, *Supreme Command*, p. 407.
24. Eisenhower to CCS, September 16, 1944, EP, No. 1964.
25. Eisenhower to Marshall, September 25, 1944, EP, No. 1994.
26. Same to same, October 22, 1944, EP, No. 2061.
27. Eisenhower to McCloy, November 1, 1944, EP, No. 2087.
28. DDE memorandum of August 19, 1947, in EM.
29. Eisenhower to Marshall, April 7, 1945, EP, No. 2399.

CHAPTER 18

1. Eisenhower to commanders, January 11, 1945, EP, No. 2234.
2. Craven and Cate, eds., *Argument to VE Day*, p. 716.
3. Eisenhower to Marshall, January 15, 1945, EP, No. 2242.
4. Eisenhower to Montgomery, January 17, 1945, EP, No. 2247.
5. Pogue, *Supreme Command*, p. 402.
6. Walter Bedell Smith, *Eisenhower's Six Great Decisions* (New York, 1946), p. 125.
7. Interview with Eisenhower, October 11, 1967.
8. Stephen E. Ambrose, *Eisenhower and Berlin, 1945* (New York, 1967), pp. 22, 33–34.
9. Eisenhower to CCS, January 20, 1945, EP, No. 2253.
10. Butcher, *My Three Years*, p. 806.
11. Eisenhower Office Diary, January 31, 1945.
12. Esposito (ed.), *The West Point Atlas*, Vol. II, Map 65.
13. Eisenhower to Marshall, February 20, 1945, EP, No. 2292.
14. Pogue, *Supreme Command*, p. 422.
15. Ibid., p. 422.
16. Eisenhower to De Gaulle, February 19, 1945, EP, No. 2289.
17. Eisenhower to Marshall, February 20, 1945, EP, No. 2292.
18. Pogue, *Supreme Command*, pp. 423, 428–29.
19. Eisenhower to Marshall, March 26, 1945, EP, No. 2355.
20. Eisenhower to Churchill, March 10, 1945, EP, No. 2324.
21. Eisenhower to Marshall, March 12, 1945, EP, No. 2329.
22. Butcher, *My Three Years*, pp. 788–89.
23. Ibid., p. 768.

CHAPTER 19

1. Bradley, *A Soldier's Story*, pp. 510–17; Wilmot, *Struggle for Europe*, p. 675.
2. Bradley, *A Soldier's Story*, pp. 511–12; Eisenhower, *Crusade in Europe*, pp. 379–80; Butcher, *My Three Years*, p. 768. All accounts of the telephone conversation use quotation marks; I have accepted Butcher's version of what Eisenhower said because he wrote it the next day. None of the accounts disagree on substance.
3. Eisenhower to CCS, March 8, 1945, EP, No. 2319.

4. These campaigns are best followed in Esposito (ed.), *The West Point Atlas,* Vol. II, Maps 65–67.
5. Eisenhower to CCS, March 13, 1945, EP, No. 2334.
6. Eisenhower to Marshall, March 12, 1945, EP, No. 2330.
7. Ibid.
8. Eisenhower to Bradley and Devers, March 12, 1945, EP, No. 2331.
9. Butcher, *My Three Years,* pp. 770–72.
10. Eisenhower to Marshall, March 30, 1945, EP, No. 2375.
11. Same to same, March 24, 1945, EP, No. 2352.
12. Eisenhower, *Crusade in Europe,* p. 397.
13. Ambrose, *Eisenhower and Berlin,* p. 75.
14. Wilmot, *Struggle for Europe,* p. 690.
15. Eisenhower to Brooke, March 12, 1945; and Eisenhower to Marshall, March 12, 1945, EP, Nos. 2333 and 2332.
16. Eisenhower to Marshall, March 15, 1945, EP, No. 2341.
17. Same to same, March 27, 1945, EP, No. 2362.
18. Summersby, *Eisenhower Was My Boss,* p. 225.
19. Eisenhower to CCS, March 21, 1945, EP, No. 2384.
20. Eisenhower to Marshall, March 26, 1945, EP, No. 2355.
21. Eisenhower to CCS, March 24, 1945, EP, No. 2351.
22. Eisenhower to Bradley and Devers, March 25, 1945, EP, No. 2354.
23. Churchill, *Triumph and Tragedy,* pp. 442–43.
24. Eisenhower Office Diary, March 28, 1945.
25. See Note 1, Eisenhower to Marshall, March 28, 1945, EP, No. 2365.
26. Eisenhower to Marshall, March 28, 1945; to Stalin, March 28, 1945; and to Montgomery, March 28, 1945, EP, Nos. 2365, 2363, and 2364.
27. SHAEF plans, September 28, 1944, SHAEF SGS 381 Post OVERLORD Planning, II, in EM.
28. Butcher, *My Three Years,* p. 788.
29. Bradley, *A Soldier's Story,* pp. 535–36. The exact date of this conversation is unclear; circumstantial evidence places it in the week of March 20–27.
30. Ibid., p. 536.
31. Cornelius Ryan, *The Last Battle* (New York, 1966), p. 241.

CHAPTER 20

1. The authoritative account is Earl F. Ziemke, *Stalingrad to Berlin: The German Defeat in the East,* Army Historical Series, Stetson Conn (ed.) (Washington, 1968), pp. 467–99. Ziemke has led me to alter my views somewhat on Soviet intentions and actions.
2. Ibid., and Ryan, *The Last Battle,* p. 254.
3. Bryant, *Triumph in the West,* p. 336.
4. Ibid., pp. 340–41.
5. Ehrman, *Grand Strategy,* Vol. VI, pp. 133–37; Eisenhower to Marshall, March 30, 1945, EP, No. 2373.
6. Pogue, *Supreme Command,* p. 442.
7. Eisenhower to Marshall, March 30, 1945, EP, No. 2373.
8. Same to same, March 30, 1945, EP, No. 2374.
9. Eisenhower to Montgomery, March 31, 1945, EP, No. 2378.
10. Ehrman, *Grand Strategy,* Vol. VI, p. 135.
11. Pogue, *Supreme Command,* p. 442; Eisenhower to Churchill, March 30, 1945,

EP, No. 2374, especially note 2; Churchill, *Triumph and Tragedy,* pp. 463–65; Ambrose, *Eisenhower and Berlin,* pp. 99–104.

12. Eisenhower to Churchill, April 1, 1945, EP, No. 2381.
13. Eisenhower, *Crusade in Europe,* p. 403.
14. Eisenhower to Marshall, April 7, 1945, EP, No. 2400.
15. Bryant, *Triumph in the West,* p. 339.
16. Eisenhower to Churchill, April 3, 1945, EP, No. 2387.
17. Brooke to Eisenhower, April 6, 1945, EP, No. 2398, note 1.
18. Eisenhower to Marshall, April 6, 1945, EP, No. 2397.
19. Pogue, *Supreme Command,* p. 444.
20. Eisenhower to commanders, April 2, 1945, EP, No. 2385.
21. Ambrose, *Eisenhower and Berlin,* pp. 64–65.
22. Eisenhower to Marshall, April 7, 1945, EP, No. 2399.
23. Leahy, *I Was There,* p. 303.
24. Eisenhower to Montgomery, April 8, 1945, EP, No. 2402, and notes 1 and 2.
25. Bradley, *A Soldier's Story,* pp. 532–33.
26. Eisenhower to CCS, April 5, 1945, EP, No. 2394.
27. Ehrman, *Grand Strategy,* Vol. VI, p. 152.
28. Eisenhower to CCS, April 5, 1945, EP, No. 2394, notes 1 and 2; and Pogue, *Supreme Command,* p. 465.
29. Pogue, *Supreme Command,* p. 466; Ehrman, *Grand Strategy,* Vol. VI, pp. 152–60.
30. Eisenhower to CCS, April 21, 1945, EP, No. 2432; Pogue, *Supreme Command,* p. 467.
31. Ehrman, *Grand Strategy,* Vol. VI, pp. 150–51.
32. Eisenhower to CCS, April 14, 1945, EP, No. 2414.
33. Eisenhower to Marshall, April 15, 1945, EP, No. 2416.
34. Eisenhower to CCS, April 14, 1945, EP, No. 2414.
35. Eisenhower to commanders, April 15, 1945, EP, No. 2415.

CHAPTER 21

1. Pogue, *Supreme Command,* p. 448.
2. Ibid., pp. 449–50.
3. Eisenhower to Marshall, April 15, 1945, EP, No. 2416.
4. Simpson always believed he could have made it; see his letter in the New York *Times Book Review,* June 19, 1966; see also Ambrose, *Eisenhower and Berlin,* p. 92.
5. Eisenhower to Marshall, April 15, 1945, EP, No. 2416.
6. Churchill, *Triumph and Tragedy,* p. 515.
7. Eisenhower to Marshall, April 23, 1945, EP, No. 2440.
8. Eisenhower to Brooke, April 27, 1945, EP, No. 2451; Pogue, *Supreme Command,* pp. 450–51.
9. Churchill, *Triumph and Tragedy,* p. 515.
10. Pogue, *Supreme Command,* p. 468.
11. Eisenhower to Marshall, April 29, 1945, EP, No. 2462.
12. See Eisenhower to Deane and Archer, March 28, 1945, EP, No. 2363, notes 1, 2, and 3.
13. Same to same, April 30 and May 6, 1945, EP, No. 2464; Pogue, *Supreme Command,* p. 469.
14. Churchill, *Triumph and Tragedy,* p. 415.

15. Pogue, *Supreme Command*, p. 459.
16. Eisenhower to De Gaulle, April 28, 1945, EP, No. 2457; Pogue, *Supreme Command*, pp. 459–60.
17. Eisenhower to De Gaulle, May 2, 1945, EP, No. 2473.
18. Eisenhower to Marshall, April 26, 1945, EP, No. 2448.
19. Same to same, April 15, 1945, EP, No. 2418.
20. Same to same, April 27, 1945, EP, No. 2452; Pogue, *Supreme Command*, pp. 476–77.
21. Kecskemeti, *Strategic Surrender*, pp. 142–47.
22. Eisenhower to CCS, May 2, 1945, EP, No. 2472.
23. Same to same, May 3, 1945, EP, No. 2474.
24. Eisenhower to Deane and Archer, May 5, 1945, EP, No. 2493; Pogue, *Supreme Command*, pp. 480–83.
25. Eisenhower to CCS, May 4, 1945, EP, No. 2485.
26. Same to same, May 5, 1945, EP, No. 2494.
27. Same to same, May 6, 1945, EP, No. 2498; Pogue, *Supreme Command*, pp. 486–87.
28. Eisenhower used this phrase a number of times in interviews.
29. Eisenhower to Marshall, May 8, 1945, and Marshall to Eisenhower, May 8, 1945, EM.
30. Eisenhower to CCS, May 7, 1945, EP, No. 2499; Smith, *Eisenhower's Six Great Decisions*, p. 229; Pogue, *Supreme Command*, pp. 488–89; Butcher, *My Three Years*, p. 834.

Index